AMERICAN BROTHERS

AMERICAN BROTHERS

SMUGGLERS, SEEKERS, LOVERS & BAD GUYS

Alicia!
Enjoy the ride from both ends! The Book!
The ebook!
    Frank

FRANK R. SAYRE

A MEMOIR

Mill City Press

Copyright © 2008 by Frank R. Sayre. All rights reserved.

Mill City Press, Inc.
212 3rd Avenue North, Suite 570
Minneapolis, MN 55401
612.455.2294
www.millcitypublishing.com

All rights reserved. No part of this publication may be reproduced, stored in a retrieval system, or transmitted, in any form or by any means, electronic, mechanical, photocopying, recording, or otherwise, without the written prior permission of the author.

ISBN - 978-1-934937-42-6
ISBN - 1-934937-42-8
LCCN - 2008937370

Cover Design by Alan Pranke
Typeset by Sophie Chi

Printed in the United States of America

CONTENTS

	Prologue	*xi*
1	Flower City	1
2	Whatta Team	32
3	The Long Hot Summer	56
4	Tell Us The Truth	74
5	Our Savior	102
6	Total Responsibility	126
7	Dissolution	166
8	Fool's Gold	190
9	The Missing Load	228
10	Five Dead Men	255
11	Self-Destruction	272

12	Jamaican Bogeyman	294
13	The Deceiver	314
14	Rage	331
15	Drought	344
16	The Loan: No Time To Quit	357
17	Modestillo	366
18	Sarah, Sweet Sarah: Soul Mate	388
19	Joy of Life	410
20	Gaviotas	432
21	Make Love, Not War	456
22	The Cardinal Rule	481
23	The Assassination	498
24	*Correctionalis*	524
25	Mother Of An Alibi	547
26	Augila: The Warrior	575
27	Piñata	597
28	Forgive The Tyrants	619
29	The Rain In No Man's Land	640
	Epilogue	663

AUTHOR'S NOTE

OUR POWER to envision is without boundary, so imagine this: God, Prime Creator, or the "Forces That Be," set forth a grand design. Everything in creation is part of that design. There are so many plans within plans going on it would cripple the mind and heart if we tried to understand them all; life is evolving and ever-changing through expansion at a mind-boggling rate. The moment a truth or perception is born it evolves, and every moment a color or a sound is born, they revise. That doesn't mean there's no staying up with the ever-expanding designing forces of the universe. Quite the opposite, for creation was designed in such a way that one only need embrace the concept of free will and the absoluteness of universal laws, and assistance will be rendered. These universal laws say "yes" to everything, even to that which we say "no" to. Understand this and you can heal anything or bring anything into your life you desire. No kidding. The universe was designed with this in mind. Check it out. In this universe, everyone gets *a piece of the action*.

ACKNOWLEDGMENTS

WRITING THIS BOOK led me down intertwining paths that others prefer not to travel. The journey has been remarkable. I learned a great deal about the various ways one can put experience to work, and that when the time came for me to enter the inner-realms of my feelings I hesitated, but entered. I owe a great deal of gratitude to all the characters in this book and to those who gave me their love, nurtured my soul, and helped me pave paths to the freedoms I longed for.

To Jessica Allen I give my heartfelt thanks for your dedication. You touched my soul by opening your/my heart as you went about typing my written words into your computer, then later inspired me to get over my fear and buy a computer. I took your loving advice and never looked back. You are an angel divine. Awesome!

And along the path, as I took the book as far as my know-how permitted, and when I felt that it was ready for an editor to judge my work, two more angels appeared.

Thank you so much Linda Bowman—editor writ large—for teaching me the finer points of writing. You too touched my heart and willingly and patiently guided me, coached me, and extended your vast knowledge. I was so lost and you directed me.

And to you Julie Clayton—my second editor—I extend my heartfelt gratitude. When I ran out of money and was in a fix, you believed in me and

ACKNOWLEDGMENTS

the book—and that there is great truth and wisdom to the concept of "two in body, one in mind."

And to you Mom: although we loved and shared, and often disagreed, we found each other before you passed away. Thank you for believing in me. Thank you for all the inspiration you gave over the years when I took care of you and was able to open up to the kind of love we came here in this lifetime to share.

All of this is so very awesome…

AMERICAN BROTHERS
SMUGGLERS, SEEKERS, LOVERS & BAD GUYS

PROLOGUE

When the opportunity to become a marijuana smuggler knocked at my door I didn't hesitate to open it. In fact, I was amazed by my good fortune to be at the right place at the right time. Had I not been, all this chasing big money would have knocked on someone else's door. Opportunity—money—is what brought all of us *Brothers* into the business: we were all chasing money. But I was also chasing a dream and money was the master key that would open the doors to freedom and allow me to fulfill dreams that had long ago captured my imagination.

I'd turned twenty-four the summer I entered into the business. I had no tangible belief system and little self-awareness. What I knew of the world didn't make much sense but my inner nature questioned life's meaning and gave me direction. Nonetheless, because of the choices I made and my naiveté, chasing my dreams led me in a direction I was not quite yet ready to deal with, but which would lead me to discover who I was and what I was made of. So it could be said that the dream I was chasing was a round-about way of getting what I wanted.

My adventures began in San Francisco, 1967—the quintessential summer of love. Perhaps it is not surprising then, that in spite of the many mistakes I made, I did one thing right: I believed in love. And because of love, I survived.

All the stories within this narrative are true, although most of the names have been changed to protect privacy. I faced many adversities, along with my older brother and the man who would become my partner. What we had to endure was not ordinary, yet our inner struggle to rise above the difficulties was not unlike anyone else's struggle to overcome their own life challenges.

Mexico was a land of opportunity during the sixties and seventies. Big money could be made by heading south of the border in search of marijuana and smuggling it into the United States. Finding the marijuana farmers was an essential piece of being successful, since it was they who could connect us with other Mexicans who could move or help move the contraband across the border. With a little start-up money—the elixir that greased the wheels—a well-organized group of American Brothers could make a fortune in no time. I wanted a piece of the action.

This book is a record of my journey.

CHAPTER ONE

FLOWER CITY

SAN FRANCISCO, CA
SUMMER, 1967

Looking out of my front window, I knew right away that the fog would stick around. I actually liked these summer "blur-outs," as we locals called them. They kept the temperatures cool, and although I loved the sun, the cool, misty air provided welcome relief. I was right with the world on a foggy day. The conditions were perfect for a ride on my motorcycle.

Cranking my B.S.A.—a bike I had rigged for dirt riding—I headed out, loaded with anticipation. My destination was the sand dunes two miles to the west. I rode down the avenues and entered the "The Great Highway," raced south a few blocks and charged into the sand, exhilarated by the flight of the bike as I put it to the test in the soft, rolling dunes.

Then I headed down to the ocean's edge for a joyride, skimming the incoming waves. I cruised along as sheets of saltwater trailed behind, watchful for cops on horseback. Under the cover of gray mist I cut through the yielding, wet sand, turned on by the machine beneath me and the expansive ocean and its pounding waves.

When I felt my batteries were charged and I was at peace, I headed to my mom's house. She was at work, but one of my younger bothers might be there. Instead, I spotted my older brother's beat-up Volkswagen in the driveway. Thinking it looked destined for the wreckers, I snickered as I pulled in and leaned the bike against the old beater.

Entering the house, I noticed the door leading to the garage was ajar. Peering in, I saw Bill standing at the workbench near the back door.

"Hey, man. How's it going?" I said casually.

Bill's head snapped around; his look of surprise quickly turned to annoyance when he saw it was me.

Unfazed, I kept walking toward him, then stopped in my tracks and let out a low whistle. "Wow! What's with all the money?"

Several piles of cash lay on the workbench in front of him along with four large glass jars. Two of them were empty and two were full of cash; each jar was covered with a thin layer of sand.

After a moment's hesitation he responded calmly, but with an agitated edge. "I'm doing okay, brother, just taking care of some business. Why don't you give me a hand?"

"Yeah! No problem! Wow! Far out! All this cash yours?" I asked, my eyes darting back and forth between my brother and the pile of bills on the workbench.

"You bet. Here, empty this and sort the bills." He handed me a jar full of cash. "Put the hundreds here and the twenties over here, like I'm doing. I want to arrange the bills, then make a count."

Eager to start sorting I picked up the remaining jar and emptied it on the counter. As we worked in silence my mind reeled. Where did he get all this loot? Christ, there's thousands of dollars here... twenty, thirty grand, maybe more.

Soon the piles took form: hundreds, twenties, tens, fives. When we'd finished, twenty-five stacks lay on top of the counter. My senses exploded. There was enough money here to pay me more than three years of wages at my present job!

A surge of power rushed through me. I couldn't believe my eyes. But yes, it was real. All that money, thousands of dollars, all neatly laid out and it belonged to him, my older brother. Wow!

As if he could read my mind Bill warned, "You're probably buzzing right now, brother. It's only understandable. Get in touch with your ego. Okay? Don't go telling anyone about this. Can you dig it?"

Bill liked to play the dominant older brother trip. Familiar with the routine I replied passively, "Sure man. You can trust me."

"Good." He studied me as I continued gazing at the loot, his vibes penetrating. Then he grinned and the moment passed.

"Everything's going good right now and I want to keep it that way—here!" He handed me a twenty-dollar bill—more than a day's wages. "Take this for your help." Picking up five of the stacks he put them in a small paper bag then placed the bag into his jacket pocket.

"Give me a hand. I want to put the rest of the money back into the jars and bury them in the backyard again, but in a different place this time. Can you do that?"

"Yeah. No problem," I muttered. "Damn, this is so unreal."

Riding home I was euphoric. What if it was mine—$25,000 in cash? What a mind-blower!

Bill always had an obsession for making money. Foolishly or not, I followed in his footsteps—but always a step behind and always not quite good enough. When he turned thirteen he got a paper route. Not long after, I landed a job selling the *Sunday Examiner*. When he landed a job at a local burger joint, I lucked into one at a local family restaurant. After high school he joined the Army Reserves and served six months. When the Cuban Missile Crisis came along, he served twelve more months. It slowed him down, but only a little. Landing a part-time job with United Parcel Service (UPS) came next, which led to a full-time job as a driver. One year later I joined the Army Reserves, did my six-month tour and then joined the United Parcel team—part-time at first, then later as a full-time driver.

He one-upped me during his UPS days when he came up with a product called Dr. Wong's, a Chinese herbal remedy used to prolong orgasms. It was one nasty concoction—that actually seemed to work—but he couldn't establish a market.

When that failed, he stretched his legs out, along with his pal Glenn, who had lived in Guatemala for six months. Glenn had "connections" and they came up with a scheme to buy a used bulldozer and ship it to Guatemala. When they tried to sell shares in this scheme no one bought. Six months ago, I ran into him at my mom's house and found out he had quit his job at UPS.

Now I knew why. He had just confided in me, on this fateful day, that he had well-established connections in the drug market. Before we split, Bill told me all about his contacts, one of whom was a Mexican living in Tijuana. Unfortunately, the contact had recently been arrested, but Bill was optimistic that he would make new Mexican contacts. He had good local contacts and a big market—the San Francisco Bay Area and beyond—to work in. He was working on two different projects, and if they came through, they would net him huge profits.

I'd been working for UPS for close to four years without making a move. It was a "go-nowhere" job and I was tired of hefting packages. I'd recently gone back to a part-time position because I wanted more time to play, even though that meant earning less money.

That evening, about half way through my work-shift, I chuckled to myself while loading parcels onto rotating carousels, captivated by the thought of money and my big brother. Bill and I had always been fierce competitors. I challenged him on everything, at every opportunity, and this annoyed him. Since he was bigger than me I had to be extra careful around him. Bill was cunning, but I had one edge: I was smarter than him. I also had a calculating nature and I knew, all too well, that he had never paid much attention to this side of me. Bill was always too busy looking out for himself and plotting his next grand scheme.

He had a ruthless streak in him that he enjoyed taking out on me—always when I least expected it. I had been a victim of his pranks and deceptions many times. Now that we were getting older, I longed for him to come to his senses and be kind and understanding. Deep down, I wanted his approval, although I didn't realize this. But it was not to be. Bill always placed me in an unwilling, subordinate position, which irritated me to no end and left me longing for some unnamed worthiness. Just lately he had eased up on me, but there was no telling how long it would last.

The *Brotherhood Movement* was the "in" thing and most everyone was embracing it; no doubt this helped to shift Bill's attitude. But the movement was more than just a fad. It offered a new way of life that seemed far more liberating and aware than the rigid roles and daily working grind that most Americans were caught up in. Eastern and Western philosophies were converging, men were growing their hair long, sex and drugs burst into the culture, protests against the Vietnam war and love-ins spilled into the streets, and the youth of the country were the ones heralding in this new era. I was reluctant to join this movement at first. Feeling awkward and uncertain of myself I was afraid of the changes and the lack of structure in my already tenuous world. But I was young and willing to learn about life, and naively hopeful that the *Brotherhood Movement* values of peace and love would trickle down into my family.

A year ago, Bill had introduced my younger brothers Ray and John, and me, to an Eastern diet known as macrobiotics. Bill explained to us the concept of yin and yang and how it applied not only to our diet, but to the laws that govern the universe. It was heady stuff and I felt honored that he took the time to explain it and to break bread with me using the precepts of Eastern philosophy. Within six months I had lost twelve pounds of unwanted body fat. Bill lost even more, as did Ray and John. Mom was abhorred, but we carried on with the brown-rice diet, defying her usual tirades. In a short time Bill had won me over. I began to trust him, which was a good feeling. Slowly, I began to embrace the changes. Once again however, Bill was leading the way and I was scrambling to catch up with him and be good enough.

The younger generation was moving forward at a fast pace. Bob Dylan only had to say it in his songs and millions had followed his lead. Most parents—adults— didn't know who we were or what we were up to. They only had to ask and listen. We wanted to devote ourselves to "love," but these adults wanted us to marry the old and decrepit system they had helped create. They didn't stand a chance against us. We were on a path of searching for something far greater than they could imagine.

In 1966, during the first "summer of love," I attended a free concert at the Polo Grounds in Golden Gate Park. Sitting on an embankment overlooking the sea of people, I could see and feel the wave of change taking hold of us all. The smell of cannabis permeated the air and half-naked bodies swayed to the beat of the music with abandoned joy. Mounted patrolmen were all around, but they arrested no one. They too were caught up in the wave of change. And on that day, the *Brotherhood Movement* took hold of me. I was convinced society would make rapid, far-reaching changes and I wanted to be in on all of it.

Uplifted by the crowd and all that was before me, in my heart I knew I would no longer have to fear change. Everything in existence was real "wow," and the words "groovy" and "far out" were terms we had invented to match the changes of the moment. And now I was part of it. Imagining myself following a path of a rolling stone was just fine by me.

The extraordinary camaraderie I felt with the crowd escalated when Timothy Leary appeared on stage. My body shivered as a mighty roar of approval resounded at the mention of his name. He was our unspoken guru and his words struck a nerve in me—and my peers. As Leary advocated, I wanted to find my path and stay on it. I wanted to find the power within to create the kind of world I wanted, and to make use of love and its power to fulfill my dreams. I believed free will would lead the way. I wanted to live in a realm beyond hate and fear, and join in with all of humanity to create unity, not separateness.

Two years before, in the summer of 1965, a serious car accident had sent me a wake-up call. High on a few beers one Sunday afternoon, I sailed my Triumph Roadster over an embankment. I demolished my precious roadster, which I had come to love, on an outcropping of rock, flipping it end over end. It landed upright, the windshield and protruding steering wheel crushed flat. The car had traveled two hundred feet down the hillside, but I had been spared. By all accounts, my head should have been severed from my body. I felt lucky to be alive. Now, with the advent of *Brotherhood*, I had more reason to live my life fully and establish myself as a free-thinking man. I'd given up drinking because it was destroying my body. Smoking pot made more sense, but what didn't make sense was that it was illegal.

My brush with death was fresh in my mind that evening after helping Bill sort and count his cash. A few months ago I'd moved into a house with my younger brother Ray and a friend. I avoided them that evening, putting every ounce of youthful energy toward somehow joining up with Bill in his money making ventures.

I knew exactly what I wanted: a boat, a forty-foot cruiser to sail in the open seas. I wanted to sail off to the South Pacific, as I had often dreamed about as a young teenager. For three days I let my visions and dreams unfold. I calculated how much money I'd need, even considering equipment, supplies, and spending money for the exotic places I'd travel to. Fresh from these deliberations and hyped to the hilt, I headed to Bill's small cottage in the lower avenues. My plans would go nowhere if he refused me. I needed a lot of money to make my dreams come true and Bill's new business was intrinsic to my success.

"So what do you think, brother? I know it must be a tricky business, but if you teach me how to handle things I can be of help," I said nervous as hell, and within seconds of asking him if I could come to work for him. "You know you can trust me to handle things. So if you have work, I can dig it."

Amused, he looked me over and chuckled. "I figured the money would get to you. It does with most everyone. Just remember, it's only worth the value you place on it and it's only paper."

"Yeah, sure." I followed him into the kitchen where he was preparing herbal tea. I waited patiently, trying to listen, but could only hear my heart pounding.

"Yeah, I have something coming up in a few weeks," he continued, pacing the floor. "I'll need a couple of reliable people to help out."

"Far out! I'd be up for it… What do you want me to do?"

"Not now, Frank. I'll tell you about it later, when it comes together."

Relief flooded through me that he had responded in a positive way. I was still pumped and had to refrain from being a pest.

"Sure... fine... If that's the way you do things. How big a job are you talking?"

"Hey, like I say... no plans right now. But if you have to know, I'll need you for several weeks. I'll also need to use your house. Think about that. If this comes together we'll make a few bucks."

Bill, being a skillful dude, was at his charming best. I was hooked and would have followed him to the moon. We sat on cushions in his living room drinking an herbal concoction called "Mu Tea." He told me about how he had gotten into the business, as we listened to Ravi Shankar play sitar. The music was soothing and helped to quell my nerves. For an eternal moment, all was right with me and my big brother. Within that peace, I felt as though the *Brotherhood Movement* was at work.

"San Francisco is a drug mecca," Bill told me. "People from all over the country come here to cop their weed. The Haight-Ashbury is where a lot of it is bought and sold, but it's available all over the Bay Area, Berkeley, and Marin County. I'm only a small man in a big market. Right now, I only care to deal with cannabis. Sometimes I sell some acid or mescaline, but I'm not into selling any of the heavy drugs. It's a karmic thing. I believe in cannabis, but not the hard drugs."

I listened attentively, receiving a brief education on how the market worked and how he dealt with his customers. When I left a short while later for work my head was still spinning with excitement.

✯ ✯ ✯

Our family had been nearly destitute when we were growing up. My father was a career service man, a master sergeant in the Air Force. We got to travel a lot, but had little in the way of material things. He had sired four sons, each of us born in a different location: Bill in Idaho, me in Oregon, Ray in San Francisco, and John at Edwards Air Force Base in the Mojave Desert, where we lived for a couple of years. Then we moved back to Frisco, then on to Florida for three more years, and then back to San Francisco for a couple of years. There was a one-year stay in Okinawa, when I was twelve and Bill was fourteen.

I didn't mind all the moving around. We got to go on trips, such as a train ride to Florida, and a one-week trip back to California in Dad's big Buick. Mom demanded Dad stop at the Carlsbad Caverns in New Mexico and all of us kids were treated to an amazing tour into the interior of one of the world's largest caverns. Then, there were the two ocean voyages to and from Okinawa. All this traveling instilled good feelings, especially the ocean voyages. I loved those moments, but what I didn't like was that our parents were always arguing over something, never giving one another a moment of peace. When we came back to San Francisco in 1956—Mom's hometown—their bad vibes were thick enough to cut.

Two important changes happened that summer: I grew five inches, from shrimp-size to man-size, and my parents ended their marriage. Before the breakup Dad had taken us boys aside and told us he was going back east on assignment, and would soon retire from the service. Instead, he retired from us. At the time, I didn't understand. It just happened. Once he was gone, he filed for a divorce. My mother contested and won, allowing her to collect a portion of his military pay. But in reality, she won nothing; Dad simply disappeared into the depths of darkness and left us to fend for ourselves.

We had a home in the lower avenues of the Sunset District, but no income to pay the mortgage or money for food. Somehow we survived. Mom got a government job. Bill got a paper route and I got a job selling the Sunday paper at a nearby supermarket. Ray and Jack, only nine and seven at the time, were off the hook for the time being.

Throughout junior high and high school, Bill and I worked. I felt strange and incomplete. A vague but ever-present insecurity gnawed at me, but I had no tools to cope with my feelings, not at that age. My only role models were sports heroes: Mickey Mantle, Hank Aaron, Willie Mays, and others. When I brought my woes to my male pals, guys I sailed with and went to high school with, they pushed aside my emotional flare-ups. We were "men," and as men were not allowed to let our feelings run our lives. So I took their advice, became a man, and kept my mind busy. But underneath the bravado I felt abandoned and my life seemed filled with moments when confusion reigned and life was incomprehensible.

My mother was a hard-liner: controlling and stubborn. She was also very short—only four-foot ten—and overweight. I hated being seen with her. It was totally embarrassing. Almost everything she said or did embarrassed me. She had been raised Catholic, so she stood by her faith and raised us as best she could. I had no idea of the pressure she faced raising four boys on her own. With no one around to help her shoulder the load she became bitter and angry, and she was irrational so often that none of us wanted to be around her.

I remember one particular incident when John and I were horsing around in the basement and I brazenly called him a "little bastard." Mom heard me from the other end of the room and flew into a fit of rage. She attacked me from my backside, slapping me senseless. I cowered in a corner trying to make myself as small as possible to minimize the damage until she was spent, and learned a harsh lesson: never again use such vile language. Years later, I found out that she had been born an illegitimate child during WWI, and the term was particularly offensive to her. Learning this, I understood her behavior better, but it didn't help me to heal the wounds.

From my perspective as a young boy in early puberty, my mother was oppressive, hateful, and dedicated to vengeance. Bill and I shared a large, downstairs bedroom and we learned to keep out of her sight as much as possible, which wasn't too hard. I'd either be outside playing with the many neighborhood kids or in my room doing homework, or just hanging out. When I started my junior year in high school I also started a six-day a week job, working every other week at a dinner restaurant. Tired of living under her roof, I left her house within a week or two of high school graduation. I didn't care. I just wanted to get away from her and away from her domination and the intrusive desolation.

In spite of living under my mom's iron fist, my imagination flourished. By the age of thirteen, I had became captivated by the beauty of the San Francisco Bay Area—the hills and valleys that spread out in molded divinity, the bay itself, with its bridges and islands and the coastal range, and Mount Tamalpais standing at the center of it all. And, all of this natural beauty offered me redemption.

At an early age I had a love for traveling and when we settled in the Bay Area this traveling bug beckoned me to explore—much as Bill and I did when we lived in Florida and would hike barefooted to the swamp on summer days, then on down to the gulf where we'd hang with pals and swim. Our life was filled with exploring in Okinawa too. Nature, I found out, had a calming effect on me—and it allowed me to get away from my parents and be with pals. Then there was the roller skating rink, the movies, the swimming pool, the hikes into the inlands forests and, of course, Boy Scouts. Bill earned "Star" in no time, while I struggled to make "First Class."

I was bewitched the summer I turned fourteen by a group of neighborhood buddies who accosted me while returning from church one Sunday.

"Come sailing with us," they pleaded, grabbing, pushing, and shoving as they egged me on to join them. Few words were spoken, but inwardly I was overjoyed as we got on the bus that would take us down to the Sea Scout Base at the foot of Van Ness. I joined that day, although we didn't go sailing. The boat needed fixing and I had been duped into helping them along, with a promise of what was to come later.

A few weeks later, I had my first sail. I was immediately hooked. The beauty of the bay was so real I could touch it. From then on, sailing on the bay was all I could think about. Every time we raised the sails and stood tall, our thirty-foot wooden lifeboat slipping out of the harbor, I felt complete and succumbed to the wonder of it all, as the vessel heeled and accelerated, as though propelled by magic. And in my glory, I often imagined cruising to exotic, far-off places, like Tahiti or Samoa—any place I chose to think about.

Sailing was not only the best thing that had ever happened to me, it offered a way of life; in fact, it was a perfect analogy to life and I would soon learn how to apply it. I especially loved that sailing meant I could venture most anywhere there was water and where the wind blew.

With visions of sailing to distant shores still dancing in my head, I jumped at the chance the day Bill called me to join him in his enterprise. I never questioned him when he said, "We're going to make hashish. We'll be starting in a few days. Brother Ray will be helping. Let's go over the plans."

The plans were basic. Bill wanted three people to work the operation. Brother Ray, who was living with me, was to be my helper and I liked that. Ray and I got along just fine.

Bill promised a few weeks of work and I impulsively quit my job at UPS, telling them to "shove it." He had already hinted he had more work and if all his plans succeeded, I'd buy the boat that dreams wouldn't and sail wherever I desired. That was all I wanted: to make enough money to buy a nice sound cruising vessel, fit it out, and quit while I was ahead.

I was charged and ready. If anything or anybody stood in my way, I'd deal with it or them. Along the way, I'd be damn sure to ascertain what was necessary by using common sense and my analytical mind: something I often had to do while sailing—especially sailboat racing, when we were really put to test by afternoon winds of thirty knots or better. One wrong move, or allowing panic to take hold, and you might just find yourself unable to regain control of the boat. Lives depended on you and each crew member depended on the other to survive. Armed with this nautical self-confidence, I felt everything would be fine. After all, I wasn't going to be doing this kind of work all my life—just a year or two.

I had my first marijuana high in late 1964. Throughout 1965 I experimented with drugs. There were a few acid trips, but smoking weed, sometimes daily, was my drug of choice. At first I smoked pot because it was hip, but after a while I became aware of how useful it was. Food tasted better, music became a new experience into the realm of sound and rhythm, and sex and erotic voyages brought intense gratification. In short,

THC opened people up to their feeling centers. It also opened doors to the conscious mind and I found that most challenging.

When my old fears would overwhelm me, I'd find a single object to hone in on and allow my mind to settle down. In a short time I would be calm again, and I'd usually have insights into what those fears were about. Approximately thirty million Americans from every walk of life were smoking pot. It was more than just a trend our country had embraced—lawful or not, it was fast becoming an elixir.

The consensus within the *Brotherhood* was that our government was out of control. I was one of many who were quite angry with our president, as well as with Congress, as they found ways to justify their bloody actions by waging war against communist insurgents in Vietnam. It was ruthless, unpopular and unlawful.

Even though we found cannabis useful, our government claimed it was addictive and would lead to a life of crime and violence. Given a vote, cannabis was a far better choice than alcohol, which was more addictive than heroin, and certainly cheaper and more plentiful. In all, contradictions abounded. The young people of our era were eager for change, but we wanted peaceful solutions to the major problems our country was beset with.

At least, that's how I saw things. As drug dealers and smugglers, we believed our job was, in part, to aid the *Brotherhood Movement* and force our government to pay attention. And the only way to accomplish such a lofty goal was to supply the drug of choice to the youth who were heralding the change and who wanted to keep on getting high—by any means possible. Risky or not, I wanted to get high as well, and promote unity and a broader awareness. I was set to take the government on, as an act of social revolution, something our forefathers said we had every right to do.

To our pot-smoking peers, we were "the good guys."

✯ ✯ ✯

Our first adventure was marred by two factors: the chemist and an angry neighbor.

John, the chemist Bill had rounded up, was a tall, lanky dude. His beard and long unkempt hair let everyone know that he was an outlaw and proud of it. In a day and age when we in the Brotherhood aspired to be mellow, he was argumentative and difficult. My brother Ray and I never knew what to expect from him when he showed up to work at our place each morning. At just past forty years old, John seemed like an old man to us.

From the start, he told us he needed to make money to pay off his lawyer. Some months before, he had been busted for making hash. So, he was making hash again to earn enough money to pay his lawyer to defend him for making hash in the first place! He stood a chance of going to jail for a few years. We sympathized with him, although we could see the irony in his situation, but his personality got under our skin. We especially disliked his hollering at us when one of the hash-paste bricks caught fire in the electric oven.

In spite our misgivings about John, Bill made it clear that John was responsible for running the operation. It was a simple, but time-consuming process. Using tri-methyl alcohol, it took us some six weeks to extract THC. First we had to break down the kilos—ten at a time—by placing the cleaned out batch in a large metal caldron, then adding tri-methyl. After it soaked for a few hours we set the cauldron on an electric hotplate and cooked the product. We used a large strainer to catch the stems, seeds and the leaves, and then cooked it down again with a second rinsing until it became a runny paste. At that point, John would decide if it was ready for the oven.

We used our basement for the first stage, then John took the paste to the kitchen and cooked it down in our electric oven. We all had to carefully monitor each step of the process. No one wanted a fire and no one wanted a burned product. John turned each blob into a semi-hard brick, which he called "Persian Rug." Bill's contacts sold the bricks as quickly as we turned them out.

By mid-October, as we were about to finish the last batch, a heat wave began to slow our work. The temperature was close to a hundred degrees and there was no wind to blow away the pungent smell of alcohol and cannabis. Just at that time, a testy neighbor showed up at our front door.

When the doorbell sounded, John and I froze. I looked out the front window to check for cars, especially cop cars, and then John asked me to answer the door. We weren't expecting anyone and Bill always called first before coming over.

Nervously, I opened the door. A middle-aged man with a befuddled look introduced himself as our neighbor from across the street, then immediately started harping on me.

"I'm tired of the noise your van makes. I work at night and I need my sleep. I know the person who owns the van over there lives here," he said, pointing to John's van.

"Yes, he does," I stammered.

"Either you get him to fix his muffler or I call the cops."

The neighbor had a point. Every morning we could hear the approach of John's van from at least two blocks away. We'd complained about the noise to him and to Bill, but nothing had been done to rectify the problem. Now that would have to change. The man at the door was clearly agitated.

"It won't happen again sir," I said respectfully and added sincerely, "It gets to us, too. I'll tell my roommate. The problem will be taken care of right away. Okay!"

The neighbor backed off and then unexpectedly said, "Your neighbor thinks you're making some kind of drugs over here."

I stood frozen for a moment as he continued glaring at me, arms akimbo, as if to say, I'm not only a conservative, I'm also a jerk. He added accusingly, "There's some real strange smells coming from your house."

Quickly gathering my wits I replied, "Oh… that would be the herbs we're working with. We're making an extraction from ginseng and gotakola. They're… Chinese medicinal herbs. We're into holistic medicine and we're selling them to the local health food stores. That's all. It smells terrible. Sorry. We're just about finished."

"What do you use those for?" he asked, pointing at two five-gallon jugs of spring water resting against the patio wall. They had been delivered that morning and we hadn't brought them inside.

"Is that what you use to make the drugs?" he persisted, letting the last word linger.

"No. That's our drinking water," I replied, thinking quickly. "We're vegetarians. That's all. Look, I'm really sorry about the noise. We'll take care of it."

Before he could question me any further I took advantage of the momentary lapse of interrogation and eased past him to one of the bottles. Hefting it on my shoulder I apologized again, then bid him a good day as I closed the door.

Bill shut down the operation that afternoon, leaving John to finish the last batch at another location. The 100-kilo experiment that we had done as a favor to John became history. Bill made a few bucks and paid Ray and I for our efforts. We barely made enough to pay the bills for the next few months. I was counting on future work with Bill to continue pursuing my dreams. We'd had a good scare, but learned a lesson about how there were many unknowns and unseen dangers to this business.

The next afternoon Bill informed me there was more work coming—lots more, he hinted.

"I've been negotiating with this man Victor for the past few days. He says he has a good connection south of the border. We're making plans to bring up some heavy amounts in the near future."

"Groovy. That sounds bitchin'. When do we start?"

"Hard to say. I just met him. He'll have to prove himself. He's all words right now. That's all. In this business you don't move 'til your man comes through. He could be just another bullshitter. We have to wait and see. If he does come through, we can expect to be doing up to seven-hundred kilos a week."

"Wow! Can you sell that many?"

"That's no problem, Frank. I've got a big market. The real problem is, can he deliver? We ought to know in a month or so. For now just take it easy and be cool. Don't go mouthing off to anyone. Keep your ego in place. That's the important thing. I'll keep you posted on what's happening. When and if this comes together, I'll have you handle the customers. You already know some of them. You'll meet Victor when the time comes."

Bill was right about this. If we were to be successful in this business we had to be discreet, no motor-mouthing. In those days we called it "ego tripping:" a term most everyone used, never really quite knowing what we were talking about. Keeping my ego in check was easy, and the news from Bill made me feel like I was on top of the world. If this guy Victor came through, we'd be major "big-time."

In the San Francisco Mission District you could get a great macrobiotic meal at the "Good Karma Cafe." I went there two or three times a week and often ran into acquaintances. Daryl, a friend of Bill's, was there one particular day in late October. As he stood to greet me, I couldn't help noticing a lovely woman sitting at his table. Daryl was a good-looking dude himself, with long brown hair. He was six feet-four inches tall and presented a big shield. I wondered why he hadn't bothered to introduce this woman, who I assumed was his lady.

She took the initiative. Standing, she said, "Hi. I'm Donna." She extended a coy smile and her hand. "So you're one of Bill's younger brothers?"

Self-consciously I responded, "Yeah… there's two more of us—Ray and John."

"So I hear." She seemed at a loss for words and I could only stare at her. She got my attention in a different way when she said, "I heard you had a big problem the other day. Bill said you handled it well. What was it all about?"

Disconcerted by her comment, I didn't know how to respond. I was also curious how she knew about our business. Bill had told me to keep my ego in check. Apparently, he had let his run loose.

I was bothered by this thought, but enthralled by her. Trying to be laid back I replied casually, "It was no big deal. We got out of it okay. Bill shut down the operation and, well, we were about finished. We were lucky."

"So what happened? Did that guy call the cops?"

Maybe she had heard Bill and Daryl talking about the near bust. Either way I was in a quandary with this inquisition. She was irresistible, so it was hard for me to remain unresponsive.

"Well, I don't know and I really can't say. Bill likes me to keep things like that discreet."

"Sure. I understand," she added quickly, then grew quiet again.

I was so attracted to good-looking women like this one, but equally confused and terrified about how to approach them. It was no wonder that my knees had grown weak. Feeling disabled and unable to keep pace with her, I could no longer withstand temptations. Daryl was hovering between us and his territorial male vibes were obvious.

"Hey! Nice to meet you, Donna." I was exasperated and begged off, "Gotta go join a friend for dinner."

Quickly making my way to my friend's table, I sucked in a big breath of air. Donna was lovely, petite, and sexy—perhaps Italian? My heart had started flip-flopping the second she had greeted me.

The following week I ran into Daryl and Donna again at Bill's place. While Daryl and Bill conversed, Donna engaged me again. I didn't know what to make of her, except that she made my heart beat wildly. Throughout our conversation I could feel my cheeks burning. As I left Bill's cottage I couldn't stop thinking about her and the way she came on to me. Or was she just being friendly?

I hadn't had a girlfriend for some time now. Several months before, I had broken up with a woman by the name of Judy (my second abysmal relationship), whom I'd "dated" for two years. Initially, Judy had broken off the relationship with me, but later after we got back together, I broke it off when she said I was being "weird"—she especially didn't "get" my vegetarian diet. As with my first girlfriend, the breakup had been an emotional drain. Since then, those familiar feelings of powerlessness and loneliness had returned, leaving me once again unsure of myself and feeling not good enough, especially around women. Donna excited and scared me.

Winter was coming and my money was running out. Bill called me one

November night and asked me to come over. As we sat in his small living room atop multi-colored cushions, legs crossed, eating rice and vegetables, I waited for the news that I hoped would be good.

It didn't bother me that Bill was in a questionable line of business. I admired my older brother. I viewed him as a cool dude with lots of friends, and as a man who had a chance to succeed. And par to the way I shadowed him, I wanted to succeed along the same lines.

Cool as a cucumber, Bill said between mouthfuls, "I got a problem, brother."

Assuming I was about to get blamed for something I asked tensely, "What's happening?"

"It looks like everything is happening at once. This guy Victor, my connection, called the other day. He's almost ready," Bill stated flatly, causing my pulse to race. "The problem is, the waves are up in Hawaii."

Bill had always been athletic. A good two inches taller than me, with thin black hair in contrast to my thick, streaky, brown hair, we were both lean with hazel eyes, and often Bill's pals at the beach mistook me for him. He didn't much like that.

In high school he ran track, played basketball, and tried out for football. We both loved sports, but he excelled. He'd have made the team as a running back, but in his junior year a gym teacher caught him when he came to a school dance plastered on beer, and banished him from sports all together. Dad wasn't around. Bill had no one to defend him. I knew Bill was still carrying a grudge about this by the way he talked about the incident.

Even though I knew of his love for big surf, I excitedly interrupted him.

"Why don't we work with this guy Victor for now? You can go to Hawaii later."

"The waves won't wait," he snapped. "Besides, Victor said he's almost ready. That can mean most anything. It may take a few weeks. I've got other plans."

"Other plans? Like what?"

"I'm leaving tomorrow for the islands. I want you to stay here at my cottage and wait for Victor's call. I'll leave a number you can reach me at. When he calls, let me know what's up."

"Christ, this is a big job. I haven't even met this guy."

"That's okay. We've been over this several times. I trust you. I'll leave you money for expenses. You can handle all the procedures when the time comes. Just make sure you see the load first before you sell. The customers I turned you on to will have the cash on hand. Just do as we planned. If there's any trouble, I'll come back and take care of things. Can you dig it?"

I could, but was shocked. "Boy! Those waves sure have you going."

"This is the season, brother. They're up and I want to move on it. I missed them last year. Let's go over the plan one more time. I don't want any mistakes."

Four days later I found myself on the defense when Victor called me from Mexico.

"Where's your bro?" he demanded, without any preliminary niceties.

"Surfing in Hawaii."

"Damn, brother. What's he up to? I'm almost ready to go."

"I have everything ready," I said, explaining the situation.

Victor was hesitant, but then conceded.

"He'd better be able to sell these as planned."

"Don't worry. He and I went over all of this before he split. I have his phone number where he's staying."

Victor was still dubious, but we ended on a high note. Victor would do the business with me, no matter what. This was all rather weird, I thought, as I hung up.

"Four or five days, tops," Victor had said, "and we'll be ready."

Two nights later a big storm hit the Bay Area. That evening, over the thunderous sound of Bill's stereo, I heard someone knocking at the door.

Not expecting anyone, I jumped up. Lowering the volume and opening the door, my jaw dropped to see Donna standing in front of me. She was shivering and clutching her sides.

"Can I come in?" she quietly pleaded.

My heart pounded. I knew that Bill had sent Daryl, Donna's flame, to India on a business trip. He was thousands of miles away and his *bella* was no more than five feet from me…and I was in a stupor.

"Uh, sorry, sure… come on in. Make yourself warm. I was just making some tea. You want some?"

"Thanks, sure, I'd like something hot. I'm cold. Bill said you'd be staying here while he's gone. Daryl's gone too. You won't mind if I hang out for a while?"

"No problem." I stumbled out of her way. "Why don't you stand near the heater? You'll be warm in no time…I'll be back with tea," I mumbled, hurrying away so that my crimson flush wouldn't betray me. In the kitchen I took a few deep breaths to gather my composure.

When I came back Donna was dancing. She wore a flowing ankle-length dress, rich with dark colors. As her body floated around the room I watched, fascinated by her carefree movements.

"You're really good," I praised, after she had stopped and sat opposite me on a cushion. She smiled warmly.

"It's like you're part of the music," I added with admiration.

"Thanks. I was taught to be a part of everything around me. I'm an artist. Did you know that?"

"No."

"I thought Daryl would have mentioned that to you."

"To tell you the truth, I don't know Daryl very well. He's Bill's friend. We just know each other from the beach. He's so into, ah…" I hesitated. I was starting to fall apart, as I typically did in these situations. The intimate proximity was overwhelming me.

Donna came to my rescue. "Well, I've been with him for the past five months and he's very difficult sometimes. He never comes on straight."

"Yeah, that's one way of saying it, I guess. He crowds me."

"What's your birth sign, Frank?"

"I'm a Virgo."

"Really! Daryl's a Virgo too, but you're much different. You're more grounded and easy-going. Daryl likes to irritate people, especially with his know-it-all attitude. He constantly finds it necessary to impress everyone he meets."

"I've seen that too." I hesitated and then exclaimed, "Wow! I'm sorry! I forgot."

"What?"

"I have to go see a friend of mine down the coast in Pedro Point. Damn, I forgot all about it. Umm…I have to see him tonight, now, as a matter of fact. He's expecting me."

"Oh, I see. Well, would it be okay if I come with you?"

"Sure. I guess. Why not? Let's finish the tea and split."

Jake was not only a friend he was one of Bill's customers. He wanted to know what was going on with this guy Victor, plus Bill had made it clear that I was not to use the phone for business. Pedro Point was down the coast some twenty miles. The ride down was anything but smooth. My little black VW bug was whipped around in the storm and my heater wasn't working very well.

Inside the house, Donna was chilled again, and hung out near the heater while Jake and I went to the kitchen to talk.

Jake was curious. "Who's the woman?"

"She's Daryl's girlfriend."

"Too bad!" Jake grinned, and wet his lips.

"I know. Boy, do I know."

"She seems sweet on you," he teased, as we walked back to the living room where Donna stood near a table peering at a Ouija board.

"I'd sure like to think so."

"Do you ever use this?" Donna asked, pointing at the board.

"Nah, not really," Jake replied.

"I've used it a couple of times," I added. "It's kind of hokey. It never works."

"Is that so? I can make it work," she said enthusiastically. Then, with contrived innocence she casually brushed back her hair with the tips of her fingers and cast us a flirty smile. Jake and I caught her drift.

Not taking the bait Jake fired up a joint, took a hit, and passed it to her.

"No thanks," Donna said. "I get overpowered when I smoke pot. Can I use your Ouija board?" she asked sweetly.

"Sure, honey. Be my guest." Jake passed the joint to me.

"Good. Now I need a second person. Frank, why don't you join me?" she entreated, looking deep into my eyes. Her request was so demure I all but floated over to the table where she had placed the board.

For more than an hour we worked with the Ouija. Jake watched, amused that we were having so much success. I was also amused but in a different way. There was so much sexual tension in the room I was about to burst. Donna was holding Jake and I completely captive.

"We're so good at this Frank," she said. "I've never had so much success. We'll have to do this more often. I have a board at home."

Bleary-eyed, Jake stood up. "I've had it. I'm crashing. I've got to get up at four-thirty and go drive a truck." Jake's wife and kids were away visiting friends down the coast, so he added, "If you want to stay the night there are plenty of beds to choose from. See ya later. Nice to meet you, Donna."

Suddenly I was alone with this enchanting beauty. I wanted to say something that would impress her, but the weed Jake had provided was high quality and I was momentarily subdued. I didn't know what to say as she sat in front of me with a capricious look on her face.

"Hmm...why don't we stay the night, Frank? It's raining still, and Jake's house is quite comfortable."

"Fine. Sounds like a plan. There's... uh... two beds in the kids' room."

"Good, one for you, one for me. I'm tired. I'd like to sleep." She said the word "sleep" with such finality, I got the message loud and clear.

Entering the room first, I stared out the huge picture window. Storm clouds had parted, leaving the room awash in the lunar beams of a near full moon. Undressing down to my underwear, I got into one of the beds and doused the lamp, erotic thoughts coming over me in bits and pieces.

Donna entered the room as I covered up. She undressed in the dark, her body visible in flashes. Stripped naked, she came between the two beds and turned down her covers. Then she turned toward me and extended a hand.

I readily grabbed it and rose to my feet.

"Come. Keep me warm," she whispered, as our bodies met. "And, please take off your underwear."

I quickly complied. Reaching out in anticipation, she grabbed my hand and gently drew me down. Lying down beside her, I quickly wrapped around her thin body. Beams of moonlight lit up her face. I was captivated, but remained silent, content to just stare at her and think how just moments ago she had drawn a clear picture. Now we were in bed, preparing to make love.

"You'd like to have me, Frank?" she supposed, in a low voice.

How could I not? She was stunning. The only thing that stood in the way was Daryl, her boyfriend. I felt a twinge of guilt, but not enough to say no.

"Yes, definitely yes," I answered.

This was a dream come true and in the dream the woman wanted me. I could feel her desire and I was fully erect, although nervous. I wanted everything to go well, no mess-ups or mishaps. Ever so gently, I drew her in and pressed my body against her. She pulled my face into hers and in no time I was in a major swoon, craving to go deeper. For a few blissful moments nothing else seemed to matter to me. Life was on hold. All I had to do was let my passions take over, passions that had not been on fire for months. This was going to be a stupendous encounter. I was still high on the potent weed Jake had supplied and making love stoned was always a trip into higher realms, where everything is touch-sensitive, smell-sensitive, and taste-sensitive.

Enraptured, my toes already curled, lips pressing against lips, my hands caressing her creamy, smooth skin and descending deeper into a heat haze, I was totally blown away when I reached down to spread her legs and she held them shut.

I was unwilling to let up and persisted, but she reached down and grabbed my arm, pulling it away. Why was this happening, my mind begged? She wants me and she's stopping me. What's she up to?

I pulled back. "What's the matter?" I asked. But the pathetic sound of my voice crushed me. I was distraught and didn't want to feel this way, especially at this moment when I so wanted to stay in this dreamy bliss.

I waited for a reply. I had no idea what to say or what to add to the moment, or how to master the situation. I was totally unprepared for this fickle behavior.

Finally she spoke. "Not now, Frank. Be easy with me. Please," she said as she stroked my face, whispering, "Come upright. Come… Yes… That's it."

Something was looking up and I was in favor of that. "Whatever you want sweetheart," I thought to myself, quickly shifting gears with her. And as I rose, she directed me to straddle her hips and come completely upright on my knees. As soon I was in position, she stopped for a moment and gazed, and then reached up and took hold of my manhood.

I let out a deep sigh as delicious waves of energy collided with my body. She had no sooner started when my orgasm began—and ended. It was explosive, but I had come all too soon. I was completely dismayed by my poor performance.

I knew she hadn't planned to have sex with me in this fashion. A part of me knew our union seemed farcical, but I was so lost in the ideal of the moment, and so delighted that she had found a way to please me, that none of that mattered.

I fell beside her, my thoughts already returning to seduction. I was nowhere near ready to end the evening in her arms and fall asleep, so I wrapped her in my arms, drew her in gently, and began caressing her.

What really bothered me was I couldn't find the words to express my feelings to her: words about how lovely she was and how she thrilled me.

Why thoughts wouldn't come I didn't know, only that my mind was blank and I was frustrated in a new way, unable to come up with simple, earnest words to let her know what it was I wanted from her. I wanted to be inside her and feel those sensations, and was ready to continue. The first orgasm had come all too soon. I could do better, I thought. I'd show her.

But she stopped me. Caressing my face she looked deep into my eyes. In hushed tones she said, "No, not now, Frank...we need to sleep. Just lay beside me. OK? Hold me. We'll have sweet dreams. Come."

She had touched something inside my heart the first moment I had met her. And now, lying here in bed with her, my awakened sexual powers ran strong and urgent. I wanted to put them to test. I wanted her to open up to me and allow me to continue, but again words failed me. I was lost, ready to consummate, but locked in fear. Try as I may, bravery eluded me. All I could do was hold on to her as my body shook, and find a way to relax and calm my energy. It wasn't in me to force her or keep on persisting. That would ruin everything. Twitching and sighing with exasperation, I remained silent. Surprisingly, it wasn't too long before I drifted off, soothed by Donna's smooth curves nestled against my body.

When I awoke the next morning Donna was beside me in a deep sleep. I was suddenly wide awake. My thoughts ran wild, especially about Daryl. Donna was his woman. Last night I had ignored those thoughts. Maybe she was tired of his egotistical ways. Would she rather be with me? If that was the case then I wanted to talk with her about it. Or was she was the type of woman who played around and was only using me for her own satisfaction?

Unsettled, I got up and dressed. Deciding it would not be in my interest to wake her, I opted to go for a walk. Opening the door, I was greeted by a stiff, cold wind. Trudging down to the beach and through the dunes, I was full of questions: "What have I gotten myself into? And why am I so forlorn?" It was a beautiful day, and although I tried to stay focused on the coastal mountain ranges, the expansive beach, and the people walking in the distance, I couldn't shake my uneasiness. I told myself, "Daryl will be back. Donna will return to him. Face it, man. She doesn't want you."

At least the twinge of guilt I had first felt had dissipated. All I felt now was the cold, annoying wind that struck my face as I walked from one end of San Pedro beach to the other—over a mile. Crisp air filled my lungs, but collapsed my breath. Again, I couldn't shake the questions. "Why am I carrying on this way? Why do I need to ponder this so deeply?" As I pushed on, I grew more and more confused.

I was overjoyed, and yet, I felt dark and sullen. Stricken by uncertainty I asked myself, "Does Donna want me in her life? Is she just a coy woman out to tease me? And what about Daryl?—he'll be back soon enough. What do I say to Donna to convince her that I want to get to know her? And what if she would come my way? I want her to come my way. Or do I? I have to be careful; I have to watch out. God this is so much trouble— beautiful, pleasurable trouble. This is a mountain of trouble."

At the house, Donna was up and dressed. She was alone and was upset with me about this.

"Where were you, Frank? I thought maybe you'd left me here."

Unprepared for her attitude and full of guilt, my mind froze and my body stiffened, but I managed to say, "No, Donna. I wouldn't do anything like that. I took a walk on the beach, that's all. You were asleep and it was nice out. Would you like to go for a walk?"

"Not now. Maybe later." Her voice was terse and she gave me a cold stare.

"Are you hungry?" I asked.

"No. Come here," she commanded. She wrapped her arms around me, then took my hand and directed me over to a small sofa-bed piled high with cushions. Pushing them aside she lay down and beckoned me to join her.

"I just want you near me right now."

"Sure! Are you cold?" I quickly took my shoes off and wrapped my arms and legs around her.

"No…well, yes, but I'm fine."

We slept for a while and when we woke she was in a strange state—

again. I could not fathom her mood. She seemed depressed about something; maybe it was the weather. There was no sun in the sky, and I too was feeling under the weather. Perhaps it was *my* mood that was bothersome.

Hunger overrode my anxiety. "I'm hungry, Donna. Let's go back to the cottage. I've got plenty of food there."

As we drove back I was seized by turmoil. It would be a good time to talk to her about my feelings but I couldn't find the words. God only knows what she was thinking. We hardly spoke. When we came in the front door she startled me. Without saying a word she wrapped her arms around me and held tightly. Eyes fastened on mine, she asked me to kiss her.

The kiss said it all. And when she gasped and pulled me into her, I knew she wanted me. Piece by piece, we undressed each another. Again she surprised me and descended to the floor, taking me with her. I did all I could to accommodate her and was captivated as she moaned and hastily guided me. Once inside her, I was enraptured.

When she clutched my flanks and pulled me into her, I lost all concentration. I had wanted to seduce her, taking my time and doing so in my way. But again, I reached orgasm all too soon. I felt as I had last night: that I had failed her even though I was exhilarated by her sighs and moans, and coming inside her…so many conflicting emotions.

All was far from finished. Still erect, I wanted more. Her beauty and sexual desire invigorated me. My urge to continue became enormous.

Prepared to continue, I froze when she whined, "The floor, Frank, it's cold and it's hard."

"Let's go to Bill's room." I suggested.

"No."

She was rejecting me. "Would you rather we stop?" I asked.

"Yes."

Frustrated beyond belief and bewildered, I obeyed. I was in a confused daze as I began to dress. Looking at her as she slipped into clothes, I could tell she was unhappy about something. I felt it had something to do with me, or Daryl. Perhaps she was struggling with guilt? But all I could think to do was ask if she was hungry.

Over breakfast I learned Donna was nearly four years older than me—and this bothered me to no end. Intimidated by the age difference, I discarded all thoughts about asking her how she felt about me and if she might want to break up with Daryl. She was much too worldly; I was raw and unsophisticated—a beginner in every aspect of life, especially with women. How could I satisfy her if I knew so little about life, or how to satisfy her in bed? And, I was a fragile male who wanted to impress her. It seemed so terribly important.

When she invited me to her parent's house just blocks away to meet them, I jumped at the chance at first, and then was stymied because I didn't understand why she would want me to. Her father was a Bay Area sculptor of great renown. He was gracious, almost docile; her mother was aloof or timid. When Donna showed me her own artwork I felt hopelessly undone, miserable in fact. Who was I to comment on her paintings, other than to tell her I liked them? Actually, I was unimpressed by her work and didn't know what to say.

Underlying my intimidation were recurring thoughts of Daryl. He would be back from India soon—all six-foot-four inches of him.

A few months back, by chance, we had met up at the beach and he had invited me over to his apartment. When he found out I had taken a few yoga classes, he told me he had been into yoga for years and was a master of sorts. He showed me a few body-bending exercises and did them so effortlessly, and with such precision, that I could easily envision how he might apply his athleticism to a woman, especially a small, captivating woman like Donna. And, with an ego the size of Mount Tamalpais, I knew without a doubt that Daryl could apply his yoga skills to the art of seduction. I was no match, not even close, and that bothered me.

After visiting with Donna's parents she asked me to drive her home. It was early evening and once inside she said ominously, "It wouldn't be wise for us to see each other." The overcast day mirrored my mood. I backed off without protest. Our tryst was a one-time happening. I was not her type.

Before leaving she kissed me good-bye, the kiss sweet and sincere. Not wanting to walk away, I did so anyway. Even before I reached my car, I was wracked by loneliness so profound that it sent shivers throughout my body. Slumped in my car, I waited for relief to come: to be able to breathe freely again and to function without the empty feelings taking control.

Over the next few days I would have fallen apart if I hadn't been busy with work. There were so many times I wanted to call her, but I felt like a fool. What would I say? Yes, what would I say when I had failed to say what needed to be said the moment I had climbed into bed with her? God, how those thoughts plagued me.

About four months after that fling Bill asked me to come to his cottage for a talk. When I arrived Daryl was in the kitchen with Bill. When Daryl saw me his face contorted, and pointing a finger at me he trembled with anger, "You know… you're lucky Bill's your brother."

Playing dumb and keeping my distance I asked, "What's with you?"

"You damn well know what I mean," he shouted. "You fucked Donna, didn't you?"

I was stunned. My mind raced. "Christ! She told him. Why did she do that? I can't deny it. Not now. I've been caught. If I lie, he'll come at me. All I can do is offer truth; I had heard that the two of them broke off.

Ready to face the music I said, "Yes, I did. She came over here and, well, she seduced me. We made love." My matter-of-fact tone surprised even me.

Daryl didn't like what I'd said or the tone I'd used because he shouted back, "You sonofabitch," then stepped toward me, ready to attack.

Bill restrained him. "Cool it, man. She isn't worth the trouble. He told you what you wanted to hear. No fighting. Let things be."

"He didn't have to fuck her. He took advantage while I was gone. She was my woman," Daryl hollered. He wouldn't give up and came at me again.

I was scared, but more to the point, put out—not only by this dude, but with Bill too.

Bill had pulled a lousy stunt on me a few days earlier and I had come to his place mainly to confront him about that. Daryl's untimely arrival had complicated matters. Or had Bill planned this confrontation to throw me off? That would be just like him. No matter. I was angry with Bill and with Daryl's attitude and I was going to speak my mind!

"Tell me, would either of you have refused her if she had come on to you? Tell me. I'd like to know."

Bill was quick to respond. Standing between Daryl and me he shook his fist and bellowed, "You're way out of hand, Frank. Cool it right now."

Daryl was either in shock or he realized that I wasn't going to back down and was ready to fight him. He didn't say anything as Bill held him and continued going on at me.

"Don't go justify what you did. You screwed this man's woman while he was gone."

Fuming, I held my ground. "Yes, I did. She's not his woman any more so why are we carrying on? She came over here and I just didn't refuse her. That's all I'm saying."

"You're being a jerk and you'd better shut up, brother," Bill fired back.

"Fine! I'm being a jerk! You got my story. You buy yours and I'll buy mine. See ya."

As I turned and headed for the door I tossed back at him, "It's not very cool being here right now. I'll talk to you later about that other matter, Bill."

I calmed down once outside. Donna had not only seduced me, she had betrayed me. I was angry, but I excused her behavior. She was tired of Daryl's bad-trip ego and she wanted to rub his face into something rock-hard, like varnishing a cold, hardwood floor to which she applied Daryl's face as a brush. I wish I had been there to witness the argument that no doubt ensued between the two of them. I knew better than to seek Donna out now. She had reeled me in without a fight. What man would have resisted? She was mine for a few exciting moments and I was content with that. And finally, I had told the truth. I hadn't backed down, or lied my way out of it. That felt good.

CHAPTER TWO

WHATTA TEAM

SAN FRANCISCO, CA
NOVEMBER, 1967

A FEW DAYS AFTER the short-lived affair, Victor called. "The load's due in any day now. Come on down to 'Boss Angles' and see our setup. We can get acquainted."

Before catching a flight out to Los Angeles International that afternoon, I called Bill in Hawaii to tell him our man had finally called.

"Go ahead without me. The waves are too good to be true. Call if you run into any problems. I can fly to the mainland within twenty-four hours."

On the flight down, I thought about how strange it was that I would be handling my brother's business affairs without him present. Bill had told me from the beginning that we'd meet Victor together, but it wasn't turning out that way. Instead, just before he'd left for "sun and fun," Bill had given me a rundown on Victor: "Watch out. He's a sly dude, prone to deception." As for Victor's partner Andy, and his girlfriend Judy, Bill hadn't told me anything, because he hadn't met them.

I was amused when Victor rolled up to the pick-up area in a big, white Cadillac convertible. It was a classic, with gigantic tail fins and chrome ornaments. Immediately, I remembered Bill's words about Victor: "He's pretentious."

Victor jumped from the car and pumped my hand vigorously, then tossed my bag in the back seat. It was his smile—insidious, evasive, and full of mischief—that struck me. At an inch above six feet, lanky, and with long blond hair and a droopy mustache, he could have passed as Buffalo Bill. He even wore a white leather jacket with tassels. Clearly, he wanted to let everyone to know he was up to something: his car, his demeanor, the way he was dressed—all a dead give-away. We drove off, top down, wind blowing our hair, and ran smack into the evening rush hour traffic.

"So, Bill's taking in some waves?" he began. "As I let ya know, the load won't be here for a couple a days. I'll show ya the setup, the warehouse location and all that stuff, and introduce you to Andy and Judy. You ever been to this part of L. A?"

"No, Victor, I don't get down here at all."

"Well, you'll get to know this place real quick. I'll take you out to dinner tonight somewhere along Sunset Strip. Bill says you're a vegetarian?"

"Yeah, for the most part, but I eat fish."

"Good. We'll go to a seafood place. Judy likes fish, too. Not me. I like meat: steaks and things."

Every time I made eye contact with him he'd respond with a grin or a smirk and usually a remark that was either funny or macho. To me, underneath his panoply, he was just another insecure male.

We headed to the warehouse first. There wasn't much to see, just a small building they'd rented. Then we drove into the heart of Los Angeles. I was lost. I thought about the map I had brought down and the instructions Bill had given me. Later, I'd have to study it and become familiar with the whole area. It was part of the job. I had to advise Bill's customers about the quickest and safest routes in and out of the area.

Moments later I was meeting Victor's associate Andy. Andy was the epitome of suave and cool: tall, lean, good-looking, with wavy dark hair, and a good two inches taller than Victor. From his handshake to the tone of his voice and the heavy vibe he gave off, I felt that all would go well between us—so long as I didn't cross him. Judy was a cutie, a regular doll with blond hair, a fine figure, and a heady attitude. I had to pinch myself after meeting them.

"God, these people are right out of a gangster movie. Maybe they're Bonnie and Clyde reincarnates," I thought, as I showered.

Over dinner, Victor and Andy gave me a rundown on how they ran their business. Victor described his connection in Santana, just below Nogales, Mexico.

"This guy knows plenty of farmers," he said. "They've lots of *mota* for us, brother. Tons of it, according to my men."

Chato, Victor's Mexican connection, could do it all: buy the load—all 700 kilos—conceal it inside a special compartment of his truck, transport it to the border, and even cross the border with it. The contraband was to be delivered to Victor in Los Angeles.

"They front us the load. I keep it stored in the warehouse," he boasted over dinner.

My job was simple. I was to contact the customers when the time was right, then direct them down to Los Angeles, meet them, collect the funds, and get Andy to load them up. As soon as the 700 kilos were sold, I'd head home.

"Easy work, man. Just stay on top of things and we'll make a fortune," Victor said as we ate. "Did Bill tell you we'll get a load a week once we get going?"

"He said at least a couple of times a month," I replied, fending off his brashness with a lie.

"Hey, we'll get 'em to run us a load once a week, man. There's so much weed down south your brother won't be able to sell 'em fast enough. Tell 'em Andy."

Barely breaking his stride while chowing down, Andy glanced up. "We saw seven, eight tons at one ranch alone, the same at another. Our connection knows several ranchers who grow the stuff." Summing things up in a cool, confident tone he added, "We'll never run out."

Surging with excitement and attempting to sound cool myself I conceded, "Right on, man. We'll have to be careful though. That's a lot of work. We don't want to get caught."

"Hey, we ain't gonna get caught." Victor patted me on the back chuckling, "All we gotta do is get it here. That's the Mexicans' job. The rest'll be a piece of cake."

The gang and I spent close to a week in Los Angeles getting acquainted. While waiting, I made it a point to study Victor as Bill had instructed. Victor wanted me to think he was tough. At the same time, he tried to come across as a nice guy. What I saw was a man who sucked up to people and tried too hard to prove he was the boss of the operation. Around me he was cordial, but at the same time, a bit gruff. Around Judy, he was sweet, but cautious. He acted the part of the tough guy around his associate Andy.

Judy was everything a drug-moll ought to be, including childish. She was also temperamental as hell, and tried to come across as dumb. But she was smart when she wanted to be, which was the case as we waited for the load and tension mounted. She let loose on Victor in front of Andy and me one afternoon, creating a timely argument over nothing. Her onslaught sent Victor running for cover.

When it was over and Victor had been notified that his brooding was not going to be tolerated, Andy, who had watched the whole scene, suggested that they do what they had to do as "men:" "Let's get off our asses, go down south, and find Chato."

Without further argument, Victor headed out the door with his partner swearing, "I'm going to grab that man by the *huevos* and direct him north. I'll kick his ass across the border if I have to… Stay here!" he ordered me sternly. "Keep Judy company."

That didn't go over well with me. I knew that seven days locked up in a motel room in the heart of L.A. would be more than I could stand. Within hours I was flying home, figuring that if and when they got their shit together, I'd return. Bill agreed with me when I updated him.

Four days later Victor called me at Bill's place, steaming mad.

"Where in the hell are you, man? You're supposed to be here with Judy. You left her all alone."

"Hey. You know where I am. I'm right by the phone waiting for your call."

"You better listen up, dude. The load's in. It's sitting in the warehouse waiting to be sold, and you ain't here. I gotta bunch of Mexicans who don't like waiting for their money. You know, the money you're supposed to take care of? You know, if you were here, you'd be doing it, but you ain't here, brother."

"OK Victor. OK. Mellow out. Everything's ready. A few phone calls and I'm out of here. I'll be there early tomorrow with cash for a hundred. You can count on it. OK? The rest of the people will be coming within the next day or two."

"You better be telling the truth brother, or I'll get on the phone and call some people and sell this load myself."

After hanging up I called Jake, Bill's customer, whom I had talked with the night before.

"Victor called. Are you set to go?" I asked.

"Everything's ready. My truck's gassed and my money's here in the house. Where do I go, man?"

"I got an idea. I'm in a bind. Victor wants me down there—now. It's getting late. I'll call the rest of Bill's people, then ride down with you. OK?"

"Sure. I'd like the company," Jake said.

"Good. See you in a few."

With everything under control I drove down the coast to meet Jake.

"We'll be there in about seven or eight hours," Jake assured me as we drove off around eleven that evening.

"Good. This guy Victor has me going."

"So you wanted to come back and play with that fine-looking lady you brought down a few days ago?" Jake teased, after I piled in his pickup.

I grimaced just thinking about her.

"No. She's out of the picture…Los Angeles was a drag. I didn't like being there. That's all."

"Yeah, but I hear they have warehouses full of grass down there," Jake quipped.

"Yeah, but right now my ass is in a sling if I don't pull this off right. Victor might sell the load if I don't get going."

"Your brother should be handling this. Is he coming back soon?"

"Hard to say. I agree though. I left a message with Bill that Victor came through, but I don't know if he's coming to L. A. or not. All I know is Victor's got the dope, so he says, and I got the pressure."

"Hey, relax, man. We'll get there in time and I'll work the first deal with you. This will be the first one, won't it?"

"Yeah. You're right. It's the first one coming up, but things aren't too groovy."

"So, lighten up. Let's smoke some of the Old Man's stuff. Here, I brought a couple of joints with me."

"Right on." I lit up, taking a deep toke. "Uh-huh, one of Roller Bill's doobies!"

"Who else!" Jake answered, smiling.

"There's nothing like the best." I took another toke and began to settle down as Jake and I launched into conversation.

Both of us were excited by our prospects. His plans were simple.

"I'm going to enjoy making some real money and cut this eight-to-five crap. It's like having to take a little poison every day. No thanks. It's hard to imagine how all those people get by thinking that's the best way to go."

"It's madness. There's nothing wrong with having a job, but it's the way in which people push themselves. They're sheep. They just act the way the system wants them to act: the usual mindless crap."

"But Frank, they need that mindless crap in their lives. They're sheep, don't forget. We all know what sheep do. They eat and shit all day, and pretend to know what they're doing."

Although Jake and I bore a certain resemblance, he was some three inches taller and close to six years my senior. We had met four years earlier at United Parcel Service. He had been a supervisor on the loading docks. My first day there, he stuck his head into the truck I was unloading and introduced himself, saying he knew my brother Bill from work and surfing.

During my time at UPS, Jake and I had gone sailing a few times and had shared a few beers. Over the past few weeks I had spent some enjoyable time with him and with his family. He had two children: Wendy, his eight year-old daughter, who wanted to learn to surf and was already a hardy swimmer; and Johann, his four year-old son, who loved monsters and playing Tarzan. Both kids were handsome and strong, as was their mother Joanne, a dedicated woman who was a cooking whiz.

After dining with them several times, I taught Joanne how to prepare macrobiotic meals. They were a friendly family, easy to get along with, and Joanne was one of the most honest and sincere women I'd ever met. I could be myself around her.

Jake had quit UPS a few months back and had gone back to his job driving for a small trucking company. The pay was better. Plus, that summer he had sold the family house. When Bill came along with his new connection, Jake had asked to come in as a buyer. He had ten grand to invest, ready cash. Bill agreed.

"If people weren't sheep," Jake continued, "we wouldn't be so inclined to be doing what we're doing. Thanks to them, we have to go to work to save them. You know...then we can spike their food with some real grass instead of that green stuff they eat in their salads all the time."

"Yeah. That would get them to thinking. Meanwhile, I've better things to do, like gettin' in some cruising," I responded, as we passed the reefer back and forth. Exhaling, I added, "People need more time to themselves. If only they wouldn't pressure themselves and would build more quality time into their lives, that would help. They've been fooling themselves all too long, Jake, all too long. Christ, some of them never think to act on their own."

"Yeah! Them sheep have been drowning themselves long enough. And them cities, they can have 'em. Too many people crowded together, like sheep drowning in a river. That's why I'm getting that cabin up in the Russian River area."

"Go for it," I said. He had told me about getting a great deal on a cabin near Jenner, at the mouth of the Russian River.

"It makes sense getting away from all these madmen. People chase dollars like dogs chase sheep. Funny isn't it," I said looking over at Jake, "we're chasing dollars too, but we have more of an agenda than those sheep do."

We talked non-stop all the way to L.A., hacking at the government and making plans for the future. The hours passed quickly as we rolled steadily south toward the land of smog and compromise. At 7:00 a.m. we stopped for gas. I called Victor to tell him we were almost there. It didn't seem to matter. He was still upset.

"Just get here, man. These Mexicans are startin' to get uptight with us. I keep telling 'em I'll have their money. And right now I have nothing to give 'em. They don't understand why I don't have anything for 'em. You got that?"

"Come on, Victor. Christ, I'm right here in town. You'll have seventy-five hundred in cash to start. There'll be more by evening."

"Just get here."

"I'll see you in less than an hour," I said, slamming the phone down, angry that he was being such a hard-ass.

When I arrived, Victor was still in a pissy mood and suggested we get moving right away.

"So, ya got some cash?" Victor's face was wry when he greeted me. The motel room they had chosen was sleazy and rundown, and Victor's room reeked of cigarette smoke. The furniture was old and offensive. I was uncomfortable the moment I walked in.

"Yeah, just like I promised." I explained that Jake was at a restaurant up the street and his truck was down the block ready to be loaded.

Andy was standing nearby and immediately asked for the keys. "Jake wants a hundred kilos, right?"

I forked the keys over. "Yeah, a hundred even," I replied, relieved that Jake would soon be underway and that Victor was no longer in my face.

"Go load 'em up, man. I'll count the dinero," Victor ordered, as I sat on the bed and pulled the bills from my jacket pocket: seventy-five hundred dollars, all in twenties.

"Ya look tired. Why don't ya get a room here in the motel and get some sleep? When's the next guy due in?" Victor asked, as he counted.

"Sometime this afternoon or early evening."

"Good! This should hold Chato off 'til then," he smirked. "Go for some zees, man. Rest up. It's not gonna be busy for a while, right?"

When my head hit the pillow I didn't wake up until the phone rang around three in the afternoon. Two of Bill's customers were calling. They had money for one hundred and fifty kilos. By five o'clock I'd taken care of them. Feeling better, but still tired, I went back to sleep.

When my phone rang again, it was Bill's main customer Mack, a man I had known from high school. He came on strong.

"Hey brother, what's going on down there? Jake just came in. I just looked at what he brought in. It sucks."

"Sucks? What are you saying?"

"The load, buddy, it's loaded—and I mean loaded with sugar."

Bolting upright I snapped, "What the hell do you mean?"

"Just what I said. Don't you know what sugared weed is? Have you looked at the stuff? It's a mess. I don't know if I can sell it."

Mack's message stung my senses. Bill had told me to check out the load before I did anything. I had failed to do that and knew instantly that Bill's wrath would come down on me. And now Mack was telling me that the kilos were loaded with sugar. Bill and I had gone over every detail of the operation, but not this one. Surely he had forgotten. If he had said something about watching out for sugar-loaded kilos, I'd have been all the more aware of how to proceed with that dummy, Victor. I didn't know what I was up against, but it sounded bad, according to Mack.

As my mind raced, I realized something else. Victor had pressured me because he already knew that the kilos had sugar in them. I'd been duped.

"Hold it, Mack. Let me clear my brain. I was napping when you called. This sounds bad. Explain what you mean—there's sugar in the stuff?"

"Boy, you don't know what's happening, do you?" Mack said, in his usual sarcastic tone. A short man with curly blond hair and piercing blue eyes, I could picture him in my mind's eye, rolling his eyes in distain as he dropped the news.

"It's an old Mexican trick. They use water and sugar to weigh down the kilos, to give them extra weight."

"I've never heard of that. Fuck! Bill told me to look at the load. Victor played a pressure game on me. Damn, it sounds like I'm in trouble man."

Mack was silent for a moment and then said in a measured tone, "Victor's the one who's in trouble. Believe me. If your brother were there, he'd probably walk away from this load."

In high school Mack had had a certain infamy. He liked to fight back then. He had decked a good friend of mine—who stood six-foot-four and weighed two hundred-twenty pounds—with one sucker punch, as he'd done with several others who'd gotten in his way. I had complete respect for him. Right now, I wanted him on my side.

"Victor insisted I take it easy once I got down here with Jake's money. He'd told me, "Go get some rest, man. Andy will take care of the load." So what do I do?"

Mack saved me from further embarrassment. "I can sell 'em, but not at the price Victor wants. He's going to have to come down a dime. Then I can move 'em."

"Great, but how can I do that? I don't know how to negotiate with him. Bill's not here."

"Hey brother, it doesn't matter. Victor bullshitted you. He knows the grass is sugared. So do the Mexicans. They know it's hard to sell. They'll gladly come down in price as soon as you tell 'em you know there's sugar in the load."

"I hear you, Mack." Suddenly things were looking up. "I'd better call Bill and tell him what's happening."

"No matter what happens, Bill's going to be upset," Mack said. He hesitated, then advised, "Hold off man. We can handle this together."

"What do you have in mind?"

"How many kilos are left?" Mack asked. We worked out a plan of attack.

After showering I headed over to Victor and Andy's room to confront them. Victor's usual grin turned sour as I walked in and said grimly, "We have a serious problem here. That is, *you* have a problem, Victor. The load is full of sugar, according to Mack. He's quite upset, and now that I'm *rested*, I'd like to go to the warehouse and see just how bad the load is. I'm not going to sell any more of them until we do."

Victor's stood silent, his grin completely gone. But Andy was cool and quickly covered his partner's inability to respond to my charges. "That's news to us. Let's go and see it."

Victor remained silent. Both of them knew the load was sugared. I didn't want to make a big scene. I only wanted to get out of this jam. "Just follow Mack's instructions," I told myself.

At the warehouse we pulled off the tarps and could immediately see that the wrapped kilos, normally light green in color, were stained dark. Opening a couple as though I had done this many times before, I saw granules of sugar. Each kilo smelled of ammonia, as Mack said they would, and I pointed all of this out to Victor and Andy while they stood nearby watching me.

"Those fucking Mexicans," Victor spat out, as I showed him a sugared kilo. "We didn't know about this."

"I can't sell them like this," I said flatly. "They're really bad." I waited in silence for a response.

Andy spoke first. "Sure you can. Everything has a price. We'll talk to the Mexicans and see if they'll come down."

"They'll come down," Victor said, acting the part of the wronged dealer, "I'll pay 'em less. Chato will just have to eat it. That sonofabitch!"

Mack was right. We had them just where we wanted them. It was my move next. "I'll talk with Jake and Mack and see if we can set a price everyone will be satisfied with."

Back at the motel I called Mack. "It worked perfectly, brother. They'll come down a dime. Are you sure you can move them? They're really messy. They lied through their teeth, but I didn't call 'em on it."

"Good work. At sixty-five, I can sell 'em, but I won't be able to come up with any front money. No one wants to put up cash for shit like that. Can you dig it?"

"I thought we were out of the woods with the price reduction."

"We are, man. Bill has the cash. Do you know how to get it?"

"Yeah, but I think he'd be pissed off."

"Well, let's go brother. I promise you I'll be able to sell them. Just get 'em to me."

"How am I going to do that, Mack?"

"You get to Bill's money, pay off Victor, and I'll get a couple of drivers down there to bring 'em back. We'll rent a car and a trailer. I'll give you all the help you need."

Early the next morning, Victor drove me to the airport. By four that afternoon, I was back in Los Angeles. I'd gone to Bill's hiding place and taken the amount needed. Victor was paid off and true to Mack's word, I was put in touch with two people, a young woman and her male friend, who had flown down that morning. The business of renting a car and trailer fell to me.

The next morning, Andy and Victor loaded up the rental trailer and Mack's people headed north with the load. Four days later, Mack handed over the money, Bill's profit and my earnings—two bucks a kilo.

Arriving home the next day, Bill found out through Mack what I had done and called me to his cottage.

"Mack told me everything." Bill's anger was obvious, his face riddled with contempt. I was nervous and wary; we circled each other like gunslingers. He practically spat on me saying, "Why didn't you call and tell me there was a problem?"

"Mack suggested I hold off. I was in a jam and had to do something."

"So you chose to use my money!" he railed. Bill then paced the room, carefully choosing his next words: "Can't you understand I use front money to buy the load? I never use mine."

"Yes…I mean…no. Look Bill, I thought I was handling it the best way

I could." I felt small and meek, the way Bill often made me feel.

He raged on, each word biting. "If I was going to use my money to buy the load, I'd be charging eighty-five instead of seventy-five. That's the middleman rate. You got that? If I pay for them, I make the dime. Where's the extra dinero for me, Frank? Where is it?"

Sighing, I responded dryly, "I guess it went up in sugar," hoping he'd grab at the humor.

"No, Frank. You're not getting it. You used my money." He harped on at me anger contorting his face.

"I know I did," I interjected, "but I came through, right? You made a good profit and I put your money back where you stashed it. I see your point. Can't you see mine, too? What would you have done if you were there?—which you weren't, Bill. You were busy catching waves. I called, remember, and left you a message!"

"Cut the crap. I'd have handled it differently, plus you never called back to tell me there was a problem."

"Fine. What can I do now that all is said and done? What about Victor? What are you going to do about him? He pulled the fast one on us."

"Let me worry about him. Number one, I'll be all over him the next time. I'll be there. You can be sure of that. We'll inspect the next load together."

The confrontation over, I felt good. I had let Bill know that had he been there this problem would not have happened, and that I did the best thing possible under the circumstances. What bothered me was that Bill hadn't admitted to being at fault for not being there from the very beginning. What also hit home was that I had successfully completed the job and had made a much-needed profit.

The next time we saw Victor and Andy was in Tucson, Arizona. At Chato's insistence they had changed their base of operation. Flying down just after the New Year, Bill and I, along with Victor and Andy, headed directly to their new warehouse. Seven-hundred red, cellophane-wrapped kilos lay on the concrete floor, a large tarp covering them. As Bill inspected the load, Victor smiled brightly, assuring him that we could expect a lot more of the same.

"They look great Bill, like the kilos we made the hash with," I said as we inspected them.

After a random inspection proved them worthy, I dropped Bill off at the airport, and then stayed behind to work alongside Andy and Victor.

Bill had a different plan this time. He planned to purchase a portion of the load with his money and allow Jake to invest his capital and profits. Bill had me collect front money from Mack before coming down and Jake would then transport his kilos north, as well as the two hundred and fifty Bill and Mack had purchased. He was also to drive back and pick up another two hundred and fifty. The remaining two hundred I was to sell to two customers. They were to come to Arizona, purchase a hundred each, then transport them in their own vehicles.

During the month of December, Jake had driven up to Truckee and found a way to skirt the California Agricultural Inspection Station nearby: the only state inspection that stood in our way. Fortunately, there were no border inspections in Arizona and Nevada.

From start to finish, it took me six days to sell the entire load. When I flew back to the Bay Area, I had a nifty profit tucked away and had accomplished the job with relative ease.

Two weeks later, Victor came through with seven-hundred kilos of the same quality. Bill flew down with me, inspected the load, spent a day, and then departed. Jake, Bill, and Mack bought most all the kilos. A lone customer bought a hundred.

Before I left Arizona, Victor assured me his man would be ready to roll every week with seven-hundred kilos. When I told Bill this he said, "We'll see. This guy Victor is nothing but mouth." I knew what he meant, but still figured we were well on our way to a once-a-week business enterprise. And I was well on my way to fulfilling my dreams. When this realization hit, a surge of energy flowed through me and shook my body.

In early February, with everything set for the next load to arrive, Bill called, ordering me to come see him right away. Our business was about to take a nasty turn.

"We have a big problem," he announced as soon as I walked in the door. "Victor and Andy are in jail."

"What?" I was stunned.

"You heard me. Judy called last night. They screwed up on the way to Arizona. They got stopped for speeding by the "Man" and Andy mouthed off to him. They had fifteen grand on them, along with some grass and hash. Judy wants me to bail Victor."

"Where did they get caught?"

"Somewhere in southern California, but that doesn't matter. I'm going to bail Victor. His bond is twenty-five grand. Judy will take care of that. All she needs is $2500, ten percent for the bondsman." Bill explained bond procedures to me, then handing me an envelope full of cash, he added matter-of-factly, "Send this money through Western Union under her lawyer's name. Here's the address."

"What about bail for Andy?"

"He's gone. Judy said he was on parole. They're sending him back to San Quentin."

"San Quentin! God! Whatta team! This is really crazy. It's one stupid story. Why in the hell speed if you're carrying? Talk about burning bridges!"

"It could get worse. Let's move on this right away."

"Won't there be a lot of heat on Victor?"

"I'm sure he'll have some. We'll see when he gets out. Just get this money to his lawyer for now."

Three weeks later Victor remained in jail. Judy told Bill that Victor's lawyer had kept the bond money as a retainer. Bill was unwilling to send another $2,500 to free Victor. Judy was mad as hell—at Bill, of course. Bill had been correct: the stupid part wasn't getting any better. Victor had blown it and would have to get himself out of trouble.

I had doubts about what might happen next as the days rolled by and

Victor remained in jail. There was an easy solution. All Bill had to do was to bypass the lawyer and send twenty-five hundred directly to Judy, and Victor would be out and back in operation. Bill was surely aware of this, but why he didn't follow up I'd soon find out. Meanwhile, I was getting tenser by the day.

Bill was also getting mighty impatient. We all were. He called me a few days after learning that Victor's lawyer had kept the bond money as a retainer and asked me to come to his cottage. We discussed the problems created by those two clowns: what were the implications of having our two associates behind bars? Bill made a decision and then pitched a business proposition for Jake and me to consider. Bill was going to pull a fast one on Victor and I was in agreement, if only to get the business rolling again. After all, Bill was the boss and in this case had invited me into this conspiracy. And that gave my self-esteem a boost, even though I knew we'd be creating a bit of bad karma. It also gave me insight about what to expect in this business between brothers. The next day, Bill and I drove up to Jenner to meet with Jake at his new dwelling.

We arrived around noon. Jake and Joanne greeted us and showed us the property they had recently rented. The previous owner had had a vegetable garden and Joanne planned to revive it come spring. It was a cool, clear California winter day—more spring-like than winter: a perfect time for what the three of us had in mind— conspiracy.

Bill laid out the plan to Jake. "I know where Victor's connection lives. He introduced him to me back in December when I went to Mexico with him."

"Victor's a very generous man," Jake said snidely. "I guess you're going to use him?"

"Let's look at it this way. Victor's in jail. Like Frank pointed out the other day, we didn't ask him to get busted. He messed up on his own. That's his problem. I tried bailing him. I'm not his keeper. I don't trust the situation and I'm not going to send any more money down south. His attorney used the bail money I sent as a retainer."

"I hear you!" Jake cracked a sly grin.

"I'm going to Mexico. I want you to come with me," he said to Jake.

"We'll meet up with this guy Chato and see if he'll work with us directly. Frank's going to wait here. If things go the way I figure, we'll be getting a warehouse in Tucson and bringing up a few loads without Victor around to interfere. Frank can drive your truck to Tucson when the time comes."

"When do we leave?" Jake was all for the plan.

Bill knew he was pulling a fast one on Victor. He had already told me he'd compensate him when he got out. Jake and I agreed to work with Bill. We wanted to get going and make money. Why not? It wasn't our fault the "Whatta Team" had screwed up.

A few days later Bill called with good news. Chato, he said, was only sorry that his good *amigo* Victor was in jail, but meanwhile he was willing to work with us until his *amigo* returned. Within a few hours, I was headed for Tucson in Jake's truck.

The next evening, I met up with them at their motel.

"That's it, guys. Everything will work out with Chato. I'm flying home tomorrow," Bill informed us. "Frank, you can help Jake find a warehouse, okay? I'll be back when you're ready."

Jake was a persistent man. We inspected potential warehouses daily. It took us two weeks of serious searching, but our tenacity paid off. We rented a warehouse in an isolated area near the southeast edge of town, away from the hustle and bustle. It was a *choice* location. Movements from all directions could be monitored.

Jake had used the ruse that his father owned a small trucking company and we had to find a substation in Tucson. It worked. The broker never asked about the business we were up to. When the papers were ready, a cashier's check to cover six months rent was handed over and we had one sweet location that was safe to operate from. Knowing we were finally in business I joked with Jake, "We're official, brother. We're the UPS: 'United

WHATTA TEAM

Pot Service'!"

The following day Bill arrived and made the arrangements. Chato approved the location and the following evening a load of seven hundred kilos was transported to Tucson. We met up with Chato and his crew at a small truck stop a mile from the new depot. The driver, as instructed, left the key on the floor. Jake made the pick-up, while Bill and I followed in a rental car.

A few minutes later we were tucked safely away inside the depot and ready to unload. Curious, I immediately crawled under the rig to check it out as Bill and Jake prepared to assist.

"God! Look at this, guys," I exclaimed, after taking a peek.

Jake moved in alongside me and shook his head as did I. Bill joined us as we looked over the simple method the Mexicans had used to conceal the contraband. The kilos were held in place by wooden slats placed across the hollow underbody of the center-frame, which formed a lip to either side. The slats were tightly attached to the lower lip of each and fit together tightly on edge, except at the end where two or three slats had worked loose. It was easy to spot the contraband through the crevices. It was a mystery how this load had escaped the attention of the customs agents.

"Yeah, I see the problem," Bill said, as we focused a beam from the flashlight on the openings.

"Maybe the slats were in place at the crossing station, then worked loose on the trip to Tucson," I suggested.

"If not, then Chato somehow avoided a sure bust," Jake laughed. "Maybe Chato pays those customs boys off."

Bill wasn't too happy. "I'll go over this with Chato. Let's get this load out and get the truck back. We have a long night ahead of us."

Within two hours we were done. Jake drove the truck back and he and Bill met up with Chato and his men at the café. When they returned, Bill had some exceptional news: Chato would deliver a double load to us in two weeks—fourteen hundred kilos!

Bill changed the investment procedures yet again. He purchased two hundred outright and Mack came up with front money for two hundred.

Jake bought the remaining kilos. Bill was fair with me when he allowed me to buy two dozen. Along with a dollar extra a kilo for driving up with Jake, I would make a tidy profit.

It was now my job to accompany Jake home, for which I was paid a dollar extra per kilo. I enjoyed the traveling. It was spring and the desert was in full bloom. During the next two months Jake and I would journey north three times, once in his truck, then twice more in a new Chevrolet van with a V-8 engine that he and Bill had purchased to handle the fourteen-hundred kilo loads. Jake wanted a sophisticated setup for the interior of the new van. He paid two cabinet-makers to convert the van's interior into two levels. The bottom section held the kilos and the top was made into sleeping quarters. Each level had its own locking doors. The new setup provided complete concealment of the van's contents; we were pleased with ourselves. Jake went all out, adding overload shocks and split mufflers for added horsepower.

A truck driver by trade, Jake loved being behind the wheel. Driving suited him well. When he faded, which was seldom, I took a turn at the wheel. We'd always leave in the early morning and arrive back in the Bay Area around four the following day, spending a night in Tonopah, a small hamlet in Nevada.

I really liked the way the three of us were willing to sit down together and problem-solve. Safety was what we wanted. In this business we had to be in sync with one another, like the night I was stopped by a police officer in Tucson because one headlight was out. The guy was a jerk. I was stoned and he probably knew it because my eyes were bloodshot and I kept smiling. The van was registered under Jake's name and the officer was all over me. What was I doing there in Arizona? How come you have this man's van? On and on he went. I gave him the phone number to our motel and Jake's room number. He had his dispatcher call. Meanwhile, I told the officer what I was up to and when he got back to his dispatcher, Jake's story and my story matched up perfectly. The next day we had the headlight fixed. Overall, we had avoided suspicion: no names were taken just a fixit ticket—we were clean. All three of us were on an equal basis and looking out for one another, especially Jake and me. When I got back to the room, both of us grinned and had a good laugh. We had passed a sudden test by being on top of things, the brotherly way.

This was just one situation that reminded us how important it was to keep our minds free: to be willing to use our imagination and be prepared with a good cover-story for our movement—and to go over this with the brother you're working with. We didn't want to learn the hard way. When paranoia surfaced, we fell into the roles we had devised: we were rock hunters, returning from vacation. Jake bought a book about rock hunting and we studied it to become familiar with the basics.

In spite of our best efforts, problems arose. We hadn't considered the emotional baggage we all pack around. Jake fell into a real funk on the first trip. While I was busy watching the scenery, he began to mope, falling into the deepest depression I'd ever seen. I related to his seriousness; I too, was serious. But I had to learn how to deal with his funks. When depression descended, there was no talking to him. He'd grow quiet, radiating "the-monster-within" vibes. His reticence would last for hours.

My first encounter with Jake's depression was a real challenge. His surliness made me think I'd done something to make him angry. But, by the next morning, his depression was gone. He remained quiet for the rest of the trip, but no longer oozed animosity.

Later, at the conclusion of the delivery, I visited Jake and his family in Jenner. When Jake was away on an errand one afternoon, I had a talk with Joanne about him. She confided that he'd had a miserable childhood. His father had abandoned him shortly after Jake was born. His mother, unable to cope, put Jake in a foster home on the San Juan Islands near Seattle. His mother would visit from time to time, but other than that, Jake had been on his own. She now lived in San Francisco, and one day I accompanied Jake on a visit with her. It was a beautiful sunny day and she was outside tending her small garden. When we walked up, she hardly gave Jake the time of day. I was shocked. Clearly, she wanted to be left alone. Although Jake knew his mother struggled to maintain her emotional equilibrium, it visibly hurt him not to be acknowledged by his own mother. Joanne had told me his mother had spent time in a mental facility and it was evident she was out of touch with reality. And, every time Jake stopped to see her, his mood would grow dark and somber.

After seeing first-hand Jake's problems with his mother, I learned not to take his moods personally. I'd just wait and try to ride out the depression. He'd always return to his usual self, most often the next day. When he wasn't locked into this lower, altered state, we often had constructive talks. For the most part, traveling with him was pleasant. We were both captivated by the desert and its desolate, mystical, presence.

Each time we headed south to Tucson, there was a waiting period. We'd get a motel with a kitchenette and pack in some food. In the morning, we'd throw the Frisbee; in the evening, we'd play cards. In between times, we'd trip out on long, dusty rides in the desert, stoned on the weed Jake never forgot to bring with him. Late one afternoon, perched on the top of the van, we watched as desert clouds turned shades of mauve and pink as the sun descended and a full moon rose. We were tranquilized by the quietness and beauty of this desert setting.

Unlike Jake, the emotional baggage that caught up with me mostly concerned my breakups with women. Pangs of loneliness and other emotional garble hit me from time to time, but never locked up my mind the way Jake's did. I had come to understand that these pangs I suffered from were directly related to my upbringing, but I lacked the tools to effectively deal with my past. Mom was one mean woman, and yet, she had a loving side to her. Why couldn't she be more at peace about life? Men were monsters, she had concluded, and she made sure to keep them at a distance. She never dated or sought a relationship after Dad abandoned her. She just ranted and raged at us, belittling us, it seemed, for being men.

The books I poked into for guidance all pointed me in one direction: your past follows you around like a shadow. You must be willing to look into your past and resolve the trauma and the hate that was imprinted on you. Brother Ray and I talked a lot about Mom. He too was mortified by women and had yet to have a meaningful relationship. We both concluded she had a powerful influence over us and we had every right to be wary of her—and women in general. Mom used guilt to manipulate us every chance she could, instilling enough guilt and shame in us to last us a lifetime. That was one of the many reasons we stayed away from her. It actually made matters worse once I'd moved out on my own, because I'd feel guilty when she'd call and berate me for not calling. If only I could get her to smoke a joint, chill out, and see life differently. The bottom line was that the best way to deal with mom was to stay way from her. No wonder intimacy with women overwhelmed me.

I wanted a woman in my life more than anything, but women baffled me. I suspected that the abuse I received from my mother was instrumental in triggering these emotions. What I wanted, and knew I had to do, was to read more books. But when I'd read self-help books I was overcome by painful emotions, which made me afraid to continue reading. It was a "damned if you do, damned if you don't," dilemma.

In late April, Jake and I brought up the second of two double-loads. Bill flew to Tucson and before Jake and I departed for the Bay Area, the three of us met in Nogales. Nogales was actually a twin city, one to the north in the U.S. and one to the south in Mexico. We then met up with Chato on the south side, along with two of his colleagues. While Bill and Jake negotiated, I remained quiet and studied the proceedings. Chato was far from serious. He joked around and constantly had a mischievous side, unlike his companions who were quiet and withdrawn. We ate together, drank a few beers, and Chato told Bill he'd have another double load sometime in mid-May.

As the meeting ended Bill slipped Chato a bag of money, telling him there was no need to count it. It was all there in hundreds: a thousand dollars in each plastic bag. Chato had come to trust us. When we left, an air of camaraderie hung in the air and I felt confident that business with this man would continue for a long time. It did, but not the way I had anticipated.

Two days later Jake and I arrived back in the Bay Area. Bill greeted us with a double-sized grin the second we came in the door.

"There's a shortage of kilos, dudes. We're going to move all of them today. You watch. Frank, I want you to work with Brother Ray. Go unload the truck in the number two garage. Ray has the keys to Mack's van. Load it with three hundred and be careful. One of you watch the street while the other loads. Go at an easy pace. Okay?"

Ray and I worked at a smooth pace and had Mack's load ready two hours later. Mack was hyped when we handed him the keys. Throughout the rest of the day and into the night, Ray and I worked efficiently. Michael, a customer of Bill's was next. He took off with two hundred. Soon, Mack returned for three hundred more. Two other customers took a hundred each. Then Michael returned after Mack was loaded. Each customer received a promised amount, and by midnight the kilos were gone and all the money had been collected.

Amazed and exhausted, I took my share and departed. Bill had once again allowed me to invest most my profits and I had a neat pile of cash.

Back in February I had purchased a sailboat, a lightweight racing vessel, extremely fast and made of plywood. It hadn't cost much—fourteen hundred dollars, to be exact. I'd been drooling over it for the past two months. It was a class boat, an International 210. Several of my sailing pals and I had been racing these speed machines the previous three years and I really wanted one—if only to make use of it before purchasing a more desirable vessel. During my time off, I'd been getting it ready for the upcoming racing season.

A few days later, ready to test a new mainsail, I headed over to the Corinthian Yacht Club. Rigging the boat, I set out on a mid-morning solo-sail. It was a weekday, so no one was out sailing. I had the entire bay to myself. The spring weather was incredible: mild temperatures with light, even breezes. In no time at all I was on course for the middle of the bay, dazzled by its beauty as well as that of the Golden Gate Bridge. After I cleared Raccoon Straits, the city shoreline came into view, as did Alcatraz, along with Treasure Island. It was all too much: the San Francisco Bay, the city, the mecca of music and drugs, and the intoxicating beauty. At that moment, I was happy to be alive—happy to be free to do the things I wanted to do. All was going according to plan and perhaps by this time next year, the business I was engaged in would be history. That was the goal. Why not stick to it?

CHAPTER THREE

THE LONG HOT SUMMER

TUCSON, ARIZONA
JULY, 1968

"I'm not going to be responsible for the two grand you gave him last week," Bill said hotly to Jake over a payphone. "That's on you, Jake. The man has problems. We don't know what they are. Go ahead and rent a warehouse in Phoenix. Get the load and come back immediately." Bill was emphatic and to the point.

I was hovering near Jake's elbow, waiting to hear what had gone down. Jake's face was expressionless as he hung up. It was the first week of July and the temperature was over a hundred degrees. We were both sweating profusely, although the heat wasn't the only reason.

"What's up, brother?" I asked nonchalantly, trying to keep my jitters under control.

I could tell Jake was wound up tighter than a coil ready to spring loose. We had good reason to be concerned. We'd arrived back in Tucson over two weeks ago and Chato had yet to deliver the promised load.

"Come on. Let's go to the park. It's easier to talk there," Jake mumbled, unable to meet my eyes.

It was a short five-minute drive to a park and Jake was close to a meltdown. Plopping onto the grass under the shade of a large tree, he gathered his thoughts.

"We're going to Phoenix after all. I'm going to rent a warehouse. Bill doesn't like it, but I'm going for it, even though Chato has problems and Bill still believes he's finished."

"Right! Tell me something new!" I said sarcastically.

"I'm ready to go back down and confront Chato," Jake said.

"You wanna go today?"

"No. We'll go to Phoenix tomorrow morning and rent a warehouse. I'll give Chato one more chance."

"Did Bill mention anything about coming down?" I asked. "We could go with him and see Chato together."

"He's not up to it. He says if Chato doesn't come through he has other people we can work with."

"Yeah. Like who?" My sarcasm was not lost on Jake.

"Hard to say. I don't like the way your brother's coming on. He should be here with us."

"I hear you, Jake. He just doesn't want to understand that he's a part of the problem. We're just his lackeys and we can't control the situation the way he could—if he were here, that is. And if he were, we could all go down and talk with Chato—and more than likely solve the problem."

"I've told him that. He says if doesn't matter. Chato's days are over and Bill wants to move on and find someone else. I don't like it Frank. Bill's letting us down."

"Don't I know! Come on! Let's throw the Frisbee. We need some exercise, man." With no one in sight, I pulled a joint from my shirt pocket, fired it up, and handed it to Jake.

It was to be a drug smuggler's version of "the long hot summer." Jake and I, as neophytes, were not well-equipped to handle the onslaught of problems. During the past several weeks we'd come to realize that the enterprise we were involved in, though stable, could turn sour at any given moment—and it had. I was so caught up in our past success that I didn't want to blow things by inserting any negative thoughts. I wanted to go on thinking that positive assertions would lead to positive results. Bill trusted us. He had sent Jake and me down to Arizona to handle the business with Chato.

But now things had turned sour. I beseeched Jake to get on board with me to fix things, just like how we fixed our boats or cars when they broke down. One way to fix the problem, and the one we complained about the most, was for Bill to come to his senses and join us. Seeing that he was unwilling to do this, Jake and I were fast losing trust and respect for the man who ran the operation: my older brother. What really hung over our heads was how uncertain we were about our future. We knew that Bill had no other connections to work with. If he had, he would have mentioned them. Chato was our only contact south of the border. Lose him, and Jake and I were as good as retired from this business. Somehow we had to accept our dilemma and fix all the problems.

Jake and I were friends: two guys who worked for Bill. We were not partners, but somehow and in some way, we had to define our friendship and make it work on a business level. He was more than five years my senior. We had to use that to our advantage. Over the past few weeks we had gotten to know one another as never before. We had to, because it was either sink or swim. We only had to put our minds and hearts to use, and figure out what to do. And during this long hot summer, while living in close quarters, we would often spend as much time analyzing our situation as we did with card games and throwing the Frisbee.

This much we knew: on one end our main connection, Chato, was yanking our strings. Bill was on the other end, yanking away. Jake and I were caught in the middle and had become puppets. It was now time to free ourselves and dispel delusions that all would go well for us. We not only had to figure out how to deal with the vagaries of a business that was going under, we had to come up with solutions. What kept us motivated was that neither of us wanted to return to our eight-to-five jobs. So, we had to be wise and patient, not forceful and over-eager.

We also had to understand the cultural differences with men such as

Chato, and find a way to get him back in the groove with his business, no matter what lies he was telling or what his personal problems were. It wasn't going to easy, but our desire to make money and to put both Chato and Bill in their place was a motivating factor. The rub was that now we were running the show, but we didn't know what decisions to make. What we had going for us was the survival instinct and resilience.

It would take us a while to accomplish our goals. Jake wasn't always open to my suggestions, and my low self-esteem and all those other abuse mechanisms that shadowed me often constrained me from saying what I wanted to say. But, more and more Jake listened to me. And so, we opened up to each other and began to plan and scheme. This interplay and exchange as equals really began taking hold after the second time we came south to work with Chato.

In total, we paid Chato five visits during the long hot summer and always came away empty-handed. Each time, we'd steadfastly keep making plans that kept us centered on our goals. The load of fourteen-hundred kilos, promised in May, had not been delivered. A much smaller load—four hundred kilos—had also been promised, but not delivered. And every time we traveled south to meet with Chato, no matter how much we prodded him, he would not reveal his problems, least of all tell us the truth. And Bill, from his end, was saying that Chato was finished. Jake and I stayed with our plans. We wanted to prove Bill wrong. We'd fix what was broken—we were adamant about that.

✯ ✯ ✯

The real predicaments, along with the first trip south, began the second week of May when Bill asked me to come to his cottage.

"Chato's ready," he said, eyes wide and his energy rippling. "He's got another double load for us. This time I'm going to do things differently."

"You always do," I said, getting a jab in before he shot me down.

"That's the way things go, brother. Each load is different and this time I want to take care of some of my smaller customers. That way I can keep them happy and in funds so they can buy larger amounts when the time comes. It's good for business and they want to make some bucks."

"Hey! I agree. Mack's hogging the market and I…"

"Never mind that. Here's the list I prepared. I want you to collect the money from each of these guys today. They're ready."

"Wow! That's over fifty-grand!"

"I want you and Jake to handle this entire deal with Chato. You guys know the procedure. I'll give you five grand to give to Chato as a down-payment on the load. Once you meet with him and he's got the five-K, call me. Let me know what day he's going to deliver. Jake can purchase the same amount as last time, and you can purchase as many as you can with your money."

"Great! Far out!"

"Good. You guys know the setup. It's clean and easy. Stay to it. If you want to make any changes let me know."

"Gotcha! Anything else?"

"Let's go over things one more time."

I was delighted that Bill was ready to turn Jake and me loose to handle the business with Chato. This meant that Bill trusted us. He was willing to let us run the business for him, and Jake was up for the challenge when I filled him in on the change of plans. My heart skipped a beat at the idea of this reconciliation.

"Hey! I like it, brother! Bill ain't gonna be there and we can handle the entire matter with Chato," I exclaimed to Jake back in mid-May.

"Well, that can work in both directions, man," Jake retorted. "But he's the boss… Yeah, I like it too. Your brother's being fair with all of us, and if he feels we can handle this without him, let's move on it."

"Good. Bill believes it will take us a week to ten days to pull this off, you know, like the last time. He said we'd stop after this load and start back up some time in October."

Satisfied that all would go well, Jake and I departed. Three weeks later, frustrated and worn out, we returned empty-handed. Chato, for some inexplicable reason, had failed to deliver the load of fourteen hundred kilos.

He had given us the same sorry lines day after day: "The load is coming, be patient, all be well."

When the excuses got old and the waiting had worn us thin, Bill called us home. He spelled things out moments after we arrived.

"Chato's like any other drug smuggler," Bill began. "At first they succeed, then along come problems. He's not going to let us in on what they are, guys. Get used to it. We may have to give up on this connection and find another one. That's what I'm up to now. You guys will have to learn these things. This business has a lot of pitfalls. I know. I've been at it for over two years now. The good money comes and goes."

He stopped for a moment and looked pensive.

"Besides, Chato has other customers. He told me the last time I was down there. Could be one of his customers is giving him more money so he's holding us off."

"Then why don't you go down and meet with him?" I asked.

"Hey! I don't work that way. If he's selling the loads to someone else for more money, I don't need to get involved."

I didn't care for Bill's overall attitude. He was the boss, and I felt he could do more about the situation, like come with us and meet with Chato in person. But before I could deliver this message he said ominously, "Meanwhile we have other problems to take care of."

"What do you mean?" I was immediately defensive. Things were getting worse by the moment.

"The customers, brother. We held their cop-money for three weeks and they're not happy.

"Well, what the hell could we do?" I panicked.

"Easy, Frank! All you have to do is talk with them. Believe me; they'll be cool, especially when they get their money back. Mack and Michael heard through some guys at the beach that we brought a load in last week and sold it. Rumors bro, nothing but rumors. I already told them what happened, but when they hear it from you they'll know exactly what went down."

When I left Bill's cottage I was bummed, but as soon as I started visiting the customers my spirits lifted. Not only were they happy to see their cash, they were also glad to learn the truth. By the time I finished, I was charged up. Each customer seemed to still have faith in us. Our efforts over the last three weeks had not been in vain.

A couple of weeks later, well into June, Bill called.

"Chato's got four-hundred kilos for us," Bill said the moment I entered his cottage. "I'm going to send you and Jake to pick up the load and come right back. I want to recoup the five grand I gave this dude, then knock off. He's got problems we don't know about. Otherwise he'd have the fourteen-hundred for us."

On this second trip south more complications arose when Chato asked us for two thousand cash; expenses to cover the four hundred kilos. When we asked why, he explained that this load of four hundred was from another source and that his money was tied up in the double load that was still due him. Jake forked over the cash and Chato asked us to wait in Tucson.

The third trip south came a week later, when our rotund friend failed to deliver the load of four hundred. Phone calls to Mexico often took a long time and once we got through, the connection was anything but perfect. This time, Jake could hardly understand Chato and we wondered if Chato was purposely using poor English to throw us off track. Discussing the matter we concluded Chato might be lying to us—about what, we didn't know. Perhaps Bill was right about this man being washed up. But we met him anyway, at the same restaurant in Nogales and Chato, ever-friendly, brought along his two *compadres*.

This time he had some surprising news. "I have trouble with the border in Nogales. It be no good for me. You go to Phoenix and get a new place. I can bring the *mota*. I cross it in Sababe."

We bought ourselves some time by explaining that without Bill's approval, we couldn't make a decision. We needed time to think it through.

On the trip back to Tucson Jake was in a quiet mood, but that didn't stop me from discussing our situation.

"Bill's going to want us to come back," I said. "But, Chato wants us to help him. He's definitely in trouble, Jake. That's what I saw. I think the load he had for us, the fourteen hundred, was popped at the border and like Bill said, Chato isn't going to let on about that. So it's like this: we either give up on Chato and go home, or stay with this and help him out."

Taking his time to consider the options Jake said, "Let's hang in. Bill wants us to handle this and that's what I'm going to do. If Chato's not willing to tell us the truth then we'll find a way to work with him anyway. I believe he'll come through, but I don't believe your brother will."

"That's exactly my point. Bill said he'd put something else together, but what? Could be he's going to find a way to work without us. And where will that leave us?"

Jake looked over at me as he drove and with quiet resolve reiterated, "Let's stay with Chato."

"I'm with you. We're caught in the middle with these two, but I'm willing to put my hopes on Chato. Somewhere along the line we have to get the truth from him."

Trip four to see our fat friend came after Chato's people pulled a no-show. It had taken Jake and I over a week, but we had found a suitable warehouse in Phoenix. When all was set, we called Chato. Arrangements were made, and on the evening of the delivery Jake and I waited at the new warehouse, but eventually gave up. The next morning, Jake called Chato. The phone connection was terrible and what Chato had to say made no sense. The no-show, along with the searing heat in Phoenix, frayed us to the breaking point. The situation had grown so desperate that we had no choice but to confront Chato—as well as Bill. We had to get a handle on things.

Bill was unwilling to understand our position and had only one goal; he wanted the five grand back that he had given Chato back in mid-May as a down payment. Our goal was to succeed with Chato. Jake and I talked it through. We had had it with both men. We had to confront both of them, and Chato would come first. Bill we'd deal with later, but we had to watch ourselves with him. One wrong push on him and he'd cut us off. That would leave us with no contacts whatsoever. Though Jake and I never broached this subject we shuddered to think about what our lives would be like if we were forced to go back to eight-to-five jobs. Furious, we headed south once again to confront Chato.

Air conditioner blasting, we left the stifling heat of Phoenix behind and our heads cleared up enough to come up with a completely sound plan of attack. We were going to trick Chato into telling us the truth. The plan was simple. Chato needed money to operate. We had the money but we were going to withhold it. We'd pounce on him, apply pressure, and then let up by assuring him we'd lend financial assistance only if he were to reveal his problems. In short, we were determined to get the truth out of him. Jake set the plan in motion before we even ordered a round of beer. My job was to listen, observe, and enter into the conversation only when necessary.

Our tactics proved effective. Jake lit into him right away, calmly and effectively.

"We know you have problems, Chato. We can help you, but only if you tell us your problems. Otherwise, we'll go back home. Bill is looking for other contacts in Mexico," Jake lied. "Frank and I are tired of all of this. Victor is in jail. We're your friends and we're willing to help you, but you have to tell us the truth."

Chato hesitated and glanced nervously over at his *compadres*. Then, biting his lip and bobbing his head, he admitted that American customs agents had found the contraband, the fourteen hundred kilos, back in May. He went on to say that it wasn't the load destined for us but for one of his other customers, which alerted me to one of two things: either he was telling a complex lie or that the other customer was wise to Chato and was unwilling to help him. Chato, from what I guessed, now had to rely on us to help him get back on his feet. Picking up on this I whispered in Jake's ear that I wanted to talk with him.

Moving out of earshot I explained this to Jake and added, "He needed us, Jake. He's only telling us the truth because we're the only ones who will listen to him. Those other Americans, they've probably lost his phone number by now."

Jake understood. And, as Chato continued his story he became remorseful. Jake eased up with the questions because Chato was on a roll now and voluntarily rattled on—he was broke, he had lost his truck, and he was out twenty-five thousand to bail his driver.

As the story unfolded, I felt satisfied. Not only had our plan been successful, but Jake handled Chato with a mixture of compassion and strength. Once Chato had realized that we were likely to split, and that Bill was willing to lose his investment unless Chato complied, he finally spilled his guts.

After the confession, Jake also got him to fess up about the no-show in Phoenix. Shame-faced, Chato explained that his plan to use a friend's pickup truck had fallen through at the last moment. But Chato assured us that he had resolved the transportation problem and everything was set to go. Perking up, he said that once he moved the four-hundred kilos, he'd have another four-hundred kilo load for us. Soon, he'd buy a new truck. Crossing the loads at the border in Sasabe would be much safer. Success was around the corner he assured us; all he needed was another two thousand dollars. We were taken aback by his request for more money. But, we had promised Chato assistance if he came clean, so Jake made good by forking over yet another stack of cash. Chato was all smiles as we broke from the meeting.

As Jake and I walked the mile back to the border we went from elated to unsettled. We still didn't know if Chato had told the entire truth. To boot, we were in doubt about his friend's truck. Would Chato really be ready to roll in a few days?

On the long drive back to Phoenix we shared notes about Bill. At this point, neither of us wanted him to come down and join in with us. We'd keep him in the dark, and stick with plans the two of us cooked up. After a good night's rest we again discussed Chato. Chances were our troubles with Chato were either behind us or Chato would fail us again. We just didn't know.

When we called Bill that day we let him know what we had learned, but said nothing about having tricked Chato into telling the truth, and nothing about the two grand Jake had forked over. Bill said to continue on—if that's what we wanted. His easy compliance was unsettling.

Two days of waiting turned into four. Chato was still unable to cross the load and with the searing summer heat again working us over, Jake fell into a major depression.

The past several weeks we'd worked hard to get along and keep our anger in check. Unfortunately, stress and pressure won out. Unable to lift Jake from his depression, a bitter argument broke out when I lashed out at him. It was late at night and the sound of our screaming at one another became alarming. We had to cool it, lest someone call the authorities. Both of us were mortified by our actions and backed off. I apologized to Jake by admitting that I apparently went a step too far in my attempt to talk him down. Also, I was sorry that I had used such fowl language and I was not only angry with him, but also with Bill and Chato. Having said this, and without resolving anything, we called it a night.

We had to find a way to endure without causing further problems between us. It was either pack-it-in and go home, or hang in with Chato and get a beating from the pressure as well as the fucking heat. Apathy was eating at us. Chato, though he promised us the small load, was once again draining our energy with lies. We were compounding the matter by refusing to acknowledge that anger and frustration, perhaps denial, was eating away at us. Our saving grace activities, like throwing the Frisbee, playing cards, watching television, and trips out to the desert, had lost their appeal. We had to find a way to relieve the pressure or our plans would derail for sure. We either had to stick to the script or give in and head back home.

The next morning, the disappointment of the previous night's ugly episode out of the way, I appealed to Jake for a truce.

"Let's stop this bickering and fighting, Jake. We're only fighting each other. Let's get out of here. The heat sucks. The mountains are much cooler. We can get out in Mother Nature, camp a few days, and think better."

It only took one travel-day to convince us we had made a good decision. In the mountains we came across a small camp area near the border between

New Mexico and Arizona. Three days there, and then two farther down near the dam at Lake Roosevelt were all we needed. Chato wasn't ready and we had to once again confront him. By now, we both felt stupid. Had we spent all this time and effort on nothing? If we failed once again to turn the situation around, we'd have to let go and return back to the Bay Area with our tails between our legs. That made us feel even more stupid, not to mention incompetent.

When Jake and I got on the second-class bus in Nogales we were the only two people aboard. Before long, it was filled beyond capacity. A severe thunderstorm hit as the bus sped down the highway. The night air was crisp and bearable, which contrasted sharply to the tension that gripped Jake and me. We sat together, neither of us speaking. The bus—and my mind—swayed precariously at each bend.

The bus reeked of body odor and was filled with shabbily dressed passengers who were packed in like sardines. As the only *gringos* on the bus, we felt awkward and out of place. The thunderstorm made us even more uneasy. Every wash we crossed was filled with gurgling, muddy water, ready to breach the banks. How many more stops would the bus make? How many villages before we reached Santana? We knew nothing about this long bus journey—and it was wearing on both of us. Finally, it came to the end. Jake and I disembarked at a large, well-lit bus station and headed to a phone.

After hanging up Jake said, "Let's wait out front. Chato will be here in five minutes."

It was now mid-August. Jake and I were at our wits end after all the confrontations with Chato and the plans that had gone awry. This was our fifth visit and this time we came unannounced. We were determined to turn the tables. Bill had repeatedly told us that Chato was finished, but we weren't ready to give up. We would have been better off heading back to the Bay Area, but we were also completely caught up in the notion that we could dig through the muck and succeed.

We had dealt with the same issues over and over again for the past three months, and now they were coming to a head. Bill was the boss of the operation, but Jake and I had done all the work. We resented Bill, yet were grateful for the financial opportunity Bill had thrown our way. But we'd had enough of his lack of support. Before leaving for Mexico we had called him. He knew we were coming here, but we hadn't revealed that we were planning to arrive unannounced. It was no big deal, really. It wasn't even a tough decision.

By confronting Chato, perhaps we were preparing ourselves for our next move; we were learning how to negotiate on our own terms, not Bill's.

After Jake got off the phone with Chato I asked, "How'd it go? Did he sound uptight?"

"Not really," Jake said tensely, trying to keep his cool. "He didn't seem surprised. He was actually glad to hear from us and glad that we had come."

Chato soon drove up. As he eased out of his Mustang he greeted us in a relaxed, easy-going manner. "*Buenos noches, amigos.* You surprise me. I no know you come. You wish to talk? *Si?*"

"Yes, Chato, we came to talk with you," Jake said, as I eyed Chato's companion Renee, a man we had met a few times before. "I want to talk with you about business."

"*Si*, Jakey, we talk the business. We talk about the problem." Chato leaned against the car, folded his arms, and listened.

"We are not happy with you, Chato." Jake started. "All summer long we've waited for you. We've been patient, and we've tried to help you, but we haven't had one kilo delivered to us—only problems."

"*Si* Jakey," Chato quickly interrupted. "I do not mean to do a bad business. You are my friends. I want to do good business."

"We know, Chato. You want to do good business, but we cannot go on waiting any more. It's costing us money and I have a family I haven't seen for two months. Frank and I have spent thousands of dollars on expenses. I gave you four thousand dollars to do this one business. We have nothing to show for it."

"I pay you back," Chato pleaded, "when we do the business, my friend. I pay you more—you will see."

Jake countered, "It's always "when" we do the business. There is no business. You have many problems. We came to tell you this: we don't want to sit around and wait any longer. *Comprende*? I want to go with you." He pointed toward the car and beyond. "I want to meet with these farmers you say will give you the *mota*. I want you and me to go talk with them. I want to understand what the problem is. Where is this man who has the four hundred kilos? Let me see this truck you say a friend will lend you."

"*Si* Jakey. You be patient with me. I have many farmer friends in the south. Soon the farmers, they have many kilos. You will see. They promise me many times. I go to the south and see them. *Mi amigo*, he say come in one month. Soon we have them. Maybe you be patient longer?"

"No, Chato. I'm impatient and I'm mad. I want to meet your people. I want us to go south as soon as possible. Tomorrow would be good."

"We go now, my friend." Chato moved toward his Mustang and opened the door. "No necessary to wait. You are mad. You no be patient. Come, we look for business together. You meet my friends. Come." He gestured Jake toward the car, an offended look on his face.

Jake and I were dumbfounded. Chato continued gesturing for Jake to enter his car. "Come. We go now." It was already late evening, past ten p.m. Chato explained to Jake that his farmer friend lived in the state of Sinaloa, a full day's drive to the south.

"Okay. Let's go," Jake said impulsively, and then turned toward me. "Frank will stay here. I'll talk with him."

Ushering me to the side Jake murmured, "I'm going with him. You heard him. We'll be back in a couple of days."

We had expected to push Chato, but we hadn't expected his cooperation.

"Damn!" I said to Jake. "This is a bit much, man. Let's go for it, anyway. Chato's cool by it. Go ahead. I'll call Bill—let him know what's up."

"Good. Get a room at the Western Motel in Nogales, OK? I'll catch up with you later. See you."

Jake climbed into Chato's car and suddenly they were gone. I couldn't help but worry about the hastiness of the decision, but suddenly realized I was famished. As I entered a small restaurant near the bus station, I panicked. I thought, "Christ, Frank, you have no problem driving a load of pot around the country, but you're too timid to order food in another country. How do I find a room? Are there any motels in this town?"

In no time at all I found a way to get what I wanted. Pointing and gesturing worked wonders, especially when the young female waitress seemed more embarrassed than me. Santana, a town of some five thousand people had very few hotels, but after filling my belly I got lucky and found a place for the night.

Getting out of town the next day was easy; everyone wanted to help the young *gringo* catch a bus to Nogales. Everyone was friendly, gracious, and inclined to smile, which impressed me. Life was a festival to them. There was no need to put on a show. As I waited for the bus the next morning, I browsed the local market. The vendors and shoppers were timid. I realized having an American in their *pueblo* was a rare occurrence.

Back in Nogales, I called Bill. He was uptight about Jake going south without first talking with him. "Why in the hell did he go? I told both of you that Chato wasn't to be trusted."

"Come on Bill, there wasn't enough time. It happened too quickly. Chato was cool. He wanted to prove to us he's on the level. Jake will be back in a few days and we'll know a lot more."

"When Jake returns I want you guys to come back here. Tell him we can work on something else. I'm getting tired of this man." Bill pressed his point, "It's time to back away from him."

I understood, but dismissed him with a quick "gotcha"—mostly because he wasn't around to manage things. Without Bill's presence, Jake and I were in charge and we had to make the decisions, right or wrong. We wanted to finish what we had come to do. Despite Bill's protests, Jake and I believed we were handling things the best way we could.

Alone and with time on my hands, I obsessed about the situation. "Would it ever end?"

The only answer was to stay the course. We could pull this off if we had the resources. We believed Chato had the connections to get weed up front, as he continued to promise. He only had to find a way to cross with a large load, as before. We even considered the idea of financing him, but that would mean convincing Bill to invest. Chato could find a good, early model truck and have it modified. Jake and I could stick around to oversee the process. We could come up with a more sophisticated way to conceal the contraband. Then we'd be on a roll and Bill would be thankful—once we succeeded. The only hitch was that Chato—like so many men—didn't like to be directed and have others sticking their nose in his business. Jake and I knew, without a doubt, that we had a long way to go to get Chato off the ground, but we were willing.

Jake showed up three days later looking tired and haggard. I did my best to welcome him. I had to. He was on the edge of one of his bad moods. "Go clean up, man," I told him, while sitting in the sun poolside. "We've got plenty of time to talk later."

Jake wandered off, looking miserable. When I saw him next, he was in swim trunks. After a dip in the pool he joined me, obviously more relaxed.

"I met this guy Jesus," he said wryly. Jake was back to his old self, I concluded. Sometimes he was my buddy, sometimes not.

"Who's this guy Jesus? Is he the farmer Chato tells us about?"

"Yeah, I met him the day we arrived. According to Chato, Jesus owns a lot of land in the mountains. Every year, he grows eight to ten tons of weed. He also knows several other farmers who grow grass. Anyhow, he lives in Guamachil, not far from Culican, about five hundred miles south of here. I don't know if they're lying to us, Frank. It's too hard to tell. He and Chato went to look for some weed. They didn't want me to come along. Chato said there aren't any kilos right now. It's growing season. We have to wait."

Wary of this news I replied sarcastically, "Terrific! How long?"

"Three, maybe four weeks." Jake stared skyward, his face vacant.

"What's this guy Jesus like?"

"He's an old guy, about sixty," Jake drawled. "He's friendly. We talked several times, but Chato had to interpret. No telling what he really said. Anyway, Jesus made it clear he would have plenty of grass for us in about three weeks. I think it may take longer."

"And what about crossing a load once Chato has a ton or two? Any word on that?"

"I don't know. Chato said he'll find a truck to use."

"Interesting. The way things are going, we ought to go back home and talk with Bill about all of this. No sense in staying on here." My insides were grinding.

Jake stalled. "Not now, Frank. Let me think about it."

While Jake chilled out, I slipped into the pool and swam.

"What was it like traveling with Chato?" I asked, climbing back into my lounge chair.

"He's got some problems of a different sort," Jake said, perking up a little. "On the way back, Chato told me about his marriage. He had a very a pretty wife, but a couple of years ago she split on him with one of his best friends. They were having an affair."

"Whoa!" I sat up with interest. "That's heavy. Happens all the time in the States; it must be scandalous in Mexico."

"I'd say so."

"That's a good thing to know. Chato must be hurting. Think about it, Jake. He's Mexican and he's *macho*. His emotions took a beating and at this stage they're still affecting him. He could hurt us in the long run. You know, the macho ego and all that stuff, running out of control. It probably affects everything he does—then he puts it on others, like us."

"Yeah. Could be true. It showed on his face when he told me the story."

"Why do you think he told you such a private story? I mean, it's his wife."

"I don't know… maybe he had to get it off his chest," Jake replied haltingly.

Through Joanne, I had learned that Jake had an affair a few years back.

It almost broke up their marriage, but Jake had broken it off and Joanne had forgiven him. Perhaps he empathized with Chato.

"So…you got pretty close down there."

After a pause Jake said, "Chato's got a mistress now. He doesn't want to get married again. So maybe you're right. Could be he's still hurting."

"Problems like that don't go away easily, even though Chato has a woman in his life. He's been jilted, Jake. We all know what that can do to a man's psyche. Let's be aware of this."

I got the impression that Jake didn't like what I had said and obviously he didn't want to comment on my sharp remarks. So, changing the subject I reported, "Bill wants us back."

"Not now, Frank." Jake looked away. "Let's talk about it later. I want to relax right now."

I stopped talking and stared out at the highway. Watching the late afternoon traffic speeding to and fro, I imagined I was sailing on my boat, watching the sun go down on the Marin County shore, a gentle summer breeze caressing my skin.

CHAPTER FOUR

TELL US THE TRUTH

THE PHONE RANG around seven the next morning, waking both of us. I rubbed my eyes open and stumbled to the phone first. Figuring it was Bill, I scrambled to come up with a script. Picking up the receiver I heard a familiar voice. It wasn't Bill.

"Hey, sounds like I woke ya."

My body stiffened as I recognized the voice. "Victor! Christ! Is that really you?"

"Sure is buddy," he sneered, "bet ya didn't expect to be hearing from me?"

Overhearing me, Jake shot upright from his bed.

"Wow, you're out of jail. Where are you?" I asked, more than just curious about this unexpected turn of events.

"Not too far away, brother—right across the street." Victor's tone was haughty.

Full of foreboding, I didn't know what to say. "So…you're here in town. When did you get out?" I asked, as Jake headed for the bathroom, a worried look on his face.

"Oh, about a week ago. I would've been down here sooner, but I had a bit of business to talk over with your brother. I needed some money to get going."

Not trusting his motives, I baited him: "He must have told you what's been happening?"

"Sure did, brother. We gotta straighten things out—that's all."

"I guess we do," I replied, realizing that he wasn't going to tell me what he knew, at least not just then. I'd have to find out what Bill might have told Victor. Then it hit me. Why hadn't Bill called to tell us Victor was out and headed here? Suddenly, I was inflamed, my mind buzzing with questions. Bill was the only person with our phone number and location. I was outraged.

"Well, don't ya go worrying about things," Victor cut short my thoughts. "We'll get Chato going. Right now I'd like to talk with you guys. Jake's there, ain't he?"

"Yeah."

"Good. Why don't ya come on over to my motel? We're at the Arizona Lodge, Room 23. Let's have some breakfast. I want you to meet my new partner."

"Sure, Victor. We'll be over. Give us an hour." I heard the sharp click from his phone. I stared at the receiver, perplexed. I looked outside, pleased to greet another sunny day and then said loud enough for Jake to hear: "Victor's out of jail. He wants us to come to his motel and meet with him. He's got someone with him. Says it's his new partner."

"I can hear," Jake said sardonically.

"How the hell did he know we were here?"

"Bill must have told him, I guess. How else?"

Jake poked his head out the bathroom and said sharply, "Then why didn't he call and tell us Victor was out and headed here?"

I slumped down on the edge of the bed. "Shit, I don't know. I can't believe he'd be so thoughtless. Maybe I ought to call him."

"No, hold off. We'll talk with Victor first." I heard the shower go on. Jake closed the door.

Three days before, Bill had asked us to stay in touch and was put out that Jake had gone down to Mexico with Chato without telling him first. Obviously, he had talked with Victor during that time. What had gone down between Bill and Victor? I'd find out later. All I knew was that Bill was the man who had disarmed us.

Does Bill expect us to negotiate with his creepy associate? He should be down here right now. And as of now, he's on my shit list. He has us in a compromising position. Now we're caught in the middle of a three-way squeeze: Bill in one corner, Chato in another, and now Victor occupying a third. We're going to get pushed around if we don't watch out. Then again, maybe Victor will be able to get Chato going. As for Bill, Jake's right, to hell with calling him.

As I got dressed I predicted to Jake, "Everything is going to change now that Victor is back."

"He's gonna be in the way of us getting our money back," Jake shot back.

"Come on Jake. I know you're set on working this thing out, but Chato is Victor's man. Besides, what's Victor going to say about us using him?"

"Don't be mistaken, Frank," Jake said from the bathroom.

"Bill's the one who used him. We're only working for him. Victor went to jail because he screwed up. No one can say anything different about that, not even Victor. And, if he has any objections to us working with his man while he was gone, let him take it up with Bill."

"I'm sure he already has. I see your point. Let's just be cool about everything."

Jake came out of the bathroom and looked me squarely in the eyes. "Look, your brother's getting to me. He doesn't bother to come here and find out what the real problem is and now he doesn't bother to call when he should have. We don't know what's happening between him and Victor. He let him come down here unannounced. That's inexcusable. We keep him informed of our moves, but..."

"OK...OK, Jake," I protested. I wanted to stop him from haranguing me about the very thing going through my mind. "It pisses me off too. You're not alone. Let's just go see Victor. We better put our energy into that and stop squabbling. We'll hit Bill about this later."

I felt trapped and wanted to break something. My brother had let us down before, but never like this. Jake was only making things worse. We were both feeling the pressure of not knowing who to trust and the fear that we might lose all the money we had invested.

We crossed the highway on foot and headed for to the Arizona Lodge, the largest motel in town. Victor greeted us with his usual sly grin.

"Lookey here. Don't you bros look fine," he mocked, shaking our hands. "Come on in."

"Hey! How've you been, man?" I asked, attempting to be casual as we shook hands.

"Oh, not so bad. That jail sure was nasty, but I got plenty of thinking done and I'm back to stay. Chato's gonna work with me this year. We'll get the best weed Mexico has to offer. We'll get your money back for ya, too, but right now we got to talk. I heard you got yourself into a mess of trouble—about ten grand worth," Victor ragged. "Hey Jim!" Victor yelled out the sliding door leading to the motel's swimming pool. "Come meet these guys."

As Victor's imperious yell echoed in my ears, I spotted a man in nylon trunks sunning near the pool. He slowly rose and moved toward us with an easy gait, as if he had the whole day at his disposal.

"This is Frank, Bill's brother, and this is Jake."

"Glad to meet ya, guys," Jim said, extending his hand. He was in his early thirties, a bit taller than me, with broad, muscular shoulders. He had jet-black hair, a thick, black mustache and large, shifty eyes. They caught mine, as his clammy hand closed around mine like a vise—he projected a fierceness that unnerved me. Deftly, he moved over to Jake and reached his hand out.

"Heard all about your trouble with that pollo Chato. Can't wait to meet this fathead," he said menacingly as he shifted his eyes, almost asking for approval. He sauntered over to the dresser and grabbed a pack of cigarettes.

"Ya gotta understand these Mexicans. They're slippery sonsofbitches. Ya know what I mean? They won't tell ya the truth." Jim lit the cigarette, greedily sucking the smoke deep into his lungs. "They like to lie and they lie like you breathe. They're heartless sonsofbitches. They put on a good show, like as if you're their brothers or something. I know all about 'em. I spent four months in one of their grimy, fucking jails down in Hermosillo."

"Tell 'em about it," Victor urged.

"Nah. Not now," Jim drawled, then shifted his eyes to Jake and me.

"They don't wanna hear it and I ain't really in the mood to tell 'em. Why don't we get us some food and talk?"

Jim looked back at his buddy and winked. "Ya want to talk to these guys, right? Go ahead and talk to 'em. I'll just listen in. Whatcha want for breakfast?" he asked, picking up the phone. "I'll call and have 'em send some grub over."

"Wow," I thought to myself. "This guy comes on like Bogey playing Al Capone." I looked at Jake, who was listening intently. I think Jake was digging the guy's act.

"Hey, why don't ya just order a batch of bacon and a dozen fried eggs," Victor suggested. "And plenty of coffee."

"Have 'em send some orange juice," Jake added.

"Tell them to bring a few slices of tomato and some cottage cheese too," I added to the order.

"Sure kid," Jim said winking at me. "I heard you're vegetarians."

Victor brought us back to the business at hand. "Hey Jake, fill me in on what that fat partner of mine's been up to. I gotta know what's been happening so we can get 'em going on the right track."

Jake walked slowly to a chair, sat down, and made himself comfortable. Victor sat opposite him on the edge of a bed, leaning slightly forward, bracing his hands on his knees, eager to hear. I remained standing.

"What did Bill tell you?" Jake inquired.

"Not much. Just that Chato's been lying and doing bad business with ya all summer, and that he lost a load at the border. Come on, I wanna hear it from you buddy. You know the details."

Jake smiled indifferently, then began explaining what had taken place during Victor's incarceration, starting in mid-May, when all the problems began.

As Jake talked, Jim slowly paced the room, smoking, and periodically looking toward Jake. When Jake got to the part about Chato's bust and the 400 kilos that were never delivered Jim growled.

"That sonofabitch is lying to ya, Jake. Those kilos were never in his possession. He's stalling ya. That's all, brother."

"You could be right. But maybe the guy who has them is the problem," Jake suggested gently.

"Come on, man. Do ya think this dude who has the kilos still has 'em? No way, brother. He sold 'em long ago and Chato's stalling, no matter what he says." Jim was working himself up into frenzy. Pointing at Jake he spat out adamantly, "Hey bro, this guy Chato needs to be talked to. He's like all Mexicans. They play little games with people. Ya know what I mean?"

Relaxing a little Jim added, "Go ahead. We can get back to this later. Chato's a screw-up. That truck that got busted at the border?—I can show you how to build a better one."

Jake described the last two-week wait: the burn-out in Phoenix, our trip to the mountains to get away from it all and our decision to return.

Jim interjected, "More than likely he's been sitting on his ass making phone calls. I doubt if he looked too hard."

Turning to Victor Jim asked, "Does this fat man do any heavy drugs?"

"I can bet if we go down there he'd have a nice stash of cocaine lying around," Victor grinned.

"A coker! That figures," Jim said, winking at Victor.

I remained quiet, watching Jim as Jake told the rest of the story—the trip south with Chato. "I just got back yesterday. Chato's in Santana. We've gotta wait a few weeks for his friend to get things together."

"This guy's livin' off ya, Jake," Jim rebuked.

"Shit, the money you gave 'em is keeping him fat. To boot, he's pouring coke down his nose at your expense."

"Maybe so," Jake agreed meekly.

Jim continued pacing, hands behind his back, looking at the floor. Wheeling around, his eyes bulging, we could see he was getting all agitated again. "He's up to something. I know he is. He's lying, and cheating, and sucking money down what don't belong to 'em. No doubt, he's scared shitless. Ya know what I mean? I wanna go down and put this roly-poly tortilla snatcher on a skewer and warm him up a degree or two!"

"Fine by me," Victor agreed. Looking at Jake he invited, "You wanna join us?"

"I'll think about it," Jake replied. "Right now I'm interested in what's happening with us: you and me and Jim."

"Jim's my partner, man," Victor said proudly, like a new father. "We'll be working together."

"What about Bill?"

"Hey, same as before. I'll sell to him. You and Frank, well, you guys can work that out. But first I gotta square things with Bill."

"What do you mean by that?" I asked, concerned.

"Now don't get uptight, Frank," Victor shot back. "Bill and I gotta few things to straighten out. He conveniently left me in jail and worked my man to boot. You guys left me sitting."

"We sent down the money to get you out Victor," I retorted. "Your lawyer kept it as a retainer. What more could we do?"

Jim quickly moved into bodyguard position next to Victor drawling, "Let's be nice about this, men. Victor here is your brother's associate. He shoulda bailed him out. Shit, it was only twenty-five hundred. Victor had to go to his mom for the money. Ya know what that's like. Victor didn't wanna put her through all that trouble."

"He wouldn't have had to if he hadn't gotten himself busted," Jake interceded. "You gotta learn not to be so careless Victor," Jake reproached. "Speeding and carrying cash and dope around don't mix in my book."

"Jake's right," I added. "You know we can't afford that kind of trouble. Look what you put us through."

"I spent six months in jail," Victor snapped, before Jim cut him off.

"Hey, bros, let's not get off the track. That fucking idiot Andy was the one who was driving. If he hadn't mouthed off at that pig none a this woulda happened."

"Then let's drop it," Jake asserted. "You should be taking this up with Bill, not us. Let's talk about what we're gonna do about Chato."

"Hey, I like this guy," Jim said, walking back to his cigarettes on the dresser.

"Jake, you got guts. So do you, Frank. Ya just don't have the know-how to handle this thing with Chato. He's a bad *hombre*." Lighting up, he added, "You guys are new to this game. Ya don't know how these Mexicans think. Ya can't be easy on 'em. They'll take you for all ya got. I nearly killed one of 'em for doing that. That's how I got myself in jail. The guy I messed with got the worst of the deal," Jim said proudly as someone knocked at the door.

Victor ushered the waiter in. "Come on, let's eat outside in the sun. Take it outside," he ordered the waiter.

I managed to grab Jake alone in the room. "What do you think about this guy Jim?"

"He's a tough one. Maybe we need him. He's probably right about Chato. We've got to do something."

Poolside, Jim suggested we drop business while we ate. "It'll give me heartburn. I don't like that. Why don't we just get to know one another? You must think I'm a bad *hombre* saying all them nasty things about Mexicans. I just don't like people who lie and steal."

Under my breath I muttered to myself, "Leave it to Victor to find a hard-line dude like Jim."

"Hey, they forgot my tomatoes!" I complained.

"You've had worse things happen to ya, right?" Jim shot back, sticking a piece of bacon in his mouth.

Victor and Jake laughed.

I cracked a smile and then laughed too. Maybe it wouldn't be so bad working with these two characters. Throughout breakfast Jim was quick with his tongue: defensive and bordering on brazen. Victor was quiet for the most part. He wanted us to be impressed with his new associate. Jake was definitely impressed. They talked about the Mexican Olympics, set to start the following month. Never cutting the Mexicans any slack, Jim figured they'd be a flop.

After we ate, Jake and I put our trunks on and went for a quick swim, along with our hosts.

Relaxing poolside, I asked Victor, "Say, what do we do when Chato gets a load and has trouble crossing it? He got popped the last time, right? Getting it across is the hard part compared to purchasing."

"Come time, we'll figure that out."

Jim, exerting his self-designated authority on Mexicans piped up. "I've worked with these Mexicans, Frank. I know how they go about crossing this stuff. It's all a matter of timin' and watchin' the border. Ain't no fun, but it works. We'll get us a good truck, and I'll show 'em how to fix it up, then I'll work with 'em on crossing. We won't move 'til everything's real right. Hey! Let's get us some beer. I'm thirsty."

Moments later, Jim and Jake arrived back from their beer run in high spirits, laughing over a joke Jim had just told. Just approaching noon, we started guzzling beer as we hung out poolside. Jim was clearly in command, controlling the tempo.

"I'm about ready to meet this tortilla. Ya wanna come along? We'd sure like ya to join us."

"Yeah, I think so," Jake answered. Wrinkling his forehead, he asked, "So what are we going to do? I'd like to hear what he has to say to you first."

"Good! The more the better! It's like this, bro: we don't wanna give Chato an edge. He may lie about what ya all been up to. That means I gotta work 'em all the harder. Am I right?"

"Why don't all of us go down? What do you think, Frank?" Victor asked, patting me on the shoulder.

"I bet Chato, crazy mother-fucker he is, ain't lettin' in on all his problems. Ya know what I mean?" Jim accused.

"How so?" Jake gave Jim his full attention.

"The sonofabitch lost his load at the border, right? That cost 'em twenty-five grand, plus he probably ain't paid for the four hundred yet. He's into you for eleven grand. Now let's just suppose he didn't have the twenty-five biggies himself and he had to go beg, borrow, or steal it from the people he's been buying from. They wanna help him 'cause they don't want any trouble. Say they gave him a few thousand, knowing he's hot. They figure, 'what the hell.' Then they refuse to give 'em anymore, figuring it's best to lose the money than to put up with bad business. But the thing is dude, they'd rather sell their weed to someone else. Chato's not the only dealer in Mexico. Ya see my point, buddy?"

"Sure, it could be true," Jake answered.

"Hey, why else can't he get any *mota*?" Jim reached for his cigarettes. "I've been in Mexico during the summer. There's plenty of weed around 'cause they ain't sold it all. Now they won't move 'cause it's too fucking hot. When that ole sun gets to scorching they like to take *siestas*. This farmer ya met, Jake, he likes to *siesta* too, but he ain't gonna give Chato any more weed 'cause they want to work with someone who'll pay 'em. Simple as that, man. Chato ain't gonna get any more fronts. He fucked up his credit. I want 'em to tell us the truth. Then we can go and find some new customers. We'll buy us a new truck, fix it up good, and put this fat man Chato to work. I'm ready to go down there."

Turning to Victor he queried, "Chato have any guns?"

"Hey, I don't know. I brought him down a couple of rifles a while ago. He said he gave them to his people."

"Well, there's no better persuader than a good weapon, like a couple of Colt 45's, and maybe a rifle."

"We'll need some money. How about it Jake?" Victor pushed.

"Don't go worrying dudes," Jim cajoled Jake and me. "It's only for show. There ain't gonna be any shootin' goin' on. When the fat man sees 'em, he'll tell us the truth. We ain't gonna work with him 'til we know what he's up to. Ya know what I mean?"

"Come on, man. That's heavy. Why would we need guns?" I spoke up. Their plans were getting out of hand.

"Hey! Chill out Frank. It's for show," Victor chimed in.

"Yeah. That's all," Jim said a little too quickly. "We show up with a couple of guns and *Chato* all of a sudden remembers what happened. These guys are *macho*. We gotta play their game. They respect ya when you do that. You can bet *Chato* has a man or two after him right now. Shit, we might get down there and find him dead. If he ain't, then he'll talk with the first man who comes at him. And I wanna be that man. We'll all know in no time what the pork-head is up to. I fucking well don't like sittin' around waitin' 'til something happens."

"Yeah. I wanna find out what the problem is," Victor concurred.

Victor and Jim had each other's backs. They had no doubt cooked up this scheme on their way down to see us. Their story sounded rehearsed, even the part about purchasing weapons. What were they really up to? I didn't know, only that their scheme seemed ludicrous.

I started thinking about the situation from another perspective. Chato was not the kind of man who could be threatened by them, not in his own country with his *compadres* around. Why would Victor want to do something as crazy as going down to Mexico with guns and threaten his partner? Andy, Victor's former partner, had had a strong influence on him, and now it was his new pal Jim Bigotes' turn. Chato might be lying to us, but with the four of us working together all we had to do was straighten things out, then get Chato back on his feet. In time, Chato would have weed. Then again, maybe Jim was right. Maybe Chato couldn't get any weed from his farmer friends and that's why Jim wanted Chato to tell him the truth.

I was totally frustrated. The long summer ordeal, including this latest episode, was wearing me thin. Chato had put Jake and me through a nightmare—and now, suddenly our drug smuggling business, which had already turned sour, was becoming life-threatening.

While Victor tried to convince me to come along to help straighten out things and once again make money, Jake discussed the gun issue with Jim. Jake was actually ready to go along with their plan. He had the money to buy the weapons and he had incentive: he wanted to know the truth and he was convinced that Jim would be more successful in getting it than we had been.

I heard Jim say to Jake, "You purchase 'em and we'll buy 'em back. They'll be ours. Not yours. How's that sound, bro?"

"How much do you need?" Jake asked.

"Make it simple, brother. Just lend me a thousand. That ought to take care of everything."

I sighed. Jake and I were caught in dire straits. There was no real need to bring guns. Should anything bad happen, we'd be accessories. I cringed at the thought, then got up and faced the three men.

Before I got any words out Jim said, "Tell ya what, guys, Jake and I'll get the guns in Tucson. Victor, you and Frank go on down ahead of us to Santana. Ya can keep that coke-head company 'til we get there."

"Sure. We can take my car," Victor decided. He was ready to go.

Resentfully I glared at Jim, who seemed to be getting us involved in yet another senseless—and dangerous—journey. "How are you going to get the guns down there?"

"Ain't nothing to worry about," Jim quipped, blowing out smoke. "We'll hide 'em underneath the bed of the van. That's an old trick I learned. Leave it to me. Let's go hunting, *hombres*."

Accessory or not, I felt pressured to go along with them. All three were set. If I backed out, I might as well as quit the whole business. I wasn't ready to do that, though it would've been smart. But, I didn't want to look like a coward. We were drug smugglers. We were supposed to be tough. Besides, after what Chato had put us through, and the fact that Bill hadn't called to warn us about Victor, I was angry as hell. "I'll come along, but I don't want any shooting," I warned.

Victor sidled up to me and put his arm on my shoulder. "Hey, do ya think I'd let Jim shoot my main connection?" he wheedled. "You make me feel bad, brother. Besides, Chato's got a lot of friends. Everyone in town knows him. We'd be lucky to get out alive. We ain't gonna hurt him. Come on, this is just a little game we gotta play before we get down to business with him. He's lying, and we need to know what he's up to. That's all."

Jake was all ready to get going and wouldn't return my stare. He was too busy talking with Jim and clearly didn't want my censure. It would have been smart to talk with Jake, but I wasn't being smart. I was shutting down the part of myself I usually listened to. I had to go along—after all, I was one of the guys, I convinced myself. I was clear, however, that if Jim got out of control, I'd go to Jake and force him to his senses. Together we'd put a stop to any nonsense. Then again, maybe the plan our colleagues cooked up would work. It wasn't as though we were conspiring to rob a Mexican bank. It was more like, as Jim put it, a *macho* showdown, Mexican-style.

Six or seven tense hours had passed since Victor and I had arrived at Chato's house in Santana. Chato had greeted us in his usual amicable manner, not realizing that a showdown was about to ensue. At about half-past seven, we heard a sharp rap at the door. Chato moved to answer it, while Victor followed him. I stood, swept up with foreboding and tension.

Jim came through the door first, followed by Jake. With Colt 45 pistols tucked in their belts and Jake holding an M-1 carbine, they brushed past Chato without saying a word. Jim came to the center of the living room, looked it over, then addressed his pal Victor.

"Had one hell of a time, bro. We had no problem gettin' what we wanted, just a bit a trouble puttin' things away. Ya know what I mean?"

As Chato closed the door Jim quickly glanced around, his dark eyes mirroring the situation. Then he removed the pistol and displayed it to Victor by popping the clip loose—it was loaded.

I stood beside Chato, silent, as Jake too brushed past us and placed a rifle against the wall behind the sofa. His animated movements gave me the creeps. He set his pistol on the coffee table as though he wanted nothing to do with the weapon.

Jim tucked his pistol in his belt, turned, and stared Chato up and down as though inspecting a purchase. He extended an arm and introduced himself, his baritone voice resounding through the room.

"Señor Chato! Glad to meet ya. My name is Jim Bigote." Jim accentuated the word Bigote, which means "mustache" in Spanish. "I'm Victor's new partner."

"*Si*. He tell me of you," Chato replied in a subdued tone.

"Good. Then you know what we came here for?"

Chato moved toward Jake, who was ill at ease and said, "Jakey, my friend, you are *bueno*?" He extended his hand. Jake was reluctant, but gave in.

Jim was put out by Chato's indifference to his arrival, and spotting the joints on the table turned to me saying, "How ya doing, brother? Why don't ya fire up one of those babies?"

Looking at Victor he demanded, "Where's the coke man—and a beer? Where's your hospitality, brother?" He gave me his signature wink. Victor smiled graciously as Jim drew out a pack of cigarettes, lit up, and casually walked to the bar area.

"Hey, bro, everything's right here at the bar. Chato's got a few beers left. I'll get ya one. We'll go for a beer run later," Victor reassured his partner.

"Good. How about some tequila too. Ya got any good tequila, Chato?" Jim barked.

"*Si*, I have the good tequila." Chato moved behind the bar, produced a bottle and set out several shot glasses. His hand was surprisingly steady as he poured liquor into each shot glass.

"Man, I can use a good brushing," Jim said as he sat at the bar. Both Jim and Jake dusted their noses and then I handed Jim a joint.

"Thanks buddy. Have a shot with me—you, too, Jake." Jim picked up a shot glass and toasted, "To *mota* and to money. We love 'em dearly." He grunted out a laugh while slugging down a shot. The rest of us followed suit. The liquor, though biting, settled me down.

"Line 'em up," he ordered Chato. "This is good Tikill'ya. Let's have another burner."

As Chato poured another round Victor added, "This year will be a great year for all of us. Here's to tons of business."

"Yeah! Right on!" Jim toasted. "As soon as we fix the business, right?" Jim looked around at all of us, then paused as he let the alcohol flow down his throat.

"But first we go straight to the *hombre* who does bad business and we ask him"—Jim's eyes fixed on Chato—"to tell us the truth."

Chato looked at Jim for a moment, then over to Victor, saying nothing.

All was quiet as we finished our shots.

From behind the bar Chato asked, "Why you bring the *pistolas*?" The rifle was understandable. Victor, on the way down, had told me Chato's men wanted rifles too. But, Jim's reply was quick and threatening.

"It was my idea. I brought 'em to fix the business. *Comprende*? Maybe you'll be able to tell us what ya been up to. Ya took money from my friends," he pointed to Jake and me while gesturing dramatically, "and ya gave 'em nothing, absolutely nothing. Don't ya try and come across with bullshit. I know ya been lying to these guys. They've been waitin' four months for you. They gave ya a lot of money, right? How much money?" He stared hard at Chato while taking a toke.

Chato answered, avoiding the stare. "My friends they give me nine thousand, but I use it for..."

"That's bullshit, man." Jim cut him off, a vicious look on his face. "It's more like eleven and change, all the expenses ya caused. And, all the trouble too. Christ, Jake ain't seen his family in two months. But ya don't care. All ya do is lie and make bad business. That's a fact, *hombre*."

"*Si*. I pay Jakey the money. You will see. I give it all back. There will be more," Chato replied, doing his best to sound convincing.

"Yeah, yeah, yeah...Ya been telling 'em that way too long. We heard it before, Chato. What about all the waitin'? It's caused all kinds of problems for 'em. Ya promised 'em *mota* and ya gave 'em nothing—nothin' but trouble and headaches, man." Jim's voice quaked with disgust. "Shit, ya wouldn't a gotten past the first lie with me."

"Soon, I make the money. I promise Jakey. I give him $10,000 American when we do the first business." Chato's voice, for the first time, quivered with fear.

"Pay 'em back?" Jim shouted, "when, man, and how? Ya don't have a truck. I heard the dumb fucking story about your border crossing. Your fucking truck wasn't ready. The customs man found it. Ya fucking blew it, goddammit!"

"There be more trucks. My friend in Magdalena, he say I can use his truck. It be good for four hundred kilos. We cross it no problem in Sabe,"

Chato protested.

Jim took a breather. All of us exchanged anxious glances while he reached for the vial of coke.

"So your friend in Magdalena has a fucking truck for ya," Jim continued. "That's just dandy, Chato. I suppose he's gonna let ya use it any time ya want. Now all we need is a few hundred kilos of *mota*, right?"

Chato sputtered, "*Si*. We must wait..."

"Pig shit, Chato! I don't wanna hear any more about waitin'. Damn, where's a cold beer? Get me a joint, too!"

Victor took off for the kitchen, returning with a can of beer. Jim fired up a joint, handing it to Jake at the bar. This is madness, I thought. Jim is enjoying this. He's working himself up and reeking hostility.

Before Jim could continue the phone rang. Silence prevailed as Chato walked over and picked up the receiver.

Jim warned, "Don't ya go trying' any funny stuff. Ya hear me? I know Spanish, Chato."

Chato spoke to for a few seconds and then hung up saying, "My friend Jorge he bring us Cerveza."

"Okay, *hombre*. That was good," Jim said, after he dusted his nose. He handed the vile to Jake and commanded, "Start from the beginning Chato. I wanna hear how ya fucking messed up."

Chato looked around the room, puzzled and obviously offended. I wondered if Jim really knew what Chato had said to his friend. I was willing to bet Jim was lying about his ability to understand Spanish. Chato could have sent a warning message. Offended or not, Chato had gained the upper hand.

"Come on Chato, why don't ya tell us the real story? We can understand," Victor prodded.

Before Victor could answer, Jim's voice ground him down again.

"Nothing to say, huh? Well, let me help. I think you're in trouble man. You're hurtin' 'cause ya screwed up. Ya have no money left. No one will touch ya. No one wants to give ya *mota*."

"It is not so," he answered calmly. "My farmer friend he give me the *mota*. I have no problem with him. He is my friend."

"Yeah, yeah, yeah! Sure, Chato..! Just who is this man you're talking about? What's his name? Where's he live? Tell me about 'em." Jim's staccato pierced the room.

I wanted to scream at Jim by this time, but Chato had regained his composure.

"The man, his name is Jesus. He live in Guamuchil."

"Where's Guamuchil?" Jim demanded, "How far is it?"

"It is one day to the south, in Sinaloa. I know this man many years. We do much business. He is a good man with many sons. Every year he grow…maybe, eight tons of *mota*."

Chato spoke deliberately, concentrating on his English. "I buy many times from him. Mostly he give it to me. I pay him when I sell the *mota*. He no have the *mota* right now. It grow. He promise me five tons. There are many farmers. They be my friends. They grow the *mota* every year. They promise me much *mota*. This year it will be good."

"Ah…I see…so all we gotta do is wait for your fucking friends to come through, huh? Well, I don't like waitin'. I don't like sitting around while ya fuck up. No, my fat friend, you're gonna tell me the truth. I wanna know what's really going on. I think your friend Jesus is holding out on ya 'cause ya owe him a lotta money."

"This is no true. *Si*, I have the problems. Not like this. You will see…"

"Don't bullshit me or I'll shoot your fucking toes off one at a time," Jim bellowed, pointing at Chato's feet. "I'm gonna let you tell me the whole story, no lying, nothin' but truth. And if ya tell me what I wanna hear then you got nothin' to worry about. *Comprende*?"

"*Si*, I tell you my story already. It be the truth," he said flatly.

"Ya have. Well, ain't that nice. Well, now that that's done, why don't we all just get good and drunk and celebrate. Come on Chato. I know you're holding back. Let's get private. Maybe there's too many ears here. Ya know what I mean? Why don't we go some place where it's quiet so we can talk."

"Let's go back to the kitchen," Victor suggested. "I need another beer anyway."

"You guys hang out here," Jim ordered, shooting a heavy stare at Jake and me. Getting up from the stool he ordered, "Bring the coke and a couple joints with you, Victor. Come on Chato."

Chato, sensing disaster, muttered to Jake, "My friend, Jake, I no lie to you. I pay you the money…" His voice trailed off as Jim tugged at him.

Jake hissed, "You have no money to pay us back, Chato. I think you lied to me. You better tell Jim the truth."

Jake stayed glued to the bar nursing his beer. I headed for the sofa to wait things out. Parts of the conversation filtered back to us from the kitchen. Jim's voice was loud and relentless; Chato was restrained, his voice almost a murmur. The wait was grueling.

Prior to Jim and Jake's arrival I had had time to check out Chato's house and assess the situation. The house was clean and all the floors tiled. The living room, sparsely furnished, was large. To the left, along the entry wall was a small bar, then an extension to the right led to a small kitchen. To the right was a hallway that led to two bedrooms. Beyond the living room was a large sliding glass door that opened to a spacious, well-kept garden.

Along three sides of the back yard were brick walls some fifteen feet high, with broken glass embedded in cement to keep thieves out. The only exit was through the front door.

Chato was ever so happy to see his pal Victor. Amidst much raucous laughter, Chato offered us beers and soon Victor asked him to bring out the cocaine. They were amused when I admitted that I had never taken coke; they insisted I try it and while we waited, we each consumed several lines. When Victor asked Chato for some weed, I was surprised that Chato refused to smoke it.

Victor began asking Chato for details about what he had been up to the past few months. I kept a discreet distance as Chato was informed that Victor had a new partner who could tell when a man was lying, a man who had spent time in a Mexican jail.

"All I want you to do is tell me the truth," Victor said, as they began to talk more seriously.

It was then, after consuming several beers and several hits of coke and high on pot that I wandered out to the garden to relax. But I could hardly relax. I was tied up inside, fearful of what was to come.

Now that Jim and Jake had arrived, twice I got up and wandered out to the garden where darkness had descended—in more ways than one. I could see Jim and Chato through the kitchen window sitting at the table while Victor stood, leaning against a wall. No one could see me as I stood in the shadows, watching and listening. Jim's voice railed on incessantly. Concerned for Chato, my stomach tightened.

Why did Jim have to use such tactics? And what was Chato lying about? Most anything, I thought. Would he break down and tell the truth, spare himself—and all of us—the consequences? Or was Chato unwilling to tell the truth? Could it be that Jim was relishing the tension and drama? I'd seen this scenario in gangster movies: killing without regard for the outcome. "Shit, we're all in it together," I swore under my breath.

During the second trip outside, my guts ached as I strained to listen. Jim's voice froze as he held his pistol to Chato's head. I couldn't stand it any longer. I had to move, do something. Without thinking, I headed back inside. "I need a beer," I said to Jake. "I'll bring you one too."

I didn't need Jake's agreement to do what came next. I headed for the kitchen and entered as gingerly as possible. With Jim's back to me I surveyed the scene and said politely, "Sorry for intruding, guys. We're getting thirsty out there. Can you grab me a couple of beers, Victor?"

Jim, highly agitated, gave me a defiant stare as I neared.

Victor, replied, "Hey, bro, there's none left. Why don't ya go and get some?"

"Sure." I lied. "No way you're going to get me out of here," I thought, as I turned and headed off.

At the bar I confronted Jake. "I don't like this. Jim's getting out of hand. He had the gun against Chato's head when I went in."

"Frank, he said he'd get tough, but he isn't going to shoot him. He's just going to pressure him. That's all." He looked away and took a sizable a gulp of warm beer.

"I don't like it, Jake. Chato's a mess. He's pouring sweat. His whole face is drenched."

"Let him sweat it out for now. We know he's lying. Jim will coax the truth out of him. It's gonna take time. Just be patient. I don't want to keep repeating this thing with Chato. He'll run all of us down. Jim will have to be tough on him for a while."

"That's what's got me worried. Jim will get out of control. No telling what he might do. He's explosive. I don't like it, Jake."

"He won't shoot—if that's what you're worried about. I talked with him about what he was going to do. He's just gonna scare the shit out of him," Jake repeated, as though he was trying to convince himself.

I took a deep breath. Exhaling slowly, I said with more calm than I felt, "That can easily change. We don't know what might happen."

"Why don't you go sit down and chill out. I'm right here."

This was unlike the Jake I had come to know. For one, we were not communicating like we could, and Jake seemed submerged in a dark side reality. I could feel it—and I was desperate. My thoughts became jagged and pierced my head. I felt as if I were going to fall apart. How Jake was handling it, I didn't know. He wouldn't move or say a thing.

Propelled by Jim's voice, I headed back out to the garden where I sucked a deep breath from the cool night air. I listened and watched. I could feel how Chato was grim and pained.

Jim's sharp voice pierced the night air. "You're lying like dog shit. There ain't gonna be any business until we have it, *hombre*. Use that fucking head of yours, else I'm gonna keep after ya 'til your head sinks down to your asshole. And none of them sob stories. I ain't in the mood." Raising the pistol to Chato's temple again he added in an exaggerated drawl, "Else I put a nice hole in that sweaty lying head of yours."

Jim cocked the trigger, then placed the pistol to Chato's head. "Shit! He's going to pull it, sooner or later—sure as cow's shit he's going to," I panicked. Jim continued belligerently, "Now tell me who do ya owe money to? Tell me how much money ya owe, tell me!"

Chato looked over at Victor and shrugged his shoulders, his round face sculpted with defeat. I couldn't hear his reply; I only sensed doom. Either Chato would tell the truth or Jim would pull the trigger. It was just a matter of time.

"He's going to push too far," a voice in my head screamed. With a quick glance at Jim, I was convinced: a contorted evil force would prevail if Chato didn't give a satisfactory answer—and soon.

Alarmed, I rushed back to the living room. Jake was still at the bar, oblivious to the explosive situation.

"Goddammit Jake, he's got that gun at Chato's head again. The sonofabitch is way out of control. Let's do something." I stood there, fearful, shaking with anticipation that any second a shot might ring out. Jake was unresponsive and stared at me with contempt, as I though I was the one causing the problem. I'd never had to suffer through what Chato was going through and didn't like seeing someone else go through it. I'd never shot anyone with a weapon, least of all been an accomplice to a mindless murder. I was not about to break that code of integrity.

Jake mumbled something about being cool. "Fuck this, man," I screeched, and headed for the kitchen before Jake could stop me.

A quick glance at Victor's maligned face further confirmed my fears as I stepped into the kitchen and stood motionless about six feet away. Jim, busy thundering away didn't see me, and held the gun to Chato's head ranting.

"If ya don't owe any money, then why don't this man give ya the four hundred kilos? Ya paid for 'em, right, with Jake's money?"

Chato's face, bathed in sweat, was indifferent and full of uncertainty. He was in shock and unable to comprehend.

Victor spotted me but didn't move a muscle. Sweat was running down Chato's forehead as he solemnly swore, "He give me the kilos when he have them."

Liar or not, he seemed ready to die. And for what? Maybe he was reliving the feelings he'd suffered when he found out his wife had another lover. Maybe he was thinking about her and the man who had deceived him, and no longer cared to live. Maybe he was going to let Jim put him out of his misery. Jim, too caught up in a pigheaded drama, would not know he was the perfect candidate to put an end to the humiliation Chato had to live out on a daily basis.

"Get on with it, Chato." Victor interjected, "Make it easy on yourself. Tell us what we want to hear!"

I detected concern in Victor's voice. It equaled mine.

"How much money do ya have left?" Jim pressed. "Tell me."

"I have not the money," Chato pleaded, his eyes darting between Jim and Victor.

"Whatta ya do with the two grand Jake gave you a couple weeks ago?"

"I use it. Some, I pay my people."

"Ya fuck. Ya told Jake the money was for weed, then ya used it to feed your fat belly. Come on ya *puto*, I wanna to hear the rest. You're fucking around with us." Jim jammed the pistol hard against his temple. "Ya feel that? Tell me the rest."

I'd had enough of this. Purposefully, I stepped forward a few feet.

Jim turned and saw me and became enraged. "What the hell are ya doing in here?" he screamed, while lowering the pistol half way.

"This is getting of hand!" I spat out. "If you pull that trigger on Chato just to prove your point..."

"You sonofabitch. Get outta here," Jim barked, teeth clenched as he lowered the pistol entirely and then faced me.

Jake came up quietly behind me and said, "What's the problem here?" His voice was calm. Relief flowed through me.

"Tell him to get the hell outta here," Jim ranted.

Before another word was said Chato made a move. He reached across the table and snatched his small vile of cocaine. We watched as Chato, totally unfazed, boldly inserted the spoon into his precious elixir and performed the operation that he had been doing all afternoon and into the night; each spoonful reached its mark, not one bit of powder fell to the table. He seemed not to care about anything, except the treasured cocaine that was now making its way into his nasal passages. His movements were so suave, I felt myself respond in kind to this unspoken bravado. Chato, unaware he'd just made a feat of accomplishment, carefully screwed the top back in place, set the vial down, and then looked vacantly at Jim.

I seized the moment. "Hold loose for a moment, will you? We know he's lying, but we can straighten all that out if we just work on getting him to find us some weed. Isn't that what we came after?"

"He's right," Jake said, as he moved in alongside me. "I heard what Chato said about the two grand. I'd like to talk with him for a while." Jake stared at Jim, then approached Chato. "Come on. We can talk in the living room."

Jim was unable to speak as Chato gladly got up and exited with Jake.

Jim glared at me and I apologized with a slight tremble, "Sorry I came on that way, man. I just think there's another way to handle this. Why don't we talk about it? Chato can get us weed..."

"Don't ya ever do that again, goddammit!" Jim glared through me, his eyes shiny and hard. "This is my game. I'm not interested in your ideas. Stay out of it."

"We're all in this together," I retorted. "Christ man, we're in Mexico. Chato's people are all around us..."

"Hey, calm down, Frank," Victor cut in before I finished. "The man wasn't gonna shoot 'em. He was just playing him along."

"You hypocrite, Victor," I thought. "One moment you're wearing the look of concern, now you're siding with your crony. You're hardly convincing. Aloud I said, "Why don't we try a new approach? So Chato's lying. We want to do some business. Let's work on that."

Unimpressed by my speech, Jim reached for the vial of cocaine as Victor placed his hand on my shoulder. He forced a smile and said, "Tell you what, Frank. When we get this mess straightened out, we'll work on it. We ain't gonna do Chato in. I wanna do business with him. Let things be for now. Come on." He ushered me into the living room, Jim on our heels, pistol tucked in his belt.

"You finished, Jake?" Jim asked, wandering into the living room after a few moments.

"He's saying the same thing, Jim. He doesn't owe any money to Jesus. Jesus owes him money. It's our money. Jesus will give us weed when he's got it," Jake explained leisurely as he sat on the sofa with Chato.

"Shit, I already heard it, man." He faced Chato and screeched, "This man has a phone, right?" Jim grabbed the phone off the table, "I want ya to call 'em. No funny stuff. I know Spanish. Tell him you want your money back… Come on. What ya waiting for?"

Jim handed him the phone, then stood back to light a cigarette as Chato placed a call.

It would take some time. We were in Mexico and the operator had to make her connections. As she did, we talked at length, me with Victor, Jake with Jim. Before long the phone rang. The operator had a Señor Roberto on the line. Chato, almost back to his merry self, sang out salutations and chided with the caller. Laughing and guffawing, he explained what he was saying, while cupping the phone.

It was Roberto he was speaking to, one of the many sons of Jesus. When he hung up Chato reported, "Jesus is no at his *casa*. His son Roberto say he come back tomorrow, maybe in the morning. Maybe he come back tonight."

"I heard ya." Jim blew a stream of smoke at him, and added, "Now I want ya to tell me everything you said, *hombre*. You talked too long for me to believe that all ya said was that ya wanted to talk to Jesus. What did you tell this dude Roberto?"

"*Si*. We talk of you Jimmy. I tell him you have many guns—that you shoot me if I lie. He say that he help me and that there be many problems if you hurt me. He say you be a patient man. His father is a man of honor. He bring the *mota* when it be ready. There be nothing he can do for now. I tell him to go see his father. He say maybe he go now. I say it is best. He find the man and he call me back. That is what he tell me. He say to me, you come see him."

Well, Jim had asked. I was elated, even smirking because Chato was out of the woods. Jim was on the decline. His evil spell had been broken. I was temped to jump up and celebrate. And obviously, Jim didn't understand Spanish. His bravado had been weakened. But Jim was not about to let Chato off so easily and resumed his threats—a last ditch effort to squeeze out the truth and soothe his bruised ego.

Satisfied that things were under control, or at least that Chato wasn't going to be shot, I went out into the garden. The fresh air helped me to regain my senses.

"He wants me ta come see him!" I heard Jim roar. "Shit! Yeah, and walk into a trap. I ain't stupid, man. What we're all gonna do is sit and wait 'til this pal of ya calls. Ya better hope it's soon. I don't like waitin' one bit."

"Relax man, we're gonna wait for Jesus to call," Victor replied calmly.

I watched from the garden as Jim sat opposite Chato on a club chair and pulled the pistol loose from his belt. He began to nonchalantly toy with it, then using his best "good cop" tone he coaxed, "I wanna know more about your friend, Jesus."

Moments later, I reentered and motioned Jake over to the bar. I fired up a joint, toked, and handed it to Jake. He handed over the vile, and after taking a hit I said quietly, "Jim is way out of balance, you know, way too much yang—yin nowhere in sight. Let's work on keeping him busy. We can head him in another direction to keep him from starting up again."

"Let's do that. When this guy Jesus calls I'll get Jim to go along with what this Jesus says. Jesus, I believe, will come through.

"Good. Get things going with Victor, too. We can move on getting some weed through Jesus—anything to avoid Jim and his monster ego. Even if we have to wait for Chato to get some weed, fine with me. We ought to go back to San Francisco. Maybe we can convince Victor to do the same. What's a couple of weeks more? Besides, sooner or later we have to call Bill."

"Victor's not going to go back. He'll want to stay here and get this business going with Chato. That's their game. I don't want to play this one either. Let's figure the worst is over for now. I'll push them to get Chato heading in that direction. Go take a rest, man. You look tired. I'll handle this. As for Bill, we'll call him when this is all straightened out," Jake advised.

An underlying tension had seized all of us, even though Jim had put to rest his surly behavior. I napped on one of the sofas while Jim hung out at the bar with his pal Victor, snorting cocaine and smoking joints. The bottle of Tequila was beginning to wane. Chato sat on the sofa with Jake at the far end. Both were quiet.

A loud knock at the door got our attention. It was well past midnight. My heart began to pound as Jim jumped up from his seat—pistol in his hand, a look of fear on his face. Immediately he pointed the gun at Chato. Victor stood, as more tension filled the room. Jake was spooked, as was I. Jake got up quickly and retrieved the pistol he had set on the coffee table.

"This better be good, fat man," Jim said in a low voice. "Send 'em away whoever it is." As Chato approached the door Jim added, "If you're pulling a fast one I'll shoot ya, *hombre!*"

"Maybe it be my friend. He bring the Cerveza," Chato said cheerfully.

"Answer it. Go on. No funny stuff either." He lowered the pistol.

Chato opened the door part way. A lone man stood near the entry. Jim moved closer to get a good look. Words were passed. A case of beer was handed over to Chato. He closed the door. With the case of beer in hand he said, "It be my friend Jorge. He go home now."

Jim moved back to the bar, picked up the vile, and doused his nose. Victor was there to hand him a fresh cold beer as he finished up.

Jake and Chato went back to sitting on the sofa. I went back to napping on the second sofa. I was exhausted, not only from lack of sleep, but from the depths of despair we had sunken to. We were all paranoid, except for

Chato. This drama was not over. Who knows what would happen when Jesus called—if he called.

Some time later, the phone rang. I woke with a start as Chato picked up the receiver.

"Who's that?" Jim growled from his bar seat.

"It be my friend Renee," said Chato, as he cupped the phone. "He call to say hello. I tell him I be fine." Gritting his teeth Jim ordered, "Tell 'em goodbye. Hang up."

Chato defied him and continued the conversation.

"Hang up, I told ya." Jim moved toward him, threatening with his pistol. The standoff continued, but only a few seconds, then Chato hung up.

"What'd you tell 'em?"

Chato looked at him and replied smartly, "I tell him I be here with my American friends and we talk. He want to come see me. I tell him no."

Bleary eyed, Jim looked over at Jake. "That what you got?"

"Yeah," Jake confirmed. He had taken Spanish in high school. I figured he knew what had been said.

"What about weapons?"

"I don't think so. It sounded like they were talking friendly."

"Ya better be right or else." He pointed the weapon at Chato, but his words lacked conviction.

Relieved, I passed out again. When I woke up, and had just returned from the bathroom, Jim and Jake were sitting at the bar deep in conversation. Jim was relating a gruesome story about his father, his voice cracked with emotion. The story had to do with his parents and his father's drinking problems—he was a brutal drunk, a man no one would want to be around. Jim snarled about all the beatings he took. He was the oldest son. Everyone in the family got beat up. When he was old enough to beat the dirty bastard up, he did. Then his dad took off. Jim had to help his mother to raise the family.

I had heard enough and wandered back to the refuge of the sofa. Jake woke me some time later saying, "Hey buddy, Chato said you can use the back room, the one on the left. Everything's fine. Go to bed."

Jim was head down at the bar, hand wrapped around a beer. He gave me a quick glare; there was pain in his eyes, his face pitiful and full of rage, and at the same time sad. I felt he was caught in a bind, unable to get out. I had unwittingly intruded on him at a sore moment. I lowered my head and went straight to the bedroom.

CHAPTER FIVE

OUR SAVIOR

MEXICO
SEPTEMBER, 1968

I WOKE TO A brilliant morning and the sound of the phone ringing in the distance. Rays of sunlight poured through the lone window, spotlighting my face. Slowly I rose and stretched to loosen aching muscles. Suddenly, images of the night before pierced my languor. Jim's heinous face hung in my mind. I wanted to laugh at it, but the face was dark and haunting. Sitting on the edge of the bed, cupping my head, I waited for the blood to start flowing. When I stood up I was racked by pain, and moved slowly toward the living room. Chato was on the phone. Victor, Jim, and Jake stood around listening, staring blankly, their eyes bloodshot from lack of sleep.

Chato hung up and said to Jake, "It be good, Jakey. We go see Jesus. He say he help me. He goes to Culican to find the *mota*."

"Then let's get going."

"Do as we planned, Jake. We'll back ya up," Victor stated. Placing a hand on his new best pal's shoulder, he warned Chato, "Don't let anything happen to these guys. You get this guy Jesus to find us a ton or so and we'll start this work. We'll be here 'til you get back. *Comprende?*"

"*Si* Victor. This no be a problem. We go look for the *mota*. Three, four days we have some. We do the business."

"We'll be waiting here, like I said, until you get back."

"What's happening?" I asked, stumbling into the room.

"Let me talk to Frank about this," Jake said.

Walking into the garden, Jake shaded his eyes from the sun. "You and I are going south to meet Jesus. I worked this out with the boys. They agreed that we should go together with Chato. That way we can see what he's up to. Jesus may find us some grass And, I want to get out of here."

"You mean out of this house? Great! Anything to get away from those two clowns," I responded elatedly. "What happened last night? You look tired. Did you get any sleep?"

"Not much. I'll tell you later. Let's just go."

"As soon as I get a glass of water. I can't even talk. My mouth tastes like I've been eating dirty sweat socks. What are Victor and Jim up to?"

"They're gonna stay here and wait for us to come back. If anything happens to us, they'll be after Chato's ass."

"That sounds ridiculous—and convenient, too. Where would they find him anyway?"

Even though I was hung over and tired, I could see the flaws in their plan. But, we'd be safer with Chato. Jim and Victor, if they did hang around, would be sitting on a hot seat. All Chato had to do was call a few of his people and tell them about the two *hombres* that he wanted removed and disposed of. But Chato wouldn't do this. He was too clever.

"Who knows?" Jake replied, with a knowing smile. Gone was the stolid demeanor that had gripped him the night before.

Chato was waiting in his car near the front door and we eased in.

Jim delivered a final warning. "I want my friends back just as they are. *Comprende?*"

As we crossed a small bridge on the outskirts of town Chato let out a pent-up howl. "*Ai chihuachua*, I be happy to be away from that bad *hombre*."

"All of us are, Chato," Jake said from the back seat.

"Jakey my friend. You be okay. You get some sleep. *Si*."

"*Si* Chato. *Si*."

"Victor's *amigo* Jimmy, he is *loco hombre*. Very *macho*, but he no brave. I think he fear many things."

"You've got it, Chato," Jake answered.

"When I come back, I tell Victor I no do business with this *hombre*. I tell Jesus you are my friend. He not hurt you. *Si*."

Finally away from Jim, I felt myself relax while Jake napped. Chato, who perhaps hadn't slept a wink, raced his Ford Mustang down the narrow Mexican highway, charging the sharp turns, the wheels sometimes screeching as though the car and its occupants were invincible.

"Chato, what's the rush? Can't you slow down? My stomach hurts and my head weighs a thousand pounds."

Chato only laughed. "It be better this way. We go to Guamochil before dark. I no like to drive in the night. There be many cows on the road. Once, I hit them."

"Yeah, right," I thought, as I let out a big belch. "Cows! You'll get us killed to avoid a cow."

At noon we stopped for gas and food in Guaymas, a city along the coast, from where we could see the rich blue waters of the Gulf and the barren mountains opposite us. Chato purchased a few tacos at a vending stand near the station and we were once again on the road, the Gulf waters disappearing from sight.

As we cruised inland through the farm country, temperatures soared. My head spun as each ray of sunshine pierced my body.

"Your country is very beautiful Chato, but it's so damn hot."

"*Si*. Is *magnifico*. Everyone know the sun. Mostly they go slow. The farmers work in the morning. It be more *bueno*."

Liar or not, I admired him for who he was. He had bounced back from the previous night's ordeal, but I hadn't. Bets were that Jim and Victor were out flat, too. By the time they escaped from their doldrums and sense prevailed, they'd be wondering how Chato had gotten away from them.

As we drove south I stared out the window watching the land, its people, and its culture moving rapidly by. The deeper we drove into this foreign land, the more I became lost in its expansiveness.

On the roadsides I glimpsed poverty. Mexican Indians, sometimes colorfully dressed, lived mostly in small ramshackle adobe huts. Small villages with bare dirt roads streaked by, and a few dilapidated vehicles dotted the landscape. There were no telephone poles, but lots of chickens, pigs, goats, and dogs roaming the streets, most of them gaunt and barely alive. A few times we passed animals that lay dead on the roadside, stiff with rigor mortis, the stench sometimes permeating the car. I wanted to understand how these people lived like this. What I saw equaled the poverty of spirit I was feeling at the moment—and I wanted to understand how to outgrow that poverty.

As predicted, we pulled into Guamochil as darkness descended. Chato dropped us off at a small motel on the outskirts of town. He was to go off and find his friend. Still exhausted, Jake and I ate a huge meal at a tiny restaurant next to the motel.

"Damn, I don't even have a change of clothes," I complained. "This sucks."

"Hey, you've had worse things happen to you, haven't you?" Jake quipped—Jim's exact comment to me within the first hour we had met still lingered. I laughed along with Jake. The cliché paid big dividends over the next few years. It reminded us that there was no situation we could not overcome. There was always a different perspective, always a choice about how to respond to situations—a portal from which to escape.

"Thanks, Jake. Like I need to be reminded," I said through the laughter. "I have indeed had worse things happen."

"Then get over the panic. We'll make do."

"Right on! I hope our boys up north are making do. What were you and Jim talking about last night? I heard part of it. Jim was telling you about his dad and all the beatings he had had to put up with."

"He's a strange man—one 'pissed off sonofabitch' would be a more appropriate. He came up while I was sitting on the bar stool and started telling me about his life in Georgia when he was a kid." Jake let out a sigh, adding, "I wasn't up to hearing what he had to say, but he got on to telling me his father was an alcoholic and that he never worked. His dad would get good and drunk, then come home and terrorize the family. Jim was the oldest. He got the worst of it. He's bitter about it and he hates his father. He couldn't stop talking about him. He just kept on telling me stories."

Jake's face contorted with disgust. I knew what he meant. I couldn't bear to look at Jim's face myself, and was spooked by the way he had glared at me from the bar.

"Yeah. He seemed a mess. Totally out of it. As soon as I saw him at the bar with you I didn't want to be around him."

"Yeah, I got stuck with him. I had to listen." Jake paused a second and then added, "It got real bad after awhile. It's too hard to describe what he was going through. You'd have had to have heard it yourself."

"I heard enough, Jake. It was enough to get me out of there. It felt as though he was dragging you in to his depths of despair."

"Yeah. He wouldn't let me go. He was begging me to hear him out. He cried a few times. It was weird. I didn't want to hear what he had to say, but man, it was hard not to. His energy was up and down. When he got married he beat his wife like his father beat him."

"Yeah, I can imagine. She must have gotten beaten a few times, as in all the time?"

"Probably. She split from him and took the kids. He hasn't seen them for a few years. He came out here to the coast and met up with our good pal, Victor."

"Well, you got to admit, they do have a lot in common. So Jim's a southern boy?"

"Yeah. He's got a monster inside him, you know, like the ones Johan is always looking at in the monster books."

Jake grinned, but the pain in his face was obvious. Jake had had to listen to Jim's emotional episode last night. Doors to Jake's unhappy formative years had no doubt been opened, and all the emotional pain Jake kept bottled up must have must spilled through.

"Well, did you ease some of his pain?" I asked.

"I don't know. I told him I never met my father and my mother couldn't handle life so she sent me off to live on a farm when I was seven. He asked me if I hated them."

"What did you tell him?"

"The truth, man. I told him I didn't, but I felt badly about what they did to me anyway. Then he told me he had been a patient at Langley Porter."

"Langley Porter? What's that?"

"A mental health clinic at UC Hospital in San Francisco. He's psychotic."

"Whoa! That's believable! We landed a loony, didn't we? Boy, he had us locked in." I added, "We're a bit loony ourselves."

"Afraid so, Frank." Jake replied, with a cryptic look on his face that was hard to fathom.

Although we could hardly comprehend what was being said, Jake and I joined in the laughter while the three of us, in addition to Jesus and his three *compadres* gathered together in our motel room the next morning. Chato, his eyes bright and face animated, was doing a splendid job of entertaining. Right hand thrust up, finger pointed out, as though it were a pistol, he played the part of gangster, Jim Bigotes, notorious bandit and part-time mental patient at Langley Porter.

A violent wind was blowing. It was creating havoc: part of a dying hurricane we were told. Torrential rain had begun to fall early that morning. The monsoon storm was expected to hang around for the next couple of days. The nearby cornfields were saturated and the once dry riverbed, a hundred yards away, swelled dangerously high. Mazatlan, 250 miles to the south, was besieged with winds up to ninety miles an hour.

Inside our motel room there was no electricity, but then we didn't seem to need any. Chato emitted enough as he bounded around like a Mexican banshee, shouting and spouting the very words that Jim had used in his convoluted attempt to corrupt him.

As the laughter abated Chato calmed down. He came over to us as we sat on the edge of a bed and said proudly, "I say to Jesus, '*Dame pistola*. I go shoot the balls off Jim Bigotes.' They say it no be necessary. He no have the balls to shoot."

"But how would you know he has no balls, Chato? He didn't lower his pants for you," Jake chirped, which caused Chato to laugh uproariously. His hands covered his belly, as he spoke to Jesus and his friends. Jesus laughed heartily, stepped forward and clasped Jake around the shoulder, and said something in Spanish to Chato.

Chato explained, "Jesus say he think you are good people. He do his best to help you. He say, tomorrow when the rains go away, he go to the mountains near Culican. He find *mota*."

Jesus, a small homely man in his sixties, stood back against the wall, appearing sincere with a pleasant smile and an easygoing expression. Soon Jesus and his *compadres* were out the door. We were asked to wait for three days.

※ ※ ※

"Jakey, come, we go soon. Jesus have the *mota* for us," Chato urged, gesturing toward us in the open entry.

"Great. Slow down, will ya? What's up?" Jake queried, quickly rising from his bed.

I awoke dazed, my stomach aching. It was mid-afternoon of the third day. I had eaten some bad food and was nauseous. Looking flushed and harried as he stood in the doorway, Chato ignored Jake's question.

"Come quickly. We must be ready. He come soon. We leave, maybe five minutes."

"What's the rush?" I asked, still in bed. It wasn't like the Mexicans to rush, not in such a fashion.

Exasperated, Chato implored, "Jesus, say we go now. He have the kilos in his truck. He hide them. You will see. Come. We must be ready or he leave without us."

"How many?" Jake asked calmly, waiting for an answer from Chato.

"He say, fourteen hundred."

I struggled to get up off the bed and began looking around for the few articles we had brought, when a horn sounded out front.

Chato poked his head out the door, then back in again and said excitedly, "It be Jesus. *Si*, he come. We must go. Hurry! We be late."

"Shit! Late for what? What are these Mexicans up to?" It wasn't the time to argue or debate the matter. Grabbing our shirts and a few sundries, we ran out of the room to get into Chato's car parked only a few yards away with its doors open. Chato gestured for us to hurry, an irritated look on his face. Up ahead on the roadside, Jesus stood next to his Volkswagen, waving at us. Fifty yards up the road was a small stake-bed truck, piled high with bundles of hay, all roped off—wooden gates held them in place.

Jake looked sharply at me and said, "Come on, let's go. This is it." We piled into the car just as Jesus took off, the stake-bed truck in the lead.

Chato chirped, "We go to Hermosillo now. We be there by the night. My friends from Santana, they come meet us. We put the kilos in his truck, *Si?*"

"Sounds good to me. Lets go!" I heard Jake say from the front seat.

Tired and my stomach cramping with a good dose of *touristas* revenge, I curled up in the back seat to get some sleep. When we stopped I woke and called after Jake nervously as he was getting out of the car, "What's happening? What time is it?"

"It's about nine. We're in Navajoa. We're going to get some food. Chato has to call his man. How ya feeling?"

Racked by painful cramps, I sat up. "Shitty. This stuff's gonna come up sooner or later. It was that fucking cheese. I can taste it." I looked him squarely in the eye and said, "Hey, does this thing make sense to you?"

"What do you mean?" Jake asked.

We were alone and could talk openly. "Something's weird, Jake. Why are they in a rush all of a sudden, and now they want to stop and eat? And that load of hay, it's kind of on the small side. I can't picture how they got the load under it. You know, fourteen hundred kilos? Come on!"

"You're not feeling well. Nothing's up. Chato wants to get to Hermosillo and get the load transferred before daybreak. That's all."

"Why do they want to transfer it in Hermosillo? Why not Santana? It's only a couple of hours more. This is silly. It just doesn't feel right."

"I don't know. I agree, but they're the ones who are handling this. Why don't you get some sleep? All I want to do is get this load north, and across the border."

"I'll sleep later. I want to check this out, Jake." Dizzy and doubled over with cramps, I lurched out of the Mustang.

"Hungry?" Jake teased.

"Are you kidding? Look, I'm serious Jake. Something's up. I want to check this out."

Inside the restaurant, Chato, Jake, and I sat at a separate table, while Jesus and his crew sat across the room from us. I ordered a hot chocolate while the others scarfed down dinner. Something was amiss. I couldn't put my finger on it. It was only a feeling, much like the one I had had about Jim.

Chato went over to Jesus' table and they talked secretively. He returned to our table and said in an uncharacteristic monotone, "Come, we go now."

We followed Jesus and his crew as they drove a few blocks, then made a right turn and parked on a deserted street. We pulled up behind them and piled out. Chato asked us to wait, then walked off to where Jesus stood.

"What the hell are they up to?" I asked, as Chato and Jesus talked at length.

"Hard to say. They're going over things, I guess."

"I don't like this."

"Just be cool," Jake advised.

I couldn't stay cool. Chato was having an agitated conversation with his associate. A chill ran up my spine as they stared over at us from time to time. There were no streetlights and not a soul around except our group. All was quiet except for Jesus and Chato who were disagreeing with one another. When Chato returned he was not smiling, and the unpleasant look on his face forewarned me that all was not well. Then he said, "Come my friends. We go now."

I wondered if Jake had picked up on the strange vibe that I had, as we climbed back in the car—my mind and body in turmoil.

I woke to unfamiliar surroundings and stabbing pains in my abdomen. "Let me out, man. I've got to puke," I moaned.

Jake quickly opened the door. I staggered out and looked around. Spotting a rest room I stumbled forward, clutching my stomach. The interior was pure filth and the smell unbearable as I stood over the toilet and puked—being careful not to fall. I somehow managed to stay on my feet and staggered back out into the cool night air.

"How you doing?" Jake asked.

"Whew… much better. God, I need something to drink."

"Here, I brought a few of these." Jake handed me a bottle of carbonated fruit juice he had purchased at the Pemex. I scanned the fuel station.

Jake said, "We're on the outskirts of Hermosillo."

"Good! Where's Jesus? Why isn't he here?"

"We passed him a while ago. Just after Guaymas. He should be here any moment."

"Any moment? Shit! Jake, I thought we were supposed to follow him!"

"We did. Then Chato decided to pass him up. Relax. They'll be here. Okay? Chato's man will be here any time now. We'll get this done."

I got back in the car and passed out, waking when I heard a vehicle pull up. Jake and Chato were talking with a man in a pickup. "It must be the guy we're to use to bring the load north," I figured. "Christ! A pick-up? What gives?"

I got out. Jesus and his men were nowhere in sight. I wanted to ask questions, but I couldn't get my thoughts aligned. Something wasn't making sense, that much I knew. Strange, inexplicable feelings took hold as I stood around in the cool morning air. To the east, the first signs of daybreak appeared.

Bleary-eyed, I stumbled over to where the others stood. "Where's

Jesus?"

"He hasn't arrived yet. Renee is here. Everything's fine."

I pulled him aside. "How are they going to get the load in this guy's pickup, Jake? Look at it. Do they even have a tarp?"

"Be easy. Chato has a place to do the transfer. We have to wait for Jesus to get here."

My head was spinning. "I don't like this. Jesus should have been here by now. The sun will be up soon and we have to consider what to do if that happens before we make the transfer. We can't wait too long for him to get here."

"Chato knows this. If he isn't here in another few minutes, we'll go back and look for him."

"Let's do it now. Come on Jake. This is not cool the way we're standing around waiting for this dude. Something's up."

"Give it fifteen," Jake replied, heading back to the pickup.

Chato gave the go-ahead moments later. We took off, the sky now filled with salmon-colored clouds.

Several minutes passed as we sped south through the rugged desert. Anxiety took over and my mind raced with worst-case scenarios. "Had Jesus had an accident? "Had he been stopped and busted?"

In the distance, a gray plume of smoke came into view. Apprehension filled the car as the three of us stared at the plume that rose up into the morning sky, like a gothic column. I leaned forward as we drove on, gripping the back seat, my thoughts running wild. I strained forward as we drove closer, on the verge of panic.

Chato brought the car to a jerking halt. At the same time my stomach convulsed, not only from the sickness, but from what I saw outside the car—a disaster scene equal to the disaster within. Scrambling out of the car, I doubled over to vomit, while Jake and Chato hurried off.

When I looked up I could see that the hay on the truck was on fire, but not the truck. Jesus stood nearby, motioning dramatically to one of his men who stood as close as they could to the fire. What the hell were they up to? Are they going to try to put the fire out? No way. They're creating a commotion to get us to believe that they're going to put it out. How stupid this is. This is a bad-news scene.

Woozy, I headed toward Jake and Chato, who stood back as Jesus continued what I considered a charade. As we cautiously approached, Jesus' histrionics became more pronounced. He began to holler and scream.

"What's he saying?" Jake asked, as the three of us stopped, dumbfounded in our tracks.

"He say someone shoot at him," Chato answered. "His truck catch fire from the bullet. He be mad right now. He say his *mota* is gone, his truck be no good, it be bad for him."

Bullshit! I screeched inwardly. A bullet? No way. Then I saw Jesus pull a small pistol from his belt.

I grabbed Jake by the arm. "Shit! He's got a gun, Jake." Craning my neck around, I spotted the truck driver and the third man several yards to our rear. Both of them had pistols tucked in their belts. Other than the six of us, there was not a soul around— no traffic either. We were surrounded by three hostile Mexicans.

Chato said something to Jesus and began to approach him. When he got within forty feet, he literally stared back-pedaling. Turning, he came back and said, "This be bad Jakey."

Terrified, I kept my eyes on Jesus and the two men to our rear. They stood fast as Jesus kept cursing, his arms and body flailing. We could tell he was only acting hysterical and out of control, but he was very convincing. Jake and I stood rooted in place with shock and disbelief. As Jesus shouted, Chato translated with great distress: "He no like what they do to his truck, Jakey."

Jake also knew that they were pulling something on us. He had to. Anyone could see that this scenario they had cooked up was a hoax, and if we stayed there the hoax would turn deadly.

"We go now," Chato suddenly announced. "Jesus be mad. Maybe he shoot us."

"He's right, Jake. Let's get out of here. Come on. This is unreal. The man has a gun. So do the other two."

Jake refused to listen to what I was saying and stood frozen, staring Jesus down as he ran around like a lunatic.

"We go, Jakey," Chato said again.

It was and us against them deal. I wanted to get out of there, so I grabbed Jake by and arm and tugged. Chato did likewise, the two of us marching him off backwards, his face full of contempt, as Chato once again gave warning.

"It be bad place for us, Jakey," Chato frowned, and shielded his face from the sun. "He shoot us if we no leave."

"Come on. You heard him. We best get outta here—now! Lets go, Jake."

The "now" word had a forever sound to it. Through the anger and hysteria, we backed away. Jake was still hedging, even as I clutched his arm.

I shouted over the ruckus. "Come on, Jake. Get with it. They planned it this way. We're supposed to leave."

I grabbed Jake even tighter and pulled at him, as Jesus continued to rant, sending chills down my spine. Agonized by this turn of events, Jake finally turned and slowly walked back to the car.

"We go quickly now," Chato said anxiously.

We piled in and Chato screeched off, burning rubber as he made a U-turn. Within seconds we were out of harm's way. The last I saw of the hideous mess was Jesus, arms flailing, acting out his part fiercely.

"What the fuck was that all about?" I raged from the back seat, my eyes never leaving the diminishing scene.

"It be good we leave. There be much problems for us," Chato said.

Jake looked at him coldly. "What is this Chato? Who did this?"

I too stared at Chato. "Yes, Chato. Who did this? No way did a bullet start that fire."

Turning to Jake he whined, "I no do this my friends," and patted Jake on the shoulder. "Maybe it be Jesus. Maybe it be the bullets. You no know this. It can be true. But I no do this to you."

I fell back and sucked in a deep breath of frustration. What else did I expect him to say? We were not about to have him go back and interrogate his cohort. And if we pushed things, Chato just might turn around and go back and have Jesus finish a job that he didn't want to do. Just what the hell did these Mexicans put together? Did they start that fire just to run us off?

"Fuming, I shouted, "I think all of them had a hand in it, including our friend here." Chato didn't respond to my accusation.

Jake leveled me with a look and warned, "Just be cool for now. I have a good idea who did this. And Chato says he didn't." He lowered his voice and added, "You and I can talk about this later." He then turned to Chato and said officiously, "Take us back to Santana."

"*Si*. We go to Santana," He flashed a false smile. "We go to my *casa*. Maybe three hours we be there."

And what about Victor I thought, not to mention your good pal Señor Bigotes? Yeah, Chato, you know they're not there. You called. The coast is clear. You're about as obvious as a rooster at dawn.

I slumped down in the back seat and put my disabled mind to work. The madness needed to be sorted out. It didn't make sense.

Two days ago, Roberto, a young student and one of Jesus' twenty-six children, had paid us an unexpected visit, along with one of his younger brothers, Carlos. He smiled brightly as he introduced himself to us at our small motel on the outskirts of town.

"I wish to get to know you. I learn English at the university in Culican. This way I practice with you. I be your friend while you are here," he told us. He had been sincere. It was another hot afternoon and we immediately purchased a few beers, then we asked him to get us some weed to smoke. We borrowed Chato's car as he napped, and drove out to the local jungle marshes, cajoling, laughing, and whooping it up as we drove along the road full of mud holes. His younger bother was mortified that we smoked the "*loco* weed" and thought we were beyond crazy. After a few beers and some smoke, Jake once again drove wildly, charging around the muddied roads like a nut in a fruitcake, giving Roberto's younger brother a fit.

That evening we were their guests. It was Friday and they invited us to the local boxing matches. The arena was packed. The first contestants were young boys, almost too small to wear gloves. The crowd roared, and cheered them on. The young boys were quickly worn out. By the time the big men came on, the arena was serious and raucous.

We were then invited us to the local whorehouse. We stayed at the bar and begged off, much to the surprise of our hosts. Some of the prostitutes looked terrific. We could have used a good unwinding, but decided to let our better judgment prevail.

So what was that all about, I wondered. Why on earth had they acted so friendly then turned on us? In Navajoa, just after dinner, they could have killed us on that dark street and left us in the gutters. Chato must have interceded on our behalf—and his own too. Had we remained at the scene of the hoax any longer they would have shot us and left our bodies in the desert where no one would have found us. Bill, Jim, and Victor would surely have come after them. Or would they?

I shook my head in disbelief just before I fell into a fitful doze, remembering what Jim had said about Mexicans being cold-hearted and a bunch of liars.

☆ ☆ ☆

We could be dead. Instead, we were camping. My crippling bout with dysentery was history, and Chato was out looking for the Holy Grail. If he found it, he'd be sure to tell us—before it disappeared of course. Jesus was not to be seen, but two young Mexican *compensianos* (farm workers) had entered our campsite that morning. The nearby river was deep enough to bathe in and that was all we wanted to do—to "cleanse" ourselves of this latest disaster. I spent a lot of time watching the small river flow along its path.

Once Chato had dropped us by his house, Jake and I returned to Tucson, picked up the van and came back to wait for Chato while he looked for *mota*.

We hadn't seen our nemesis since. We didn't care where he might be or what the partners in crime might be up to. We were just glad to be alive and to charge our batteries. For all we knew, California had fallen into the ocean taking with it one Jim Bigotes, "The Impostor," and his much overrated crony, Victor "The Bleak."

We had no desire to let Bill know what we were up to and we did not care to call him. We only cared about the next moment and the next track of music on the small portable stereo that was blaring away, as we chased the Frisbee.

Our new friends suited us well. All morning long they hung around our campsite when they should have been heading west to gather cucumbers, to make money and to feed their families. We had corrupted them—for a while, at least. It was nearly noon when they left for the fields. They thanked us for the huge breakfast we had fed them and for sharing with them the game of Frisbee.

We had other visitors too: people from town, other travelers, like the two who had departed. The night before, we had been invited to a wedding by a friend of the groom. Jake begged off, but I went. They were friends of Chato's. His pal picked me up. When we got there I was warmly welcomed and enjoyed some of the best Mexican food I had ever eaten, as we feasted at the house of the betrothed.

The past three days had been taxing. But now, Jake and I had time to open up to one another and discuss what we had been through the past several months. We concluded that the business we had gotten into was a bitch of a game, mainly because Bill, Chato, and Victor had failed us. We too had failed. What would we do if Chato was truly washed up and Bill decided to go his way and cut us off? We were looking for answers, solutions to this mess we had gotten into. There was only a glimmer of hope that Chato would come through—yet we waited, and talked and thought about a future.

Could I really find the freedom I wanted? Could I remain in this business *and* learn how to empower myself and overcome the flow of painful thoughts that would sneak up on me the second things went wrong, or that just came at me out of nowhere? I reflected as I sat near the river one afternoon while

Jake napped. I had thought in the beginning that I could gain insight into all of this, but now that I'd spent a year of my life involving myself with men who I had thought to be my brothers I had to ask myself, "Just how stupid can you get?" There was one question that was becoming apparent: had I chosen this line of work in hopes that my self-esteem would rise? Well, it did and then it didn't; my self-worth went up and down like a seesaw. Was I chasing dreams through my own filters of poor self-worth? And if so, would the outcome of my dreams be equal to the "sometimes" low opinion I had of myself? And what about guilt and shame? Where did they fit in all of this? And what of fear? How does all of this work? I didn't know.

My thoughts became so tangled, I couldn't see straight. I longed to be home and at peace. Perhaps then I would find solace—certainly not here in a foreign country where I felt out of place. I wanted my books, especially the one that I read most often: *Education and the Significance of Life*, by Khristnamurti. The moment I'd open the book, his words always soothed my mind and heart. But I hadn't read them in so long I could hardly remember what he said that had endeared me to this unique man. "Follow no one," he had proposed, but what did that mean? Don't follow them; just learn from them? Was that what he meant? In that case, Jake and I had learned a great deal and we had to find a way to co-exist with the type of people we worked with. But it was as though all I had read and learned the past two years could not be of use to me or to my friend Jake.

Bill would be angry with us for not calling. Our credibility with him would take a deep blow, as had our self-esteem. We even thought of quitting the business. Jake and I considered the possibility that we'd never find a way to deal with the problems that seemed to be inherent in this line of work. We could retaliate against the man who had screwed us, but that wasn't our nature. So, we had to figure it out or quit.

Sitting with our legs crossed on a grass knoll by the river, I asked Jake one afternoon, "Are we any different than the ultra-slaves, consumed by nine to five jobs? Then I laughed, adding, "How much longer should we hang in like flies on a turd for Chato to come through?"

We didn't have an answer to any of these outstanding questions but we had to come to a decision about what we'd do next, and soon.

Shortly after the *compensianos* departed, Chato arrived. It was a short and convoluted visit before he flew off again with more promises that he would soon find *mota*. He left us on a high note, but we were sullen within minutes.

Arriving back from town after picking up food supplies, we were surprised to find Renee, Chato's *amigo*, at our campsite. We were also surprised that he spoke English, though not as well as Chato.

"*Buenos dias amigos.*"

"Good day, Renee," Jake responded.

"My English no good," he added, as he shifted his feet nervously. "I talk, you listen. It is good. *Si?*"

"Sure. What's happening?" Jake asked, as we stood in the shade.

"Chato know you be here. He no come 'til you leave."

"Yes. That's maybe true. Why are you telling us this?"

He stammered a moment and then replied in his broken English.

"Chato not my friend. He do bad business. He lie to his friends." Renee placed his finger to his chest, and then pointed to us in turn as he spoke. "He lie to you. He no get the m*ota*. You not hurt him for what he do."

"Yes, we know he lies to us," Jake answered.

Choosing his words carefully Renee said haltingly, "Chato no have money. He owe many people. Two years I work for him. I make business for him with the farmers. They give us *mota*. Sometime he pay. Sometime he no pay. They no give him the *mota*. There be trouble. Soon someone shoot him. He a bad *hombre*."

Jake quickly agreed. "Yes. Chato is a bad man. I know what you say, Renee."

More relaxed now, Renee smiled and continued.

"I want to do business with you. It be good?"

"Sure. We do business, you and me and Frank. Is that what you want?" Jake looked at me for approval and I nodded,

"Sure, Renee." Sizing up the situation, I added as our eyes met. "We do business. No Chato."

"*Si*. No Chato."

"Tell us what you want to do, Renee."

"*Si*. I have farmer friend. He have nine hundred kilos maybe two, three weeks. Two months more he have three, maybe four tons. He sell them to me every year. I sell to you. It is good." He stammered again, looking pensive.

Jake put him at ease. "*Si*, you sell them to us. We won't say a thing to *Chato*."

"Good," he continued. "I have friends. We put the kilos over border. There be no problems. We use the airplane." He mimicked a plane with his hands and his voice. We chuckled.

Jake said again to confirm the agreement, "*Si*. We do a business, Renee. You and me and Frank. No Chato."

Having established this, we sat down to work out the details with our new friend. Phone numbers were exchanged. Schedules were worked on. Agreements were made. When we were finished, we let Renee know once more that Chato would be kept out of this arrangement. When the meeting ended we were all smiles.

Elated by our turn of luck I shouted with joy, "Far out, man! Can you believe that? This guy just walked into our lives. You have to admit now there was good reason to hang in here."

"Yeah! He just may have saved our asses."

"Well, there's no sense in staying here. Let's break down camp and head home."

"I'm with you. We've got a lot to talk about."

Jake was poised, unlike me. I liked to let my mind rip; my feelings would explode and I was jubilant about our good fortune. It was as if we had created it and I was not about to let anyone tell me different. Yes, no doubt about it, we could now turn things around, and we would, whether or not Jake showed emotion. "We're both caught up again by the lure of this business," I thought, as we packed up. Renee walked right into our lives just when we needed him. We were on such a natural high we all but forgot that we had been "bitten" many times and Renee had yet to prove himself. We just feasted in our good fortune, knowing that we had earned it. Renee was our new connection, and our attention was on the good news he had passed on: he knew a few *mota* farmers, but more importantly, he could connect us with two *Americano* pilots.

Jake and I indeed had a lot to talk about. With our lives now in a major transitional upswing, there were still major obstacles facing us. We began immediately. With paper and pen at hand I wrote down what we needed, as Jake drove. Money was the key issue. Jake had about eight grand left and I had three. To pull the first deal off we had to come up with at least ten grand more. Bill was considered, but would he be willing to join us? We had to think beyond Bill. We could, if we chose, find another investor. And as we went over this we concluded that Bill would indeed be a problem. He had failed us and we found it hard to forgive him. More to the point, we wanted to do this on our own. We deserved the opportunity. If Bill acknowledged that Jake and I had saved the day by hanging in for him, the door of opportunity to join us would be open to him.

We began to search our souls. In most ways we knew that we wanted to continue with this business, but didn't feel confident about how to accomplish our goals. Guilt and fear had to be acknowledged, but the one unresolved issue was that we wanted to change the relationship we had with Bill. He was my brother, and as we bashed him I also felt obliged to defend him, but soon realized I was only feeling sorry for him and the pitiful way he had treated us.

"Bill will most certainly be interested to know that we gained a new connection—at our expense, mind you—but will he acknowledge our accomplishments? Would he be willing to let us partner with him?" I asked Jake.

"Frank, I think it's about time you realize that your brother is not the person you think he is. He treats you like you're something less than him. Seriously. He's got a big ego and I think you've always known that he's going to use you. Let's work on our plans—without him. If we back away from Bill and the rest of the "Bad Karma" crowd, we're free to plan and act on our own.

The truth of Jake's words hit me square in the chest. Of course I knew Bill always put himself first, brothers or not. Still, I so wanted to believe that things would change, that Bill would become the caring brother I wanted and needed him to be.

"Let's give him one more chance. Bill's my brother and that makes it hard. Let's put him through a test and put everything we've done for him over the past year on the table."

"How so?"

"By asking him to explain why he failed to call and let us know that his associate Victor was on his way down."

"That would be a god place to start."

"Good. Then let's confront Bill as soon as we get back. If he admits he was at fault, let's reconsider working with him."

Thinking things through Jake replied, "I don't think he will. It's his ego we're up against…and you being his younger brother… he's not going to let on that he made a mistake. Let's go one step further. How about you and I being partners in this new business? You've earned it. What do you think?"

Momentarily stunned I said, "Damn! I hadn't thought about that. Sure. Let's be partners. I'd like that. We're already partners in a sense. We almost got killed together. That says a lot to me."

"Good. Then let's start thinking as partners, partner."

Later the next day, after Jake and I had gone over what we would do together as partners, I thought about how Bill might react when he was confronted. Jake and I had worked out the details but I was nervous.

"I see the way he treats you, Frank. He could do a lot better—you deserve better," Jake had said earlier, and I felt the same way. Bill always made me feel less than what I was. It was his habit and I was getting tired of the egotistical override. Bill was so involved with his self-image he was unaware that I was on to him and was now ready to deal with him. It was time to rise up and face him. With Jake behind me as my partner, I no longer felt alone or powerless in confronting Bill's shoddy behavior of treating me as though I was not good enough.

✯ ✯ ✯

A burden had lifted when I let my new partner in on my concerns. But my relief was short-lived, for as we approached Bill's cottage the next day, my heart ached and my mind was in a state of despair I had never before experienced. Bill wanted to remain separate from me and in many ways, separate of others. He had introduced me to a spiritual path, a path of love and unity, but he wasn't living it himself. When Jake and I had gone to work for him, Bill had always been fair to us and shown loyalty to his customers. That was just a show. Underneath it all he lived in denial of how his actions betrayed his hollow words. His spiritual path was, to me, fraudulent. Were he true to what he espoused, like loving me as a brother, we wouldn't be in this position. Why couldn't Bill see all of this and reach out—or let me reach out to him?

The afternoon was warm and an autumn-like feeling hung in the air. Bill opened the door and his face turned from astonishment to relief. Then, in a flash, a frown of irritation furrowed his forehead.

"Christ, why didn't you guys call?" he demanded, as we entered and he closed the door behind us.

One thing was certain: he'd failed the first test. His sordid comment grated on me, as we brushed on by him, none of us willing to shake a hand, let alone give one another a hug to show we cared.

"We were busy with your pal Victor," Jake replied, his sarcasm bitter and prickly.

"What's that mean?" he challenged.

"It means we're alive, no thanks to you," I said, staring him down.

"Hey, mellow out guys," Bill snapped, then stepped back. Averting my stare he changed tactics and began to gather himself. In a calm voice he said, "Victor told me all about the situation. You went down there with guns. What the hell was that all about? Then you went with Chato down south. He figured the Mexicans had killed you. Now, why didn't you call?"

"We'll answer that as soon as you tell us why you didn't call and let us know your associate Victor was coming," Jake countered.

"Did you really believe what that jerk Victor had to say? How about hearing our story?" I said accusingly.

Bill didn't like being confronted on two flanks. He fidgeted and then replied heatedly, "First you tell me why you didn't call."

"Because it was on you to call us, man," I spoke up. "We work for you. It was your responsibility to let us know your associate was out of jail and coming down to see us."

"Back it off," Bill said, his eyes fixed on me, a finger pointing in my direction. "I just told you he came here and I sent him down there."

"Then why didn't you come along with him?" Jake questioned.

"What is this? I didn't need to. You guys were there. Chato is Victor's man. He decides who works with him. Besides, Victor said he'd go down and work with you guys to get his man going. There was no need for me to call."

"Without even calling to give us a warning or to give us instructions, not to mention he had a new partner? That's a lot of crap, Bill," I said, as sarcastically as I could.

"The way we see it, you ought to have come down and worked with all of us to get through all of this. We had no idea what you wanted us to do," Jake chimed in. "It's your end of the business. We worked all summer doing your work..."

"Hey!" Bill yelled, now turning his loaded finger at Jake. "Don't go telling me that I messed up by not coming down there. You guys were to call. You didn't. That's the way I see things."

"That's just great, Bill," I spat out. "Just great! If you want to stand by that, then we've no choice but to stop working for you. We made a new connection down south with one of Chato's people."

Jake added, "He can get us some good weed. We can all work with him if you want, but we're not going to work with you unless you're there each and every time we do a load."

He stared us down and then said arrogantly, "I'm not interested. I've been making other plans. I told you we had other connections. You guys go work with this man. I'm going elsewhere."

"Fine! Then you don't mind if we work with this guy?" I asked, still looking for approval.

Through clenched teeth he hissed, "Victor and Chato are history. Work with this dude if you want. You're not to use my customers. You got that?"

"Sure do," I said casually. "Is that all?"

He looked me squarely in the eyes, "I've things to do today. Just remember, don't go near any of my people. Now clear out of here. I've got some people coming over."

The confrontation hadn't lasted long, nor had it gone the way I had hoped it would. Then again, it had. Bill had shown me his true nature and it was as if I was really seeing this for the first time. I was in shock and my heart was heavy. Jake and I left as abruptly as we had arrived. I groaned as we climbed into the van.

"What a bummer. Shit! He didn't even want to know about the new connection."

"What else did you expect?"

"Shit, I figured he'd at least admit he should have called us. God... I can't believe he'd be so defensive... I've never seen him like this. Did you see the look of concern on his face at first when he opened the door?"

"Yes. It was there. He couldn't hide it—but he also couldn't acknowledge it. As for his defensiveness that's always been there. You didn't see it before. Believe me, it was there. You just had a wake-up call, brother. That's all. Remember the times are changing. You got to be ready for the change. Bill's not who you think he is. Everyone's got a gimmick."

"Yeah, everyone's got a gimmick!" I repeated, my heart and mind in a haze.

"Hey! You're beginning to notice."

"Yeah! I'm beginning to notice—and what about Brotherhood, Jake? Where's all that going to these days?"

"Lets go home."

"Yeah! Sounds cool."

CHAPTER SIX

TOTAL RESPONSIBILITY

SAN FRANCISCO, CA
OCTOBER, 1968

WE WERE ABOUT to become Manny's new best friends. Manny was involved with Scientology. He was also involved with dealing drugs. He claimed that his market was every bit as big as Bill's. We had met him several months before, while in Tucson. Gary, one of Bill's small-time customers had introduced us.

On three separate occasions Manny had bought a hundred kilos from Bill, through me. Bill had no idea we had met Manny. He wasn't one of Bill's regular customers, so we figured it was okay to use him. Manny was interested in what we had to offer him. He was also interested in recruiting us into his cult known as *Dianetics*. The word alone conjured up deep, esoteric thoughts, and in my naiveté I was more than curious about how *Dianetics* worked.

Each time Manny had made a trip south to pick up his contraband he lectured Jake and I on the attributes of this Scientology organization. Their claim was that they could fix most anything that troubled the human mind. "Aberrations" were what the *Church of Scientology* referred to as the "problem within each and every soul." L. Ron Hubbard, its founder, was something akin to a deity according to Manny and the rest of the members.

What we were mainly interested in was Manny's money. Along with Jake's ten grand and my three, we needed an additional ten grand—maybe more—to get our new business off the ground. In a preliminary visit with Manny, he had indicated interest in lending us the funds. Without Manny's money, we didn't know where to turn.

In the aftermath of the dissolution with Bill, Jake and I had taken a couple of weeks off to think things over. Jake had gone back to Jenner to be with his family and I had returned to my small apartment I shared with an old friend in Marin County.

On the way back from Mexico, both of us had poured out our feelings and thoughts of quitting the business. The psycho-drama we experienced had jaded us, and our fears about life, what we were doing, and what we wanted, had taken over on several occasions. By the time we got home we had mostly worked through those troubling thoughts. We had come full circle and acknowledged that our minds and hearts were indeed troubled. The bottom line was obvious; we had to find a way to overcome our fears, which meant we had to find the courage to deal with any bad boys who might happen along. And, to overcome fear we had to look at who we were and what each of us had to offer the other. I felt we had already created a measure of "togetherness" while working in close quarters throughout the summer. And now that we were partners, we could address one another as equals. I talked to Jake of this and a good many other shards of insightful knowledge that I had picked up on over the past couple of years. This was my time to open up and I did—no matter how I came across, I spoke out.

"It's all comes down to self-abnegation, partner," I told Jake.

Jake laughed loudly. "Self-abnegation? Where did you come up with that word?"

"Krishnamurti. I got it from him. It means to admit the truth—or something like that. So if you're afraid of something, admit it."

"I got you. But, you also have to know how to deal with what it is or why it is you fear something."

"I know. It's all a part of the experiment, you know, how to deal with life and all the shit that it brings up each and every time you walk out the door."

"Frank, you're my partner and we have to deal with everything that comes at us."

"Then let's put our total effort forward and work as a solid unit. If we create a close-knit arena of solidarity we'll find protection as we go about our jobs."

"Man, are you ever serious," he chided.

"So are you when it comes down to it—and don't go telling me anything different."

Giving what I said a moment of thought he replied, "You're probably right. What I do know is that I can trust you. That's the main reason I want to partner with you."

"I know. When you keep level with me, I'll be level with you. Just don't cross the boundary with me. You've seen me in action," I chided back.

That's when a bond of "trust" began for Jake and me. Amidst all the lying, cheating and deceit we had experienced, we realized how paramount trust was. It had been Jake who had said we should do this together as partners, as we drove up through the dessert, our hearts and minds heavy. From that point on we opened up and began listening to one another. It was a novel experience to be treated as an equal and to be allowed to express my thoughts with another male who would actually listen and respond. Jake and I had worked together under intense pressure and had succeeded. Now I knew that I could trust him and that together we could go on building trust.

It wasn't until several days after our return that I remembered that this dude, Manny, might be in a position to help us. Excited about the possibility, I made a special to trip up the coast to visit with Jake and family at their cabin in Jenner. After reminding Jake that Manny, who we figured to be a bit eccentric, was a primary candidate, we laughed with relief. Manny just might indeed save our asses, aid us in clearing our "aberrations," and propel us back into business. No telling what he and his Scientology buffs could do to straighten out our warped souls.

What was saving my ass at present was simply doing whatever came next, otherwise known as "living in the moment" as much as possible. I hung out at the place I called home—a small apartment in Marin County that I shared with one of my sailing pals. Once again, I began to enjoy listening to music and cooking fresh foods—getting back to my old self. Being gone so long over the preceding year, I'd fallen out of touch with friends. Most of my sailing pals were still available, but there were others who thought I was too radical. They came across as phony to me. I had to let go of them.

I had missed having the time to read, so I hit the books in search of knowledge, otherwise known as "think-your-way-through-it" time. When time allowed, I went sailing, which helped soothe most of the hardened thoughts that had entered my psyche. I spent a lot of time outdoors, hiking, and riding my dirt-bike—which I did until I was either contented or exhausted.

Ironically, during this time pot had an adverse effect: too many heavy feelings came up when I smoked, so I let up. When the desire for a woman to complement my life came up, a melancholy came about, but then abated when I realized that these emotions were proof that all the desires of life I was attracted to were there for the asking. I had only to work on how to achieve what it was that I wanted. This came to me one evening when I read a passage about all thoughts being noble, and how "wanting" is something that all of us feel, and that we can have what we want simply by thinking it so. In short, all things we desire will come— just lighten up and let them come.

Karma could be the number one issue, I concluded. Karma was everyone's issue these days: definitely an over-used word. I had come to accept Karma as a belief system, but failed to understand it. Karma, a Sanskrit word, means "action:" nothing more, nothing less. Every action is subject to reaction, either of a negative nature or a positive nature. Within positive action there is also negative, and vice versa. Whatever action one takes there is an equal and effective reaction. It's the law, the order of the universe—simple, yet complex.

The complex part had to do with all the components of yin and yang—the two driving forces of the law. One had to learn how these two components blended and how to blend with them, no matter how complex all life becomes. So, I began questioning the karmic direction I had taken—my *dharma*. Besieged by the complexity, I questioned whether or not I was hurting myself as well as others by what I was doing: smuggling drugs. Do I really have what it would take to run such a business? Would the people we dealt with attempt to destroy us, one way or another? And if so, was this the karma—the universal reaction to my choice?

At the end of this two-week sojourn I concluded that life was choice, and that within everything we choose, there is a valuable lesson to be learned. All of humankind has lessons and tests to look forward to. It's part of what is referred to as "being responsible to one's life."

I had my karma and everyone else theirs. Jake and I would just have to learn how to accept all the karma we created—good, bad, or ugly, and know that those around us would have to accept theirs in turn. As for the bad guys that we might encounter along the way, Jake and I figured that if we joined forces, we'd keep them off balance. We'd deal with them from strength of unity and experience—gained at the hands of slimy lunkheads like Victor and Jim Bigote, as well as Bill, Chato and Jesus.

※ ※ ※

"Hey, good to see you guys," Manny effused, as we came through the door to his apartment. Manny was big on hugging and we each received a short, casual embrace. "Come on in. This is my wife, Marlina. Sit down. I'll get you some tea." Beaming, he added, "I've some good Nepalese hash."

We sat down lotus-style on cushions and relaxed. Manny returned with three cups of tea on a platter and a hash pipe dangling from his mouth, and sat down next to us. He fired up the pipe. Passing it to Jake he began. "Tell me more about this problem you had with the Mexicans. I'm real interested in hearing about them."

Jake unfolded the story as I listened and added pieces.

Manny was close to Jake's age. He stood five-foot-six and there was no body fat to be found on his frame. Light brown curly hair covered his crown. What was odd about his features was his nose, which was somewhat large and slightly bulbous, as though it didn't really belong—a cosmic mistake. Other than that he was a picture of perfect health. Like us, he was a vegetarian, but a rather eccentric one.

"I can well understand why you guys want help," Manny concluded, as we finished relating the fiasco. "So, you believe this guy Renee will be able to handle the job and get a load flown over for you?"

"I don't see why not," Jake replied. "I've called him a couple of times. He insists it will only be a matter of days now before he gets the nine hundred kilos. And he has pilots—Americans."

Marlina entered and began setting down pots of steamed vegetables in front of us. Manny insisted we eat as we talk. She had prepared a vegetarian feast for us: beans, potatoes, and veggies, all cooked to perfection, as well as cloves of raw garlic. I watched with great curiosity as Manny occasionally popped a clove of garlic in his mouth. I had never seen anyone eat raw garlic like it was an appetizer.

"Frank said he already talked with you about investing money," Jake mentioned, as he too popped a clove of garlic, "We'll need ten grand."

"No problem," Manny looked up, smiling as he chewed.

"Good. How about investing with us and we'll sell everything through you?" Jake began setting forth the plans we had discussed.

Manny, quiet for a moment, came back with a startling proposition. "How about a partnership?" he suggested, his tone lucid. Jake and I shot a quick look at one another.

I shrugged as if to say, "This is a complete surprise to me."

Jake turned to him and said, "I don't know about that. Frank and I are partners already. Just what do you have in mind?"

"Big business." He beamed again.

The proposal lingered in the air. Then Manny added whimsically, "I like you guys. You're good people. I think we'd work well together. Have you ever thought about creating an organization, not only for smuggling, but one that would encompass using your potentials to their fullest?"

"Sounds far out to me." Curious, I urged him to go on.

"I have things to offer you guys other than just selling and front money. I have a way of life I believe in rather strongly. Frank, I talked a lot with you about Dianetics down in Tucson."

"You mean Scientology, 'getting clear' and all that stuff?" I asked.

"That's the idea. Getting Clear and taking responsibility in your life is what it's all about. Don't you think?"

"Sure. Jake and I discuss responsibility all the time. Tell me, how does one take responsibility for the people who come into their lives, like Victor and Jim?"

"You have to learn to take total responsibility for your own actions. You can't really do that until you've cleared away the aberrations that are stopping you."

Manny looked back and forth at each of us. Popping another clove of raw garlic into his mouth along with a huge spoon of beans, he added while chewing, "I've learned how to draw in the things I need and *avoid* those people who try to stop me from getting what I want. Anyone can do this. They only need to be 'Clear'— and that's what Scientology does. They have procedures for doing this."

"Just how do they do this?" Jake asked, staring intently at Manny.

Manny's eyes brightened as he explained how the process worked. He told us what "E" meters and "auditors" were, and all about traumatic problems stemming from our past: areas we could well be stuck in that were affecting our present behaviors. I listened intently as he added that the auditors are trained to release our hold on past traumas, thus clearing away aberrant behaviors.

"It's important to get Clear," Manny reiterated.

This was the very message I had tried to bring Jake and others; our past had everything to do with how we lived our present day lives. Manny had talked about a lot of this when we had first met him down in Tucson. Now it seemed even more important to listen to what he had to say about *Dianetics* and the organization he belonged to, and what he had in mind when he suggested a three-way partnership. Maybe we could unite and start our own organization based upon Scientology precepts.

"What you say makes a lot of sense, Manny." Jake looked over at me. "What do you think, Frank?"

"It sounds groovy to me. I'd like to read some of your books. I'd be interested in trying it out to see how all of this works."

"Good!" Manny continued, "All of us need to work on our past. Scientology offers this to anyone. There are lots of big name people: doctors, movie stars, and affluent people with money that are into it—and plenty of people joining the 'Orge' all the time."

"Where's this 'Clearing' stuff done?" Jake inquired.

"At the Orge in San Francisco and also in Los Angeles. Soon I'll finish up with the Clearing stage at the S.F. Orge. Then it's on to higher levels. The beauty of it is that all three of us will have the money to go through the Clearing process. That's what I want to do: help Clear the world. We can do it ourselves first. Think of the far-reaching possibilities. We can create a dope smuggling organization that will have the ability to survive by overcoming repressive people that stand in our way. We can bring up huge amounts of dope."

Leaning over, he grabbed Jake's arm. "Think about it. I want to make money. So do you guys. We can make what we want, but we need to set goals. That's what we learn in Scientology. Set goals and keep them, no matter how high."

"I have some big goals," he continued, "and you have the connections down south to get going. Add my money to the total and we can all have what we want; a three-way partnership that will flourish. We can have this Jake." Turning to me he repeated, "We can have this, Frank."

One thing was for sure, Manny was convincing. Everything he said made sense. His ideas were grandiose. I listened as he explained how we could set up an organization: hire drivers and helpers, purchase planes as we saw fit, and modern electronics for protection. He covered all the bases in an intelligent and realistic manner.

I'd never imagined having a sophisticated smuggling organization the size he was outlining. My mind was reeling and I found myself seriously interested in what he had to offer. He seemed sincere except for one small, but very obvious, detail. He was too confident.

Was I listening to a man who was just full of exaggeration and full of himself? Maybe. But that thought didn't stop me from agreeing that a partnership with this eccentric man just might launch Jake and me back into business in a positive and substantial way.

After going over all the details with Manny and listening to him pour out his feelings, Jake and I went outside to confer. I told Jake that Manny did not come across as a man who would overpower us, or deceive us. Scientology was worth digging into and we needed Manny's assistance, his money, and his market. When I expressed that I was interested in digging into my past and all the traumas that I might be stuck in, Jake hesitated. Perhaps he was not ready to delve into his past—an emotional drag that even thinking about might deplete his energy. But he got on the bandwagon with me anyway. We were back in business.

Manny was so overcome by our decision to take him on as a partner that he shed a few tears. He sure was an eccentric dude. I didn't even know the exact meaning of the word; only that Manny seemed to fit the description. More important to me was that his proposal would get Jake and me off the ground. After we gave him the thumbs up, Manny proceeded to organize us into areas of responsibility.

"There's three main parts to this business: negotiating the purchase and crossing for starts, then the pick-up and delivery, then the selling," Manny outlined. "Jake would be the best bet for handling the Mexican end. I'd like to take care of making the pick-up and transporting our goods. That way I can move to L.A. The Orge down there is much bigger and they offer more Clearing classes. Frank, how do you feel about handling sales?"

We each agreed to our roles.

Manny added blithely, "We'll all know each other's jobs down to the last detail. Everything we do will be communicated so that each of us knows what the other one is up to. We'll hire good people, set goals, and get what we want."

"So, you think communication and responsibility are the keys to creating a good organization?" Jake asked.

"Well, actually there is one more ingredient that keeps things from breaking down and that's 'affinity.'"

"Affinity? What does affinity mean?" I asked.

"It's the concept of caring for something, or someone: the concept of being at peace with everyone and the things you are doing."

His explanation sounded empty. Maybe it was the way he delivered it. I pushed the thought aside. "Lack of communication was what got Bill into trouble with us. You heard the story. Communication is essential, but it's got to be good, strong communication: clear, rational, on time, no lying, or game playing."

"Of course!" Manny said, staring at me. No matter who was talking, Manny looked directly at them and focused intently on what they were saying. I found it to be kind of creepy, actually.

Still staring, Manny added, "That's the beauty of Scientology. They teach all of that. We can teach this to the people who come to work for us. They'll know what we know in most all respects. We can teach them how to handle themselves in all situations."

Completely hooked by Manny's rhetoric and his irrefutable positive energy, we talked matters over until we were satisfied. We knew just how we were going to start our new partnership and how to put it to work. Jake and I departed on a high, ready to merge with this strange man and his high ideals.

My first job was to rent a house. I found a good one in a quiet, conservative area in San Francisco near Twin Peaks. Near the middle of October, Jake and Manny left for Mexico. A few days later, Manny called to inform me that everything was groovy. He and John had a load and were to arrive that evening. All was well.

They pulled in to the garage that evening and Manny immediately jumped out and hugged me. "We met the pilots, Frank, a couple of American dudes from Indio. They want to work with us and they have more connections for getting grass." Manny was pumped up, his face glowing.

Jake took the whole matter in stride, saying little.

Manny continued prattling on as we unlocked the doors to the lower compartment. He and Jake had picked the load up at a small, dirt airstrip located inside a grapefruit orchard at the upper end of Choachella Valley. Manny explained the landing procedure and about meeting the pilots, as I pulled out one of the cosali sacks. Immediately a rank smell filled the air when I opened the sack and extracted a kilo. The wrapper was wet and the smell of ammonia and alcohol permeated the garage. Unwrapping the packet, I was further dismayed.

"Wow! This is bad, guys, really bad," I lamented. "Look at the weed. It's good quality, but it's tainted. Sonofabitch! What the hell are the Mexicans up to now?"

Holding it close to his nose, Manny exclaimed, "Smells like alcohol!"

"God, why do they do have to do this?" I smelled it again and sighed. "Maybe you're right, Manny. It smells like wine or tequila."

Thinking quickly Manny said, "Get the customers to pay our full price for them anyway. Seventy-five is fifteen below what I usually charge on the open market."

"I don't know, man. These are especially wet. Sugar is one thing. This is new, whatever it is the Mexicans are adding. The customers might complain."

"Stay with seventy-five anyway," Manny pressured.

I knew I might run into difficulties, but agreed. "Let's get rid of these in a hurry. The next load might be just as bad. We promised our customers dry kilos. Seventy might work for a quick sale. This is really crap weed."

"Be patient, Frank," Jake spoke up. "Go for high dollar. We can always lower the price if it doesn't sell."

Again, I complained. "And what about our man, Renee? He lied to us. He said the kilos would be of good quality. We went over this with him."

"Then we'll talk with him," Jake said in his easy-going manner. "The kilos were not available to inspect when we met up with Renee in Nogales, and we didn't have time to inspect them when the plane landed. We had to get off that man's property, *pronto*. The pilots picked them up. So, you're right! The next load may be just like this one. You'd do better by not complaining. Just take care of business, partner. We'll do okay."

Manny was quick to follow suit. "In that case we may not be able to refuse the next load. These new pilots—wait 'til you meet them, Frank—they're really great and they know what they're doing. They have connections with a Hispanic dude from Indio. This guy can get us weed too, plenty of it according to Mel and Gil."

"Yeah! I guess you guys are right. Besides, we need to get underway and, well, this load sucks but I'll go to the customers and let them know what's up."

"Good. The next load will be ready in a couple of days. Jeff and Mike will be bringing them up," Manny replied.

I had yet to meet Jeff and Mike. Jake had. Manny had met these guys at the Scientology Orge in L.A. They were of good character, according to Jake. He had given the go-ahead. They were to be our new drivers.

While unloading the truck and over a meal I'd cooked, Jake, Manny and I went over plans for the next load. We discussed the pilots as well as what they and their other connections could do for us. We were all in a jubilant mood when they departed, leaving me to take care of the soiled kilos.

I began selling the kilos and soon become dismayed. Manny had introduced me to his contacts in Berkeley, a man by the name of Ben, and his pal Berkley Bill. When I showed them the kilos and informed that we may have one more load, they promptly refused to handle them. I couldn't make use of Mack or any of Bill's customers, but did contact a younger dude by the name of Jim who I knew from the beach. He had let me know a while back that he had a market. I connected with him, but he too refused to handle the wet bricks. Irving, a Jewish dude in Marin, saved the day. He could sell anything that had THC content, but immediately suggested a price reduction. Irv was the go-to man.

"Irv said sixty-five would work," I reported to my partners. Jake consented, but Manny stalled. We argued. He thought I could do better.

When I had had enough of his criticism I called Jake and asked him to intercede. Reluctantly, Manny agreed. Jake pointed out our position: sell these bad-ass kilos quick and get on with what we wanted. We'd soon have good quality dry bricks—we hoped.

Even with the lower price sales were slow. When Jeff and Mike showed up the following week with another load of crap weed, less than half the first load had been sold. Our new drivers were shocked when they saw the bricks. They had never seen a sugar-brick, let alone whatever it was we had dared to accept. As soon as the load was stored, I called Manny.

"They're the same. I've got Irv selling the last load. He isn't gonna like this."

"Frank, just sell 'em. Don't reflect on negativity. We can't do anything about this problem right now. You know we can't check the load until it comes in." Manny sounded disgusted with me.

I reminded him, "Communication, brother. Communication! This is tough work for Irv. We've sold less than half the load and it's taken more than a week. You guys know we'd already have this load sold if we had the good stuff. So, let's make this the last one—as we agreed. Irv would certainly appreciate this. Everyone would."

"Well, it's all we have. It's that simple. We have to work these things out. I know the market. You can do it. Stay with it."

I was unsettled after hanging up. We knew to expect a crappy load, but Manny's attitude was bothersome and left me feeling cold. My gut instincts told me to be wary of him. He was a weird dude.

I called Jake. "What's up with Renee? And how about the man from Indio, the pilot's connection?"

"I'm meeting with the man from Indio soon. His name is Ramon and he's anxious to meet with us. He's down south and will be back in a couple of days. As for Renee, he has another load for us. It's hard understanding him. All I got was that this shipment will be different."

I sighed. I'd heard that song before. "I sure hope so, partner. I hate it when we expose ourselves with this crap. You know what I mean. If we had a dry produce I'd have them sold."

"Without a doubt. And we'd have good profits to boot. This guy Irv, you let on that he's the only man who's willing to sell them. What about Mack?"

"No, Jake. He's Bill's man."

"Then do what you can with Irv. The main thing is they're selling. Just be safe. We'll work through this and get the good stuff."

"You can plan on that. Irv is one sharp dude. Working with him is easy." I then let Jake know about Manny's strange attitude.

Manny and Jake had both moved to Los Angeles to be closer to their work and also, as Manny put it, so that he could immediately attain the level of "Clear" at the nearby Scientology Orge. Manny had chosen an expensive house up in the Hollywood Hills; Jake got a nice place in Venice, a couple of blocks from the ocean.

Jake and Joanne also started taking Scientology classes. She told me over the phone, "I guess it works. It's kind of weird, though. The people there are really different. I don't know. Maybe it'll help Jake. He goes there a lot when he has time."

Joanne wasn't much on philosophy or any of the other esoteric subjects. She was of Portuguese blood with a strong, trim body, along with a thick head of long flowing dirty-blond hair. She was an attractive woman, very much in love with her man. Jake was reluctant to talk about his beliefs, but Joanne was a mother first and foremost, and knew how to listen to what wasn't being said. She didn't hesitate to give her opinion.

"I don't know about Manny," she intuited. "Something isn't right. He gives me the creeps."

The following week a third load arrived. They were wet and I flipped out. Totally frustrated, I called Manny.

"This has got to stop right now. Didn't you and Jake talk with Renee about this? Didn't you tell him we don't want this shit anymore? I'm sitting on more than four hundred kilos when these arrived. Irv is the only one who will handle them. I promised him we'd have dry kilos this time. What the hell do I tell him?" I ragged on.

"Frank, if the other customers won't help out, find new ones," Manny said casually.

I didn't expect him to reply this way and was shocked over his apparent lack of understanding, and again the cold way he conducted himself.

"Sure! Like I'll just walk down to the Haight-Ashbury and find a few guys willing to sell this crap."

"That's the idea," Manny retorted, cutting through my sarcasm.

"You've got to be kidding."

"No, not at all. You can do it. I got going that way. I got contacts all the time."

Angry at the absurd suggestion, I lashed out at him. "I don't know where you're coming from, man. We have a huge market. I'm not going to bring down any heat on us. You guys are in charge of receiving them so I'm gonna put it back on you. I'll make it worth your while to pay attention. I'm gonna drop the price on these."

"Frank, I'm not in agreement with that."

"I don't give a shit. I'm not in agreement with you. Take these fuckers and shove 'em. I'm tired of them."

"Frank, we're having a communication breakdown."

"Glad you noticed. Have a nice day!" I slammed the phone down.

It kept ringing, but I refused to answer. I wanted Manny to stew for a while. That'll get them all off their asses, I thought. Mostly, I was steaming over Manny's shoddy attitude.

Sure enough, Jake and Manny flew up the next day to meet with me. By that time, I'd calmed down.

Manny was polite and cordial as we held court.

"It's stupid to deal with this type of merchandise," I said vehemently, as we sat down in the living room. "The proof is sitting down in the basement. Over eight hundred kilos remain out of the thirteen hundred and fifty we received."

"Let's drop the price and get rid of them," Jake insisted.

"I don't think we need to," Manny objected. "If the customers are balking, we can find others. I've sold lots of sugared kilos in the last couple of years."

"That's not the point," I countered. "We agreed, as partners, from day one, not to accept any contraband unless it was good quality. This is the third load and it's shit. It's not what we agreed on and I move we settle this by dropping the price and by never again accepting bad weed. A promise is a promise. It's a major part of the total responsibility code. One load of bad weed is questionable, a second is outrageous, and a third is irresponsible. Where do we stop? How can I trust you if you accept this crap, not to mention the customer?" I looked directly at Manny. "We're smugglers, brother. If we don't demand the best, Renee will just keep rubbing our nose in this kind of shit."

"He's right, Manny. I've been through this before. Let's cut it out. We've got too many good things going right now to mess up."

Jake looked over at me with approval and then added a surprise, "I've been talking with Glenn. He wants to do a load with us, five hundred of the Old Man's kilos. I talked with him last week and promised him I wouldn't talk on the phone. That's why I didn't tell you guys."

"Damn! That's great!" I said, also aware that Glenn and Bill were good friends. But we had never sold any of our kilos through him. Would Bill be outraged if we used him? I put the thought aside.

"Can the pilots handle that much? You know, those are big packages."

"No problem. Mel said he's going for another type of twin engine, an Apache Navajo. They already have some new places in the desert to land. They're set."

He looked at Manny. "How about you? Let's say we drop that price and you and Frank get back online."

Jake and I waited for Manny to reply.

"Sixty a kilo doesn't leave us much profit," he drawled.

He looked first to Jake, then at me. Lacking conviction he finally replied, "Okay, I agree. Let's lower the price and start fresh with some real quality product. Jake, that's good news. Frank, I'm sorry that we had a communication breakdown." He extended his hand. We shook firmly.

There was more I wanted to say, but I held my tongue.

"Good. Let's not forget we're running a business here," Jake said with calm confidence.

We made plans for the upcoming move with Glenn. Then Jake delivered more good news. We were to begin making use of the new contact named Ramon. Jake pointed out that this man was an entrepreneur who could get us large amounts of *mota* from many different sources.

"He has connections for airstrips down in Mexico as well," Jake related, as I listened intently. "They're located near the border. Our pilots are already familiar with them. Ramon is due to call me back. He may be ready to go in a couple of weeks. And yes, Frank," he looked at me seriously then broke out in a silly wide grin, "I told him we want good, clean, dry weed." The sound of our laughter filled the room. "This deal with Glenn is of course fifty-fifty. We'll get two hundred and fifty and share expenses with him."

"Sounds great!" Manny and I agreed.

Glenn was Bill's contact. He was also a friend of Jake's, and was a member of the beach crowd. He was also a crafty dude, hell-bent on making a fortune. Two years before he had stumbled onto a connection down in Mexico referred to as "The Old Man." The Old Man was a connoisseur; his weed was the best by far. He carefully selected tops and then he pressed them so the weed would not be harmed, which meant his kilos were larger than normal. His prized packages were referred to as "Telephone Books" by the locals. We were going to be smuggling them for Glenn and that was a great boon—Glenn never dealt with anyone outside his business. We were, of course, impressed by Jake's ability to negotiate a deal with him.

It was agreed that we immediately halt all work through Renee and his people. We had plenty of good contacts for what we wanted.

"That's far out, Jake," I exclaimed excitedly. "We're going to bring up The Old Man's Telephone Books! Wow! We can sell them for well over two hundred a pop."

As for Bill's customers, we weren't tampering with them. We were supplying a service to men we already knew.

Jake called me a few days later. We met up in Golden Gate Park that afternoon. He delivered more good news. "Mack wants us to fly a load over for him."

"Damn! Unreal! How did you work that? He's Bill's man."

""He found out through Glenn we had pilots and he asked Glenn to have me give him a call."

"That's cool. By the way, when am I going to meet these pilots?"

"Soon. Let me tell you what's up first."

Apparently Mack, my brother's number-one man, had made a good deal of money during the preceding year. He had put together an organization of his own and had purchased a *granja* (a small, walled farmhouse and *casa*) just outside Guadalajara. He had gained these new contacts through a Spanish-speaking associate.

"He says he's got some very high quality cannabis. He's going to get his own pilots soon, but for now he wants us to haul for him. He's got eighteen hundred pounds right now," Jake explained.

"Right on. Good news." A tingling sensation ran through my body. "Looks like we're underway, big-time."

"There's more. Ramon has a load for us. I'll be going south tomorrow to hook up with him and the pilots. How are sales going?"

"Okay. There's about two hundred left. Irv is crabby, but I'll tell him that we'll have the good stuff soon. We owe him."

We were kept busy. Ramon came through next. A load of four hundred and fifty regular kilos was delivered to the house within a week. The drivers and I celebrated the fact that the merchandise was free of sugar and mescal.

Two weeks later, the first week of December, Glenn's prized load of Telephone Books arrived without any hitches. Jake was congratulated. He had arranged the whole thing and had, along with Manny, carried out the job flawlessly. I had informed our customers of the good news and sold these gems at a very high price.

Jake confided in me when we next met up at my place. "Glenn's very difficult to work with. There won't be any more through him this year. He says the supply is limited. Mack is ready to go. I'm flying down to Guadalajara with the pilots in a few days. If everything goes right, we'll have them up here before Christmas."

A few days before Christmas Mack's load came through. He came to my "safe house" the day they arrived. Both of us were giddy as we stood in the basement inspecting the eight hundred plus, brightly-wrapped kilos that lay neatly stacked against the wall. They were high quality and would fetch a good price.

"We kiloed them ourselves to look like Telephone Books," Mack proudly explained. He then went on about how he had special presses made and how his people had transported them in a big camper truck to a small airfield outside the city of Navajoa, in Sinaloa, where our pilots had picked them up.

"We did everything but grow it," he said with an ear-to-ear grin.

"Maybe that's next," I bantered.

"That's a ways away, brother. Right now I'm going for higher quality. This stuff is good, but there's better. We'll have another load ready in early January. Tell Jake he did a good job. Let's load up. My customers are waiting. Hey, let me sell some of these for you. I'll give you a dime more," he bargained.

Manny had a friend in the Seattle area who was a small-time dealer. I was asked to front his pal fifty pounds of our regular. When he arrived by car, I loaded him up. A few days later, he flew down and gave me half the funds. He was to fly back down in one week with the rest. When he called back, I held him off. Instead, I told him, I'd fly to Seattle to pick up the remainder.

A few weeks prior, my mother informed me that she had obtained my father's address from the military. At the time I paid little attention, but I got to thinking about Dad and why he had never gotten hold of us all these years. I asked her for the address. She and I argued and I won—he was my father and I had every right to visit him. I had to find out why he deserted us. Mom told me I was making a mistake, but I wanted to find out what my father would say when I showed up unannounced at his house.

Two days before Christmas I flew to Seattle, rented a car, and checked into a motel. The next morning I met with Manny's friend and collected the money. Then I took off for Enumclaw, a small town southeast of Seattle.

I found the street my dad lived on and drove slowly down the road looking at addresses, getting more and more nervous. When I spotted the house I saw a Buick in his driveway. Dad had always loved Buicks. There was exhaust coming from the muffler. I pulled to a stop directly in its path, turned the engine off, and got out of my car. There was snow and ice on the ground. Living in San Francisco all these years I had no experience with icy winter conditions and had to be careful. No way did I wish to slip and fall on my ass, not in front of him.

He slowly rolled down his window as I made my way forward. For all he knew I was an intruder: a young, unknown male in his neighborhood, blocking his path and approaching his car. At least that was what his look told me until we made eye contact. Then it hit home. I was his son, there was no denying it.

As I looked at him, I saw a frightened man who did not know what to say or what to do. I waited for him to say something, anything—some reaction that would be positive. Finally he said stolidly, "Which son are you?"

"It's me Dad—Frank." I felt deflated that he would have to ask or say such a thing, or worse, that he wasn't happy to see me.

He looked me up and down. "I figured either you or Bill would come see me. Did your mother send you?"

"No. I came on my own."

He was uncomfortable and turned to look at the woman who was sitting next to him—his new wife, I guessed. Then he looked back at me and said without conviction, "Why don't' you get in the car? We're on our way to see friends."

As I walked back to my car and moved it my emotions swirled. He hadn't greeted me, not the way a father should after a long hiatus from his son. God, he could have gotten out and hugged me. Instead, I found myself easing into the back of his car, unprepared for what might happen next. It was Christmas Eve day and one of his sons had just shown up, and just in time to crash his party.

What came next was even more heart-shattering. "Why didn't you or Bill ever write me?" he asked, as we drove down the block.

At first I didn't know what to say or how to react. How could I write him? I didn't have an address. Why hadn't he written us? With this rolling around my mind, I said rather pathetically, "I just got your address from mom a few days ago. She got it from the Air Force."

"Still, you could have written me."

"Not without an address."

Could it be that he was upset that I showed up unannounced? Had my sudden appearance thrown his mind out of whack?

He saved me further discomfort by asking what Bill was up to. I lied and told him that Bill was driving for UPS and added I owned a small boatyard in Sausalito. He was content to hear this and asked about Ray and John. I lied about them also. I had to, and as I did, I felt small. Actually, I didn't know what I felt other than being upset that this reunion was not going well and that he hadn't even bothered to introduce his wife. She was Japanese and had not said one word.

By the time we reached their friend's house on the edge of town, we had already run out of things to say. His friends were dairy farmers, and greeted us warmly at the door. Other friends were inside, celebrating Christmas, and when my father came in with Miyako trailing, his friends gave him a hardy greeting.

"And who is this?" the hostess asked as she moved toward me.

"This is my son Frank," my father responded, though his voice lacked enthusiasm.

"Your son? Bill, you never said anything about having a son," she said, while looking at me in a different way, with a confused and forced smile.

"I'm not his only son," I was quick to add. "There are four of us. I'm the second born." She didn't know what to say. Neither did the others who were listening in.

"Well, you're welcome in our house. Come with me. Would you like an appetizer?"

She attempted to regain her composure and played the perfect hostess while my father made busy with his male folk. The hostess and another woman asked me about Bill's four sons, and although I answered politely, I found it hard to believe my father had hidden these facts from his close friends. What kind of man was my father? What had he become over the past twelve years? Nothing was asked about why I had not seen him in all those years, or how he had left us one day, never to return. They knew what might be up, but Bill was their friend and a good man by their standards—or at least, that's the impression they gave.

Back at my father's house, he and his wife did their best to make me feel welcome. I was shown the guest room and later we sat around and talked. No matter what we said, my dad did his best to control the conversations. Nothing was said about my mother. He told me he was a school custodian and that his military retirement pay helped a great deal. His wife worked at a local pickle factory, and she had once been our maid when we lived in Okinawa, Dad reminded me. As soon as he said this I remembered her: Miyako.

One day, Mom announced we would have a new maid, and the next day Miyako failed to show. Mom and Dad had had several arguments about her: Mom banished her from the house. After getting a Mexican divorce, Dad had gone back to Okinawa and brought Miyako to the States and married her. Mom had suspected as much when she got the dissolution papers several years ago.

By the time I was ready for bed, Dad had opened up. He was the dad I had missed, the man I had cried for after he took off. But deep down, I felt forsaken. When I woke up the next day, I had reason to feel awful. Nothing felt right. Miyako was stubbornly quiet. Dad was remote, but he did show me his hobbies. He had built model ships out of wood and loved to craft leather. I was given a fine leather wallet for Christmas that night. Dinner that evening was solemn. I had no gifts for them and I felt terrible. What they thought of me, I had no idea. They were not the kind of people to express feelings or to get all pushed out of shape over anything. At least that was what I detected on the surface. What was really going on for them—and me—was a mystery. It was Christmas day, but there was not much to celebrate, even though one of Dad's sons had come home for the holidays.

The next morning I was so sick I couldn't get out of bed. Dad was as alarmed as Miyako. They brought me medication and took my temperature. It was well over a hundred. For three days I slept and sweated out the flu, or whatever it was that attacked me. I had never been so sick. On the fourth day I came around. What I came around to was that I no longer wanted to be in my dad's house. He couldn't give me what it I was looking for: inner peace of some kind. But I wasn't thinking along those terms. All I knew was that I felt bad being around the man; he had emotional problems and there was no way this man was going to open to them. He was shut tight, as in get-outta-here-son-you-remind-me-of-my-past.

Mom told me long ago that Dad had been abandoned by his parents. He was one of fourteen siblings sent to foster parents or to relatives. His self-worth was crushed as long as I remained in his house: a constant reminder that he had run from his past. Amazingly, he didn't drink but had paid a price: he had a bad heart—no surprise there. When these and other realizations hit home, I found the strength to get well and leave, knowing that I'd never be back.

To excuse my hurried departure I lied to them, saying I had to get the rental car back to the agency and that I had things to do down in the Bay Area—which was the truth. They were relieved. I departed as I had arrived—emotionally uncertain. Once I arrived home my energy returned.

Over the next few days I sorted through all the feelings and came to a conclusion: my father had no real desire to be with his sons. He had abandoned us as he had been abandoned. There was no coming back home for either of us. When I related the entire story to Brother Ray he agreed. Still, I wanted to accept my Dad for who he was—a very confused man who could not accept love. I knew I had a lot to learn from his mistakes.

After the contaminated weed had been sold, my job became routine. That was the way things had been when we worked with Bill. We were now on top of things. L. Ron Hubbard would approve our efforts, though not the contraband part, I thought, as I chuckled over the matter. In between the work schedule, I read some of L. Ron's writing and his theories—or better to say, dogmas. Mixed feelings erupted.

"L. Ron is indeed brilliant," I told Brother Ray one day, "but his dogmas are hard to swallow."

Ray and I questioned how L. Ron had gotten most of his data. He was an acclaimed science fiction writer, we knew. He had also been an U.S. Army Intelligence Officer. Manny freely disclosed that L. Ron had procured top-secret data from Army files, mostly Army psychology studies. He had contrived to borrow from them and then added his own personal touch. This intrigued me. On the other hand, his organization didn't. I went ahead anyway and made plans to purchase auditing sessions. Why not? I had the money and maybe more clarity of mind would bring peace of mind.

By the time the New Year arrived, the freezer compartment of my refrigerator was constantly filled with frozen money, carefully counted and stacked in thousand-dollar bundles. Everything the three of us had carefully planned was going accordingly. I believed, too, that we were operating in a safe manner. Every precaution we had considered had been implemented, and was working. Only a handful of people knew where the Safe House was located. Everyone else was kept away, including the big customers: Irv in Marin, Ben in Berkley, Jim in San Francisco, and people Manny had introduced me to back in October.

They were a safe group to work with and I learned to make life simple. I'd front them from fifty to a hundred kilos at a time, deliver them with no problem, and then go collect the money. When the customer ran out, I fronted them an equal amount until the load was sold. Usually, I'd make sure everyone received an equal amount.

During the months of December and January I was often aboard a jet headed for Los Angles to deliver profits and to attend Scientology sessions. Joanne was right—the Orge-groupies were real L.A. types: pretentious and full of glorified hopes that gave me the shivers. L. Ron was their guru and they made no bones about it, saluting his picture every time they came out of an auditory session. I'd get caught in these brouhahas myself after coming out of an audit.

These audits were quite the celebration. Announcements assailed the crowd. Everyone and anyone in the vicinity would come forth to clap and to praise the recipient, not only the auditee, but L. Ron too. His picture hung everywhere. There was no escaping his Lordship or the fact that were it not for him, we dire people would have nothing. Even though I readily joined in the celebration, later, after the initial effects of the audit ran thin I cringed at the thought of all the rejoicing. There was just a bit too much veneration going on there. Jake and Joanne felt the same way. At their place in Venice, we compared notes. A spiritual element was missing: Scientology had no soul. L. Ron had yet to discover, along with the rest of the believers, how to reach inside the soul of a being and instill love. And that's what I was looking for: LOVE.

December and January had been especially successful months in the drug smuggling business. After Glenn and Mack's load, Ramon came through with another load of four hundred and fifty. This load was now sitting in my basement. After I sold Glenn's load and Mack's, I had plenty of profit money lying around. Not yet ready to consider the purchase of the boat I wanted, I decided to buy a car. I chose a 1966 Porsche 912 and bought it for thirty-five hundred cash. I was excited beyond belief. I'd always wanted a car like that, and the fact that it had become a reality was mind-boggling. At the rate we were going, I'd have the money to buy the boat of my dreams by summer.

A couple of days later, itching to go for a long drive, I took off, with no particular destination in mind. A large Pacific storm had moved in. As I passed by the Cliff House restaurant, near Ocean Beach, I spotted a young female hitchhiker on the Great Highway. She was dressed in a thick navy P-coat, long skirt, and boots.

I stopped and she got in.

"Where you headed?" I asked. She was a flower child no doubt, maybe twenty, cute, with child-like features and a pug nose.

"Big Sur."

"Nice place to go. I haven't been there in a while."

"I've never been there," she said, looking tentative. "But, I'll get there. Where are you going?"

"Just going south, out for a drive, don't know where. I'm just enjoying my new car."

"It's nice. What is it?"

"A Porsche," I said proudly. "A German sports car. It handles really nice. What's your name?"

"Christine. And yours?"

"Frank."

We were quiet for a while as we cruised down the Great Highway and then on to Highway One. The ocean was busily churning waves; Christine looked out at it curiously and said, "Isn't it wonderful? I love the ocean. It looks so good right now."

"You're not thinking of swimming in it?" I joked.

"Oh no. It's just that it's so real—so full of things." She turned and looked at me. "It's immense."

"Why are you headed south? It's ready to rain. Do you have friends to stay with in Big Sur?"

"No. But I'll find a place for the night."

Her eyes were perhaps her best feature, but every time our eyes met I wanted to say something less than flattering. She wore tons of make up, mostly eye shadow, as well as eyebrow and eyelash make-up. It made her look cheap.

"So what do you do, Frank?" she asked, looking around the interior of the vehicle.

At first I didn't know what to say. If I lied, I knew it would be okay. Instead, I told her the truth. "I'm a drug smuggler."

"Really!" she scanned me. "You don't look like one."

"What are we supposed to look like?"

"Ummm...hard to say."

"Well, that's what I do. I sell grass, to be more accurate. That's how I can afford this car. Do you work?"

"Not right now. I'm staying with some people out in the Haight. I'm from Southern California, San Fernando area." She looked forlorn when she said this.

"And you've been living up here awhile?"

"Yes. I like the area, especially Berkeley." The more we talked the more relaxed I became. Our conversation livened as we passed through Santa Cruz. I had no plans other than to drive and I had plenty of money on me. Christine wanted to go to Big Sur and I decided to take her there. She didn't bother to ask why I was driving her this far, nor did I say that I would. We just drove on, talking and getting to know one another as the storm moved in closer and the rain threatened.

By the time we reached Monterey darkness was closing in and a pounding rain began to fall. I chose a place to pull over along the oceanfront beneath some cypress trees. With the last light of day, we sat and looked at the ocean.

She looked over at me and said, coyly, "I love the sound of rain, all that splattering as it hits the car. And look at the ocean." She craned round, then back, and added, "It's so wild."

"I'm right there," I replied. "And what makes it so wild?"

"I don't know. I think everything is wild. Don't you?"

Unable to check myself, I reached out and touched her face. Then I brushed back her hair and drew her closer. Our kiss was long and passionate. It had been a long while, so I literally sucked on her lips and smothered her face with kisses.

In no time, we were hot and bothered. I drew back. "How about if I buy you some dinner? Are you hungry?"

She smiled, caressed my face, and said, "Yeah. I'd like that. I'm hungry."

"And after dinner, how about doing something wild?"

"Sure. What do you have in mind?"

"Join me. I'm going to get a room at one of them fancy motels."

"Great."

Trying to sound casual I added, "Boy, I'd like to make love to you."

"Hmmm... I'd like that. Sounds wild."

Score! I zoomed off and got us a room in Carmel, where our hormones took over. We decided to eat later.

Beneath the dress and the thick coat was a slender, smooth body with small breasts and long, shapely legs. She was an explosive lover. I hadn't had a woman in a long while, and with her I made the most of it. And, this time, I was able to pace myself. Both of us were swept away, especially me. I enjoyed her child-like innocence and her thirst for pleasure.

Lying in bed with her legs wrapped me I said in a soft, sweet voice while stroking her, "You're a very nice looking woman. You also have very pretty eyes, but the makeup is heavy. You'd look much better if you took most of it off."

She shrugged, and then smiled demurely. "If you think so, I'll do it."

Later, we ate a huge meal and then returned to the room. Our appetite for sex returned, and we started all over again. We spent the rest of the weekend together, making love, driving around visiting sights and eating—then drove home in a hard rain. After spending the night at my house, I drove her to the Haight-Ashbury where she gathered her few possessions. She was moving in with me.

I hadn't seen Bill for quite a while, though we had crossed paths a couple of times. Back in November he let me know that he was going to take time off to make a movie about surfing. The filming had already begun, but he was to go to Barbados to surf and to finish filming. He was also planning a trip to Sweden to find a sweetheart.

Two days after Christine moved in, I left her at my place while I flew down to L.A. for a meeting with Jake and Manny. This included a bit of auditing at L. Ron's cerebral fortress.

When I returned, Bill was at my house, along with his new girlfriend Inger. Brother Ray was also there. Surprised and happy to see Bill, we embraced. When he introduced me to his new woman I immediately took a liking to her. She was slim, blond, pretty, and had blue eyes. Most of all she was friendly. She seemed nervous, but was perhaps overwhelmed just by being in the United States for the first time, and meeting all these new people. Also, there were a couple of hundred kilos in the basement. She had every right to be nervous.

Bill told me Inger spoke six languages. He was proud of this and that her English was near perfect, with only a slight accent. While Inger and I talked Bill hung out with Ray in the living room. He wandered in moments later and was seemingly indifferent towards me. I had had what was referred to as a "power release" that morning at the L.A. Orge, and I was in a way, bulletproof. I tempered myself and asked him as he poked his head in the refrigerator, "What're you going to be doing now that you're back?"

Inger and Christine were just leaving the room so Bill took his time answering.

Crouched over, head hidden as he snooped for food he replied, "I'm going down to Mexico to join Mack. We're going to be partners." The word *partner* had a ringing quality.

"Good. I hope it works out. We're bringing up his weed, you know. I'm sure he's told you all about it," I said casually, careful not to overemphasize this point.

"Not for long, you won't. We'll going to get our own pilots. You guys will be history in a couple of months."

His reply was vicious. I watched him carefully as he paced the kitchen eating a hunk of cheese and a slice of bread. I knew he was still angry with me over our dissolution, and perhaps now angry that we were working with his people. But he said nothing about this.

"We have a good thing going right now," I responded. "We've been highly successful. If we can help you guys to get your weed up here then let's go for it. I'm sure you and Mack will find pilots in time, but right now we have a couple of good ones you can make use of. Plus we have a reliable connection to transport large amounts of pot down south. He can pick up Mack's load in Guadalajara and move it up north if you guys are interested."

"That's really great, Frank." He gave me a quick glance then looked elsewhere as he continued. "We'll see. Mack can take care of moving his weed. He's got a pilot lined up."

"Great!" I figured Bill was lying. "Mack's got some very high grade weed. We're going to move another load with him in about two weeks."

"I know." He stopped pacing and looked at me. "I'm going down to help out."

It was awkward and quiet for a moment. Then he sprang on me.

"So, you think Scientology is going to help you make a fortune?"

"Let's just say I'm into it right now. It's working. I feel confident." I was agitated by his tone.

Bill paced the kitchen again. "I don't like organizations like that," he hissed. "I've heard about them and none of it's good. I'd watch out if I were you."

I said to myself, "What about them, Bill? You're pissing me off right now. Lighten up. I'm your brother, not your enemy. I'd rather hug you, not override you or drag you down."

Instead I replied, "I'm well aware of their limitations," annoyed by his narrow-minded stance. "I'm taking in what I need. They have a few good points."

Walking out of the room he replied sarcastically, "That remains to be seen."

The next day Bill and his new Swedish girlfriend departed for Mexico. "We'll be in touch," was all he said.

Jake called me a few days later. I was excited. I was to fly to L.A., meet with him, then we'd fly south with the pilots. Manny was tied to his Scientology classes and wouldn't be joining us.

The next day I met with Jake at the L.A. airport and early the next morning we drove to the Santa Monica airport. The pilots had rented a brand new Piper Navajo. Mel and Gil were there to greet us. They were each well over six feet, heavy-set and very friendly. Mel was much older; Gil was Jake's age. Both were family men, eager to make money, also eager to be a little crazy. They clowned around like a couple of little kids and bragged that they were the best pilots money could buy.

Mel commented as we walked up to the plane, "We should buy this baby. It only costs a hundred and sixty grand. It's a real good deal and it's perfect for our needs. It cruises eight hundred miles, but we can modify it to go a thousand."

Gil nodded enthusiastically. "We could partner up—go five ways. We'd have it paid for in no time."

When I climbed aboard I was impressed by the amount of room and all the seats. Mel and Gil said that this baby could carry near to a ton of weed without compromising the plane. I believed them. I was also impressed by the way our pilots handled the plane. When we took off and flew south I felt safe and relaxed behind their confidence. These guys were good-natured and real pros. We were lucky to have them and I pictured a prosperous future for all of us as I looked out my port to the earth below.

A few hours later we landed in Punta Chivata, fueled up, and took off for our destination—Puerto Vallerta. By early afternoon we approached land.

"Hey you two, here's what it's like to fly the border," Mel said, as he brought the plane down to a few hundred feet above sea level.

Mel lowered the altitude even more as we approached thick tropical jungle. As he did, my adrenaline began to pump. At a speed of just over two hundred and thirty mph we skimmed treetops by fifty to a hundred feet. I gripped my seat and held on. It was a thrill never before experienced and I was scared shitless, mainly due to the air pockets that rattled the plane.

"This is real 'bush pilot' flying, guys," Gil shouted at us, as his pal Mel grinned. They knew we were impressed.

I was. As for Jake, I didn't bother to ask or to look his way. I was busy looking at the flight our plane took. The jungle below seemed awful close and one small mistake by Mel and we'd be dead in an instant. Three or four minutes later we were over the water and with my adrenaline pumped to the max, I sighted Puerto Vallerta up ahead.

"What ya think, guys? Is this a good plane or what?" Gil asked rhetorically.

Still bragging, Mel added, "When we fly the border we're down low for a good forty-five minutes. We're used to it. You guys got a good picture. We earn our money."

Mel leveled off at a thousand feet and headed for the airport where we fueled up, caught a taxi to town, and ate a hearty seafood dinner. The next morning we flew to Guadalajara and rented a car. Mack was expecting us and had sent his associate George to meet us. We followed him to Mack's new *granha* a few miles to the south.

Mack had not met the pilots but gave a thumbs up on their visit. Knowing Mack's need for ego stroking, I figured he wanted all of us to see his set-up. He was all smiles when we came in, as was his girlfriend Cathy, and his two *gringo* helpers. Immediately, he took us for a tour.

The *granha*, surrounded by high walls made of stone and cement, was about a quarter of an acre, consisting of a main house and several smaller stone structures. Out in his blockhouse where he stored the weed, he showed us the setup for the press and the way they went about making the kilos.

How Mack had managed to put all of this together amazed me. It was one hell of a good setup. Mack knew this and his ego soared while he entertained us over lunch.

Later that afternoon I paid a visit to Bill and Inger, who lived in town. Bill was more receptive this time. Perhaps he felt threatened in my domain and was secure in his, along with the fact that he was back at work.

As we ate, Inger and I did most the talking. She told me about life in Sweden and how she had met Bill.

"I answered his ad," she said. "He was looking for a model to come to Barbados with him to film a surf movie. My friends told me not to answer it but I did."

"I'll have the load ready in a few days," Mack said the next morning when he met us at the airport. He wanted to check out the plane and to make plans with Jake and the pilots.

Three days after I arrived back in the States, Manny called. Mack was ready, and Jake and the pilots were underway.

Mack came to our stash house the day it arrived and picked up his half of the load. "We'll have another load ready near the end of February. It'll be the same high quality," he promised as he left.

Ramon also came through with another load of good regular. After it arrived in mid-February, Jake paid me a visit. He informed me, with his usual nonchalance, that we had had a near disaster down in Mexico.

There had been a communication breakdown between our pilots and Mack's people. The fault lay with our pilots. They had let Mack's people know that they'd be at the pick-up zone by sunrise, but Mexican law didn't allow a small plane take off before sunrise and our pilots were over an hour behind schedule when they took off.

Mel and Gil, who usually fly a hundred miles into Mexico when picking up our loads from Ramon, then back, had this time flown several hundred miles below the border to make this pick-up. Having forgotten they could not take off before sunup and unable to arrive on time, they devised a crazy plan. While they flew to the area they scanned the main highway. When they spotted Mack's camper they buzzed it. When they came back around, Gil let loose a piece of cardboard with a map drawn on it and a message for the camper driver to follow them to a spot they would land in.

When the pilots hadn't show up on time, Bill and his crew had gotten the willies and had taken off, but were pleasantly surprised when the plane buzzed them. After they retrieved the cardboard message, Bill, who was in charge and in a lead car, ordered the driver to follow the instructions. Somehow, they connected up at the new landing zone.

"Jake," I said, "the pilots told me that they couldn't take off before sunrise. Remember? They told us about this when we went down south with them."

"Yeah, I know. I had a good talk with them about this mishap, but mostly over the good job they did. That field they landed in had farm workers. They saw the plane land and watched the whole thing go down."

"No shit!"

Jake started laughing. "Yeah, Mel said the Mexicans cheered them while the plane was being loaded and clapped and waved at them when they took off."

I joined with him in the laughter. "No kidding! Obviously the Mexicans knew what was going down."

Although we were laughing, there was also need for concern. Jake would have to make sure that communications between the pilots and the ground crew would be safer on future runs.

✯ ✯ ✯

Toward the end of February we prepared to move Mack's next load. When I learned that Manny would be attending Scientology classes and wouldn't be available for the next several days, I called him.

Manny was smooth but forceful when I confronted him.

"Once I start these classes I can't stop. I have to be there every day until they're over. I told you about this. Jake knows. When you or Jake take these classes, I'll fill your spot. I've gone over everything with the pilots and drivers. They know what to do. This is not a time to worry. You can come down here and work with them to make sure everything goes off as planned."

"Manny," I interjected. "I know you told us this. I also told you I was not in agreement with you. You could take these classes later. I…"

"Hold on Frank. Jake's in agreement. You need to get *Clear* on this matter."

"I am. You're the one who laid this on us and you expect complete cooperation."

"Everything is taken care of, Frank. I've talked to my crew extensively. Gil is to handle the drivers. Just call them when everything is ready and make sure they're under way. Everything is set. Don't go putting a bad charge on this."

I was unconvinced and thought of calling Jake. However, that was next to impossible. He was down south in Mexico doing his job, nowhere near a phone. All I could do was chill out and call the drivers when the time came. But the next day I was alarmed, as I listened to weather reports and learned that a massive storm was expected to bring torrential rains and high winds to northern and southern California. Rain, accompanied by high winds, had already started in the Bay Area. Southern California was going to be hit hard.

I called Manny but was unable to get him until late that night. I warned him, "There's a storm headed your way and it's a big one. The load is due to be picked up tomorrow afternoon. I have no way to get in touch with Jake to let him know."

"Thanks for informing me, Frank. Those storms hardly ever get down to Southern California. The desert should be fine. But let's be aware."

"This is a huge storm, Manny. You're in class. I've been watching the news. The storm is going to hit southern California and bring floods."

"I'll call the drivers and let them know."

"One day, Manny, take one day off and…"

"You're over-reacting. There's no problem except the one you're creating. You know what I've told you about this kind of thinking. It gets people in trouble. Why don't you come down for some auditing after your work is done? You need to get *clear* on this issue."

Fuming with anger I spat out, "Tell the drivers to call me when they're in position."

By noon the next day I was beyond concerned. Our operation was underway, but so too was the weather. The storm had penetrated Southern California. Heavy amounts of rain were falling. Flooding was imminent. Manny had told me the night before that he had talked to the pilots and the drivers. They were in position and were to call me if any problems arose. The pick-up was set for sundown. The pilots, drivers, and Manny knew the landing zone.

By three o'clock the news was bad: flooding in Riverside, high winds in the desert, as well as flooding. Interstate10 and other major highways were closed due to flooding. I quickly analyzed the situation. Our landing area would be a disaster, but Mel and Gil would know how to handle the situation. They were pilots. They know weather is a major factor— they'd have alternate zones to land in and find a way to get the drivers to the load. Why they hadn't called the drivers to call off the day's work off was puzzling. That was either a problem or a blessing. Bad things were taking place and I had to believe all would go well, in spite of the weather and my fears.

I was relieved when the phone rang an hour later. It was the drivers. "We can't get through Frank," Jeff admitted. "All the major highways are down."

"Wait a minute! I thought you were already in place down there. Manny said he dispatched you last night."

"He did, but we didn't expect the flooding to be this bad."

I groaned, knowing they had messed up by failing to realize the true impact of the storm. They could have driven to Palm Springs long before the flooding started.

Jeff continued. "Gil called us late last night after we talked with Manny. He told us meet him at the Denny's restaurant in Palm Springs around four this evening. We're about sixty miles away, but we can't get through. We checked our map; there are no roads available to us, none that will get us there in time. What are we supposed to do?"

"Wait a minute," I snapped. Why were you supposed to meet Gil at Denny's? He's with Mel in the plane."

"No he's not. Gil is in Indio. They switched things around the other day. Mel is flying the load up himself. Gil is supposed to meet us and tell us which landing strip to go to. No way we can be there in time."

I was confused by the plan changes and said heatedly, "Who the hell told them to make the change?"

"I don't know, man. Gil called me and said I was to meet with him at Denny's around 4:00."

I was outraged. "So, Manny doesn't know the pilots changed the plan?"

"I don't think so. We found out last night."

"Shit! This is fucked! Give me a moment to think."

I knew Manny would not be at home. Jake wasn't unavailable either. Mel was en route and Gil would be at Denny's at 4:00 to meet the drivers. He must know by now that the flooding would cause the drivers to be late or that they'd be unable to get through.

"Where in the hell is Gil?" I asked. "We need to get hold of him ASAP."

"I don't know. That's why I called you. We called him, but his wife said he was out doing errands."

"He can solve this problem. He knows what to do, even with all this rain. He's probably running around making preparations. Get a room and call me back. Call Gil's house again and tell his wife where you're at. Okay? That way Gil can be in touch with you as soon as he gets back. Call me the minute you hear from him. If the highway opens up, get on the road. Go to Denny's. Okay? No matter what, tell Gil to call me immediately."

"Sounds good to us."

"Good! We're in trouble and we need to act wisely. The way I see it guys, you're going to be late no matter what. Mel and Gil will have to use their heads. That's why I want to talk with him. We have to save this, man—we have to! If Mel lands and has to leave the load in the desert, Gil can connect with him then get to you and lead you to the landing area."

"Gotcha! That's what we figured. There's a few motels nearby. Catch you later."

I called Manny. He was not expected back until late. I called Gil. I was cordial with his wife, but learned that Gil was unavailable. I could only figure he was headed to the landing area. He would be there when Mel landed. He and Mel could unload the contraband. They would hide it then bring the drivers to fetch the load. We were caught in an absurd situation; Gil was the only one who could save the day—as long as he knew where to meet up with Mel. All we could do for the moment was to sit tight, wait, and hope this matter would correct itself.

It was not the time to smoke grass. Paranoia would set in. Christine snuggled up to me while we sat on cushions in the living room watching the tube, and the rain poured down. I kept turning things over in my mind. What were the pilots up to? Why had they changed things around and not let any of us know? Had Manny had been there to oversee them, Mel and Gil would have let him in on their plans. Yes, if Manny had been there…this thought lingered, leaving a bad taste in my mouth.

I had never been so worried and restless. It was now 5:30 p.m.—pick-up time. The only two people I had a positive location on were the drivers. They had called. They were worried. All we could think to do was to keep in touch. Where was Gil? What could he be up to at this most important moment? Was he stranded? Most certainly, he could not get to a phone. Was he stuck in the sand? We were at a loss about what to do. We just had to hang in and wait for Gil to call.

When 8:00 p.m. rolled around, I began to sense disaster. I felt like a man stranded in a jungle with a broken leg. I began to hope everything would be okay. Christine tried to console me, but nothing could lift me from the fear that surrounded me at that moment.

When Gil finally called at 9:00 p.m. he was panicked.

"Frank, I think Mel's gone down."

I was so wound up I ignored his comment and began interrogating him. "You got to tell me what happened. The drivers said you guys changed the plans. Why did Mel go south alone? That's what I'd like to know. And why didn't you call sooner?"

"I don't have time to explain. It's too complicated."

"Shit, Gil. Why didn't you call me personally and tell me about the change you guys made? "

"Calm down. We have a problem here. Mel didn't call like he said he would. The weather got out of hand and I couldn't get him on the radio."

"He was to radio you? I'm confused. Where? You mean from the plane?"

"Yes, but the sandstorm came up this afternoon. I went up in the plane and couldn't get him on the radio. The storm ruined everything. Mel was to put down at one of three different spots and I don't know which one he used. After I landed, I got in my truck and drove out to all the areas. I covered them twice. I couldn't locate him. That's why I didn't call you. I was busy."

I was totally disoriented. "This sucks, Gil. I'm sorry I got mad at you. You think Mel crashed the plane? Where could he possibly be? Is there a chance he didn't fly today? I mean what with the sandstorm maybe he knew better than to take off. Weren't you guys aware of this storm front? What gives? This is madness."

"It sure as shit is, man. Everything was fine until 3:00 or 4:00 this afternoon. Then it started blowing like hell. I've seen this kind of thing before. About once every four or five years we get a bad sand storm. It's calm now, but..."

"Did Mel fly today?" I interrupted. "That's what I need to know."

"Yes he did. He called me from Mexico before he took off this morning. He was to be in around dusk."

"Would he cancel?"

"No."

"Gil, I'm still confused. Why did you go up in the plane? What was that all about?"

"It was part of the plan. Mel was to fly, and I was to radio him and let him know if there was any activity going on and which location was safe to land at."

"God, that's complicated. I'll talk to you about it later. Boy...I wish I was down there to help out," I said, exasperated. Unable to think of a solution myself I asked him, "What can we do?"

"I don't know. I've pretty much run out of steam. I'm at home now. I'm thinking about driving out in my truck and looking for him again, but like I say, I've already checked all the areas twice. He's not at any of them. He's landed elsewhere and I haven't a clue where. There's a good chance he crash landed. That's what I'm worried about."

My mind was running in circles. "I hear you, Gil."

"If Mel is okay I know he'll get out of this. He'll hike out of where he's at and call me. Maybe we can save this."

"That's what I'm hoping for, but if he's injured or worse, then there's no way we can get to him?"

Gil was quiet for a moment then added, "I'm afraid not, Frank. I'm lost as to where he's at. I have to stay here and hope he calls."

Again I searched for an answer. "Let's concentrate on a solution, Gil. Go ahead, stay by the phone. I'll call the drivers. I'll have them move down closer to your area when they can."

"Yes, but no worry. I've already done that. If Mel calls we'll be ready to come to where he's at, even if it's in the middle of the night. The drivers and I will take care of things."

"Good. That's all I can think to do right at this moment. I'll call you if I come up with something else."

I hung up in a state of despair. Mel, Gil's close pal, was out there somewhere.

We had no idea where. There was a good chance he was badly injured or had been killed. How had things gotten so messed up in such a short period of time? I wondered.

As I brooded, I considered calling Manny. Anger stopped me. We'd only get into an argument anyway.

I called Gil just past ten—my guts twisting. No news.

When I went to bed I had little desire to make love to Christine. I slept fitfully. My instincts told me we were in deep trouble. It was midnight. The phone remained silent—unlike my mind.

CHAPTER SEVEN

DISSOLUTION

SAN FRANCISCO, CA
FEBRUARY, 1969

A PHONE CALL woke me. It was just past 6:00 a.m. In a haze, I hesitated answering, considering last night's circumstances. When it rang a third time, I hoped it would be Gil calling to tell me that Mel was okay: that he along with the drivers had retrieved the load and the drivers were on their way home. It was a positive thought, but far from the truth. We were in deep trouble.

"Mel's been arrested," Gil declared—his voice loud and clear. "He just called me from the El Centro jail. He needs a lawyer. His bail is going to be high."

"Oh shit!" I expelled a deep breath. "What else did he tell you?" A rush of adrenalin hit as I began to come out of the morning stupor.

"The plane went down in the sandstorm…" He hesitated. "Mel tried to land…and he crashed. That's all I know. He didn't want to say anything else. He just wants a lawyer to talk to."

"Okay, Gil, you got it. Give me a second to think… Hang in with me. We'll get one for him. I'm going to see Mack, but he lives across the bay and it'll take a while. Stay at home, or at least, stay in touch with me. Christine will be here to take messages. Call Manny, okay? Tell him what's happening."

I hung up and began to dress. As I did, I woke Christine and let her know that our pilot was in jail.

"Honey, I'm sorry, is there anything I can do?"

"Just stay here and take messages. Write them down, okay? I have to run off. I'll be busy."

I kissed her inattentively and headed for the shower.

Within minutes I was in my Porsche on the bridge that would take me to Marin County. Mack lived at Stinson Beach. I had two dozen miles of twisty road to cover. When I cleared the city the only semblance of peace was the day itself. The storm had disappeared. The sky was a rich blue and a few cumulus clouds had rolled in. The day was cold, but crystal clear, and all I wanted to do was drive and enjoy the sensational beauty—hoping it might calm my mind.

I knew it would be difficult to approach Mack. Trying to construct the best way to approach him I considered the options. Should I reveal the true story to him—everything I knew? Would that be unwise? I settled down and decided to tell him the truth. But where was the truth? Was this really happening? I barely knew what was going on. I need more info.

Mack would know what to do about this mess. He'd had legal problems before, and I needed him to help me to get Mel out—and soon. Mack would see the importance of this, but would he react poorly and blame all of us? His bad temper was foremost on my mind as I whipped the Porsche around the mountain roadway.

Secondary was Manny. The problem had occurred on his end of the operation where he failed to do his job. He had brought havoc on all of us. I was not about to let him walk free of his responsibility.

In a state of calm anger, yet with abject fear, I pulled up to Mack's house and took a few deep breaths as I sat in the car and collected my thoughts. Not only do I have to face Mack, there was the law to deal with. No matter what happened out there in the desert last night, the bust could put an end to all our efforts. Everything had been going so well—now this. What would happen to us?

Feeling more together, I got out of the car. I had to wait a while, but Mack soon appeared at the door dressed in a bathrobe, a furrow on his brow. He knew something bad had happened. Why else would I come here in the early morning? His face turned sour as I walked on into the living room and faced him.

"What's happening, brother? Anything wrong?"

"Plenty, Mack. The load's been busted. Mel's in jail," I blurted out.

"When did this happen, Frank? I want to know everything. Is he talking? We have to get a lawyer to him right away or we'll be in trouble. Do you understand?"

"Yes, I know. He's already requested one. As to what happened, I don't know all the facts yet." Mack paced as I ran the story down, his hands in his pocket and head down.

When I finished he looked up. "I suggest you use my lawyer. He's as good as they come. Have you got any money for bail?"

"Yes—it all depends on how much the bail is going to be, but I've plenty of money available."

"Good! We'll get to this later. I'll give you the lawyer's number." He found a pen and wrote down a message.

"This man got me out of a big jam a while back. He managed to get the evidence in my case suppressed. Maybe he can do the same for you. His name is George Chambers. He lives in Orange County. That's close to where the bust occurred."

Handing me the number he cautioned, "You better start using pay phones. This is a big bust. The narcs are going to be all over you. They may tap your phones."

"I'm sure they will. That's why I drove over."

"Good. That's smart thinking, brother. We just gotta hope your pilot hasn't started talking yet."

"I hear you. Mel's not the type. I figure he'll be cool."

"Maybe so, but get him out soon or that may change. Have George go see him sometime today. That's the best way to start."

"Yeah! I'd say so. I've got to get back, Mack. I've got to call Gil back and Manny too. There's a million things… and I have to get going. I'll keep you posted. When I call, it'll be from a pay phone.

"As for losing the load, let's discuss that at another time. That's not my concern right now."

"Good! Hey, I appreciate that, brother." Looking him directly in the eyes, I added, "Thanks for being cool about this."

When I returned home it was nearly 9:00 a.m. Christine greeted me.

"Manny called. He wants you to call him first thing. Gil also called. He said that he has something important to tell you."

"Thanks, honey."

Biting the bullet, I called Manny first.

"Manny, it's me. I guess Gil got through to you about Mel."

"Yes, Gil communicated with me. I know the whole story. Why didn't you have him go look for Mel last night? And why didn't you call me first thing this morning?"

His condescending tone put me on the defensive.

"Because he and I decided that it was not necessary to go out and find Mel. That's all. If Mel had gotten to a phone before he was arrested, Gil would be at home, ready to help out. You were unavailable. Remember?"

"That doesn't matter. You shouldn't have given up so easily. Mel was out there all by himself. If Gil had gone out there with the drivers helping, they might have found him. Why didn't you call late last night? I'd have told you to send Gil to go in search of Mel."

"Back off man. I just got back from seeing Mack. I had to drive over to his house to seek legal advice. He's involved in this, too. Besides, you don't get my point. You were unavailable. I was in charge. I chose to handle the matter with Gil. Now stop harassing me. We've got problems."

"You're supposed to communicate with me first. We might have been able to solve this together," he droned.

"You're pissing me off, Manny."

Obviously he wanted to hang the blame on me.

"You were supposed to be in charge of these people," I shouted. "You're the one who handles the middle position. Christ, you didn't even know Mel and Gil had changed things at the last moment and took matters into their own hands. Apparently, you haven't got the information I have."

"Frank, we're having an 'Arc' break. You'd better come down here and talk with me in person."

Manny was so full of restrained anger, a chilling sensation ran through me. I snapped.

"I know I have a break with you. I don't give a shit right now! We've got a man in jail. I've got the phone number of a lawyer, thanks to Mack, and I'm gonna do what I can to bail him. I've got calls to make, so get off my back. I'm hanging up."

I slammed the receiver down. Sitting down for a moment, agitated by his insolent behavior, I decided to call Gil.

"It's me. Sorry it took so long."

"I've got some more bad news, man. Your brother Bill is in jail. They caught him early this morning."

"Whaaat?" I couldn't believe what I'd just heard. "How can that be? He's down in Mexico."

"No he's not. I heard it on the radio. It's also on the tube. Believe me, they got both of them: Mel and Bill."

It was too much. Exploding, I exclaimed, "This doesn't make any sense!" Fighting back the panic I fell down on a pile of cushions, completely shaken, my energy depleting as the news sank in and Gil's voice buzzed in my ears.

"Believe me. They have him. There was a massive search for them in the desert last night. Mel was caught first. They got your brother a few hours later. All hell is breaking loose around here. My phone won't stop ringing. Mel's wife is totally out of her mind. His brother just called me. He wants to know what's up."

Bill's job, I knew, was to help Mack's people run the load up to the pick-up zone where they were to meet Mel and Gil. For whatever insane reason, Bill must have gotten on the plane with Mel. Why would he do that?

"Okay, Gil. Okay! God! This is so absurd!" I interrupted in a huff, then regained myself and sat upright. "We've got to sort this out, so cut me some slack... First of all, Mack gave me the number of a lawyer, but I don't know how to go about this. Guess I ought to get in touch with the lawyer first. Damn, it's hard to say how much money we may need. All I know is that I have a good deal here at the house, and I'm gonna use it. Let me get back to you. When I do, I'll be ready to fly down that way. Okay?"

"Fine. I've already contacted a lawyer here in Palm Springs. He's gonna go see Mel. He said he'd know very shortly what the bail will be. He'll find out what happened. The news is that the plane went down near an old mine that had a landing strip. I know where it's located." Hesitating, he continued, "Frank, I don't want to talk right now, not over the phone. Had I known he landed there...well, never mind. Let's talk soon."

"Yeah. I hear you. Let me get to a pay phone." In a state of confusion, anguish being the better part of the moment that had me spellbound, I said hopefully, "Let's hope Mel will hold up."

"Mel ain't going say a thing to the Man. We talked about this a while ago. Got me?"

"Yes. Call you later."

Plagued by questions about why Bill would get on the plane, I drove to a pay phone and called the lawyer. He was not in. His associate, a man by the name of James Morrissey talked with me.

"Why don't you come on down here?" he recommended, after I told him about the bust. "We'll get these guys bailed first thing. It may take a day or so. Bring plenty of cash for the bondsman and a couple of grand for a retainer."

Next, I called Joanne. I'd talked with her late the night before. She was aware that something bad might go down. "We're in deep shit. Mel's in jail. So is Bill."

Joanne never hesitated from cursing if it were warranted. "Boy, this is a fucking mess. What can I do to help?"

"I'm coming down there. Can you meet me at the airport? I need a ride to the lawyer's office."

"No problem. Do you have enough money for the bail?"

"Hard to say."

Fighting the maelstrom of confusion I made a reservation. At home, I gathered up all the money in the freezer. Fortunately, I hadn't made a run south in several days. There was well over a hundred grand—our profits. Placing the loot in a small suitcase along with some clothes, I readied myself. Then the phone rang.

Christine answered. It was Manny. "He's out making calls," I heard her say.

"Thanks for covering for me. I just don't want to talk with that sonofabitch right now."

"I know, but he sounded very pleasant, sweetheart. Not like what I expected."

"Well, he's not a complete tyrant. It's more like he's a man who knows how to blame others. Bye sweety. I'm headed out. I've got to take care of this. It may take a while. I'll call you. Take messages please. There's money in my dresser. If my brother Ray calls tell him to come over, then let him know what's happening. Tell him to stay in touch."

Calling Gil from a pay phone at the airport, I asked him to meet me at the lawyer's office that afternoon.

"You wanna hear how much the bail is? I just found out. They've been arraigned already."

"Not especially, but I guess I'll have to. Shoot!"

"Sixty-two thousand, five hundred dollars each. That's one hundred and twenty-five grand. You got that kind of money?"

Shocked, I replied, "Most of it, Gil. Most of it. We'll have to put something together. Let's talk with the lawyers. They'll tell us how to handle this. Just meet me at their office."

I made one more call to Mack to inform him that his partner and close friend had been busted. He was shocked and concerned, but indifferent when I told him the amount it would cost to bail him. No monetary assistance was suggested. "Just get him out. We'll talk about this later," he said. This time there was a telltale sign of anger in his voice.

George Chambers, Attorney-at-Law, was a slight man with an air of intelligence and a boyish face. James, his P.I., was tall, balding, distinguished and bearded. They looked like Mutt and Jeff. Greeting us they led Gil and I, along with Joanne, into a conference room. Gil and I told them our story.

George peered over at his associate, then back to us.

"The problem here is with your pilot. He's the weak link. The authorities are not going to go after Bill right now. They'll put their efforts into Mel and try every trick in the book to coerce him into talking. He may be talking with them right now."

"No way!" Gil blurted out. "He won't talk."

"I understand, but we have to let everyone know of this possibility. These agents know how to threaten people. It's their *modus operandi*. They could offer him immunity against prosecution as a device to further sway him to talk. If he talks, more charges will be filed. They'll want all of you. They'll be after everyone who's involved. Let's approach things from this angle. That's why you're to bail Mel first. I'm going to put you in touch with some bondsmen."

He handed us a card. "I recommend you make use of them—today." Turning to me he added, "As for your brother, we can get his bail reduced if he's willing to wait a few days. I suggest you go to Palm Springs or Indio and have the bondsman come there and work with you. You can use my phone. Just explain the situation to them. They'll understand. I'll fly down tomorrow and meet with you. Gil, make sure your lawyer pays Mel another visit tomorrow morning to let him know you're out there helping him. I'll also visit with your brother Bill while I'm down there. Any questions?"

"How many days will he have to wait for a bail reduction?"

"A week, maybe ten days. We'll talk more about that tomorrow when I meet up with you and Gil."

Gil was quiet as we gained the highway, the shock of the bust still upon us. I was full of remorse. Bill was in jail at that moment. I was sure he'd be climbing walls, scratching at the concrete as he waited. With all the good plans Jake, Manny, and I had made when we first started the venture, not one of us had thought to hire a lawyer to protect us, or to counsel us about what to do before things went bad. To boot, George Chambers had stalled us when we had asked about suppressing the evidence. He needed more information. So did we. We could only hope that Mel and Bill had used their heads. If they had secured the load and had left the plane locked, we might stand a chance. Then we'd see just how good the lawyer was.

Meanwhile, I had to break the ice with Gil who was rambling on about the bail.

"...Add ten percent more for the bondsman and we won't have enough money to bail both of them," he worried.

Everything was lost. I could only agree with him.

"Well how about that Gil? One week we're buying stock in asparagus, and the next week we're buying stocks in bail bonds," I said, making a feeble attempt at humor.

He knew what I meant. On that trip south to Guadalajara, Mel and Gil had approached us about plans to invest in farming asparagus with them. "It's a ten year crop. We can make a killing. We have use of the land and the people to farm it. All we need is money," Mel had said. Now we needed all the money we could lay our hands on to bail Mel and Bill out of jail.

Laughing, he said, "Yeah. We'll spring 'em with our asparagus money. No kidding. Mel and I put up twenty grand last week. I'm sure we can get it back. We know these people quite well. They'll understand. It's not too late."

"Sounds terrific."

"What do you think about the lawyer?"

"Mack said he'd be good. We'll just have to see."

"Don't worry. Mel ain't gonna talk. I know him too well. He hates the authorities."

"I hope he knows better than to say anything. What I'd like to know Gil is what it was you and Mel worked out with the drivers. How did that all come about?"

Rolling his eyes he groaned, "It was my idea."

Mel and he had wanted to take turns at flying the loads over. They felt it was safe, but hadn't told Manny for fear of refusal. Gil's job was to fly over the landing areas and check out which zone would be best suited for the day. Using their radios they'd make contact an hour before the landing. Gil would let Mel know which one of the areas was safe. They had figured that if the landing site they had chosen to use that particular day was unsafe, they could correct the problem.

"What screwed it up was the sandstorm. I couldn't get Mel on the radio. That can happen sometimes during a big blow."

What I couldn't figure out, as he explained the complicated movements, was just how they'd get the drivers into position on time. It wasn't necessary to know that now, and I didn't have the heart to ask him. Instead, I listened to Gil carry on, not bothering to mention that their plan seemed overly complicated. Then I turned my thoughts back to Manny: Mister Tardy. His pilots had changed their plans and he hadn't been there to oversee them.

The Imperial County courthouse in El Centro was a bleak-looking building. Its architect must have had that in mind when he had designed it several decades before. Jake and I were waiting in front of the scourge of a structure for Bill to come out, and were fighting back depression for many reasons, the building being one of them. It was early morning, the sky a mucky blue, and I couldn't help but think what it would be like living inside the walls of that hideous icebox that someone had dared to paint loathsome yellow. Weather and time had stained and tainted its exterior by several shades. Even the molecules that gave the building the illusion that it was yellow were in the state of revolt. Maybe the city's pioneers knew that we would be there that particular day to see that particular inexcusable mess they had created. For them, it might have been worth the effort to see us sit there suffering through that tormenting moment. They would also be happy to know that we were all but broke.

On the previous day we had been successful. Gil had come up with the extra twenty grand we'd needed. One hundred and thirty-seven thousand dollars had been handed over to the bail bondsman. Through our lawyer, we had found out that Bill had not wanted to wait for a bail reduction. We were requested to get him out immediately. No one argued. We just handed over the necessary funds and everything had been taken care of in a very mysterious manner.

The local papers had more bad news for us. A mining engineer on his way home from work had spotted the plane about 4:30 that afternoon, and had called the local authorities on his citizens band radio to let them know a plane and its occupants were in need of assistance. The local sheriff entered the area and found the plane abandoned and full of contraband: 1,757 pounds of marijuana. With no suspects in sight, the sheriff had called in a posse. A manhunt began. Mel was apprehended eight hours after the crash: Bill, four hours later.

When Bill came down the courthouse steps I was elated: we could now leave. Jake tooted the horn. Bill swung around and walked toward us. He looked terrible. I could only imagine. I wanted to hug him, but remained in the car.

Falling into the back seat with a troubled face he grunted, "Let's get out of here. I don't want to spend another second around here."

"Right on. We're with you," I answered.

All was quiet for a while as we cleared the dusty little town, then Bill let loose.

"Man, your pilots sure didn't have their shit together. They messed up, brother. That's all I can say."

We were prepared for an outburst like this. Still, I felt guilty that because of our failures, Bill was busted. I sat in silence.

Jake had no guilt and asked him directly, "Why did you get on our plane, Bill?"—with a strong emphasis on "our."

Immediately, his defenses rose. "I don't wanna talk about that right now."

There was silence. Jake and I figured on that, too. He'd find some sort of excuse. We'd have to wait for the right moment. Time was on our side.

Then we heard him lament, "I'm not gonna hang around long, I'll tell you that. No way am I gonna spend time in jail. Three days was enough. Any longer, you can forget it."

"Not now, Bill," I said, not bothering to look at him. "It's too soon."

"I know it's too soon," he responded with agitation. "But I'm telling you now so you'll know. I've already made up my mind. I'm gonna split when it's time."

"Fine." Jake cut him short. "We're meeting with the lawyers at our motel as soon as we get you back. Let's hear what they have to say first."

Mel didn't look like the Mel I had met a few weeks ago. All the cocky confidence was gone and he appeared to have suddenly aged a few years. Both he and Bill stood at opposite ends of the room, each in a corner and as far away from one another as they could get. We'd soon find out why, and why they were shamefaced, whether they were aware of this or not.

Mel was asked to tell us his story; Gil, Jake and I, along with our new lawyer listened intently, as did Bill, standing steadfast in his corner. Manny would miss this grand, fiasco of a story. He was at the fortress looking for the Holy Grail. He might just find it, but not in this lifetime.

As the tale unraveled Mel had all of us in state of suspense, for the tale was extraordinarily sad, and most certainly twisted. As he began talking his eyes darted all about. He was nervous about what we would find out and he had every reason to be ashamed—what had happened between Bill and him out in the desert immediately after the crash was pure foolishness.

"We came close to getting killed," Mel started, then back-tracked. "Before landing I was worried when I saw the sandstorm up ahead. I knew I wouldn't be able to find the landing area Gil and I had agreed on, so I went for this one. I was familiar with it and thought I could land okay. I would have if it hadn't been for a sudden gust of wind. I had to correct-out to keep the plane level. We almost landed on our side but came upright and landed hard. When we hit the ground the gear collapsed. Sand flew all over the place, but the plane took the beating. When we came to a stop every muscle in my body hurt. All I thought about was that we had survived. When the dust cleared away, I thought about the load. We had to get it off the plane somehow. Bill didn't want to. He and I had words. I knew we were both in shock and not thinking straight, but I figured that we'd be better off if we got all the bags off the plane and found a place to hide them."

"Then Bill took off. He was angry and I was too, but, shit, I was hurting all over and after I removed a few bags I stopped. I just couldn't finish up. No one was around so I thought about hiking out of there and getting to a phone to call Gil. I tried a few times to reach him on the radio but came up with nothing so I took off, figuring it might take some time, but we'd somehow retrieve the load even if it took all night."

"All I wanted to do was get to a phone," he added after a short pause, "and call Gil and let him know to bring the drivers. But, shit, I was way out in the boonies. The nearest phone was at least twenty miles away. I knew something was up when I saw the posse crisscrossing the desert."

"Jesus. If it hadn't been for that mining engineer, we'd have gotten out of this fucking mess," Gil added, in support of his pal.

Everyone agreed.

Bill was next. I was already upset with him after learning that he had argued with Mel. Why had he taken off, leaving Mel to take care of the mess?—It was just like him though, to do something like that. Plus, his rash decision to board the plane put all of us in a deep hole. And why did he take off and leave Mel to fend for himself? Did Mel go berserk and Bill couldn't deal with him? Or, did Bill put blame on us for screwing up and felt he had every reason to clear the area and avoid being arrested. Troubled by his decision to leave Mel to take care of the problem, I readied myself for Bill's side of the story.

Before Bill got his chance to defend himself Chambers asked Mel if he had locked the plane before leaving. He couldn't remember and finished up with, "I don't think so."

Visibly upset and quite nervous, Bill began telling his tale.

"Gil wasn't on the plane when Mel landed. It was strange so I asked him why. He said they were taking turns. Gil was going to fly the next load up so I asked him if I could come along. He said 'no problem', so I got on. I thought it would be simple, you know, land the plane, drop off the load, and fly back with Mel to the airport in Indio."

I thought, "God, Bill. Why are you telling this to everyone in the room? Gil had already informed us that Mel had told him that Bill asked to come along. The lawyer couldn't care less that Bill hitched a ride, only that he was an accomplice. Then it hit me. Bill wanted to make it seem it was okay for him to get on the plane down in Mexico. He was directing blame at us. Had everything gone according to plan, he'd be safe and on his way home. You're not going to get out of this, Bill, I thought.

After his confession a melancholy descended over him. In a subdued tone he said, "Mel mentioned we'd have a problem landing. I could see the sand storm and figured we were in trouble. All I could do was wait and see what happened. Man, I was scared shitless. And when Mel tried to land and the plane almost flipped over I figured we were going to die, especially when the plane hit hard. Man, it was something, and by the time the plane stopped every joint in my body hurt. It was unbelievable. Why we weren't seriously hurt was beyond me. Boy, did we take a pounding."

He continued in a more upbeat manner. "Once we got out of the plane, Mel wanted to remove the load. I advised him not to. Then he got crazy on me. I was hurting and I didn't want to put up with him. That's all. He just didn't want to take my advice. When he said something about finding Gil and getting the driver to come and get the load, I figured he'd handle that so I told him I was going to get out of there. There was no reason to stay. "

"When I saw the posse scouring the desert, I freaked out. It was shit-ass cold out there and I was tired and hurting. They knew how to find me. There was nothing I could do, man—nothing. They got me cold and I said nothing to them. Gave them my name and that was that."

"How about you, Mel?" Chamber's asked. "When they found out you were the pilot did they get tough on you?"

"Not at first. They wanted to know where I had gotten the contraband, but I acted as if I didn't know what they were talking about. I know a few sheriff deputies and I know the law. I didn't have to tell them anything. After they got me to El Centro they tried again and later that day a few detectives came in and put me through a grilling, that is they tried to, but I told them I had nothing to say. Gil sent a lawyer in and I told him the same thing I'm telling you now. They tried and I said nothing. They got heavy and made a bunch of crazy threats, but I tuned them out."

"Good," Chambers replied. "That goes for the both of you. You don't have to say anything to the law enforcement agents. Let them investigate all they want. That's their job. Your job is to remain quiet. We have the upper hand on them here. They'll need cooperative evidence from the both of you to get a federal indictment. Right now I'm concerned about the State. They have a lot of evidence and we have to make sure they don't get anything else on the two of you or anyone else. Is that understood?"

Mel and Bill both agreed.

He added, "I'll do what I can to file a motion to suppress the contraband. It doesn't matter that they found a few bags outside the plane; they had no business searching the plane. I'll find out if they got a warrant and what kind of warrant. These things matter, but until I have all the facts there's not much I can do. We'll keep in touch. Here's my card." He handed one each to Bill and Mel. "Call me after the weekend, say Tuesday. I'll have more evidence. For now, rest up and get clear on what went down. I'll talk with both of you together in my office when you're ready. Okay?"

I'd heard enough. The dispute between Bill and Mel, though upsetting to us, was of no consequence to the law. Our only chance to survive this blunder lay with our attorney. Chamber's motion to suppress would have to have a million Hail Mary's attached to it in order to get a judge to go his way. I believed in my heart that he would not succeed. The evidence was overwhelming. Their fingerprints would be all over the plane and Mel had rented it. And the part about the sheriff not obtaining a proper warrant didn't mix with what I knew about compelling facts. The sheriff must have found the bags of weed outside the plane and after opening the bags and discovering there was contraband, he had every right to look inside the plane. Locked or not, the sheriff would readily spot the same kind of bags in the interior. It didn't seem possible a judge would overlook this fact. And the prosecutor would most definitely back the sheriff up.

As the meeting drew to a close, Jake and I pulled Mel and Gil aside.

"Hey guys," Jake said, "we've got a tough situation to work through.

We'll handle all lawyer fees, Mel. Don't be concerned about that. We'll cover everything. Frank and Manny and I will work this out with Ramon. He's already promised help and he has a pilot for us."

Gil interrupted, "You mean Nick? Hey, I can still fly. Let me go with him. We know Nick. He's a good pilot."

"No Gil." Jake squelched his crazy suggestion. "I already talked to Nick. He wants to fly alone. You'll have heat all over you and that's one reason Nick wouldn't let you come along."

Mel remained quiet, but Gil protested. In the end he conceded. His flying days were over and so were Mel's—at least for now.

"Lets not give up on this," I said, adding a positive spin to this grim situation. "It doesn't look good, but Chamber's might get us a break."

"What do you think guys?" Mel asked. "What's the chance the lawyer can suppress the evidence?"

"I don't know, man," I said, withholding my true feelings. "You heard him. He needs to find out what the sheriff did out there. Mack sure thinks highly of him. Mack got caught with a steamer box full of pot on a train. They had him dead cold. He had checked it in and they opened it up and found the pot. But Chambers got the evidence suppressed and Mack went free."

"We'll stay on top of this, Mel," Jake affirmed. You think about what you want to do. Maybe it's time you become an asparagus farmer."

We all laughed but Mel said, "Fat chance. We got our money back, but our friends were sore, even though they knew we used the money for bail."

"Then keep busy with your family for now. We'll be in touch with both of you. Let's use the pay phone. Frank and I have a system all set up."

I eyeballed my brother. He had just finished conversing with Chambers and was now hovering about. He looked in our direction, and I sent him a hand signal to hang in. Then I let Jake know that we better talk with Bill before he decided to bolt. Saying goodbye to our two pilots, we focused on my older brother.

I said to Jake sardonically and in a low tone as they took off, "Well, now that we're officially wiped out partner, let's make sure Bill understands our position. Chambers wants thirty grand to handle the case. And there's the bond money we put up for Bill. What do you think?"

"We're going to have to ask Bill and Mack for some help. Does that answer your question?"

When we turned to face Bill I was shocked. I'd never seen him so out of place and uncomfortable. Bill knew he had to face the music and lend a hand with the finances. And, because of what he had just gone through, my heart went out to him. But, I also knew enough to be aware of his cunning tactics. If Jake and I had to get on his case about his responsibilities we'd do so. When Jake had arrived yesterday afternoon, he and I had gone over every aspect of the bust, including any possible excuse Bill would come up with. He had no excuse, really. Jake and I, along with Manny, were the bosses of the operation. We concluded that Bill had acted on his own when he no right to board our plane.

Jake came right to the point. "We know you have a lot on your mind. But so do we. You got on the plane without our permission and you need to come to terms with that."

Without hesitation Bill said, "I'll work something out with the both of you about the bail money. Right now I need to consider what to do with my money."

Before Bill said another word Jake pressed him harder. "There's the bond money and the lawyer's fee to pay."

Looking Jake straight in the eye he asked, "What's that come to?"

"Well, for starts," Jake stood his ground, "the bond is sixty-nine grand and the lawyer wants thirty, maybe more."

"Thirty grand! That's too much," Bill whined.

"He's Mack's lawyer. What can I say, other than that he's now your lawyer," Jake retorted.

Eyes darting, he replied, "I'll make arrangements to give you a portion of the bond money sometime in the near future. As for the lawyer, you know where I stand."

"Not really," Jake said, deflating Bill's posturing. "You have an obligation to us and to Mel, not to mention Mack."

Looking askance he fidgeted, then let loose a reply true to his nature. "I don't want to talk about this right now. You'll get the bond money and as for the lawyer as soon as I can put things together I'll pay a portion of the fee. Right now I want to get back up to the Bay Area and see Mack."

"That's it?" I asked, as he was already turning at the heels to leave.

"That's it!"

As he disappeared out the door, I turned to Jake and said, "I don't think he ever thanked us for bailing him out."

"You'd be right, partner."

"He's so outta here, he forgot to ask us for a ride to the airport," I sighed, sad to see my brother in this state of affairs.

Jake drove, and I brought the subject up of our partnership with Manny. "He tried to blame me, Jake. No doubt about it and I'm not going to put up with his shit. He's gone man. He's outta here. I don't want him as a partner. I said this to you yesterday and I feel the same today."

For most of the drive to his house Jake had to listen to my rag-on-Manny routine. I even grew tired of listening to myself. But Jake was adamant. He'd call Manny and request a meeting to be held at Jake's house, saying, "I want to hear what he has to say before I make a decision."

I filled Joanne in on the day's activities as Jake made a beeline for the shower. When she found out I wanted to kick Manny out of our partnership, she was all for it. She never liked the man. He was disgusting. When Jake rejoined us, she recounted the story about Manny's Thanksgiving Day theatrics.

Manny had invited all of us to his house for a Thanksgiving feast. He insisted we come. Although I was reluctant, I flew to L.A., met with Jake and family, and we drove to Manny's house. Marlina cooked a turkey with all the trimmings—everything organic, of course. Manny ate three plates piled high with food. After finishing the first plate he left the table and went to the bathroom. We could hear him vomiting. When he came back we all looked at him, concerned. He let us know he wasn't sick. In order to make room for the food he wanted to consume that day, he felt it was perfectly fine to continue to fill his belly and then heave it up. After the third helping, and another trip to the bathroom, we were all totally turned off, especially Jake's daughter, Wendy, who was old enough to know what was going on.

Joanne concluded her rant by saying, "Manny is the one who should have been there to run the pilots. You heard Frank. The pilots knew Manny wouldn't agree to their plan so they changed things without telling Manny."

Backing up Joanne's sentiments, I argued, "Jake, if they believed in him, you know, affinity and all that shit he preaches, they would have brought the matter up with him."

Jake listened to our outbursts, but was steadfast. He'd call Manny and arrange a meeting.

When I got up the next morning, Jake confirmed his plan. "I got through to Manny late last night. He'll be here tomorrow night about nine."

"Tomorrow?" I cried out.

"He's got one more class to go to, then he's done."

Eyes bright and brimming with energy, Manny arrived late and promptly greeted us with a hug. His star-studded demeanor did not impress me.

With the kids long ago put to bed, Joanne made busy in the kitchen. She was my ally and she believed Manny was the biggest creep she had ever encountered. She was greatly relieved when I let her know Manny would soon be history.

But it wasn't going to be easy and I was uneasy when Jake spent several minutes explaining what had happened during the previous few days. When he informed Manny that all our money had been used to bail Mel and Bill, Manny spoke out in mild anger.

"Why wasn't I informed of this? You had no right to use my profits to bail your brother, Frank."

"Never mind the fact that you weren't there to oversee all of this," I accused silently. But I remained quiet, allowing Jake to take care of this matter.

Jake knew that Manny might attempt to manipulate us and was ready with an answer. "It was necessary. Bill made a mistake. We had to cover him. He owes us. Simple as that. We talked to him about his responsibilities. He's going to pay us the bond money and we'll collect attorney fees from him."

Manny, not ready to back off demanded, "When will he pay us?"

"Hard to say," Jake said. "We'll have to keep on him. Frank and I figure he'll come up with a good portion of the money—but not all of it."

"You should have insisted he wait in jail for a bail reduction."

"Put yourself in his shoes," Jake insisted. "We did what he asked us to do. Bill's out and the money is now in the hands of the bondsman."

Irritated, Manny retorted. "Still, you used my money without my permission. You and Frank should be responsible and pay me back. Why should I have to wait for Bill to pay up when you don't know when he'll pay?"

I thought, "Dig a hole, Manny."

"I feel you should pay this money back," he barked at me.

"Even if I had this money I wouldn't," I declared, unable to keep quiet any longer. "Can't you get it through your head, man? It's gone. We used it up to pay a debt you helped to create."

Jake was irritated too and said pointedly, "Just how much do you think we owe you?"

Patiently I waited for Manny to stick his foot farther down his mouth.

Focused on Jake, he replied, "All of it. The profit portion I was to receive was thirty to forty thousand dollars. All of that was used to bail Bill."

"And what about the lawyer's fees to cover Mel?" Jake asked.

"We'll split that of course, three ways as usual," he said, his eyes darting about. "What you owe me is more like twenty-five. We can figure it out."

Jake produced pen and paper and began writing down figures.

"Hmmm…looks like we owe you close to thirty-five grand in profits. Minus the bail money, and the money we owe to Chamber's; that leaves you next to nothing."

"That can't be correct."

"Yes it is. If you take away the money we used to bail Bill, then you'd be in the plus column by over twenty grand.

"Fine! Pay me off as soon as possible and you guys can collect the money Bill owes you. That's the best way to solve this problem."

"Not really," Jake countered. "There are up and coming lawyer's fees to consider. That's thirty grand to start, but you know lawyers. Chambers will want a good deal more, especially if the Feds get involved."

"So, for now it's back to ten thousand or so. Okay. We can figure out the exact amount over the next few weeks. What I want to know is how much money we have between us. We have to get back to work. Let's head in that direction. "

I was ready to explode, but Jake saved me the trouble. "I don't think so, Manny."

"What are you talking about?"

"We have to resolve the main issue before we talk about what we'll do in the future."

"And what would that be?"

"Your responsibility, Manny." Jake answered. "You were in charge of the pilots and the drivers. You assured Frank and me that they would handle their end. The pilots changed things around and I'd like to know why."

Calmness settled over me after Jake asked this question; I could hardly wait for Manny to reply.

"The day before this came down, I called Frank and suggested he fly down and oversee the lower end," Manny rationalized. "He refused, even though he knew that I was busy with classes and could not get away. He said that as long as I had control of the pilots and driver and they knew how to handle everything there was no need for him to oversee them."

"Yes, I'm aware of all of this," Jake said. "What you need to tell me is why did the pilots change things around without telling you?"

"Jake, I don't have an answer for that right now. I have to talk with them."

"Bullshit, Manny." I all but shouted and started tapping my finger on the kitchen table in cadence with my words: "You know why they did. It has everything to do with 'affinity.' They figured you'd put their plan down. That's what Gil told me. So they went behind your back and did things their way—because you don't have a line of affinity with them. You created this mess just as much as Mel and Gil. I know that you know why these guys went behind your back, but you can't admit that they don't respect you, nor do they trust you. If they did, they would never have changed things."

Joanne overheard me as she rattled around in the kitchen. With a broad grin of approval, she raised an arm in a clenched fist of approval behind Manny's back.

Unfazed by my outburst Manny replied, "I'm going to remind both of you that we had an agreement." Looking over at Jake, he added, "Surely you know what I mean. You said it was perfectly fine with you that I attend classes while the two of you took responsibility for the business."

"You were the one who was in charge of the middle position," I said boldly. "I made a request for you to stop going to class and take over the middle position. You declined, and now you have to pay for it. Mel and Gil took things into their own hands. You readily assured us nothing would go wrong."

Jake pushed, "What can you say to that, Manny? Mel and Gil took over and changed things. They're your responsibility, no matter what. "

"Not when I turn that responsibility over to you and Frank." He pointed a finger at me and began to lose some of his control. "You never came down to take over. I asked you to, but you said…"

"Fuck you, Manny," I interrupted. Staring at him just like he stares at others I added, "Be a man. Live to know that you had a choice and you made a bad one. We're all paying for it now. Shit, come off with something better than just a poor excuse as to why your end went down." I stood over him and lowered my face into his, pointing a finger almost into his chest. "It went down because you weren't there to attend to your crew—our crew. Accept it. Get humble, or something, man. Go back to class and find out why you can't face responsibility."

Disgusted, I backed away. "I'm finished with you. No way do I want you as a partner."

Trying to keep his emotions in control Manny countered, "Frank, the way I see it you're the one who is out of touch with your ego. We could address this matter if you come with me to the Orge tomorrow and go before the ethics director. This is how these matters are handled. This is a major ARC break (Affinity, Reality, Communication) we're having and it can be settled."

"Fat chance," I spat out, as I stalked off. I wondered with amusement what we would say to this ethics officer about the type of partnership we have.

Jake had finally heard enough. "That's not going to happen, Manny," he declared with finality. "Responsibility falls on you. You failed to oversee your end and Frank and I are going to dissolve the partnership. We discussed this the past two days, but I wanted to hear you out before I made a decision. And now I have. We'll divide the expenses and figure out what's owed. As for you, you still have use of everything the three of us put together."

"Wait a minute, Jake. I don't understand. Why don't you want to work through this? I don't understand your reasoning..." Manny halted. As suddenly as that, he was emotionally spent, and lowered his head and began to cry. He muttered, "We can learn from this. I know how to make things work. We can do this."

I was taken aback by Manny's lethargy and walked over to the kitchen area to talk with Joanne. Jake asked Manny to go with him to a small anteroom near the foyer.

Manny's eyes were swollen when they emerged from their meeting two hours later. Emotionally withdrawn and obviously depressed, he hugged Jake and departed without saying a word to me, or Joanne.

I was on pins and needles while waiting. But when I saw Manny leave I was overcome with guilt. I don't know why I felt guilty. I had pushed to dissolve the partnership and had prevailed. With this reality sinking in, I was relieved, even if I was also a little shaken up by the whole messy business.

Jake's energy was also depleted. Without saying a word he retired to his bedroom. The next morning, before I took off for San Francisco, we talked at length about our future. I cautioned, "Let's be extra careful. Manny might try to seek revenge. What frightens me, Jake, is that his kind never let up, and we have to deal with him if he decides to turn on us and create more problems."

CHAPTER EIGHT

FOOL'S GOLD

SAN FRANCISCO, CALIFORNIA
MARCH, 1969

THE U.S. GOVERNMENT would be happy to know that we were broke and on our knees. But on the other hand, we had all the resources we needed and the drive to continue. Understandably, we had to be extra careful and not fall prey to disasters such as the one we had just suffered.

Jake had ten grand left. I had five. Bill and Mack owed us a bundle. We had to collect from them and it wasn't going to be easy. Then again, it would be a damn sight easier than trying to get our money back from the system the government used to take our money in the first place.

When I called Bill from a pay phone a few days after the fiasco and asked him to meet with us along with his partner Mack, Bill blithely informed me that Mack didn't like Jake. *Aloof and arrogant* were the exact words he'd used.

Aloof and arrogant! Christ, everyone plays that game, including you and your pal, I thought after hanging up. Aloof and arrogant were getting to be much overused terms, and most certainly had misleading implications. More to the point, guys like Bill didn't know what the hell they were talking about.

To be sure, all humans are aloof and arrogant from time to time. I had come to realize that insecurities hamper everyone's ego and are always at work. To protect ourselves we create a façade of arrogance—a cover-up what will suit our needs during the time we are feeling less than secure. All four of us were caught up in our insecurities. All four of us would choose a nice suit of armor to protect ourselves while we battled over who owed what to whom, and how much was to be paid.

The night before the four of us were to meet, I got good and stoned. It wasn't the smartest thing to do and I paid for it. Over-sensitized by the THC, my emotions began to rock me out, sending me into a fit of anger. There was no outburst. I was just locked into anger that had been building up and had not been released. I had to calm myself and reason my way back into a clear state of reality.

I was mad as hell. I knew that Bill and Mack would find a way out of their responsibilities and would do whatever they felt necessary to cut Jake and me down. At the core of this anger was that Bill—my older brother—was suffering. I wanted to reach out to him and had made an attempt a few days back, but he was closed off. I wanted to share with him my thoughts about arrogance and how all of us are insecure at times: how we all hide behind a mask to cover up our insecurities, and in so doing, we often become arrogant. But, I knew from experience that Bill would shoot me down, mainly because he had not been the one to come up with the idea. Talk about being arrogant! What happened to the *Brotherhood Movement*? What happened to the bond of being brothers?

To be safe, everyone had moved. Bill and Inger found and apartment in Santa Cruz. For the interim, Jake and his family had moved to San Mateo. Christine and I were out of San Francisco and back to Marin County. I had found a small hillside house in Mill Valley with a terrific view of the bay.

On the way to the meeting I offered as much information as possible to my partner about what to expect: Bill's attitude about our success and that we might have infringed on his business when we worked with Glenn and Mack...shit, even Manny, was a major concern. There was little doubt in my mind that Bill was harboring bad feelings toward us. Maybe he felt our recent success was due our using his people. Adding to that, he wasn't exactly exuding happiness after Jake and I had quit working for him. Maybe he figured we'd fail. Instead we'd been very successful and in a very short period of time. Then Bill jumps on our plane, without our permission, gets busted and tries to blame it on us as though we're a couple of idiots. Not a happy ending for a man whose self-image is so fragile, he's afraid to admit that he has foibles. Whatever he'd packed around about all of this had caught up with him in a hurry. No doubt he was feeling slightly envious—and maybe vengeful too.

After explaining all of this to Jake I added, "He's going to play the-wounded-dog act, Jake. He's in misery and unable to confront the mistakes he made. And I don't understand why he chooses to shut down at a time when he ought to open up and admit the truth."

"I think you're really becoming aware of Bill's pitfalls," Jake observed. "And, if what you say about the ego being a façade to cover our fears we can't face is true, then you have your answer. He's afraid to let you see him as he really is: one scared dude. And you're his younger brother. He's not going to let on around you. And if he's seeking vengeance, we'll have to put a stop to whatever he tries to pull on us."

Jake had given me these same messages about my brother before, and I could only figure that he wanted me to get over my unrequited hopes for brotherly love and let Bill be who he was.

"I'm on to his act, Jake. And he doesn't realize I'm on to him. Or maybe he does, but no matter what, he's caught up in a vicious cycle. It's going to destroy him."

"Oh, he's on to you alright. So watch yourself. He may drag you into his game."

As expected, Bill showed us just how much of a shit he could be at the meeting.

The meeting was to be held at a friend of Bill's. Mack made it a point to arrive late, forcing Jake and I to hang out with Bill for nearly an hour.

He arrived in a truculent mood, which gave fair warning of just how Mack would react to our request for financial assistance: poorly. Forcing a smile, he shook our hands. I'd have to keep my distance from him.

Jake, relaxed and ready, after going over a few facts and details about the bust, got right to the point by informing them that we were no longer partners with Manny, and that Scientology was no longer part of our lives. Bill and Mack had little interest in these matters.

What did seem to matter was that all of us chose to sit a safe distance from each other. Jake and I sat in the middle of the room, while Bill sat on a dining room chair facing the room. Mack found a club chair at the far end of the living room. Then the battle began.

Jake said kindly but firmly, which I'm sure was interpreted as arrogant, "What we'd like is some help from both of you. This bust has flattened us out. Frank and I have a lot of debts to pay and we don't want to take on all of them. We don't feel responsible for…"

"Hold on," Mack interrupted, "right now I wanna work out what we owe each other. Let's do that first. I lost 1,750 pounds of some really nice pot. You pay for that and we'll go from there."

"It's covered, Mack." I quickly answered and looked in his direction, wondering what he was up to. "We paid you for our portion before the weed even left Mexico, sixteen grand, to be exact. So the load is paid for on our end."

"I could have sold those kilos for well over two hundred each," he complained, staring back at me.

"They never made it here," Jake said. "As you know, the local sheriff now owns them. We'd like to talk about who's responsible for what and figure out who owes whom as a result."

"Hey look, I came here figuring you guys would accept all the debts," Mack burst out. "Now I have to listen in while you pull some fucking kind of a responsibility game on us?"

"What about Bill's bail money and paying off the lawyers?" Jake fired off calmly. "Your partner got on that plane against our wishes. He created a big problem for us and we think the both of you have to look at this."

"Bill is not my responsibility," Mack said, leering at Jake, then at me. Bill remained noncommittal. "You guys owe me for…"

"Wait a minute, Mack." I interrupted hotly, looking at him then at Bill. "Bill's your partner. We're dealing with both of you. Why are…"

"I'm not Mack's partner," Bill interjected calmly, before I could say another word.

"You're not his partner!" I exclaimed, giving him a third-degree stare and then firing back, "You were back in January when you told me you were headed to Mexico to join *your partner.*"

"That was just a figure of speech," he responded craftily, eyeing his pal and not bothering to face me. "We're associates. We work together. That's all."

"Great, then how do we straighten this out," I quipped sarcastically, "if he's not your partner?"

"Simple. I owe you the bail money. Talk with Mack about what you owe him."

Jake jumped on this. "Good! When do we collect?"

"We're going to have to work that out." Bill was just as quick to respond.

"And the lawyer's fees?" I asked.

Bill stared hard at me for a second and then replied arrogantly, "We can split it for now. When I'm gone, I'm gone. No more money."

"And what about the money to keep Mel quiet?" Jake asked. "He may have screwed up, but we have to protect him." Jake looked at Bill, then over at Mack, and added, "Who's going to cover him if he has to go to jail? And what about you helping us with lawyers' fees, Mack?"

Incensed, Mack stared harshly at Jake and cursed. "What the fuck are you talking about? How do you figure I owe you for Mel?"

"Simple," Jake stared him down. "We're all in this together, partners or no partners. We're all responsible. We can blame Manny; we can blame Bill or Mel, or even Gil. The fact is that all of us put this deal together. All of us have to pay up."

"No way, brother," Mack shot back, pointing his finger at Jake. "You guys fucked up and I'm not going to cover for you. That's the way I see the situation, Jake. You got that?"

"We're asking for help here." I calmly offered, attempting to soften things up. "Do you want us to pay for all of this?"

Jake added in a concerned manner, "You owe us, Mack. You and your partner have to see that."

"Where do you get off coming on like this?" Mack's voice rang out, his face stained red with anger.

My adrenalin began to run. Fastened to my seat I figured it would only be a matter of time before Mack started a fight.

"Right now, I stand as good a chance as anyone of getting indicted, thanks to your fuck-ups. You were the ones who brought Mel to my ranch in Mexico," Mack accused, again pointing a finger at Jake.

"That was with your approval, brother," Jake shot back, with calm anger.

"That doesn't cut it, dude. If he spills his guts I'm gonna be on the indictment list. That's fucking reality to me," Mack thrust a clenched fist at him.

"Then why don't you help keep Mel quiet?" Jake countered. "That would help keep him from talking. As you well know, money talks."

Jake had him there. Mack had walked right into the trap we had set. As the realization hit home, Mack gripped the ends of the small club chair, eyes fixed on Jake.

Ready, in case he made a leap at my partner, I cautioned, "Hey, why don't we calm it down here?" Glancing toward Bill who was watching the proceedings and remaining uncommonly quiet I added, "We didn't come here to fight with either of you. We came to solve some problems in a brotherly manner. We've got to see what it takes to keep all of us from going to jail."

"Apparently, they're not ready for that," Jake said, and then looked over at me.

"I've had enough of you." Mack sprang from his seat, the veins on his face standing out as he again pointed menacingly at Jake. "You talk to me like a man. Don't go talking behind my back like that."

"Calm down Mack!" Bill finally spoke up. "Let's settle this. No more arguing."

That must have been the cue Mack was waiting for.

"I'll settle this right now, right here." Mack looked around the room, then over to me, then announced in a most arrogant way: "I'm gonna to bring up another load in about a month. A portion of it'll be yours." He pointed at me. "I'm not gonna deal with your partner, just you. I'll take on part of this, mainly because of Bill. Forty-grand worth ought to take care of it. I'll be in touch, Frank." Looking back at Jake menacingly, he added, "That's it. No more. This meeting is over for me. I'm leaving." He turned, gave Jake a final ugly stare, and stomped out the door.

Glaring at Bill I said with a good deal of sarcasm, "That was really brilliant, brother. Thanks for the fucking support."

Bill stood nonchalantly then came to the center of the room. "You heard Mack. You guys talk about responsibility, so take it. He gave you a good deal."

"Yeah, great deal, Bill! You guys had your way with us. You strong-armed us into accepting your terms, right?" I stood a few feet from my brother, my heart still pounding from Mack's fierceness.

"Get over it, brother," he hissed. "Mack's got a lot to lose. See it his way."

"I'll get over it when you decide to take responsibility for getting on our plane, brother," I jeered back.

Yeah, and if you hadn't gotten on the plane we wouldn't be here negotiating over a bond for seventy grand, streaked across my mind, as Jake came to the center of the room.

"When are you going to make good on the bond payment?" he asked Bill.

"You're going to have to wait 'til I decide. I'll need a lot of money when I split. Meanwhile, I'm going to invest money with Mack. After we run a couple of loads up I'll work something out." Deliberately ignoring Jake, Bill turned to me and said, "I'll be in touch with you, Frank."

Jake and I headed to the Golden Gate Park. Sitting on a small bench overlooking Spreckle's Lake, we consoled one another. Although it was a pleasant spring day, our minds and hearts were elsewhere. We had every reason to be angry at those two baboons. After a prolonged discussion, we agreed to find a way to get these two worms out of our lives as soon as possible.

"They're fucking stupid, man. They're treating us like idiots. Did you catch what they did towards the end when Mack, and then Bill, made it a point to suck up to me instead of you? It was their way of creating a degree or two of separation between you and me. Shit! So much for Brotherhood! We've got more to learn about how to handle people. If we use force or coercion it will just come back at us. To hell with them! Let's just get busy and keep our heads together and figure out something that will work for us and the rest of our organization."

In agreement, Jake leaned forward and rested his forearms against his thighs, hands clenched together. Gazing out across the lake, he predicted, "I think Bill's going to hedge paying the bond money to us. Maybe even the lawyer's fee. He made a lot of money last year. He must have plenty."

"I agree. When and if Mack comes through, there'll be no more help." Hesitating a moment, I added, "Bill told me he had fifty-five grand to his name. Hard to say if it's the truth. Last week he mentioned he'd give us twenty grand. Now, he's stalling us. All I saw was two men acting out their insecurities: Bill, and his cohort Mack. Both of them treated us poorly today. They were nothing but ruthless. Too bad for them they can't see that they're only showing us their weak side."

"Yeah, I saw it too. It's a bad act, man. In the beginning I really liked your brother. I had a lot of respect for him. Now he's just another rat in the crowd we have to watch out for."

"I hear you," I said, then paused to collect my thoughts. "When Bill turned me on to macrobiotics and Eastern philosophy, he opened up. I saw him as loving and wanted to believe he had changed, you know, had become the brother I wanted, not the conniving person that I'd learned to keep at a distance. The turd would always take advantage of me when I least expected it. But now that I think about it, even when he was being so kind and loving, shit we'd cook meals together and share ideas, he seemed somehow remote."

Considering this revelation I added, "I see all that now. I see how he runs from everything, how he pushes me away, how he uses me to further himself. He's always been this way and now he wants to run off and become a fugitive. Christ, he's running from life and he's running from all of us—the family, the people he cares for. It's what my father did. When I let Bill know that I had visited our dad, he didn't want to talk about it. He said the man was a bummer and he left all of us to take care of ourselves."

"He's hurting, Jake, I just know he is," I stood up and paced in front of Jake. I was hot and I lamented further. "He got on our plane to save time and a few bucks, and thought he'd have a joy ride flying with our pilot. Then he fucked things up by arguing with Mel after they crash-landed, and then ran away like he always does, leaving Mel to fend for himself. Now he thinks that by running from all of this, he'll be doing the right thing, you know, by *doing his thing*. Now he's screwing with us just like I figured he would. He talks big about Brotherhood but all he does is project his ego on us and…his concept about money and power…he's a phony, Jake. He doesn't practice what he preaches."

Jake looked up at me and concurred. "Then get past him. You know he's got an oversized obsession about self-image to consider. He's dragging you down, Frank. Back off. He's not going to come around and straighten himself out. You know that. He's too busy running. What we have to consider, partner, is to make sure he doesn't drag us into his trip—so get a grip, man."

"Yeah, I hear you. I got to mellow out here. Those sonsofbitches got to me. Those big time egos they pack around are just crap—image crap, Jake. And images like Bill and Mack's won't keep us out of jail. And I'm tired of talking about egos and who's responsible for what."

"Most certainly, partner. I'll be glad to get out of their way. But we're one man away from going to jail and I don't want to have to split, like Bill.

What's your take on Mel?"

Jake changed the subject and I didn't mind. It was time to invest energy elsewhere. "I think Mel is like any other man. He may be cool now, but as we proceed with this court case, well, we'll see. He's a family man. Do you think he'll do three years in jail—for us?"

"That's too hard to say. I called Gil the other day. We talked about it. He's strong on Mel. He thinks everything will go okay, and Mel will hold up just fine. They're still close and Gil let him know that we'd support Mel's family if he has to do any jail time." Jake hesitated and then added, "We'll just have to see. Meanwhile let's support him completely. I want to let him know we're behind him."

"Yeah, everything we can possibly do. So let's keep together with our plans." Sighing, I grumbled then let out a snicker, adding, "You know I think *separation* sucks. But it's a constant. So, you're right. We have to understand that Unity works—isn't that the change we're all fighting for these days? But, the people we work with are not embracing real change. Why, I don't know." Shaking my head, I looked out at the lake. "I believe we have to keep on finding clever ways to survive in this business. Not that we're unaware of this. It's just that we have to hone in on this, Jake. Seriously. We have to see what it's going to take to overcome the odds, even if we have to get a bit ruthless ourselves. If we don't, we'll be the fools...By the way, good job on Mack. He bit on your gambit."

"Right on," he smiled. "The rat race is not about to end. Let's talk about getting the next load up here."

In order to survive we had to keep on working. More accurately, we were trapped in this line of work. We also had to reason that we had a battle on our hands on two flanks: one with the government and the other with our so-called brothers. How much more trouble could possibly come our way? But we backed away from trying to troubleshoot like this when we realized that we could only plan and envision so much without overwhelming ourselves. What we did know was that was there was no room for failure. And to avoid failure, we decided to put aside our animosity and not to put blame on anyone.

"Let's go back to basics," I said, as our meeting progressed. "If we keep things simple, like Bill did, we can stave off paranoia."

"I'm all for it. Come on. Let's go look for garages for rent," Jake smiled.

"Yeah. But first, I'm hungry. Let's go to that Russian deli up on Ninth Avenue."

Three days later, after we had scoured the city and rented three garages, Jake decided it was time for him to head south. Our contact man Ramon had a load for us and Jake wanted to handle the entire matter. He was going to meet with Mel and Gil as well, and have a long talk with them about legal strategy and the plans he and I had made concerning our new operating procedures.

I was to remain behind, as a safety precaution and to monitor Bill and Mack. If Jake ran into a problem and was arrested, I'd be available to come to his rescue.

Jake called a few days later. "Hey partner, everything's fine. There's no heat around and Gil wants to fly for us."

"Funny, Jake, real funny. What else is new?"

Jake felt certain he was not being watched. He had met with Mel and Gil and told me with uncharacteristic exuberance, "We got a new pilot. He's going to work out just fine."

"That's real good news, partner."

"I met with him a few hours ago. He's top notch—trained by the U.S. government. He's going to rent a single engine plane and Ramon is ready to go with a load of four-fifty."

"Good job. Everything's falling into place. I like that."

"So do I. See you in a few days."

Jake arrived back in the Bay Area with four hundred and fifty regular kilos. Nick had flown the border without a hitch and had landed in a new desert location. Jake was there to greet him. Using our Chevy van to pick up the load, he arrived back with little fanfare. We had to let go of the two drivers who had brought our loads up when we were working with Manny. Jake was now our pick-up and deliveryman until we hired new drivers.

I greeted him when he pulled up to the garage. "Mack called me the other day."

"No kidding? How about that?" Jake responded. He was in a good mood.

"Yeah, no kidding. He's got a load in. He's going to call me and let me know when he'll deliver two hundred kilos."

"Mack, a delivery man. Too hard to believe."

"Well, for your information that's the way we set things up. I asked him if he'd be so kind to deliver. He jumped on it when I told him you were busy."

Without wasting time we unloaded the kilos. To keep with our plans, I used my VW bug to deliver fifty kilos apiece to our waiting customers. Two days later, I met with Mack at one of our garages and took possession of two hundred kilos of super weed. By the end of a week Jake and I had over fifty grand. We were financially safe for the time being.

Jake flew south to pay the pilot and to once again talk with Mel and Gil. He handed them ten grand for the lawyer and two grand each to Mel and Gil to keep them happy.

How much contraband did we want to bring up before we got too carried away? This was one of many decisions Jake and I had to make. We felt Manny had gotten inside our heads and we had allowed him to lead us down the path of greed. So, we devised a plan to work one load at a time, keeping in mind that it was unnecessary to bring up several loads. Ramon, who was now our main contact, promised us he had access to several tons of weed. A few days later when Jake talked with him over the phone, Ramon changed his story, saying that he wasn't sure when he'd get us another load. What bothered us most about this was that Ramon refused to elaborate. Disarmed by his inability to be truthful, Jake and I decided to look for connections among our customers, as we had done in the past, just in case

Ramon failed us. Mack was out of the picture, but Glenn was around. Jake would go see him and I was to see a man who claimed a friend of his might have a connection in Guymas, Mexico.

Jim was a young surfer dude who approached me at the beach one day and asked me to front him a few kilos. For the past few months I appeased him. He was a high-energy dude I came to believe in, because he always came through, so I rewarded him by fronting him more kilos each time we did a business. He was one more man in our business we could depend upon to sell our products. Aware of our bust, he had offered assistance. I had turned him down at the time but was now ready to meet with him and discuss what he had in mind.

When Jim introduced me to a big galoot by the name of Harvey, Harvey clarified that his contact had only "mentioned" to him he knew several farmers who grew marijuana. I was dismayed, but after much talk we decided to check out his contact. Guymas was just below Hermosillo in the Mexican state of Sinaloa, where Ramon got most of his weed. Harvey's contact spoke Spanish and was an American. If this man had any contacts at all I could connect him up with Ramon and the two of them could work together. It was worth a shot.

Underlying reasons also motivated me: I wanted a vacation and I had the money. Christine was also ready for a vacation. When I told her I'd be heading south and wanted her to come along she was visibly relieved. Over the past few weeks she had had to put up with my problems and my coming and going. Our relationship had been put to test, and frankly, I didn't know where we stood. Scientology had scared her and so did the bust. Adding to that, she was reluctant to open up and discuss her past, and I had been unwilling to take our relationship seriously because she wouldn't let me get any closer to her. The little I did learn was that she had a mother living in Los Angles who was not very kind to her and a stepfather she loathed.

A vacation would bring us closer, I hoped. With this in mind, the three of us took off the last week of March and headed for Guymas in my Porsche.

On the way down I got to know Harvey. The back seat was hardly the place for him, but he made do and I was impressed by the way he looked at life: simple, keep everything simple. He wasn't overbearing and never put me on the spot with self-image trips.

When we reached Guymas we headed for the beach where Ralph, the contact, owned a small sports fishing business. Ralph was Japanese, but born in America. He made no bones about being on the lam for failing to pay taxes and told us his story. He'd been living in Mexico for the past ten years and I guessed his age at sixty. When we told him that we had come all the way to Mexico to see him and to discuss business, he stalled us. Dinner was offered and we accepted. Afterwards he let on that he knew a few people…who knew a few people…that farmed the *mota*. He said he'd think about the matter and let us know later. Meanwhile, he invited to us to come fishing with him the following day.

His boat, a twenty-foot fiberglass runabout, was small but efficient. No matter where we anchored the fish took our bait and by days end we had a boatload of Sierra" mackerel. "Good eating," Ralph said, "especially when it's fresh." He gave his deckhand most of the fish, but kept a few for us to eat that evening.

Throughout the day, I sensed Ralph's fear. After dinner, when I raised business matters, he quickly folded; even though I let him know that all he had to do was connect me up with these people. I'd get names and a phone number or two from him and would give this information to my associate who spoke Spanish. There was nothing Ralph had to do beyond that, plus we'd pay him a "finder's" fee. Nonetheless, he refused my offer.

That evening the three of us headed for Mazatlan. Ralph was history and we were in the tropics and the temperatures were near to perfect. As darkness descended I thought about when *Chato* had told me about how he had hit a cow, so I drove sensibly. This was Mexico and I didn't know how I'd deal with hitting a cow or some stray horse, or worse, a deer. When a bus passed me I decided to keep up with it and let it "hit the cow." When I grew tired, Harvey drove. He was in heaven driving the Porsche and got us there just before dawn.

A few weeks earlier I had approached Stan, a Sea Scout friend I'd known since age fourteen, and asked him if he'd like to bring my International 210 down to Mexico. Stan was an elevator rigger but was going through a nasty divorce and was now working at the yard Al and I owned in Sausalito. Stan had more energy than he knew what to do with and he immediately accepted my offer. He was so enthused he took over and made plans to borrow a boat trailer from mutual friends. I borrowed an older pickup from one of my customers and let him take my motorcycle as collateral. Stan was now in Mazatlan with my boat and I had told him that somehow, some way, I'd get down there.

Stan had described the harbor where he was located and we made our way there as the sun came up. Spotting the pickup we got out and walked over. Stan was in the back wrapped in a sleeping bag. He almost flew out of it when I said gently, "Hey Stan, we made it. Come on. Let's go have breakfast—on me."

Out came the stories. Stan, who had a way of making friends, had met Carlos who was the boss at a molasses exporting business. Carlos was a sailor and had helped Stan launch the boat. We met him later that day. He was a refined man and most definitely upper class. Several times he had gone out with Stan, but this day he was busy. Stan had also met Tuko, a fellow Californian. We met up with him and plans were made to go sailing.

Harvey was anxious to fly home, so we took him to the airport where I bought him a ticket and waved goodbye.

Back at the harbor, Stan had the boat ready. Libations were purchased and shortly we set sail. I was soon in a sailor's dream state and could hardly believe that I was aboard my boat, sailing in Mexican waters in a fair breeze that was all so perfect, along with my lover and my good friend. Stan's new pal was a character. He was a mountain man from northern California and his hair looked like a walking mountain range: long, straggly and completely unkempt. He and Stan provided lots of laughs over the next few days as we loaded the boat with cold beer, fresh fruit, and whatever else we needed for the day's outing. One day, we started with an early morning sail and that evening watched a nearly full moon come up as we slid along in a light breeze. When the wind crapped out, we paddled back to the harbor.

Easter, we found out, was Mexico's Holiday of all holidays. Every

Mexican takes it seriously. And everyone who had a few bucks took the week off and came to town to celebrate and to chill out, Mexican style. We had arrived just in time but had I known, I'd have stayed away. Only by a minor miracle did we find a motel room—call it persistence and the Yankee dollar. This room was sufficient but lacked luxury.

Christine was irritated about the dismal quarters as was I, so we spent little time in the room. She wasn't much into sailing so we drove around a lot and got acquainted with Mexico. We discovered mangos and delectable fresh fruit juices that left us wanting more. In the center market we wheeled and dealed with the jewelry vendors, but they were more experienced than me at that game.

When Monday arrived we rolled out of town for the long journey back to the Bay Area. Even though we had come to Mexico to have a good time, I had learned that Christine was comfortable at home, but had trouble adjusting once away. A spell of miserable-ness had descended on her. Driving became a chore. At the border the next morning, customs decided to give my car a thorough search. When Christine mouthed off at them they took offence with vigor and made us stay put as they took their time. Adding to this that the both of us had the trots, my mood turned fowl.

The real problems started when she said to me, "I'd like to visit my mother while we're down here. Can we do that?"

"Honey, you've let on several times that you hate your stepfather. And you really don't get along with your mom. Why do you want to see her?"

"I know. I just want to stop off for a short visit while my stepfather is at work."

I tried to persuade her otherwise. "This is not good, Christine. When was the last time you talked with her?"

"I called her just after I moved in with you."

With a deep sigh I cajoled, "You know, I wish you'd talk to me about the way they treated you, especially your stepfather. What did they do to you that makes you hate them so much?"

"Maybe I'll just call her. Can we stop in L.A.? Would you please give me some money so I can at least call her?"

She didn't have to ask for money, not in that way. As for stopping in L.A., that was not a hassle like a visit would be. "That's no problem, honey. The problem is you refuse to talk about them. We've been together a few months now and you know all about Scientology and how it helps people get clear on their past. You know I believe that past traumas affect us. But you have to be open to talking about them."

"I know, I know. You've made that very clear, Frank. And I've told you that my mother is okay most of the time. She's good and mad at me because I'm such a renegade. She was never that way before I left home. I was only fourteen and she constantly worries about me. I haven't seen her in for such a long time. I'd just like to see her."

Recalling what I had gone through when I visited my dad I counseled, "I don't want you to do that, Christine, no way. I just don't see how you'd profit from a quick visit with your mom. It would bring up bad memories and you don't want to talk about bad memories, let along deal with them. See it my way. Jake and I are stressed out in most ways. You know that. I tell you most everything that's going on. I don't hide things from you that are happening to me. No, Christine. Call her. We'll stop in L.A."

The call to her mother turned into a disaster, leaving Christine to fall from miserable-ness into deep depression. I tried to get her to open up, but when she rebuffed me then I, in turn, ignored her.

When guilt ran its course I asked myself, "Where is my understanding and compassion? Why am I so reluctant to reach out to her and take her sorrows to heart?" I wanted to reach out but couldn't. What haunted me had to do with my father and my brother. Was I caught up in past trauma and was acting out my life in much the same manner as my father and older brother?

And what haunted me haunted her. We remained remote and shortly after we returned home, she came up to me one afternoon and asked me to take her to a friend's house in Berkeley.

I helped to pack her few possessions. When I dropped her off, she took off without hugging me. She was angry, but angry about what?

What I did know was that I was not in love with Christine. Even so, seizures of loneliness rolled through my body, and no matter how hard I tried I couldn't find a reason why. Why would I feel this way if I didn't love her? Stressed out and locked in this inexplicable state, I fell into a relationship with depression that was all too familiar.

I was momentarily lifted from it when Jake let me know that he had met with Glenn and things were brewing.

"I'm gong to be meeting with a friend of his by the name of Todd in a few days. He's down in Mexico right now and wants someone to fly his load up. He knows it's a fifty-fifty deal."

On the verge of an emotional downspin, I became sick. The sickness had everything to do with my emotions and I was soon to find this out, but first I had to find a way to get to a doctor's office—any doctor. Confused and more vulnerable than I had ever been, I called Christine and let her know that I could hardly get out of bed. She rushed to my side and was immediately alarmed. Using the Yellow Pages, she called a doctor. That afternoon I learned I had hepatitis, though the doctor was bewildered that my skin had not turned yellow. Either way, a urine and blood test revealed the problem. The doctor wanted me to spend a day or two in the hospital but I turned down his advice and had Christine call us a cab. She spent the night, then headed back to Berkeley the next day.

For the better part of three weeks I lived in my living room on a mattress I had somehow dragged upstairs. When I wasn't sleeping, I'd watch the tube and think of nothing, which didn't matter because I was as useless as a boat with no rudder. On the third day my skin began to turn yellow and so did my stool. When I let everyone know that I had hepatitis, no one wanted to visit. Brother Ray had heard hepatitis was contagious, but he reluctantly helped. Every three or four days he'd come by and drop off fresh fruit and bottles of fruit juice. I lived on protein shakes. Nothing else was remotely appealing. I shed fifteen pounds and looked terrible, but survived. Ray bought me a book from the health food store that had information about hepatitis. Reading it was a chore. Short-term memory loss was to be expected; full recovery would take months. Ironically, what I learned next brought relief. Hepatitis is a virus that attacks the liver and the liver controls emotional centers. This, to some twisted degree, explained why tears flooded my eyes and I'd get all choked up when I watched movies with maudlin scenes. I'd lie in a stupor, thinking, "Why am I so sad and why am I crying?" But now that I knew that this disease attacked emotional centers it made tearing up okay: I had plenty to be sad about.

Bill had always had "hyper" Taurus energy, and Jake possessed high-power, Aries energy. How he managed it so well was a mystery. I liked that he was calm and reassuring. But when he made plans he'd take action long before he fully envisioned what he was doing. That's where I came in. I relied on the use of my imagination. I wanted the big picture to form before I took any action. Before the hepatitis bug hit, I had described this to him, and how our combined talents made us a good match. I'd calculate a matter, get a clear picture formed, and then bring this to him. Together we'd clarify what course of action to take.

But Jake would often keep hidden his thoughts. He was the epitome of the "strong, silent type," and I'd have to extract information from him. Now that I had lost a good deal of my ability to concentrate and use of my imagination, I appealed to Jake to keep all business activities even more straightforward than they were before.

I loved the house I had rented. Christine had helped to find it. We posed as husband and wife and I claimed I owned a boatyard in Sausalito, which was the only truth I told during the application. Credit reports were almost non-existent in those days, and for three hundred dollars a month I had a wonderful, modern, hillside home with two bedrooms on the lower level and a good-sized living room and kitchen on the upper, as well as a big picture window and a balcony that ran along the back side of the house. The view was spectacular. I could see most all of Richardson's Bay and on out into San Francisco Bay. Fog would often finger in and I spent many a moment gazing at the wondrous, ever changing vista, be it morning, noon, or evening. I couldn't get enough. Perhaps it was this wondrous view that helped restore my energy.

I wanted to live! And that was the main reason healing took place. After my convalescence, I broke free and visited Jake and family. He had not bothered to come around. There was no need. We had no work. Ramon, for whatever reason, had not come through. My trip to Mexico turned up nothing and Glenn's friend was still in Mexico putting things together. Our services had been recommended and we were on a holding pattern. Still, we had to find a way to get going.

We were in deep trouble and we had every reason to fear our future. Chambers had called. He had requested a meeting to discuss the motion to suppress. Jake and I were convinced it would meet with complete failure. Either way, we had to fly south and discuss important up-and-coming legal matters.

When Jake and I flew to Ontario, CA, my mind was plagued because I still had so much trouble thinking clearly, but Jake seemed okay when we met up with Mel and Gil at Chambers office. The motion to suppress was on the agenda first. It had indeed been over-ruled. The sheriff had every right to open the plane and search for evidence. In short, we had no case. Mel and Bill would either have to plead guilty and ask for leniency, or go to jury and be convicted.

Chambers added something we didn't want to hear: "The local Federal Grand Jury will probably hand down federal indictments."

"On who?" Jake asked.

"Mel and Bill," Chambers responded, "and very likely Gil."

I was beginning to dislike this strange little man who sat behind his desk with a pompous air about him. He seemed condescending, which made my guts tighten as he rattled on about the case. Mel and Bill, who originally had been charged by the State of California with possession with intent to sell marijuana, were being investigated by the Feds. They had every right to bring conspiracy charges against Mel and Bill. They'd need corroborative evidence from only one party to get a jury to convict. Bill, who had elected not to attend the meeting, was not a prime target to rat out. The Feds and the

State wanted Mel and Gil to do the dirty work and they'd pressure them in any number of ways. Both of them would be offered immunity. If either or both talked, then the Feds would indict Bill, Jake, me, Manny, and anyone else they thought was involved.

It was obvious that we had more to fear from the Feds than from the State, which had a rock solid case on Bill and Mel. When and if Mel and or Gil folded, the federal indictment list would reach shocking proportions.

Shaken by the news, we did our best to remain composed. After Chambers left the room we talked with Mel and Gil. Mel, once again, reminded us he was not about to cave in. Gil added his resolve as well. Both were sincere. They were not about to send any of us to jail for something they had created. Nothing was said about the likelihood that Bill would go on the lam, or that Mack might seek revenge if he was indicted.

Federal agents had already been to Gil's house. He had sent them on their way, knowing full well not to start a line of dialogue with them. All of us agreed that if no one talked, no one, beyond Mel and Bill would do any jail time. The State trial was scheduled for late October. Sentences of five years, three and a half mandatory, would be handed down. Federal charges of conspiracy would be about the same: five years. I cringed at the thought.

When Chambers reentered and heard our story, he advised, "Make sure you have bail money handy."

With the latest bad news at hand, Jake and I had to come up with more capital and very soon. Our working capital was dwindling and with summer coming on, we had to make something happen. Weed was often scarce during the main growing season. Desperate, I paid Glenn a visit.

I'd always believed Glenn to be on the heartless side. And, I figured him to be the kind of guy who'd run if you were hot. But he surprised me when I called and asked to meet with him. "Come on over," he said graciously, "and we'll talk about things." I was soon to find out one of the reasons he was being so kind.

Several days before, Jake and I had met with him at his apartment in Sausalito and appealed for help, even though his pal was more than likely going to use our services. He had responded evenly as he sat in a large lounge chair, dressed in a bathrobe.

"As you know, the Old Man is out. He doesn't have any good pot this time of year. Maybe we can do something in October or November. But, I believe Todd will be interested in having you guys move his weed through you. I talked briefly with him the other day. He needs someone to transport his goods out of the area. I told him you guys had the means and that you could also have the load flown across. He was somewhat reluctant when I told him you wanted a fifty-fifty split, but I got him to come around."

"What kind of weed are we talking about?" I had asked, though I already knew.

"His contacts are down in Acapulco."

"Great. That's far out. It ought to be good, maybe Acapulco Gold," I said.

Then Glenn added casually, "He may very well get the good stuff. That's what he's down there for and it's taking him a long time. He's a reliable dude, guys. I've known him for a while. He speaks Spanish."

Glenn was known as "Carrot Head" because he had a thick head of bright red hair. Even though he was short, one could spot him in a crowd of a thousand people. He was weird in many ways, especially about his good looks and fine features. Woman loved his red hair and he had a knack for parading around as though he were a *prima donna.*

When I met with Glenn that afternoon, he confided that he had been afflicted twice with hepatitis. He had not mentioned this before, I figured, because Jake had been with me. Now that we were alone he opened up and wanted to help. But first, I had to listen to how he almost died when he was living in Nicaragua. What saved him, other than his will to live, was his diet.

"I got back on my feet by eating plenty of protein. You ought to consider eating meat. That's what saved me."

I had to give his advice thought. I wanted to stay a vegetarian. My body was conditioned to it. On the other hand, I was open to anything that might help me to heal, and get my body, emotions, and brains back on track.

Glenn knew what I meant when I complained about the long-term effects of the hepatitis. "Some days I simply feel helpless. Other days I'm on top of things—but not really. I can't work with Jake down south because I don't want to be in the tropics, not now. "I sighed and added, "Adding to that, I broke up with my woman a few weeks ago and you know how that goes; it's a real bummer, man. I can't focus or concentrate worth a damn. It sucks."

"Sure do. It's like riding a down-bound train, man. I know. It's a long, nasty ride. It'll be months before you're back to normal. Don't give it too much thought. Let's go down and get a couple of good steaks. I know just the place."

The smell of the meat cooking on the barbeque started stirring me. When we first entered the restaurant I felt guilty, but I overrode the guilt and ate the steak. The bond I had once had with veganism was over. The steaks were the best I'd ever had. I had to go easy and not get carried away, but at that moment, I wanted to eat meat like never before. After that meal I considered at least incorporating fish and chicken back into my diet. Jake and Joanne were quick to join me. Jake and I had stayed tight with the vegetarian diet we embraced and had altered over the past two years. Eggs, dairy, nuts and legumes had become our chief source of protein. Joanne confessed that she loved her man and would cook and eat what he wanted, but that she was never big on our choice of diet.

Todd finally showed up. Jake got him to come our way with our fifty-fifty service. Future work was also discussed. It was now late May and Jake and Todd were to leave for Mexico in a few days.

Before leaving, Jake urged me to pay Bill a visit. I felt the same way—Bill needed prodding. *When* would he pay the bond money he owed? Mack had paid his dues, we concluded. Bill also had to be updated about possible federal indictments and that wasn't going to go over well with him.

With my mind in a fix and uncertain about to how to confront Bill, I headed south to his apartment in Santa Cruz. Inger was there and greeted me warmly. Bill, on the other hand, was guarded the minute I walked in. He knew what I was there for so I chose to bring him up-to-date on legal matters rather than whine about the money that was owed. No more than ten minutes later the phone rang. Inger answered it and looked over at us as we sat at the kitchen table. Bill had just heard from me that indictments would come down and when Inger said a James Morrissey was on the line, both of us froze.

"It's a Mr. Jim Morrissey. He says he's an investigator from your lawyer's office. He says it's important."

Bill and I looked at each another. Fear shrouded his face. If I could have seen my own expression, I would have seen the same fear.

"Tell him I'll call him back in a few minutes. Okay, honey?"

"Come on. Let's see what he wants," Bill said, getting up. Scurrying to a pay phone, Bill called as I stood nearby.

"What's up?" Bill asked, as I listened in to bits and pieces of information. "Uh-huh! Yes! They've been arrested? No shit! When? This morning?" There was a pause as he listened in. "You want me to turn myself in. I don't know. I have to think about that... Yes, I understand. I just can't do that, not right now. I see! Well maybe we can alter that. Fine... Let me think it over. I'll call you back later. What's the bail?"

Bill was in a daze when he got off the phone. So was I. Mel and Gil had been arrested and I all but forgot about asking Bill about the money he owed us, not when we had pressing matters to attend to. Mel and Gil's bail was twenty grand each as was Bill's who had an arrest warrant out for him. If he failed to turn himself in, in due time, his State bond would be rescinded.

"Shit! Gil too!" I said, the words rolling off my tongue as I stared at Bill, his face ashen by the shocking news.

"Chambers wants me to turn myself in. No way, man, no way!" He gasped.

As the news sunk in, the enormity of the situation took hold. Mel and

Gil were in jail. Jake and I would have to find a way to bail them out. I had to go see my partner.

"We need cop-money to pull this deal off with Todd," Jake said shortly after I arrived. "Let's figure Gil will be able to use his house as collateral. That'll free up twenty grand."

Fear and anger still running its course, I added, "Yeah. I agree. But we'll still be plenty short. We have to be careful about Mel, more so than Gil."

"Then let's bail Mel right away."

We no sooner had it all figured it out when Jake and I ran into another problem: Jake's attitude. We had not had an argument in a long while and I was undone when he agreed to the plan, but ragged on me for not talking with Bill about the money he owed.

"The timing wasn't good," I argued. "Back off, man. Come on. We'll be tight for money but we have the money to put all of this off, cop-money included... so don't let the pressure get to you. That's what the Feds want. They'd love to see us arguing—over who owes who money and that we might not have enough money. So, get off it."

"Then let's get Manny involved."

"Yeah, right, as if he has any money. When was the last time you talked with him? "

Jake rolled his head back and laughed. "It's been a while. He's still busy with classes, I would think."

"Even if he did, he'd find a way to weasel out."

Fed up with the entire matter and ready to burst, I growled, "Screw 'em Jake. We don't need to keep on bitching about who's responsible for what. Let's take all of this on ourselves, the government included. Let these jackals we call our Brothers sweat it out. If Mel and Gil start singing the blues to the Feds because we don't have the money, and Mack and Manny won't help out, all of us will be on the next indictment sheet. But, if you and I agree to take the problem on ourselves, we can beat this thing our way. That's what I'd like to do. Let's just be responsible to ourselves. That's more direct and it gets us out of the hole on our own."

Jake didn't say a word. He was transfixed, waiting for me to continue, so I added, "Don't get me wrong, partner. We can still press them for money. Hard to say if they'll come up with any, but we can. I'm ready to come up with all that it will take. Let's rise up to that level and feel good about it, you know, like put aside the blame and get down to taking care of everything. I feel better just thinking about it, Jake. It's a 'if we don't succeed, at least we'll have gone down trying' deal. What do you think about doing something as cool as that?"

"You got something there. I like it. Amen, brother. Let's go with it. But we've got to come up with something fast…yeah, I'm tired of getting on everyone's case. Right now, we'll probably need another ten or fifteen grand to pay the lawyers for the additional work. When this load with Todd comes in we'll have the money. Ramon will come through sooner or later. I'm gonna call him. He keeps saying he'll have some shortly."

It was early evening, perhaps 6:00 p.m. Marin County weather was at its best, with no fog around to cool the evening. Mel and Gil had been released on bond. Jake and Todd were in Acapulco waiting for the Mexicans to come through with fifteen hundred pounds of high quality weed. We were to get half and I was excited. I was also ready to head out the door to go out to dinner with Glenn in Sausalito when the phone rang. It was Bill.

"Hey, I'm in the area. I'd like to see you. I need to talk to you." He kept it short.

"Fine. How long we talking? I'm headed out, right now."

"I'll fly by in a few. Okay?"

No more than ten minutes later he and Inger showed up. Before we even sat down Bill said, "I'll have twenty grand for you in a few weeks."

"Great! Far out! How'd you arrange that?"

"I have a deal going with Mack. That's about all I can say. I was in the area and I wanted to let you know I'll pay off some of the bond money."

Content that he had come to let me know, I changed the subject and let him know how we had gotten Mel and Gil out on bail. Bill appeared to be relieved, but about what I didn't ask. His sudden good demeanor had caught me by surprise. For the first time in a long while, I was impressed by his willingness to treat me in a friendly way. We were all smiles when we headed out the door together.

As the three of us stood next to my Porsche, a four-door sedan with four men in suits drove slowly by and continued up the narrow road way. Another followed with four men dressed in suits.

Suits! Shit, they're Fed's! What the shit! The men inside the second sedan craned around and peered at us. Just then the first sedan came to a halt beyond the driveway; the second sedan came to an abrupt halt in front of the driveway. The first one began backing up. Doors began to open.

Without saying a word, Bill took off. The men in suits quickly exited. Four of them flew by Inger and me. It all happened so suddenly and Bill had only one exit: my front door, which was locked.

With my heart pounding I stood frozen, along with Inger—the proceedings all too predictable.

"Federal Marshall's! Stop where you're at now," shouted a hulking man as he caught up with Bill. Three followed and within seconds Bill was boxed in. We found out later that his State bond most definitely would have been rescinded had he found a way to escape.

Before I could react, Bill had been cuffed and the agents had barely flashed their badges as they whisked Bill past Inger and me. We remained frozen, completely stunned by their actions. The agents from the first car stood around a moment or two, staring at us coarsely, saying nothing. Inger and I couldn't do anything but watch as Bill was hustled into one of the sedans.

Shaking with fear and anger, all I could think to do was clench a fist at them as they drove off. No more than two minutes had passed and in that period of time, all my senses had been shattered. Inger, ironically, helped ease my mind when she threw her hands to her face and began trembling, followed by hysterical sobbing as the sedans disappeared.

Seeing her this way, I was bound to comforter her, and felt her tremble as I wrapped my arms around her. And, although in shock I said firmly to her, "Calm down, Inger. Calm Down. Everything's going to be okay."

"He's gone. He's gone. They've arrested him," she sobbed.

"Don't worry." I held her tight. "We'll get him out. Believe me. We'll get him out. I promise. Okay. Calm down. Let's go in the house. Good..."

I provided a box of Kleenex and as she wiped her eyes, she asked, "Can you get him out?"

"Yes," I lied. "I'll have him bailed out in a couple of days."

Where I'd get the twenty grand to set him free, I had no idea—twenty-two grand actually, counting the bondsman. "You can stay here for the time being."

I sat down next to her, my mind fixed on the problem. My mind also fixed on how the agents knew where I lived. And, how did they know Bill was here? They must have my phone tapped, I figured, either that, or my Mom's phone. She had called earlier that afternoon. If the Fed's had her phone tapped, they could have gotten my address from Ma Bell. Either way, they knew where I lived and that realization gave me a rush of fear.

My dinner had to be canceled. Inger and I comforted one another. She told me about her childhood in Europe and described what it was like to live in a land with long summer days and short winter nights while growing up in Sweden. She perked up when I let her know that one day, maybe soon, I'd fly to Europe.

"Bill told me about his trip to Europe and I've been thinking about going. Bill's gone twice; the first time he was gone for a couple of months. I'd like to go to Germany and then on up to Sweden. I've heard so much about your country and I'd like to spend time there and then head on down to the Netherlands and on into France."

This kept our conversation going for over an hour as she let me know that she'd connect me up with her friends and family.

Inger didn't know where Bill had his money stashed. Mack was not around to help. Glenn, one of Bill's close friends, was not in the mood to assist. I'd run out of options and had only one left—a last resort and a dreaded one: Mom.

What else are parents for? Bill needed to be rescued and I had to find the courage, which meant I had to get humble and suck in my guts when I asked her to help bail her son out of jail. It would be a very difficult task indeed. Mom had worked for the IRS for several years. She always fretted about the controlling power our government wielded. She knew they were ruthless. More than anything, she fretted over her job status: she could lose her job. And such was the argument she gave when I showed up at her house several days later.

Bill's bond had been reduced to ten grand. News about his bust had made the papers, real back page stuff. But that didn't cut it with Mom. Without a trace of a greeting she lashed out at me, using all the pent-up rage she could muster. I had to remain humble through the denuding and listen to the sound of her diatribe that could skin a catfish at lightning speed. Her voice, shrill and full of vengeance, was directed at me as if I were my father returning after being AWOL. I stood there, ashamed to be alive. Or was it that I was ashamed of being her son? I'd have had an easier time with my old platoon sergeant.

First she laid the shame trip: "What are my neighbors going to think?" They should give a shit, I wished to say, but of course didn't.

Then she did the guilt thing: "I can lose my job over this." If that's the kind of outfit you work for then quit the sonsofbitches.

Finally she delivered the knockout punch: "I'll lose everything."

This actually reassured me, because I knew that wouldn't happen. Her tactless barrage was just more of the same that we boys had lived with growing up.

"Can't you see this, Frankie? This is our home. I worked so hard to get this place and it's all I have."

I had to act. I had to say something to bring her around to my side; I had to give her a reason to live through this. I also had to be cautious. Mom was purely irrational. Raised in the Catholic faith, she relied on guilt and shame as tools for manipulating us. I'd fallen prey to this very tactic time and time again. Before arriving, I had given careful consideration to how she would react. If she chose to use guilt and shame I'd turn it against her.

Easier said than done, I thought, as I listened to her carry on about our father and the fact that he wasn't present. As she poured out her grief, I thought she might start crying. Caught up in her mix of emotions, I actually almost shouted at her.

"Mom, Bill has the funds to cover the entire bond. He can pay you back the money as soon as he gets out of jail."

"How do you know this?"

"I know he has the money, mom. He's got it stashed somewhere and I can't get to it. Trust me."

"How can I?"

She lived for revenge and in so doing had taught me well how to stand up against tyrants. Knowing my job here was to find a solution, I stayed to the plan. "He's your son, Mom. He's in jail. You have to help him out. He'll give you the money to pay the bond as soon as he's free."

"But I don't have that kind of money," she whined, in a state of confusion. Apparently what I was attempting to get across to her wasn't getting through. "You know that. You don't care what happens to me. You're nothing but a bunch of punks. You think you can get away with this drug dealing. The government will get all of you."

"Yes, Mom, I know. I hear you. But right now they have your son Bill. You have to come to his aid. I have no one else to go to."

"If your father were here you wouldn't be doing this. This is his fault," she lamented for the billionth time—heart-crushing condemnation we'd all heard before. Next, she'd usually bring up the past and how our father was a coward and that we were all following in his footsteps.

Oddly enough, she bypassed this one. "You can't kid me, Frankie. You drive that expensive sports car and wear nice clothes. I know you're involved in selling drugs. I'm your mother." The words trembled out of her mouth and into my guts. For a brief moment, guilt once again found its way into my soul.

Rebounding from the onslaught I answered her charges. "Okay, Mom. I'm doing it too, but there's nothing you can say or do that would stop me from continuing. Will you come downtown and sign the bond? I have the ten percent payment, but not the collateral. You'll have to put up your house. Bill will back up the bond. All you have to do is understand this. Bill will take care of the matter as soon as he can."

"I'm going to lose my house," she wailed again.

Ever so carefully, I explained in detail how this would not happen. Somehow avoiding her flack, for the most part, I was finally able to convince her that it was the maternal thing to do: get her son out of jail and away from the Blue Meanies.

I hadn't seen my mother much in the preceding year and a half, so this little bout of intimacy cost me dearly. I had to absorb all of the verbal abuse that she couldn't pass out to her other disrespecting sons, as I drove her down to the federal building the next morning. A day later, Bill's bond, having been dropped to ten grand, he was sprung. I was exhausted and beaten. If only he knew what trouble he had put me through.

I soon found out through a Private Eye that my mother's phone had been tapped. And now that the narcs knew where I lived and also had the phone number, I had to figure they'd tap my line, perhaps even follow me as well. To offset that probability and the fear it instilled, I decided to find out what they were up to.

So I came up with a plan. When I went by my good customer Irving's house and asked him if he'd be willing to carry out a rather crafty solution, he immediately agreed. We worked out a scheme we felt the narks would bite on. Later that day, as planned, he called me at my house. Careful not to be overzealous and tip the narcs off, we set up a mock drug deal. I was to meet him and deliver fifty units. A time, at the usual place, was agreed on. I stayed at home for over an hour then met up with him. We did this three times over the next two days and no one showed up, nor did anyone follow me.

Everything, I presumed, was safe. I could operate as long as I took precautions and stayed with the pay phone system Jake and I used.

Jake and I were caught up in the latest dilemma. It had been going on for the past forty days and forty nights. No, it was not a sabbatical, and for the most part it was Jake's dilemma. But, it was mine too, as well as Glenn's and Todd's.

It was late June. Glenn and I had, at one point, flown down to Mexico to check out problems that were keeping us all waiting for the deal to happen. When we arrived, Jake was so lethargic and whacked out that Glenn badgered him into going to a doctor for a vitamin-B shot. After the treatment, the three of us relaxed on the beaches for three days. At night, we took in the discos.

Todd was close to my age; he was sincere, intelligent, and confident that all would go well. He informed us that this region of Mexico had three growing seasons. The upcoming crop, he was told, had been planted in early April. Soon it would be ready and we had only to wait two more weeks. His people would come through, as they always had. Glenn and I left our encounter satisfied that we'd soon have our pot of gold.

Toward the end of June, Glenn called me to his house. Everything was set and he was to head down to the desert with a helper to pick up the load (he was to sell Todd's portion.) Ramon, as planned, was to meet Jake and Todd in Acapulco and move the merchandise north in his associate's moving van. Nick would fly it across.

A few days later Jake called and said rather rudely, "Come pick me up at the airport."

He looked as though he had been on a drug binge for the past several days. When he got in the car he let loose.

"We got burned, Frank. The fucking Mexicans did it again." Jake didn't curse much. It had to be bad.

"I don't understand. The load's on its way back. Glenn's due in tomorrow. What are you talking about?"

"Well, the load made it out all right, but it was more like eight hundred pounds than the fifteen we paid for."

"You mean we paid for fifteen and got eight? What the hell

happened?"

"Todd's man ripped us off. It was more like he took candy from a baby. We're lucky to be alive."

"Christ, I can't wait to hear this one. Tell me the story."

"Todd's man said he was ready. I had Ramon come down with his van. We went to where we were they told us to go. It was up in the mountains outside of Acapulco. We waited, and when the men with the donkeys showed up we started counting bags. Something was wrong. Todd saw it. So did I."

Jake hesitated. He looked terrible as he related the rest of the story.

"Todd counted the bags and told his people that only half the load was there. All of us stood back, but Ramon let me know what was going on with Todd and his people. They insisted everything was there, fifteen hundred pounds. These bandits were well-armed and there were seven or eight of them. There was nothing we could do, so we loaded up and got out of there."

I sighted and said, "Shit! All this waiting and they took us to the cleaners!"

"Yes. We didn't press them and they took off after Todd paid them the rest of their money."

"Right, like who's gonna argue with seven or eight armed bandits?"

"It's been a long six weeks, buddy. Just get me home, will ya?"

"How civilized of them. They could have shot you guys' right there and walked away with the money and the weed," I said, adding more mockery to the moment.

"Yeah. I know. I'm fed up and need some rest."

Glenn also arrived home in a fit of anger. The load was not only half what we counted on, it was far from mature; however it was of decent quality and there was an ongoing pot drought in the entire Bay Area. We asked for, and received, a handsome price for our product. No one complained.

Shortly after I finished up with sales, Ramon had a load of four hundred and fifty regular kilos for us—his first in over four months. When I met up with Jake in the park to discuss this, he sprang some news on me: Manny had called.

"What's he up to?"

"He says that we owe him money and he wants to get back on his feet," Jake reported.

"Did he say anything about assisting us with lawyer's fees?"

"We went over that. He'll help out, but he has no money. I let him know we'd assist him, partner. That's the agreement we made when we broke up with him."

Jake had spent two long hours in the anteroom with Manny that evening, and only now I find out he had made a deal with Manny—and failed to fill me in on the details! I was in a mood to tell Jake that Manny would have to find his way out of this problem.

Instead I said, "I don't know, Jake. He's way too crazy for me. I don't like the idea of favoring him just because he thinks we owe him a favor. Ramon has money and he'll have plenty once we finish this deal. Manny can work something out with him."

"I already thought of that. Manny's going to keep on pestering us. If we do this one-time thing with him we'd get him off our backs for good. What do you think?"

Bill had paid us twenty grand. We were pretty tall on money and this load with Ramon would get us through the rest of summer. Plus, Ramon had new connections. When Jake last talked with him, Ramon promised that he'd have plenty of merchandise, come October.

I was getting weary of all the manipulating. "On one condition, Jake. Let's handle the whole thing ourselves. I don't want Manny around. Plus he'll us owe us a favor."

A few days later the load Ramon promised arrived. Jake and our pilot had taken care of everything. After selling the load for a handsome price, arrangements were made. Manny, without lifting a finger was to receive half the profits. I didn't feel good about this, but it would be a deterrent to keep people like Manny at bay.

When we met with Manny at his friend's apartment in San Francisco he was the picture of good health. Rippling with energy and as exuberant as a dog in heat, he hugged us. He was especially friendly with me and immediately began droning on about Dianetics training. It had completed his life. "I'm not only Clear, I'm a Free Theta Being. I'm now free of all earthly aberrations. My potential is unlimited. Scientology is going to lead the way, guys. I wish you would join me."

"We still use Scientology principles," I informed him, turned off by his rhetoric. "But only for our own gain. That's all I need."

"That's great." He beamed a smile of approval. "I see you guys so much more clearly now. Frank, I know why we had our breakdown. I had an aberration with you that involved my father. I was unable to detect it at the time, but it's gone now. I'm no longer at the mercy of it. I've become total cause."

"That's terrific," Jake said sarcastically.

"I'd really like you guys to consider coming back into a partnership again. We could really have a great organization. You don't have to make your minds up now, but consider it. Come October, with the trial and everything, we could band together and beat the oppressive government."

"We're not into it," I reminded him. Not now. Not ever. "But thanks anyway. It's nice to hear that you've come so far with Scientology. It must feel great to have reached the O.T. levels so soon."

"Yes, I thought it would take longer, but I went beyond my goals. In a few months, you'll see some astounding changes in me."

"Well, what's that? Just how far can you go?" Jake egged him on.

Eyes wide, exuding confidence, he dug in and delivered. "For instance, at night, in the alpha state I leave my body at will."

"Sounds impressive," I interrupted. "But, I figured you'd be capable of doing things that people would consider impossible, like what we talked about in the past."

"I agree with Frank," Jake responded. "You have new powers now. You can make use of them in a very wise manner."

"Right on," I added, as Manny looked at us searchingly. "Remember how we talked about the yogis of India and their ability to dematerialize themselves and reappear elsewhere?"

"Sure. That's all very possible."

"It most certainly is," I stated, in phony excitement. "Wouldn't it be groovy to use your power for that? Say you're in Mexico with a couple of tons of good weed. You could dematerialize yourself, along with the load of course then rematerialize wherever you chose. Right?"

Jake added to the subtle bashing. "The narks would go crazy. Even if they found you, you'd disappear, like that." Jake snapped his fingers.

Manny didn't miss a beat. He smiled knowing that we were chiding him, but added anyway, "I have that potential. It's very close. I'd use it that way. It'll come soon. I know. I wish you guys would join me. We'd make a hell of a team."

"No thanks, Manny." Again, I fended him off and forced a smile. "We're done for the year. Jake and I are taking a few weeks off. After that we'll start up our business. You've got Ramon at your disposal. Finding a pilot ought to be relatively easy for you. You've got money now. You can run your business your way. That's the way I prefer doing things."

"Come on, let's go," Jake said abruptly. "We have some people to go see."

Outside, Jake and I let loose our stifled laughter. "Did you see the look on his face when I mentioned he could dematerialize the pot? He really thinks he's going to be able to do it—in this lifetime, no less."

Jake chuckled and added, "But what if he does, brother? What if he does?"

"Well if he does, we'll just have to join him. Wouldn't you?"

"Yes. But, that's the only way he'd get me to join him." We laughed until our guts ached.

Like a man on the lam, I flew into Frankfurt, Germany seeking shelter and a much needed vacation. I'd sold my Porsche to Glenn and planned to purchase a nice, used 911, with a six-cylinder engine.

Down in Mexico, this year's *mota* crop was just coming to fruition. Harvesting would soon begin. Ramon had assured us he'd have plenty of work for the coming year, and we had enough money to not only pay for a load, but for a vacation. Everything was online for our business to roll as soon as we got back.

Jake and family decided to head to Washington. They were to visit with people Jake knew from way back. Before they left, Joanne informed him that she was pregnant. The baby was due in September. Her doctor had told her she'd never have another baby. It was a miracle of sorts, since she had only part of one ovary left.

Inger had been full of excitement when I told her I'd be heading for Sweden after purchasing a Porsche in Germany. Pulling out her address book, she wrote down phone numbers and names of close friends. "You can meet all my friends in Uppsala, and Lena, my very good friend. I'm sure you will like each other."

All I could think about was how to put myself far and away from the maddening circumstances. We had had another disastrous year. Mistakes had taught Jake and I to realize that taking responsibility was only a part of what it would take to overcome our problems.

I offered Jake a few ideas about how we could make use of "harmony" to deal with the insurmountable odds facing us. We needed to be willing and prepared to work under pressure. How much pressure we had yet to come to terms with, and how to handle the pressure was part of the unknown we had to face. Mostly, we had to admit we were under pressure, and self-abnegation, I assured him, worked wonders. We were well aware there were two opponents to consider: authority-beagles and the people around us. We were up against tyranny, envy, greed, and people who worshiped power and misunderstood the true concept of how to use power. Any number of people might strike out at us. Jake and I had a bond that others could only wish for. And I let him know that we had to be on the watch for those who might envy us: Manny, for one.

Mel and Gil were our main worry. We had no choice but to stand behind them. Would they hold up under the pressure and would either of then be willing go to jail while we remained free? Would pressure, exerted by law agents and their family and friends, win out?

We were not the type to threaten anyone with violence. We were going to exert the brand of *brotherhood* that Jake and I had embraced—no matter what. Come October, we'd find out where we stood. The trial would be most telling. Would we have to consider fleeing, as Bill was intending?

We were no longer neophytes in the business. Jake and I had become accomplished smugglers, all too aware of how to do our jobs, which meant it was hardly time to quit. We knew we had to envision a future. Harmony on all levels would show us the way, along with careful planning. We had fought both foes and we had survived up to this point. The authorities, who were breathing down our neck, had money, agents and know-how, plus lots of time and resources on their side. They could wait us out, remaining hidden until we made another crucial error. They were the foxes; we were the hens. Somehow, we had to keep managing to find ways to avoid them.

For the moment, the trip to Europe was mighty inviting. I was to land in Frankfurt. Was that symbolic? "To me it means Frank's Fort," I chuckled, peering out the window just as the jetliner hit the runway.

CHAPTER NINE

THE MISSING LOAD

SAN FRANCISCO, CA
OCTOBER, 1969

"Her name is Heidi," Joanne said, as I held her three-week-old baby. Even with the blanket wrapped tightly around her she squirmed, kicked her legs, and resisted the unfamiliar grip. Unprepared for the encounter, I did my best to comfort her child. No more than a minute later, the baby's eyes closed tightly, and then her tiny body shuddered. Opening her eyes she let out a yawn, then began howling.

"She looks like Jake," I managed to say, then exclaimed awkwardly, "Shit, she's crying. What did I do?"

"Boy! Wait 'til you have children!" Joanne flashed me a grin. "You'll find out. Here. Give her to me."

Embarrassed, I handed her over. Suddenly, Joanne disclosed some shocking news: she had given birth to twins. Then she told me that the baby boy had died. Before I could commiserate she said, "I can live with that. Heidi's healthy. That's what's important to me. The boy was a stillborn."

I sighed compassionately and then Joanne continued with more unsettling news. "Joey was our first son. He died in the crib when he was only nineteen months. That was before we had Windy."

No one had told me. Neither Jake nor Joanne had ever mentioned they had had a son. I thought Windy was their first-born. Joanne then cut the conversation short, saying she needed to feed her child.

"Joanne, I'm so sorry to hear this," I said, feeling awkward. "You never mentioned that you had a son, you know, before you had Johan...I'll talk with you later....and congratulations. Heidi looks perfectly healthy. Go feed her. I'll talk with Jake."

Jake was keeping busy, stacking wood near the fireplace. Greeting me with a firm handshake and a meaningful look, we reconnected. Having both just returned from our month-long vacations, we were refreshed and eager to get going.

Jake had decided to move to Lake Tahoe, near the California-Nevada border. Situated in the mountains, their new home offered a place to raise his family away from the prying eyes of the law. When we sat down to confer, Jake fired up a joint.

The State trial was to start in three weeks. We had to jump-start our organization and get going as soon as possible. Our plans were set before I left for Europe. Everything was ready to go. We only had to connect with Glenn. He had hired us once again to bring up a load of the Old Man's weed. All I had to do was drop off fifteen grand to Glenn as soon as I got back to the Bay Area.

We were going to upgrade our organization. Nick would remain lead pilot and Ramon our main suppler. Three other men had been recruited. Howie, a good friend of Jake's, was more than interested—he was ready to drive for us. Dan, an old high school friend of mine said he would join us. Randy, a friend of my younger brother Ray, was also available.

Nick decided it would be safer to move our operation to Arizona. The three of us had poured over aviation charts and came up with four good locations. Jake and Nick had flown over the areas. We had yet to make sure which ones would suit our needs; at this point we knew only that all of them were accessible by road. The drivers had to get in and get out without being detected, and Jake was to take care of this job within the next few days. Walkie-talkies were considered, but Nick assured us he could spot any problems long before he landed.

"Hey guys. That's what you pay me for. I don't just come in and land. I make a first-hand check, then land real quick. It's a real slam-bang procedure I was trained to do. I know how to drop bombs, guys. Trust me."

As soon as possible we'd purchase a single engine, Cessna 206. It was known as an aerial workhorse and could haul a thousand pounds of cargo, along with fuel and a two-man crew. Once we had enough money, we'd buy two more pickups. Later, we'd purchase a suitable of piece of land that we could use as a base of operation, instead of landing out in the middle of a potential trouble zone.

Willy, who was an acquaintance of mine, and a former Special Forces sergeant, was to go along with Nick as the designated "kicker." Both Nick and Gil had told us that the government was using Beachcraft Baron's to patrol the border. The Cessna was slow compared to the government birds. Should it become necessary, Willy was to kick the load out the door: better to lose the load than suffer a sure bust.

We wanted every advantage we could think of. We were going to sit down with our people and put them to test. Everything we had learned would be passed on to them.

"Just stay to a mindset," I told them, when they met with Jake and I the following week.

"It worked for Jake and I. The law won't know you're carrying a load of weed, so just pretend you're on a hunting trip or coming or going to camp. Make something up before hand and agree on it. If for any reason you get busted, say nothing, no matter what. Okay? Above all, didn't argue with one another. Do all of this and you'll do just fine. Also, don't get too friendly with anyone while you're working. Just come straight back, be cool at all times and everything will go as planned. Don't smoke pot. You can do that when you're done. Just use your heads. And come back safe."

They were a great bunch of guys, and like us, they were risk takers. We expected them to get along just fine.

Jake and I went over every aspect of our business, including our situation with Mel and Gil. Jake said, "I talked with them last week. They were restless, especially Gil. He asked me again if he could fly. I told him to be patient and for now it was out of the question. Mel was cool and said he knew we were behind him and eventually we'd finance him."

Toward the end of our meeting Jake announced that he wanted to take flying lessons. Every time he and I flew with the Nick, Jake always sat in the co-pilot's seat. He was fascinated with flying and Nick took ample time to teach him the basics. As for me, give me a boat and a body of water. Small planes didn't interest me at all.

Heading out that afternoon, I felt we were ready.

It took four hours to drive back and although I started out relaxed and full of hopeful energy, anxiety set in—nothing specific, just the resurfacing of stress. Prior to leaving for Europe, I had moved from the Mill Valley house I had come to cherish. In my haste, I had rented an apartment in Terra Linda, and had only enough time to throw everything I owned on the floor. When I pictured all my possessions lying scattered about, I was overwhelmed. Sure enough, arriving at my new digs and looking around I cursed. What a fucking mess. Then my resistance gave way to the inevitable and I began to arrange things so that I could at least have a decent sleep. The rest would fall in place later.

Going about my chores, fear kept creeping in and finally I had to take a break. I kept thinking about getting busted—what if the narcs know where I live? It seemed possible, and it was an intrusion of the worst kind. Searching my memory I went over all the precautions I had taken to rent this place and whether or not I'd arrived undetected. I'd used a false name to rent the place, I knew that for certain. But try as I may, I couldn't remember all the precautions I had taken. And that was what was bothering me. And, if I allowed fear to hamper my thoughts and gain control I'd be of no use to anyone. That bothered me too.

Lying on the sofa I suddenly sat up and said aloud, "That's why you're so tense, man, don't let your fears take over. Call Irv and set up another mock delivery. Christ, if the narcs are on to me they'll show up."

Positive thoughts began to flow freely then. By the time I was ready for bed I had unpacked most all the boxes and felt at home. With my energy on the rise, I thought about a young woman I met on the plane from Chicago to San Francisco. She was a flower child, about nineteen, cute, short, blond and buxom. I invited her to a friend's house down the peninsula. She was more than happy to come along. I was more than happy when she crawled into my sleeping bag. All she said was, "I'm cold. Can I sleep with you?"

We'd had a love marathon. I was sure she would have come home with me if I had asked, but she was headed to the Haight-Ashbury District. And although she had never been there and didn't know a soul, she carried on as though this was not a problem. After all, she was the essence of free spirit and was a fox. No doubt she probably hooked up with a group of flower children within a couple of hours. But she had swept me away. I was not only forlorn over the way she let me take her that night, but also by the fact she was so experienced.

At nineteen, and already sowing oats, she would have crushed my heart in one breath. She was also carrying excess emotional baggage. We had spent most of that day together before my good friend Fay showed up in my VW Bug to bring me home. And what tore at me was this woman's sadness. Christine had taught me a good lesson: I could ill afford to put myself in this position, not with all the troubles that Jake and I were facing. No. I had made a good choice. Still, I yearned to hold this woman and soothe her sorrows—if only to have my own sorrows soothed.

The next morning, I headed over to Glenn's and handed over fifteen grand. Shortly thereafter, the trouble started. It came on fast and it came from every corner. When the dust settled, Jake and I had won. But it was one hollow victory after another and was akin to warfare: a war that everyone knows no one will win. What we did win was the strength to carry on under pressure by banding together and taking our so-called brethren on, one at the time. I, for one, could not have ever imagined that we'd have to endure the abuse that was cast our way. But we did. We had to.

The first person to run a sham on us was Glenn. After holding our money for a week he called me to his house one morning. He brazenly informed me that the deal that was underway was off. When I asked him to explain, he refused.

When I demanded he return our money he said that it would take a few days. Outraged, I argued with him. How could he call me over, call off the deal, and be unprepared to give our money back? Throughout my fit of anger he stood his ground. Our money would be returned as soon as he could manage it—no time frame was given.

I wanted to drag him out of his house and beat the crap out of him. Instead, I departed in a huff and called Jake.

"The sonofabitch has just put a royal hurt on us, Jake. We no longer have cop-money and Glenn knows this. I wanted to beat the shit out of him."

"You know he can be this way. Let it rest. I'll call Ramon and let him know. Maybe he can help us."

"Better yet, let's drive down and talk to him, and pay a visit to Mel and Gil. They need to know what's happening."

✯ ✯

"That's bad news guys," Ramon said. "I have a load for you but I need the money to pay for it. Why don't I move it through Manny? He's ready to go. When he pays up I'll have enough to pay for the next one."

When Mel and Gil learned of the problem they were ready to beat Glenn to a pulp, at least Gil was. Mel on the other hand seemed far off. His face was riddled with fear, but he assured us he was ready to face the government. If anything was up with these two, we figured Gil would know. We trusted him and when we talked to him separately from Mel he assured us everything was going well.

But it wasn't. We'd no sooner returned home when Jake received a call from Gil.

"I think Mel is going to turn on us." With those words ringing in our ears, we hustled south again and met with Gil.

"Chambers is fucking up. He's handling the case all wrong. Everything's wrong," Gil told us upon meeting him at the airport in Ontario. "I think Mel is talking. I know he is, I just know it."

Gil was in quite a state, and Jake had to get him to calm down and tell his story slowly.

"I've been pushing Chambers to get me a federal lawyer to handle my case. Shit, he's been stalling me for the past two weeks…I didn't know or at least I can't figure why he'd do something like that. You guys know what I mean. There's no reason for him to stall. He's up to something. Mel's gonna talk. He won't even talk to me. I…"

"Be easy, Gil, " Jake said. "Just tell us what you learned."

I'd never seen Gil in such an emotional bind. His face was red and puffy and now my guts were tied up in a knot as I listened to his story.

"Yeah, you're right. I'm so pissed off right now I'd shoot Mel if I had a gun, maybe even Chambers, that sonofabitch. Anyway, I went to Chambers the other day and he sent me to see this guy Max."

"Why didn't you mention this when we were down here?" Jake asked.

Unable to meet Jake's eyes, he replied, "I don't know. But that's not important. Let's go see Max. He's expecting us. He's only a few minutes from here. Max can explain everything. All I know is that this is bad, guys. Max believes Mel's talking or he's going to talk. He says Mel had been granted immunity and he has to talk—something like that."

As we got into Gil's car Jake asked, "When was Mel granted immunity?

Chambers had told us months ago that Mel might be granted immunity. Nothing of late had been said. Now that we knew, I was furious. How could this happen? Why would our lawyer withhold intrinsic information from us? What the hell was going on?

"I don't know," Gil said, interrupting my thoughts. "Max figures Mel might have been granted immunity a couple of months ago. He'll explain everything."

Gil then launched into berating his good pal Mel. "Mel started acting real weird the day you guys left. I called his house that evening but the asshole wouldn't answer. When I went over to his house his wife asked me not to disturb him. He's never been like this, neither has his wife. She wouldn't talk to me either. I finally caught up with him yesterday as he came home. The sonofabitch said he had nothing to say."

"This is fucked," I cursed.

Jake asked calmly, "Who's this lawyer, Max?"

"Like I say, Chambers hired him. I think he's cool. I like him. He says Chambers has been withholding information from us. He knew Mel was talking but he didn't tell us. What the fuck is that all about?" He added desperately, "We've got to do something, guys. If Mel talks, I'll..." His voice trembled. He looked over at Jake with a wrinkled brow. "I'll kick his fucking ass."

Calming down he reminisced, "Christ man, I've known Mel since I was sixteen, when my dad died in a car accident. He took me in. He was my other dad. He took me everywhere. He even trained me to fly. We smuggled cosmetics into Mexico together. He was the best man at my wedding. We dined at each other's homes and now the sonofabitch is selling me out. Can you believe that?"

I'd already learned of Mel and Gil's close relation from Jake. What Gil was saying was repetitive. Because their close relationship was unquestionably safe and sound, Jake and I were convinced from the start that Mel would hold up. And if Mel was going to talk, Gil would know. Even when Mel seemed insincere the other day, we paid it little attention. Jake and I figured Mel was just scared. Everything had changed now. The information Gil had given us convinced me that Mel was going to rat on us. Federal laws required only one cooperative witness. Mel could bring all of us down—so why hadn't we been indicted? That was also very confusing.

"Fuck the government!" Gil shouted. "They can kiss my ass. They're not gonna get me to act like a coward like Mel. I'll die first." He looked over at Jake, and added, "You guys stand behind me and I'll keep quiet. I'll put all of them down. Screw'em!"

The moment we entered Max's house I felt comfortable. Max was amiable and unpretentious as he brought us to his office. His desk was large and awash with papers. He had a grass-roots approach. I favored that.

"Just listen to Max, guys," Gil said. "He'll tell you. Mel's gonna blow everything."

"Well, I'm new on this case," Max said. "Chambers called me the other day and asked me to handle Gil's Fed case. Occasionally, I get work from him, but this case I have to question. Chambers never informed you, nor did he say when Mel was granted immunity. That's unethical"

Getting no reaction from us, he continued, "When someone is arrested, the government, requires all the information the prosecutor has received, including witnesses, evidence—everything—to be handed over to the defense well before the trail begins. The process is called 'discovery.' Okay?"

Jake and I were aware of this. We shrugged and waited for Max to continue.

"Well, yesterday I got on the case and called Gil to let him know that he'd better come talk with me. I told him that Mel was granted trans-axial immunity shortly after he was arrested by the Feds. That means he has to talk or go to jail. If he refuses, he'll be cited with contempt. The Feds can hold him for eighteen month. If he again refuses, well, it starts all over again 'til Mel caves in."

Now *this* was news. Jake and I had listened to Chambers when he let Mel and Gil know that trans-axial immunity could well be granted, but he had never said anything about it since then.

"Exactly when was Mel granted immunity?" I asked Max.

"My guess is shortly after he was indicted by the Feds, which means he may have started talking right away. But I don't know. He may have caved in a few days ago for all we know, but you can bet he's talking now."

"Wait a minute. If he's talking, why haven't all of us been indicted?" I asked.

"Good question. Hard to say what Mel has told them. And if he caved in a few days ago you guys might get indicted when the next grand jury sits. But now that we know he's been granted immunity, when he's convicted by the State in a few days there's a good chance the information they want will indict all of you. The big question is why didn't Chambers inform you guys about all of this? He's up to something. Have you paid him all his money?"

"No." Jake said and added, "We paid most of Mel's bill, but we owe him plenty for Gil."

I added, "We paid him half the money shortly after the bust in February. But we told him we didn't have any money and asked him to wait. We explained our position, but I doubt he believed us."

Jake added, "We paid him more money in August. I brought ten grand down and gave it to him, but he was upset. Could be he feels we were holding out on him. We owe him another ten."

"Hmm, Chambers has to have reason to withhold," Max said. "Could be this whole matter has to do with the money that was owed him. But that would be rather strange. It doesn't really explain why he'd withhold information about Mel and immunity. One might believe he's on the side of the government."

Max reflected a moment then looked at Jake and me. "We need to investigate him. That's your best bet. Let me handle Gil's federal case in the meanwhile. I don't care for Chambers. Never have. I'd like to know what he's up to."

Max looked all of us squarely in the eyes. "Are you with me, guys? Mel's definitely going to talk. Once they have Mel's testimony they'll start working on you, Gil. They'll offer you a deal and force you to join them. That's how they work. You're sitting in the hot seat. I'm sure all of you understand what that means."

There was a collective sigh. Gil spoke first. "I'm serious. I'm with you guys. Mel can squeal all he wants. I'm not like that. I'm not a coward. I'm gonna hang in and stop these assholes. If they think I'm easy, they'll find out what kind of person they're dealing with. My wife is cool. She knows what's up. I talked with her this morning. She'll hang in for me."

"Three years in jail is no piece of cake, Gil," Jake replied.

I added, "And right now I believe you. Mel dumped on you and you have no choice but to believe in us. Jake and I will come up with whatever it will take to keep your family going. "

Gil responded dejectedly, "That's secondary. I trust you guys. I know you'll come through and I want to prove to you guys that I'm going to put a stop to Mel and the law."

Pounding his fist on Max's desk he added, "I'm going to get to Mel every way I can. I'll put it all over town what he's up to. He's got lots of friends. He won't have a single one left when I'm done with him."

Gil brightened up as Jake came over to him saying, "Come around, big boy. Let me see you stand on your feet." Embracing him he added reassuringly, "We'll have the resources to take care of you. Mel may have blown things, but we won't. We'll fire Chambers for starts and give Max what it will take to cover your federal trial come January. If any more problems arise in the next few days call us."

"You bet, man. Let's get these guys. Mel will pay for this. So will those asshole prosecutors."

We had to move fast. We said goodbye to Gil and arrived in San Francisco in time to see a lawyer Jake had met and consulted with back in March. Ryan was overconfident: a typical high-powered city lawyer.

Shaking hands, we sat down as Ryan opened the conversation: "What can I do for you? How's the State case coming? When's the trial?"

"A few days away," Jake said. "That's what we came to sound you out on. We have a big problem."

"What's that? Your pilot's talking?" Ryan said, as though he had some sort of inside information.

"How'd you know?" I asked.

"Hey, come on guys. Who else? He's your only problem. Your brother certainly isn't."

On the flight to San Francisco Jake and I had talked about how we had messed up by not consulting Ryan after the federal indictments came down.

THE MISSING LOAD

Ryan blasted us after we explained part of the situation "You come to me for advice when the State came down and now you forget to come to me when the Feds come down. Where do you think your lawyer lives half of every day? I'm here, not in China. And now you have a problem. You guys are smarter than that. Now what happened? Is the other pilot talking and you guys are on the next indictment sheet? If so you have a major problem, not just a problem *per se*."

"We don't know everything yet, but we just found out Mel was given trans-axial immunity." Jake explained the rest of the story and added, "The other pilot is cool."

Leaning back in his leather swivel chair Ryan said sternly, "Mel's talking and the other one is not far behind. Bet on it, guys. He's not going to hold out. Don't be foolish."

Silence filled the room and Ryan got on our case again, "I told you guys to keep me informed, didn't I? Too late now! This guy Gil, he's saying one thing and will do another. He's just buying favors for now. You don't really think he's going to spend three years in jail for you, do you? I deal with this shit all the time. It's highly improbable."

"Yes. I believe he'll hold up, thanks to Mel," Jake replied. "We've talked it over with him."

Ryan, who had just delivered a wake-up call, had my attention. "Maybe you're right."

"Don't count on him," Ryan warned. "And this lawyer Chambers, you're smart men so get up and go after this slime ball. I'll help you."

As we sat fast in our seats and unable to reply Ryan added, "Come on guys. I don't want you hanging around my office sulking like this. This Chambers cat needs to be investigated—right away. Here."

Ryan grabbed his Rolodex, fingered through it, wrote down a name and number, and handed it to Jake.

"If I had the time, I'd jump right in on this. This is the best I can do. Call this lawyer in Los Angeles. He's sharp, but watch out. Make sure of him. Let me know what's going on. Now get out of here and take care of yourselves. Later, brothers."

The next afternoon, we were back in the southland having lunch with a sharky- looking Los Angeles attorney by the name of Joe. When we ran down the entire story with him he replied efficiently.

"Leave everything in order for now. Don't push any buttons on this guy, Chambers. Let everything go down as planned. This pea-brain is a nerd. I'll nail him for negligence. We'll get a new trial."

"What about Gil?" Jake asked. "How can we protect him?"

"Just keep him under your wings. He may just hold. He's facing a three- to five-year sentence. You never know. God gave us brains, but people develop their own courage. Maybe he's an exception, *maybe*. Well, it was nice. I have to go. I'll get a Private Eye on this right away."

Jake slipped him two grand as we departed.

Three days before the trial Bill showed up at my place with Inger, loaded down with suitcases. Bill had been informed that Mel had been granted immunity. Over dinner we did our best to avoid the subject, but it eventually came up. Bill had figured all along that Mel would bring all of us down. He had experienced a side of Mel we hadn't. And Jake and I had not listened. Bill was also livid about Chambers.

"Burn his office down. That will teach him a lesson."

"We thought about that," I responded. "We'd also be hurting his clients. Let his actions catch up with him."

Bill looked long and hard at me. "They do with everyone. It's the law."

Bill should know. He was paying the price, as were Jake and I.

When morning rolled around, Bill and Inger readied themselves. As they did, all the unruly thoughts I had harbored over the years concerning the bad blood with my brother dissipated. He was my flesh and blood and for some inexplicable reason, I loved him dearly, but couldn't find the words to express myself. We were brothers who had yet to understand how to allow one another to be the person we were. All we could do was stand about, squirm, and grope for words that would not come. How and when we might connect back up never came forth. Bill wanted things this way. I didn't. That summed up the difference between us.

Inger let her tears flow as we stood out front and a cab pulled up. Not so with Bill and me. We embraced awkwardly, then backed away silently, crushed by passions we could not express. There was significance to this moment and I waited, hopeful that Bill would break down and shed a tear. But the moment passed us by. One last look, a last wave, and they were gone.

The guy I called "Brother Bill" was no more. All I had left were memories. He was the guy I wanted to be friends with—a real, true-blue brother. But he was also the guy who pulled rank tricks on me, the guy who "piled up" on me when I least expected it; the guy who tried, but failed, to "pants" me; the guy who pushed me off my bike time after time to keep me from tagging along, while he and his buddies laughed as they sped off to be on their own. A millions times or more he had made me angry, but never would I cry, not in front of him. Never would I let him know how he much he hurt my feelings. But he was gone now. Who was I to get mad at? And why couldn't I free myself up and shed a tear? One doesn't lose a brother every day.

And, not every day was trial day. I got the satisfaction of calling Chambers.

"Bill's gone. He split yesterday." Thanks asshole.

"What!" he exploded. "This blows the whole case. Mel's gonna be granted immunity. He's gonna talk. Where's he at? Can you stop him?"

As if you don't know he was going to talk, you shit. "No. I can't. It's out of the question. He's gone." I listened to him rant and rage for a while then hung up.

As we predicted, Bill's absence from court caused a major stir. The duty-bound judge had no choice but to call off the trial and re-schedule it for late November.

When Chambers informed Gil that Mel had been granted immunity,

Gil listened but remained quiet as instructed. He said over the phone to Jake, "Chambers knows something's up, but he can't do anything about it, that fucking jerk. You don't know how bad I wanted to tell him to go screw himself. Letting him sweat it out for as long as possible is what kept me from blowing it"

A few days later, Jake and I flew to Ontario and met with Gil. We immediately went to Max's house. We had good news for them.

"We've got ourselves a dirty lawyer." Jake delivered the privileged information as we sat in Max's office. "It seems George Boy was in jail for tax evasion. He served two years. That's where he met his bodyguard, Jim. Jim was in jail for extortion."

"Really!" Gil exclaimed, and let out a whistle. "The sonsofbitches were in this together."

"Yes, really, Gil!" Jake laughed and added, "They were after our money—anyone's money. That's what we discovered. George Boy has been close to going under for quite some time. He can't seem to make enough money. He's got quite a track record of unpaid bills and he just lost a piece of property."

"So Chambers withheld information about Mel until he could no longer keep it secret," I surmised.

"Had he told us in the beginning that Mel had been granted immunity, he knew we'd stop paying him. He needed money and we were good targets. His associate Jim kept us off the track with his smooth talk," I added, looking over at Gil. "You remember that afternoon Jim mentioned to you and me that he was going to Laguna Beach to hear Tim Leary talk? That's when he sold me. He said Leary was their client and also a personal friend, and what a cool person he was, and would we like to meet him sometime? Remember?"

"Yeah! Boy, what a fucking buttering job that was," Gil bellowed. His six-foot-two, two-hundred-and-thirty-pound frame shook as he let out a loud howl and pounded Max's desktop. "Those shit heads. I'd like to punch their lights out. Damn, this is hard to believe."

"So would we," Jake replied. "Frank and I talked about this. We were the ones who were stupid. Had Frank and I stayed on top of things we'd have uncovered this problem long before it became a problem. Remember, Gil, Jim was in jail for extortion; that's another way of saying 'con man.'"

"So let's hire someone to fix 'em up," Gil burst out. "They fucking deserve a good lesson."

"No, Gil. They'll get what's coming to them. We got conned and we have to live with that. They're going to go under anyway. Why bother?"

"Come on, you're being too easy!" Gil was furious. "Something should be done."

"Something is being done," I replied. "We're going to beat the con-boys. We'll have your "going away" money for you and we'll pay Max to defend you. We'll even hire another attorney if necessary to help Max."

"Let it go Gil," Jake pitched in. "All of us got taken and even if we hadn't, Mel was destined to fall. Georgie-Boy became a separate issue. And now we have to help prepare you for what you're about to face."

"Put your energy into to that," I quickly added. "Don't play into them."

Gil sighed. "You're right. We'd playing into their games and I don't want to stoop to their level. So, let's do this together."

"Good. If we concentrate on your defense instead of going after these bandits we'll be the ones who come up winners," I offered.

"They're right, Gil," Max said, who had been mostly just listening up to this point. "Jake called me the other day. He let me know what was happening and I'm ready to proceed with your case. Jake and I agreed on an amount and he offered more funds to bring in another attorney. I've just the man in mind."

I added reassuringly, "We're also committed to the truth. You work with Max here and we'll force the truth to the surface. Whatever Mel and George are up to, we'll use against them."

Gil, who was our weak link, had to be coddled sincerely if we were to succeed. Jake walked over to him and put his hands on his shoulders.

"That's why we're behind you, buddy. We know you're for real. Let these guys go. Concentrate on what you're about to do."

Gil was quiet, then responded.

"You can count on it, guys. I haven't even begun yet. Mel's gonna be eating dirt when I finish with him. Maxie and I know just what to do come trail time in February. Mel's gonna to have to testify against me. That ain't going to be so easy. Maxie figures he'll have to lie on the stand."

Max agreed. "I've concluded that Mel has already lied to the authorities. He'll have to come up with a story that only involves Gil. I'll have to expose his lies. Once this is apparent, I'm going fry him and then rely on some good character witnesses. Gil's got several lined up. Mel may just blow this Federal case wide open."

"Sounds terrific," I piped up.

"For now, yes. But what about later, Gil, when the real pressure is on?" Jake pushed. "Max's defense scheme seems solid, but what if you're convicted?"

"I know what you're getting at Jake," Gil said firmly, pacing the room. "I won't alter my stance. I'm tired of the law harassing me and I'm very disturbed by the karma, as you guys always say, of my good ex-friend Mel and the asshole prosecutors. I'm gonna fight this thing. I don't care how many times I have to say this, but I'm gonna put the law down and put Mel in his place."

Jake embraced him. "Okay. We really needed to hear you say it that way. But I caution you Gil, we've got some ground to cover."

"Speaking of ground to cover, remember, I can still fly." Gil was deadly serious.

☆ ☆ ☆

Brother Ray stopped by with some interesting news. I hadn't seen him in quite a while and he was very talkative. Manny was preparing to bring up a load. Ray and Dodge, Manny's younger brother, would be driving it up.

Ray, who was still into Scientology, and because of his easy-as-it-goes nature, was vulnerable to men like Manny. So I laid an older brother trip on him. "Manny's not a stable person to work for."

But Ray wasn't to be deterred easily. "Dodge and I are aware of that.

We're going to work with him, make some money, and then keep away from him after we do."

Hesitating a moment, he then asked meekly, "Hey, I was wondering if you had a spare garage we could use?"

"Yeah! Sure. I got one. You're in luck." I liked the idea of having Ray close by during this operation. My analytical mind went to work in a second: through this favor to Ray, Jake and I would be able to collect data from my brother about Manny's movements and we'd also have an avenue of control if Manny decided to pull any fast tricks on us. I simply didn't trust him.

"Thanks, Frank. I appreciate it."

Ray was an honest, easy-going man. We never fought, mainly because he was passive. We would rather sit, talk, and share information, which we often did whenever we got together. Over the past three years we had learned much from one another, but Ray was reclusive and I had to let that be. Besides, it was Bill and I who had all the fights.

After he drove off, I started thinking. "Hmmm, so Manny's getting a load and we're not. Ramon knows we have cop-money now that Glenn paid us off. Ramon has some explaining to do."

I called Jake. "Hey Jake, have you talked to Ramon lately?"

"Yeah! This morning! He said he had no raisins for us. He may have some next week."

Ramon was in the almond and raisin import business, and we used the "raisin" word as cover up—no raisins, no weed.

"I think someone's playing games with us." I said, and then ran down my encounter with Ray.

Ramon's legitimate business, importing raisins and almonds south of the border, kept him financially safe. He wanted to work with us and export weed, but he had yet to prove his worth to us. To me he had been all promise and not much else, but he was still our main supplier and Jake believed he'd come through. He was also just another questionable man, willing to take a risk to make big money. He was a likeable guy about Jake's stature, a family man with two teen-aged sons. Ramon had a gentleman's demeanor and from what I knew of him he wanted to keep everyone content, including himself. That made him easy prey for someone like Manny. Manny could be manipulating him.

"I believe we have a problem here, partner."

Ramon, who had yet to come through this year, had also told us the load he had two weeks ago had gone elsewhere. Although he had promised us we'd get the first load, we were wary of him, and at the same time mighty anxious to get going. Learning that he didn't have a load for us, I was ready to strike back if necessary.

"Tell you what, Jake. I'll stay in touch with Ray. We'll find out soon enough, two or three days at the most."

After placing several calls to Ray over the next few days, he finally answered.

"Good to hear you're back. Everything go okay?"

"Yeah. We just got back. What's up?"

"Not a whole bunch, but I'd like to talk with you."

"I'll be busy. You know, with things I have to do for Manny."

"Yeah. Listen, I'll catch up with you in a couple of days."

As soon as I hung up I headed over to the garage I had turned over to Ray. He didn't know that I had a spare key. When I opened the garage Manny's load was stacked neatly against the far wall. Backing our pickup in, I loaded the merchandise and took it to one of our other garages, then called Jake.

"Hey, I was right. There was a load of raisins in the garage. Let's go see Ramon."

After meeting up in Ontario we rented a car and drove to Indio. Jake had called Ramon from the airport to let him know we were coming. Usually I like to blab right off and let on about what I had done, but I was enjoying the moment. I waited until we got on the freeway and then said, "Looks like we have Manny on this one, including Ramon. We have something to bargain with."

Jake, momentarily serious as he drove, replied. "Oh yeah. What's that?"

"I took the load, Jake."

Looking over at me he grinned widely. "You took the load?!"

I started laughing. "Shit yes. It was just sitting there. You don't think I'd leave it? It's in our garage over on Sixth Avenue."

He started laughing again. I couldn't stop laughing either.

"That dumb shit," Jake hooted, as he slapped the wheel.

I added between laughs, "Don't tell Ramon."

We laughed harder. "No way! Let him stick his foot in his mouth."

"This is great," Jake exclaimed. "Far out! We have Manny's load."

"Yeah, I'm sure he'll want it back. Feel better, Jake?"

"Yeah. Boy, this is just what we need. Let's see what Ramon has to say."

"Hey, good to see you guys. What's so important to bring you down here so suddenly?" he asked, as we entered his house.

His wife served refreshments as we sat in the living room.

"We gotta big problem," Jake said as soon as the room was clear.

"No kidding? What's up, Tell me about it," Ramon patted him on the knee. He liked to be likable. His house was clean and comfortable, just the way he wanted it to appear.

"Well, we think someone's playing games on us," Jake answered, then fell silent. Both of us stared at the man we felt was a culprit.

"Oh, yeah. You think maybe Gil is talking," he suggested in a hushed tone and a serious face.

"No, it has nothing to do with Gil." Jake paused for dramatic effect and then asked earnestly, "Ramon, why aren't we getting any loads through you?"

"Hey, come on. I'm doing my best. I'll have a load for you guys any day. I've got a man down south now who's lining it all up. I told you this a few days ago. Everything is going to work out just fine."

"Okay. If you say so, but I'd like you to be honest with us," Jake appealed.

"Sure, I have nothing to hide."

"Good. Then explain to us why Manny just got a load of weed from you two days ago."

His eyes bulged and darted around. He was momentarily quiet, then said flatly. "Well, he needed it, or at least he said he did, so I got him a load."

"What about our needs?" I asked. There was a strained silence.

"Look, I know you guys need some help. It's on its way."

Jake cut him off, saying calmly, "Why are you playing games with us?"

"Jake, everything is going to work out. Really. In a few days I'll have some raisins and we'll get you guys back on your feet."

"Fine, but why didn't you offer the load to us first as you said you would?"

Ramon was lost for words so I walked over and stopped a few feet away. Jake and I had planned this approach: I leaned over and stared Ramon right in the eye. I said in a composed manner, as I paced each word, "Manny is more than a persuasive person. He's ruthless, Ramon. He's non-stop cold, as in "ice-cold." He puts up a friendly front, but he only cares for himself and I know he used his Hitler-like charm on you."

When I stepped back Jake took over.

"Let me point something out to you. Gil will be going to trial here come February. You know we're standing behind him. I told you we're footing the bill."

"And, I'm gonna help with that," Ramon whined, as I hovered nearby.

"Yeah. We hear you," Jake continued. "Now, if Gil doesn't get some money come trial time, he may think we're backing out."

"But, Jake, we'll have the money."

"No Ramon," I injected. "We're playing games here. Manny is pressuring you. We know him."

"If you want to play a game, here's one," Jake said, coming at him from another angle. "Gil talks, blows the whistle, and suddenly we're all indicted. You included." Ramon was involved. Mel and Gil had used a ranch down in Mexico that belonged to one of Ramon's people. "Your sons are going to hear all about it. Your wife will be devastated, not to mention that you'll be spending time in jail."

"Do you think I'd refrain from ratting on you?" I cut in from the left. "What are you up to with Manny? How did he pressure you?"

Jake jumped in again. "We want to undo this game. It's going to get us into trouble if we don't."

"Look, all he wants to do is some business with me. A lot of business," Ramon wheedled. "I told him I'd help him out."

"What else? Give us some details," I demanded, sitting next to him on the edge of the sofa.

Rolling his eyes he took a breath and began. "He's into this Scientology thing. He even wants me to join up—said it would be good for all of us to be in it. He wants to bring up tons of weed, as much as he can and he's got the people to help him. He's ready to go with pilots, planes, everything."

"And how do you fit into this plan?" Jake asked.

"What did he offer you?" I snapped.

"He wants me to partner with him."

"And what did he say about us?"

"He said we'd give you guys enough to help out." Ramon looked sheepish.

"Christ, don't you think this is a dangerous man you're working with?" I countered.

There was no reply, just a blank stare.

Jake spoke up. "Well, you only have one choice here. You either both back off and help us now, meaning *right now*, or there's going to be a big problem."

"A very big problem, I guarantee it," I added hotly, staring directly at him. "We can't stop you from working with him, but we know how to create a bit of havoc. You'll be hearing from us soon. When you do, you'll come running. Come on Jake, we got some business to talk about."

✯ ✯

Nervous as hell, I called Manny.

"Hey, nice to hear from you. You guys okay?" He was being friendly.

"Not exactly, Manny. We have a problem."

"Well, what's with? Anything I can do?" He was being cooperative.

"There sure is." I fell silent.

"What's the problem?" He was being cool.

"The problem I have is with you, Manny."

"What are you talking about, Frank? I can't possibly understand why we would have a problem. Please explain yourself."

His words were tidy, but clearly he was confused.

"Sure. Jake and I paid a visit to Ramon this afternoon. We found something out that's rather disturbing. Any good guesses, Manny?"

"No, none whatsoever." He was annoyed now.

"Well, I have a good way to help you remember what you should be talking to us about."

"What on earth are you talking about?" he said with irritation.

"Manny, right now if you were in this room I'd attack you physically with every bit of anger that's in me. I'd love to take all of it out on you, just you, no one else, you sonofabitch."

"Whoa. What's the heavy threat about? What are you withholding from me?" He was now being "Mister Dianetic."

"You damn well bet it's a threat, you asshole. You're trying to manipulate Ramon. We know all about it so I suggest you get off your ass and meet face to face with Jake and me on this matter."

"Oh, sure! I'll be right there, like I'm shaking with fear." He was now the village idiot.

"Listen and listen carefully, dude. You and your partner, Ramon, are going to come talk with Jake and me about certain matters regarding our survival. You got that? You make arrangements with him to meet us at one of the airport hotels in San Francisco and we'll sit down and work this out. If you don't, I'll keep the fucking load I hijacked from you no more than eight hours ago. You got that, you shit?"

"What are you talking about?"

"The load that Ray and your brother just came in with. He stashed it in one of our old garages. I took it. Get that through your head. It's mine. Didn't Ray tell you that I gave him one of our old garages? He should have. You know what I mean. Now move it Manny or I'll keep the sonofabitch. You have no idea where I've got your load stashed. I'm going to hang up."

He was fuming.

"Stop ranting. Just call Jake. Make it soon, very soon. Within twenty-four hours."

A few minutes later Jake called. "Boy is he pissed at you. But don't worry. I calmed him down. He'll talk with us tomorrow evening."

"Good. It's like I tell you Jake, when we run into these types of situations, we've got to get a handle on these people and shake the shit out of them. Manny and I don't like each other, and in this case you can use your influence with him to get what we want. I'm sure Ramon is a bit pissed at me for being so heavy with him."

"Maybe so. But I don't think he's the type to hold a grudge. Let's just concentrate on Manny. "

The next evening, as we entered their hotel room, Manny and Ramon were laughing about something. After a strained but civil greeting, we got down to business.

Jake opened the conversation. "Thanks for showing up. Manny your load will be returned this evening. Frank will make arrangements with his brother after our meeting here."

"That's fine with me." He was so very kind—too kind.

"Good. Then let me tell you why we chose to do this. It's obvious to us, Manny, that you're getting way ahead of yourself. We knew when we broke off from you that sooner or later you'd come back into the business. We told you that Ramon was a connection that the both of us would share as well as the customers. Now Ramon tells us that you want to be partners with him and do a lot of business. Is that correct?"

"I'm going to do a lot of business through him. I'll need his services for the type of organization I'm setting up and I want him to be my partner. That's what we talked about a few weeks ago."

"Well Manny," Jake continued, "we know you also said to him that we would be happy with a few loads every once in a while, and apparently you think this is fine. I'm gonna tell you, it's not. We're in this business together, and Frank and I won't tolerate any of your manipulation games."

"That's right, Manny," I interceded. "We can argue this all day, but it wouldn't get us anywhere. Ramon is ours to share no matter what. He is not to be persuaded into anything that would cause us harm."

"That's our main point here, Manny. Ramon, are you with us here?" Jake asked. "Good. The next load is coming to us, the next three, actually. We need the money to take care of Gil, something you said you'd help with, Manny. We're open if you are. We just want to warn you though, that if you try any more games with us we'll respond in kind."

"Actually it will be worse," I broke in. "Whatever you do, remember, I'll come up with a better plan. Are you *Clear* on that?"

Manny refused to respond.

Jake added, "We hope we'll never have to do that. But if we do, you can be sure I'll be involved too."

"You once told me several months ago, when I couldn't find people to sell the bad-ass weed we were bringing, to find new customers. Well, I'll say the same back to you. Go to Mexico and find new connections if Ramon is not enough. Surely you know what I mean by this. You have far-reaching powers now. So use them wisely without interfering with us," I ordered.

He stared at me, his vibe ice-cold, doing his best interpretation of the L.Ron stare. His words were cordial and agreeable, which only told me that he was up to something.

We received help on two fronts: Ramon came through and the U.S. government unknowingly aided our cause by establishing a new drug deterrence program dubbed "Operation Intercept," to be implemented along the fifteen-hundred-mile border. The plan had been a complete mishap. That was the consensus from the media and from anyone paying attention to the daily news reports. Legal businesses on both sides of the border had suffered. Traffic at every major location had been backed up every day for weeks. For all the effort, only a small amount of contraband had been confiscated. Relationships with Mexico were strained. "Who are the morons that came up with this idea?" was the consensus.

It didn't matter to us. We were concerned, but as the weeks rolled by and our first load arrived in mid-November, we were delighted. The price of kilos, normally $90 to $100 skyrocketed to $150 per kilo. Our profits were enormous. We even gave our workers a raise.

Before Christmas we managed to bring over three loads, fourteen hundred kilos all total. Nick did a fine job, arriving on schedule each time. Our new drivers proved their worth. They delivered the loads safely to me in San Francisco. Selling them went smoothly. Our operation was back in full swing and the last of the imposers had been beaten back—for now, at any rate.

On two separate occasions Jake and I had flown over the Arizona desert with Nick at the wheel searching for new areas in which to operate. Plus, we worked with Willy, our ex special forces man, on new ways to communicate between the drivers and the men in the plane. Nothing too complicated. We simply wanted to prevail over any unexpected problems.

With Gil's trial approaching in early February, we were well satisfied with our success and had money to pay for additional lawyers to help the cause.

The Porsche I had bought in Germany arrived about the time the first load came in, and once again, I was behind the wheel of a Dream Machine: a six-cylinder, one-hundred-and-fifty-horse power beauty. Shortly after it arrived, I hooked up with a young woman by the name of Jane who lived just below Glenn's apartment in Sausalito.

In early December the two of us headed for the snowbound mountains of the Sierras. Jane was of Scandinavian origin, a true blond with blue eyes, who wore no makeup. She was cute, but also kind of floppy-looking. She was quite independent and very promiscuous, which was a major plus. Her lifestyle equaled her love for sex: she let me know from the day I moved in that her boyfriend was in jail, and would be out in six months, and she planned to be with him. Meantime, she felt perfectly fine to let me fill her with love juice each night.

Our relationship was mostly physical. We made love often and for prolonged periods. Come Christmas, I had plenty of money and plenty of her. I'd need the infusions of love in the coming months: Manny, as was his nature, tapped into our business from a different flank and began manipulating our people in a deadly fashion. Jake and I were prepared to stop him, but we received vital information about his exploits too late.

CHAPTER
TEN

FIVE DEAD MEN

SAN FRANCISCO, CA
JANUARY, 1970

THE STATE COURT upheld Mel's grant of immunity by the Feds back in November, and shortly after he fired Chambers and hired a local attorney to take over the job of defending him at the federal level. He had yet to be sentenced because he was to be the star witness for the Feds in the February trial. They were counting on him, big time. If Mel delivered and Gil was convicted, they'd expect Gil to fold. A rash of indictments would follow. The problem was, their tactics stank. Little did the Feds know how much they had embittered Gil.

Jake and I had grown to like Gil. At heart he was a little boy. And true to his heart, he refused to let anyone control him. He constantly goofed off and made annoying remarks. Always ready to engage people, he often brought us to laughter as he put Mel or the law down. When he told us in a whimsical manner how his wife actually ran his life, Jake and I readily agreed. He played the tough family guy, who underneath it all loved his kids, his wife and life itself. The faith and assistance we extended to him was immeasurable—well worth the effort.

The night before his trial we were at his side. After taking him to dinner we handed over fifteen thousand in cash, a partial payment on the fifty promised.

In high spirits he proudly announced, "Hey, you have nothing to worry about guys. I'd keep quiet with or without this money. Mel's a phony and we're gonna prove it."

He was right. The tactics the Federal prosecuting attorney chose were dreadful. Gil's attorney's saw right through them, as did the judge and jury.

At Gil's request, we had hired an additional attorney, an aging man by the name of Jean Parsons, who had defended Sirhan Sirhan several years before. Discovery evidence provided proof that Mel had implicated two men: Gil and Bill. Max and Jean knew the prosecutor had a one-dimensional approach; each day at the trial Gil listened quietly as his ex-pal testified under oath that Gil had met all the dealers and handled all negotiations—that Gil was the boss, and Mel was his employee. Gil took care of everything, including the Mexican end. He collected money and paid it out, he lied.

Gil was ready to barf. Mel's demeanor on the stand was pathetic, but he stayed to his well-rehearsed story and buried his pal in a sea of false testimony. The prosecutor had no idea Mel was lying. We figured Mel lied because he feared one of us would have him killed, plus the State, as well as the Feds, would go easy on him; after all he was not the kingpin—Gil was. By the time the prosecutor finished up the damage had been done.

Gil's lawyers could not get Mel to yield on cross-examination and spent little time on this. They relied on several character witnesses to vouch for Gil. These men and women testified that Gil had always been an employee to Mel and that Mel in all cases was the boss. Mel was several years older. He had been a surrogate parent to Gil.

In the closing arguments these discrepancies were pointed out: Mel was lying to save his ass, and that testimony clearly indicated that Gil, in business and in friendship, had always been Mel's subordinate. While the jury was out deliberating we hoped for an acquittal, but we were mistaken. They returned a guilt verdict. Gil was immediately incarcerated and Max immediately filed an appeal.

A few days later Gil was granted an appeals bond: thirty-five thousand.

All of us were elated. Jake and I immediately came up with the ten percent for the bondsman. Gil used his home as collateral and walked out a free man—for the time being. Appeals bonds are somewhat rare, but in this case our lawyers did a good job; the judge had been made aware that the Feds had put a questionable man in the stand. It would take several months, perhaps a year before Gil would have to return to court. We had won a major victory and Gil was in position to win on the appellate level.

Jake and I flew down the day Gil was released. We took him to dinner and discussed hiring another attorney to help Parsons and Max on the appellate motion.

As for Mel, he was sentenced to a three-year term. Where? We didn't know. In a way, I felt sorry for him. He not only had a long prison term, he had lost his best pal and perhaps many close friends.

As a unit, we had gone up against the big boys and had come away with a victory. Although we were completely overjoyed by the results, we were still cautious. We had beaten the system for the moment, but they could lose all the battles they wanted. If we lost but one, we'd be food for the fox.

With the trial behind us, Jake and I put full attention on upgrading our business. Through our good customers Ben and Bill in Berkeley, we had met Bert, a trainer pilot. Jake and I wanted to purchase a plane. Bert, who was to be our back-up pilot, located a used Cessna 206 in Palm Springs. He and I flew down on a commercial jet and checked it out. It was a beauty, a single engine plane with plenty of horsepower. That afternoon I called Jake. He flew down with a cashier's check for nineteen thousand, five-hundred.

Two brand new Dodge pickup trucks with camper shells were purchased from the state of Nevada. We did this to gain an advantage. The trucks would bear neutral license plates as the drivers traveled between Arizona, Nevada, and California.

After the trial, through my brother Ray, I obtained information that Manny had bought a ranch in Arizona back in December. It was large and remote, and it came with a usable airstrip.

That prompted Jake and I to make a move. We hired a real estate broker who was also a small-time customer I had met through Bill. In February we sent him to Arizona to look for a piece of property that would suit us. A week later, he reported back. He had found a perfect piece of property. It was dead-center in the middle of the state, and was completely surrounded by Federal property. It was an eighty-acre ranch; sixty acres a long flat meadow.

"You can hire a man to run a blader down the center and put a road in," Marty suggested. "It's not unusual. Tell him you're just dividing the property. Once he's done, you'll have your strip and a terrific location."

I flew down with Bert in our Cessna and checked it out from the air. Marty was right. The ranch, situated inside a Federal Forestry Reserve was ideal—no one around for miles. Though there was only one dirt road leading in, we had access rights. When we returned, we had Marty purchase the property for twenty-five thousand dollars. Ryan, our S.F. lawyer, put the land into a trust along with our plane.

Once the paperwork was completed, Jake and I drove to the ranch and inspected the area. Winslow was to the north by thirty miles, Payson was to the south by sixty miles, and there was nothing much in between. If we were cool, we could operate out of this prime piece of property for as long as we wanted.

Jake decided to hang out on the property, but I wanted to go back and mess with Jane. Her lover was still in jail and that was fine by me. All I wanted to do was use her as a sex device. She never seemed to get enough and neither did I. Besides, there was work to do at the ranch, and Jake was willing and able to get it done right away. He had three men with him, all of them young and work-ready.

Even though Ramon had come through and we had brought up three loads in January, expenses had taken a toll and we were low on money. Pressure was no longer a foremost factor and we were anxious to get going, but couldn't. The new ranch offered such good protection it would be foolish for us to use a landing place anywhere else. With that decision made, Jake hired a man to blade our property, but we had the infernal wait for the permit to go through. Jake reported that it would take four to five weeks

Jake hung out at the ranch with our crew, worked, and waited. While I waited in the Bay Area I found out through Ray—bless his heart—that Manny was having a field day out at his new ranch. Ray spilled the news that Manny had brought across a load a day, six straight days during the month of December. He'd crossed several loads in January and in February while we sat waiting.

It was now mid-March. No telling how many loads he and his Scientology crew had managed to cross. I would rather admire people for their accomplishments than let envy take over, but in this case, boy, was I envious. Manny was rolling along and we had to wait. It wasn't fair. But my envy turned to curiosity when Ray came by one day and told me that Manny had had a strange mishap. Ray was not privy to all the details, only that Manny's new ranch was now hot, and Manny could no longer use it. He was planning to move his operation to New Mexico.

Jake called about that time. The road had been taken care of and we were ready. "Come on down," came the message. When Jake picked me up in Winslow, I let him know that something was ailing me and was in high gear. "I don't know what it is. Maybe it's the hepatitis. Or maybe it's a flu bug. It's weird, man. I didn't know what's going on."

He listened, but didn't really hear me. We had more important problems he told me, as I finished relating my concerns.

"Well, partner, we're ready, but Nick's not."

"What do you mean? What's happening?"

"Nick's been flying loads over for Manny. I found out through Ramon two days ago."

"Ah man, shit, this is crazy. How many times have we told him that Manny's a problem? Why can't he see this?"

"Well, we can't stop him, Frank," Jake replied sardonically, adding, "I called him and talked with him about it. He said Manny doesn't get in his way and pays him, so he's got no beef with Manny. I don't like it either.

Anyhow, Nick will be ready soon, maybe tomorrow. Ramon's ready. He's got two loads for us at his ranch down south."

"Great. That's a relief."

The distance to the ranch in Mexico where the loads were stored was a mere two hundred and fifty miles from our ranch. Nick had only to fly from his base in Arizona, enter Mexico, land, refuel, load up and fly back underneath the radar. Landing on our ranch would be a snap for him. Jake and I were anxious. We'd be back in operation in no time. Maybe my lethargy, or whatever it was, would go away.

Jake was in a strange mood too, bordering on one of his funks. We were silent for the most part as we drove to our ranch, but made plans to have a serious talk with Nick. We wanted him to work with us and drop Manny like a hot rock. We'd promise to keep him busy. He was too good to lose.

Out at the ranch the next day I worked alongside the crew tearing down an old shack. Come early evening, Jake and I headed back to Winslow to check in with Ramon. After making the call, Jake came back to the truck with disturbing news.

His face pallid, he broke the news. "Manny has a plane load of people missing."

"What?" I rose out of my listlessness to pay attention.

"Ramon just gave me the details over the phone. He said they're late. Manny's worried. So is Ramon. It doesn't look good, Frank."

After Jake got in the truck he turned and added, "Nick was on the plane. So was Gil."

"Oh shit." Expelling a deep sigh I wailed, "I don't believe this. Gil's on board the plane? He promised not to go near Manny. And Nick too?"

"Yes, Gil and Nick," Jake replied soberly. "There were three other men; a pilot, who works for Manny, Manny's father, and step-brother." They left early this morning from Manny's ranch and were due back this afternoon around 5:00 p.m. at the latest. Manny called Ramon a few minutes ago."

"Five people!" I once again expelled a deep sigh and gazed out the window. It was half-past eight. The sun had gone down near an hour ago. Analyzing the situation I quickly came up with some frightening scenarios.

If they had put down somewhere for any reason, they'd have called no matter what. And no matter what they would have been back before dark at Manny's ranch. There was only one answer to the mystery: the plane had gone down.

"Ray told me a couple of days ago that Manny might set up in New Mexico."

Jake started the truck and as we took off he replied, "That's where they were headed. They were to fly that way and return to the ranch before dark."

"This is ugly. I don't like the sound of this one bit. I just don't."

"Maybe they put down somewhere."

"They would have called."

"Yeah. I know," Jake said, and became silent.

Later that evening, we drove back to Winslow and called Ramon, hopeful that the plane had landed at a lit airport, and Manny had received word that everyone was safe. But when Ramon told Jake that the plane was still missing, our hopes vanished. Manny had called the FAA, and a search would begin in the morning. We were mortified. The lethargy that had gripped me came on strong, as did an angst that tore at my guts. I wondered how Jake was dealing with the news. But, I was having difficultly breathing and sleep that evening was almost impossible.

The next morning both of us were in a reality far from what we knew as everyday reality. It showed on Jake's face and in the way he carried himself and it made me feel eerie. Something bad had happened and we both knew it. I wanted to be upbeat, but in my heart, I feared the worst. Each and every time I gave thought to the situation, negative thoughts came up. Five men and a plane were missing. They had not called. It meant only one thing. The plane had gone down—and my body systems were shutting down as well. There was little I could do and when I looked at Jake, he too remained in a daze as we headed to Winslow, ill prepared to call Ramon and get the latest word.

Jake got out and made the call while I waited, anxiety biting at me.

"Still no word from them," Jake said, as he got back in and looked into the distance.

I sank into my seat, unable to respond. We were in the midst of a tragedy and we were in deep shock.

"This doesn't look good," Jake frowned.

"Not in the least."

"I'm really worried."

"So am I."

"Let's go back to the ranch."

"Fine by me."

But it wasn't fine by me. I was all tied up inside. Anxiety had taken over and once we got to the ranch I was at a loss. Drained of energy, I told Jake I wanted to go home. I could regain strength there, I was most certain, and repeated my earlier lamentations.

"Something's wrong with me, Jake. I'm as useless as that rat the cat caught yesterday."

We had both pickups at the ranch and Jake no longer needed his car, so he asked me to drive it to Tahoe for Joanne to use. Driving off, I was simply overcome with fatigue. I had to stop and rest several times before arriving in Tahoe. When Joanne learned what had happened she was terribly concerned—for me as well. Five men were probably dead, and we could only to wait for the search team to verify our belief. It was gruesome and I was tied in knots. With her, I could let out my feelings.

When I arrived home and told Jane the bad news, she consoled me. The listlessness continued anyway. When Jake called two days later he reported, "I sent the crew home. I'm on my way to Tahoe. Ramon's going to shut down for now."

After a week-long search the FAA called it off, but Manny refused to give up. He hired a psychic, and a few local pilots volunteered to go on a search mission. Five days later one of them spotted the wreck. A rescue team was sent in. Five bodies were on board. The plane, mostly intact, was perched on a rocky outcrop near the summit of an eight thousand foot pass. Investigators, including FBI personnel, were sent in. They concluded the accident was due to pilot error. Gil had been responsible. His burnt body was in the pilot's seat. The canyon was narrow and Gil must have entered at low altitude. Pinned in by canyon walls, he had no room to turn, nor could he gain enough altitude to get out. And, as the canyon walls closed in on them, Gil and the others, all of them no doubt terrified for their lives as he tried to maneuver the plane out of harm's way, met a fiery death.

Ramon, who provided us with this news, added that he had visited Gil's wife. Manny, who had lost his father and a step-brother, was taking a month off.

When Jake called me I moaned, "How could this happen? There were three pilots on board."

"Gil screwed up. He entered the canyon at low altitude."

"Yeah, but he should have known. Nick should have known. They're good pilots."

"It doesn't matter, Frank. They let Gil fly and he took them in and one thing led to another. Then it was too late. Gil didn't know the canyon would close in on them, otherwise he would have entered at a higher altitude."

Jake was right, but it didn't make things any better. Gil and Nick and the other pilots knew how to make use of air navigational charts. One of them must have had a chart out and seen that Gil was at low altitude. And if that were true, Gil would have had time to turn around as he entered the canyon. But as Jake said, none of this mattered now. Whatever had gone wrong, we'd never know.

I had met Nick a few times. He was a pleasure to be around, a man's man with unique vitality, a man you knew you could trust. He made me feel that I was alive: part of him and a part of everything we were doing.

There had been only one incident involving Nick that gave Jake and I a huge amount of grief. It started when Nick came to us back in December and asked if he could fly the border without using a kicker. Jake and I granted him permission.

"Christ, I can put the plane on autopilot and kick the shit out myself. We can bring across an extra sack of kilos and make more money."

I could still hear his confident voice the day he insisted he fly alone. But on this second run, unknown to us, Nick had a problem at the airport and got off to a late start. Unable to make up lost time, he came up with a plan that would work only we had no way of knowing he would be late or what his new plans were. Our ground crew, who waited as long as they could, took off when the sun went down and returned to their motel. Jake and I, as we had done on several occasions, had rented a room in a motel. When the drivers called and said, "No Nick," we had had a major fit and immediately called Ramon.

"My men said that he loaded up down there, but he was late taking off."

We told the drivers to hang out at their motel and wait for further instructions. Nick would know where to find them. If he were alive, he'd call. It was all we could do for the time being and as we waited we had visions of Mel and the desert fiasco that had brought us to our knees. Stuck in our motel room, ours fears running out of control, there had been nothing we could do but fret and worry.

Finally the phone rang about 9:30 p.m. that evening. It was the drivers. They were on their way home with the load. "Nick will call and explain what happened. See ya soon."

When Nick called, he said, "Hey, sorry guys, but it was dark and I couldn't land at our regular spot so I flew around for awhile, made sure everything was right, then landed at the strip in Scottsdale. It was good and dark by then so I taxied right up to my usual spot, went down to the rental agency and got me a van, drove back and loaded it. Then I drove it straight to the motel. Yeah, your drivers were quite surprised when they opened the door and saw me. We had a good laugh and a few more when I told them the hard part now was to get the bags from my truck to their truck without anyone seeing us."

He was gone now, as was Gil. We were all prone to being rebellious. They wanted things their way, but had lost their lives as a result.

Suddenly, my lethargy dissipated. When it did, I questioned the synchronicity. Had my intuition picked up on what had happened at the time of the crash and my body had simply reacted to the fact that five men had died a terrible death? I had no way of knowing and I'd never find out, but there was a good possibility.

Suddenly, it hit me. Now that Gil was dead, he could no longer give evidence against us if he were to have changed his mind. This, of all things, felt odd. When Ramon called Jake and asked us to join him in declaring a two-week moratorium, we immediately agreed.

Four weeks after the disaster we made use of our ranch for the first time. During the downtime, Ramon had turned us on to a pilot who had worked for Manny. Jake had met with him and was very impressed. He was known as Las Vegas Benny, an older man of Korean War vintage, a damn good pilot with a perverse nature, who no longer wished to work for Manny. To Benny, Scientology was perverse, especially the way Manny pushed it on him. He had had his fill. Thanks Manny.

His female companion was his co-pilot. They were not only a sound team they were a machine, well-oiled, well-prepared, and mighty expensive. They demanded top pay and we coughed it up each time they flew loads over—three in three weeks—always on schedule. Our profits were lower, but the job was being handled by a Korean War veteran, trained by the U.S. Government.

Our drivers, Howie and Dan, picked up the loads and brought them safely home. And after each delivery Jake and I rewarded our entire crew. Three times we took them out to a high class Japanese restaurant in San Francisco and celebrated.

While all this was going on, Jane asked me to move out. Her lover would soon be free and there was no love between Jane and me, just good, wholesome, libidinous pleasure. Packing up, I headed over to Corte Madera to live with Ed and Fay. They were friends of Jake's whom we had hired to rent a house and receive our loads. We had struck up a good friendship over the months and I looked forward to living with them.

✯ ✯ ✯

May rolled around and when the last of the kilos had been sold, my energy restored, and confidence once again on an upswing, I felt supremely proud about what Jake and I had accomplished this year. I had over forty grand in my pocket and our organization was in full swing. Swept away by good thoughts I went for a ride—to my favorite beach of course. Though ecstatic, something was nibbling away at me as I made my way along the water's edge. Whatever it was had everything to do with the way I perceived love and how I dealt with fears that attacked me when I least expected them.

"What's up?" I thought, as I listened to the pounding waves. As I stood taking in the expansive view my body loosened up, and the internal angst, those infernal surges that so often took hold, began to wane. Earth was my rightful partner. It was a part of the whole and that whole was a part of me. A change was coming and I was listening. I began to think about what my partner and I had been through since October. There had been unimaginable complications. We had confronted what life had thrown at us and now there was a new future to deal with.

At this point, Jake and I could head in most any direction. I, for one, could call it quits, back off, and buy the vessel of my dreams. But this deeply earnest ideal refused to take hold—not at this moment. There were too many other things to consider. What did stick was that I needed a respite from this business. A much-deserved vacation was in store and the more I thought about it, the more my energy soared. Yes, it was time to take a long holiday and escape from the frightful experiences we had waded through these past several months.

In a day or so I'd head to Tahoe to meet with Jake, and pass over the money share due him. We'd have a talk, as usual. I would have the chance to go over everything that was on my mind and how I longed to gain back the freedoms I had lost—him too; freedoms that had fallen by the wayside. Freedom at this juncture would be a luxuriously long summer break. It would certainly be most welcome and I was hopeful that Jake would be eager for a break himself.

The year had started badly. Glenn had pulled a heartless stunt on us. I was outraged all the more because I knew his potential. Glenn was a jackal.

His nature was to strike out and he brought pathos in the picture when he served notice on us. We became merely one of the obstacles he wanted moved out of his path. And when he cleared this path there was little we could do to stop him. Let him go, regroup, and move beyond him was the path we carved. It was our nature to avoid animals such as Glenn. There was no need to punish him. Jake and I chose wisely and summed up the whole episode as a "no bitch, no complain, no blame, just get-on-with-life" trade-off.

As for Manny, we knew how to handle him, but he was a pain in the ass because we had to pay close attention to his moves. That was mostly my department and I mostly succeeded, but we were shocked when we learned that Ramon had joined up with him. They attempted to beguile us, but we outfoxed them and matched them step for step. In the end we had disarmed them. There was no need to brandish a gun and make hollow threats, nor take Manny aside and beat sense into him. We just brushed him off and stayed alert, aware that he might strike again.

When we learned that Mel had been granted immunity and that Chambers and his associate were grifters we felt like fools. At least I did. Jake and I had failed to take care of rather obvious details, such as going to our San Francisco lawyer and consulting with him. And, come to think of it, Jake and I had not talked in depth about the predicament Chambers and Mel had put us in—either before the incidents or after. But we did a remarkable job of steadfastly working together to overcome the problems. Had we consulted with our lawyer it would not have mattered in Mel's case. Mel was our weak link and we knew deep down that he might fold.

Chambers' con job made us realize the cost of stupidity—does one always have to learn the hard way? But fortune had been with us. And, everything happened did so the way it did because we created that reality. Chambers and his crony would get reamed by their own creative vices, right up the old woozier.

Gil was a man we could trust, even though our lawyers told us to *get real*. His death, and Nick's, had spooked me. They wanted to do things their way. We respected them, but for some convoluted reason they separated themselves from us. Had greed consumed them? If only they had taken our good advice, they might be alive and well. But whey had to die from their mistakes was hard to grasp.

When I thought about Bill's decision to run from the law, at first I really believed that it was the right thing to do, even appropriate. But then there was his attitude. He became arrogant, another cover-up job to cover his real feelings. The few times we were together before his departure I saw through him. I felt his fears and his anger. He was running long before he went on the lam. He was running from the law and running from all the things he loved, which had everything to do with his family and close friends. A hidden, inner aberration that had to do with his past was eating at him, I'm sure. And no matter what kind of corrupt behavior Bill applied to life, he was my brother. That I loved him, I could not deny. I could also not deny that I was in many ways ashamed of him.

When I told him that I had visited our Dad he was completely unreceptive to the idea that Dad's past may have damaged his mind and heart as well. He saw Dad as a man who had failed his family and wanted us out of his life. Dad could go to hell, as far as Bill was concerned. Dad had run from us because he perceived life was being cruel to him, and Bill chose to run from the father who had let him down. Where was the difference between these two?

Thinking about Bill was distressing, so I sat on the beach and watched the waves and wind patterns rippling the surface. Waves never stop. They are countless, but not as countless as the thousands of dollars Jake and I had paid out to keep afloat, or so it seemed. No one other than Mack and Bill ever gave us any funds. We paid the bills and were damn glad to have the money. And now we were flourishing despite all the damage. We were no longer troubled by a "we need to work–to-save-our-asses" anxiety. We were sitting pretty. We had a perfect ranch with a perfect landing base, two perfect trucks, a perfect plane and a top-notch pilot. What more could we want? All was in order for us to reach out and gain a new pinnacle.

And this, among other things is what I said to Jake shortly after I arrived at his house in Tahoe.

"All in all I'm satisfied with what we've accomplished this year," I said, summing things up. "Ramon will have plenty of work for us come October and I want to knock off for now and wait 'til the new season starts."

"Not a bad idea. Why the sudden change?"

"Lots of reasons, Jake. Like I say, I want to get back into the things I miss. Playing this game takes away the freedoms I love. You have a family and I don't. I want to normalize my life and be with friends. Maybe find a girlfriend. Christ, I haven't the time to sail and you know how important that is to me. Al wants me to work at the yard. He hates paperwork and the business is falling apart because of it. He's a stubborn man and I feel it's my obligation to keep the business together even though we're not making any money."

Jake took a moment to consider my plans. "Ramon said he hasn't got any work right now and he's thinking along the same line. Maybe we all need a good break. Let's go for it. That will free me up to get some flying in. I'll have Ben fly the plane up to the Truckee airport and *get serious*. I've already got a few hours in, and over the summer I'll have time to learn to fly. I can go for a pilot's license in no time, and get in a few hours of solo fly-time each week. Come October, I'll be ready to go along as a co-pilot. Benny can put me through some heavy training and I'll fly a few loads over."

"Far out, Jake. Benny's not going to like it, but we'd sure make out. Besides, Benny ran several loads over for Manny. He's sitting pretty at fifteen-K a load. Go for it, man. You got my support. We'll have more control of our operation."

Most of our problems stemmed from our pilots. We would do better if Jake flew our merchandise out of Mexico to our ranch. Going over our future plans from top to bottom, we were satisfied that next year would be a successful one. Jake had the time, the resources, and the willingness to learn all the necessary flying procedures. By January Jake would fill in as pilot, with Benny as our backup. Willy would fly with Jake as a kicker.

"Hey, you're going to make a lot of money, partner," I said, as we wound down the meeting.

"I know. That's what I'm planning on."

At the wheel of my Porsche, I felt more at ease than I had in a long time as I drove out of the mountains and back to the Bay Area. All things considered, it made sense to take a long break. Besides, I had other areas to concentrate on.

Back in February of the previous year, prior to the desert fiasco, I had invested fifteen grand in a boat yard in Sausalito. Al, my good Sea Scout pal had hounded me and had made all the arrangements while I was busy working. We bought out the original owner. Essentially we bought a shop, all the power tools and equipment and materials to run the place. Rent on the worn down WWII property was very affordable and we had plenty of customers.

Al had been running it in my absence. He now wanted me to invest more time and perhaps more money. My racing sloop had arrived back from Mexico in one piece. It was in need of repair and I arranged a haul out at the yard. After removing the mast, Al showed me how to remove the keel bolts. After we turned the vessel over and set it on a dolly, I began a daily work routine. When I wasn't working on the boat I tackled the paperwork that had piled up.

It was pure drudgery. No wonder Al wanted me there. One day I let him know we had two grand of disposable income hanging around. He promptly chided me that quarterly taxes were due.

✯ ✯ ✯

I was to turn twenty-seven that summer. With time off to think about things, I now allowed myself to once again open up to just how close I was to the goal I had set when I first entered the business. I had the money. I even had a boat in mind. It was a forty-foot woody: both a racer and a cruiser. And as I came to work each morning there was a rush of anguish. Should I keep with the smuggling business or keep to my plans about the goal I had made? Did I want more money just to have more money? But when I thought about making more money, money won out.

What actually won out had everything to do with excitement. Excitement was the name of our game. Even the detestable dramas that had come and gone over the past three years were exciting, or at least, exciting the way Jake and I had challenged them and had won out. We were a team. We knew what it took to run our business. We knew how to plan each run. And now that we had a perfect ranch, we could control the action on down to the last step. All would go well. The drivers would pick up the load, return home, and all I had to do was to be careful when fronting the kilos to our good customers. Collecting the money was a huge rush. Jake would learn to fly. We'd be ready, come October. In that, I was beyond excited—I was at peace.

Living with Ed and Fay was an added bonus. They enjoyed life and we were a good fit. Fay was a kind-hearted woman with countless friends. They came and we partied, sometimes sensibly, sometimes not. But always we had a good time, either playing cards, throwing Frisbee, or getting stoned together and listening to good music. We took in a concert every now and then. And Al had a racing sloop and I'd often crew. I had my motorcycle repaired and rode the local hillside trails, usually on warm summer evenings. Life was stupendous. And living with Ed and Fay, life was full of the unexpected. Dull moments were non-existent, not with "Hotai" her Lahasa Apsa and her two uncommon tabby cats around to further entertain us. As I settled in, life became anything but dreadful.

But the relaxation I so longed for didn't last long. Manny, along with his Scientology entourage, decided that self-destruction would lead them down a speedy path to Nirvana. He did something that not even we would have thought he could do: he brought down his entire organization.

There would also be another rumble, an unexpected one that would become a source of much angst. Someone very close to me would have a change of heart and cause a great stir, laying waste all the good plans that had been set forth.

CHAPTER ELEVEN

SELF-DESTRUCTION

CORTE MADERA, CA
MAY 17, 1970

"Wow! What a day! Another out-of-sight morning, no overcast, nice big blue sky," I thought, as I drove to the store. Standing in front of the newspaper bins, ready to purchase a S.F. Chronicle, I glanced over and caught the Marin Independent Journal headlines: "Big Drug Bust in Fairfax."

"Well, who'd they get today?" I said out loud, amused.

Purchasing both papers, my jaw dropped when I spotted Manny's name.

"Whoa! Damn! He did it! The turd got busted! He's locked up in the Marin County jail. His bail is thirty-five thousand dollars."

Manny, along with six others had been busted while selling eleven-hundred pounds of weed. Several thousand dollars had been confiscated.

Who were they selling to, I wondered, an eleven-hundred pound deal? That's ridiculous. Manny wouldn't sell that much all at once. He liked to sell small amounts, like us, and make big profits. This didn't make sense, and as I read the article I wondered if Manny had an informant inside his group. Maybe the paper had their facts wrong; either way I had to contact Brother Ray right away and talk with him.

Without wasting any more time I called Jake. Joanne answered instead.

"He's out right now. He'll be back any moment. What's up?"

"Manny was busted in Fairfax yesterday with 1,100 pounds of weed."

"Shit! No kidding! "

I explained what I knew and then said, "Tell Jake to call Ramon and tell him what's up."

Next I called Brother Ray.

"I don't have the time to meet with you. We're working on getting him out. Call me later," Ray said, uncharacteristically intense and business-like.

Jake was cool and indifferent when we connected up, even cynical about the news. "What did you expect? He kept pushing and now look at him."

"Jake, this is going to bring some heat."

"Yeah! Some! I let Ramon know. He feels okay for now. The narcs know we're doing things. They just can't catch us, buddy. You know that. As long as we keep to the pay phone system, we're cool. Go relax. Keep me informed. Okay?"

Heading home, I got caught up in a sudden rush of paranoia and went over everything I could think of from top to bottom. I began with the fact that the narcs didn't know where I lived, and the system Jake and I had worked out on the pay phones was so complex, sometimes we had a hard time figuring it ourselves. No one had a chance at intercepting our calls as long as we stuck with our system. There were always the mock-deliveries, but it didn't matter: we weren't working right then. But what kind of heat and how much would come our way, I had no real way of knowing.

All the names in the paper were unfamiliar, but Manny, I figured, must be selling to some questionable people—maybe even to The Man. Did the authorities know if we were connected to Manny? It was too hard to say. If they caught on to Ramon through their investigation, they'd be all that much closer to finding out that he was the connection who supplied Jake and me.

In a pensive mood, I spent the weekend at home monitoring what was happening. Bother Ray's insider information would be handy, but I couldn't reach him.

Monday the real bummer hit. Once again I went out to fetch a morning Chronicle, and once again I froze in front of the newsstand.

"HUGE POT BUST IN LOS ANGELES. Eleven Arrested. Five Tons of Marijuana Confiscated."

Christ, what's going on here? I asked myself. Who is it this time?

As I scanned the paper I could hardly believe what I was reading. Manny was the main catch of the day. He had done it again. It was the biggest pot bust in the history of the West coast: five tons of marijuana—*ai chihuahua*. The newly formed DEA had apprehended the smugglers as they unloaded their contraband that was aboard a barge docked in San Pedro Harbor. Again, the story reeked of an informer, but I let out a pent-up laugh when I read that Manny and the Captain of the vessel, who had towed the barge in, had jumped into icy water in an apparent escape attempt.

Then another bad note hit at the end of the article. In the list of names of all the lesser characters was my younger brother, Ray. Oh shit. It was pure madness.

Friday, Manny had been arrested and thrown in jail. How he possibly could have gotten out so quickly was mind-boggling. It usually took me three or four days to spring someone, plus it was the weekend. What was going on? My thoughts went on automatic: work on this later. Get to a lawyer and see what Ray's bail was going to be.

I called Joe, our attorney in Los Angeles. "Let him know that I'm gonna bail him out, okay?"

Next, I called Jake. This time he was more responsive, but insisted we were cool.

"What about Ramon?" I inquired. "The narcs are going to investigate Manny and find out that Ramon's the main man. When they do, they'll find out about us."

"He had nothing to do with this," he said. "He may have sold some of the raisins to Manny. That's all. As for the narcs investigating Manny,

Ramon told me a while back that Manny uses the same kind of phone system we do."

"Fine! But that doesn't cut it, Jake. This is a major bust. We're going to have heat all over us."

"Probably. But we can work around all of this. Come October, we'll know how to handle this. Why don't you get your brother out in the meantime and find out what you can."

"That's what I figure on doing. It's underway. I'll have a long talk with him."

"Good. Get back to me when you feel it's necessary."

"I'm finished with Manny," Ray said, head slightly bowed as he sat with me at the kitchen table at my place in Corte Madera. A week had passed. His bail had been reduced to five grand. I had used my own money to free him.

"It's a bit late—but good." I didn't want to press on certain issues, but we needed facts. "Tell me what happened, brother. The last time I talked with you, you were busy bailing Manny."

He cracked a smile. "Well, we got him out just in time to go get busted again."

"Apparently." We both chuckled. "This is a confusing story. Start from the beginning."

"Manny's had this big one ready for quite some time. I thought he'd call it off when the first bust went down. But he couldn't really. We had to get going on this project. After we bailed him he got together with us and told us everything would be okay. Manny was sure he wasn't being followed and the other bust had nothing to do with this job."

"How did you feel about going down to do this, what with all the heat?"

"We were concerned, but Manny insisted. You know how persuasive he is."

"Yeah. He really likes to lead a crowd. This whole thing stinks of an informant. Any ideas?"

"You're right. No I don't." His head shaking side to side and with a silly smirk on his face he added, "We should have known better. The narcs really got us. Someone had to rat on us."

"The narcs had to have been using radios to communicate during the bust. Didn't Manny think to use radios to monitor the airways, like that dude from Berkeley we worked with?"

A little over a year before this happened, I had sold 200 kilos to a guy from back east through our Berkeley customers. Cautious of the law, he had hired a young, hip, radio ham to monitor police calls. Bringing a rather sophisticated machine to the motel, the man had monitored the airways for several minutes before I took off to load up the vehicle. I was impressed. So was Ray, who had helped me.

"Yeah, but Manny didn't do a thing about radios. Nothing."

"That's crazy, considering all the circumstances. It wouldn't have cost much for a good monitor. Damn, he just doesn't think along those lines. He could have prevented this."

Ray was looking dismal, so I dropped the heavy rhetoric and asked,

"Where did Manny get the load? Christ, five tons at once!"

"Through Mack, mostly. I heard that Ramon put up some of it."

"And somehow it got transported up to San Pedro on the barge," I added.

"Yeah. The barge was towed into Long Beach on Friday evening. That's why Manny wanted to get going. We were told we had better get the barge unloaded and out of there before any problems arose." He shrugged his shoulders. "Manny convinced us we had no choice."

"Uh-huh. The pressure game!"

"Yeah. The pressure game."

"And the narcs were sitting in the bushes all the while. I bet they were laughing. Tell me about it."

"They were. We moved in right at midnight and parked on the pier, four pickups all together and started unloading. I wasn't feeling too hot about it, but after several minutes, I figured everything was safe. We saw a couple of helicopters nearby, but that didn't stop us. The next thing I knew, the narcs were all over the place."

"It must have been a scene?"

"Yeah." Ray's grin was wry. "It was comical. The narcs were more paranoid than we were. They came out of the bushes yelling and screaming and running around in confusion. They must have thought we had guns the way they acted. And that's what got me shook up—their paranoia. They calmed down after a few seconds and that was when Manny jumped in the water and started swimming away."

"I can picture it; narcs scared to death and Manny seeing that, then making a break for it. Not a bad idea. Maybe I'd have done the same." We laughed at Manny's expense. "He didn't get very far."

"Not at all. We could hear all the commotion from where we were. The narcs started hollering, 'Harpoon them dope fiends.'" We rolled over in laughter. "When they pulled him out they brought him over to where we were being held. A bunch of them started jumping up and down like kids yelling, 'We got Manny! We got Manny!'" We laughed again.

Then I added, "God, this is so crazy, Ray. It's hard not to laugh."

"Yeah. The narcs even gave it a code name: 'Operation Elimination.'" We broke into another fit of laughter.

"So true. So true." I said, "They totally eliminated him. I'm beginning to feel sorry for the guy."

"The way he's been pushing things, something bad was going to happen real soon. Dodge and I saw this but we didn't think it would happen this way or so sudden."

"So, who's the informant, Ray? There must be one. Think about it. Jake and I would like to know. The narcs are going to investigate and you know what that means."

"I'm not familiar with all the people Manny deals with, but it could be the new guys Manny's been selling to in Marin."

"Hmmm, but you don't know anything about them?"

"No. Nothing. Never met them. I'm only going by what Manny told us after he got out and what I learned from Dodge."

"Who does Manny use to sell his weed?"

"This guy Brian. He uses two other guys to help out, but I don't know them very well. I stay away from them. They're a bunch of loud mouths, especially Brian. He's got a giant ego."

"Really! Could be this guy Brian connected up with the wrong people and passed info to them about the barge in L.A.—giant egos are apt to do things like that."

After covering the matter thoroughly, we talked about litigation. Ray and the rest of the lightweights would more than likely receive light sentences. Some of the heavyweights would talk and or be granted immunity. As for Manny, his free days as a Free Theta Being were numbered.

Ray commented, "Manny's organization was getting out of hand. Even his brother was upset with him, mainly because of the crash that killed his father and half-brother."

"I bet, but guys like Manny never stop."

"Not at all. He wanted everybody who worked for him to join Scientology. Everyone. He didn't pay us good wages like you guys do. He told everyone that they're part of his family and promised them recognition through Dianetics. That kind of stuff."

"What a power trip. Think of where he might be had he been "clear" about what he was doing. So much for the Scientology training he paid for. Little good it's done him. Too bad Dianetics bypassed "Ego Trips 101" on their curriculum. Then again, guys like him are in denial about their fears. No amount of training would have been sufficient."

A smirk spread across Ray's face. "You know, he's reached the first O.T. level with his Dianetics training: O.T. means Free Theta Being. His brother said it's more like Out of Touch." We laughed then began howling.

"Yeah! He's out of touch all right," I said. "What a perfect description of Manny. Wherever he goes, whatever he does, he's out of touch with everybody and everything—he hasn't got a clue."

Around the first of June, Jake called.

"What's up brother? Everything okay up there in Tahoe?" I asked from a pay phone ten minutes later.

"Sure is. We're doing good. Got in a few hours of fly-time last week."

"Far out. I'll come up soon and visit, okay?"

"Maybe sooner than you think. Ramon just called. He's got some raisins. Three loads, he says. He wants us to run them over."

"I don't think so, Jake."

"I know you're set on not working, but this won't take long."

As Jake rambled on, I was soon juiced up, but quickly reminded myself of the firm decision I had made. "Come on, Jake. We made a verbal agreement not to go back to work yet."

"Ramon's got everything ready. We'll be done in about two weeks."

"You know as well as I do Manny has put heat on all of us, Ramon included. The informer is not known yet. We don't know what kind of heat is on us. It's too risky, Jake."

"Ramon had his phone checked a few days ago. It's not being bugged."

I wasn't convinced. "It's too soon, man. We're hot. No, I don't like what's happening. Come October, this thing with Manny will have cooled off and we'll have more info on what might be happening. Let's hold off like we planned."

Quiet for a moment, Jake then pushed again. "I figured you would change your mind and come back and do this work. It'll be easy money."

"Nothing is ever easy in this business. You know that. I'm not changing my mind. That's firm."

"Well I'm gonna do it with or without your help. You can join me any time you want."

"What the shit is this, Jake? We're partners. I'm saying no."

"Things have changed. Ramon has the raisins. I'm not afraid to go for it."

"Jake, you're not getting my point. Half of everything is mine: the ranch, plane, trucks and all, and I'm not going to give you permission to use them."

"And you're my partner. I'm inviting you to join me."

Hastily I asked, "So you think you have the right in this case?"

"Yes Just join me and everything will go well."

"No, Jake. You don't get it. Absolutely not! I'm usually the one who gets antsy. Now you're all hopped up."

"It's business. It's there and I'm not afraid to get it done."

"Fuck this, Jake. That's twice you've implied that I'm afraid to do this. It's not fear stopping me. It's common sense."

"I'm gonna go with or without you."

"And I'm not gonna change my position."

"There won't be any problems, man. Everything's ready." Jake's arrogant attitude reached home. "The work will be simple. I'm not going to argue with you. Call me if you change your mind. I'm going now."

Hanging up I exploded and cursed out loud. "You arrogant shit! You think I'm afraid. Fuck you. I'm being smart. I'm being patient for once!"

Overwrought with anger, I had to find a way to clear my head and put a stop to this. Jake had never put me in such a predicament. And now that he had conveniently backed out of our agreement, and also wanted to make use of my half of the equipment, without permission, I had to make a move. Should I drive up and talk some sense into his head? And if he decided to work without me, should I charge him a user's fee? No way. I don't want anything to do with this and he's not going to get me to change my mind. Screw him. Let him bring the loads up on his own. More than anything I had to remove these bad-ass thoughts from my mind. But I was so angry I couldn't think straight.

I decided to keep busy and spent the next several days at the boat yard in Sausalito working on my light-weight racing sloop. Making it a project, I peeled the fiberglass from the bottom and was to re-glass the entire hull. The work would take a month.

While eating lunch one afternoon, Al walked over. "Crazy Bill is on the phone."

"Hmmm. What does he want?"

"He says he can't go to Canada. He wants to know if you want to go in his place."

"Hell yes!"

Al looked doubtfully at me as I headed for the phone in the office. When I came out, he and the work crew were just finishing lunch. I sat down on a small bench and Al looked over and asked again if I was going.

"You bet. I wouldn't miss it for the world."

"What about the yard?" he inquired.

Al was a workhorse. He was also handicapped. He had always loved to drink the hard stuff. A few years ago he got good and drunk at the yacht club one night. He wrecked his car and his life and had spent over a year and half in a hospital recuperating from second-degree burns over seventy percent of his body. Most men would have chosen a wheelchair. Not Al. He out-worked the crew. He was an angry man with a big heart and an intelligent mind, but he despised paperwork. I ran the office for the first month, but gave up even knowing our boat yard business might flounder.

"Like I told you a month ago Al, get Fay over here. She needs the work and you need her good smiley face around here." I smiled. He had been procrastinating. "Four or five hours a day ought to do it. She'll have this place in good order in no time." From the beginning, Al agreed he'd run the place. I was to put up money and join him if possible.

The "if possible" was of course where the consternation lay. Crazy Bill, a mutual sailing comrade, had just invited me to Canada. Every other year they sailed the family boat, a classic, varnished hulled thirty-three foot cruising sloop, north to British Columbia. Al had gone to Canada twice with Crazy Bill and his bothers. I'd heard zany stories of their adventures and how outrageously beautiful the fjords were. I'd dreamed about going.

The timing couldn't have been better, I told Al. He backed of by giving me a side-winder smile and regretfully adding, "Good luck."

In two weeks, I'd be leaving for Canada. The vessel was already in

B.C. and the crew and I were to meet with the parents at the B.C. Yacht Club in Vancouver, take delivery of the boat and sail it back to the Bay Area—after we cruised the fjords for a month. Bob and Tom, the father's two younger sons, Stan the Man, our crazy salt of the earth sailing pal and I were the crew. We were going to have a blast. They always had in the past and now it was my turn to join in on all the fun.

I'd been enjoying life for the past two months. I had time to sail with Al and time to party with Ed and Fay. But the pressure was mounting. Jake hadn't finished his job yet and the informer inside Manny's organization had not surfaced.

What was supposed to take Jake two to three weeks was now into its second month. One load had been brought up. I'd called Joanne to get this news and also that Jake and his crew were in the process of bringing up the second load. I'd remained adamant about my decision. Jake had remained adamant about his. But there were times when I felt mighty foolish. Perhaps I had not made a wise decision concerning Jake. I had instead chosen to hide out, keeping negative thoughts at bay by keeping busy—so I could "do my thing."

And day-by-day, dark thoughts crept in. Even though I was enjoying life, internally I was hurting, partly because I knew Jake was screwing up. He needed me. I was the organizer, the analyzer, the one who saw the big picture. He was the energizer and the authoritive sheer plank that anchored the ribs of our business. Each of us acting alone was incomplete—our individual strengths complemented each other and made for a whole, a team that functioned together as one. Yet, I had steadfastly refused to go to him and muster unity.

Several times I considered why I'd refused him, and had come away with a few reasons: one of them had to do with my desire to quit the business. Another had to do with my pride. And, I was angry with him, which tied into pride. And within all of this, I was pretending to be happy when in actuality I had a serious problem that was going unattended.

I was up against the wall and refused to admit it, which allowed denial to take the driver's seat and lead me down a new path toward self-destruction.

I didn't take the time to notice this. Had I taken the time and gained proper insight and desire to confront my pride and the anger within, perhaps I'd have realized the course I was on. Because I didn't and I chose to ride it out, the resistance I'd created was being served up. It was an enfoldment of my karma: push things out of the way and run from them and they'll eventually run you down, no matter how fast or far you run.

So, even though I had given a certain amount of thought to the decisions I had made concerning Jake's actions, these thoughts were far from pure. Impure thoughts have a grip on all of us. They are the very reason we self-destruct. Impure thoughts about how I might get back at Jake came quite often. I'd grow frightened by these thoughts, would drive them away, only to have them pop up again. Finally the thoughts manifested into form, as they always do only I was unaware that I had created these denials. My mother openly sought revenge; I was unconsciously seeking revenge. And so it was that revenge came knocking at my door—literally.

It was a Saturday. Three weeks after, Jake had gone to work without me. I was out back when Fay called to me.

"What's up?"

"There's a strange, little man at the front door. He wants to talk with you."

"Really? Did he give you his name?"

"No. And I didn't let him in. Could he be a narc?"

"I'll check it out."

Cautiously, I approached the front door. From the living room window I could see a powder blue Porsche parked at the curb. It was Manny's, and he stood at the door waiting.

"Manny! What's up? Come on in."

I couldn't believe it. What was he up to? How did he get my address? Ray must have given it to him.

"I know this is unusual," he said after greeting me, careful to not offend me with one of his hugs. "But I want to talk to you. Your brother said you might be of help."

"With what?"

"My bail bond. I need cash and my bondsman won't take my house as collateral."

"Really."

"Ray said you have a good bondsman."

We did. Our attorney Ryan had turned us on to Barrish Bonds and we had used Jerry a few times. He had handled Gil's bond, as well as Bill's and Ray's. And as Manny stood in front of me I thought about the informer. I'd make a trade with him.

"Yeah. He's a good man. If you want we can call him. My dime," I added, as we headed over to the phone.

Placing the call I said, "Hey Jerry, it's Frank. I've someone here who needs help. His name is Manny."

I walked away as the two talked. A few minutes later Manny came back to the living room. He immediately and sincerely thanked me. "I really need some hard cash and he can take my house as collateral. I owe you, Frank." He looked sheepishly at me and added, "I've some other matters to talk to you about and, well, let me tell you what I'd like to do."

"Okay. But first of all, I want to know about the informant that's inside your group, Manny."

"So do I," he said, and began to explain.

Manny's preliminaries in the Marin County case had been delayed several times and his lawyer was furious, but could do nothing. This was highly unusual—and speculative. The judge and the prosecutor were behind the matter. They obviously were coordinating a legal conspiracy to keep the defense from finding out who the informer, or informers, were.

"And you have no idea who it might be or if there's more than one informer?"

"Not really. I think it's the new people we were selling to. The man who takes care of my sales had just met these people. We cut ourselves off from them right after the Marin bust. The rest of my people are totally cool."

"Manny, someone is talking. "

"It's a fact, but we won't know 'til the preliminaries."

"Man! That's something—and your lawyer can't do a thing? That sucks."

"Not entirely. I can still do business. I've good people to work with, but I need some investment money. How about it?"

"I don't think so, Manny."

"Hear me out. I have two Scientology dudes who have a mine sweeper."

"Christ! A mine sweeper! They're over a hundred feet."

He beamed and quickly added, "That's right, and these guys are cool. They spent over a year on L. Ron's yacht in the Mediterranean. They want to work with me. I have two tons of primo weed down in Mexico and they'll bring it up. They want to get going, but they need to haul their boat out and I don't have the money. I need four grand. If you invested with me, I'd pay you back double and let you sell four hundred pounds at a good price."

"Not interested, Manny."

"You wouldn't have to do a thing, just put up the money."

"You'll have thirty-five grand soon. Use your money."

"Jerry said it would take a while, probably a month."

When I again hesitated he coaxed, "Let me give you my number at the house. Call me if you change your mind."

A few days later, I called. Manny's offer was not the entire reason. I wanted to penetrate his group and see if I could come up with who the informant might be. Even as I cooked up the scheme I questioned how I would accomplish my goal without putting heat on myself. And what good would it do me to know who the informers were? I went forward with the plans anyway, knowing that my motives were impure. Something was egging me on. It had to do with Jake and it had to do with some kind of convoluted vengeance trip, and I'd soon find out where that would lead me.

I wasn't surprised when I arrived to see a half a dozen young hippy-type men and women working in Manny's large vegetable garden, terraced in front of his house. The house was on a small hilltop and had a long circular driveway. Manny was out front and greeted me warmly. With him was a man by the name of Brian. Ray had told me this man was in charge of selling Manny's weed. Brian's wife had just given birth to a boy. Brian was holding him. The baby had no clothes on and Brian began bragging about the size of his son's penis, which totally put me off, especially when he held the newborn up for all of us to see.

"Greg and Mark are on their way," Manny cut in, as the swaggering continued. "What do you think of the garden? It's been feeding us for the past few weeks. Come, I'll show you the setup."

It was hot out, but I took the tour and was impressed. Shortly, a car came up the driveway, a vintage red Ferrari. Two men got out. The four of us converged at a patio area where it was shady.

"This is Greg and Mark," Manny introduced us.

They were Manny's age, and they quickly engaged me. They knew all about me and were quick to mention that their minesweeper was at Anderson/Kristofferson's in S.F., waiting to be hauled out.

When the four of us began talking shop about how they'd smuggle the two tons of weed north, I learned they were not only knowledgeable seamen, but were also very capable men. By the time the meeting ended I was convinced they could pull it off. These two were solid in every way. When Manny once again brought up the fact these two had been on L. Ron's yacht for over a year, they didn't brag. They were confident—more so than Manny, and they were ready to go though with their smuggling plans in a way that spoke volumes to their character. I could understand why Manny wanted to work with them.

As to whether or not these two were beyond reproach, as Manny had said, I wasn't certain. They were capable seamen and they had a vessel, and by all accounts it would do the job. When I had asked about possible breakdowns and others matters, they said they had a repair shop set up in the engine room and that one of their crew was a diesel mechanic. Drawn into their plan, I decided to go along with Manny's offer. Arrangements were made and the next day I turned the four grand cash over to Manny.

But the project I invested in several weeks ago was now in limbo. The boat had been readied, but the weed, which was in Mexico under Mack's control, had suddenly disappeared. So had Mack, who had sold the load to Manny four months ago.

The clincher that sent me reeling came a few days after Manny let me know that the entire deal was in jeopardy. Manny did not deliver this news. Brother Ray did, and it brought an end to my dealing with Manny and at the same time became a serious wake-up call.

As the twisted tale unfolded, Manny had been successful with my bondsman and had brought home thirty-five thousand in cash. Two days later it was gone. Ray said that Manny was in a super fit. It appeared that one of his trusted people had gone into Manny's bedroom where the cash was stashed and had made off with it.

I was willing to lose four grand and eat humble pie for a while rather than further jeopardize my position. I'd become a fool who knew how to get out of a bad situation when the time was right.

In the realm of love and gratification, I hadn't done much better. I had met Sharon, a woman my age, tall and quite pretty, who had a four-year-old son. Sharon was a user—on the verge of becoming a grifter. I met her one afternoon when she came over to visit Fay. Before she left I asked her if she'd like to dine with me sometime. She took me up on the offer. Returning to her house after dining at an upscale restaurant, we made love.

Sharon, it turned out, was being kept as a mistress by a man from L.A. who was her "Pamper Daddy." He gave her enough money to live in the style she demanded, so she rented a large house in Tiburon—waterfront dock included.

She wasn't my type at all, but she was available for what I wanted. Her Pamper Daddy showed up only a couple of weekends a month, which gave her ample time to play around, not only with men like me, but also with her Daddy's business. Her gay brother played into this. The two of them ran a retail audio electronics store for him: one of several he owned. Most of these stores were in the L.A. Basin, but the brother was in charge of the one here in Marin Country. He pilfered stereo equipment and sold these items at half price. I found out what he was up to when he offered me a deal on a new tape deck. I bought it and realized afterwards, when he offered me a deal on a new stereo amplifier, what he was up to.

Shortly after this incident I broke off with Sharon. It happened on a Saturday, when the Pamper Daddy showed up unannounced. Sharon and I had come back from a dinner date and were getting amorous in the bedroom—the one he was paying for—when there was a rap on the door. Sharon knew it was him, but she hushed me. He kept pounding and I got nervous. My Porsche was parked in the driveway and I asked her if he had a key—or why it was he didn't have a key to her house. She kept things that way, I was told, and she admonished me to remain calm. How could I? Was he a big dude, I asked? No. He's short and pudgy and he can't run a step without running out of breath. Was she telling me the truth? I didn't know, only that he kept pounding and we lay there, both of us scared and unable to function. When he stopped and she had gone to the window to check that he was gone, I got out of there and never returned. The outcome of this relationship was an obvious wake-up call: I had better come to terms with my fears about Jake working without me—and Manny.

I had made mistakes and I didn't know if it'd be too late to undo any of the circumstances I'd created since Jake and I had parted company. I'd have to find out. Meanwhile, I decided it would be wise to let bygones be bygones and start fresh. Jake was a rational man. We were both understanding people. All we had to do was get together and talk about our follies and get back on track. I'd approach him, not from fear, but from the heart.

I prepared myself to meet with him prior to leaving for Canada. Jake had moved his family to a summer cabin near the Russian River. It was only an hour or so north of Marin County. Letting go of lingering anger, I called and got Joanne on the phone.

Right away I ran into a brick wall. There'd be a few more before this day ended, and my anger toward Jake would return and ripen. Jake had plunged his life into a soap opera. Joanne revealed to me how he had compromised his life the moment I called.

"I couldn't care less where he's at, that sonofabitch... I should leave him…"

"Whoa! Wait a minute, Joanne. What's up? You sound terrible. What did Jake do?"

"He's driving me crazy, that's what. He's with that bitch Jane and he's fucking her. He's been fucking her all summer long. I'm ready to kill her, Frank. She's nothing but trash."

"Hold on, Joanne. Tell me what's happened. Jake is screwing Jane and you just found out, I guess?"

"Yes. He's not only fucking her, he wants her to move in with us."

"Holy shit! What do you mean, move in?"

"Oh God, Frank, I don't know. He's in love with her or she's in love with him. I can't think straight right now."

"Hold on, Joanne. Just be cool. I'll come up and talk with you. Okay? I'll be there as soon as possible."

When I arrived her face was swollen, so I drew her in and gave her a long hug. As we broke, she began sobbing.

"Windy is inside taking care of Johan and Heidi. Let's sit over here." She pointed to a seating area outside on the small patio. In a trembling voice she said, "Jake's been having an affair with your ex-girlfriend, that fucking bitch Jane."

"When did this start?" I asked, waves of anger taking over again. Joanne had already painted a clear picture, but I had to be cool and not blow things, not now, even though Jake had put a wrench in my plans.

"Sometime during the summer. I don't know. I don't care. He's been fucking her and he says she's in love with him."

"She's in love with him! How sweet! Boy, I knew she slept around, but this is too much. Jake hardly knows her. She once told me she couldn't stand the arrogant SOB."

Forehead furrowed and a sour look on her face, she continued. "He hired the bitch to do some work for him. That's what he told me. Now he wants her to move in with us."

"Pardon me! Am I hearing you right? Jake wants Jane to move in with you and the family?"

"Yes. He called me the other day and told me all of this over the phone. Everything. I had no idea and now she's to move in with us."

"What the hell is he up to, Joanne? How can he be so cruel?" I began to pace the patio. "First he messes with me and now with you and the family. Who the hell does he think he is anyway? God, he's pissing me off!" Another stream of anger rolled through. "What did you tell him?"

"We argued." Tears were rolling down her cheeks now. She sobbed. "I told him I didn't know. He said I'd have a few days to think about it."

"A few days? That fuck. Do you know where he's at right now?"

"Yes. He's got a house rented in the city. He's there. They just brought in a load and he's selling it."

"So the second load is finally in?"

"Yes," she stammered, weeping uncontrollably.

Caught up in her emotions, I asked, "And what if Jane was to move in here with you?"

Her Portuguese blood running hot, she said with vengeance, "I'd kill her. I know I would. She's a fucking bitch. I can't stand her. Shit, just the thought of her drives me crazy."

I was moved. In all the years that I'd known them, I felt I knew Joanne better than Jake. Jake, as Mack stated, was aloof and arrogant a good deal of the time. He withheld things. She didn't. She was a truthsayer and delivered stern, often hot, messages— sometimes rational, sometimes not.

"What about your kids, Joanne?"

"I told Windy. She's angry at her father, very angry."

"If Jake gave you a choice, what's he going to do if you say no?"

"He said he'd leave us."

"Bullshit Joanne. I can see through that. Really. Jake may be a shit but he loves his family. Jane's nothing but a tramp. She'll only last a while, no matter what. Can you see that?"

"Yes. But he's done this before and come back. It's always so shitty to have to deal with it and put up with him. I'm tired of it."

Sitting next to her, I placed a hand on her shoulder. "Do you love him?"

Still sobbing, she caught her breath to reply. "Yes, I do." Hesitating, she added, while her face contorted, "I do and I don't. He's got me so pissed right now." She clinched her fists and shut her eyes. Face straining, she cried out, "Yes. I love the sonofabitch. I just do. I don't know why. I just do."

"I think I understand where you're coming from, Joanne. He's a shit, he's got me totally pissed at him, especially right now, but he's also like a brother to me. Why don't you call him on his bluff? Give him an ultimatum. Can you dig it, Joanne? Call his bluff."

Wiping her eyes she said, "You really think that's what he's up to, bluffing us?"

"I can only suggest. He loves his family. He needs you. That's one reason why he wants Jane to move in. He wants her and you at the same time."

"But what if he does leave us?"

"Joanne, I'm your friend. I'll always be that. I'm blown out angry at Jake, but I can't interfere in this. Please, you have to make the decision. I only know what I would do if I was in your place."

Blowing her nose she gave a partial smile. "Then I'll tell him no way. I don't want that bitch living here. I'd probably put poison in her food, or something worse."

"I can only imagine." I smiled at her.

"If that's what you want, then stay with it and believe in what you're doing. Jane has nothing over you. Believe in that, just like I have to. He's my partner, remember? And right now I'm going to go find him and have a heavy talk with him."

On the way to Frisco, topped off with anger, I stopped off at Jane's small apartment. She was surprised to see me and before she could say a word I blasted her but good. She was destroying a family just to satisfy her pussy.

"Don't even say a word, you cunt. You stay away or I'll make trouble for you. You got that?" I departed as quickly as I came.

When I arrived at Jake's stash-house, he was not around. Willy and the boys were and were hard at work. Willy showed me the load in the garage and I was immediately repulsed. In front of me was a huge pile of loose marijuana laid out on a large plastic tarp. It was ugly.

Willy said jokingly as he came up behind me, "It's taco time, man. Why don't you join us? We can use the help."

"What the hell is this? It looks terrible."

"The Mexicans are putting the whole plant in, stems, roots, maybe even a dead rat or two." He smiled and added, "That's why we have to clean the weed. We're losing about twenty percent of the weight, same as the last load."

So this is what Jake and Ramon have been up to—accepting trash like this. I'd have put a stop to this after the first load.

I sighed and shook my head. "And Jake accepted this shit?"

Will nodded, with a glum stare.

"Have Jake call me when he gets back."

A chill ran through my body as I drove off. The work crew appeared to be about half done with cleaning out the sticks. Lord only knows how long they'd been working.

Jake called the next day. "What's up?"

"Let's meet. We have to talk."

"I don't have the time. I'm running around trying to sell this stuff. Ramon's ready with another one. I'll be going down south in a day or so."

How convenient. "That's just great, man. There's a lot for us to converse about."

"Maybe so, but I can't do it right now."

"It would be best for all concerned if you made the time."

"As soon as I get back, we'll talk."

"Is everything okay, business-wise?"

"What do you mean?"

"Just that, Jake. I'm your partner. I want to know. I don't have a clue about what's happening with you, other than that shit Ramon and you brought up."

"Everything's okay. There are a few small problems out at the ranch, but it's being taken care of. Don't worry. I'll tell you about it soon."

"I hope so. This work has lasted more than a few weeks, man. I want an explanation of what's going on."

"You will, as soon as I get back."

"Make it soon. I'll be leaving for Canada in about ten days."

When I arrived at the yard the next day, a surprise awaited me. Brother Bill had sent a letter. Al handed it over immediately. Excited, I ripped it open. The message was timely and short. He and Inger were living in Mexico. When I read that he was looking forward to doing some business, I made a decision. If Jake didn't soon come to his senses, I'd break from him. Maybe it was time. I had just enough money to buy my dream vessel. If Bill could buy a load of high grade and fund my movements, I'd put together a crew and bring up a load myself. To hell with Jake and the pilots! I didn't need them! One good load and I'd have all the money I'd need to take off and sail wherever I wanted. Sibling rivalry or not, the prospect of working with Bill looked far better at that moment than working with Jake. I was ready. It was as good as done.

What I wasn't ready for was the phone call I got a few days before leaving for Canada.

"It's a lawyer by the name of Ryan," Fay, my good roomy said. She smiled and handed me the receiver.

Tensing up I asked, "What's up Ryan?"

He had never called me before. Without greeting me he replied in a haughty tone, "I have some bad news for you. Jake's been busted. He just got through to me a few minutes ago. Can you bail him out?"

CHAPTER TWELVE

JAMAICAN BOGEYMAN

CORTE MADERA, CA
AUGUST, 1970

T HE FJORDS OF British Columbia are, without exaggeration, utterly astounding. On the afternoon of the third day, we set the spinnaker. Though there was a high overcast, a good breeze had set in, enough to reach maximum haul speed. Mountains surrounded us: forested peaks as high as eight thousand feet. I was awestruck by the beauty and the serenity. It was breathtaking—mind-boggling.

Astounding, breathtaking, and mind-boggling were the exact words that grabbed my emotions when our lawyer Ryan informed me that my partner had just been busted.

"Busted! How? Where?"

"At your ranch in Arizona. He wants you to work on bailing him out. He says you know where his money is. Can you handle it?"

"Yes! Sure! Wait! Christ, give me a few details first. Who else did they get?" I was picturing a complete disaster, pilots, drivers, and caretakers, all in jail.

"Jake and three others. That's all I want to say for now. We'll talk later. Good luck."

Even though I was in shock, I now knew quite well what to do next.

Jake had entrusted his money to a close friend. To get to his money, I needed to get hold of Jake's wife. As I called her, confusion set in. What the hell had happened? Jake and three others kept running through my mind. Which three?

Maybe Benny and his girlfriend, and a driver? Shit, the pilots. It had to be. They were busted on the ranch. Shit, the ranch is lost. We can't use it. Jake's fucked up big time. Damn, what did he do to get caught? Boy, he's got me good and pissed, that sonofabitch. We're screwed, and I have to wait to hear from Jake to get the story.

Joanne already knew about the bust. She was calm, though angry, as we discussed the situation over the phone. She'd get to Jake's money and meet me at the bondsman's office in San Francisco the next morning.

Jerry and Jeff, who I was getting to know rather well, were into one of their time-killer card games when we arrived. "Come on you guys. Break loose and let's count some cash," I requested lightheartedly. This was serious, but at least I knew how to handle this part.

Jake's bail was thirty-five thousand. "It's all here, including your ten-percent."

"We're on the case, buddy. We'll process the bond right now. He'll be out by tomorrow, promise."

We were getting good at the bonding game. In the past, it had sometimes taken us three or four days to spring our people. But now that these guys were almost our employees, we got top-notch service; one of them, Jeff, was an old high school acquaintance.

Joanne and I hung around while they processed the bond. They cheered us up as best they could.

The next afternoon I met up with Jake at the airport. I wanted to greet him as he came off the plane. But Jake was in a foul mood, unshaven and in soiled clothes, and he brushed by me without even a handshake. He was abrupt and contemptible.

"Come on. I want to get out of here and get a shower."

"Sure. Just slow down. Lighten up a bit, will ya?"

He wouldn't. I practically had to jog to keep pace with him as he marched quickly through the crowd. It wasn't going to be easy. He was being a total arrogant prick. "Keep your cool man," I told myself. "Don't let him get to you. He's the one who ought to be humble." But Jake doesn't do humble very well. He streamed through the parking area at an ever increasing rate with me still at his heels, my anger building.

When we got into my car he demanded, "Take me to San Mateo."

Shaking with rage and a how-dare-you–treat-me-this-way attitude, I retorted, "Look Jake, I'm gonna take you to Joanne's mom's house, but I want you to know before we talk that there's a good chance I'll dissolve this partnership unless you come to a complete understanding with me. That's all for now. Once you're cleaned up, let's talk. I'm leaving for Canada tomorrow morning and I don't want what's happened to you to stop me."

"Fine. Just get me there." He wouldn't look at me. He had regressed into one of his funks. What else did I expect?

We drove in silence, his mother-in-law's house a short ten minutes away. Joanne was there to greet her man, but Jake brushed by her too and headed directly for the shower.

"He's being a complete ass," I told her. "I've never seen him like this. If he doesn't cool it, we're finished." I told her the reasons I was considering breaking from Jake.

She was even more worried. What would Jake do if I didn't lend them my support?

Ever since hearing of the bust I'd considered the situation from every possible angle. What stuck most in my mind was that if I dissolved the partnership, Jake would just mess things up all the more. The problems he had created would compound. The pilot would talk. So would his woman, maybe even the driver. Common sense and wisdom told me to stay with Jake, straighten this damnable mess out, and keep myself off the indictment sheets. Find out what happened first. Proceed from there. Be calm. Be understanding. Jake's ego had just taken a heavy blow. So had mine.

"Tell me what happened? Who got busted with you?" I asked, as we sat at the kitchen table alone. Jake was more relaxed. A good washing perhaps had cleansed away the sordid moments he had recently experienced.

"Just me and the drivers: Dan, Howie, and Randy."

Shocked but relieved I asked, "What about the pilots?"

"We didn't use the plane."

"I'm confused. Explain."

"We didn't need to use the plane. We used a camper. Ramon crossed the load at the border near Sasabe. It's a new method. Howie and Dan made the pick-up. Everything went fine until we got to the ranch."

"Jake! Why would you need to go to the ranch? And what the hell were the narcs doing at the ranch? What gives?"

He rolled his eyes. "It's a long story."

"Go for it."

"We'd been going to Winslow for gas and supplies and we got familiar with a few people in town, this one guy in particular, a gas station attendant. He's a nice dude, a Vietnam vet with long hair. I told him we had a ranch."

"Wait a minute. Why would you tell him about our ranch?"

"We come in there all the time for gas. I had to say something to him. It's strange otherwise. If I didn't have a sound story, he'd get suspicious. He's local, and in a small town news gets around. I wanted to let him know what we were up to out there, so I told him we were dividing the property and putting up a nice ranch house for starts and we'd be building a few houses in the future. He wanted to know if there was any chance we would hire him on as a carpenter. Dan and Howie got to know him also. He was the only one in town who knew where the ranch was. He must have been the one who informed the authorities. That's the only thing I can think of."

Upset that he had been so foolish, I said sarcastically, "You told him where the ranch was located?"

Without even looking shamefaced Jake replied, "Yes. I was going to hire him to do some work out there."

Be nice, Frank, I instructed myself. This was ugly. I let out a sigh of exasperation and did my best.

"Shit, Jake." Falling back in my seat I reprimanded him, "That's the very thing we talked about from the beginning. No one was to know where the ranch is except our employees, the guys we know, the men we trust. It's hard to believe you'd do something like this and not let me know."

He was silent. He had had his reasons for doing what he had done and I had to accept this, no matter how convoluted the story. And what rang loud and clear had everything to do with Jake's ego. He had given information out about the ranch simply to satisfy his ego—that part of him, or any man, who felt insignificant. His insecurities had gotten in the way, sure as hell. The gas station attendant could have been waved off with any story that would have satisfied anyone's curiosity about why Jake and his people were coming around—so what that it might be a lie?

Standing up, I paced the room. "Go on, man. Tell me the rest."

"I'm sure it was him. I talked with Joe, our Los Angeles attorney. I'm going to have him handle the case. He'll find out what happened through the courts. He's pretty sure they screwed up with the arrests and had improper search warrants."

"Great!" I said sarcastically again. Taking a moment to think about the whole matter I began to lighten up. Things didn't look so bad after all. Maybe we'd catch a few breaks and get out of this. As for the ranch, we could no longer use it, but we could sell it and find another choice piece of property.

"What rights did the narcs have coming on to our property in the first place?"

"Joe figures that's where we got them," Jake explained. He was out of his funk, but sullen and defiant. "They had no rights."

"Jake, if you got the load at the border why did you go to the ranch?"

"I wanted to weigh it and repack it."

"I see. So if you hadn't gone there they wouldn't have caught you?" I was upset because I wouldn't have chosen such a procedure.

"The narcs were on to us. They would have gotten us sooner or later."

I agreed and switched my line of questioning. "Tell me about the bust. How'd the narcs pull it off?"

"Complete surprise, man. They waited until we were well into weighing and boxing, then they sprung out of the woods, screaming at us not to move. One of them was filming us with an eight-millimeter movie camera. Not much more to say than that. They arrested us and brought us to Winslow."

I was quiet for a moment, reflecting on what Jake had just told me and deciding what to say next. We'd been through so much together and at that moment I was terribly angry, but I didn't feel it would be wise to come down on him.

I looked directly at him. "I'm only sorry you didn't heed the advice I gave you when we first bought the ranch. You could have simply started going to Payson if things got hot in Winslow. You could have taken the time to do that."

"I'm not so sure going to Payson for supplies would have solved the problem."

"To me, it would have made all the difference. I'm just pissed you didn't see this."

"If you'd have been with me in this you would have."

Annoyed and feeling a strain of guilt, I retorted, "Yes I know. That crossed my mind more than once over the summer. Right now we have a ranch we can no longer use and a court battle once again. This time it's you they want and they have you unless our smartass lawyer gets you off the hook. And we won't know why and how the narcs got on to you until the preliminaries."

"How about you? Why don't you stay here and help out. Cancel the trip to Canada? Ramon will have plenty of good merchandise. We can get going."

"Just what I didn't want to hear from you Jake," I said, doing my best to be calm. "Put yourself in my shoes for a moment. You'll see that I'm the one who got screwed here. Before this bust came down, I was damn close to breaking up the partnership. It's what I had wanted to talk to you about when you said you didn't have time to talk with me. I think you sensed this and that's why you squirmed and avoided me. Surely Jane told you I gave her a word of warning."

I had the floor and Jake had to listen. "I've been thinking about why you went against my advice. You even put me down and I couldn't make you see the truth. I had a hunch the work would take longer than two weeks.

But you went against me and worst of all, you went against yourself. Now you're hurting. So am I. We no longer have a usable ranch and we have three people in jail. The narcs will want them to talk. What's gonna happen down the line when it comes time for a trial and all of you are facing five to ten years in jail?"

"I hear everything you're saying. They won't talk."

"But if something bad happens, they will. And I'm cooked, brother, just the way you are right now. And that's the main reason why I'm gonna remain your partner. I'm here to work with you and to protect my own interests. If I walk away from you and from them, it would be a big mistake, so I'm going stay on and work with you. But things are going be different from here on out. I want you to agree that we'll work together to make changes that will aid us in regrouping. We can work things out when I get back from Canada. I'm going. I won't be back until the end of September."

"Fine. I'm with you, but Ramon's got more work. I want to get some revenue. This bust wiped me out."

"Come on, Jake! Back off. Did you hear what I just said? Go on a vacation. Shit, go fly the plane like you said you would. Find a few mountains to climb, something other than this work. Can't you see you're letting this life take charge of you? We came into this business so we could have the time to do the things we wanted to do. That's why I'm going to Canada. Does that make sense to you?"

"Sure does, but put yourself in my shoes. We need to get out of this mess. I want to get going. Join me now."

"Don't push me. Just don't. I'm not into controlling you. I can only hope you'll respect my advice, like getting rid of Jane. She's just another bad-news affair and I well understand that you're enjoying screwing her. She's great in the sack, but your family is angry with you and hurting, man. Think about them first, not about pussy. Be with them and enjoy life with them. When I come back I'll be refreshed and ready to work with you. We can figure out how to get out of this one. Let's just get ready to work together as we've done in the past."

Jake looked miserable as I drove home my point. He always clammed up when hit with the truth, which drove me crazy. Why Joanne and I liked this man was a mystery. As Joanne had said to me a few days back, "I love him, I don't know why, I just do."

Standing there and looking at him I wanted so badly to sock him in the face—so that it might jar his senses. Maybe it would wake him up to the fact that he was a self-centered, arrogant, shithead. People, I had learned, can only handle so much in the way of truth being thrown at them. Jake was not ready to hear all that was on my mind and in my heart so I let things be. All I could think to say at this juncture was, "By the way, I'm in touch with Bill. He's in Mexico. He wants to do business with us."

The day we departed in the doctor's van, not more than two hours from the city, we passed a Volkswagen van that had a sign "Oregon or Bust" in big bold letters on the back. Two bikini-clad foxes were inside.

"Whoa! Did you see that? Slow down! Let 'em catch up!" Stan, the prankster, shouted. So, the cruise had begun. Stan was in top form.

In Vancouver, Canada, we met up with Bob's parents. Two days later, under auxiliary power, we reached Captain's Island. The next day we were in Princess Louisa Straights. It was while staying there for the next three days that I truly began to relax. Relieved for the time being, I joined my pals. We hiked on the local trails and feasted on the dense forests that were ever present, as were the mountains that rose up eight to nine thousand feet. There was not much time to think about the problems facing me at home. Nature called and played its part to perfection. Each location we visited had the same effect. Two buckets of fresh oysters were gathered at low tide from off a shoal one afternoon. When we ran out of beer, we cruised off to a trading post in search of libation. At the end of the third week, we headed for Vancouver Island.

The following day, we joined up with a couple the three of them had met two years ago then we headed home. It took five days but we sailed into San Francisco Bay on a picturesque, Indian Summer day with a *primo* wind, moored the vessel, washed it and headed home.

Forty days had passed. There had been several hangovers—mostly Stan's—lots of laughs, a full day filled with exasperating fog conditions, but the cruise was now history and the voyage had been everything I wanted it to be. Pressing problems that had weighed me down had mostly been held at bay. And with no partner around to get me cross, I greeted Fay with a big hug as she met me at the door. Tired and in need of a shower, I carried my gear in, ready to tell them about the good times.

Facing me with an uneasy manner she said, "We're fine, honey." She hesitated and added, "Jake called us a couple of days ago. He wanted me to tell you something as soon as you came home."

"What's that?" I had been cautioned; her soft-hearted words carried more than just a simple message.

With a look that reeked of disappointment, she replied. "There's been another bust. Not with Jake. He's okay, but he wants you to call him right away."

"Unbelievable," I thought. "What's he up to now? He said he wouldn't work while I was gone." Fay was sorry and I was livid—my breath once again taken away.

"I'll call him as soon as I shower."

✯ ✯ ✯

"Jake, I'm back. Fay gave me a briefing. What the hell is up?" I was not in the mood to be formal.

"We've got a lot to talk about, brother. We should get together first thing tomorrow morning. I've some good news to go along with the bad news."

"Nice welcome home, man. Who's in jail this time?"

"I'll tell you now so you can prepare yourself for tomorrow. There were two busts; three people are in jail. Ramon and I are working to get them out. Bob and Jeff were in the first bust and your friend Dwight was in the second."

I was no longer in shock because numbness had taken over. "I need to think about this. All of a sudden I'm fucking pissed, man. Let's meet in the park tomorrow at ten—our usual spot."

"Fine. I'll be there. Get some rest. You sound tired."

The next day was weather fit for Paradise. Starting my Porsche up for the first time in over a month, I took off, my mind in tatters, wondering just how in the hell Jake and I were going to work our way out of these maddening circumstances. And how I would find a way to co-exist with this man? Once again I thought about disconnecting from him. Those thoughts didn't last long. I had no choice but to hang in. Jake and I were a unit. If we were going to survive this racket, we had to find a way to work together as before. But, it was going to take a supreme effort on my part. I'd have to put up with him and in doing so I'd have to truly learn what it meant to be open-minded.

Jake greeted me with a strong handshake and began talking as we took a seat on a park bench. "It'll be rough putting things back together."

"Well, I was hardly expecting the grisly news, especially since I advised you not to do any work while I was gone. I hope you have some decent news about what happened. I don't want to have to puke," I replied, humorlessly.

"That's up to you, man. No matter what I say, you're not gonna like it, but I've got lots of news, both good and bad. I hope the trip to Canada did you good because you're going to need it. First of all, I didn't work alone. Berkeley Bill came in with me on this. Also, Ramon's hurting financially. Manny's been completely wiped out and we're sinking fast. We do have some financial support from Berkeley Bill."

Berkeley Bill was Ben's associate; both were men I'd sold a lot of weed to over the past several months. They were solid people, older dudes, who had been around quite a while: men we trusted.

"How'd he get involved in this?"

"I went to him and Ben right after you left. Ramon called and had a load for us. I needed investment money and Bill wanted in. He lost a lot of cash on this bust too, including his camper truck. Now he's helping us to bail Bob and Jeff."

"Bob, Stan's brother, and Jeff, my brother Ray's friend?" I repeated.

"Yes. Both of them are cool. We'll have them out soon, maybe today."

"How did they get popped? Give me the details."

"Okay. Ramon was using his new location to cross, the one down by the border between Nogales and Sasabe. He crossed it to us okay, but in order to get out of the area we had to get past the roving customs checks they set up. We knew that would be our only hard spot. Once past the customs boys, it's drive home safely. Willy was the lead man. He and the drivers were in touch by walkie-talkie. The problem was, customs set up shop in a very smart place, on a blind turn. Willy said he was completely taken by surprise. The customs boys were all over him and he couldn't pick up his radio or else the agents would see him and know he was up to something. The drivers were hanging back a couple of miles and drove right into the block. The customs boys found the load and took them straight to jail."

Exhaling a deep breath, I replied. "No more border crossing at Sasabe, Jake. I don't care how easy it is for Ramon. We gotta plane, let's use it. If you don't agree to this I'm gone—as in, out of your life."

"Okay. You got it. Ramon's gonna say a thing or two, but I agree. We'll use the plane."

"What about the second bust?"

"That's touchy man. Dwight was driving a load of four hundred pounds. The batteries in his radio went dead and he didn't know it. He drove right into the customs stop. Willy was in the right place this time, trying to tell him to stop." Jake looked over at me and pondered. Something was up. "Frank, the bad news here is he was in your van."

Springing to my feet I cursed out at him. "Fuck! That's Marty's van, too!" So much for being cool! Is this what I get for being nice? Marty, my real estate broker and I had bought a beautiful custom van several months back. It was loaded with special features. We used it for camping trips. I had loaned it to Jake before leaving for Canada. He was to use it for its real purpose: camping.

"I know. Calm down."

Although on the verge of flying into hysterical rage, I stood silently, my body getting more and more tense, until I was shaking. Taking a deep breath to expel the rage I responded with deep, satisfying contempt, "How... could you do this, Jake? How...how could you possibly be so fucking low? I told you to use it for camping, remember? Not to run a load of fucking weed across, you fuck."

"Listen Frank, Ramon had the stuff. We needed to move. Your van was there. It was all we had."

"It's not my van, you fucking shit. It's registered in Marty's name. I bet you haven't even called him. Am I right?"

"Yes. I didn't think to. Not yet."

"Jesus Christ, man. Where's your head?" I screamed, my arms flailing. Hate poured through me as I looked at him. I was close to striking him. The look on his face was sorrowful, yet his mouth showed defiance. I continued my verbal attack.

"You had no right to use my van no matter how you look at it. Didn't you consider that? Do you think Marty would have let you use it? Did you even consider giving him any compensation had you been successful? Did you, Jake?" My Mom had taught me the guilt manipulation trick well. She'd have been pleased.

"Calm down, will ya? I told you we needed to get a load over. I didn't think about it. You're right about all of it. I was..."

"Fucking desperate!" I interrupted. "Right, Jake? You were desperate, just like you are right now. What the hell is happening with you? You don't give a shit about anyone but yourself, man. You're probably still fucking Jane, right? Maybe Mack and Bill are right: you're arrogant. You put up a facade to protect yourself, to hide all those insecurities you pack around. That's what I see. You're a shit, man. A real fucking shit."

In a huff, I walked away, my mind broken. I was falling apart. So this is life. This is taking responsibility. This is what being open-minded is all about? Where are you God? We gotta talk. I kept walking, Jake at my heels saying something I didn't want to listen to.

"I'm going to get Jane out of my life and get back with my family.

Okay? I made a big mistake using your vehicle. I'm paying for it now. Go ahead. Get angry." Jake trailed behind, attempting to console me.

Not bothering to look at him I berated him further. "I'm the one who's paying. You put the screws to me."

"I'm waiting to hear you say that I brought down your whole life, Frank. You can only put just so much blame on me. The rest is yours. I asked you to join me. You never did."

Great! Everyone had justifications for their screw-ups. Jake's stank. "Terrific, now we're going to argue that I didn't do as you asked?" I stopped to glare at him. "Is that what this is?"

"No. Only that you didn't join in with me when you could have. Think about it, Frank. You had that choice, but you didn't want to for whatever reasons, so I went to work without you. I wanted you to join me. You're my partner."

Walking away again, my mind in tatters, I considered Jake's statement as we headed around the lake in silence. I didn't want to say anything in response, but he initiated the next conversation.

"You're not the only one hurting. Ramon's hurting too. He brought a good-sized load across for Manny. Manny's people got it across okay. They got it north to Nevada and were ripped off. Ramon said the drivers came out of their motel room the next morning and the truck was nowhere in sight."

I stopped in my tracks. "What? Manny was ripped off again?"

"You could say that. Ramon was the one who got ripped off. He fronted the entire load to get Manny operating capital."

The oddball story caught my attention. Momentarily shocked, I forgot about our differences.

"Who ripped him off? Do you know?"

"Two guys who were working for Manny—Greg and Mark."

The second those two names spilled out of Jake's mouth, scenes from two months ago flashed in front of me. I felt my knees go weak as I recalled how these two had taken me in. Guilt and shame hit at my core, as this realization hit home.

"Holy shit! I met those dudes. They seemed solid. Tell me more. I want to know everything. Did Ramon tell you this?"

"Well, they were solid alright. They were the ones who informed on Manny."

"They were the informers?"

"You got it. I'd say these guys were heavyweight. They weren't narcs. They were more like mercenaries and when they found out Manny was into smuggling drugs they went to the DEA. I guess the DEA let them act as informants—and it worked.

"Jake, I met these guys two or three times during the summer!" I told Jake about the deal I'd worked with Manny. "I was taken in by them too."

"Well, you weren't the only one, man. They fooled Manny all the way," Jake said. "They were in charge of the load and they drove off with sixteen hundred pounds of weed. And easy day's work, wouldn't you say?"

Exasperated and feeling like a complete fool, I let out a deep sigh. "I had my doubts about them in the beginning, but Manny said they had been Scientologists a long time and they had been on board L. Ron's yacht for several months. They were beyond reproach." Then in a stilted voice I added, "I was helping them set up a drug run."

"So, they got to you too?"

"Those sonsofbitches, they must be laughing about this. Sixteen-hundred pounds! Scott free! At a hundred and fifty a pop, that's over three hundred grand. We're in the wrong business, Jake. Let's become mercenaries and paralyze guys like Manny. He's easy prey."

"Yeah, I got you man, but that's not our thing."

"You're right, but what a joke on all of us." I laughed disdainfully. "Manny must have felt like a complete fool when he got word these two drove off with his load. He was so high on them. They were his salvation—and they turned out to be the informers. What a total bummer. They destroyed him, man, totally destroyed him. How's he going to bounce back from this one? And how is it that Manny, with all his Scientology training, couldn't pick up on them?"

"Well, you well know he's out of touch with reality."

"Yeah. Jesus, it might have been these guys who ripped off Manny's bail money." I explained how I had helped Manny and about what Ray had told me.

True to his character Jake mocked me, "So the master charmer got to you, too."

When I failed to respond, Jake added," Well at least I have some good news."

I waited, my mind and heart loaded with thoughts about Manny and his demise.

"Wanna hear it?"

"Of course," I said, but holding my breath.

"Berkeley Bill and his pal Ben want us to help them haul some *gunji* out of Jamaica. It sounds really hot, and they're good people to work with. He knows we're hurting. He wants us in on this. Bert wants to fly for us also. We're to meet with them tomorrow."

I exhaled with relief. "Good! Fine! Terrific! Let's join them. Is there any more news you haven't told me about yet?"

"Nah. Just that we stand a chance of getting the whole case thrown out of court. That kid was the one who did the snitching all right. He went out to the property on his own and snooped around and found a kilo that Bob had stashed there. He took it off the property and turned it over to the sheriff. That's how they got us. Joe said the guy had no right to remove the weed and he's planning to suppress the evidence."

"I don't know if that's good news or bad news, Jake. What the hell was Bob doing leaving grass to be found?"

"He was stupid, that's all. I don't know. Why did the kid come out and snoop? It happened."

I pointed my finger at him. "No more, Jake. No more. We're running a fucking silly circus here. There are too many people around. Let's go back to basics: drivers, pilot, you, me and Ramon."

"We ain't got any drivers left. They're all in jail."

"Funny, Jake! Funny! I've got a sound plan about the future and I want you to hear me out."

"Hey, go ahead. I'm all ears."

"First of all I want us to consider working with Bill."

"Good. He's one more connection for us. More than likely he can get us the good weed."

"More than likely, yes. We can figure on that. The other plan is more for the future, hopefully around January. Let's get a few loads over now with the plane. Are Ben and Betsy still available?"

"Yeah."

"Good. Let's use them. Let's bring a few loads over, pay off all the debts, then sell the ranch and the plane and buy a forty-foot sailboat. I have just the one in mind. It's lightweight and has a big interior, Jake. We could bring up to a ton at a time—nothing but super weed."

"Boats take too long. We could fly a ton across in a couple of weeks, man."

"I know that. I'm looking at better control. There'd be no pilots or drivers, just you and me and a couple of crew members. Profits would be huge."

"I can't consider doing that right now."

"It's for the future, Jake. Think about it. Two loads a year. We could make two hundred grand each with one trip."

"Let's use the plane and talk about this later. Berkeley Bill comes first. Let's get this Jamaican operation going."

"Tell me what you know about their plans."

Ben and Berkeley Bill were our best customers, along with Irving. Both were well over six feet tall. Bill was in his forties and was considered a beatnik. During the previous two years I had fronted them quite a bit of business, mainly through Ben. Ben was safe to work with and calm under pressure, and always paid quickly. Bert, a pilot we had met through the two of them but hadn't used yet, was to be the pilot.

The three of us arrived at Ben's house in Berkeley around noon the following day. We were introduced to an older dude, Ralph, a close friend of Bill's, who was a journalist and a former CIA agent. He was to be the central man in the operation. I was impressed with him; he kept all of us on the edge of our seats with smart rhetoric. He too was a sailor. We would use his fifty-foot schooner. Tim, a friend of Ralph's, had flown in from Jamaica where he'd been living for the past few years.

"Right now we're sitting on eighteen hundred pounds of top grade Jamaican *gunji*," Tim related.

Ralph brought out aviation charts and pointed out Kingston International airport, and began describing how the operation would work. "Seventy miles away and across this mountain range," he pointed out, "is an old WWII airstrip. It's huge and it's unused. I saw it from the ground with Tim a month ago. It's the pick-up zone."

Tim added, "We have routes to get in and out of there through the jungle. My people say no one uses the strip."

"What's kind of condition is it in?" Bert asked.

"Lots of grass growing up between cracks, that's all. There's no real problem with the strip itself," Ralph insisted. "Once you pick it up Bert, we fly it to a small island off Bimini right here," he pointed. "It's got a small, uncontrolled airstrip on it. There are a few natives around and I know the British families there. They live away from the strip. We'll be coming in at dusk. We land the plane, wait 'til dark, and unload. My schooner will be nearby. I have a twelve-man raft. We can load it at night and be in Miami the next evening. Bill and Ben will be renting a house along the waterfront and will take it from there."

We poured over the details all afternoon: cost of the weed, transportation, who would handle what, and how the expenses were to be covered. Everything fell into place. No one differed with the plan.

All in order, we ended the meeting. We set a timetable of a week to ten days to get everything in place. Excitement took hold. This was one sharp group of brothers.

Jake couldn't leave the state or his bond would be rescinded, so I got the go-ahead to depart for Miami, along with Bert and Bill. Tim had flown back to Jamaica and Ralph was already in Miami. Leaving four days after the meeting, we took a commercial flight to Miami and checked into a motel. Ralph showed up. We went over strategy. Bert, as planned, was to charter a Piper Apache for a three-day period. He and Ralph were to make a dry run. They were to fly to Kingston and go through customs then go check out the old WWII airstrip.

Ralph updated us as we gathered around him. "I'll let the local authorities in Kingston know I'm on a journal assignment. Bert is my private charter pilot. British customs is quirky, but I know how to handle them."

The next day they took off for Jamaica to stay overnight in Kingston, planning to leave the next morning, land on the old strip and check it out, then return to Miami. We wanted to be sure our plans were going to work.

Two nights later Ralph and Bert showed up, tired, weary, and ill-tempered. We had already received a brief call from them when they landed in Miami. "The plane's out. We got caught," was all they had said. We had to sit tight until they arrived.

"What went wrong?" Bill asked, the moment they walked in, still blown away by the acid message Ralph had delivered an hour before.

"If I hadn't been there I'd find it hard to believe," Ralph said bewildered. We were all ears.

"Well, get on with it," Bill said anxiously. "Tell us what happened."

Ralph began. "We flew in yesterday and met up with Tim in town, and discussed what time to meet and at what end of the strip. Tim said everything was fine. He was ready. So was the airstrip. The next morning Bert and I cleared customs no sweat, flew off and headed for the landing site. Just as we were ready to come in for a landing, both of us noticed that the grass on the center section of the field was mowed down. Someone had recently landed there."

"Had any of you seen it," Bert interjected, "you'd have noticed it right off. It was a big plane that made those marks, very big."

"We put down as planned," Ralph continued. "Tim and his people drove out in a jeep. He was upset. So were his people. He said a big four-engine jobber had just been there and taken off. Whoever it was loaded about ten tons of grass into the plane in about forty-five minutes. There was something like four army deuces carrying the stuff and about eight or ten Jamaicans helping six or seven guys from the plane. After hearing this, we got out of there real quick."

"Then we got rousted out of the sky," Bert chimed in. "Right after we took off, a plane comes out of nowhere. It was a small prop job with the Royal Air Force emblems all over it. He wanted me to land, so we put down in Kingston. Customs was all over us the second I taxied up. They searched us and the plane, every square inch."

"Then they interrogated us. They wanted to know why we landed on the field," Ralph added. "I told them I was curious and had my pilot land the plane. I doubt if they bought the story, only that they let us go. Now they have information on us. We're suspects. We can't operate out of Jamaica, guys, not with a plane."

"Wow! That had to have been a government job," I interjected.

"Without a doubt," Ralph agreed. "The RAF pilot spotted us in the area. He had to make sure we would not interfere with the operation. I know how they work. They run an operation; they watch over it to make sure everything goes off as planned. We were not part of the plan. They're pros, and considering the size of the plane, I'd bet the government used one of their own. The British run this place. They're aware the Jamaicans grow weed all over the island. They're soft with the natives and it's a well-known fact that the people of Jamaica grow up smoking the stuff, so why not make the best of it? Ten tons, that's big time. The government is the only outfit capable of running a sophisticated operation like that."

With the room abuzz with talk and our plans crushed, Ralph began talking with Bill. He wanted to handle the entire trip from Jamaica to the mainland by boat. We were to be phased out. I sat and listened for a while. It was late and Bert and I were tired. We excused ourselves and headed back to our rooms.

Back in San Francisco the next day, I ran the story by Jake and added sarcastically, "We got run out of Jamaica by a Boogeyman."

It was a bleak moment. With no immediate alternative plans to work on we had to count on Ramon. It was early in the year. Ramon would find a way to get things going, and Bill was a solid second. Whatever our next move was we had to make it work. The Jamaican venture had cost us a good deal of money and had eaten up precious time.

CHAPTER THIRTEEN

THE DECEIVER

MARIN COUNTY
NOVEMBER, 1970

THERE WAS A POSITIVE SIDE to our next move: I was to take a trip to Mexico. The downside was that Jake had to go to Arizona and attend his preliminaries.

The trip to Mexico came as a surprise when Al informed me one day that he was to sail to Mexico aboard a thirty-seven foot racing sloop. A crew member had to cancel at the last moment and Al asked if I'd be interested in going along as a replacement.

I gave him a nod and immediately sent a telegram to Bill. A day later he called me at the yard. The race was to start in Long Beach and end in Mazatlan. As luck would have it, Bill and Inger were living in Mazatlan.

"Mack's going to turn me on to his super-weed connection in Guadalajara," Bill let me know after I told him I'd be there in mid-November.

Ramon, who was having problems procuring contraband, had me in a fit. Financially, he'd taken a beating and had no money to purchase a load. He'd lost over forty-eight hundred pounds of weed the past three months and he told Jake he owed money to the people he worked with. He was strapped and desperate, as we were, but he steadfastly refused to let on what his real troubles were. Out of desperation, I suggested to Jake that I would go south with Ramon and see firsthand what problems he was facing. Jake wouldn't agree with my proposal.

When the sail race came up, and with the imminent prospect of getting the high-grade connection from Bill through Mack, I backed off.

Four months ago I had over forty grand. When Jake went down I had less than thirty. Joining back up with him, the Jamaican operation, and the bond money, had left me with less than five grand. Jake sold a Harley Davidson Roadster that he'd bought several months back and now had a few grand left from that. Essentially, we were broke, but both of us had low overheads. Jake had moved from the Russian River to his mother-in-law's house.

With no money to cop a load, pressure was mounting. We composed ourselves and made plans to find new connections and alternative methods to get out from under our problems.

The government wanted to put our asses in jail and the first step in winning the battle against the giants was for Jake and me to come together as one. Both of us had made foolish decisions in the past. Now we had to pay the price.

We had to count on good fortune to come our way. We believed that eventually, we'd once again rise up and dig out of the hole we had both created. But our good fortune, as we were to find out, would go by the wayside, and problems of an even graver nature would besiege us over the next several months. And each and every time problems arose, we had to find a way out or else go down with the business.

As for the law authorities, they had a job to do just like us, and we had to come up with clever ways to keep them off our backs. With a multitude of drug rings operating in the Bay Area, the DEA was kept busy. And, seeing that they were a newly formed law enforcement body they had little manpower to keep surveillance on us. In our case, we presumed the DEA counted on the courts to win out.

There were over forty racing machines at the start line for the eleven hundred mile trek from Long Beach to Mazatlan. The weather was perfect Southern California conditions: small seas and a ten to twelve knot breeze. The big machines took off leaving us with the smaller boats. Come nightfall, only few boats were in sight and as morning came around, not one was in sight. But the wind held fair and we sailed downwind with strong breezes in the afternoons and light winds throughout the evenings.

The owner of the boat took care of the navigation and his pal did all the cooking. He had stocked the boat with food from the three supermarkets the captain owned, so we were a well-fed crew. Al was on watch with one other crew member and I was on the second watch with a man who was prone to sea sickness. I didn't mind. I got a lot of helm time in.

What I especially enjoyed was the waxing moon. On the fourth night out I witnessed a celestial delight that made me remember the goals I had set would be mine—if I could find a way out of this mess and make money.

The sunset that evening was spectacular. Clouds covered the western horizon, speckled with gold, purple, and mauves of all hues. And, as the sun fell a full moon rose, seemingly climbing up out of the depths of the rich, blue ocean. Moonbeams made their way across the water and as darkness took over, the deep blue sea became silvery gray.

The vessel, with its spinnaker set, was clipping along at a steady six to seven knots through a body of water that was near perfect: a long, gentle, rolling swell, cast in silver beams that were becoming more pronounced by the rising moon. The wind was warm and welcoming. We were in tropical regions and were dressed for the occasion.

By the time Al came on watch at 4:00 a.m. I was transfixed. I could not get enough. The warm wind had held steady, and as the boat slid downwind with purpose and ease, I became a stargazer. I had to take hold of the moment and let it burn into my soul, where it would lay in escrow for the day I'd need to bring it forth.

So I stayed on deck to indulge in the ever-changing effects of all that was before me, highlighted by the moon that cast reflective trails of silver upon the liquid gray mass, and the silver patterns creating dark shadows that marked our path as we sped south.

Shivers shot throughout my body as the descending moon turned orange. When celestial darkness fell upon us the heavens above came alive; millions upon millions of stars gave us a show to behold, all of them transmitting light into my soul, and sweet scents of an unknown nature captivated my senses.

Then the sun began to rise. When a crack of sun appeared it brought with it colors of deep red, which soon turned to orange as the orb made its way up. Peering to the west, darkness held on and the Milky Way was still visible. But soon the light took over and Al admonished me.

All I wanted was to soak in the splendor of the moment, but I had to bargain with my duties

"Hey. Get some sleep, Frank. The sun's up now. You have to stand watch in a couple of hours."

Begrudgingly, I slipped below to the comfort of a sleeping bag.

On the seventh day out we spotted Mazatlan. By 4:00 that afternoon, with the spinnaker drawing and a stiff breeze on our quarter, we sailed into the mouth of the harbor, dropped sails, and anchored.

Ashore at the yacht club, a party was under way. When the boat was made ready a water-taxi took us ashore. With hardly any room to move about freely, I had just grabbed an ice-cold beer when Don tapped me on the shoulder.

"Hey dude, good to see ya. How was the race, man? Kind of excitin', I bet."

Don was one of those do or die Northern California surfers who didn't know enough to get out of the water on a cold winter day—the kind of dude I admired for his singular dedication to his one true love, the surf. We'd known each other since grade school.

Surprised to see him, I gave him a hug. "Yeah, man, it was great. Damn, I thought that was you on the jetty...You dink. What are you doing here?"

"Just hanging loose, dude. Getting high and enjoying the rays and visiting with your bro."

"Where's he at?"

"Outside, waiting. He didn't want to come in. You know, he's being cool—wants some distance from the crowds."

"I can dig it, man. Let's go. I got no business here."

We made our way through the throng of yachtsmen, already drunk and getting more belligerent by the second. Just beyond the club gate I spotted Bill leaning against a car. As we approached a smile spread across his face, and we embraced for the first time in over a year. Dressed in shorts, tank-top and sandals, he looked great. "You look like life's treating you well, brother, " I said. "Boy, what a tan."

"Part of the daily deal, bro. All a part of life. Man, you look tired."

"I'm exhausted. It's a lot of work out there and not much sleep. A couple of nights of rest and I'm back at it. Good to see ya'. Where's Inger?"

"Not far, man. Right up there." He pointed up to the cliffs to our north.

"Wait 'til you see the sunsets."

"Awesome, man. Awesome," Don chimed in.

"Come on let's go. Inger's anxious to see you."

When I came out of the shower, Bill called me to the railing of the front deck and handed me a cold beer. Don joined us and we talked as the sun slipped from the sky. Inger had prepared a meal and the four of us dined with the French doors open, tropical trade winds blowing in whispering breezes that kept us refreshed.

Everything I had been through for the past year was brought to Bill's attention. I was careful not to mention all that had gone down between Jake and me. I felt Bill wouldn't understand my motives, or be accepting of the way I live my life. It was better to put more emphasis on other matters, like letting him know that Mel had blown the whistle on Gil and that Gil was now dead. By the time I got to Manny, Bill had heard enough.

"Watch out for Jake," he cautioned. "I told you he was arrogant and he's going to bring you down."

Careful not to fall into his trap, I cut the subject off. "Jake and I are in need of new connections. That's the main reason I came as soon as possible. We only have Ramon. We're hurting. Can you help us?"

"I'm waiting for Mack to get a hold of me. He promised he'd turn me on to his man in Guadalajara who's the super-weed connection. Mack also turned me on to Tambor, who's a go-between man for this guy Modesto. Tambor can get me weed, but I'm reluctant to use him."

Curious, I asked, "Why not?"

"Don and I just finished up a small run. It was a total bummer. This guy Modesto is a heavy dude. He was a bodyguard for a former governor and now he's probably one of the biggest middlemen in Mexico. He's got in excess of tons of weed."

"Did he rip you off?"

"No, but the weed he showed me was inferior. I'd rather wait and get connected with Mack's man in Guadalajara. The man has the good stuff."

I added, "So, Mack is not in touch with anyone from what I gather. This is bad, Bill. Any idea as to what he might be up to?"

"No. I last heard from him back in May, but he'll show up, and when he does, I'll have access to some really fine *mota*."

I wasn't so sure about that. Mack hadn't contacted anyone for the past four months. Where he might be was more than I could handle. No matter what, his sudden disappearance was a disturbing mystery. Deeply concerned by this and knowing that Bill wasn't about to delve into the matter, we cut short the talk after I once again asked him about this man, Modesto.

I was curious about this man and that he was a heavyweight. When I asked Bill if we could connect him up with Ramon he refused. "No way. Mack's not here and I can't connect Modesto up with anyone without his permission. "

I was tired from the trip at sea and couldn't think straight any more. The next morning I wasn't much better. Had my trip been in vain? Not entirely. Mack might show up any day now and if he did, Bill would have access to tons of good weed. And if Mack was dead or in jail somewhere, all of us were in trouble. Beset with fatigue and bad news, I stayed away from Bill.

That afternoon, Inger and I renewed our friendship. A trip to the center marketplace did wonders, but I noticed she was reluctant to talk about what she had been through the past year. So, we shopped and made small talk. That evening, the four of us dined out. The next day, I flew home frustrated with this business.

On Jake's front the news wasn't so good either. I was vexed as he explained his litigation problems at his mother-in-law's place.

The young hippy dude from Winslow, Arizona, who had gone out to our ranch without permission was another enemy. Jake's lawyer, the shark from the City of Angels, had filed a motion to suppress all evidence, which included the original search warrant. The informer had entered our property without our permission, had taken on his own to searching our buildings, found contraband and had taken it off our property without consulting us. Then he had turned it over to the authorities. The case should have been dismissed, but the judge was an elected official and he refused. What would his constituents say if he had he gone our way?

Infuriated with the judge, Joe used another well-planned tactic by attacking the State narcotic agents who had filmed the entire event with an 8-mm camera. Jake and our workers were not captured on film, but the narcs were. Jake said that when Joe charged the bench and ragged on about who was in possession, he shouted at the judge to have the narcs arrested on the spot and the judge all but charged Joe with contempt of court.

"I saw it. The narcs were in possession of contraband. If they show it come trial time, Joe knows he can win on appeal. He can also win an appeal on the suppression charges," Jake related.

I had met Joe on two occasions. He was brassy and full of himself, just the kind of lawyer you wanted on your side.

"Joe tore them up," Jake continued. "He wouldn't let up even after the judge told him he'd cite him for contempt. He made fools of them and kept carrying on. It was a pleasure watching him work. He was enjoying it and he had them crying for mercy. And the judge kept pounding his gavel."

"Just like in the movies," I said. We laughed.

"Just like it. They were damn glad to get rid of us. Joe was so high-powered the judge didn't like him from the beginning. You should see the suits he wears. He's flashy and he's L.A. style. The judge cowered every time Joe raised an objection. They're small town people, partner, and Joe let them know this and he didn't care. He had already figured the judge would throw the suppress motion out. This trial may go on for years. Anyhow, he spent so much time badgering them the judge had to call off the preliminaries because we were taking up too much time. He had to reset them for sometime in March."

"Great! So Joe bought us time and beat them up at the same time. Any other good news?"

"Well, it's not good news but it's positive in a weird sort of way. We have to revamp things. Benny and Betsy have decided to retire. I guess he's getting a bit old. Anyhow, we have two new pilots, Gary and his pal, Tom. Gary is an old friend of Gil's. He contacted Ramon a couple of weeks ago. I connected with them last week. They're both ex-Marine Corp pilots. They want to learn to fly the border. And their friend Dave wants to drive for us. We're set to go."

Jake assured me they'd work well together and added, "We still have our Cessna and one pickup truck. That's all we need. Ramon said he'll have a load for us in a few days.

True to his promise Ramon called, and Jake and I headed to the deserts of southern California and met up with the new crew at a restaurant in Palm Springs. Gary and Tom were tall, robust man in their early thirties. Gary was boisterous, much like Gil, his good pal. Dave was full of fun, an ad-libber. Tom was quiet and reserved and looked like an All-American boy.

"Remember," Jake cautioned, when we returned to our motel room, "no one has been caught while in flight. That end is quite secure. It's what happens between people where problems occur."

Jake began giving them a rundown on the flying procedures the two of them would have to employ. Navigation charts that would help them find the landing areas in Mexico were brought out and gone over. We'd need new landing areas on our end. Gary knew just where to look for them. He'd been making plans for this event ever since Ramon told him we might make use of him.

The next morning we gave our neophyte crew a more intensive rundown on the business. We once again brought out aviation charts and went over air routes. We considered locations for landing the load and the exact location of the ranch inside Mexico. Ramon was on hand briefly to help pinpoint the area on the chart.

Taking off, Ramon announced, "The load is at the ranch. Everything is set. Let me know when you're ready."

Gary, unfamiliar with our Cessna, had another plane in mind, a strange looking twin-proper that would do the job. Jake and I conceded. Going to the airport, we rented the plane under Gary's name. An hour later they took off to practice landing on nearby lakebeds until they felt satisfied.

The next morning, the pilots took off. Around five, we got a disturbing call from Gary, who was back at the airport. He was angry. They had gone all the way down only to come back empty, unable to locate the ranch down in Mexico.

Jake called Ramon. Within an hour a meeting was held. Ramon came up with a quick solution. He would call his people and have them set up a more reliable way to find the ranch. Word came back later that evening that special orange-colored tires would be used as markers.

"We've been through this type of stuff," Jake pointed out. "It's nerve wracking for all of us."

By late evening, we were squared away. The next day, with everything set to go, the pilots took off once again. Shortly after, Jake and I drove off to meet up with Dave in 29 Palms. There wasn't much else for us to do but wait. Around noon the three of us headed out to the landing zone.

A few miles from the touchdown zone, Jake found a good spot to park off the main road. We hiked out to an area with low-lying hills and sat down on boulders. From here, hopefully we'd be able to spot the plane when it came in, even though the lake bed was six miles away.

The day was warm and clear. A small low front had dropped a small amount of rain during the evening. We could see for miles in all directions. Our energy soared as the three of us stood fixated on the expansive view. Surrounded by mountains and valleys, and with the desert floor covered with sagebrush and cactus, the desert seemed timeless and wise. Noises could be heard for miles. Distant planes left streams of vapor in a cloudless, blue sky. It was still early, and the three of us sat cross-legged on the rocky formation, tranquilized by the surrounding mountains and boundless desert.

"Hey, do you feel how we're blending in here, man? This place is so bitchin'," Dave mused, gazing out at the enormous expanse.

"I'll take this spot any day," I responded. "No telephones, no cars, no taxes, and best of all, no government agencies to look up your asshole."

"It's back to basics," Dave pointed out. "Back to hunting, digging your own shitters and worrying about whether or not you're going to make it through the winter. And if you do make it, what's to stop you from climbing that mountain over there?"

"Yeah, and what's to stop us from just sitting here all day, or a couple of days figuring out how we sold ourselves so short?"

"Yes," Jake mused, "we have a lot to learn. This would be a good place to start."

"It's time to close the gap, dudes," Dave replied, gazing. "There's miles of open desert out there. You place your mind in the center and the universe opens up. Boy, on a day like this, these mountains, this desert, they're happening for us, right guys?"

"So true, Dave," I agreed. "Life feels real good right about now. If only we had a way of keeping these feelings going."

Indeed, there was something gentle and tantalizing about the day—nothing to make us suspicious of anything.

While I was taking a short nap Dave headed out for a hike.

Jake hung out and asked at one point, "Where's your Frisbee, Frank?"

"It's not here. If it were, we'd be throwing it. Besides, when was the last time you threw one?"

"Can't remember, man."

"That's the problem, Jake. We're losing all those little freedoms."

"Nah, we can have them anytime we want."

"That I know. But, that's part of our problem. We don't know any better most of the time. Stupid isn't it?"

"No. Not really. It's only stupid when you don't bring the Frisbee along." Jake began tossing pebbles at me. For several minutes the two of us playfully cast stones while we waited.

Dave joined in upon returning. We continued the spontaneous friendly game of dodge the stones.

When the sun started departing from the sky, we gave Dave a last minute pep-talk and told him to head for the landing area. As soon as he left, Jake and I got back in his car and started driving back and forth along the stretch of highway from which we had entered. From there, we could both observe traffic and also hopefully spot the plane coming in. With hardly a soul around for miles, we were content that all was well.

Then it got dark, seriously dark. We hadn't spotted the plane coming in for a landing. "Think they came in from a different direction?" I asked Jake, already knowing he answer.

"Hardly likely!" He fell silent.

"Maybe they couldn't find the landing spot again?"

"Could be. Maybe they're not too smart."

"Marine Corp captains? Nah."

"You're right. Something's wrong, brother."

"Yes. And they can't call us out here. Let's get to a phone."

"Gotta wait for Dave to come out."

A few moments later, he pulled alongside. Rolling down his window, he said offhandedly, "No go, guys. Nothing."

"Yeah. Listen, Frank and I are going to get to a pay phone and call Ramon. Why don't you head to your motel?"

Immediately, we headed off for 29 Palms, a long forty minutes away. Doing our best not to be pessimistic, we traded bits of conversation. When we called Ramon, we had to wait a long ten minutes for him to reach an outside pay phone.

"There's been a no show," Jake informed him.

"Ah... really. This is bad, boys. My people said they made it. They got the load and left. They said it was late, though."

"Any idea what time? Did they say?" Jake asked.

"No. Just that they said it was late."

"Why don't you call down and get an exact time?"

Jake hung up. After he let me know what had happened, he added, "Come on. Let's meet with Ramon in Palm Springs. We can be there in than an hour."

Before departing Jake called our motel, just in case the boys had called. There were no messages.

"Let me have the water bottle, would ya? This is cruel," I said, besieged by fear as we headed off.

"Yes, we might have a crashed plane and a couple of dead bodies." Jake too was deeply worried. Had our new pilots crash-landed?

"I don't even want to think about it," I brooded, as anxiety took hold.

Somber, we discussed the situation as much as we dared, as we sped toward Palm Springs. Odds were good that we had another major problem on our hands, this time with two very inexperienced men.

An eternity passed before we got to our motel. Ramon was there waiting for us as we pulled up, shortly after nine. We had a tough decision to make. Should we call the FAA, and if so, when? A plane was missing and one of us would have to account for it.

"They could be out there and be okay," Ramon suggested optimistically.

"That's what we're figuring on," Jake concurred. "Let's give them a chance to work their way out of where they might be stranded and call us."

To us, it was a familiar scenario. We'd withstood similar calamities: one had turned into a disaster, the other a hearty laugh. We were batting five hundred. That would be good—if we'd been playing baseball.

Ramon added, "It's too soon to call the FAA. Let's pray they're okay. I'll hang out here for a while and wait with you."

In spite of our concern, Jake and I were hungry so we ordered food and quietly ate. Meanwhile Ramon decided to check the aviation charts. There wasn't much out there. There were no towns, only a few gas stations, but mainly desert and lots of it.

When half past ten o'clock crept up, Ramon decided to go to his home in Indio. He left with a false smile of hope and a short message. "Call me when you hear something."

Jake turned the tube on. Both of us lay on our beds watching patterns pass across the screen. Neither of us wanted to let the other know just how wrangled our minds were at that moment. Sooner or later, Jake would have to call Ramon to ask him if he'd be willing to call the FAA come morning.

When the phone rang, Jake lunged. "Hello. Yes... What's up?"

Jake cupped the phone. It was Tom's girlfriend, Janet. We had a new problem.

"Yes, Janet. What can I do for you?"

"I'm really scared, Jake. Tom's not back yet. I just talked with Gary. He gave me your room number. He told me I could talk with you. He's upset, too," she rattled on.

Jake stopped her. "Wait a minute, Janet. You said that you just talked with Gary. When? Where?" Jake shot a quizzical glance over at me.

"He's in his room."

"Janet, where are you?"

"I'm here in Tom's room at the motel."

"Good. Why don't you come over to ours, okay? Room 246. Yes. See ya. No. Don't worry about him."

Jake hung up. "Gary's in his room. He didn't fly to Mexico. Tom went with a guy by the name of Gino."

Standing up, I exploded. "Holy shit! What's going on here?"

"Calm down, man. We'll know more when Janet gets here. Let's get ready to handle this."

We had just enough time to make a few comments when she knocked at the door. Both of us had met Janet two nights before. She was a striking woman, full of laughter and smiles. Now she was understandably disturbed, a woman in distress. Jake had her sit on a chair as we sat on the ends of our beds, facing her, while she poured out her concerns.

"Gary said he told you that he was sick and that you said it was okay for Tom and Gino to go today."

"Well that isn't so, Janet," Jake replied.

"Why would he tell me that?"

"We'll have to find out."

"Where's Tom and Gino?" she whined.

"First of all, we don't know Gino. Tom left late down there." Jake left it at that.

"Then everything Gary said was a lie. He said he called the people he rented the plane from and the FAA, and told them the plane was missing. Do you think he lied about that?" She was anxious for information. Her eyes darted back and forth between Jake and I.

"He's really acting crazy," she continued. "I don't believe he's so concerned about Tom and Gino. Gary said you'd know more than him. Is Tom okay? Why isn't he back?"

Jake and I shot a look at each other. Jake calmly told her, "Look Janet, we have a problem here. Right now we have to talk to Gary. Okay? It's important. Tom is somewhere between here and Mexico. We really don't know."

"We can only hope that they're okay," I added. "They may have landed after dark and will call us as soon as they can. They took off late on the lower end. There's a good moon out tonight, plenty of light to land by." With Janet listening to every word, I had to struggle to contain myself. Gary was up to no good and we had to confront him.

Putting her hands to her mouth, she cried out softly. "Oh God! That means he might be hurt. Do you think he's crashed?"

She was a flight attendant. No sense lying. Jake said, "To tell you the truth they could have landed safely. Could be that they put down on another dry lakebed. If they did, then he and this guy Gino will have to get out of the area and find a phone."

Surprisingly, there were no tears yet, just an immense amount of concern. She was poised. "Are you going to look for them?"

"We thought of that and decided to come here and be by the phone. Why don't you go back to your room? We need to see Gary right now. Maybe he can help out." Jake stood, walked over to her and added gently, "If Tom calls us while we're out of the room, he'll call you next. Let's figure on that. Okay? Frank and I will consider what you said. One of us can drive out that way and search for them. Dave can help out, but first we have to talk with Gary."

On the way to Gary's room, I was cautious. "He's a big boy. You heard Janet. He's acting real weird. This could be dangerous. He's probably in some sort of out-of-control state right now, and if we pressure him, he may not be able to cope. Handling him physically could be a problem."

Jake agreed. "Don't worry. We'll go lightly on him."

In shock over the evening's events, and further compromised by the latest news, Jake knocked and the door opened almost immediately. Gary, clad only in briefs, stood before us, shame-faced, a deep frown on his forehead as he first peeked out and then opened the door for us to enter. Turning, he headed straight back to his bed.

Leaning against a backboard, he drew up the sheet as we approached and stood near the end of his bed. On the nightstand was a container of Kaopectate. Trace smells of alcohol, maybe whiskey, permeated the room, along with cigarette smoke, leaving the room stale and musty.

"I'm sick, guys," Gary stated, not bothering to say hello. "I couldn't go today. My ulcer is bleeding, but I didn't want to bother you with all of that. Hell, if...if I had gone to work today there would have been a problem. I mean, I think that it wouldn't have been safe to go. Christ, I'm sorry man. I should have told you. But Tom and Gino wanted to go so I figured it was okay. But they're missing Jake, and I think we ought to do something."

"Yes. I agree, Gary. We'll do that. We'll take care of it. Don't concern yourself. How are you doing? The ulcer really hurting?" Jake asked with a calm tone.

"Yes. I think I need to go to the doctor."

"Fine, but right now I want to discuss a few things with you."

"Like what?"

"I want to reinforce that we're running this operation. We've discussed communications with all of you guys. You're the lead pilot. We're open to all possibilities, no matter what."

"Jake, I didn't want you to think I was afraid to go." He lowered his head.

"We would have understood the problem, Gary. Fear is something all of us have to deal with. We don't put people down because they're fearful or sick. We want you to understand this. Okay?"

He blurted out, eyes darting, "It was a tough decision to make. Really. Tom agreed with me. That's why he went without saying anything to you about it. We called Gino last night and had him come down. We all figured it was okay."

"Look, Gary. What's done is done. We can talk about this later. Right now those guys are out there somewhere. We'll have to go find them. Let me bring you up to date first. Ramon's people said they got off to a late start down there. They probably landed after dark, maybe on another lake bed."

With a bit of enthusiasm Gary offered, "Maybe they had a bad landing. The gear on that plane is not too strong. You're right. They could be somewhere out on one of the dry lake beds."

"We've considered that. Then again, there could be other problems. If there are, we'll call the FAA in the morning," Jake baited him.

"I was thinking the same thing. I didn't do it though. I told Janet I did only to make her feel better. I figured I'd wait until I got a hold of you."

Yeah. Sure Gary. We're used to guys like you. You're in denial right now and you don't know that we're on to you. You're a sick man, all right.

"We'll wait and do it in the morning. They won't be able to do anything until daybreak." Jake was firm and believable. Now was not the time to call this deceiver out.

"Fine with me," Gary said meekly.

"Frank and I are going to discuss all this. Get some rest. Call us if you have any questions or suggestions."

"Nice job, Jake," I said as we were leaving. You handled that really well. Did you smell the room? He's been drinking, with a bleeding ulcer no less. I think he has no guts, and he's being torn apart by guilt. He's afraid all right. He's afraid to tell the truth, man. I saw it over dinner the other night, the way he kept bragging and carrying on. Gil was the same way sometimes, but he was more capable, or something. I don't know, Jake, he's a man with personal problems and right now he's our problem."

"Right. Do you think he'll give us anymore right now?"

"I doubt it. He seemed contained to me. We took a lot of pressure off him in a very short time period. I think he's telling the truth about the FAA thing."

"That's the way I see it," Jake said as we entered our room.

"There's a near full moon out. Maybe we ought to drive out there. I could go and leave you here to keep Gary and Janet busy."

"It's getting late. It's almost midnight. Let's talk this out first. It sounds good to me, but let's be sure."

No more than a few minutes into our discussion, the phone rang. As Jake grabbed for the phone I reminded him, "That's probably Janet. We forgot to call her back."

As Jake picked up the receiver he said, "Hello," and then paused. Then Jake broke out with a big smile as he looked over at me. "Tom! Where the hell are you?"

CHAPTER FOURTEEN

RAGE

SAN FRANCISCO, CA
DECEMBER, 1970

As it turned out, all was not well. As a matter of fact, nothing was going well. What, I wondered, was happening to us? Were we complete fools, caught up in chaos being created by others? And just what the hell kind of chaos were we creating?

This latest drama had me in an emotional tailspin. I wanted answers to those questions and others right then, not later. But my emotions were flowing fast and they were far from benign. They were the rage within my subconscious that had to come to the surface. Total ruination was but a scant distance away. Depression, caused by negative thoughts had ensnared me.

What I wanted was to find a way to work free of the negative thoughts, but I felt trapped, as though a dark shadow had been cast over me. Right in front of me were answers—but I couldn't see them; couldn't touch them, or even call out for help. I only knew I had to break up the doom and gloom, the sheer hopelessness, and the rage within that had me by the balls.

It was mid-December. Hopeful that a long ride would ease my apprehension, I drove south in my Porsche, directly into the eye of an approaching storm as huge as the trouble within, smoking grass and blasting music, suspended in the moment, my thoughts too rigid and forbidden to comprehend. It was my way of escaping, my "right" to escape, and evasive action that was as necessary as breathing. This was not my last breath. Not by a long shot.

Several days ago, Jake, Ramon, and I had to confront Gary, the pilot who had deceived us. We came face to face with each other in an Oakland apartment belonging to Gino, Tom's good friend, a man we hadn't even met until after he had gone to work for us.

We had intended it to be a forthcoming confrontation, but it got out of hand. A fight broke out between Gary and his pal Tom. He had accused Gary of being a liar and a coward. The only injuries were a broken lamp and a small cut above Tom's eye, but all of us in the room had been shaken. We pulled Gary and Tom apart, while Gary kept screaming that he wanted to get paid in full, insisting that he was the boss on his end of the operation and would pay Tom and Gino what they had agreed on before leaving to get the load.

After the fight, Jake had coaxed Gary to come to another room. There, he had read him the riot act. He had told him to back off—that we had no place for a man like him in our organization. We gave him two grand and told him to keep quiet. He left with Ramon immediately, all of us keenly aware that he had enough information to destroy us.

Apparently, arriving late with the plane full of contraband, Tom landed hard, and collapsed the landing gear. Fortune was with us: we hadn't used our own plane. Dave had driven out to the desert to a small juncture called Amboy, where Tom called us from, and met Gino and Tom. Retrieving the load, he brought it home safely. To clear the matter up with the insurance company, we asked Gary to tell them a fictitious story we had cooked up. He had taken care of this before coming to meet with us.

Additionally, the fronted load Ramon had accepted was another pile of "stick-shit" as we had begun to call them. Along with a couple of helpers, I spent a good deal of time cleaning out the debris. Profits would be low. After expenses, there would not be enough money to pay our lawyers and little money to give to the men who had been busted. Plus, our customers were quite upset by the prospect of selling stick-shit.

As if that weren't enough, we had been ripped off. Our driver Dave had arrived five hours beyond the time we had figured he'd be in. We counted the load as soon as he got in, and we were short forty kilos, over eighty pounds. We called Ramon and he said his people had put four hundred and forty on board. Questioning Dave, we got nowhere. He denied taking any, but did so in a way that led Jake and me to conclude he had. We fired him just after the confrontation with Gary. He left peacefully without arguing his innocence.

To boot, Jake had gone into one of his arrogant funks. We argued mightily over nothing and everything, pent-up rage being our common foe. This had happened just the day before, as I had stood over the pile of contraband helping the crew to clean out the spoils of our efforts. Leaving in a huff, I told him where he could go—straight to the pit.

Some of my worry receded as I cleared San Francisco and headed down the Coast highway. Even so, it was time to keep letting my mind rip so I could begin to open up to what my mind/heart wanted. It was indeed time to let Mother Nature draw me forth to heal what was causing me to go mad.

Big Sur was a welcome sight. It helped quell the waves of anger inside: thoughts about Jake and his aloof attitude, and the terrible mistakes he had made over the past several months. Pounding the steering wheel I screamed out, "Where in the hell is Brotherhood? Just who in the hell are you guys anyway, you shits, you're nothing but a bunch of sham artists!" As easily as that, I blamed Jake. It was his fault we were suffering. I didn't stop there.

On and on I went, lashing out at Ramon, who had accepted the weed, and the Mexicans, who had dared to put this inferior product in our hands. How utterly fucking stupid!

I attacked Manny with unkind words, as well as Bill. More images came into focus. Victor's face loomed large as did Jim Bigotes as well as Chato's. I was having a field day. Glenn's face came, as did my parents; the mother and father who had forsaken me. All of the liars and deceivers I'd come across the last several years fell prey to my outbursts. Everyone got a good licking—except for me. I was the good guy who did no wrong: the victim of kindness, caught up in a den of starving wolves. I was also caught up in self-righteous pity—no matter, I screamed and howled, raking every one of them, cursing them for what they had done and blaming them all for the screws put to me.

Why not? My reality told me they had done this to me. I lived on a planet of misfits and cretins who saw fit to trample on the Brotherhood.

When all was howled about and driven out, my reality shifted. Just how did a nice guy such as me fit in with these charlatans? I, who had preached to those around me that life is all about "choice," was at this moment face-to-face with what I had created— the choices I'd made. "This is the hard part," I said aloud, the part each we all fight with; we deny the truth even when it confronts us. Not me, we say. Not me. I am perfect. Just ask God. He'll tell you so.

I went deeper and deeper into this altered state. It was crucifixion time. It was time to invest awareness where it didn't really want to go. It was time to admit that I was no different from any of my brothers I had chosen to surround myself with people and situations that would allow my shadow side full reign. In a weird way, we brethren had all chosen each other to play out our internal and unresolved insecurities. Oh God, I didn't want to admit this but self-abnegation was upon me, I'd ushered it in. It made perfect sense, and the second I gave way to this I began to expel the negative emotions that had been harboring inside of me. I began to see the deeper reality of life.

I had gotten into this business to feel better about myself and I realized that I was not feeling better about myself. I was feeling worse. I was heading in the wrong direction—getting further from my dreams of unity and connectedness. These brotherly characters I had chosen and my lifestyle were opposing forces to resolving my internal conflicts. I felt even more powerless and alone than ever.

"What is it that you want?" a voice within reached out. "Peace of mind," I answered back without hesitating.

Why had I brought corrupt people into my life? Why the lies and all the head games? And on down the coast I drove, driven by rage. Were they just reflections of my inability to be honest with myself? Was I making myself out to be a victim? Maybe that's what I was doing? It had to be, but I had learned along the way that there was no such thing as a victim. But that was what I was becoming, a victim, and now I had to release from it. That's all. I'd failed to see this. I'd allowed my emotions to overwhelm me, but even so I knew that there was no single conclusion as to why I had fallen prey to my emotions. Things were the way they were because of the choices I had made, and still I didn't know why.

"She knows there's no success like failure and that failure is no success at all," Bob Dylan sang out on the tape cassette. He has that one right, I thought, as I listened to every word. How timely. I have to deal with what I've chosen, wallow in the mud for a while until I tire of it, then let all it go, like a bad seed.

As I drove on, saddened by confusion and anger, surges of relief began to fill the void.

"I want this," I said to the land that came into to focus. "Be in the moment," a voice beckoned. "See that all is beauty, and all is well."

I gave into it. All about me was beauty: the land and its contrasting form blending in with All-That-Is. So what if I'd made unwise choices, choices we humans call failures? Let these failures show me the path to what I truly wanted. Let the beasts within leave. Tomorrow is another day. Each day we're reborn and we're given the chance to make new choices.

I pulled over. Parking the car on a bluff overlooking the ocean, I reached for my coat and got out. The beauty of the land drew me in. So did the dark rainy day; the dark overcast reflecting a somber mood. Standing in the cool breeze, the vast waters of the Pacific, filtered in more relief as I gazed at the broad expanse. I was awed by the splendors that surrounded me: broad mountains jutting up into massive gray clouds, mountains shrouded with green grass, mountains in full foliage. And in the far distance were the majestic cliffs jutting over the depths of the ocean—the ocean that steadily beat against them.

Before me was God's creation. Ever so divine, it drew me in, mitigating the self-pity and the rage within. There was no reason to think of myself as a failure or to blame the others for their foolishness; I acquiesced. There was no need to become what they were. I had only to see who I was: a man caught in the game of life—one invented by me and all the characters that I'd invited in. "It's your life, and even failure can be an opportunity to learn and grow from," came the messenger.

"And what is it that I had failed to see?" I asked my inner voice.

When no answer came I stood there as before and waited, allowing no interfering thoughts to penetrate my mind. Nothing else mattered as I stared, my eyes searching the beauty of the land, combing its luster, drinking in the contrast as I studied each feature, each mountain rising up, waves as they pounded against the cliffs—more at peace, more comfortable with who I was and how it was I had chose to come here and stop at this precise setting at this precise moment with this precious segment of All That Is.

Somehow I deserved this moment, had created it and had allowed this moment. And I wanted it to last—forever, if I could. And when I thought about that a realization shook me. Answers don't always come in words, but come from letting go, surrendering to the moment and allowing it to move through you. Yes, I could have this moment any time I wanted it even though the moment I drove away, this setting would be gone, never again to be seen, not like it is now. I could create anything I wanted. I could even create peace of mind any time I wanted.

An hour or two earlier I was about as low as I'd ever been. Now I was surfacing. What had happened to free me from depression?

I was caught up in the things I didn't want, and now, after this respite with nature I was more where I wanted to be. Was that what choice was all about? My mind questioned. Could I simply choose to be free of an emotion and be entirely free of it? Was it that simple? I didn't have a true answer, but nonetheless I had been led down a path to freedom at least for a moment—a glimpse into a probable future.

What became clear was that I could choose what it was I wanted instead of getting stuck in what I didn't want. And if I stayed with that premise, little by little, I would and could come to terms with the rancor, and with what I though were mistakes, and perhaps too all of life's traumas that I'd yet to heal—the very negativity that would so often control my mind. I didn't have a true answer, only that my mind was on to something and that *something* had opened me up to something never before considered.

My body was infuriated by the cool wind, so I sought warmth. Slipping back into my car, I turned it on as well as the heater. Turning off the music, I settled into the stillness.

Was this the lesson I sought? Could it be that Jake and I really *weren't* trapped in this game? Could I work free of my negativity simply by applying positive thoughts no matter how many depressing thoughts stood in the way? It was true that one more bust might finish us, put our collective butts in jail, but there was also truth that my partner and I could find our way into a realm of higher thought without destroying ourselves and each other.

In a higher mode, but still overwhelmed by all the issues that swarmed my mind, I drove off again and kept heading south, my mind and heart still at odds, but the dam was breaking.

"The very negative thoughts that I had created and that had gotten me in trouble, were going to become positive thoughts that would ease me out of trouble." I pondered this for a while then ceased to think about all of this as I drove in peace, once again subdued by the scenery and the music, knowing that here too was an answer.

As the daylight faded, I entered the Los Angles basin in a positive mode. Slowly but surely, I was finding peace of mind. I decided to call a young woman I had met just prior to leaving on the Mazatlan race. Surprised to hear from me, she invited me over. I accepted the invitation, glad to have someone to talk with and share my new insights.

Marcy, a sweet, young woman with a four year-old daughter, had a husband who was never around. She told me he was the abusive type and quite readily shared with me her grief and hardships. There was no support from her spouse. Her mom helped her out, but she struggled to make ends meet. We spent the night together in bed, comforting one another, neither of us bothering to make love. When I left in the morning I knew that my problems were somehow less then hers. I'd survive, no matter what.

Christmas and New Year's passed. The stick-shit load was finally sold. Our people who had been busted, and who expected us to pay for their lawyer, had only our good word we'd come to their aid. They knew our past history and trusted us, but they were starting to waver. Over the past several weeks we had gone to each of them several times and had carefully explained our problems. We asked them to be understanding and be patient. What more could we do? They knew if we had the money we'd take care of them. But for us, time was running out.

Jake and I began to focus on our main problem: Ramon, a man who was under a good deal of duress and unable to assist us. He was near broke and we were down to being frugal with the little money we had left. I was reluctant to work with Ramon anyhow, considering the kind of product he had come up with, fronted or not.

No one else was available to help out. Though we'd asked around there was only one glimmer of hope beyond Ramon, a customer of mine whose friends were in need, and we had the resources to help them.

In January, just after I had talked with that customer, Jake informed me that Ramon had four loads lined up and that he wanted to meet with us at a motel near the San Francisco airport. We figured the meeting would result in a raise in price of the fronted kilos.

When we arrived Ramon was quite cheerful. He was cheerful most of the time. "I've got two tons of weed promised. My people will be picking it up any day now. We'll use the ranch in Mexico and fly it over as usual. Okay? Not all of it is for you guys. Manny's going to get half. There are four loads, two for you and two for him."

"Good! We'll be ready!" Jake exclaimed, as I remained silent, waiting to hear what more Ramon had to say.

"Fine," he replied as he sat relaxed in a small sofa chair. "I'm also making a few price changes on the kilos. They're costing me more so I have to charge you ten dollars more."

Jake and I glanced at each other. Five dollars would have been proper. Ten was too much, and Jake said so.

"That's more then we anticipated."

"I've got a lot of expenses. Things are getting tough down there with Operation Intercept and these people are fronting me. If anything goes wrong, I'm responsible. In the past few months I've gone from having lots of money to none. I've helped you guys and I've helped Manny, and now I'm ready to work a different deal with all of you."

"Bullshit," flashed through my mind. Operation Intercept was being used as an excuse— another manipulation.

"What do you mean?" Jake asked.

I didn't like the tone of Ramon's voice and the way his eyes were avoiding mine.

"Well, on top of the forty-dollar price, I want one third of the profits. For this, I'll drop the usual charges on my end."

The idea repulsed me. To be business associates fine—partners, no way. He was under pressure. All of us were. I wondered if he was making these intense changes because he figured he could get away with it, as if we were a couple of starving dogs, panting for food, ready to eat anything that was thrown to us.

I cleared my throat. "A one-third cut! Ramon, that's pretty unreal along with the raise in the price of the kilos."

"Yes, but I need to do this because I have so much responsibility. Manny's in agreement. We've already talked."

I'd kept my cool thus far but growled sarcastically, "So essentially, Ramon, we'd be partners?"

"In a manner of speaking, yes."

"I don't know," I said, getting up off the end of the bed. "This is very sudden. What can we expect in return if we agree?" Standing a few paces away, I looked him directly in the eyes.

He averted mine and looked toward Jake.

"You have my services."

"Yes, but what about quality control?" I retorted.

"My people always check the load."

"But do your people see the whole load?" Jake asked, supporting my concerns.

"My people are shown samples." He leaned over to Jake to avoid my presence.

"They see samples!" I exclaimed in a coarse voice and began pacing. "But not the whole load. Why not the whole load, Ramon? You know yourself that your fellow Mexicans are full of tricks. They show your man a sample of weed and you say okay and pick the load up. You bring it to your ranch and find out it's full of sticks. You've been tricked, but you can't return it, so we get it. And you want us to be partners with you on stick-shit?"

"This is not that kind of product," he answered calmly, still unable to meet my eyes.

"How do you know? You haven't seen it," I rebuked.

"We'll get good *mota*. That, I promise." He leaned forward, fending me off again. "Remember this stuff is being fronted."

Always the promise; I was getting tired of the false promises.

"Yeah, sure. Will you go look at this load before you accept it?" I asked, glaring.

"I don't know if I can. Be reasonable," he said with disdain.

"We are being reasonable. You're buying a product aren't you, fronted or not? That's what this is all about. We're in business together. I don't know of any businessman that would be so reluctant to see what they are getting for their money. Come on. Get real!"

"It's being fronted!"

"That's just great," I retorted. "You want us to pay you a one-third cut in our profits and you won't go look at the loads. That's a complete farce to me. You've been sending us stick-shit loads and you think I'm suppose to believe it's gonna stop. No Ramon. No way. Take your shit-weed and give it back to them assholes that are doing it and tell 'em I said so." Walking toward the door I added, while pointing at him, "Clean up your act and I might work with you. Jake, I'm done here, are you with me?"

"Whoa! Hold it! Stop right there," Jake said, coming toward me. "Let's talk here and now. Out back if you want privacy." Jake pointed to the small patio. "Why are you so uptight?"

Outside the room I spat out, "I'm tired of this shit. He's offering us nothing and he wants a big cut. We'd be working for him."

"We need work right now. He's offering to help. He says this load is fine and he said he can't go see the load."

"He said that about this last one, too. Right? How can you believe him?"

"I'm looking at the fact that he's got work for us and we need it right now."

"You see what the pressure is doing Jake? You're caving in to it and I bet Ramon has too. I don't want to play into this position of being his partner under these conditions."

"We've got to get back on our feet and this is a start," Jake wheedled.

"You can believe that all you want to Jake, but I don't. And I don't care if you don't understand that."

We were face to face, a few feet apart. Rage had taken hold, the same rage that had seized me just a few weeks ago. As soon as I recognized it, I did all things possible to mitigate it.

"Look, we came into this business with high hopes in the beginning. Both of us talked about what we wanted. Freedom seemed to be the common ground on which we stood. I wanted to sail off someday in a boat and fuck the eight-to-five jobs people are so caught up in. You wanted the same thing. No more kiss-ass bosses, no more kowtowing to the asshole supervisors who extend their authorities over us. We've shared those beliefs for all this time and there are a lot of other brothers and sisters who think the same way…I want a freedom born of my own design. This deal with Ramon is far and away from all of that. It's a step backwards. I want to go forward, my way. Not according to his rules or anyone else's… It's hard to say how the pressure is affecting him or any of us…And maybe this has less to do with him than I think. All I know is I'm angry and I don't want to work with him right now."

"Okay. You said a lot. He is asking for quite a bit. I don't side with him, but we have to get some work going."

"Fine. I told you on the way over I've been negotiating with Jimmy for the past two days about a load of eight hundred kilos of high quality Michoacan weed. Let Ramon do this business with Manny. That will put him back on his feet. Then he'll have the money to purchase something other than the stick-shit. On our end, one load of this good weed from Jimmy's people and we'll be back on our feet."

"Right. I see your point. We just have to figure Ramon and Manny will succeed. Let me talk with him and smooth things out."

"You better. Remember Jake, he doesn't need us right now. He has Manny. He's just keeping us around because he's concerned for us. I think he's sly underneath all that concern. What if he goes down? I'm sure the narcs are on to him. They pick him up, he talks, and we're fried. He's a family man. That comes first."

"Yes. Let's work this out with him. I'll tell him we're backing off for now. Let's keep the doors open."

"By all means, yes. We may have to have him move this load of Jimmy's up for us. Also, there's Bill. I'm gonna have another talk with him to see if Mack got in touch. When he does, Bill will have the man in Guadalajara, the super-connection."

Jake and I had withstood pressure many times. But how does one not fold under pressure? How do you hold onto high ideals when your life keeps handing you garbage? This is what we were up against. Along with all the animosity that had come and gone over the past few years, I knew pressure and rage lurked in my psyche, like a venomous snake ready to strike out. Though I had put out some of the fire, desperation had a grip on me and my mind and heart were heavy. Keeping an open line of communication meant that we had to share our feelings all the more, and share the fears that hampered our minds. But, what man wants to acknowledge that their life is in the pits and that they are desperate?

And as we drove back to Jake's mother-in-law's house in San Mateo, I thought about all this and wondered if Jake was truly supportive of me—or was it that he just needed a partner around him he could trust? Trust was indeed our mainstay. But, I sensed that he was holding back because he was afraid to open up his feelings. I was afraid too, but I was more afraid of what would keep happening if we didn't open up. When I tried to talk with Jake about the positive aspects about life I'd learned he never seemed to grasp my true intent, or how important all of this was to our survival. He'd just listen quietly, not really responding. I realized that sharing thoughts about our fears with others has its limits, and not everyone is open to let on what they fear most.

Putting my theories to the test, I described to Jake what Ramon had gone through with Manny just a few months before.

Back in November, just after Ramon had done business with Manny, they had met up at the Ontario, CA airport and had a drink. Manny had passed him money and Ramon, while driving home, said he was besieged by strange sensations. He had told us that he thought a flu bug had hit. After a short while, he pulled off the highway. "It was the colors that gave it away. I could see them when I closed my eyes. I knew Manny had slipped me a drug, so I parked for a couple hours, napped then drove home when I felt okay." Later, Manny confessed he had put a tab of mescaline in Ramon's soft drink when he had gone to the bathroom.

"He thought I needed some conscious awareness," Ramon had told us with a queer grin on his face. I had been livid and found it hard to believe that he hadn't come down on Manny for endangering his life.

Cautioning Jake, I asked him to think about that act and just how far Ramon might go in deceiving himself about the pressure and fears that were eating at him. Just how much did his Hispanic world of *machismo* rule his life and feed credence to his denials? I looked over at my partner after saying this, and wondered if Jake was really listening and taking it to heart. Jake drove on, not bothering to give much of a comment about the dirty bit of treachery Manny had pulled on Ramon.

It was at that moment that I knew: if we were to screw up once again, the law wouldn't have had to fry us. The ingredients necessary for a true partnership didn't exist and we'd fry ourselves.

CHAPTER FIFTEEN

DROUGHT

MEXICO
FEBRUARY, 1971

ALL TOTAL, it took five hours in a grungy Mexican jail for me to learn the next lesson: let Ramon handle transporting our contraband. It was a cheap lesson to learn, all things considered. The four men who were crazy enough to be with me were unquestionably in agreement.

It had all started in early February. Ramon had not been successful in obtaining the two tons that had been promised, but he was looking for more work and said he had a line on a ton of decent *mota*.

Through contacts with my customer Jim, I had entered into yet another ring of conspiracy. One of his close customers had a great source for "Michoacan Green," a prized, high-powered weed, worth lots of money. Jim's people had lost their connection to transport their product safely out of Mexico. Appealing to me for assistance they had offered—and we had agreed upon—a fifty-fifty split on eight hundred kilos. The sample I had been shown was of good quality. I was assured the rest of the load would be the same excellent quality.

Jim's people stalled when we told them that Ramon wanted a high price to transport their contraband north to his ranch, but I came up with a possible solution. It involved our plane, two pilots, and one rather large dry lake bed two hundred miles south of the border.

I had two missions. I was to fly to Mazatlan and meet with Bill, then head North to Guaymas and connect with Jim, who planned to drive down. Our pilots were to fly our Cessna down and meet us. We'd then use the plane to check out the dry lake bed.

In Mazatlan, Bill had the same old story—his pal, Mack had not called. Don, his surfer pal, was hanging out and when he got wind of what I was up to, he decided to head north with me. If the plan I had come up with was successful, he wanted us to fly a load he was to purchase north for him.

In Guaymas, Don and I connected up with Jim and our two pilots. Early the next morning, the five of us took off in our Cessna and flew north to the lake bed. I'd told them from the beginning that the main problem would be finding a safe route out to the lake without being observed. There were dozens of roads coming and going to and from the lake, and without a doubt smugglers had used it in the past. No matter what, we had to check it out. How to get a load of contraband safely up the Mexican highways and out to the lakebed also had to be considered. Don had a few ideas, as did Jim's connections. That was why we had come this far. Today we were to look the lake over and come to a decision.

What we observed from up high hardly answered our questions. There was indeed a maze of dirt trails leading in and out of the area. And the lake bed was so huge, one could get lost in no time. After circling around for a good hour we were unable to come up with a solution to go about the plan I had suggested. Had we been able to, we'd save a great deal of money. But money was not the issue. Safety was, and we decided that Ramon would have to move our contraband.

When we landed at a small airstrip near Guaymas, a group of four Mexicans dressed rancher-style greeted us. One of them, a short, burly *hombre* approached. As he flashed a customs badge he said in broken English that we were to stand aside while he inspected the inside of our plane. As the four of them inspected, we sharpened up our story about why we were in Mexico.

Finished with the search, we were made to wait, but they wouldn't say why. It was close to an hour later that Don got antsy. The rest of us watched as Don approached the men who were just a few yards away. At his best, sincere and smiling, Don hailed Mr. Burly and asked him if we could buy him and his men a beer.

He refused Don's offer, so Don asked, "Why are you holding us here?"

Don's friendly gesture, along with the question, seemed to insult the burly fellow. Mister Burly decided to lecture us on diplomacy. It gave him the perfect opportunity to show us how a Mexican male must act in a macho situation.

Striding over, he stopped just short of our group. Pulling open his dirty hunting jacket, he displayed a nasty looking weapon. Tucked inside the belt of his pants was a U.S. Army issue, ivory-handled, Colt .45 pistol. He couldn't have been more proud. Hands tucked in his belt, a deep menacing scowl on his face, he geared up and fired off what he thought were some damn nasty words. "You are in my country, *gringos*. You learn what is patience. This is Mexico. We do things different. That is our way. If you no like this, you no come to Mexico."

His immature antics only served to amuse us. We had been waiting patiently for well over an hour. We had also been searched and interrogated. We didn't like the man. Even though we were in Mexico, Don couldn't resist showing Mr. Burly just how a surfer dude handles *machismo*. Standing directly in front of Mr. Burly, he pointed at the weapon and snidely said, "Hey dude, that's a far out *pistola* you got there. You must have bought it from John Wayne. Did he give you a good deal?"

All was quiet as Mr. Burley stared defiantly at us. Then we started laughing. The joke was on him. He knew it and we continued to jeer him. Looking meaner than ever, and twice insulted, he looked us up and down. At this point, all of us were waiting for him to draw his pistol on us. His pals were only a short distance away. The laughter came to a halt.

As we quieted down, he turned and walked off. It was his turn again. We discussed the situation, while our instant enemy talked with his posse.

One of his men was sent off. Before long, a small van bearing a Mexican customs insignia showed up. Mr. Burly came over and ushered us inside with only a few protests on our part.

They took us the local jail in Guymas, a citadel of Spanish architecture just like ones seen in the movies. Unceremoniously, we were asked to get out of the van and were deposited in the holding tank of the citadel; no phone calls, no mug shots, no reason given.

Within ten minutes we started complaining to the office staff only a few feet away. We wanted out of there. They couldn't care less. It wasn't much of a standoff, especially when we started hollering that we were "Americanos." That was that. They'd hear no more. They simply herded us out of the tank, through the main gate, and into the main yard.

Immediately surrounded by a multitude of nasty looking prisoners—it happened to be the house of the hard timers—they were as astounded as we were that five *gringos* would be thrown into their quarters. Asking them if any of them spoke English, we were happy when two came forward. They promptly told us what we didn't want to hear. We'd probably be there a few days. We were being investigated, they insisted. Great! Where's a toothbrush and bed for us? They didn't know. They didn't give a rat's ass. The five of us consulted. Money talked and we had to get it talking.

Within an hour we had a plan worked out with an old drunk who was in for two weeks and had only been there for two days. He had lived in the United States a few years, and his English was passable. He wanted out as badly as we did— more so, because he wanted to get drunk. When we asked him to help us out, he was all smiles when we explained that we'd pay his bail, two-hundred pesos, and add the same amount if he could get us out. He had already informed us he knew where the warden of the jail lived—he called him the *Alciadia*—and would let this man know that we were being held in jail for no reason. We embellished this. This *Alciadia* was to be told that one of us was a Captain in the U.S. Marines. That would be Tom, who was a reservist, but they didn't know the difference. With the drunk frothing at the mouth, we handed over the bail money. In no time he was at the main gate, pleading with them. Soon he was let out and we began to loosen up a bit.

Three hours passed with no results. The sun had gone down and the temperature was dropping. Three of us were without jackets and no sleeping arrangements had been made. We now figured that the drunk had gone off and left us. We did manage to purchase some food from one of the inmates who ran a small restaurant in his hut, which he called a *caraca*. Jim had made himself at home, playing craps with a few unkempt inmates.

As 9:00 p.m. rolled around, we were dismayed and in a fix. Much to our delight, we heard someone call out from the office for a "Capitano Tom." Brightening up as the main gate opened, Tom headed out. A few minutes later, they called to the rest of us. They led us into the office where there were a few officious-looking officials, all dressed in khaki uniforms. Tom was in the middle of them showing them his ID when we entered. Soon they asked us a few questions: Why had we come to Mexico? How had we met up? And so on.

Interrogation finished, one of the officials shook hands with Tom. He spoke some English and apologized to him. He had a short conference with his fellow officials and then told us we could all leave. They even showed us the door.

Mister Burly was outside. We had found out he was not an official but a bounty hunter. Not bothering to pay him any attention, we spotted the old drunk. Beaming us an I-wanna-get-drunk smile, we handed over his well-earned prize money. Don even gave him and extra hundred pesos for good measure. Relationships with their neighbors to the north having been settled—thanks to Uncle Sam—we got out of there post-haste. If they only knew!

Low on cash, I decided to ride home with Jim, along with his girlfriend. On the way back we discussed using Ramon to transport the eight hundred kilos north. Jim was up for it. He called his people as soon as we crossed the border and let them in on what all of us had been through. They wanted their weed brought safely to the U.S. and were still willing to go fifty-fifty with Jake and me. In two weeks or less, I figured, we'd have our first good load of weed and we'd be out of the doldrums.

Jake had some disturbing news when I returned. Howie, his good friend and one of our drivers, had been talking to the Feds. It was a money matter. The IRS wanted him to pay the fine for possession of illegal drugs. Though it was an absurd penalty, by law, they had every right. The fine, a hundred dollars for every once of cannabis, was astronomical. Sixteen hundred pounds times sixteen, times one hundred equaled two point five million and change.

Howie was the only one arrested who owned any property: a home he had built with his own hands. The government wanted to take possession. We didn't have the money to hire a lawyer to fight them off. Jake and I were now ensnarled as government agencies applied pressure. It was obvious why the FBI wanted Howie to talk; Arizona had a weak case. If the Feds got Howie to blab, along with one of the other drivers, they'd have a strong federal case against Jake and me, along with Ramon and several others.

We wanted and needed to protect Howie and keep him on our side, but we didn't have the money to accommodate our good intent.

"I told him to hang in with us and to hire a lawyer with his own money for now," Jake said somberly, as we sat at the kitchen table at his mother-in-law's house.

"How did he take that?"

"Not too well. He'll do it, but I noticed his reluctance."

"I bet. I'm sure he's fine for now, but not for long if these IRS guys get to him. We'd better work on getting this load up here for Jim and his people."

Howie was a long-time friend of Jake and his family, an outgoing dude, very brotherly, seemingly solid. He had gone back to his old job—printer—but he had a family, a good wife, and two teenaged daughters. Both of us trusted him. Then again, everybody has a breaking point and Howie was the weakest link in our efforts to fight off law enforcement agencies.

Dan, an old high school pal of mine, was the second weakest link. I knew him quite well from school. We had once shared an apartment together several years back, and his wife and I were also quite close. We'd have meals together sometimes and I always informed him of our business, including the bad parts. I felt he was with us for the long haul. He and Howie had both gone back to their previous jobs. With no money coming in Dan could become another weak link.

Bob and Jeff, the two drivers busted in the first truck, were single dudes. They were willing to hold out no matter what the issue. They were not part of the main bust, and their lawyers had informed them they'd only serve eighteen months, so we weren't too worried about them.

Dwight, whom I'd known over the years from when he had worked at the Tiburon yacht Club, was married, had a young daughter and a heady wife who looked askance at us whenever we'd visit them in their small rural house. She was a bit of a problem, but Dwight loved his pot and was an anti-government advocate. That was the main reason I'd chosen to go to him in the beginning. He was also a true hippy. Supporting him and his family, although they lived frugally, had been a burden on our depleted finances. Dwight was only facing eighteen months, but didn't want to do jail time. He assured us from the beginning, that if we paid him enough money, he'd split for Canada come trial time.

Willy, we figured, could be a problem. He'd been in the main bust and was upset with us in general. He and I had never been close, but he assured us he'd hold out like the others so long as we gave our support. The underlying problem with him was that he had an older brother who was a San Francisco police officer.

Jake, like me, was showing signs of wear and tear. "Yeah! Let's get this job done with Jim," he agreed. Howie said that the federal narcs had come by a couple of times just after the IRS had come over. He said he closed his door and didn't say a word. He's upset. He doesn't understand all the problems we're having even though I keep him informed."

"Shit, we don't even understand why we're having such problems," I jawed. "All we can do is stay in close touch with all these people. Meanwhile let's get going with our plans. Is Ramon ready to pick up this load?"

"Yeah. He's down south right now. He's getting ready to pick up the two tons he was promised last week, and to look at some other loads. I'm in touch with him by phone."

"I thought the two tons was history."

Jake rolled his eyes. "This is a new deal. All I can say is he's looking for weed."

While Jake and I set things up, we made our rounds to look in on our people. Someone had to stroke their psyches in order to keep faith. Five months had passed since the busts and we'd only brought across one measly load.

This next job was mine to run. Jim was my contact. Jake had never met him, so shortly after contacting Ramon, who said he was ready any time we were, I connected up with Jim and assured him all would go well. I didn't have enough money to go south and meet up with Ramon, so I decided to make the whole job as simple as possible. Jim's people, who were already in Mexico, would only need to connect by phone with Ramon, who was already in Mexico chasing phantom loads.

When I received word that the two parties had connected I knew all would go well. All Ramon had to do was go meet them at certain motel in the state of Nyarit, in a town called Del Rio.

Two days later, I received an irate visit from Jimmy.

"Your man screwed up. My people said your man called, set the whole thing up, and then didn't show. What the hell is up?"

Jim, a swarthy, short, stocky and truculent man, was fuming. So was I. Ramon knew how important that load had been to us.

"Hey, I don't know. My man wouldn't do that unless he had a problem. Let's wait and find out. Tell your friends to hang in."

Two days after that, Ramon called Jake to apologize for everything. His truck had broken down in a very remote area. He and his people had gotten stuck in the boonies. Jim's friends were notified and forgave us, due to the situation. Then they readied themselves once again.

Fortune, however, was not on our side. It hadn't been all year. Once again, Jimmy called, livid, and ordered me to come over to his house right away. "Your fucking man really blew it this time, buddy. My people don't wanna ever do any business with you. They're asking two-grand expense money this time and I'm not going to pay it."

The force and anger of his delivery frightened me. "Okay! Tell me what you know."

"Well, your people showed up all right. But your main man didn't. He sent three guys and a moving van. They fucking got paranoid and split, leaving my people and the load in a bad predicament."

"This doesn't make sense, Jim. You know that!"

"Your man was supposed to be there. He wasn't. That's all I know. I believe my people. As far as I'm concerned it's over brother, and you're gonna have to pay me."

I sighed as I sat down in a chair. Looking at him, I said, "I haven't got the money right now, Jim. Also, I have to find out what went wrong. I'll get back to you."

According to Jake, Ramon had a different story. "That's a bunch of crap. Those people were not ready. We had our vehicle in an impossible situation. It was too narrow a road for my truck to make it up and the other people refused to believe it. They argued with my men and insulted them. My men simply took off because they couldn't back up the narrow road and these people wouldn't bring the load to them."

When Jake had asked him why he wasn't there, he said, "Because I had another lead I was following at the time and I didn't want to lose it. I talked with your people on the phone and they assured me it would be no problem to make the pick up. I'll be there this time."

✯ ✯ ✯

Maybe it was the pressure. Maybe it was sheer lack of fortune or karma. Whatever it was, Ramon hadn't shown up in person when he said he would, totally disregarding our request. I was furious. The next message I got from Jake was about the so-called load Ramon had been chasing down was no longer available. We ended up empty handed. I came unglued when I met up with Jake at his place.

"He just fucked us, Jake. He fucked himself, too. Everything's falling apart. He isn't doing anything right. It's the pressure, man. It's eating at him."

"No shit. We weren't there either to make sure the load was picked up."

"Don't defend him, Jake. I'm not in the mood."

"I'm not. It's what's happening. He made a huge mistake. So did we."

"How so?"

Jake cracked one of his silly smiles. "Because we didn't go down there and take care of things. One of us should have been there."

I sighed. He was right. Even if I had to go borrow a few bucks from Jim for the trip, I should have gone down. Shaking my head I replied, "You got me there. I figured he'd show up as promised."

"He didn't and we have to live with it. We've got to overcome his problems. We've also got to get something else going. So calm down and let's put something together. Ramon's still down south looking."

"Yeah. I'm sure he is. Christ, I'm so short on money I won't be able pay my rent next month. Your preliminaries are coming up next week. We're all but finished. All I can think of doing is borrowing money from our good customers and buying a load through someone, maybe Bill. I sent him a letter a few days ago."

"Maybe it's time we ask our customers for help. Right now we have to depend on Ramon. Let's give him a few days. By the time I come back from Arizona, if he's not together, we'll move on getting some help. Your brother even looks good about now."

Jake had to go to Arizona to attend his preliminaries. When he returned from Arizona, the news was indifferent. Joe, his zany attorney, once again was unsuccessful at having the evidence thrown out. The trial was set for early September.

"I've got some good news," I said to Jake over the pay phones upon his return. "I'm in touch with Mack."

"Far out. I guess Bill came through."

"Big time."

"Tell me about it."

"First of all, Mack was in jail."

I heard Jake laughing. "No kidding?"

"No kidding!"

"What for?"

"For being stupid."

"If that's a crime, we all ought to be in jail."

"We are. It's called life on planet earth—paradise or hell. Whichever way you want it," I joked.

"No wonder no one could reach the dummy."

"Yeah! He did five months—in a Mexican jail, no less."

"Mack in jail! I can hardly imagine." We laughed again.

"This is hot news, partner," I said. "Bill just told me about this afternoon. There's more good news. As soon as I get a hold of Mack, I'm to drag him, if necessary, to the phone and have him call Bill."

"How did Bill find out?"

"Simple! He called a friend in the States. This guy had been in jail with Mack. He let Bill know what happened. Now listen to this. Bill says he wants me to get Mack to call him so he can turn him on to the man in *Guadalajara*, you know, the super-weed contact."

"Terrific! Let's get to Mack."

"I'm on my way. I wanted to talk with you first. All I have is an address. Let's hope he's around."

Mack had me laughing shortly after I arrived. Maybe that was to be a breakout day. It sure seemed like it. What I noticed most about Mack was his paranoia. He even admitted as much. He was through with the dope business. Too much stress, dude, too much on the body, he lamented. I was surprised and dismayed, but proceeded anyway. Mack needed to rest, was all, then think about what he'd do next. In the meanwhile, he didn't mind telling me about his adventures.

His problems had started when he put $25,000 cash inside the air-conditioning unit of his hotel room.

"I wanted to hide it. Shit, I'd done it before. How'd I know the fucking maid would come along and turn it on?"

We laughed, knowing what was coming. The picture was clear. "She wanted to be cool; she got cool. So did my cash. It wasn't tied down and it came flying out."

Jaws agape, I asked, "And she didn't keep it? Unbelievable!"

"Maybe she kept part of it. All I know is the next thing I was in jail trying to explain where I got the loot and the pound of grass I had stashed. Brother, you don't ever want to be in a Mexican jail. Believe me, it sucks. Five months was enough. The warden hated me in the beginning, but in the end, he and I were pals. Really! From hate to love, all because I made him rich."

With a wide grin on his face, ego soaring, Mack leaned forward and said almost in a whisper, "He let us set up a drug deal right from his office phone."

"Unreal. I've heard you can buy those guys off, but that's original."

"Yeah. He wanted money. I wanted out. I met this guy Jimmy in jail, a young Mexican from a family of dope growers. His brothers came down to see the warden about getting him out. Jimmy and I had already talked the warden into the deal beforehand. He didn't want me in on it, but we got him going when we informed him I was the only one who could pull this off and sell the load once it got to the States. At that point, he handed me the phone. I made a couple of calls and put things together. The whole thing took about three, four weeks. The cash was brought down and the warden, shit, he could have cried when he saw the loot. He even hugged me the day I left."

Both of us howled with laughter. Finishing his story, I broached him with the possibility of work. Why not use the same guys who got him out? Mack came round very quickly when I told him we'd do all the work. All he had to do was to make the calls. Money moved mountains, and he was nearly broke.

Immediately, we began conspiring. One load of four hundred and forty kilos was agreed upon. No more. Mack would make a buck, then ponder life for a while.

Within a week everything was set to go. The last phone call made, Jake, the pilots— Tom and Bert in this case—along with Tim, our new driver, headed to Arizona and set up shop. I was to stay in Marin with Mack.

Three days later, success came. Tim, our new driver, arrived with the contraband. As soon as I saw the load I freaked out. It was another load of stick-shit. Where's God? I need to talk with him again. This just isn't fair.

Glad to have revenue coming in, we cleaned up the load. But when it came time to count our profits, Jake and I had just enough to last us a few months after we paid debts and doled out to Dwight.

All this had eaten up a month. It was now May. Despair was creeping around but we now had Bill and his connection. It was time to go to our people and beg for a loan.

Bill had moved to Guadalajara. After I sent a letter, we connected up at a *larga distancia*. He spoke highly of his new connection a man by the name of *Aireberto*. "I've been to his place several times. This guy's definitely got the good stuff, brother. He gets it year round. Get your loan together and get your butt down here. He'll get us what we want, though you might have to wait a few days."

CHAPTER
SIXTEEN

THE LOAN

GUADALAJARA, MEXICO
JUNE, 1971

SHE WEIGHED A LITTLE over seven pounds and her head was covered with what I imagined would someday be blond hair. Her eyes were midnight blue, like her mother's. I was totally unprepared for her infant beauty. No sooner had Inger placed my nine-week-old niece Kerstin in my arms, than she began to cry. This was getting old. I felt helpless not knowing what to do, or if I ought to talk and soothe her, or maybe sway her back and forth, cuddling her to make her feel more comfortable.

I did neither. Bill was looking on, as was our old friend Don and his surfer friend Terry. Being one of the guys, I didn't want to show my sensitive side. Not there. Not at that moment. It was too much pressure. I just held her, said hello and looked at her, then waited for Inger to rescue me.

"Oh, she must be hungry," Inger cooed. This was exactly what Joanne had said to me when Heidi was in my arms nine months ago. I was relieved as she took her baby daughter away and began breast feeding her in the back room.

I had just arrived in Guadalajara and had taken a taxi to Bill's new apartment. I had barely had time to greet them, when Inger, the proud mother, had placed her daughter in her uncle's arms. Already under a huge amount of pressure, even holding a newborn baby was difficult for me. Bill realized my awkward demeanor and promptly handed me a cold beer. In the living room, I spewed out my story as our good friends listened in.

Our organization was collapsing; all those protective walls we had so carefully constructed were now pressing in upon us, even though we were doing all that could be done. We had made mistakes, but others had usurped us. We'd triumph however, with the pending deal through Bill. We'd wrench loose from this deadly drought.

Making money soon was key to overcoming the situation, I pointed out more carefully. No genius was needed to figure out that much. Just that morning, Jake and I had discussed in detail our immediate problems and how to solve them. I didn't know how truly effective our efforts might be, even if we were to succeed.

The narcs, the DEA, the FBI, and the IRS were closing in. Their tactics of preying on the weak links had all but made us want to throw up our hands and surrender. Howie, Willy, and Dan were each beginning to show signs of folding under pressure. Howie, the Feds' prospect and Jake's close friend, was at the end of his rope, and was beginning to avoid us. His wife, a close friend of Joanne's, had told her that Howie had been talking with the feds lately.

Howie swore he would never rat on his buddies, but that was before the IRS came down on him. Just how much longer he'd hold out, we didn't know—we only knew that if Jake and I were delayed much longer it wouldn't matter how successful we were in the next month or the coming months: time will have run out.

It had taken Jake and I four long weeks to procure a loan of $15,000. We had estimated two weeks, tops. We had used our plane and our ranch as collateral, when we approached several people, most of them dealers, two of them lawyers. No one loves you when you're down and out. That was part of the problem. The other part was that we were not alone with problems. All the other drug dealers had sob stories for us. They either had had major busts in their ranks, or their money was tied up in pending drug deals. Glenn, the Telephone Weed Man, was on the run as was his associate,

Todd. Over the years, Jake and I had met or heard through our lawyers of other large drug rings. All of them were having problems, or had had problems similar to ours.

Our timing was poor and knowing that we were not alone with our plight didn't really relieve the pressure. Our persistence paid off, however. We managed to get the loan from three different sources: one was a lawyer whom we never met and who was a friend of Fay's friend Ben, an ex-Hell's Angels dude. Our good customer Berkeley Bill had also invested, as had Irving. We were to pay all of them back double their money within four weeks. In order to work the loan with Berkeley Bill, we first had to pay off a debt to the lawyer he had hired to defend our drivers, Jeff, and Bob.

There was only one solution to solving the problem: give up my Porsche. Bob and Jeff's lawyer accepted the offer. Suddenly my dream car was gone. Along with it, a part of me was missing. We got the loan, but I felt empty. Jake had said to me as I dropped it off at Berkeley Bill's, "You can't take it to jail with you."

"Thanks," was my sarcastic reply.

So, we owed thirty grand to the people who were willing to take a chance with us. They were banking that we'd overcome our streak of misfortune and pay them back their dividends.

Now we had to deliver. We now had the means to buy a load, and all the other parts to our smuggling operation were still in working order. There was no room for excuses or for failure.

After giving Bill a synopsis of our situation, he told me that my arrival was poorly timed.

"Yeah, I saw him earlier today. He just sold the last of his good stuff to someone else. He has some good regular if you want it, but I'd hold off for the good stuff. Don't worry. It'll be here in a few days. Don and Terry are also waiting for the high grade."

My stomach tightened as I attempted to adjust to the news. The only thing that looked good right then was the cold beer in my hand that was already getting warm.

"Any exact time on that?" I wondered.

"No. He tells me it will be soon. I'll drop by and see him tomorrow and give him the twelve grand. That will put you on his list. He's got a large clientele, brother. Don't be surprised if we have to wait a bit longer. But don't worry. *Aireberto* is a big dealer. Like I told you before, he's got tons of *mota* year-round. Relax. I know you're under pressure. We'll have our pot soon enough. Let me tell you what's happening. Then you'll see what I mean."

Bill, sitting in a small club chair with a beer in his hand, looked quite casual. Don and Terry, sitting on the sofa opposite him, also sucking down beers, listened in.

Preferring to remain standing I said, "Fine, Bill. Tell me what I need to know. I hope it's good."

"It is. Like I say, tomorrow I'll go see him and place an order. Don and I are going in on some of the same stuff. All totaled, we've got enough for eight hundred kilos of high grade. Plus, I talked Aireberto into doing a front of four hundred more, twelve hundred all together. All we need to do is pay him double on the four hundred. Here's the good part. We want you guys to handle the whole thing. That's three loads of high-quality pot that we want you and Jake to handle. You guys can fly it up for us. Will that straighten things out for you financially or what?"

Suddenly, I felt better. "Yeah. Sure. That'll fatten us up, but I wish I had been here a few weeks ago to get the load he had then."

"Patience, brother, patience. He'll come through. Guys like him always do." Bill got up, patting me on the shoulder on his way to the refrigerator to get another beer.

"How'd you get so friendly with him so soon?" I asked as he returned, smiling. "I mean, why is he willing to front you kilos? He barely knows you, right?"

"Frank, this guy's been around for years. He knows what he's doing. You've heard of the Old Man, Glenn's connection? This guy knows the Old Man. They do business together and Mack's done a lot of business with him too. I was introduced to Aireberto with good references and we get along. What more can I say?"

THE LOAN

"Okay. Don't mind me. I'm on edge. I want things to go okay. We can't afford to screw up. We owe thirty grand and I don't like it, Bill. The pressure is on. I had to give my Porsche to a lawyer a couple of weeks ago, and I'm feeling shitty about that and a lot of other things that have happened lately."

"Well, that's life brother. It comes and goes that way. Things will change around. Come on, dinner's ready. Let's eat."

"Thanks for the cold sermon, brother," I thought. I'm all too familiar with the rhetoric. Still, I found it disturbing. It's just fatigue, I consoled myself. Lighten up and get some rest.

The next day I called Jake to let him know what was happening. "As I say, there's good regular here, but none of us want it. If we purchase now and come back later for the good stuff we'll have to get back on this guy's list. No telling how long we'll have to wait. So you're in agreement; we'll wait and go for his best?"

"Yes. Let's wait. We can't make enough profit anyway, and the investors want the good stuff. Tell me more about the twelve hundred units of raisins."

Explaining the deal I added, "Yesterday I was tired and cranky. Today the deal sounds mighty good. If we can get these loads up north by the end of June we'll be out of debt and sitting pretty."

"That's great, man, but I still think you ought to find out all you can about this guy Aireberto. Pump your brother on it. Don't let Bill suck your energy like I've seen him do. See if you can go meet this guy and see what you think of him."

"I'd feel better if Bill would agree to that, but I doubt it. Today he's going to place the order. I gave him the twelve grand last night. That will start things. Hopefully in eight to ten days we'll have what we came for."

"Good. Let's hope so. I wish Bill had a phone."

"Send a telegram if you need to. I'll call you back in few days. Okay?"

Later that night I asked Bill if I could come with him to meet his man.

"No way, brother. No one is to meet him unless Mack approves."

"Okay. But I want as much information as I can get about this guy. We want to know who we're working with."

A few days turned into two weeks. It was mid-June and the Mexican monsoon season got underway. Like clockwork, it rained in the afternoon, sometimes in torrents, leaving the streets in the low-lying areas flooded for a long time. In the mornings, Bill and I often walked a mile or so to the Centro Mercado for breakfast.

It was a new "complex" with several food vendors to choose from. Bill had it down pat. We'd get a fresh glass of orange or carrot juice from one vendor, then head over to the bean vendor and get a *frijole* soup, then on to another for eggs and rice- and finally to another for small freshly cooked corn tortillas. Up in the *brujho* shops, one could purchase any number of hallucinogenic drugs, including fresh green peyote bulbs. Twice we purchased those belly-benders. Cleaning and cooking them down to a paste, we were completely put off with the vile taste. Tequila helped get it down.

Don and his buddy Terry usually showed up about noon just as we were finishing our morning routines. The four of us would head off, either to a local outdoor swimming pool or to the Rio Caliente to the south of town for a hot soak.

Finally, we got word that Aireberto would have two tons of very good weed in a couple of days. Calling Jake, I gave him the news. He replied. "It sounds like the old game of wait while I lie to you and if you're stupid enough to believe me, then you're stupid enough to wait." We chuckled.

"Well, it's a little different this time, Jake. Instead of it being just you and I, Don and Bill are included. We're all in this and we're committed to bringing up the best. No matter what, it's kind of stupid, especially after turning down the regular grade."

I reminded Jake of the decision we had made two weeks before and that everyone had agreed to hold fast. Now I wasn't so sure we had made a good decision. Had we taken the regular weed, we could have had the loads over and gotten a decent summer price. It would have gotten us out of debt, but the customers wanted the good stuff.

When I got off the phone with my partner I felt powerless, even though I'd delivered good news. The news was easy to see through. Jake's black humor spelled it out. It left a terse taste in my mouth and I shuddered. Were we being fooled again, this time by Aireberto? I didn't know, but my energy was low and past experience suggested this might be an indication of things not going well.

Over the next couple of days I experienced dysentery—or at least I'd thought it was dysentery. It was difficult to say what it was because of the pressure I was feeling. All I knew was that I was sick. While Bill and the guys ran off and played, I stayed at the house with Inger and the baby and read or slept. Consumed with worry, I knew that time was no longer on our side. When I tried to rid myself of the apprehension by putting it out of my mind, I couldn't. Thoughts concerning our demise plagued me, but strangely enough it helped me to think about them. Maybe I'd get some relief. Then I couldn't think at all. To concentrate on anything became nearly impossible. I didn't dare smoke grass. When I attempted to drink more than two beers my body revolted. It was as though my mind and body were dividing up into little pieces.

As we waited, slowly but surely, the sickness dissipated. Bill kept me informed about the deal. He reminded me how the system in Mexico worked: corruption at all levels.

Aireberto, as I found out, had been a colonel in the Mexican army and his father was a general. Their military status helped put Aireberto in a position to become a drug entrepreneur. He was also a pilot, trained by the U.S. government. He owned a small plane, which he used on occasion to visit his connections in the mountains. He'd been in business for ten years and had only fallen once, several years back when he was into growing and smuggling Mexican heroin. He had narrowly escaped a long prison sentence, and had turned to growing and selling marijuana. There was no telling how many connections he had made in the mountains over the years.

Aireberto was at the head of a large army of *compensianos*—the labor force. As their protector, he paid the *mordita*, the Mexican system of "I-pay-you-to-look-the-other-way-while-I-do-something-questionable." Actually it means "a little bite." He also supplied his *compensianos* with rifles, pistols, ammunition, and gifts of radios, appliances, cosmetics and other sundries they needed or requested.

According to Bill's information, each state in Mexico was responsible for supporting a segment of the national Army—the *Federales*. Each state had its own set of rules governing *mordita*. This depended on the way in which the governor or the *commandantes* wanted matters to be handled as each dealt with the central government. Corruption in Mexico was expected. One learned to live with it at birth. Any attempt to alter the system for the better usually resulted in death by assassination.

There were some exceptions to the *mordita* rule. The U.S. government had "Operation Intercept" in full gear, and it was putting a strain on people like Aireberto. The m*ordita* he paid to the *commandantes* usually kept the troops away from the fields he was operating, but special force groups operating under *commandantes* outside the field of *mordita* could strike. So far, Aireberto had been fortunate.

There was another catch to this cat and mouse game—once the grass was harvested, it had to be safely removed from the fields and brought to market. Bandits inhabit the mountain trails leading out of the jungles. They scored big-time and sometimes on a regular basis, although Aireberto told Bill that such things didn't happen to him and his people. Most of his people were well-armed and trained to protect themselves. As for the federal troops, if they came across a truck loaded with *mota* bound for market, it was confiscated and yet another *mordita* collected. One had to pay for being careless or stupid. Once concealed, the chances of the loads making it to Aireberto's warehouse in Guadalajara were good.

No matter how many people Aireberto paid off, he was still vulnerable to "Operation Intercept." Our government had placed a fleet of helicopters at the disposal of a select group of Mexican *Federales*, a highly skilled special task force trained to raid where and when they wanted to destroy the grass fields. But money knows no boundaries. Corruption had even leaked through that elite group. Through Aireberto's grapevine, he knew where they'd be next, but he couldn't stop them. Local *commandantes* were given advance warning, that's all. The raids were going on daily and being kept out of the local papers. The only people who knew about them were military people, and of course, the farmers whose fields were set on fire.

"It's a game they play," Bill informed me out at the Rio Caliente one afternoon. "The fields they burn are mostly those of people who are not paying the *mordita*. They don't hit the big boys. They knock out the small man, to make things look good. The U.S. government is content and the Mexican government charges more *mordita*, forcing the price up once again. But for now, there's some fields being burned and Aireberto is a bit uptight."

One afternoon, after Bill returned from seeing his man, we received some good but outlandish news. According to Aireberto, the Governor of Aqua Caliente, a state just to the north of Jalisco under the protection of the local *Federales*, had just set up a deal with Aireberto. He was asked to sell some eighty tons of *sensemillia*, a very potent grass that grows well in the state's mountainous regions. It was to be harvested come October. Aireberto would have complete access to the entire amount.

Aireberto had told Bill on two occasions, "If you wish your money back, I will give it to you so that you can go elsewhere." We hadn't. We'd held on. Two weeks had turned into three-plus weeks. The two tons of superior weed that had been promised a few days before was in jeopardy. Everything was in jeopardy. The loan was past due and litigation matters were coming to a head for Jake and the rest of us.

"Aireberto's load just got popped," flew out of Bill's mouth the moment he walked into the apartment the next day. Don, Terry and I were there waiting for his return. Bill's face was as bewildered as I had ever seen it. The energy in the room took a sudden nosedive.

CHAPTER SEVENTEEN

MODESTILLO

GUADALAJARA, MEXICO
AUGUST, 1971

WHEN JAKE PICKED me up at the airport the next afternoon the first thing he said was, "You look tired and worn out, pal." He had asked me to return. We were facing severe problems at home and my mood was somber as we drove to his mother-in-law's house.

"How've you and Bill been getting along? Has he been working you over with that older brother crap?" Jake asked, leering at me. I'd seen the look before. It was part of his dark humor, his way of getting us to open up.

With resignation I replied, "Yeah. I guess so. We don't talk much, just business mainly. He's been good about giving me all the information I want. Other than that, he treats me good at times then makes himself unavailable at others. Don and Terry are around, so he mainly pals with them. I'm kind of invited along."

"But enough of that, Jake. We gotta make some good decisions quickly or we're lost. I've told you a few times that it's best that I make the final decisions because you have more pressure being a family man. Now I'm not so sure that's correct. You have a good woman to go to. I don't. Look at you. You seem more relaxed." Staring out of the window, I added in a tone that spelled gloom and doom, "I'm not so sure about anything at this point, Jake. I feel like we're either incredibly stupid or incredibly unlucky, or perhaps both."

"You need to come down to earth, Frank. Bill's got you in a fix. Chill out. Let's get on this and figure out the next step. Tell me the whole story about this Aireberto dude. We'll figure out what to do."

I reported everything about Aireberto, *mordita*, the politics of growing weed and finally the latest fiasco.

"Aireberto told Bill that the two tons of weed was busted at the Mexican customs (*aduana*) station coming from Nayarit into Jalisco. We were even given a Mexican newspaper with the story in it. Inger interpreted it for us. Bill also said that Aireberto could pay a *mordita* to get the load back, but the asshole *commandente* wanted way too much for it and that was that. We could still get our money back or wait until Aireberto gets the next load of "super weed" in two weeks. We could also go to this guy *Modesto*. Bill took off for *Mazatlan* yesterday. He's going to check with his connection to see if Modesto has any good regular weed. *Whatever we do, Jake, we have to make the right decision*. We have to make something happen."

"I hear you," Jake quipped as he parked the car in front of his mother-in-law's house. As we sat in the car and talked he continued. "You need to rest and be away from your brother's influence for now. I know you think he's doing a good job because he's given you lots of information, but he hasn't produced and I think he could have."

"Hard to say, man, hard to say. All of us created the problem. We were committed from day one to bring up the best weed possible. Bill, you, me, Don, all of us decided to pass on two tons of good regular four weeks ago. Shit, we could have had that stuff up here and sold by now."

"That's part of it, buddy. All of us made the decision, but I think Bill ought to have seen what was coming. He's the one who knows *Aireberto* and how he operates. Bill tells you his version about what's going on with *Aireberto*, and you have to go along with him and his pals. Now we have a busted load on our hands."

"But, we all made a decision, Jake. And no one knew that something like this would happen. Aireberto made an offer—and we let a sure thing slip by. It's group egotism."

Alarmed that I had so boldly spelled out the truth, I stumbled on. "Well, we'll be in fat shape next year. Aireberto is going to have tons and tons of "super weed," but we need work *now*. Shit, I don't think it's Bill's fault. And it's not Aireberto's. It's all of us. We're in this together and we're screwing things up. Maybe we're all a bunch of greedy shits and we don't have the sense to admit it? Think about that, Jake. How are we going to get out of this mess we put ourselves in? We're thirty grand in debt and the law is really close to putting our asses in jail."

Exasperated, I continued. "I'm stumped. Jake. I am truly unable to figure out what move to make next. I'm sick and tired of thinking we might to be finished, you know, all washed up and ready to hang out and dry. It just isn't so." I rambled on, looking straight ahead.

"Aireberto tells us he'll have some weed for us in two weeks. All we have to do is wait. Be patient, we say. It'll come. It's all so stupid, man. We're relying on someone else and they don't understand our needs."

"I hear you, Frank. We'll get on top of things. These aren't the only problems we're facing. I think Howie has cracked."

"Are the narcs back on his case?"

"It's worse than that. Ryan called me just yesterday. He told me he heard through a reliable source that a Federal Grand Jury in San Diego is ready to subpoena him and several others. He says someone is talking and there may be some indictments coming down. He wants us to lay low."

"Shit. It's already too late." My head bent low, I let out a huge sigh.

"Everyone else seems to be cool, including Dwight. I don't have any more money for him, but he's got a part-time job to help out."

"And the customers, how are they?"

"Cool for now, but we'd better make the rounds to reassure them and promise some sort of bonus to them."

"Anything else I ought to know? If not, I'm headed back to Marin County. Give me two days to rest Jake, and I'll be ready to go."

"Nah. Just that Joan and Donna both miss you." Jake started laughing.

I managed a smile. Both of them were good friends of Jake's. They were mother and daughter. Joanie was a paralegal at a law firm and Donna had placed second in a beauty contest before I left, and Jake knew I was hot for her.

Fay and Ed greeted me when I came on the front door, but when they heard the news about our failures they changed the subject. It was dinner time and we talked about more pleasant matters. The next morning I took off early and headed to Muir Beach in my little VW Bug. As always, the State Park was pristine as was the weather. A few people were about as I crossed the small wooden creek bridge and made my way out to ocean's edge.

In front of me was the vast sea, with two very prominent points of land—one to the south, one to the north—separated by a half mile of beach. Flanked by cliffs, I began to walk north where the creek meets the ocean. It was landlocked this time of year, and I stood there a while, gazing at the clear pool. The tide was out, so I continued north out along the edge of the cliffs until I could go no further. I studied the land and the ocean and the sky above to keep my mind free of heavy thoughts which I knew would come, but at this moment I wanted freedom from them. The waves were small, yet somehow perfect. And the color of the water was a perfect green. But, the feelings I held inside were far from perfect.

I continued to walk and was soon at the far south end of the beach. Among all the thoughts that came and went, one stood out. I was grief stricken. Up to now, I had only been thinking about the terrible situation I had gotten myself into. Now, thoughts about my younger brother John flooded my mind. Resting against a large boulder a few feet from the ocean, I started to feel the pain John had suffered over the past two years.

My youngest brother had a huge problem. It all started back in 1966 when he began hanging out with a couple of questionable beach dudes. Bill, Ray and I had cautioned him, but John refused to listen. One day, my mother called. She was in a fit. Bill and I knew John was taking acid trips with his pals, but he was not coming down. The day she called, Mom told us that she had taken him to the Presidio to see an army psychiatrist. She had him admitted for thirty days. Midway through his stay I paid him a visit. I was totally blown away by his condition.

He was nineteen and his mind was somewhere in the ethers. I did my best to get him to talk sensibly, but he only wanted to talk about the strange visions he saw and the macabre thoughts he so often had. His mind was stuck in alternate realties that were too deep to comprehend. I was scared and wanted to shake him, if only to shake loose those thoughts, but couldn't reach him. He and I had never been close, but when I felt his confusion my heart went out to him. I did what I could to reach out to him. Fear and grief hung over my head when I left.

Ever since John's admission into the psychiatric ward I had lived in fear of what had happened to him. He was my blood, and when the psychiatrist told me that my younger brother was schizophrenic, I feared not only for him, but for myself as well.

"He's a passive schizophrenic," the doctor said, explaining that this mental disease usually comes to a head early on—about age eighteen to twenty.

I recalled what my father had said when he took Bill and me aside one day before he departed for the East Coast. Mom and Dad had gone to an army psychiatrist when we lived in Okinawa. The psychiatrist had told him Mom had schizophrenic tendencies. She was irrational, Dad told us. She was mean and angry and he could not live with her.

Ever since learning that John was schizophrenic, I had lived with this stigma and the fear that accompanied such a stigma. I questioned my own sanity. Was the disease genetic? Would I one day come face-to-face with it myself? I had no real answer for this, and when the fear came in, I shut it out. Only time would tell. Right now I had to be strong and ready for the upcoming ordeal Jake and I faced.

I wondered how John was doing now. Although I loved him, I lacked the courage to go and see him. With all the problems I was facing, he'd feel my pain and I'd only hinder his recovery.

As for Mom, she was a strong woman. I knew she'd be fine, even though she was terribly worried about her four sons. All of us were in jeopardy in one way or another, and our lives were in turmoil. And that haunted me, as did my guilt about not having the courage to face her and let her know that I was about to be indicted. She'd find out eventually, and that would weigh on her. John, who needed proper care, was still living at home with her and was still going to the doctor who fed him Throizine, which he hated. I'd visited them every so often and always came away feeling pained by John's condition and overwhelmed by my fears.

I guess that's why I was thinking of John now. I was overwhelmed by my fears—just fears of a different nature. Some day I'd find the time to be with him, I decided. Right now, I had to let go of these heavy thoughts and think about my partner and how he was withstanding the pressure. He seemed to be handling it well, which was unusual, but most certainly welcome. Reassured, I wanted to be part of his strength. I had to. We had to survive and the best way to do that was to stay united and at peace with one another.

The following day, Jake and I paid a visit to our attorney in San Francisco who advised us to make ourselves scarce. Afterwards, we paid a visit to our customers to reassure them we were going to do our best. After we visited our people with much the same reassuring story, Jake and I and his family packed up our camper truck and cleared town. Word had come down that the Federal Grand Jury indeed had subpoenas for us. No way were we going to hang around and get served.

All our moves had to be carefully planned. In a matter of weeks indictments would come down and we'd be fugitives, just like Bill. Neither of us talked much about fugitive status; we talked about future work.

A couple of years ago, Jake and I had come across a place near the New Mexico, Arizona border when we had camped out before heading to Mexico to confront our old nemesis, Chato.

Appropriately named the Blue Mountains, we set up camp at the exact spot Jake and I had camped. The kids loved it. There was plenty of shade and a stream that had small pools, deep enough to sit down and cool off in. Even so, Johan, Jake's son was unhappy. He was seven now and he was confused about our predicament, and because he was unable to comprehend what was happening he became frightened in a way that young kids do when confronted by an unknown nemesis. We tried to get him to play around with us, but the effect was nearly devastating. We had to leave him be and carry on as though all was well. Ironically, a lot of the pressure I had been packing around the past several months lifted. I believe the same was true for Jake.

That evening, Jake and I talked about our situation in depth. Howie was definitely talking. We figured Willy was also talking. Who else might turn on us was unknown, but the Feds only needed corroborative evidence from one person. It would only be a matter of time before a host of indictments came down on us. One mistake and we were finished, and with no available bail money we had to keep on working, no matter what. For now we were safe, so it was imperative that we succeed in the coming weeks. And to succeed we had to make first-rate decisions.

The next morning Jake and I located a phone booth. Bill had given me a number in Mazatlan and a pre-set time each day to call. I was overjoyed when he picked up the receiver—our communication was back on line. I asked right off if he had good news.

"Hey, it's good guys. Relax, man! Aireberto will have a load of his good stuff for us in a week. If he stalls, I'll get our money back. I talked with Tambor. He says Modesto will help us. Either way, we'll get a load of weed. Why don't you come back down here in a few days? We can meet up in Guad."

"Well, at least he was optimistic," I said to Jake after hanging up. "He's moved to Mazatlan." I explained the rest and added, "What do you think? Should we trust this thing with Aireberto, or get our money back and go with this guy Modesto?"

We decided to relax and talk the matter over back at camp.

We had less than three grand to pull this off. Jake had two credit cards as backup. If we fell short we could go to the customers when the time came. They'd cover expenses but only if we had the product in hand. *Ramon*, who was to help us move our load to the border once we had it, had little or no money nor had he been able to come up with a load. All things considered, Jake and I agreed to stay with Aireberto, and that I should take off in two days.

We got a good night's rest and spent the next day with Jake's three siblings. Joanne always amazed me. She carried on with little assistance from us. She loved to cook and we loved to eat whatever she put on the table. It was always fabulous and well balanced, and the tastes were so good it drove away the maddening moments.

At this point, Jake and I, along with his family were about as close to one another as we'd ever been. The setting we shared was almost perfect. The weather was ideal: not too warm during the day and cool at night. Johan had come out of his funk, so we goofed around with the kids and were stabilized further by Joanne's cooking.

Then it was time to call Bill to let him know that we'd stick with his man Aireberto.

On the way in from the airport I gazed at the cornfields. When I'd first come down to Guadalajara back in mid-May, the freshly planted corn was six inches tall. Now it was well over six feet. The sight of the corn stalks annoyed me. We'd had to wait, but the corn had grown, undeterred by human frailties. Only the farmer had to wait, who would harvest it come September. How ludicrous time worked. It was a constant. Why wasn't it working for us?

Don was at the motel when I arrived. Bill showed up two days later. He'd stopped by to see Aireberto and was pumped up.

"Everything's set, guys," he said before greeting us, "The grass had been cut and is dry. The load should be here in about three of four days."

Don thought waiting was funny. He thought everything was funny. He'd wake up every morning with an affectionate grin on his face and start his day off with a plunge in the pool. He was quite a character and had it not been for him I'd be singing the blues. He shrugged things off, but then again, he was not facing the problems we were, nor did he have an older brother to deal with.

While waiting for Bill to show up, Don and I had an encounter to remember. It started early—the morning after I arrived.

Don had a way about him that women loved. They trusted him. I knew why, but could hardly duplicate what he did to win them over. This morning and later that afternoon, I got a good lesson on how he charmed women. It was his attitude, the way he stood, the way he smiled, the way in which he had no fear of the opposite sex.

When Don arrived back from a morning walk, three young women trailed in behind him. They carried schoolbooks and each of them was no more than sixteen. I was in bed, nude, with just a sheet covering me as he ushered them up close.

Startled, I sat upright and stared in disbelief. "Don, what gives?" I cracked a smile and got out of bed, quickly grabbing my shorts.

The girls got a quick look at my bare ass. Don just stood there grinning as I turned around and stared at the three teenagers. They stood fast, clutching their books and giggling.

Don looked at me and smiled. I looked back at the girls and smiled. They in turn smiled. All was quiet. Everything was happy, funny, and quiet.

"Do they speak English? I asked.

"I don't know."

I asked them in English. They looked at one another, confused, said a few words in Spanish to each other, then looked at us for a response.

The girls wore expensive clothes and make-up. They were obviously from families with money. I was still in a morning stupor and couldn't comprehend what was happening, but that didn't stop me from drooling as I slipped on a shirt, while the three lovelies stood by my bed fidgeting and holding on to their books as if their lives depended on it.

"Don, please tell me how they got here? Where did you pick them up? They're cute as hell, but way too young."

"They were at the bus stop when I walked by. They stopped me and asked me where I was going or where I was from, something like that. So I pointed to the motel. They started laughing and, well, I signaled them to follow me."

"And they came along, just like that?"

"Yeah. They followed me here. They probably want to check me out."

"Yeah, and we don't speak Spanish and they don't know a word of English," I replied, then turned to our sudden guests and asked them once again if they spoke English. All I got was muted stares and nervous vibes.

"Don, this is nice, but I'm sure their parents would disapprove. We're *gringos*. This is Mexico. We could be in a shit load of trouble in no time."

Before Don could reply, the three lovelies sat on the edge of my bed and began to address one another. They had no clue what we were talking about and we had no clue what they were saying, or what they might be up to by coming here.

"Maybe they want to cut school, Don said. "We could take them to breakfast."

I asked, "Hey girls, would you like to go to breakfast? Don's paying."

They looked up at me and stared, then looked at one another, and started giggling and began speaking in Spanish.

"Did you get that, Don?

"Not a word."

"Didn't think so. What's the fun in this? They're school girls." Turning to the girls I said, "I know you're supposed to be in school. I sure wish you were a bit older and could speak English," to which they giggled again. "Please, Don," I said half-laughing, "get them back to their bus stop. This isn't cool."

"Hey, they followed me. But yeah, it's time to get you to school. Come on." He motioned them toward him.

They obeyed. As they departed, I laughed once more as he herded them back to where they came from saying to myself, "Just how do you do it, Don? Amazing! Next time make sure they're more our age, will ya?"

"Hey Frank. Look who's heading our way," Don said as he grabbed my shoulder.

"Damn! That's Carman and Rose."

"Yeah, and they haven't spotted us yet. Lets' be cool."

"Unreal!"

We were in downtown *Guadalajara*. It was mid-afternoon and the sidewalk was crowded. Don and I stood still waited for them to come to us.

We had met them several weeks back at the motel swimming pool. We hit up on them the first day, but they would have nothing to do with us. On day two they lightened up. On the third day they let us know they would be moving into an apartment. They were from Texas and were here to take a few classes before moving on. Don had hit on Carman. I had done everything in my power to get to know Rose. Before taking off she let me know that she was engaged.

When they were a few feet away, Don turned on his smile as I stared at Rose. She was exquisite, and when they spotted us smiles broke out.

"Oh my God! What are you guys doing here?" Carman asked, as the two of them stopped in front of us.

"Just hanging out," Don said casually.

I added as I looked at Rose, "We just got back in town the other day. Hey, how are the classes going?"

"We're done. We're on vacation now. We'll be leaving for Mazatlan in a couple of days. How about you?" she asked intently.

"We'll be here a few days, then its back to California." I said, and then began to ask her about her classes, as Don talked with Carman.

What became apparent was the way Rose was addressing me. She had not been this way before and now seemed excited. I remembered what she had said several weeks ago, but played into the moment.

"Hey! Would you like to go out for dinner this evening? I know a great place to eat," I offered, braving my fear of rejection.

"I'd love to. What did you have in mind?"

Not expecting her to accept, I choked up a second. But when she added a comforting smile I said, "How about Carlos and Pancho's? I've been there a couple of times…"

"So have I. That would be fine."

"Good, uh … where you living? Should I pick you up?"

"Yes. Let me give you the address." She jotted her address down on a piece of scrap paper. "Here, pick me up about seven. Okay?"

"Great!" I said, nervous as hell. "Carlos and Pancho's it will be."

"Sounds good! I like that place. See you soon." She batted her eyes and smiled again, then tugged on Carmen's sleeve and asked, "Are you ready?"

They left as suddenly as they came and we stood there dumfounded. At least I was, as Don mentioned casually he had made a date with Carmen.

"They wouldn't date either of us a few weeks back. I wonder what changed their minds?"

Don, hands in pockets, relaxed and grinning, replied, "They want to celebrate a bit, man. Kick back. School's over." He winked and added, "Hey, I don't know. They're women."

"Yeah. They sure are," I chided. "Just don't go to the same restaurant I'm going to. Okay?"

"Hey, no problem, man. Carmen's cooking me dinner."

"Shit. How do you do it, man?"

"Like I say, they're women. I like 'em," he mused.

Rose was petite and most definitely a full-blooded Hispanic. She was also very much in control at every junction as we ate and talked non-stop. I did what I could to keep from drooling over her long, dark hair, her large chocolate eyes, and her smooth complexion. At ease with her I soon dropped all my worries, as we shared bites from each others' plates, flirted, laughed and drank beer. I also completely forgot about the fellow she was engaged to. She had not said a thing about him, and I in turn was not going to mention my line of business. She didn't ask. She wanted to be with me and that was ever more apparent as time slipped by.

"How about a walk?" I invited, as we left the restaurant.

"Good idea. I know a nightclub within walking distance. They play live jazz."

"Here, in Guadalajara? I'm impressed. Let's go." I had put down a few beers and was up to doing anything she suggested.

On the way there, she held my hand. When we entered the club she led me to a table in a dark, intimate corner. Except for a few patrons, we had the place all to ourselves. Then she moved right beside me and rested her side against me as we listened to live jazz.

By the time our drinks arrived, her eyes were fluid and bright as she gazed at me and squeezed my hand. She was seducing me. It was obvious and I allowed it, feeling content and without a worry in the world. I wasn't even concerned about her need to be in control.

We ordered another drink and by that time the nightclub began filling up. She was getting drunk and I was ready for her next move, when she fell into me and we started kissing: long one's, short ones, then with full passion. When she reached in my pants and found my erection I let her stroke it 'til it was too much. I then drew back and said in a whisper, "Lets get a cab and go to my place."

"I think we'd better."

In the cab we resumed our passions. By now I was beside myself. Fearing Don might be back I paid for another room and the second we came in the door we began shedding our clothes. Then I attacked her. I was so horny that I forgot I was horny and did what came naturally. She was a woman and she wanted me to take her, so I took her. And the heat and the passion continued beyond the norm. I felt lust driving me, but knew that what we were doing went beyond lust. I wanted to know her. I wanted to be with her, and to be fascinated by her. I wanted her to charm me as she was doing now. I wanted to stay inside her until the dawn came, and then some. Our lovemaking became a "keep-me-I'm-yours-sweetheart, deal"—at least for me.

As for her, I could only hope she felt the same as the lovemaking continued and I climaxed a second time, still ready for more. But soon we were sore and couldn't continue, even though we wanted to. Laughing over our predicament, we agreed it was time to sleep. Cuddling, we drifted off.

In the morning, I woke excited and carefree as she slept. "What a beauty, and such a ferocious lover," I thought. She stirred after a while, awakened by Saturday morning sunbeams streaming into the room. She had to do some errands, she whispered. Getting up, she quickly dressed. Shortly after, she was on her way out the door.

I asked her, "How about dinner again tonight?"

"Yes. Come to my place. I'll cook for you," came the answer I was hoping for.

Our lovemaking that evening just wasn't the same. It was more like a "good-bye screw." Stupefied, I wondered where her heart had gone.

In the morning she asked me to leave, no address, no phone number, just a curt, "I've got to get ready to leave with Carmen for Mazatlan."

Fine. I understood, but I didn't. It was heart-wrenching. I wanted more, but she spurned me. She saw my anguish, yet started busying herself, figuring I'd soon get the message and leave. I did. Heading out the door, she gave me a quick goodbye kiss. I walked out trying to make sense out of her sudden change of heart.

She was off to vacation and to have fun. What kind of fun, I could only imagine. If only her fiancé knew.

Back at the motel with Don, I offered this explanation, but it did nothing to ease my pain. Carmen had been sure to tell Don that Rose's fiancé had cheated on her. Rose was out for revenge. I had been chosen. I was the lucky fool. In a very short period of time I had fallen for the woman.

Exasperated, I looked at Don. "Yeah, they're women all right."

"Hey, don't take it so seriously, man. You had some fun. That's all she wanted. Now she'll go home and tell her fiancé all about you." He grinned widely as if that were all there was to the situation. Where's the Goddess? I needed to talk with her, too.

Don and I were sitting poolside when Bill returned from visiting Aireberto. Bill, usually cheerful, no matter the situation, walked up with an inexplicable look on his face, then blithely announced, "Aireberto's gone."

Two days had passed. All three of us had been waiting for the news we figured would be good. Snapping upright I barked, "Gone? What the hell does that mean?"

Don demanded, "Yeah. What are you saying, man?"

"He's gone, guys. He's unavailable." Bill's voice was full of consternation, his face riddled with fear.

"Jesus, Bill, can you be more specific?" I stood up to face him. "Is this real? I mean is he gone or just out of town?"

Worried and somewhat tongue-tied he replied, not looking at us, "I think he split. That's what it seems like."

"Split. What the hell for?" Don asked, as he too stood up.

"Come on. Let's talk in the room," Bill grumbled.

Standing in front of Bill as he perched on the edge of a bed, he seemed all the more nervous and unable to function. Unable to look us in the eye, he continued. "I went to his workplace where he usually is. His secretary said he wasn't in and that he's not available to anyone. Not today. Not tomorrow or anytime. From what I got, she was not sure where he is or when he might be back."

Both Don and I were silent for a moment as Bill continued haltingly. "I…know where he lives…and I went by his house. No one was home. No wife. No kids or servants. Nothing. The house was shut down."

"Fucking-A!" Don cursed. "This is too much. What's this dude all about?"

"Come on, Bill. You know him. What can you tell us? Shit, he's been around for years. Why would he just up and leave?" I all but screamed at him.

"How about going back and seeing what his secretary has to say," Don hounded. "Maybe he went on vacation."

"No, he's not on vacation. He's gone. That's all." Bill looked directly at us this time, but his voice lacked certainty. "He may be on the run. I don't know guys. I don't think he'll return." The vacant look on his face startled me.

"Fuck, man I'm not going to put up with this shit," Don spouted out. "Let's go over to his house."

"No. I won't do that. It's not necessary. The man's gone. That's it. His house is empty. That says a lot. He's not going to be back."

"Wait a minute Bill. This is crazy," I said, attempting to grasp the enormity of the situation. It just didn't make sense. The very thing we didn't want to happen just happened. "Could have he just gone away a day or two?"

"Not by the looks of his house."

"Then do something, man." I was hot. "This makes no sense. I don't believe what's going down here. Let's all three of us go over and talk with the secretary."

"Yes." Don chimed in. "Let's go."

Bill, looking sheepish, complied. We got into his clunker and headed out.

※ ※ ※

Over the next two days, Bill, Don and I visited Aireberto's place of business. Each time we entered the furniture store, his secretary looked askance at the three of us. She was tired of us invading her domain and kept conversations short and terse. Because she was unable to speak a word of English, Bill used his limited Spanish.

"*Señor Aireberto no está aquí,*" she would dribble out, then return to her work.

Bill always asked when he'd be back.

The reply was always the same: "who knows," or in Spanish, "*quien sabe.*"

We had driven out to his house. Bill was right. The place was, as we could all see, locked and shut tight.

After leaving the office on the third day, Don let some pent-up anger rip loose. I listened in as he blew his cool at Bill. It was over money of course; money that we had fronted to Aireberto; money that kept all things running. Don wanted Bill to pay him back. Bill was reluctant at first, but soon conceded. They worked something out while I stood back, thinking about the mess we were in. Contingency plans had been if Aireberto didn't show—but the plan was a long shot—Bill was hopeful that his man Modesto would front us a load of contraband. If not, we were in deep trouble.

Don was dropped off at the airport later that afternoon and Bill and I headed for the coast in his old clunker. Mazatlan was eight hours away. Ten, if you're in a clunker. Twelve if you're in no rush, and just then, there was no reason to push. We arrived in the middle of the night. It was a silent journey. I didn't have much to say to Bill and he had even less to say to me.

Along the coast the monsoon season was at its peak. The daily high was ninety-five degrees. The daily low was ninety-something, with the humidity somewhere in between. The heat awoke me. It was late, perhaps 10:00 p.m. Bill and Inger were out shopping. I showered, dressed, and headed down the hill. Walking down the Malacon, I passed the now archaic restaurant "Cope De Leche." I was already sweating. It was hard to breathe or relax in the stifling heat. I walked alone, my mind wrangled by our situation, heading to Tambor's restaurant for breakfast.

Tomorrow, I would call Jake. Thinking of him and his family camping out in Arizona, I wondered how Jake was going to react when I told him the news. With these thoughts running through my mind, I glanced up and was completely astonished by what I saw. Rose and her good friend Carmen were headed straight in my direction, just as they had in Guadalajara a few days before. What gives? I asked myself. The first thing that went through my mind was, "Are they narcs? Nah. This is just something that's supposed to happen. Weird!"

As I hugged her she said, "What on earth are you doing here?"

"Well, I'm not following you. Honestly, I'm not." Still stunned and having no answer for her at that second, I simply told her I had come down with my brother and that he had just moved here. "I'll be hanging out for a couple of weeks—Hi, Carmen. Boy, this is such a surprise. I mean, I knew you were going to be here, but this is unusual—you have to admit." I rambled on nervous, "Hey, I was headed for breakfast. Can I take you with me? I know a nice place. I go there all the time."

"Well, sure. We haven't eaten yet," Rose replied.

Over breakfast, Rose and Carmen acted superficial. Already I'd picked up the vibe that I was intruding on them. They made this apparent when they mentioned they wanted to run off to the *marcato* and there was no invite. But we did make a date to meet up at the beach later that afternoon.

When they failed to show I took my woes to Inger, who was a hopeless romantic. Any story of this nature made her a captive audience for hours. Add a couple of bars of chocolate and she'd hang in a day or two. After telling her the twisted tale I said, "So they pulled a no-show, Inger. Why do women do that?"

She looked at me coyly as she rattled around the kitchen. "Oh, women will do those things. They are not beyond that. Besides, she has the fiancé. And he's to pay the price. She was good to do that. She paid him back."

Inger was a feminist, but had yet to figure out how to make use of her liberty with Bill. They had had a few good fights and she always got mad and stormy, while Bill just stood back, avoiding flack as he worked his cruel ways on her. I often confided with her as she struggled through these times. We agreed on most occasions; Bill had a way of bringing out the worst in us. We couldn't really figure out why, only that we had to find a way to not let him get our goats up. Sooner or later, we agreed, his karma would catch up with him. Then we'd continue whining and moaning about the injustice of the situation we'd both been caught in.

"Perhaps you were getting to like this woman." She changed the subject.

"No kidding. Without a doubt. She's lovely, fun, smart…I could go on."

"Well, it may take some time, but you'll get over it."

"Shit, I just love it when people say that." I hated the truth of the matter.

"What else is there to talk about?"

"Bill is with Tambor this afternoon. He's arranging a meeting with Modesto and he wants me to come along."

"To be the interpreter?"

"But of course," she said proudly.

"Inger, did you persuade Bill to do this?"

"Yes, I'd like to meet his man. He is very famous here in Mazatlan, you know."

"I've heard his name, but I don't know him."

"Yes. They have a song about him, "Modestillo." He was once the bodyguard of the Governor."

"Yeah, I heard that. So you're going to come along. I'd like to meet this guy, too."

Two days later, all was arranged. We were to meet Modesto just before lunch. Tambor, our contact and the middleman, was to be present. It was his job, but on that day, Inger would also interpret. Decked out in her knit hot-pants, both Bill and I were taken back by her choice of attire, but she only smiled and said, "Let's get going," as she whisked past, holding the baby securely.

Tambor drove. He took to the back streets of Mazatlan and in no time I was lost. Shortly, he pulled to a stop in front of a rundown building in the middle of a block. The interior was quite homey. A couple of older men, along with two women of different ages, greeted us. Inger talked to the young one right away, and found out she was one of Modesto's wives. The woman approached and took the baby from Inger. She was to watch Kerstin while we met with her husband.

A few moments later, a big pickup truck pulled up out front. Four men got out, all of them with pistols tucked in their belts. They looked like ranchers—hats, boots and belts.

When he entered, Modesto greeted the others warmly as his men stood by quiet. Modesto laughed over something said to him, as we were introduced around. Cordial to us, he was charmed by Inger's presence, as she informed him that she too would interpret. Continuing around the room, he guffawed with Bill as they shook hands, the two of them looking at one another as if they were friends. It was Bill's fourth meeting with him.

"*Mucho gusto, amigos. Mucho gusto.* You are my friends. Welcome to you. Let us talk," he said in Spanish.

Modesto, cool and apparently ready to negotiate, remained standing with arms behind his back, looking at Inger as she told him our heartbreaking story. Once he learned about, *Señor* Aireberto, the busted load, and Aireberto's disappearance with our money, Modesto's face became sad.

Inger seized the opportunity and asked him for assistance. We wanted him to front us a load of four hundred and fifty kilos of regular marijuana and would be willing to pay him more per kilo if he agreed.

I could tell that Inger was pleased with the outcome.

"*Señor* Modesto is very sad to hear of our problems and says he would like to help us. He will give you the *mota* under one condition. After you do this one business, you must come back and purchase more from him. He says there is nothing available at this time. In one month he will have plenty. Then he'll give you your *mota*."

"Good. Ask him if he expects any high-quality weed this year," Bill requested.

"The answer is yes. He will expect several tons of a good quality from Nayarit in the coming weeks," Inger told us. She was in her glory. We might just be out of the woods on this one, I thought.

A few details were worked out, and Tambor was to inform us when the load was ready. Modesto, apparently pleased by the outcome shook our hands, then departed with his bodyguards.

So we had to wait a month. What the hell! We'd been doing that for the past few years anyway. There was nothing else for us to do but wait.

I informed Jake of the deal with Modesto and he was greatly relieved. "We're tired of the Blue Mountains, buddy. We're coming to Mexico. I want to talk with Bill and maybe meet this man Modesto."

"How you doing with money?"

"As much as I loathe the system I'm still making use of the credit cards. I can hang in for about another grand. Then they'll cut me off."

Three days later, Jake showed up in Mazatlan with his family. With time to kill, we headed to the beaches almost daily while Joanne and Inger became fast friends. They shopped, cooked, and doted over babies.

When my birthday came in late August, for some ungodly reason, Jake and I downed a bottle of mescal: poor man's tequila. We were celebrating, or so we thought, when actually we were out to get ourselves sick. Friggin' pressure, that's all. Jake and his family came down with the *touristas* during the first week, but managed to survive them. To us, Mazatlan was an unholy sweatshop.

Toward the end of August, as promised, Modesto came to our aid. Tambor, dropping by Bill's apartment and told us that *Señor Modesto* would have the *mota* ready for us in two days.

Jake and family packed up and departed the next day. He was to handle the lower end with Ramon and the pilots. We wanted to oversee the entire project as much as we could. When Ramon arrived on time, along with two of his men and their van, I began to believe this would happen. The next morning, along with Ramon in his car and the van following, we sped south following Tambor along the main highway.

Exiting the highway a few miles out of town, we stayed close as Tambor turned on to a dirt road. A truck was waiting for us. Quickly, large sacks—the Mexicans call them *cosali*—were loaded into the van. Moments later we took off with Ramon and I following the van. In Los Mochis, we watched as the van passed safely through the *aduana* station with no problems. As planned, I got out in Hermosillo and took a motel room.

Two days later, when I heard we had been successful, I flew to San Francisco. It was the first of September when I landed, ever so happy to be back, at least for the moment. Jake met me in front of the terminal and we took off immediately. Craning round, he gave forth a strange stare, then announced, with an equally strange grin, "Hey, congratulations!"

Before I could respond, he added with good humor, "Yesterday the Federal Grand Jury in San Diego indicted you and eighteen others for conspiracy to smuggle."

Somewhat stunned I said, "Good for them. They'll have to catch my ass first. Who's on the list? Howie must have been very cooperative."

"We'll find out soon enough. Come on. Let's get out of here. We've got a motel room in Ben Lomand. Ben lives nearby. Dwight is due in with the load sometime this afternoon."

"Jake, it's already afternoon."

"I know."

CHAPTER EIGHTEEN

SARAH, SWEET SARAH

SANTA CRUZ MOUNTAINS, CA
SEPTEMBER, 1971

Jake's State trial, which was coming up in another few days, was going to have to take place without him. As for the federal narcotic agents and the federal prosecutors who wanted us, we were unavailable to them as well. Both of us were officially fugitives, wanted for conspiracy to smuggle marijuana into the country. Some of the details we didn't know, only that the narcs had arrested everyone involved except the three main characters: Jake, Ramon and me.

We found a safe base to operate: the Santa Cruz Mountains, a one-hour drive south of San Francisco. Ben and Bill, our good customers from Berkeley, were living in the area. Our relationship with them had been strained, but they greeted us cordially when Jake and I stopped by the next day at Ben's new digs off Highway 17. We arranged a place to store the load and Ben agreed to sell most of the weed as a bonus.

Irv, my Marin contact, was as happy as an elf with a golden flute when I called to ask him to pick up his portion of the contraband.

When we found time, Jake and I met with the lawyers on three different occasions over the next few days. One of the O'Bryan's, a well-known San Francisco father and sons attorney group, planned to litigate for our attorney, Ryan, who was out on bail and in a very bitchy mood.

"He doesn't want to meet with you, nor does he feel it necessary," Patrick stated. He then asked us for as much information as possible to successfully defend his client.

Later, he assured us that Ryan would not go to jail and charges against him would be dropped. "Pure harassment, guys. They indicted him because Howie said he was your attorney."

Howie was indeed the main informant, along with Willy.

After the meeting, Jake and I headed back to our motel hideout in Ben Lomand, pleased to learn that those who had been indicted were out of jail on bond or had been released on their own recognizance. My good friends Ed and Fay were among them. As for Howie and Willy, we figured they'd have to live with themselves. We were angry. We also knew the drought had everything to do with our demise.

As for Jake and me, we were getting along just fine. We had to, and we communicated most of our moves every day. Neither of us wanted to make a mistake. We'd be totally ruined if we got picked up. I shuddered to think about the consequences and pushed the paranoia aside. It was tough. Both of us were running around without false ID's. Should we get stopped for speeding or for something trivial, such as a burned out brake light, we'd be served up.

During the first week, I got up early one morning and took Windy, Jake's young daughter, to the store with me for a few groceries. I had my old VW, and returning from the store, still groggy, I made an illegal U-turn, thinking no one had seen me. The highway patrolman even said I'd have gotten away with it if he hadn't just come around the bend off my rear. Sweating it out while he considered checking my driver's license, I was relieved when he backed off with a stern warning. In this case, I was daddy taking his daughter to school. Windy, age eleven, played the part well.

When I returned, I confessed this to Jake. We were out of there real quick—twenty minutes, tops.

It took over a month to sell the load. The money to pay Modesto, Bill and Tambor had arrived safely down south by courier, and a sizable portion of our debts to our colleagues had been taken care of, but not the dividends. We were kind of smug, even though we hadn't much money. The drought had ended, so we believed.

When I connected with Bill, we were informed that Modesto would have the good Nayarit weed in a couple of days. At the moment there was only more of the same regular weed. We passed because Ramon finally had a load. He was hurting financially and Jake insisted we help him out.

Cautious, I told Jake. "I don't like moving unless we know what we're moving. You know he never looks at the loads, and he'll do anything to get going. Let's have him move Modesto's stuff when it's ready. Two loads and we're all back on our feet, Ramon included."

"If he goes to look at it, I'd like to move it for him." Jake didn't want to give in so easily.

The following day, Jake told me Ramon had agreed to our request. The load was of good to decent quality. "I'm gonna move on it, Frank. He's set to go. It's at his ranch in Mexico."

He and his family had moved to the foothills some two hours to the east. I had found a perfect little hideaway in a canyon near Los Gatos, only three miles from Ben's house. It was a small, rustic, summer cabin situated in the redwoods up a very steep canyon, a peaceful place to dwell, and much to my liking.

I contacted my brother Ray and asked him to retrieve my personal possessions from Ed and Fay. He arrived one afternoon, and we hauled my stuff up to the cabin. After a short visit, he was gone. He seemed more disturbed than concerned. It didn't matter. I had more important things to think about. I had a place of my own for the first time in several months. I rolled up a joint, cranked up the stereo, kicked back, and began to set up the living quarters.

Jake called a few days later to let me know Dwight was on his way back with Ramon's load. I only had to wait for his arrival.

I drove to meet Dwight the next day in my new, used VW. I had sold the old one for fear of being stopped by the law. When I arrived at Toby's house—a customer and friend of Ben's—he and Dwight were outside. Something was amiss. I could tell by the long looks on their faces.

"Hey, you guys look dismal. Anything wrong? How's the load? Ramon said it would be good."

"Well, take a look at it. Tell us what you think?" Dwight was obviously not happy.

Heading to the garage, I opened up a kilo, and was immediately enraged. "Oh, man! Sonofabitch!" I yelled. "He promised us good reg. I can't believe this." Turning to Toby and Dwight, I said, "This is inexcusable."

Toby was to sell most of this through Ben.

"Ramon flat out lied to us, guys. Don't mess with it right now. I'll call Jake and talk with him about it."

Speeding off to a pay phone, I contacted with Jake and complained bitterly. "He fucking lied to us, man, all the way. It's another load of stick-shit. Toby doesn't want to sell it. I have half a mind to tell Ramon to come pick it up and sell it himself."

"Okay, man. I hear you, but we can't do that. It's not that simple."

"Jake, I don't want it."

"Be easy. We've got to do something with it."

"That sonofabitch, all this movement for this crap. Jesus, Jake, this is ugly. You're gonna have to do some heavy talking to me on this one. Come on over and get a good look at it. It's in the garage. I had a feeling he'd pull something like this."

"I'll come over tomorrow and see it. Besides, I haven't told you the worst part of it yet."

"It can't possibly get worse."

"Oh yeah? Listen to this. I held off telling you so there would be less pressure. The people who fronted this to Ramon are holding him hostage until he pays them off."

"Jesus Christ. He's a birdbrain. He's putting his life on the line for this crap. That's the pressure I talked about that he's under, Jake. This is bullshit. If he lied about the load, he's lying about being held. God, what an idiot. He knew we had other work for him through Modesto."

"I don't think he's lying. He's never said this before."

"Did he tell you this after you got the load?"

"Yes."

"Then tough shit, Jake. I'm not buying into his problems. You come over here and we'll discuss what to do with it. It's the only way."

"I'll be there, but you need to realize that we have to sell this stuff." Jake was firm.

After Jake looked over the load with me, we decided to call Irv in to help. A price was worked out. We'd also gained new customers in the nearby San Jose area through Joanne's sister's boyfriend. Those people agreed to help sell too. The cleanup began at Toby's place the next day.

"This is it, Jake. Ramon's on my shit list. No more of his weed. We'll have him transport our stuff through Modesto. That's all we need him for."

"Fine." Jake shot me a quick look, and added. "You know I'm in agreement about this guy, Modesto. We'll stay with him. Let's just sell this stuff and get Ramon his money. We'll have a few more bucks of operating capital."

Ramon's stick-shit load was selling very slowly—two weeks and counting. Coming home one afternoon to my cabin for a short break and a bit of lunch, I sat down to eat. Ten minutes later the phone rang. I guessed it was Jake, who was due to call. I became thoroughly annoyed when it was Ramon.

"Hey, glad I caught you. How's it going?"

Jake must have given him my phone number without telling me. I had no desire to talk with this man, "Slow Ramon, very slow." I was thinking to myself, "He's got a lot of nerve calling me after what he pulled." I didn't like the intrusion one bit.

"When do you think you'll have some money for me?"

Further annoyed, I answered, "Talk with Jake about that. He'll be able to tell you."

"Hey, take it easy. I need to know. Jake's probably told you my situation here. These guys want their money."

Outraged to the hilt, I replied, "No one told you to do this. And you lied, flat out bullshitted us about this shit."

"Hold it," he interjected. "These guys are serious. I don't get out of here unless they get their money. I need to know."

"Get off it, goddamnit. Don't go putting your crap on to me, man. It was your choice to do this. You lied to us all the way."

"Frank. They're holding me here. Just give me some sort of time frame. I need to say something to them."

As I listened in, I couldn't pick up any fear. Quite the opposite, he sounded cool, almost relaxed. I shot back, "Jake will call you by this evening. I've nothing more to say to you. You got that?" I slammed down the phone and returned to lunch. A minute or so later, the phone rang again. Figuring it was Ramon calling back, I prepared myself for another argument.

"Is this Frank?" asked a male voice.

The voice was vaguely familiar, but I couldn't pin it down. Cautiously, I said, "Who's this?"

"Please don't ask. I'm a friend of Joan's. Okay? I have a very important message for you." By now I knew who it was—a lawyer whom I had met at the office where Joan worked as a paralegal.

"Fine. What is it?"

"Jake Larson was arrested in Carson City, Nevada, two hours ago by Federal Narcotic agents. I was informed of this only a few minutes ago. I was asked to let you know as soon as possible. He had his phone book on him. I'm sure you understand what all of this means."

"Is this for real?"

"Yes. It's very real. I can only advise you to proceed with caution. I'm sorry. I know this is a big blow. Do what's right and keep it together. I have to go. Stay in touch with your people. Peace, brother!" He hung up.

The voice and the message lingered. I was dazed. Looking vacantly around my cabin a fury hit me. "Get out of here," my mind screamed. "Get out now. There's no time to waste."

In an instant I grabbed my jacket and headed for the door, but stopped. Think, Frank, think. What do you need here that's of any importance? Jake's gone. Fuck! Pack some clothes. Turn the stove off. Jake's gone. Sonofabitch! Why is this happening? Get out of here. The narcs have his phone book, and even though he codes his numbers they may figure them out. Get your ass out of here. Leave everything and get going. Jake's gone. Ah fuck! This can't be. They can't do that. Get out of here. Jake's gone and you're alone now. Go on. Get going.

Hastily, I packed a few clothes and sundries, threw them in my Volkswagen and raced off. Within moments, I was on Highway 17 headed to Santa Cruz. Tears were flowing uncontrollably, making it difficult to see as I drove the twisty uphill portion. Suddenly, I found myself pounding the steering wheel, screaming in anguish, "Why Jake? Why did you do this? For God's sake, why? You didn't have to do this. You just didn't need to!"

The night before, Jake had called to check in and let me know everything was okay. He had mentioned that he had had a few good ideas concerning our future and would talk to me about them that evening. "I've got some errands to take care of first, but I should be there in the early evening. We'll have dinner and talk."

I had hung up without asking what those errands were. Now I knew. We had had our pilot bring our plane in for a mandatory 100-hour check-up. It had to be done at an FAA-controlled airstrip. We chose Carson City, even though the authorities would know in no time that it was there. We had great concerns about that, but after some discussion decided it would be safe for the pilot to fly it there, come back, pay the bill, and then fly off to an airfield that had no FAA control status. The worst that could happen was the feds might seize the plane. Then we'd rent one—simple as that.

Now I was driving down the highway, pent up and bitter, knowing that Jake had gone there to pay the bill himself. That was the only answer. Again, I pounded the wheel. "Jake, you didn't need to do this! Why did you go, man? And why didn't you tell me you were going there? Oh Christ man, you're fucked. You're completely fucked. They have you and there's nothing I can do. Nothing, man, but I'll get 'em, Jake. They won't get away with this. Stay cool, brother. I'm out here. I'm free. I'm bringing these assholes down. That's a promise." Pounding the wheel again, I screamed out loud, tears streaming down my face. "I'll get you shits. I'll get you!" I was so worked up I had to pull to the side of the road.

"Calm down, Frank. Calm down. You're safe—for now." Leaning forward I rested my head on the steering wheel. Blowing my nose, I said aloud over and over again, "Why Jake? It makes no sense. Tell me why you went there? Tell me. Give me one good reason! Oh God man, look at what you've done. Why Jake? You're not stupid. You knew to send the pilot to do the job. We talked about it. I want to know, dammit. I'm pissed at you. Give me one good reason." I pounded the wheel again and again. "There was no reason for you to go there. You piss me off, you turd. Why can't you be here so I can to tell you this?"

Slowly, I calmed down, but breathing was difficult. I needed to regain my senses, so I sat there for several minutes. Finally rational thoughts replaced panic. "I've got to help him. I've got to do something to help all of them. I've got to keep Brotherhood afloat. My brethren would want me to. Oh God, Jake, why did you do this to yourself, to me, to your family, to all of us? We needed you to be here with me. You're my brother. This is so unfair—so stupid. Yes, that's what it is, and stupid doesn't work. I have to get with it. I have to keep the campaign going. Screw you narcs. I'm gonna keep on working. Let's go, man. Let's go. You've got work to do. Yes. There's work to do. Think. How are you gonna get going? Get back on the highway. That's it, one step at a time."

Starting the car, I headed off. "That's it. Get a motel in Santa Cruz near the ocean. Go ahead," I coaxed myself.

Within an hour I found a motel with a room about as close to the beach as one could get. The day was beautiful: no fog and the sky clear and blue. Checking in, I immediately headed out for a walk on the beach. "Come on brother ocean, soothe my spirit," I said aloud, as I walked south on the beach along the water's edge. Already I had glimpses of how to deal with the situation. I knew it would take very careful planning and real heavy decisions. Walking barefoot, I allowed the cool ocean water to awaken me.

The plane was out of the picture: the narcs had it anyway, plus, Jake had the pilot's number and Ramon's. No way could I get in touch with them—more stupidity. Ramon could go screw himself as far as I was concerned. It was my ball game now, with no one to advise me. I was free to act on my own. No Ramon. No Jake. I began to like the feeling. I could do the work my way. I'd have only myself to answer to. Working with Ramon would only be a problem anyway.

Joan, Jake's good friend, had warned me a few months back. She told me that it could come down to me taking care of myself. She was right. She knew something would happen. So did a few of my close friends. So I'd have to go it alone. I'd seek help from the universe.

It's okay. You've earned this position. Jake would understand—he had to understand now that he had screwed up. "Why, Jake? Why on earth did you go there? It makes less sense every time I think about it. How are you doing, partner? I'm angry at you, but I have compassion for what you did. It's hurting, Jake. It's hurting. I'm gonna keep on working. That's for sure."

I need a boat. I'm gonna do this next one with a sailboat, the way I've always wanted to. I'll just figure it out. That's all. I need money and a crew. I have a load of weed here. There's enough money there to pull it off. I hope. Shit, not really. I have to pay everyone off and after that there won't be enough for what I need. If I buy a boat I'll need at least twenty to twenty-five grand. I have five on me now from the last deal. I'll need another five grand to outfit the boat and get it to Mazatlan and back. I'll need expense money—money that I don't really have. I'll have the money, but it's Ramon's money. Money to go to Ramon for the shit load he sent us. That's it. That's the key.

Stopping on the beach, I let these thought run through my mind. At first I was shocked at myself, then a bit ashamed. The very money I would need was within reach, only it was Ramon's money, or better yet, the people who had bought the shit and sold it to us. If I paid them back, I wouldn't have the money for the boat. To boot, I'd still have to work with Ramon. That idea repulsed me. I could do the boat thing, no problem. Then it really hit me: I had no choice. It was survival time—time to take care of myself, like Joan had said. Ramon would have to eat his shit load. He'd have to survive as he always had. The people who were holding him, if that were true, would have to deal with what I was about to do.

"Fuck you, you stick-shit turds. I'm sticking it to you. I'm going to survive this one on my terms." Then it dawned on me. I hadn't called anyone to let them know Jake had been busted.

Furious with myself, I turned around and made my way back to the motel. Two hours had elapsed since I'd received the shocking news. Ben answered the phone. "It's Frank, Ben. I've got bad news." I told him all I knew and added, "I want to move the load from Toby's place."

"Yup. Right away. You want me to call him?"

"No. Check in with him in a bit. Let me call him first and make the arrangements, though."

"Okay. Sorry about your partner. What are you gonna do now?"

"Haven't time to talk Ben. Call Berkeley Bill, please. Sorry, but this is going to put heat on you guys, too. See ya."

I reached Toby next, who was both concerned and annoyed, but agreed to move the load to his girlfriend Barbara's house. "You stay put, man. Relax. Dwight and I will handle it. Go make some calls. Talk with your people. Give me a call later. *Ciao!*"

Next I placed a call to Tambor in Mazatlan. Luckily, he was at home. "Tambor, go to Bill's house and tell him to come to the phone at your house in two hours. I must talk to him. I have a big problem."

"*Si*. I will go to see him now. Are you *bien*?"

"Yes. I'm okay. Hopefully I'll see you soon, for the good stuff. Right?"

"*Si*. For the good stuff. Later, man."

Heading back to the room, I found a pen and a note pad. Figuring for the pilot's pay and investment returns to Berkley Bill, Ben, Dwight the driver, and other small expenses, I had $28,000 leftover. I had close to five of my own. That's enough to pull this off. I knew Bill would have a few thousand, Tambor, a couple. If Modesto went according to his word, he'd front us the same amount we purchased. Bill had mentioned that possibility before I had left.

"Good. That's the deal. That's the way I'm gonna pull this off," I said aloud.

Ramon and his cohorts would be the odd men out. Feeling utterly strange about my decision, I headed for Barbara's. Toby and Dwight were there when I arrived. "We just finished storing the weed in her garage."

"Good! Dwight, come with me. I've got a call to make."

Dwight began questioning me about our immediate future the second I drove off.

"Be patient. I'll have an answer soon. I have to call Bill first."

When I reached Bill, I was cautious over the phone.

"Hey brother. What's up?" His voice was cheerful as I began the dialogue.

"Something heavy, Bill. Jake was picked up by the man." I quickly explained.

"Damn. I'm sorry to hear about this."

"The airways are out. Okay? So is Ramon. I'm prepared to come to you by water. How's that sound?"

"Fine, man. Are you sure you can pull it off?"

"All I need is your support on this. I can put the rest together. How many units can you purchase with your money?"

"No problem. Let's see, not counting the front, about seven hundred. Tambor's right here. Hang on." A moment later he said "He can get it transported out to you if you come by water and he knows Modesto will front another seven. That's fourteen hundred pounds altogether."

"That's all I need to know. Let's connect tomorrow at the long distance place—same time."

"I'll be there waiting."

Heading back to the car I said to Dwight, "We can talk now. I have the go-ahead I need."

"Damn, Frank. What's up? Jake's gone and you say everything's up in the air." Being a fugitive had rattled him, and now this.

"We're going to keep on working, brother. I'm gonna do this one by boat. I'll need you to help me. You'll be well paid and in the end, you'll have the money we promised you. I plan to buy a forty-footer and sail to Mazatlan. We're going to smuggle fourteen hundred pounds. That's the picture. I need a crew and I'm asking you to come along."

"That's far out. Yeah! Yeah, sure. Count me in. Nancy may get pissed at me, but I'm in. Where're you gonna get a boat?"

"Look Dwight, I'm gonna do something heavy. I don't want any judgments. Okay? Don't try to change my mind on the matter."

He nodded affirmatively. The plan was laid out. "Call it a sly loan, an inconvenience to a distraught man, or a rip-off. I don't care. I want to survive. You see the circumstance we're under. I can't work with Ramon, and Jake has really hurt all of us. So this is it. Are you still with me?"

It took him a moment, but he came around. "This is really heavy man. But they're your plans, not mine. Yeah, I'll join you."

"Good. I'll need you."

"When are you planning to do this?"

"As soon as we sell the weed, brother, we're outta here. I'll put things together in the meantime. Right now I figure it'll take a month to get ready. If we get out of here by the first part of December we'll be back maybe before Christmas."

When I contacted with Bill again, I worked out a deal. We agreed on approximately fourteen hundred pounds of contraband. Modesto would front half. Acting officious with him, I stipulated that Tambor would receive ten dollars per pound; Bill would receive a third of the profit. My people and I would receive two-thirds. In a few short minutes, we haggled out some other problems and all was set. He wasn't exactly happy. Then again, I had expected him to be angry.

"What about the pick-up? Who's going to get it off the boat for you?" he asked.

"Let's work on it together. Maybe some of your surfer friends can help.

Why don't you check with them?"

By early November, I had the necessary funds to purchase a boat. I let Dwight know all was ready and headed south in my VW for Los Angeles. Dwight was to come down as soon as he finished selling the last few pounds. I contacted two friends before departing, Dale and Mary, to join in the crew. Everything was falling into place. Arriving in Los Angeles I checked into a motel in Venice.

The next day I made an appointment to look at three different K-40 vessels. One of them had a new two-cylinder diesel engine with a power cruising range of six-hundred miles. "It burns about a third to a half gallon an hour. How about that?" the broker asked cordially.

Yeah. How about that? I thought, licking my chops in silence. "Well, that's no big deal to me, but it's nice to have—and diesel, too. That's safer isn't it?" I asked, playing it naively.

"Sure is, young man. Make an offer and you'll have the best of the three."

Two days later, after a sea trial and a haul out to paint the bottom and at the same time have the boat surveyed, I walked into the brokerage with a small briefcase full of cash. I had gone to the bank and gotten a few money wrappers to make the cash look like it was fresh from the vault, all twenty-five bundles. "Hope you don't mind, I brought cash with me. Is that okay?"

"No problem. That's how Peter Fonda paid for his schooner—all cash. That's the way he wanted it. Cash is for real."

While his secretary counted the loot, I signed the papers using my new alias: Steve Allen Walsh— I had no ID, and had made up the name. Besides, this was not the DMV and no ID was required. A few moments later the broker shook my hand and handed me the title and the key. "Good luck. It's a fine vessel. Remember, you have to be out of the berth by December first."

I checked out of my motel room and spent the evening on the boat. I wanted to get acquainted with my new vessel, and did so like a miner inspecting the vein of gold he'd just discovered. Poking my head into every corner of the craft, I gave way to passion. The marine surveyor had found two small problems and both had been corrected by the former owner during the haul out; otherwise the K-40 was in excellent shape. And, indeed all was well. Not a flaw to her, no broken ribs, no doors or draws that would not open or shut properly, no lights that would not turn on, no halyards or rigging that needed immediate repair. Her bright work and hull as well as the wenches and the sails would need future consideration. After the first run was over, I'd purchase new equipment. For now we'd go with what we had.

She was made entirely of wood; oak frames, mahogany planking, and bronze fastening. She had ten feet and six inches of beam, drew an even five feet, and weighed twelve thousand pounds: five of that a cast iron, bolt on, keel. She had a wheel, as opposed to a tiller, and the rudder was spade. Kettenberg had designed this class of vessel in the late fifties: light-displacement sailboats capable of planing downwind.

When I went to bed that evening, thoughts about love overwhelmed me. Perhaps this had to do with the very attractive young woman I spotted walking down the dock as I inspected the exterior of my new boat that afternoon. I stopped what I was doing and when I fastened my eyes on her, she caught me and unfolded a heavenly smile that sent shivers up my groin. As she disappeared from sight, libidinous thoughts came streaming in. She was twenty at most, trim, with dark hair and face that one could look at and cherish.

I wanted a woman in my life, but for the past few years I'd been stymied. I didn't have the time, what with running around smuggling drugs and playing dodge ball with the law. Now that I was a fugitive, my chances of finding a good woman were even less. I had packed around those negative thoughts all these years and accepted them as truth. But the smile she gave me was a message. Had I been on top of things I'd have spoken out to her, gained her attention to let her know she was attractive. Women love that because they are women, and the creator designed them that way. My self-esteem was low at that moment, and the negative thoughts that came to me in a flash said that she was too young; too innocent and sweet, and not to tamper with her. Regardless, I had let another opportunity walk right past me.

The next evening I fell into another weighty emotional state as I lay in my bunk. I was alone and would be until Dwight arrived in two days. I'd just bought the boat of my dreams, but had used other people's money. My partner was in jail and I was a fugitive. The future, though uncertain, looked bright, but in no way curtailed the emptiness I'd always had to live with.

Jake came into view in my mind's eye; he was not the same man I knew. His shoulders were slouched, his face worn and haggard. He was beaten, remorseful, depressed. He was a living example of the horrid mistake he had made. And that put fear in me for the few seconds his apparition was visible. And when the apparition faded and then disappeared all together, what was left was the truth. Jake had self-destructed because he could no longer deal with the fear that had been mounting over the past several years. It had to be that. He'd succumbed to all those pitiless moments in his past he'd suffered through and had been unable to let go. He'd lived with these lies, and I'd sensed many a time these withholdings; that was why he could not tell me he was going to Carson City to pay the bill. I'd have stopped him but deep down Jake wanted the authorities to take him away and put him in irons. Maybe then he'd release the pain, and the misery, and all the fear that was at his core. "Jake, "I spouted out as the whole of my body shook, "you could have come to me. I'm your partner, the closest thing to being a brother. How many times did I tell you that truth frees us?"

Exasperated and in turmoil, I let the moment proceed and soon Ramon came into view. He was okay, but a bit on the side of worrisome or something akin to that. When Bill came into view he was dancing, maybe he was thinking about going surfing, anyway he was buzzing with energy. Manny, Mack, and Glenn, came and went in a flash. They didn't want to be seen, it seemed.

After those people from my past had flashed before me, an alternate heaviness swept over me. We all pay a price for the harm we do to others. And for whatever reason, I felt shameful about what I was doing to Ramon and his people. I could only hope he was no longer in danger. Sooner or later, I'd find out. As for Jake, I wanted him here with me, and yet I was relieved that he wasn't. I had a newfound freedom, even if it was taxing me. And at that moment, as I lay in the forepeak of my new vessel, I was uncertain about what I was about to do. Everything depended on my ability to captain the vessel, and the weight of that pressed down on me.

Finally, along with the intense emotional stress, came the realization that I had to believe in myself. The good crew I had assembled was essentially solid. Bill would be awaiting us, and Dwight would soon be here with the rest of the money. Dale and Mary would arrive in five days. We'd outfit the boat, sail south, pick up the load, sail north and all would go well. It had to. There was no room for mistakes. A bad storm could ruin things, the mast might break, or the engine falter, but I had to believe that I could do this.

A few days after Jake's bust I had contacted Jake's wife. I learned the horrible details from her. Indeed, Jake had gone to pay the bill even though he knew better. The Feds had the place under surveillance. Their efforts paid off. Joanne, Windy, Johan and Heidi had all witnessed the arrest. Jake had further compromised his situation. The narcs had found a stash of grass, some hashish, and a small vial of cocaine in Jake's pickup. The State of Nevada was pressing charges. If what I was going through brought about depression for me, Jake was probably being raked over the coals of hell. I talked with Joanne about all of this, and concluded on an up-note.

"I'll be back in late December with a load of contraband. One-third of the profits will go to Jake, and our good people. You can use the money to pay attorney fees. The lawyers will be happy to hear this."

The next evening, I walked the beach as the sun set. And as darkness descended over the basin I'd dubbed "The Badlands," I began to settle down. I somehow had a better fix on the future—there was hope. A message from within said, "Flow with it, man. You deserve the chance to make your word good." And indeed I would reach out to my friends. They were my brothers and it was my chance to help them. I'd never been in such a position and

I felt uplifted, and I knew it was in my very nature to make such a choice. I had to succeed, but that was not the point at this moment. The point had to do with the life I had chosen and the resulting karma. I had been given a chance to come to the aid of others so that I might give assistance to myself, and a chance for me to feel the sheer joy of giving.

"We'll figure out how to deal with the celestial navigation on the way down. Getting a latitude shot is a snap. Longitude will be a bit of work, but we'll get it done as long as we have a good sextant," Dale said to me as we stood at the navigation table. He and his wife, Mary, had arrived on schedule.

Dwight had also shown up on schedule, along with his wife, Nancy, and their young daughter. The money to outfit the boat was in hand.

Dwight had been acquainted with the boat and was impressed. Twice we had taken the boat out for a sail, once in a moderate breeze and again in a stiff breeze. Dwight took to sailing readily. As for the vessel, she'd do just fine.

Dale and Mary were part of the auspicious mix. I had met the two of them at the boat yard in Sausalito several months back. Dale was in his early twenties. He stood six feet, was lithe and muscular—an athlete. That he was quite smart, not to mention a master seaman, and a second-generation shipbuilder, was a *bona fide* plus. Plus, he had served four years with the Coast Guard and was familiar with how they operate. That made him indispensable. It was the same with his wife, Mary who was a quiet woman, independent and strong of mind, always there and always a seaman. She was to cook for us, and sail when she wanted a turn at the helm.

"I've got plenty of money, Dale. We can buy a good sextant and all else we need. Let's make a list."

The next day Dale inspected the vessel. He anticipated every possible need and over the next few days we made numerous trips to the local marine stores to purchase charts, a good sextant, books on navigation, a good chronometer, plastic jerry-jugs (to hold additional fuel to extend our cruising range to nine hundred miles), repair kits, spare parts, a first aid kit, flares, lines, and a radio-directional finder. The list seemed to go on and on, but we found everything.

As Thanksgiving approached, Dale and I readied for a post-holiday departure that would put us right on schedule.

"It'll take a week or so to get to Mazatlan; three, four days to rest, load up, then head home; then, two weeks or a little less to get to our destination. Hey, that puts us home around Christmas." Dale's estimate matched mine.

"How sweet," I joked, "Christmas presents for everyone except for Uncle Sam and the FBI."

Everything kept falling into place, including getting in and out of Mexico. I learned through a "Yachtsman's Magazine" ad that I could use a local customs house broker. All I had to do was submit proper paperwork, ownership papers, and crewmember names. The broker had visas and would fill them out. For a small fee, they'd do the work, all without having to show them identification.

Two days before Thanksgiving, as I drove back to the boat from running an errand, I recalled meeting a young woman at my yard in Sausalito who had impressed me. It was months ago, but she was cute, gregarious, and friendly. "I'm looking to go down Mexico way. If you ever hear of someone heading that way, let me know. I'll be ready to go in a flash," she had said.

"Call her, man," my inner voice rang out. "Don't miss the opportunity." Decision made, I pulled over to a pay phone and placed a call to Al at the yard. I knew next to nothing about her other than her name was Millie and she was Crazy Bill's girlfriend, or at least she was hanging out with him. Al answered the phone and in a minute I had Crazy Bill's phone number. When I called, he was at home.

"No, I'm not with Millie anymore. She'll go, but I haven't seen her. I'll give you her number."

It was a number for her parent's cabin in Inverness, a small town in Marin County near the coast. I was amazed when she answered. She even remembered who I was. "Frank! Well, nice to hear from you."

"Crazy Bill gave me your number. He said I might reach you here."

"Haven't been around lately, but I'm here with my family, home for the holiday."

"Listen up, Millie. I have a K-40. I'm sailing to Mexico right after Thanksgiving. Would you like to come along?"

"Wow! Gosh! I sure would. But, I have this new boyfriend."

Not prepared for that detail I faltered, but added, "Well you can still make it, right? But yeah, I agree, with a new boyfriend he may not want you to go."

"Yeah! Damn, I'd really like to. I have school of course, but hell, I'd go anyway. How about my sister, Sarah?"

"Come again? What about her?"

"She'd probably like to go. As a matter of fact, I know she would. She's a sailor, too—very good at it."

"This is sudden. I mean, ah…I don't know your sister."

"Oh, you'd like her. She's older than me. She's tall, gives a good massage and likes to sing. She's great fun."

All sorts of pictures began floating through my head. Who was this woman? Should I invite her along, with only a brief statement from her sister that she was a fun-to-be-with kind of gal?

"Boy, you got me there. Sounds great, but I need to think about this. Ask her. Make sure she's interested first."

"No problem. She's right here," Millie stated. I heard her holler for her older sister to come to the phone. I could hear them talking and it sounded like Sarah wanted to go.

"No kidding? Mexico? Who is this guy? A K-40? Boy, sounds great."

"He's a friend of Crazy Bill's. He owns a boatyard in Sausalito. He's cool, and he's ready to leave after Turkeyday. He wants you to make up your mind right now."

The rest was muffled. Millie cupped the phone to talk girl stuff, I figured. Soon she came back.

"Hey Frank, she's coming. She wants to know when you're leaving."

"Hold on Millie," I faltered. Damn, she wants to go. What do I do? Without thinking too long, I decided.

"OK. Let's do it all the way. If your sister comes, why don't you and your boyfriend come, too? I've a crew of four counting myself and seven people will be okay."

"He wants all of us to go," I heard her shout across the room, followed by a collective "Yes" from the background, then, "Where do we meet you?"

"All right! Terrific! I'll be at the Long Beach Marina at the departure dock." Going over final directions and what they might bring along, I hung up, sighing as I did so.

When I informed the crew of this sudden change in circumstances, understandably, they seemed apprehensive. But, they were still with me. We were set to go.

✯ ✯ ✯

It was late afternoon, a day after Thanksgiving. Dale and I had fixed, adjusted, replaced, or calibrated everything. All was ready.

Sitting in the cockpit talking with Dwight, I spotted Millie getting out of an older model Mercedes. Unloading their gear, our three guests headed down the ramp toward the guest dock. Millie waved as she and her sister Sarah, arms around one another other's shoulders, sang and danced a sailor's jig as they bounded down the dock, looking like two drunken sailors. Stopping in front of the vessel with their gear slung over their shoulders, they sang out in unison. "We're here and we're bound for Mexico."

Mary and Dale came topside to greet them as William, Millie's boyfriend, walked up. All of us stood around awkwardly staring at one another, then the three of them started climbing aboard. Suddenly, I was transfixed.

"This here is my sister, Sarah; I'm Millie and this here is my honey-pie, William the Prince," I heard Millie say, as I stood there in a daze. Sarah, who was so demonstrative coming down the dock, was now quiet and introspective. I caught myself staring at her as we introduced ourselves all around, shaking hands.

Overwhelmed by this unexpected vision of beauty, I made myself busy while the three went below to get squared away. As Mary began the evening meal, I planned. Sarah was going to be on my watch. Being Captain had its rewards.

That evening, we were entertained by a young man from another boat—persuaded with the help of good pot, he played his guitar, and we sang, cajoled, smoked reefers and downed beer for hours. Keeping my eyes off Sarah was nearly impossible. She certainly was tall, more precisely, exactly my height. She had long brown hair and blazing blue eyes, which were deep-set. They were inquisitive and had an intensity that personified intelligence. She had fine features, a square jaw, and a smirky smile, much like one I'd been accused of having.

We didn't talk much. She too was self-conscious, as was I, but she let loose around her sister and William. I discovered that the three of them liked to chide one another, constantly teasing each other with harmless and hilarious ridicule. An hour into the evening, Millie decided to put her older sister to test by pushing her to play the guitar and sing a few songs. For her own reasons, she wouldn't—Sarah, wanted only to slug down beer as a way to ward off the brow-beating her younger sister was so aptly dishing out.

But Millie wasn't about to give in easily. She kept up the castigation until Sarah had to tell her to stop it in no uncertain terms. The scene almost got nasty and Sarah sank into an unpleasant mood. The young musician saved her by striking up a tune. The challenge was soon forgotten, but I had been given notice. Sarah did not want me to get to know her that well, so soon.

As the evening wore on, I found myself thoroughly enjoying their company. They enjoyed life and pushed for laughs like no one I'd ever met. William, the shy one, was also full of puns. He had pet names for everything that existed, cute names for the things around us that most people didn't bother with. Puppies were dimples. Buns were smiles. Woogies were messes: hairballs and things that people don't like. "Gilguys" were for when you couldn't remember the name of a boat part. They were all about gagging and poking fun. Nothing was serious to them. Life was all a big farce, and going to Mexico was a day off when they should be elsewhere being serious. "Who cares," was their philosophy. They just wanted to enjoy the moment.

When we got tired, everyone found a spot to crash. This will more than just be fun, I thought before I dozed off. From the first moment I had met Sarah she had enthralled me. *Was she the one I had been waiting for all my life?* I didn't know only that I was completely attracted to her. And the fact that we had the time to get to know one another put my inner demons to rest. It was wise to invite these "brats," as they called themselves.

Well rested the next day, we were ready to depart. Last minute runs to the store for fresh foods and ice and we were set. I called Bill at Tambor's house that afternoon and told him we'd be there in a week. He assured me all was ready down in Mexico. Starting the engine, my zany crew hollered and gagged as we let loose the bow and stern lines.

Beyond the breakwater we were greeted by an unusually stiff breeze: fifteen knots and gusting from out of the northwest. Setting sail, my vessel slid through the water and down the coast with a wind off its bow making a steady seven knots, bound for the land of sun and fun, along with a crew of seven young souls. Dwight was the old man at thirty years.

CHAPTER
NINETEEN

JOY OF LIFE

MAZATLAN, MEXICO
DECEMBER, 1971

L IFE IS FULL OF IRONY and this was especially true in this case: our guests had no idea we were preparing to smuggle a load of contraband. All they knew was that they'd been invited along for a cruise and would depart when we reached our destination. It was definitely not wise to tell them what we were up to. From what I could tell so far, the seven of us were going to get along just fine.

Before the brats had joined us, the four of us had been somewhat consumed in our workload, figuring it best to focus on the tasks at hand. Those nut heads added much needed levity, relieving the tensions that had accumulated.

Underway now, I was smitten by what we were doing. Everyone was out on deck and the vessel, about eighty-degrees off the wind, close-reaching in a stiff breeze, was sliding along at hull speed, sailing away from shore to fetch the night winds on the outside. I'd been waiting all my life for such a moment. Everything was perfect, even the quietness in which we were communing.

Someone had to be captain. I knew it was my job, but it seemed frivolous. No one wanted officiousness that came with the title, certainly not the "brats." But someone had to be in charge, so I set to it.

Setting the watches within an hour of departure, Dale and Dwight were on watch from four to eight. Millie and William were to come on next. Sarah and I would to come on at midnight. No one objected to the decision, though Mary commented wisely as she prepared dinner with a tell-all grin, "Hot Brandy for the midnight crew? If you don't want something to warm you, tell me now."

Dale and I were to navigate, but Sarah jumped right in as we set up the nav-station with the coastal charts about the time Mary was set to cook.

Sarah declared that she'd taken a celestial navigation class while at Cal Berkeley. "But I flunked it, and now is as good a time as any to prove that the teacher was wrong."

"Yeah, right. Well I haven't had any tests to flunk yet," I said gingerly, as she hovered over us.

"Well, this is serious business, Captain," Sarah said playfully.

"It can't be too serious. Not according to this guy," Dale added to the teasing. He showed her a book that we had gotten at the chart store: "The Kindergarten to Celestial Navigation!" Sarah replied with a grin, "Perfect! Wow! This is great!"

"Yeah, just what all of us need," Dale chided. "It's a step-by-step book. You know, go find the sextant first. Then, here's how you use the damn thing."

"Hey, the author was a Trappist Monk," Sarah said with a chuckle. "It's right here in the preface."

"Oh really!" I jested, as she put the book down for us to see the page.

"Yes, really, Frank." She picked it up again.

"This guy's great. He's funny." She started flipping through the pages. "He makes things real simple. I'll show this to Millie. She'll love it. Look, he says this is your present position: *Quien sabe?* That means, "who knows?"

"Yes, who knows?" Dale laughed. "We're all trying for that one."

"Yes and who cares," I added, my nose to the chart as they chuckled. "Right now all we have to do is get it straight with this dead reckoning stuff."

The most preferred method of navigation is dead reckoning. It's a simple process. At the start of a voyage one presumably knows their location. The beginning location is plotted on the chart. A compass course is laid out and a course is given to the person at the helm. Every four hours, the crew logs the average speed and plots the information on the chart. Allowances for current are later applied, and presto, one comes up with a mean location. Backing it all up is the radio directional finder. A daily latitude shot aids in correcting. Longitude shots are somewhat difficult and needed practice to make perfect.

We joked around with the technical stuff for a while and decided that in the ensuing days, we'd have the entire process down pat.

When Sarah and I came on at midnight the steady breeze had dissipated. With a cold, moist wind off our quarter, the vessel was sailing along at a steady four knots. We were both a bit nervous; hot brandy helped. Mary had made a thermos full and I poured a cup to share with Sarah. We had four hours to spend together, with no one to interfere but our own shyness.

I wanted to know more about this woman who beckoned a sense of tranquility. The troubling fears that had pestered my heart and mind the past few years were not here. I felt renewed, on top of things, as though divine energy was coaxing me along. It was quite cool outside, so I took a good gulp from the steamy liquid as Sarah sailed. She had asked for the helm and I readily complied, but soon she was struggling to stay on course. The more she struggled the more embarrassed she became. The vessel's metal wheel, rather than it being a tiller, challenged her and she complained in a lighthearted fashion, "I've never sailed a boat with this arrangement."

"You're over-steering, that's all," I assured her, amused that she found it difficult. I knew she would soon correct the problem. "Relax. Use less movement. I had to get used to the opposite movements myself. It's like driving a car, only it's a boat. You learned to steer with a tiller by going left to go right. And now it's a wheel and it's left to go left. You're confused. That's all."

Attempting to use the wheel as instructed, she was soon all over the place. Coming up alongside, I put my hands on the wheel along with hers. "Here. Have a drink," I said.

She released one hand and took the steamy liquid, as I helped her hold the helm. As she drank, I sailed the boat with her, one hand holding onto the wheel. "See. That's all it takes, short movements, just like a tiller. You just got up and you're still a bit sleepy."

The vessel was steady now and she eased her hold, and then berated herself. "Yes, God, what's wrong with me? I know better."

"I suppose you do."

"Really, Frank. I'll be fine. I'll take it from here."

"Good. I'll leave you be."

As I sat down on the weather side bench she said humbly, "Thanks for inviting us, Frank. This is truly a pleasure. I've never been on a long voyage. I can't wait until we get into the warmer climates. Have you ever been to Mexico before?"

If she only knew. "Lots of times, but only once by boat."

"Tell me about the boat trip. Was it a sailboat?"

"Yes. It was a sail race to Mazatlan, aboard a thirty-seven footer."

After I told her of the night I had experienced, the rising and the descent of the full moon, and how special it was she replied, "How wonderful. Maybe we'll have the same experience on the way down. But what am I saying? The moon won't reach full for over a week and by that time we'll be in Mazatlan."

Sarah had a certain lack of self-confidence. But when she was on top of things she was provocative, steady, and sure of herself, but I had only seen brief moments of this. Now, holding a drink in her hand, she steered with the other. Gone was the angst that had gripped her. Gone, too, were the nervous vibes.

Soon we began asking one another more personal questions. She was well-educated, with a BA in liberal arts and music from Cal/Berkley. Her parents were affluent and from back east. Her father was a well-respected physicist. Mom was a well-educated, rather bossy mom who at one time taught French. "She's an uptight woman, but we've trained her to be a brat like my sister and brother and I are," Sarah mused.

"So you probably speak French?" I asked. In the dark, the soft-pink compass light outlined her face, making it easy for me to observe her expressions.

"Not really, but I speak Spanish pretty well. That's more fun. I lived in Puerto Vallarta for six months. That was a couple of years ago." I found out later she was being modest: she was fluent. "I got to practice and picked it up. It's a wonderful language."

"Ever do any protesting?" I asked, after she told me about living in Mexico.

"Sure!" She grinned. "I was dragged off a couple of times. My parents were quite happy when I graduated and when Millie decided to go to a small college in Oregon."

"I bet. How about sailing? Where did you learn that?"

"God, I was born in a boat. My dad said he took us sailing before I could walk. The same was true with Millie. We have a 110 in Inverness and we sail the bottom off it all year round."

She described what it was like living in Inverness. She had grown up with a number of spoiled, but very creative rich brats who lived there.

"What about you? When did you learn to sail?"

"At thirteen when I joined the Sea Scouts. We sailed the woody lifeboats. Our engine was our arms and a 14-foot oar."

She giggled. "I've heard about you guys. Tell me about the Sea Scouts. I bet you have some tales."

She heard it all then; Stan the Man, the tower, the summer cruises, the capsizing episode, the theft of the oar lock bases and countless other stories. We laughed and cajoled through all of the tales, then I took the wheel for the last two hours.

"Another hot toddy?" she asked.

"Sure, I'm ready."

Pouring us a drink she said with sincerity, "I've always dreamed about deep water sailing, going off to Mexico or the Caribbean, even the South

Pacific. It's what I'd like to do for now. It's in my blood."

My heart took to this kindly, pounding with anticipation, but I didn't want to leap to any conclusions. "Same here. I was probably fifteen when I began to dream of sailing off to exotic places. And now I have the boat. In high school, all I ever did was draw pictures of boats and read seafaring tales while I was in class. Well, most of the time anyhow. I graduated knowing more about sailing than anything else. I was kind of a cut-up, you know, the quiet, sneaky type. My friends' parents always thought I was the nice guy. They said they wished their kids were like me, that kind of thing."

"Oh yes. My mother doesn't know what to make of us. We have an older brother, but we call him Sister Carla. He's gay and my mom's a straight arrow all the way. She never hears the end of it."

What excited me most about Sarah was the way she treated me. She wanted to know everything, which was a perfect delight. No woman had ever asked so much, so sincerely, within such a short time. She was charming me and I wanted her to continue—every moment was genuine and precious.

And as time wore on, like the ease of the wind that pushed us downwind, we talked about politics, the war in Vietnam, her love of music writing, and more. "Music is my true vocation. I play the guitar, but I revel in the flute." She had played in a few concerts in Pasadena where she'd also lived. Now she was a waitress at a coffee house in Inverness, where she often sang folk songs. Life suited her well there. It was away from the Badlands.

Suddenly, it was four o'clock. Our watch had ended all too soon. Dale and Dwight came on deck and Sarah and I slipped down below. As she headed for the forepeak, I headed over to the nav-station to plot out our mean position.

There were two places for me to crash—the small upper berth a midship or in the forepeak with Sarah, which was crowded with spare sails to one side. I decided it was not the time to approach her, but had to head to the forepeak anyway to fetch my sleeping bag. I found her awake.

"Sorry. I need my bag. Damn, I can't see a thing up here. I should have gotten a flashlight out of the nav-station."

In a soft and welcoming voice she replied, "That's all right. I laid your bag out for you. Come on in. There's enough room."

"Hmmm, barely enough" went through my mind. Stripping to shorts and T-shirt, I scooted in alongside her in total darkness, the berth warm and womb-like.

As I struggled to get in my bag she asked, "Are your feet as cold as mine?" She was only inches away, though I couldn't see her. She was only a voice in the dark.

"Boy, are they ever, now that you mention it."

Unknown to me, she had placed the bags so the zippers were facing each other. "Let's get our legs warm," she said.

Unzipping her bag, she moved about. I was stunned when she shifted her legs alongside mine. I couldn't help but touch her as I wiggled around. And as I did she let out a sharp laugh. "Boy, you're not kidding. God, your legs are ice cold." She was facing me then, and I could smell her sweet breath. Then she laughed again, a sweet, provocative sound.

As we rubbed our legs and feet furiously, bodies touching, I reached out and drew her closer, discovering she was totally nude; totally inviting. And, as she continued giggling about the absurdity of cold limbs, I could not yet give way to my desires. I was so cold, I was shivering. So was she. But that soon changed when she wrapped her arms around me and I followed suit.

"That's what's nice about using bodies to warm each other," she said, only inches from my face. "We find comfort no mater what." Seconds later she whispered, "Why don't you get naked?"

She helped me by using her toes to catch the garment and with a few thrusts they slid down my legs. She laughed softly the whole time as I fell back beside her in the darkness, laughing along with her, and we once again wrapped around each other. By now I was ready and so was she.

And as I opened up to passion, I discovered something new about seduction. It had everything to do with desiring what made the other person want more. With Sarah all I had to do was to let go and indulge. The pursuit of a conquest would come. There was no need to prove myself by way of aggression or overzealous bouts of manly display. I only had to make love to her and in doing so, our lovemaking became more akin to what love had to offer, like a night of a rising full moon, or a day when rain fell, and I was discovering the joy it brought. I was ready for her and what's more, I had always been ready for her.

Her breath was sweet, her lips responsive, and her womanhood soaking wet. When I climaxed in her it was not an enormous explosion; it was a warm and receptive sensation. The aftermath brought me a feeling of completeness that was a beginning with no end.

And, after the consummation came the searching: the caressing, the tips of our fingers touching, the running of fingers down the length of her neck and her back then on over to her small breasts. And, as I found a nipple she ran her fingers through my hair and grasp my head as I began sucking—all of this in total darkness. Somehow the darkness of the moment made sense: there was no need to see one another. We only had to feel and respond naturally to what was there.

In time, we coupled again and soon became lost in the pleasure, the sensation much like a new sense of purpose. I had the woman of my dreams in my arms and she had me, and I believed at this point the guessing was over. We were a love match that I'd never before thought was possible and it wasn't the least bit frightening—not at this moment.

In the morning, she was all smiles when we heard Dale come to wake Millie and Willie for the eight to noon watch. With light to see by, I looked at her and drew her in enjoying a fresh kiss. I was refreshed, even though we'd only slept a few hours.

"Time to pee, sweet friend," I said springing from the bed, and hurrying topside to relieve myself.

When I entered the main cabin moments later, Sarah was just coming out of the head. Millie, who was getting dressed, looked at me, then her sister, then unloaded one of her verbal shockers. "Boy, you guys sure smelled up the cabin last night."

Sarah, who was completely nude, stood there and looked at me, then at her sister. She smirked, backed up, placed her hands on her waist in a strutting motion and retorted, "Well you had your chance to do the same, sister. You blew it. We beat you to it."

"Tonight sis!" She pointed her finger with mock menace. "Willie and I get the forepeak."

"Oh really!" Sarah leaned forward. "You'll have to ask the Captain, Deary."

"No way, sis. That forepeak's ours tonight."

"We'll see," she mocked, "I do have my ways about me."

"Then you better watch yourself today," she responded as I stood there grinning at these two jesters—all of which brought to mind and heart that I wanted to find a way to live my life as these two did.

✭ ✭ ✭

And as the temperatures rose each day and the wind stayed fair, each night Sarah and I made love much the same as we had the first night. When we came off watch, she'd head to the forepeak. After a few minutes at the nav-station, I'd join her, not always in the forepeak; sometimes at the settee table, which adjusted down into a large double berth.

Everyone was in the best of spirits. It was collective chemistry at work. It was also the feelings Sarah and I imparted as new lovers. No one complained about their duties, nor did anyone get vexed or irritated. There was only one small crisis and we handled with it with aplomb.

It happened on the fourth day out with Dwight at the helm. The afternoon breeze had kicked up to twenty-plus knots and we were having a good old surf-ride. Most of us were down below talking, eating and gagging, when Dwight hollered, "The spinnaker's ripping!"

"Hold your course," I hollered, as Dale and I came running out of the main hatch and headed forward. He manned the pole and I went for the halyard. When I looked aft, Sarah and her sister were manning the sheets. "Let go the pole," I hollered to Millie. I let the halyard loose the instant the spinnaker collapsed. As Dale disconnected the pole, Sarah, Willy and Millie gathered in the sail. The big genoa was brought out, hanked on, raised, and set to weather with the aid of the spinnaker pole.

We had saved the spinnaker from being torn to shreds. We were in sync. And I was caught up in this harmony as the days passed by and Sarah became all the more real.

On the evening of day five, we were abeam of Cabot San Lucas, the tip of the Baja. As we sailed east towards Mazatlan, a magnificent lighthouse showed the way, along with a strong twenty-five knot breeze.

Dwight woke me about one in the morning to let me know that Dale wanted to change the headsail. When I came on deck with Sarah, the moon was ready to set. The sweet smell of desert sagebrush enticed our nostrils. Though the wind was strong, it was warm and pleasant. Dale, now dubbed the Mad-Sag, had an at-a-loss look on his face that was fierce, yet friendly. He was enjoying the moment even though we were overpowered by the wind. We were on a beam reach, the vessel streaking along at high speeds.

Assessing the matter I said, "I don't know, man. I'm too lazy to go up there and change the headsail. Besides, it's dark and dangerous." I was referring to the bow. Should anything go wrong someone might fall overboard. "Let's ease the main a bit more. How's that?"

"Better. I can live with that, but if the wind comes up anymore, it'll be a bitch on the helm."

"Let's ride with it for now, okay? I'll stay up awhile. Maybe we're on the edge of this wind-line and it'll ease up once we're inside." The vessel bolted into a wave as I said this, drenching both of us with warm seawater.

"Yeah, I know what you mean," Dale replied sarcastically. "This could settle down in the next few minutes."

The crew was up and ready to make the change, and also unwilling to go back to sleep, so we gathered in the cockpit. The stiff evening breeze was exhilarating, but put a strain the vessel, as it raced through the warm tropical water at speeds up to nine knots. Decked out in foul weather gear we began howling, laughing, and cutting jokes as we huddled together to avoid the heavy spray while the vessel plowed into the waves, parting the waters. It was madness, and at times like these, one can only have faith that no objects are in the water that would result in instant disaster.

Captivated by the elements and the mania of the moment, we all shrieked when sheets of saltwater found their marks. And shrieked again, as sudden gusts of wind took hold, and the boat in kind would respond—the knot meter cresting at ten-plus.

Dale's expression continued to grow ever fiercer, causing Sarah to remark, "Look, he's a fiend. He's become a mad-Sag fiend."

In time the wind settled down, and Mary, loyal to her job, surprised us. From the main hatch, she handed out a stack of grilled cheese sandwiches. All of us hollered in unison, "More! More! More! We want more!" Hastily eating them, we passed around a bottle of brandy. Mary grinned ear-to-ear when she came up with a second plate. "I know better. You guys are easy. There's more. I'll keep 'em coming."

No one went hungry that night. The mast held up, as did the rest of the running gear. Finally, we crashed. Come daybreak the breeze was still strong, but had veered toward our stern. We winged out the genoa and set course for, Mazatlan, now only a hundred and fifty miles to the east. It was time to tell Sarah my secret.

I was nervous. It had everything to do with the deep feelings I had for Sarah. I wanted her in my life and I didn't know how she would she react to the news. One thing was for certain: our relationship had regenerated my life, and now I was afraid she might leave me when she heard the truth. As far as she knew, I owned a boatyard in Sausalito and had recently bought this boat. She never asked anything about money at all. That was one of the many reasons I had begun to trust this woman. In spite of my fears, I had to tell her everything. She'd want that. She deserved that.

I waited until our evening watch from eight until twelve. With everyone else below deck, all was set. We had just feasted on a beautiful sunset, and with a pleasant breeze off our quarter at work, my K-40 slid downwind at a steady relaxed pace. It was time.

Sarah beamed me occasional smiles as she stood at the helm, glancing over her shoulder at the sun as it made its descent.

"There's something I need to tell you," I said, as I slid beside her at the wheel focused on the compass course. "It's really important." Kissing her behind the ear, I left her side and sat on the cockpit seat, becoming quiet as I stared earnestly at her.

"You're being so serious. What is it you wish to say, 'Beast'?"—my new pet name.

"It's very important and I'm lost for words right now. I want to tell you because you've got to know. I've got to be fair with you and with me."

"My word! This is important." She looked me over, her brow wrinkling. "Tell me, what's on your mind, dear man."

"Well, I wouldn't need to tell you this if you weren't so special to me. You see, I've had to lie to you in order to cover my butt."

"Lie about what?" She became serious again.

"Sarah, I'm not who you think I am," I struggled.

"But who would you be otherwise?" She gave me a serious grin.

"It's a long story. You may not like it. It's difficult."

"What's so difficult? Come to the point, Frank. You're confusing me. Tell me. I want to know." She was now frowning now and in a state of anticipation.

"Okay. Fine! It's like this, I'm a drug smuggler." There was a moment of silence.

"You're a drug smuggler!" she exclaimed, mouth slightly ajar.

"Yes and my partners are in jail. I'm also a fugitive."

"You're not kidding me are you?"

"No. Not at all!"

"Oh boy. I don't know what to say."

"Say nothing. Let me tell you about it."

I laid it all out to her: the story about my partner Jake; his unwise mistake; my brother Bill, who was in Mazatlan and also a fugitive... "And that's why I lied. I couldn't just up and tell you, not until now. And now, I'm wondering what thoughts are going through that head of yours."

She was quiet for a moment, her face somewhat sullen. "It's hard to believe. That's all." She attempted to smile. "I do see you differently, but I still have the same feelings toward you. God, this is too much, Frank. I'd never have guessed."

"And I'd never have told you if I didn't feel so strongly about you. I'm going to be sailing a load of contraband back to the states in less than a week. You need to know this. I..."

"Frank," she interrupted. "I haven't told you everything either. I'd better tell you now." She halted a moment then added somewhat tensely, "It's about Roger, the man I've been with for four years, the 'chronic' artist. Well, I've yet to break up with him and I haven't exactly been straight with you."

My heart sank.

Continuing, she said, "He's flying down to Mexico and will meet me in Mazatlan. We're to stay in Vallarta for a week." Sighing, she added, "I fully intend to break up with him while I'm there. I mean this. I really do. Our relationship has been on the verge of collapsing for the past few months. He knows this."

My heart stopped sinking. After spending so much time in close quarters with this woman, we had formed a bond of trust. I believed her every word, and at the same time felt supremely relieved that my confession had not brought about ruination. A thousand monkey's had been lifted off my back. I could now move on with her and shape a life.

Getting up, I held her from the backside. Using well chosen words I responded, "We're both in a big mess right now. God, I wish it weren't so. I wish I could make more plans with you. But, I have to take care of this job and bring up this load of contraband to the States. There are people depending on me. I'm going to be in the Bay Area for at least a month selling it. If you do break up with this guy Roger then I want to see you. But I want to warn you that I'm also going to go back to Mexico for another load of contraband. Beyond that, it's all open."

"Good. Roger is as good as gone. I'll be available, too. How about that?"

I was more than pleased beyond words. I hoped she would respond in this way and she had, and I could feel the stretch of the smile that spread about my facet. "Yeah! How about that?"

She turned around so we could look at each other. As I gazed into her deep blue eyes, she fidgeted a moment, then shocked me. "Well what are you waiting for? You're supposed to kiss me, Beast. That's what I want."

I smothered her. She came up for air saying, "Ummm. Nice Beast. Just make sure to make it back home safely. Damn it! You really are a fiend."

"That makes two of us." I responded by pinching her bottom.

"Ouch! Stop it! Now, tell me more. You went over your story so briefly. I want to hear everything. This is great."

Relaxed now, I chided her with. "Then tell me once again that Roger is history."

"He's history! That's a promise."

We arrived in Mazatlan about five the next afternoon. Sarah, Millie and William packed their gear shortly after we anchored in the main harbor. The Avon was inflated and once we were all ashore, Sarah was disappointed when I told her that she'd have to wait to meet my brother and Inger and Kerstin. As we walked up the dock and out into the parking lot, I suggested I'd meet with her and the crew as planned, over a celebration dinner at Tambor's restaurant.

With a sad, silly grin she rested in my arms. "Seven wonderful days we've been together and now you're leaving me. What a cad."

"What can a man say to that?" I jested.

"Nothing! Come by when you can. I'll be hanging out at Tambor's having beers with my friends."

Sighing, I gently kissed her. Feeling terrific, I entered the first of two cabs we had called. I listened as she rattled off directions to the motel in impeccable Spanish to her cabby. Boy, was I proud to know her and more so, that I had fetched her. Immediately, I felt strange that she was not with me.

On the other hand, I had to let my cabby know were to go street by street, go left, go right, all by hand and singular mutterings that only confused him. But we managed to get to Bill's house and Inger met me at the door, with Kerstin in her arms. Bill greeted me warmly. After some small talk, he and I got down to business. I related the latest news, including telling them about Sarah.

Inger said, "So, you have a girlfriend once again. Tell me all about her."

It was late when I arrived at Tambor's. He greeted me and winked. He had had *carte blanche* service ready for us. When I spotted a man sitting next to Sarah, I was immediately annoyed. Suddenly I was shaking hands with Roger, who was tall, handsome, and lean. How in the hell had he gotten there so quickly?

Though predisposed, I was quite hungry. Sitting opposite from me for the next hour Sarah kept giving me reassuring glances. Roger's presence didn't seem to matter that much.

As we walked out and all of us were standing about, I was surprised when Sarah came right up and wrapped her arms around me, everybody, including Roger looking on.

"Sweetheart, I told Roger everything. He was here at the hotel when I checked in. It's over between us and I want to come with you and spend the night. Tomorrow I'm going to Vallarta, but tonight I'm yours."

Using cockpit cushions as a mattress, we made a bed outside on the foredeck. Putting our sleeping bags together we crawled in for a private outdoor evening. All was calm and pleasant inside the harbor.

As we lay side by side facing one another, Sarah smiled and said, "Roger thought Dwight was my new lover. How about that?"

"I think Dwight's wife would have something to say about it. Besides, Roger hadn't met me yet. I'm sure he knows now."

After making love we talked about meeting in Inverness, once I arrived back in California. I was in awe of her sensitivity. She'd be there waiting. Soon, we were fast asleep.

In the morning she was first to awaken. I was in a deep sleep, which was very unusual. She shook me, "Honey, wake up. Wake up. Look at the day."

Rubbing my eyes, I could hardly believe what I was seeing: numerous colors emanating from the sky, catching my eyes. They were breathtaking, and the moment beyond exquisite.

"Oh God... that's incredible, Sarah. Wow! It's hard to believe." Sarah and I clutched our sleeping bags and gazed at the beauty around us.

"Isn't it spectacular? My, oh my! Owwwie! Never have I ever seen a sky such as this." She was unable to take her eyes off the wonder.

The morning sky, covered entirely with a thin layer of upper-level stratus clouds from horizon to horizon, radiated shades of pink and mauve so brilliant they brought tears to Sarah's eyes. The harbor water, mirror-like, reflected this spectacle in its entirety. I choked up as she embraced me.

"Sweetheart, this is our morning, you know that? This is for us." She planted a sweet kiss on my neck, and reached up and caressed my face. As I turned to meet her eyes, tears were streaming down her cheeks. She looked at me intently and said, "I'm afraid I've fallen in love with you, Beast."

I was stunned speechless. I had never before heard those words, never. Not from one who truly meant what she was saying. Sincerity went a long way with me and I panicked..."Respond, Frank," an inner voice cried out. "Tell her what you feel. It's the perfect time."

But still I hedged, lost in distress. It was too soon. She was too soon. If she had said it a month from then, maybe I would have thoughts of love. Then, in a nano-second, came the thought, "But you love this woman, you're enchanted by everything about her. She warms your heart like no other woman has. That's love."

I came to my senses. Reaching up, I wiped her tears away. As I did, her eyes waited. Still in a daze I replied, "I love you too, sweet thing." I shuddered then kissed her lightly on each cheek. An awkward emotional wave took hold of me and I said, "I don't know why it's hard for me to say this, but it's true. I've never said 'I love you' to anyone."

"I believe you, sweetheart", she sniffled. "I love you and I believe in this morning." As I wiped tears away again she added sincerely, "It truly is our morning, Frank." Her eyes met mine. "Honest, I love you and I want us to have this morning. Look at it. It's our beginning. It's our new morning."

Again, I wanted so badly to say the right thing to her, but words failed me. Finally, I said, "I'm stunned, honey. Right now I'm just blown away by what you've said. But I do love you. I know I do. And yes, this is our new morning."

"You'll come back. I know you will. I want you to. I want us to be together. You're the one I want to be with."

"Believe me, sweetheart, I'll be back. I'll call you and we'll be together. You're the best thing that's ever happened to me," I said, still wiping tears away.

"Then kiss me, you fool." She broke into a sad smile.

Ever so softly and gently we made love as the sky above changed colors. Soon it was grayish and the sun peaked its head above the horizon as we lay content, the crew down below having missed the magical sunrise.

Two hours later, we headed ashore in the Avon. Again we declared our love and promised to meet up in Inverness. She waved as she drove off in the taxi. As it headed up the hillside, I wanted to run after her and tell her one more time how truly I loved her. Standing there, I felt like a mad, crazed fool; a man caught up in the suddenness of it all. But she was far from sight by then. I was left with a joy I'd never experienced before.

Over the next three days we made ready. We purchased supplies and worked out the pick-up with Tambor and Bill. After we paid a small fee to the broker to handle the boat's paperwork, to our surprise, no officials came out to the vessel to check us out. To customs, we were just paperwork, a paper boat with rich *gringos* and pretty *gringas* aboard. There was no apparent need to snoop.

On the evening of the fifth day at anchor, we slipped quietly out the mouth of the harbor. In the dark of night, we safely anchored in a small bay to the south side of the main breakwater. An hour later, Tambor and two fishermen arrived in an open boat, having come from the river that runs past the main harbor. Hardly a word was said as fenders were laid out. Tying alongside, they unloaded the *cosali* sacks in less than five minutes. Tambor waved goodbye as they powered off. Working furiously, we threw the sacks below, up-anchored, and powered out of the small bay into the open ocean.

The sun rose an hour later as well as a strong breeze. Sails were set. Within and hour we had to make a sail change from large headsail down to club footed jib—a *Santana* wind was blowing and we were flying to weather at a steady six knots.

We got our butts kicked for nearly three days by winds gusting up to forty knots; the added weight of fourteen hundred pounds worked as ballast and kept our bow into the sea. We had anticipated this, and the boat charged to weather without hobby horsing. By the time the Santana blew out, we were completely exhausted, but the strong winds had favored us. We had passed Cabo ahead of schedule.

The next day was kind. With the strong winds gone, a gentle breeze filled in from offshore. We sailed directly up the coast, hugging it. But this favorable wind soon collapsed and a light breeze filled in from out of the northwest.

On the fourth day, we anchored in a bay off Punta Lazaro, a quarter of the way up the Baja. Dale and I knew it would do us well to rest and rearrange the cargo, and I was still exhausted when Dale woke me just before dark. Slipping out the mouth of the bay, a steady breeze filled in from well off our bow. Within an hour we were sailing a course directly up the coast.

"Man! This is so uncommon," I mentioned to Dale. "What do you make of this wind? It keeps veering around to the northeast."

"Good luck, I suppose. Let me check." Going below, he consulted charts he had thought to purchase, which indicated weather patterns during given time periods. "Look here." He pointed with the tip of a pencil. "This area we're in now, there's a twenty-percent chance the northeast trades will come right inshore."

"Wow! Far out! I hope they stay awhile. This is cream with strawberries on top right now."

To our amazement they hung in for three long days. It was a gift from the gods, we figured. We sped along on a beam reach with winds up to twenty-five knots making incredible time, sailing a course that brought us straight up the coast. Another boon was that we didn't have to fight a head wind.

But there were minuses too: a never-ending grayish overcast that was quite forbidding, even depressing, kept us company. No one minded, but at night it was terrifying. With no moon to cast any light, nights became impalpable.

On the second night out in that blackened arena, I relieved Dale for the midnight-to-four a.m. watch. We were down to a single person: four on, eight off. Dale, completely decked out in foul weather gear, tired and wet, went below immediately while I stood watch for four horrifying hours.

The wind, still dead-abeam, at a steady twenty-five knots, thrust my vessel forward at a steady eight to nine knots into nothingness—no horizon whatsoever to fix my eyes on. Blackness was omnipresent, except for the wake of the vessel; which dispersed a brilliant, silvery, luminous wave that spewed off the lee bow and tumbled aft, only to disappear into the murk. And, all during this four-hour trek it seemed as though I was in a dark cave with absolutely no lights to guide me. Except it was the ocean, a liquid mass, and we were sailing along at incredible speeds.

At night, illusions take over. Nine knots seems more like twenty. For four harrowing hours, I fought fatigue; an equilibrium that went unsettled as I attempted to stay on course.

Dwight saved me at four o'clock. About ready to go mad, I cautioned him, "Just believe everything will be okay and take a few deep breaths while you're at it."

As suddenly as they'd started, the northeast trades died out and the ocean turned into a giant gray mirror. The overcast remained but the wind ceased to exist. The diesel auxiliary had been employed. Again we were able to head straight up the coast at a steady five knots.

On the evening of the eighth day, some seventy miles offshore, we reached the latitudes of the border between the United States and Mexico. That, too, was a boon. We could then use the long dark night as cover as we made our way north.

The sextant had been of no use, and we now employed the Radio Directional Finder. Homing in on local radio stations, we got an exact fix. From here our plan was simple: head north until we were safe. Using the overcast sky as cover, and with the long dark night ahead, we plotted a course that would bring us directly to the backside of the Santa Barbara Islands.

As I stood watch that night from twelve to four, something extraordinary took place. Alone on deck, I thought about all that had happened the past three months. Jake, Joanne and many others came into focus. Sarah, too, was there, as was Bill and Inger. I sent out a verbal message to all of them. "We're safe, guys. No need to worry about us. We're on top of things, and we're getting the job done. We'll be back soon." I was exhilarated and could almost see them. All was well.

Suddenly, from the port quarter, a lone porpoise leapt out of the water, no more than two boat lengths away then dove under the boat. It emerged one more time then disappeared. Stunned, I knew it was a portent. "Wow!" I said aloud.

Porpoises, most always traveled in packs. This porpoise had come alone to deliver a message that all was indeed well.

The following morning, we were a full eighty miles above the border and in sight of the Anacapas, the southernmost island of the Santa Barbara archipelago.

While crossing the channel the crew watched carefully for any vessels in the area. We saw little or nothing at all as we powered along in a mirror-like sea. By days end, we were just to the west of Santa Catalina and headed for our next rendezvous: the Straits of Santa Barbara. From there to the mainland was Gaviotas State Park, our destination.

The day passed without any problems, though we spotted two large military planes. Dale said they monitored coastal activity, which worried us. If we'd been spotted, the Coast Guard might come out and check.

Listening to the Marine A.M. radio the next morning, we learned that a Pacific storm was due to hit. Already, breezes out of the south made presence. By noon, with a strong southerly blowing, we were making a steady eight knots under full sail and had just cleared the straits between the islands of Santa Rosa and Santa Cruz.

As Dale and I sat in the cockpit I marveled, "Unreal the time we're making, just unreal, brother. I think we've done it. We're safe. Gaviotas here we come."

Not more than an hour later, Dale, spotted a vessel with the binoculars, and said with great trepidation, "Shit, there's a Coast Guard eighty headed right for us. Look." He pointed to a position off our weather bow.

I stiffened. "Damn! You're right." The vessel was still a speck, but we estimated they'd be on us in about five or six minutes.

Dale quickly headed below to check out the Marine Band. My adrenalin was running wild and a decision had to be made and quickly. Perhaps aerial surveillance had picked us up. We didn't know, only that the eighty-foot Coast Guard cutter was closing on us, and no more than two minutes away. Finally, Dale popped out of the main cabin and said loud and clear. "It's the Pt. Judith out of Ventura station. They're looking for a twenty-six foot sailboat that's overdue and in this area. They're talking to the Marine Operator about it."

The Coasty, only a half a mile away and closing at high speeds, was still on course to cut across our bow.

"Let's hope this is the Pt. Judith," he added, as he took a seat next to me. The two of us sat tense, unable to speak as the big cutter passed no more than a hundred yards away.

Both of us waved. As their stern appeared Dale said, "That's the Judith. Don't worry if they come back and stop us. If they don't find that sailboat, they might want to ask questions."

We worked out a story should that occur. "If they knew better, they'd let that little lost boat stay lost for awhile," Dale smirked. Gradually, my heart rate began to slow down.

CHAPTER TWENTY

GAVIOTAS

GAVIOTAS, CALIFORNIA
LATE DECEMBER, 1971

WE WERE GLAD to be ahead of schedule, but we still had many concerns—the storm being one. Based on his knowledge of the Sailing Directions Manual, Dale was confident we'd find a good mooring. As we came into the narrow channel, we used binoculars to search. None were available and we had to motor around for a while.

Finally, two fishermen in a thirty-five foot woody hailed us and insisted we tie off their stern. We didn't hesitate. Making fast with double bowlines, we were soon riding safely in an onshore swell two-hundred yards from shore, with kelp beds a scant hundred yards off our bow.

To our stern and to starboard lay an aging wooden pier that extended out two hundred yards. Brother Bill knew this place well and had said it would suit our needs.

Dale and I headed ashore in the Avon within minutes of mooring to check out the State Park. A small loading dock lay alongside the pier and we docked and made our way up the gangplank. Both of us laughed as we lopped along like two drunks, doing our best to gain our equilibrium. Gazing at my boat, it seemed helpless as it rolled around in the long swell.

"The kelp beds to the outside will keep the sea from breaking," Dale pointed out as we stood fast in the stiff southerly wind. "But it won't stop the swell on shore."

From where we stood, we could see the true height of the waves that were pounding the beach. They were a good four to five feet, but were bound to get bigger when the worst of the storm front hit. Uncomfortable with what we saw, we knew that to attempt to unload in those conditions might prove disastrous.

As we approached the main gate, park rangers were nowhere to be seen. Except for the rising surf, all looked good for the unloading process.

Walking the beach, we discussed our concerns. Surfer friends of Bill's were due to arrive in a few days to help us unload. We had arrived a few days early, and I thought to call them. But with a storm brewing, we agreed there was no rush. They'd only tell us to "hang in" anyway.

Dale added, "We'd better be out of here before Christmas."

We had four days. Heading back as darkness descended, Mary had a huge hot meal waiting for us. Appetites run big at sea. Dale and I wolfed down all we could eat then settled in with Mary and Dwight. There'd be no rest that night. We didn't want to chance things, so I put us on moorage watch should the double lines give way. We didn't want to end up on the beach.

Shortly after setting the watch, as all of us were lying around relaxed as could be, we heard what we thought was a log bumping against the hull. Within seconds, the sound came again, only it was more defined.

Dale and I jumped up at the same time. I said, "It could be them."

Flashlight in hand, I exited behind Dale who shined his light to port where the sound had been heard. We spotted two surfers sitting on their boards.

"Is that you Matt and Dick? I asked in anticipation.

"Yeah, it's us."

"Unreal! How'd you know it was us?" I asked

"We saw you before dark," one of them said.

"So you came out in the surf anyway."

"Yeah. Why not," said Mat who identified himself, then added, "Your bro told us what the boat looked like. We wanted to make sure, so we came out."

"You guys are too much. Come aboard," I said.

"You can use the stern pulpit, guys. Hand me up your boards," Dale directed.

Once below, we were all smiles. Their easygoing bravado assured all of us we stood a good chance of completing the final phase of the voyage—storm or no storm.

I poured them a brandy while Matt and Dick, both longtime friends of Bill's, made themselves comfortable. I'd never met them, but Bill spoke highly of them, especially Dick, who was considered one of the best surfers along the coast. He was also the quiet type. Matt wasn't and insisted on looking at the contraband. He came on strong, so I appeased him. They were to be paid in product and Matt said that our weed wasn't as good as he had been led to believe. Not to be discouraged, I told him that we'd get a good price anyway. The quality was not the best, but the way we had packaged it would help. Matt wouldn't accept our reasoning and proceeded to be a boor.

We made plans anyhow. Maybe he'd settle down and be more at peace. Dick, quiet and unfazed by the situation got seasick: even a joint didn't quell him.

They had brought all the equipment we requested: their eighteen foot runabout, a large, inflatable, black navy life raft and plenty of plastic bags, as well as enough duffels bags to put all the kilos in. After spending a good hour aboard making plans they headed ashore, both of them looking green by then.

Come morning, we were fine. The wind had subsided considerably. The storm had passed through during the night, but high surf conditions would remain for several days, peaking at about eight feet, according to our friends. Tonight, we were to off-load. Matt and Dick didn't want to risk hanging out there once the storm ended, huge waves or not.

Dale woke me about eight that morning with some disturbing news. We were safe, but someone else wasn't. "Those fisherman who got off the mooring last night might be dead, Frank."

"That's not good!"

Just as Dale and I had arrived back from our tour of the State park, for some inexplicable reason the fisherman wanted off the mooring. After we exchanged spots and were secure, they had drifted off with their engine out. We yelled at them, "Do you need help?" They had waved us off. They were drunk as hell, rowdy and egotistical. Moments later, darkness had enveloped them. Dale had turned on the radio to find out if they were calling out. They hadn't, and we figured all was well.

Tension set in as we listened in to the marine radio. Heading out to the cockpit with binoculars, both of us observed the high cliffs to our north. The fishing boat lay ashore, wrecked on the rocks. Someone had called the Coast Guard as well as a rescue helicopter. For the next few hours, we hung out watching as the coasty-thirty ran about. Shortly, we learned that both men were dead. We felt shitty. Drunk or not, they'd needed help, but they had been so macho the night before, cursing, hollering and being abusive. Now they were dead. Nothing we could do to change that. We just wanted the coasties out of there so we could unload.

"The coasties may come by and ask us how we're doing," Dale reminded me. "Let me talk with them."

Sure enough, about two that afternoon, when the coasty-thirty had finished up, they pulled alongside. Dale was there to greet them. He became family after announcing he was an ex-coasty. After a brief conversation about the fishing boat, they took off.

As Dale and I headed below for a shot of brandy he reassured me, "They'd never have come aboard. It's not their policy in this type of incident."

By late evening, all was ready. Just after dark, Matt put his eighteen-foot runabout in the water using the electric hoist on the pier, and brought us the equipment we'd need. We put twenty kilos each in duffel bags, and then a double wrapped them in plastic bags.

Matt and Dick mentioned as they helped, "The surf is up to eight feet, guys. We'll pull through okay if everyone does their job."

The crew filled the navy raft with nineteen bags of contraband and headed toward shore. They were to tow it with the Avon and remain just outside the surf line. Dwight would have the pleasure of staying in the Avon, while the crew went ashore with the tow line attached to the Navy raft. Dale, who had donned a wet suit and given a surfboard, was to join them. This was not his job, but he insisted on helping. He and Dick were to go ashore on surfboards, while Matt ran the runabout back to the hoist. Dick and Dale were to take one end of the towline from Dwight and run it ashore. Matt would join them and the three of them would work together and haul the twelve-foot life raft through the eight-foot waves. Hopefully the raft wouldn't capsize. Even if it did, the bags would float and come ashore on the beach. Mary and I were to stay aboard and ready the second half of the load.

Time ticked away, three hours plus, and the guys had yet to return to the boat. "Damn! They're having trouble and we have no way of knowing what the problem is, nor anyway to go help them," I fretted to Mary.

Another hour passed. What was taking so long? If they'd been caught, we wouldn't know.

Some five hours after they'd split, Dwight and Dale arrived back in the Avon. Dwight was wet from head to toe, and so cold his body was shaking. "I went over the falls, man. Pissed me off. I came real close to drowning, man, real close."

Ignoring Dwight's near-drowning for now, I almost screeched at them. "What happened, guys? Is the load safe?"

"Yeah, but the fucking engine on the outboard isn't." Dwight said crossly as Mary put a blanket around his shoulders, "The fucker died on me just as we were ready. I drifted into the surf and came ashore with a belly full of salt water."

"Too much. So you went through the eight-foot surf? I think I felt what you went through," I chided as Mary handed him a shot of brandy. "You guys were late and I was going through hell worrying. I knew something bad was going down. Sorry man," I said looking over at Dwight who was still shaking. "There was nothing I could do from here. I'm only glad you're okay. So you came through the surf, huh? Shit man you could have died. How did you get out of it?"

"I'm cool, but those waves were more like twenty feet in the dark," Dwight barked, still angry. "Dale dragged me out in the end. They knew I was coming when the Avon came in with the raft."

"The fun part came when we had to run up and down the beach and collect bags," Dale added. "It took us a long time. We got 'em though and everything's fine."

"How's Matt going to finish up?" I asked Dale, as he stripped away his wet suit.

"He's coming out in his boat. He should be here any moment."

Heading topsides, with binoculars, I watched from the cockpit. Matt and Dick soon arrived on the pier with their truck and trailer. It was five-thirty. We had to hurry before the early-bird fishermen arrived.

Although no one else was on the pier, we were anxious as we watched them lower the runabout off the hoist. All went well and Matt pulled alongside, adrenalin rushing, and hollered, "Let's go man! Let's go!" Within moments we had tossed the remaining bags on board. Dick covered the load with a single tarp as Dwight hopped in. The three of them sped off. Moments later, Matt and Dick hooked the runabout to the hoist. We watched as the full weight of the small craft lifted, hopeful that all would go well

"Don't break, baby, don't break," Dale and I said in unison.

We finally breathed easy as they swung the craft around and set it on its trailer. A couple of minutes later they drove off.

The first light of day was coming on. We were relieved that the job on this end was finished. Dwight and the others were on their way to Santa Rosa—his wife had rented a house to store the load—and we set about to depart.

Under power, we headed to Santa Barbara and arrived shortly after the noon hour, replenished but exhausted. Dale and I proceeded to the Harbor

Master's office where I rented our berth for a month. After cleaning the vessel, we spent the night aboard. The next morning, we rented a panel truck and headed north, all of us euphoric. The journey had been remarkable—near perfect, except for Dwight's brush with disaster. I didn't know what we would have done if Dwight had perished.

On top of our success, it was December 23. We'd be home for Christmas.

We arrived late in the afternoon at Dale's houseboat in Sausalito. Immediately I called Joanne.

"I'm here. We made it. Merry Christmas!" I said, and there was pandemonium in the background. Joanne, her kids, and Joanie's kids were in a frenzy. "I'm at a friend's house. Come by. Pick me up. I'm taking everyone to dinner. Let's celebrate."

My friends lavished me with praise to the point of embarrassment. I didn't mind. I was home, safe and sound, with my dearest friends. It was perfect timing. Joanne shed tears of joy, then tears of sorrow, when she told me about Jake and Ramon who was fine and had turned himself in to the authorities. Jake would be uplifted to hear what we had accomplished. He'd be depressed and envious too, Joanne said, because he hadn't been with us to pull it off. "He's okay, Frank, but he won't talk about what happened. He dwells on the future and how he's going to survive. I'm frightened. It doesn't look good."

"If the lawyers are good, they'll work out something good for Jake, I really believe that. He has no priors. Let's hope the charges from Nevada are dropped. And if they do, who knows? Maybe he'll get lucky and Arizona will drop charges if Jake doesn't insist on a trial. Most anything can happen." I had thought long and hard about all of this over the past few weeks. What little I knew of the law I knew charges could be dropped but two—we'd have to wait and see.

"But it's the shits, Frank. Jake doesn't deserve to sit in jail."

"Yeah, but society doesn't understand this." I was stuck for the right words, but added awkwardly, "Joanne, one reason why we became smugglers was our belief that sooner or later the system would pay attention. Maybe when the jails are full of drug smugglers and dealers, they'll start reconsidering. To me it's the only way, and Jake will just have to endure. By the way, I have a girlfriend. Her name is Sarah."

Joan and Joanne were happy for me, but immediately ganged up on me and cautioned and haggled me: these two women who cared for me wanted me to be sure. I understood their concern. This woman and I had met in a moment of rapture. They felt I was vulnerable and although they used other words of caution, the point was made. I repelled them but they came on even stronger after I told them she was the woman I'd always been looking for and that I was incredibly content.

"You'll see. You'll meet her soon then you'll know what I mean. She's a catch," I boasted, to ward off their errant advice.

The day after Christmas Joanne drove me to Santa Rosa to check out the load with Dwight and to get my little Volkswagen from him. When I contacted all the customers, they were overjoyed and ready.

With all my work taken care of, I now had time to call Sarah. Though the better part of me craved her, another part hesitated. I was a fugitive and Joanne and Joan's advice fell upon me. They were only being protective. Even though I was feeling terrific about recent success, I gave thought to their warnings. I'm not the melodramatic type, but I was living in a melodrama anyway. Perhaps I was caught up in a moment of rapture and was unaware of it. So what! It felt good.

Regardless, I would be in the Bay Area for the next several weeks before heading south. I had some time and would use the opportunity to be sure about Sarah's true intentions. She had come into my life so suddenly; we had now been apart for several days. I'm sure she was worried about me and anxious to hear from me. I owed that to her and to myself, and decided to call.

When she answered, I uttered ever so softly. "Hi, Sweet Thing. Merry Christmas! I'm home. I love you and I want to see you."

"Oh God! You're here! I was so worried I haven't slept well. You're okay aren't you?"

"Quite well."

"That's wonderful, sweetheart. Yes, I do love you. I want to see you. Can you come here?" she asked.

"Yes. Where do I go?"

"Inverness! I'm in Inverness, but of course you know that. Oh, I want to see you. There's so much I want to say. And your trip, how was it?"

"Wild and crazy. I'll tell you all about it. You'll love it. Give me directions and I'm on my way."

When I arrived at her parents' cabin, she clung to me. There were no tears, just joy as we hugged, kissed, stared and smiled, then laughed.

"It was worth the trouble, honey. We made great time. Here, I brought a little something for you and Carl." I handed her a bag of smoke. Grabbing my hand, she led me into the kitchen to meet her older brother Carl, the mad suffering gay-artist whom Sarah and Millie called Sister Carla. He looked every bit like Sarah, high cheekbones, deeply set blue eyes, heavy eyebrows and square jaw. He was the male version of her. Right away, I saw they were close. He was friendly to me, but cautious. I knew he'd be checking me out over the coming days.

Sarah began making hot toddies as Carl rifled through the weed stash. "My, you have no idea how nice this is Frank," he said, as he sat a helping of pot on a plate and began cleaning. "I haven't had a joint since god-knows-when. Can't afford it right now. You know how it is—parents, Christmas, all the brouhaha. It's enough to drive an insane man to sanity."

We partied for about an hour. Even though it was cold inside their cabin, Carl was ready to keep on trucking, but Sarah shooed him to bed. With bold, swish histrionics he announced, "Well dearies, I'm gonna tuta-lu and drop into one of my macabre dimensions. You love jays have a great evening and don't make too much noise. There's nothing more exasperating than having to hear that racket. I'm sure you're hip to what I mean. Nice meeting you, Frank. Ciao, Sister." Looking us up and down he smiled, hugged Sarah, then me, and headed out to his cabin.

"Don't pay any attention to that, sweetheart," Sarah wrapped herself around me. "He's always demonstrative. Come here. Now I have you all to myself. Let's go to bed."

As she pulled a hide-a-bed open, we griped about the freezing cold. We were so frigid we yanked off our clothes and jumped under the covers. Naked and shivering we clutched each other until we stopped. Wild and anxious, Sarah then wasted no time devouring me. We had been quiet lovers on the boat, but with no one around now I found it difficult to keep up with her hunger and strength. She smothered me with her passions and made sounds that almost frightened me. She was strong and she used her physicality to subdue me.

Soon I was her equal and surrendered to her desires. When we had had enough, we collapsed exhausted, and fell into a deep, relaxing sleep.

The next morning we had breakfast at the coffeehouse where she worked, then headed up to "The Ridge," as they called it there in Inverness. We stood at Vista Point, overlooking Point Reyes Peninsula, both of us admiring the view of the coastal mountains and the waters of the Pacific,

"I'm going to leave for Mexico as soon as the load is sold." I said, interrupting the moment.

"I want to go with you, Beast. I'll quit my job. We can go together. I'd like that."

"Are you sure this is what you want to do? You know I'm going to bring up another load."

"That's your business. I just want to be with you."

"After I finish, we can make other plans. How's Hawaii sound to you?"

"Oh baby, Hawaii—anywhere! I love sailing the way I love you."

"Then I want you with me all the way."

"All the way, fiend. All the way." Looking into those ice blue eyes, so full of passion, the deal was sealed. There was no need to worry or fear. She'd be there for me, for us.

Over the next few weeks I met with the customers and collected money, while Sarah moved us into a friend's place down in "The Hollows." There, in a quaint old cabin with a small potbelly stove, we set up shop. The place had "country" written all over it. For the better part of thirty cold days and thirty freezing nights, we hunkered down, made love each night and got to know one another.

We didn't go out much at night, but I did meet several of her friends. They were much like her, except for a woman named Barbara. They called her "Rapid Transit" because she never stopped talking. Her boyfriend, of course, was a pussycat. They planned to crew for us on the trip south, along with a passive sailor named Michael.

Benny, on the other hand, was not a passive person. There were old debts to pay off. By mid-month, all but one had been paid: five grand we had borrowed from a lawyer we'd never met—make that ten counting the profit margin.

My good roommate Fay had introduced me to Benny, an affable ex-Hell's Angel. He had arranged the loan, but I hadn't called him in months. After learning that he had stormed into Ryan's law office and demanded that Ryan make-good our debt to him and the lawyer who had loaned us the money, I was reluctant to call, but I could put it off no longer. When I reached him one afternoon, he was livid.

"Benny, it's Frank. I have your money and I have a bonus. I even have an excuse if you're willing to listen."

"You sonofabitch, why didn't you call, man? Tell me that first."

"What, and tell you some ridiculous story you'd never believe? I just couldn't. I have the money and I apologize. Can I bring it to you without you doing any damage to me?"

"All I want is my money back. You can tell me what happened in person. Fay told me about your partner and that you got indicted. Okay? Nothing will happen. Just bring the whole amount."

Later that evening, Sarah and I drove into town and met Benny at the office of the attorney who had lent us the money. When I handed him two kilos of our weed, along with his ten grand cash I added sincerely, "Thanks. Enjoy this, brother. Once again I'm sorry."

He gripped my hand hard, looked me directly in the eyes and trembled with anger. "Boy, you made me feel like a sucker, listening to all those hard luck stories in the beginning and lending you money afterward. You've no idea how uptight you made me. Now, I'm glad you came through. I was ready to kiss it off as a bad deal. Sit down, man. Tell me what happened. I want to hear about it."

"Sure. This is Sarah. I heard our lawyer got an ears-worth."

"Ryan! Shit, he's just another goofy attorney."

For the next several days everything went according to plan. Sarah and I hung out in Inverness in a cold cabin, found time to go sailing on the 110 she loved so much, hiked on the beaches, and made love. We couldn't get enough of each other, but we did manage to have an argument during the holidays. It was over the friggin' Super Bowl. She wanted to go sailing. I pleaded with her that it was the sporting event of the year.

"Who cares? It's gorgeous out and I want to go for a sail. You said you'd come."

"But I haven't watched a football game all year."

"Then stay and watch it. I'm going sailing with or without you."

She stormed off and I followed her like a pussycat. "You're right sweetheart. I did promise. Let's go. I'm with you." It was a gorgeous California winter day and we made the most of it.

"Unbelievable! What's Harry doing out here?" I thought, as I stood in a phone booth near the center of town ready to make a call. He was driving ever so slowly as though he were looking for someone. As he came abreast of the phone booth and began to pass it, I gave out a holler.

"Hey Harry! Over here." Harry, a lawyer and a good friend of Joan's, stopped and stared over with a look of bewilderment.

"Damn, what are you doing out here?" I asked, as I strode over to his vehicle.

He was all smiles as he parked and got out to shake my hand.

"Hey man. How you doing? Joanie sent me out here to see if I could find you."

"I'm doing fine. So, you found me. That's amazing. What's up?"

"Yeah. You saved me a lot of trouble. I figured I'd come out here and have to go back without seeing you."

"Yeah. But you know how things work. This is no coincidence."

"Got'cha! I'm here to tell you the narcs know you're around."

"Shit! How? Who's talking?"

"We found out through Howie's wife. That's all I know. Joan is worried. You better lay low."

"For sure, but how would Howie know? Who's got the big mouth?"

"Hard to say. Someone might have talked over a hot phone."

"Great! That sucks." Taking a breath, I added, "Thanks, Harry. Your coming out here really helped."

"Don't take this lightly. The narcs will put some heavy surveillance out. Stay away from Joan's house."

"I hear you. I'm about done with things anyway. Guess I'll get out of here soon, real soon."

"Good. I got to get going. Take care, brother. Good luck. See you someday."

Harry sped off, leaving me standing there shaken by the news. I headed over to the coffee house to see Sarah and pulled her aside to tell her the upsetting news.

Knowing I'd be leaving that evening, she blurted out, "I'll quit. I'll give notice today. I'm coming with you."

"Not right now, honey. Give it a couple of days. Dwight and I will finish up here shortly. I'm going up to Santa Rosa to see him right now. Everything else has been taken care of. Meet me back at the cabin later. We'll figure out how to get you down to Santa Barbara."

Dwight was annoyed by the news, but agreed to finish up and join me down south in a few days.

I said goodbye to Sarah then headed out using the back roads. Once again I was without her. Arriving in Santa Barbara, I was happy to see all was well with my vessel. She needed a new paint job, a new headsail and main, and some varnish work. Relaxed, I was also lonesome, so set about the task of preparing for the trip south. When I called Bill he agreed to line up our next purchase with Modesto, through Tambor. We would go for one ton, and haggle out the new deal after I arrived. "Expect us sometime in late February," I signed off.

※ ※ ※

"Sweetheart, no wonder you seem so frustrated. When did this happen?"

"Two days ago. I called Dwight and got his wife, instead. She's been bitchy lately and came on strong. There was nothing I could do. She knew I was in Santa Barbara so she let me have it. Then she hung up on me. I called back several times: the next morning, and that afternoon. No one answered. I got hold of Dale and asked him to go up there. When he arrived, he found the house empty."

Four days had passed. Sarah had just arrived by bus, and I barely had time to hug her before letting her in on the latest news. Dwight, my friend and employee, along with his wife and daughter, had left town with a good portion of our profits, nearly thirty grand. Half was mine, the other half was to go to Jake and the others to help pay for their defense.

She was stunned, "Oh God, Beast! I'm so sorry to hear this. What will happen now?"

"It means our people are going to suffer." Sitting in the cockpit now, looking toward the distant mountains I added, "Had he wanted to, he could have ripped off the entire load."

Turning to face her, I moaned, "I don't know, baby. I just don't know. I'm blown away. I gave Joanne close to fifteen-grand to cover our people. I had planned to give her another ten or more. Now I'm way under what I thought I'd make. Odd isn't it? I took Ramon's money to save my ass. Now Dwight takes us to the cleaners. He's a fugitive. He wants to start fresh in Canada. Together with all the other money he made, he's probably got over fifty grand on him. He knows this hurt us. He just didn't give a shit. Plus, I needed him for crew. Then again, why work when he can rip me off?" I lamented.

Sarah gave me a long hug. "I'm so sorry, sweetheart. There were times when I saw him being jealous of you and I never thought twice about it. Maybe I should have."

"Maybe so, but I didn't set the best example for him when I ripped Ramon off," I replied, staring vacantly into the distance. "Now I'm paying for it. Bad karma! It comes around and I got it good."

"Make no mistake. He did something very evil. He'll have to pay for this. But what now, Frank? Can you still do your work?"

"Yes. We're still going south. Everything's set. I'm just feeling shitty right now."

Clutching her hands I professed, "I'm so glad you're with me. That's all that matters. I have you, baby."

"Yes, sweetheart. You have me."

"Good! It's time to move. This is not going to stop me. I'll put a crew together somehow. Dale and Mary aren't coming. They've made all they need. I respect that. Dale is going to find some other people to help out."

Sarah listened without commenting. I knew she would just as soon we sail off to Hawaii and forget the unpleasant business. But I was obligated to make one more run. I'd made a promise to Bill that I would, plus I wanted to complete payment to the lawyers for defending Jake and some of our other people. Then I could sail off with my dreams: Sarah, the boat, and a large stash of cash

I failed to ask her what she really wanted so I had no way of knowing how she truly felt. I was a fugitive and my goal was to get out of the business with a good deal of money in my pockets. One more run would see to that. Bill was also depending on me, as well as the others. Without more being said, I asked her if her friends Barbara, Franco, and Michael were coming to Mexico with us.

"They're ready, Beast."

We took our time on this trip. Dwight had brought down our morale, but we were determined to lift it back up. The next day we purchased three harbor charts at the local marine store and made plans for a leisurely sail south, with stops at Tortugas Bay and Magdalena. From there we'd stop off in Cabo and then on to Mazatlan. After our crew showed up, we spent the following day buying provisions. The next morning we sailed out of Santa Barbara and by days end berthed in Long Beach, where we had left from back in November.

Sarah's parents lived in Pasadena. I'd met them during the holidays and I wanted them to go for a sail with us. Sarah took care of the arrangements. The day after we arrived they showed up. Our crew was asked to stay ashore at the yacht club while Sarah and I took her parents out for a sail.

Her parents had been everything Sarah has said they would be. Mom was on the stuffy side and dad was tall, distinguished, and an outgoing man who loved to talk about most anything—every bit the scientist. I enjoyed him immensely, whereas I did what I could to be nice to her mother. The wind that day was stiff and cool—a winter breeze out of the northeast—so we kept the sail short. Afterwards, I took them out to dinner, along with the crew. They all knew each other—Barbara had gone to school with Sarah in Pasadena and Mike, who was an excellent sailor, had raced against Sarah and her father many times in Tamales Bay.

The next day we powered out of Long Beach Harbor under overcast skies and a very unusual lumpy sea. I'd never experienced such strange conditions and didn't like it one bit. There was no wind and my craft was soon bobbing around, making life difficult for all of us.

Soon after we had departed, Rapid became seasick, or so she said. She was going to die if I didn't get her ashore immediately. I wasn't buying it. No one ever died from seasickness, Sarah told her, as Barbara lay in the quarter berth, face pale.

Going below to console her, I told her she'd live through it, but she begged me, as she had begged Sarah, to head ashore. No way. The guilt trips didn't work on me. I've seen this before. She just had to hang in there. Her angst was so great she pulled me down on her. She was sick, but she wanted to be played with. No way, honey. No way. Then she lived up to the billing of, "Hell hath no fury like a woman scorned." I was on her poopsheet. So was everyone in her vicinity.

Franco soon felt the pinchers and became rapidly obsessed himself. Rapid, full of embarrassment and rage called out to him, pulling him to her side as she lay there in the berth, dying. Franco, gravely concerned, turned to us for advice. Sarah, who knew Rapid well, took Franco aside and talked with him. For the rest of the day he was on our side, but would come and go to attend to her false requisites.

Out in the cockpit, I conferred with Sarah and Michael. We agreed to band together and do what we could to bring Rapid out of her funk. Meanwhile, we'd ignore her. She was unable to stand watch so we rearranged them to fit ours—two on, six off, but always with two people on during the night.

Sarah and I kept busy in the galley that afternoon. We wanted to have a wonderful time on this cruise and were off to a slow start. Keeping busy and promoting love was a key point. We put together lunch and later cooked dinner, all the while cajoling as Rapid slept and the lumpy seas gave way to normal swells.

The next day the weather was primo and Rapid, who had refused to stand watch the day before, gave in and stood watch with Franco. But she was in a reticent mood and hardly said a word.

We kept our distance. The weather turned fair and we were on course for Tortuga Bay. By the time we reached our destination, Barbara had let go some of her animosity. When we entered the harbor in the early hours of morning, we anchored near a small cannery town.

The Baja is a desolate land. Its mountains have no forests, but the colors are catching: rustic reds, shades of gray, tans of dark and light. We feasted on all of that, including the deep blue sea that gave so much contrast to the land.

There was not much to do here, other than gawk at the terrain, so we sailed off the next morning with a fair breeze that came up that afternoon.

Magdalena Bay resembles San Francisco Bay in many ways, and just outside the entrance, with a good breeze off our stern, hundreds of porpoises streamed alongside as we made for the opening. They are joyful fish. They seem human and appeared to smile at us as they swam in bursts and leapt from wave to wave. We were all on deck for this treat. We began shouting for them to continue their friendly welcome. I felt safe with them around and said as much when Sarah joined me at the bow pulpit, with camera in hand and grinning madly.

We were dismayed when they disappeared as swiftly as they had arrived. I asked Sarah with a silly grin, "I wonder which one of them orchestrates the departure?"

"Well, dear, when it's time to go, it's time to go. All animals know when it's time, especially these friendly beasts. My God! They're so charming.

After we were well inside the bay we spotted a huge gray whale. Sailing alongside, it paid us little or no attention, while we observed its graceful path and were overjoyed to be so close to such magnificence.

We sailed up the north shore and anchored underneath a mountain range. A large fishing boat anchored nearby that afternoon. Sarah and I powered over in the Avon and purchased a large lobster and a kilo of shrimp.

Two day later we arrived in Cabo San Lucas. Anchoring, we went ashore in the Avon. Rapid had yet to return to normalcy and still had all of us on edge. The five of us dined at one of the beach restaurants.

We headed for Mazatlan the next day. The weather was fair but Rapid wasn't, and when she decided to bitch about some petty matter, I told her to stay away from me and away from any more watches. I'd had it with her.

An hour later, now calmed down, I said to Sarah, "Remarkable isn't it, how one person can be so unruly." Sighing, I added, "The first trip down not a one of us ran control trips or got out of line. She's afraid, honey. I can feel her fear. She's not a sailor like you and I and Michael. She's just afraid to be out on the open ocean. All that arrogance is just a cover. She doesn't want us to catch on to her and she knows we're on to her bad act. Believe me when I tell you I've dealt with her kind before."

"I do, Frank. I see her fear. She's always been high strung. I should have known…"

"Please don't go there, sweetheart. You're not to blame. She has choices just like anyone else. It's just that she chose to deal with a side of her self she's never dealt with before—and how were you to know how she'd react so poorly? Really!"

"I agree, Beast. She's still my friend and she'll be going home right away. Then we'll let this whole episode go. I'm looking forward to being in Mazatlan with you and meeting your brother and Inger, and Kerstin, too."

Arriving in Mazatlan the next afternoon, Barbara and Franco were packed and ready to go ashore shortly after we anchored.

"Dracula couldn't have sucked as much blood as she did," I said sarcastically to Sarah, as Michael rowed them ashore in the Avon.

I loved introducing people to Sarah. This was especially true when we arrived at Bill's and Inger's apartment in Mazatlan. Kerstin, now eleven months old, was soon in my arms. This time I felt very capable with her. And despite the feuds Bill and I had in the past, everything was put aside for the time being. I was with family and with the one I loved most.

While talking with Bill, I watched and marveled at the ease with which Sarah and Inger became fast friends. First, they doted over Kerstin, and then Inger showed Sarah her new weaving machine, which she used to make bikinis, hot pants and halter tops. She sold them at a consignment store in town and boasted that she made enough money to pay her own way.

I told Sarah to pick out what she wanted—the late Christmas present I had promised.

My next order of business was to reach and agreement on the upcoming business with Bill, who felt he had been more than generous in giving Jake and my people a fair share on the last trip. But I was now in charge of running the show, so I told him that as long as I had to do most all the work, the deal was to remain the same: one third for him, two thirds for me and my people.

Of course he fended me off. He was the one who could get us good weed. Cautious, I mentioned the money he still owed us from way back and the money we had put up with his ex-contact Aireberto. Bill, as usual, said little to this, only that he'd think about everything.

If Bill wanted time to think about what he was going to do, so did I, and each time we met I'd tell him that I wanted to think about things before I made a decision. Watch out brother, I got your cunning tactics covered—just as a sailor must do at the start of a race. Besides, there was no immediate rush and we had no crew. Bill put little emphasis on this. Perhaps he thought it would be easy or he knew people who might go—his surfer buddies for instance. He knew I'd need three qualified man. And tomorrow would be another day to conspire.

Meanwhile, dinner was served. Inger had cooked Swedish meatballs and creamed spinach. Cold beer was offered, and we set about to relax and enjoy a family gathering.

The next day I called Dale. He agreed to find us a crew when I offered him two grand and an equal amount once we arrived back.

Over the next two weeks, Bill and I, along with Tambor, headed out to Modesto's ranch most every day to oversee the job. There were gags galore working with the helpers and jaws agape as we sorted through the tons of weed that lay around under cover of trees, guarded by two men.

Two days after the kilos were ready, Bill and I quarreled. It was about who was running the operation and his reluctance to talk about the amount he owed or would pay on the old dept, especially since Jake was out of the picture. Again, I insisted that a portion of the load should go to Jake and our people to aid in their defense. Standing firm, I left his place upset over the fact that I was doing most of the work while he was to sit on his butt in Mazatlan. Bill, hedged at first, then hinted he'd go along as crew in order to rectify the situation. We were both fugitives and on equal grounds, but that made little or no difference to him.

If only he'd lighten up and tell me how he honestly felt. But, that seemed all but impossible with him. He was too full of himself.

All we needed was an able crew. Part of the problem was that we had to rely on Dale to find worthy people. I called him back after the tangle with Bill and offered him a bonus of five grand if he came through with a couple of able crewmen.

Back at the vessel, I found solace with Sarah. She listened as I told her about the ordeal with Bill and the way he asserted his powerful male ego.

"Jake and I had our problems, but we just took care of business in an orderly fashion and seldom mixed egos or laid control trips on one another. We had fights, but we knew better than to manipulate each other. With Bill, it's the only way he knows how to operate," I lamented to her as the sun began to fall, shading the harbor.

As late March approached, Bill and I were still at odds. Then Sarah fell sick. She was rushed off to the hospital and had her appendix removed. Two days later she was back on the boat, but had to convalesce for a week. All the while, Dale was looking for crew, but was at a dead end. I found it hard to believe that no one wanted to make a run with us.

"You come along Bill, and with two good men, we can pull this off. Somehow I'll work this deal with you; otherwise we can't go. Simple as that," I told him that afternoon.

Over the next several days Bill called his surfer pals and made inquiries. Both of us came up empty.

By the end of the week, after all but begging our friends to help I told Bill, "Be patient. Sarah and I are going for a short cruise."

It was her I wanted to be with, not Bill and his inimical ways. That afternoon as we sat in the cockpit I told her, "Remember the trip we talked about two weeks ago, the one to Puerto Vallerta? Let's make plans to go."

We had just returned from a five-day trip to Culican to visit some friends she had met in Vallerta two years before. For several weeks now, we'd laid at anchor in the main harbor. A mountain, some 900 feet tall, stood guard at the entrance to the west casting a welcome shadow over us. A light breeze was blowing, and six, maybe seven yachts, were anchored nearby. Sarah had been entertaining herself with a book and a young tabby kitten, a stray we had picked up near the central marketplace a few days before. We'd named her "Chicken of the Sea," because she was always so ravenous and had one day eaten part of a fish I had caught.

"Oh boy. You're on. Jualapa included?"

"You bet. We'll see it all like Bogie and Bacall: San Blas, Vallarta, and Jualapa. It would be nice to have some crew. Let's keep our eyes open. But first I want to haul the boat out and paint the topsides and the bottom."

"Fine. I'll help. We can have the new name painted on too," she added, revealing her fabulous smile. She picked up the cat, held it to her face and said, "And you get to come along too, Chicken. We'll have all sorts of fun."

We made arrangements and hauled the boat out at a yard a short distance away. I'd purchased the paint and material before leaving the States. Within a week the two of us, with some help from a couple of young Mexicans, finished the job. Lastly, the sign painter showed up and painted the vessel's new name on the transom: *"New Mornin."*

It took a few days, but we found two people for the crew while out at the beach one day; George, a surfer and Sara, his girlfriend, a very attractive woman who lived in her bikini. Neither of them were sailors. They just wanted to come along and enjoy the ride.

The four of us sailed south in early April with a gentle breeze on our stern. Sarah, in true form, took the first turn at the helm, humming and singing a tune, clad in her bikini, with a large broad-rimmed straw hat atop her head.

We arrived in San Blas early the next afternoon and anchored near the mouth of a small river, rich with jungle growth. The coast had been mostly flat and unremarkable on the way down. But in Santa Cruz Bay, where the Mexican Sur began, the mountains stood close to shore, the foliage dense, and palm trees lined the coast for miles.

"We can go to Hawaii first, sweetheart. Then off to Fiji and on to Tahiti."

"Millie and William will help us sail the *New Mornin* there, for sure," she replied as we lay in the Avon tied to the stern of the boat. Sipping a cold beer, still wet from a late afternoon swim, we romanticized sailing anywhere we pleased.

The next day we hugged the coastline. With a gentle breeze off our quarter, we passed long stretches of lush tropical beaches and small villages lining the way. Huge mountains served as a background. We gazed for hours and drooled at the sights as we sailed by them. Along the cliffs off Punta Mita we set the spinnaker on a reach in yet another light breeze, then powered when the wind collapsed that afternoon around four.

Come morning, we were anchored in the bay off Puerto Vallerta. Up early, Sarah and I headed ashore for breakfast, picked up some fresh fruits, and hung out in town. Sarah loved to stop at each vendor and talk. I was delighted that she spoke the language so well and loved to banter with the Mexicans. They loved her too, and would often ask where our babies were, unable to comprehend why we didn't have children.

Upping anchor that afternoon, we sailed a scant twelve miles to Jualapa, a small, but famous off-the-beaten-path village. No roads lead to this piece of paradise, just paths and water routes. Anchoring there was tricky due to the depth of the water. Tying off in the cleavage between two tall cliffs, we dropped the hook to keep our bow in the open water. We stayed two full days, taken by the tropical setting.

The next morning we spent the day by the waterfalls, basking in the sun along with our crew. We lay on granite; partially submerged pools of water, formed by the fall, formed perfect swimming holes. We brought food and drink and dined in the most divine setting we'd ever seen. Tourists were our only distraction. They came ashore by the boatload about noon.

Roberto and Patty came into our lives the next day when they arrived in the harbor aboard their thirty-eight-foot double-ender. As we sat in the cockpit of the *New Mornin*, they anchored their boat some two boat-lengths away. It was an eye-catcher, a classic, yet funky sloop called, *Whippoorwill*. Even though he didn't know us, Roberto called over to us. He had caught a good-sized fish early that day and wanted us to come help him eat it. Invitation accepted, we swam over; George and Sara electing to stay aboard while we partied.

Roberto, it turned out, was Jacky Coogan's brother. Because Sarah felt their family was one of the best vaudeville acts to come out of Hollywood, Sarah gave him accolades— attention which he laughed off. Roberto, of course, was an actor, though an aging one. At six-foot-three and three hundred pounds, he was a one-man show. And we were his captive audience, as well as his newfound friends. Through endless prattle, we drank, yelled all evening, and then sang out when a full moon rose above the mountains where we were anchored under. Later, we got crazy and swam in phosphorescent water with our two nutty friends.

Several beers and some shots of tequila later, we lowered ourselves into the tropical liquid and oozed our way back to the *New Mornin*.

"See ya' back in the harbor," we said to Roberto the next morning, who was to sail to Mazatlan in a few days. Standing on his foredeck, clad in a huge pair of loose fitting swim shorts that looked more like underwear, he clutched a beer in his hand and waved goodbye with the other. He was that kind of guy—always ready for fun, but always in need of an elixir to sort through things.

CHAPTER TWENTY-ONE

MAKE LOVE, NOT WAR

MAZATLAN, MEXICO
MAY, 1971

As the days and weeks passed without finding a crew, my frustration with the business grew. Instead of the usual past problems of not getting good weed, a ton of prime marijuana, bought and paid for, sat at Modesto's ranch, useless until we found a crew. Our contacts produced nothing. Bill and I even considered looking among the sailors and surfers who came and went with the boats and at the beaches, but found no prospects.

The good side of the delay was that Sarah and I were having a lot of fun. We had days on end of leisure, a wonderful boat at our disposal, and not a care in the world—other than finding a crew to bring the contraband north. Sure, I was a fugitive in the States, minus a crew, and the monsoon season was fast approaching, but that all seemed distant and unreal being with her. I had some important decisions to make, however, and I had no idea how important they'd prove to be.

Bill came down to the docks one afternoon where Sarah and I were hanging out. He reminded me that I was supposed to be preparing for war, not love. He didn't use words, but his demeanor was quite clear.

"Honey, your brother's at the dock," Sarah said, as I sat in the cockpit playing with our feisty young cat. "He's waving to us."

It was early afternoon and the wind had come up. Sarah had gone forward to tighten a loose halyard that was slapping the mast.

"I'll go talk to him and be right back."

Heading ashore in the Avon, I found Bill standing next to his old clunker out in the parking lot. He looked annoyed as I approached, but wore his usual sly grin.

"Hey Bill, how's it going?"

"Okay brother, but no good news. Matt just doesn't have anyone who's willing to crew with us. How about Dale? Did you call him again?"

"Yes. It's the same. No one's available. I don't understand it. I don't think he's trying too hard. Either that, or we're not pushing him hard enough."

"Would you be willing to go back to the States and find someone? We've got to get this thing going."

"No way, Bill. I told you that before."

"Tambor came by. Modesto wants to know why our kilos are still out at his ranch. He wants them removed, or a date when they will be."

"What can I do? Our hands are tied without a crew."

"I'm going to make a couple of more phone calls and see what I come up with. Would you call Dale back? Offer him a better finder's fee or something. We've got to get going, man," he said seriously, looking troubled and impatient. "Ask Sarah again."

He'd asked before whether Sarah would be willing to crew. I flatly refused to discuss the possibility. He seemed to be getting desperate while I grew more at ease.

"No way, Bill. Not a chance. Like I told you, even if asked her to come, I wouldn't let her take the risk. If anything happens, it happens to me, not to Sarah!"

"Well brother," Bill said firmly, "we have to do something."

"Yeah, I know." I didn't really want to talk about it, which was difficult for me.

Finishing the conversation without resolving anything, I went back to the boat and discussed matters with Sarah, not mentioning that Bill wanted her to crew for us.

"Bill's pushing the trip again. It's crazy. I can't believe that with all our contacts we can't come up with some good men. All we need is two!"

"You said before maybe this wasn't meant to happen." She snuggled against me. "If you don't have a crew, what will happen?"

"Well for starters, Modesto will be mad as hell. He wants us to move the load off his ranch. If we don't have a crew before monsoon season, we'll have to find a storehouse for the kilos. Shit, I'm almost broke now. I have about three grand and that won't get us very far. If I were to sell my portion to Bill I'd have another fifteen grand."

"That would be good. Wouldn't it?"

"Yes." I looked across the harbor, my mind searching for answers. "Right about now, it would be plenty to keep us going."

"Then talk with Bill about what's on your mind. You know if you can't find a crew you're going to have to do something. Tell him you've run out of time. Honey, we've talked about getting out of here before monsoon season starts, and that's only a few weeks away. I wish I could be of more help."

"You already have. And now it's time for me to make a decision. That's all there is to the matter. I really believe we're not going to find a crew. Look at the harbor. For the past several weeks we've seen dozens of boats come and go. Now there's only Roberto and us. We've become fixtures. I need to think about things."

"I'll fix us something to eat while you're thinking," Sarah said, springing into action.

A little later she called to me; the settee was set for dinner.

"*Hamburguesa con queso* for my Beast," she announced with a joyous smile.

"I think I've got it figured out."

"Good. Eat and tell me about it."

"Well, it has mostly to do with you and me and this boat."

"I hope you're including the cat, Beast."

"But of course. The plan is for all of us." Leaning back, I said gravely, "When I first got into this business the goal was to buy a boat and sail off some day, with a certain amount of money, of course. I never much thought I'd sail off with a woman, not one like you. But here you are Sarah, and I want to be with you. I want us to sail off and live out our dreams. It's what both of us want."

"I'll be with you honey, if you want to sail off. You know that."

Reaching out, I grabbed her hand. Looking at her I reminded myself of my good fortune in finding this woman. "Yes, but there are lots of obstacles in our way. And as you know, we're running out of time, which means only one thing. We ought to take off for Hawaii now. If we do, I'll need support from you."

Looking up, she gave me that big smile that made my insides melt. "Well, praise the Lord, as my old nanny would say. This is for the better. Let's work on it. Tell me what I can do."

"Just be here and make plans with me. You're my soul mate and I need you to know that there's a great deal troubling me. Mostly it has to do with Jake, and the people who need help. I promised them more money. And there's Bill, too. He's depending on me. I'm in a quandary.

"You have to think of yourself too, Frank. Don't forget Jake and those other people got themselves into trouble. You've already given them tremendous help. Really. There's only so much a man can do. In my eyes you've done it and then some. You've succeeded. I understand what you're up against. I see it from the outside while you're on the inside. I know it's hard for you to make a decision about all of this while you're free and Jake is rotting in jail. I bleed for their cause. It would hurt to have to make such a decision myself, but I know you can. It may bother you a bit, but this 'holy vendetta' of yours is up against some pretty bad odds. As for your brother, he'll be fine. He's a survivor. I've seen that."

"Those are the very thoughts that have crossed my mind. My life is different now that I have you. And since I do, let's plan to sail off to Hawaii."

"Yes, yes, yes." She squeezed my hand. "I'm for that. We can leave right from here. Just sail right out of the harbor. I'm sure Millie would go, and William too. I could get us some other people from Inverness. There are plenty of people to choose from."

"Good. Now, for the hard part. I have to tell Bill about this decision, plus we'll need some money, more than what I have now. If I ask him to buy my portion, that would give us fifteen grand. Bill will balk. I know him."

"But we don't need much. We only need to sail to Hawaii. We'll be safe there. We can find work. I'm behind you all the way. It would mean the start of a new life. Think about it."

"I already have, sweetheart. In the morning I'm gonna tell Bill that it's over, and I want my money back. I've made my decision."

✳ ✳ ✳

It would be nice if life was simple, but it never is when you're up against the odds. It would be so much easier to know what you want from life and then go after it without compromising yourself. I was caught between love and war. To end my war, I needed to negotiate a peace treaty with Bill—and with myself. And Sarah was now a big part of that. Someone was going to get hurt, but I couldn't foresee that yet.

After having breakfast ashore the next morning with Sarah, I headed for Bill's apartment, leaving her to do some shopping.

"Hey Pancho," he greeted me, smiling. "What's up?" He was holding Kerstin as I came in feeling calm, confident, and resolved. Sitting down I replied, "I've made some decisions. I want to talk to you about them."

"Go ahead." He remained standing, holding the baby.

"What we're doing isn't working. Neither of us wants to go back to the States to find a crew. If we did, I know we'd find someone. That tells me that we're not all that interested in doing this work. Right?"

Bill didn't reply. His face began to cloud over as he sensed what was coming.

I added, "The monsoons are only a few weeks away. I've decided to sail to Hawaii with Sarah as soon as I can put a crew together. We can..."

"Hold it," Bill interrupted hotly. He put his daughter down and she went off to find her mother. "You can't do this now! We're too close." He held up a thumb and forefinger, so close one could hardly see between them. "Number one, we've got a ton of weed here, Frank!"

"You can buy my portion. Shit, I'll sell it to you at a much reduced price. You can pay me later."

"Oh no! No way, brother," he moved closer. "That's out totally. I'm not going to buy your share," He hesitated a second and added. "Look, you called me several months ago when your partner Jake went down. You asked for help and we agreed together that we'd do two business deals this year." He accentuated this by pointing a finger in my face. Dropping his hand, he demanded, "Why do you all of a sudden want to take off for Hawaii? And why don't you want to do this one run?" He looked down at me, with his big-brother guilt trip.

"Simple, Bill. I have everything I want right now—a boat and Sarah. Not much money, but that doesn't seem so important. Does that answer both of your questions?"

"Frank, this is foolish." He began pacing in front of me, turning every now and then to stare at me. "Really. Think about what you're doing. You're deserting all your friends for one. You're also breaking an agreement you made with me." He came on heavy, using guilt to leverage his arguments, going on and on about my promises and how they affected not only him but his family too, then more guilt about Jake and our people.

I began to falter. Bill knew how to apply pressure and even though I knew his technique, the guilt was sneaking up on me.

"And what are we going to do with two thousand pounds of weed?" he continued. "We've come this far. With a little more effort, we can pull this off. We need two guys. That's all that's stopping us." Going over to the kitchen table he grabbed a small note pad and a pencil. Returning, he announced, "It's coming up summer. You know what happens to the weed market. Prices go way up. I see no reason why we couldn't get two hundred a pound easily, probably more. Times that by two thousand pounds, that's four hundred thousand."

Working on some figures he added, "We already own the weed. Tambor gets twenty grand. Add two crewmen, that's another twenty. Off-loading with Matt is twenty-five tops. That leaves three hundred-twenty thousand, minimum, brother, minimum. Split fifty-fifty, that's one hundred sixty grand each and I'm paying you twelve thousand from the Aireberto deal, to boot. That's one hundred and seventy thousand bucks you're walking away from. You stand to make more money than either of us has ever made at one time. We can do it in one trip, brother, one trip! We're two people away from making a small fortune. You can't back down now. You can't. You can always go to Hawaii after we sell the load. You and Sarah can go in style, not as paupers"

I knew all of this, but Bill wasn't hearing me. "Bill, you don't seem to understand. The trip is not coming together. We've made all the calls and no one's available. Maybe we should find out what that's all about?"

Rolling his eyes he replied, "What if I came up with someone in a few days, or if we run into someone here?"

I felt I had him there. There hadn't been anyone; there wouldn't be anyone. Time was running out. "That would be a good sign. I'm talking two good people. No turds. If that were to happen, I'd go with you," I blurted out, then cringed, torn between guilt and the prospect of making a small fortune.

"Good. Then stay with it."

"Fine! We only have to the end of the month then I'm out of here. June first is the deadline. Is that a deal? That gives us less than three weeks." I was exasperated.

He tugged at his beard and paced. After a while he said, "Yes. If it comes to that, we'll store the load and I'll find a way to bring it up later."

Meeting Sarah at a beach later in the day, I dreaded telling her what I'd negotiated. "Sweety, the chances on us coming up with someone are slim to none. We've been in the harbor two and a half months. No one has shown up yet who's crew material. With the monsoons coming, each day makes the chances all the more remote."

"It's your decision," Sarah said, but she wasn't pleased. "I agree the chances are slim, but what do we do? Should I call Millie or not?"

"Can you put her on standby?"

"I don't really want to do that, but if you think it's best."

"Yes. Call her and let them know there's a very good chance we'll be going to Hawaii the first part of June. She doesn't get out of school 'til then anyway." Attempting to smile, I changed the subject. "Hey, do you think Roberto and Patty are going to make it to Hawaii with no booze aboard?"

The day before, Roberto had told us he was serious about quitting drinking. The only way he'd do it was cold turkey. We had partied hearty with them. Roberto had consistently sucked down beer and hard liquor at an alarming rate. He once killed a six-pack right in front of me one afternoon as I varnished the toe-rails on the *New Mornin*. It hadn't taken much more than an hour. Every time we were invited over, he'd pour us shots of tequila and we'd have to beg off. Now they wanted to take off without any liquor aboard. They had two young adults with them who were neophytes. His plans had major flaws. We saw it. They couldn't. "Patty and I and the kids are going to take off for Hawaii in a few Days. No booze, baby," he'd boasted, "no booze."

"Good, God no!" Sarah's laughter was a welcome sound. "Not a man like that. The way he puts it away!"

"It's a forgone conclusion, I'd say. If only we could find a way to talk him out of it." I said.

"Did you see the look of misery in Patty's face when he told us? I give him three days. Four, tops. He'll be sailing in and heading directly ashore!"

Eight or nine days passed. Two yachts remained in the harbor. A month ago there had been several. Monsoon season was approaching. Sarah and I were caught up in daily routines. Returning back from town one afternoon, we spotted three young dudes in a funky old Avon coming ashore. Powering up, they tied off at the dock, right next to our Avon. Right away, they were friendly.

"Hey, how's it going, man?" the blond dude said as he climbed up on the dock. All three wore shorts, sandals and T-shirts. I introduced Sarah and myself.

"I'm Mike," said the blond fellow, "this is Dirk and Patrick. Where you guys from?"

Shaking their hands, I replied. "Uh, San Francisco—Marin County, just to the north, actually. How about you?"

"We sailed down from Long Beach a few weeks ago on that thrity-two footer over there." Mike pointed to a small ketch in the harbor about two hundred yards from *New Mornin*.

Dirk, who was about six foot, swarthy, and broad shouldered with a deep frown, remarked, "Actually we've been here a few days. We anchored in the cove by the marine biology lab a few days back thinking it would be a great place to stay. A few hours ago, some shithead fisherman got tangled up in our anchor line and cut it. Our boat came ashore in the surf."

"Yeah, then he split," Patrick added. He was lean and tall, about six-one. His long, brown hair was tied back in a ponytail. I looked him over as he added, "We came back from breakfast just in time to save it from going on the beach."

"But you saved it?" I inquired. "I mean…it looks like it's okay."

"It's a shallow-drafter with twin keels." Mike added, "The surf was small. A couple of fishermen came along and helped us out."

"We'll feel safer with our boat here in the main harbor." Mike inquired, "Did you come down on a boat?"

"Yeah. The K-40 over there." I pointed.

"Hey! We'll talk to you later. Gotta run. The bus is coming." Mike was looking up the hill. A cloud of dust marked the progress of the old vehicle as it made its way along the edge of the cliff. We stared at the three of them as they ran off. Mike was more my height and outspoken. All three were around twenty-three to twenty-five years old.

"Well, how about that? Three prospects for crew." I said, flippantly, as we pulled away from the dock in the Avon.

"Yeah," Sarah replied, in a serious manner that caught my attention, "They certainly look the part. They're all big, strong and handsome, especially Dirk. He's your tall, dark and handsome type." Her tone lightened. She grinned.

"I figured you'd notice."

"We women always do, my dear," she teased. "We're just more subtle than men. We know how to look without looking."

"Well, aside from that kind of look, they're definitely the best looking prospects yet. I'll tell Bill," I added. Though excited by the prospect, a deeper thought took hold; it would be just as easy to never mention the incident to Bill.

The next morning I did what any good brother would do: I informed Bill, although reluctantly. The prospect of making all that money had won out. Many a time the same kind of challenge had put me to test. The end result was "damned if you do, damned if you don't." Bill was delighted by the good news. He had resigned himself to finding a warehouse and storing the weed, and was clearly on top of things when I laid out the favorable crew prospects. If anything, he was even "brotherly" as we figured out a plan.

That afternoon he came down to the harbor about four. Picking him up at the dock I told him, "They're aboard their boat now."

"Good. Let's head on over."

Coming alongside the ketch a few minutes later, Mike invited us on board. Down below there was a mess: crap everywhere. No one seemed to mind. I introduced Bill, and we talked about surfing and cruising as we drank beer.

After a while I asked them, "How about coming over to my boat for some chow? Sarah's cooking. We have cold beer, too."

Two hours later, all us of were sitting around the settee, slurping down a good spaghetti dinner and drinking cold beer. I brought out some of our good Nayarit weed shortly after dinner, and even started cleaning some right in front of them.

As I passed a joint to Mike he asked, "Where'd you get this?"

"Ask Bill."

"Got it from a good connection in town."

"Can you get more of this in quantity?" Dirk asked, while inspecting a few buds.

Bill nodded. "No problem, brother. Why? What's up?"

Dirk looked at his two buddies for approval. "We'd like to get ten or fifteen pounds, enough to pay for our trip down. Can you get that much?"

"That's no problem. I can get plenty. How are you going to get it back to the States?"

"That's easy," Dirk stated. "We have three surf boards and some glass and resin. We'll cut the boards open and stuff the weed in, then glass 'em back up. No one's gonna check 'em out."

"Good idea." Bill added, "But there's not much money to be made doing that. If you're going to smuggle some weed in why not bring a lot more?"

"Yeah, like where do we put it?" asked Mike. "We don't have the room. Besides, a few pounds will do."

Sarah made herself busy as Bill popped the question. "How about crewing for us? We're going to bring some of this up to the States."

"Keep talking," Mike said, eyes darting at his pals. All three seemed game.

"We'll pay you ten grand each, payable in weed at one-fifty a pound," Bill informed them.

I added, "You can sell it for a lot more than that, more like two to two-fifty a pound in LA. It's summer time. There's not much around."

"Sounds hot. What do you think guys?" Mike asked his pals.

Patrick, who was the quiet one agreed, along with his buddies.

They were ready, even grinning at the prospect of selling it as they calculated that they could most certainly sell that produce for much more than one-fifty.

We went over all the details and they agreed to the terms.

"So you got a ton of this stuff sitting at a ranch ready to go. Too much man! Too much!" Mike was in awe, as he passed a joint around. "That's nice stuff, real nice. It will be easy to sell in L.A."

"When do we leave, brother?" Dirk brought up.

"As soon as possible," Bill quipped.

"In less than a week, if all goes well," I added.

Whippoorwill departed for Hawaii the next day with their crew of four. Sarah and I waved and hollered to them as they headed out under power. Three days later, as predicted, they sailed back in and anchored far away from the sport fishing dock. Roberto and Patty made for shore in the Avon within minutes, not bothering to stop or look in our direction.

"That's so sad," Sarah offered, peering through binoculars as they rowed. "They look miserable, especially Patty."

"Oh well, at least they'll get some liquor in them to calm themselves down. Too bad they hadn't stuck to their resolve; but I'm glad they turned around before their "cold turkey" cruise turned into a 'bad trip'.

We were about ready for our own departure. Sarah planned to fly back to San Francisco. The *New Mornin* had been fueled, and just a few more repairs and it would be ready to go except for last minute supplies.

As Bill drove us to the airport the next day, Sarah was quiet, her mood hard to decipher. She was troubled by something. I tried not to let this affect me and acted as casual and loving as I could.

"I'll call as soon as we come ashore, probably around the middle of June, sweetheart."

"Okay, honey." We kissed. She was pensive and didn't want to share her thoughts. Neither did I. We gave one another a last-second hug. "Goodbye, Beast," she choked, and then turned and headed out the gate toward the jet that would take her home.

Both of us wanted the moment over with, as if it were all wrong. Perhaps we should be on our way to Hawaii, carefree on *New Mornin*, instead of parting at an airport in a crowd of bustling strangers.

Suddenly, I felt terrible—even more so as I walked back toward the main corridor where Bill stood, silent and waiting.

Later that evening while waiting for the crew to come aboard, I sat alone in the cockpit, holding Chicken of the Sea. She was playful like any four-month-old kitten. But no matter how much I appeased her, both of us were lonely. Since Sarah had departed, I'd thought a great deal about the venture ahead. As I gazed across the harbor, Roberto's boat came into view.

Days had passed. They had returned to their vessel, but had once again been on a binge. Considering the ordeal they put themselves through, they probably wanted a good dousing to jump-start their systems.

Earlier I'd told Sarah, "He probably feels guilty as hell about what he did, not being able to make it without alcohol."

But there I was, alone in the cockpit feeling just like Roberto and Patty had three weeks before. In a way, I had made the same decision—to go cold turkey. It weighed heavy on me, especially since Sarah had said she would stand by me no matter what. There was no need to doubt her, not one bit, yet I'd allowed Bill to talk me into doing this one last load. And I had weakened by letting money lure me back.

I could preach responsibility to others, but I couldn't apply it to my own life. I was in a quandary though. I'd made my choice and unfortunately it was too late to make a change.

If I kept on obsessing over the situation, the pressure would get me. There was a job to be done and the best way to get it done was to be positive.

"You've had worse things happen," I said to myself. I laughed softly, if only to remind myself of my intentions.

"Everything will go well," I said to Chicken of the Sea, since there was no one else to listen. "You and I and the crew will get this work done then we'll sail to Hawaii. We'll do it in style."

It was a long three hours before rendezvous time. When the crew showed up, other matters took precedence.

At midnight, we broke free of the anchor and headed outside the main harbor. We were to pick up the load in the same spot. The plans were straightforward: receive the load from Tambor, stash it aboard then sail north to Gaviotas beach. The unloading ought to go easy. At that time of year, there'd be no rainstorms, just strong summer winds as we made our way north. Matt and Dick would be there to receive us. Should the beach there be unusable, we needed only to sail down the coast to escape the prying eyes of the rangers who manned the station during that time of year. Should we encounter some problems along the way, well, that was the game we were playing; we'd just have be prepared, like good boy scouts.

Making the pick-up presented no problems, but the *New Mornin*, weighed down by 2,000 pounds, responded poorly and was sluggish under power. The sea was odd and lumpy. At best, we would make three and a half knots with our little diesel.

When the sun came up, we were still within sight of land. By ten, a breeze filled in and sails were set—full main and large headsail. Soon we were making a good six knots to weather and heading straight for Cabo San Lucas, 180 miles to the west.

When the breeze crapped out around four, we lumbered along, making three to four knots under power. The day was no surprise. To the north of us the lay fair weather and strong summer winds that would kick up to twenty-five knots or better. The crew was aware of the weather factor, but for the time being, we loved our little diesel.

Paying close attention to the engine's oil pressure gauge was especially important. Before departing, I'd gone over as much of the engine system as I understood. I had changed the oil in the transmission and fuel induction system, and cleaned the water separator system. Basic maintenance was all I knew, and it wasn't enough. After running the engine for several hours, it suddenly shut down while I was calculating our position.

"What the hell happened?" I asked Mike, as I came out the companionway and stood in the cockpit.

"I didn't do a thing, man. It just stopped dead. I checked the gauges a moment ago and everything was fine," he replied defensively.

"Okay. I'll check it out."

From under the main steps I removed the engine hatch, and crawled in to check the induction system. Sure enough, the oil reservoir was empty. It worried me because I had filled it the night before we left. I was stumped, even fearful. I filled it again, and bled the engine; a simple enough process. Then I announced to the crew, "Guys, I don't know why, but the induction reservoir was empty. We'll have to stop the engine every hour and check it. I brought plenty of oil, so fill it whenever necessary." I showed all of them how to do this, then restarted the engine. Minutes later, it came to a complete halt once again. Cursing, I checked out the bleeding system. It was full of air, the reservoir empty again.

Mike, crowding around the engine with me, asked, "What do you think it is?" We rested on our knees, while peering into the small engine compartment.

"The induction system is malfunctioning and I don't know shit about it. I'm going to bleed the system again and see what happens."

After I repeated the process, the engine ran for another twenty minutes then stopped. I was completely stumped when after an hour and two more attempts, it failed again.

Exasperated and fearful I might screw things up with the induction system, I addressed them. "We're going to have to shut this engine down for now. That means we can't use the batteries, guys. I'll go over this system in the morning and check out what the manual says. Maybe the gasket is leaking."

"Got any gasket material?" Patrick asked.

"No. I'm not sure I'd know how to fix one, anyway."

Morale was low, even though the engine, which had been out for three days, was once again operating. The problem had been the water separator. Before leaving, I had cleaned it, but had put the bottom on wrong, allowing air to suck in. I had gone over the damn thing twice. The third time, on the fourth day out was the charm. The top had been out of alignment ever so slightly. It had to be exact. In the small area I had had to work, it was difficult to see the tolerances. Even though we now had the two-banger running, the crew and I were put off by the whole affair. Sitting becalmed for up to half a day, for three days in a row, had taken its toll. Lethargy had set in.

Mike, who was always friendly and high-spirited, was quiet and unsettled. Patrick was friendly, but Dirk was aloof, as was Bill, who was out of his element. Bill would go about his four-hour watches, and not much else. It would have been so much easier if the crew were more affable and supportive instead of moody and tense. "We've got the blahs, that's all," I told myself.

We were coming up midway in our trip and sailing north against stiff summer breezes; the blahs were bound to happen.

We were eight days out now and a stiff summer wind that morning had been a forewarning that the day would be like the last two. We had to put the small headsail up early, and were sailing with a single reef in the main. *New Mornin* was enjoying it, charging like a stallion into the breeze, making a steady six knots to weather, doing well on one tack, getting a beating on the in-shore tack. Waves were four to seven feet between crests and would hit the vessel at odd angles, many of them breaking over the deck and coming aboard.

Come early evening, Mike was on watch as the rest of us hunkered down below. Appetites were low, so I just made sandwiches and hot coffee for the crew. It was one of those kick-ass days no one liked; a day when you dream of sailing downwind in a moderate breeze, yet knowing on the morrow you'll be going through the same kind of kick-butt weather. It was hang-in-there time; time to carry on and find a way to endure the heavy afternoon winds. There were jobs to be done: standing watch, cooking, navigating and whatever decision-making came along.

But we were all tired, especially me. Suspended in a strange state, I pondered how to pull us out of the low morale that was eating at us.

For now, it was time to go over the navigation: Dead Reckoning. I began to update our assumed location as the sun was slipping from the sky.

Going topside land was visible, though barely, for the first time in thirty hours. We were on course and were only some seven hundred miles from our destination. Time-wise, we were doing just fine; Gaviotas was a week to eight days away.

After checking the horizon off our bow for a few moments, I headed below and checked it against the charts topography. The two prominent mountains I could see; one broad and cresting; the other, Table Mountain, flat and desolate, all checked out. Going topside with a special bearing compass, I took two azimuth readings from between the centers of these two reference points. I then plotted a fixed position on the chart, and noted that we were eight miles off the assumed position; not bad, not good. Calculating that we were about twenty-five miles from land and were coming up the shore at a thirty-degree angle off true north, I came to a decision, then went topside to let Mike know our position.

"Let's keep on this in-shore tack until...eleven. OK? We're about twenty-five miles out. At this angle, we'll only be coming in fifteen miles, maybe less. This breeze will start crapping out shortly after dark . At eleven, tack out. If at any time, the wind goes below ten knots, or the boat goes below four knots, turn the engine on and sail under main and engine and head north at 315 degrees. That will take us on a parallel course up the coast."

"Sounds good to me. It looks like we're well offshore," he responded.

I went below and logged instructions for Patrick, who would be coming on watch next, then for Bill. With nothing more to do, I fell exhausted on the upper berth to port, thinking it would be good to escape the punishing effect of the wind. Coming in-shore would help out. My only concern was keeping the diesel running properly. Exhausted, I fell asleep.

It was a fitful sleep. I woke several times, confused and sweating. The interior of the boat was dark, and I couldn't even see what time it was by the ship's clock on the main bulkhead. Later, I woke in another sweat to the smell of diesel and the sound of the engine. I needed to know the exact time and our heading. In a daze, I rose up out of the bunk and headed to the companionway. Stepping up the small ladder, I slid the main hatch open and peered out. Clouds obscured the evening sky making it an eerie night. With Patrick's face aglow in the soft pink compass light, I asked him as I stood in the companionway in briefs and T-shirt, "What time is it?"

"About one-thirty," he replied, matter-of-factly.

"What's your heading?"

"Three-fifteen, due north."

"Good. How long has the engine been on?"

"Mike said he ran it the last hour or so of his watch."

Satisfied, I noted that the sails were down, furled and in ties. All had been taken care of as requested. Nonetheless, I was still uneasy.

Then the unimaginable happened.

In a calm sea, *New Mornin* shuddered and crunched as it hit a submerged object. Fear and pain shot through my heart. At the same time, the jarring impact pushed me up against the frame of the companionway and the *New Mornin* came to a complete halt.

Frightened beyond belief, I drew loose the companion boards and raced forward along the wash rails on the starboard side yelling to Patrick, "Point her out to sea, point her out to sea." I spotted the problem, as I looked out over the bow where the sea churned, revealing the submerged object. My instincts took hold. "Jesus, we've hit a reef. Get out of here. We're safe for now, but get the vessel turned around and head out." Waves of panic hit as I raced toward the helm. Pushing Patrick aside I yelled, "Give me the helm, man! Move over!" Lights came on from down below, as I put the wheel to port.

Dirk's face appeared in the companionway. "Check the bilges, man. Check 'em now. And turn out the lights. I can't see!" I yelled, as the vessel responded ever so slowly. Reaching for the throttle, I revved the engine. Inside, I was dying, in a panic, my thoughts exploding. "Get the hell out of here, now. Why are we moving so slowly? The vessel is floating. The object's out of the way. Come on, turn boat, move out of here! Come on! Turn. Move. Time is precious. Move boat, move."

It was, but too slowly. Why? What the hell was the matter?"

Looking once again to starboard as the boat slowly came round, the dreaded object we'd hit, though submerged, was still in sight. The boat, by then, headed directly out to sea, was near dead in the water. "What was happening?" I fixed my eyes straight ahead, but I was greeted by darkness. Again, I throttled the little two-banger, and revved the engine up and down.

"Move boat, dammit, move!" I yelled, to no avail. "What the hell is wrong?"

Confused and in total disarray, I heard someone yell, "The bilges are fine." Then Bill's face came into view. He was asking me something, but I paid him little attention. I did say in a panicked voice, "We've got to get out of here Bill, but we're not moving."

There was no time to lose. What's happening? Why aren't we moving forward as we ought to? Had the propeller been damaged? A maze of questions flew through my mind, as Mike and Dirk bolted through the companionway. They stood frozen, eyes wide, looking at me, then out to sea. They were in shock.

"Don't pay it any attention. Just get out of here," I told myself.

Patrick asked the same question. "Why aren't we moving forward?" I didn't answer him. I knew we'd hit a reef and for some godforsaken reason the vessel would not go forward. "Jesus! What have I done? You came in-shore too far. But how? God this is forbidden. But it's been done. Now you've only precious seconds to get away and out to sea where all will be well."

Precious seconds passed by. At that moment, I existed in a world of my own. The crew surrounded me, frozen as if on the edge of a cliff. Once again, I cried out, "Come on boat! Get going! Get going!" Every second counted. We could get out of the mess if the boat moved forward, but my knees and my mind had gone weak. My thoughts were wild and out of control. "How could I have done this? How could have I been so stupid? Or maybe it isn't what I think it is. Maybe it's a small offshore reef, overlooked on the chart. Oh God! Move boat, move. Please move. Come on."

As we inched along the crew kept trying to talk to me, but I shut them out. "Just get out of here. I can answer you later. Fear has you by the balls. I fucked up. I'm trying to undo the problem, so leave me alone."

With my eyes still fixed forward, a dark form moved toward us. In a fraction of a second it struck without hesitation, breaking a few feet off our bow. It was merciless: three feet of gut wrenching seawater pounded the *New Mornin*; taking me, the vessel, and the crew onto the reef. Its force was so strong that I gripped the wheel with all my might as it swept us sideways, dragging us across the reef. The angle of the vessel was so steep, and the sounds and shudders so deafening, complete panic shot through my heart. Every fiber of my being was fighting off the obvious, but I knew; I had felt the keel of my vessel being knocked clean off, like a plane landing too hard and its landing gear shattering.

Suddenly, another wave of water struck. I shrieked in agony. But it was of no use.

The *New Mornin* fell backwards, shuddering, scraping and dragging. My heart was crying out for the onslaught to stop.

It wouldn't. The ocean, pitiless and omnipotent, sent another jarring wave, sweeping the vessel around as though it were a toy, sending it further onto the reef.

The crew was now attempting to get my full attention, but they couldn't. I was unable to respond or fully comprehend what was going on. I felt worthless, drenched, and useless. My body and mind had gone elsewhere.

"Come out of it, man. Come out of it," Bill screamed, clutching my T-shirt. I stared back at him with wild foreboding, fear and rage having taken over.

"Snap out of it!" Bill screamed. "We've got to get ashore. Come on. Snap out of it."

I heard Dirk's voice ring out in the background. "I'm going to inflate the Avon," then I saw Bill rush to assist him. Mike and Patrick joined the effort. Transfixed, I clung to the wheel, caught in terror.

I watched the crew wrestle with the bulky bag as they cut it free from its perch atop the main cabin. All I could think was to look to sea for incoming waves and cling to my dream vessel, as it careened forward again as the next set of waves hit. The shuddering, the pain, the shuddering was endless. Why is this happening? Why had I come in-shore?"

"Hang on!" I screamed to the crew, as another wave descended, then another seconds later. As I clung to the wheel, a portion of my mind struggling to surface. But I couldn't. My mind wanted to stay in the abyss, even so, the crew worked furiously. But to me they were just forms moving in the dark.

I wanted to break free and help them, but I was unable to leave the helm though it needed no tending. This came to mind as Bill shrieked at me again.

"Snap out of it, Frank. Come to your senses."

I couldn't. "Go away. This isn't happening," I answered in my head.

I refused to speak, holding on for dear life as another wave hit. The pounding continued, my heart sank deeper, and the *New Mornin* kept dragging and scraping across the bottom. Insanity had taken over. I could no longer cope.

"Oh God, if only I could undo this."

Suddenly the spreader lights came on. Someone had thought to do that. Helplessly, I watched the three men fill the Avon. Bill's face came at me again. In his black, turtleneck and denims, he grabbed at me and shouted, "Get hold of yourself, man," his voice full of concern, full of rancor. "Come on. The boat's a goner. Let's go. We gotta get out of here! Get some clothes on! Move man, move!"

I felt an arm pulling at me, tugging me away from my precious helm, as yet another wall of water pounded the vessel. Stumbling forward, now free of the wheel, I regained some of my senses. Racing forward to where Dirk, Mike and Patrick were working furiously, I tried to assist. What could I do? There was no room to join in.

Suddenly, I felt cold. Suddenly I was present, drenched and shaking, humbled beyond words, struck cold by the ugliness of the moment. Turning, I headed for the safety of the companionway, my brother urging me on. I wanted to live, but I couldn't control the vessel's movement or stop the constant shuddering. I moved anyway, but it was not me moving. It was someone else. It had to be. I was not there.

I descended into the main cabin and looked in horror at what awaited me down below. I stumbled and fell to my knees as another wall of water hit.

Senses once again shattered, humiliation redoubled as I tried to regain my balance as another wave sent me to my knees. As it passed I regained myself and spotted my sea bag. The pounding was endless. So was the debris floating all around my as I extracted clothes from my sea bag, including kilos of weed clad in plastic wrappers, drifting past as I struggled to dress. Nothing made sense. All was wet. All was lost. Even my shoes were missing. Nothing would go right. What was I to do now?

I headed topside and was greeted by a wave of water that sent the *New Mornin* rocking forward, screeching and grinding. It sent me backwards, down the companionway, and into the water. I fought, freeing myself and climbed the stairs, and held fast as another wave hit.

Shattered and beyond humility, I joined the others and helped hold the life raft, worrying about what might be awaiting us. "Was there a beach? Would there be cliffs? Were we doomed? Then I realized something odd. I was holding the Avon with one hand, and clutching my sextant with the other. Why was I bringing it? Why was this happening? Why was Chicken of the Sea clinging to the mainsail atop the main boom, terrified?

"Hang on for another one!" someone shouted. I held onto the raft—almost full now—for dear life. Dirk pumped the billows, furiously putting air into the hull. Another wave hit, sending the vessel screeching over the reef, the grinding and crunching as unbearable as the cold and pain in my heart. Somehow my senses steadied and I readied myself for a launch. "Help them. Help them," I pleaded to myself. I wondered if I were a balloon being released into the atmosphere, soon to be lost to the darkness.

Confronted by Bill again, a wild, furious expression on his face, I heard him say, "Let's get ready to go, Frank."

I heard myself say, "I can't find the flare gun. I've got to go find it!"

"No way, man! Get a hold of yourself," he raged, as another wave hit the vessel. "We can't fire any flares. Not with all this weed on board. Get with it, man. We're going ashore."

Consumed by fear, I could only offer, "It may be safer to stay aboard."

"No! We're leaving," Bill insisted, grabbing my arm and shaking me. "All of us together. You got that? We're getting in the Avon and going ashore. Collect your thoughts, brother. You're in shock. Realize it. We're going ashore, man. Your boat is finished. It's wrecked. Come to your senses, goddammit."

Another wave pounded my dreamboat. It was less violent. The vessel slid further ashore, and I hung on through the rocking and scraping, every crunch, every grind. I felt cursed and I wanted it to stop. I wanted a foothold.

I whined at Bill, "But we don't know where we're at."

"It doesn't matter. We're going ashore. We've all agreed. We're going ashore," My brother voice was loud and piercing, "We're in white-water now. Let's go."

I looked on as the Avon was launched, then rushed to get in with the others, still clutching the sextant, as we pushed away from the vessel.

Adrift in the Avon with the others, all was calm for a several seconds, then I felt the Avon lift. As it did a rush of water caught my shoulder, instantly dumping me out of the raft, propelling to the bottom, and water entered my lungs. A new fright set in: I was alone. I had been sent to the bottom where sharp edges of the rocky reef struck at my feet. I might die in the sea, along with my dream.

Unnoticed in the melee, the sextant came loose and slid to the bottom. At the same instant, all my survival senses came into focus and I began to fight for my life. I was in shallow water and I used my legs and sprang to the surface and screamed. Instantly, I was creamed by another wall of water and went under, and fought to gain control on the shallow bottom. I wanted to survive, no matter what. I cried out, and again another wall of water hit, bringing more water to my lungs, taking my breath away. I needed help. Would it come? Would I survive?

Suddenly, I heard my brother's voice and was relieved. He called out to me and was suddenly alongside me.

"Relax, Frank, relax," I heard my brother say reassuringly, as he grabbed my arm. "We're okay. Don't fight the backwash. Go forward when I do."

I relaxed as instructed. In the lull that followed we progressed forward. "The beach is close. Come on, keep it up," I heard Bill say. Already we were in three to four feet of water. "Hold on, man! Here's another one. Go with it."

Finally, I was wading in one or two feet of water. Bill had released my arm and we were safe now, but the ocean floor was tearing at the flesh of my feet. Losing my balance I began crawling, the white-water sending me forward, keeping me on my knees, rolling me toward land.

Distance and time seemed never-ending, and the crawling and pounding constant. But suddenly there was sand. I stopped crawling, too exhausted to go any farther. On firm dry soil now, I rejoiced in finding I had survived and I knew insanity had not completely consumed me.

Still, I was in a state of incomprehensible fear. I had destroyed my dream and my future was unknown. I could only wait and see what it would bring, but being on the beach, safe and sound, was all I cared about for the moment. I was glad to be alive, but was also aware enough to know that we were all in deep trouble.

It's hard to say how long I lay there, unable to move, only that I heard voices around me saying all was well. No one had died. For the moment, that was all that mattered. I heard distant waves and knew that *New Mornin* lay dying. Sleep was what I needed.

"You okay, Frank?" Mike asked, approaching me.

I opened my eyes and spoke, the sound of my own voice shocking me. "Yeah. I'm wiped out. That's all." My mouth was incredibly dry. I wanted water—cool, mouth watering, drinking water.

"We found some sand dunes to rest on," Mike said. "Come on. Why don't you get up and come with us?"

Half-staggering up the sand dunes, I followed him. Cold and wet, we all crowded into a protective mound of sand. Stacked body against body, we pulled the Avon over the top of us.

Coming around now, shivering and tense, I listened as Bill said, "We can go out at first light and get the load off the boat."

"Yes," Mike replied. "There's a small village not far south of us. I saw the lights on my watch."

"We have to be careful to remove all the kilos," Bill emphasized.

"Let's get some sleep," Dirk said.

Subdued, I was in complete agreement. "Yes, let's sleep and dream this didn't happen." Still shivering, sleep came and I drifted off into complete oblivion.

CHAPTER
TWENTY-TWO

THE CARDINAL RULE

MEXICO
JUNE, 1971

I T WAS A NIGHT I prayed hadn't happened. But reality doesn't work that way. The sun always comes up and the night's ugly ordeal was before me at the first light of day.

Still wasted, groggy, and thirsty, I stared up at an overcast sky from beneath the shelter of the rubber craft. I stretched and looked at my watch. It was five-forty. Though still fatigued, I was ready for the day. Or, at least I thought I was. The previous night's events still weighed on me heavy. And already I was late; everyone else was up.

Spotting the crew standing around talking a few yards away, I headed over. Without wasting a moment, I informed the crew, (minus Mike, who was on the beach) "I'm going out to survey the boat. Can someone come with me?"

I presented a plan and they agreed it was sound. Bill was standing in front of me, bleary-eyed, exhausted, and put out. I could only imagine what Bill thought of me as I gazed into his eyes. I wanted him and the others to be receptive to my ideas. Right then, I felt like a total screw-up, but knew I had to clean up my mess and I was not about to give in to Bill or any of them.

Just then Mike came running up carrying a pair of shoes. "Hey, are these yours?"

I felt an eerie sense of relief as he handed me my topsiders. "Thanks, man."

As I slid into them, Mike added, "There's quite few articles coming ashore. I've got a pile of them. Come on down." He trotted off to the beach some sixty to seventy yards away. The rest of them followed him slowly, Pat and Dirk dragging the Avon behind them.

I stood there a moment and studied the terrain. There were sand dunes everywhere, green tufts of grass sprouting from their tops. In the distance lay the desert, an expanse of brackish sand, spotted with saguaro cactus and sagebrush. Chains of mountains jutted up in the background, including the ones I had used the night before to get a bearing. Table Mountain stood to the south, the cresting mountain to the north. They held some sort of meaning. The night before, inexplicably, I had made a huge error in calculating our position.

I had told Mike to keep heading to shore, but I should have known better. At an early age, I had learned the Cardinal Rule: *never make an inshore tack at night*. I had gone against that rule. "You knew better," I told myself. "It was brainless."

Before those depressing thoughts overpowered me, I turned away from the mountains and desert terrain and made my way toward the beach to join the crew. When I spotted the *New Mornin*, she sat upright, in a tide-pool some eighty yards from shore. Small ebbs of water surrounded the hull, making it appear she was safe or at anchor. It was deception at its best. I had to shake the notion and tell myself, "This is real, Frank. Face it."

The crew was readying the Avon as I walked up. "The boat's in a perfect place for off-loading. Come on, Mike. Why don't you join me?"

I steeled myself as I turned to face them, giving orders: "I'll tie some lines together from the boat. Mike can bring the lead end ashore. Find a place to make the lead end fast and we'll ferry the load ashore in the Avon."

"We've found a good spot to stash the load," Dirk added.

"Shit, I'll drag it up the dunes myself if I have to," Bill added, the first hint of humor since last night's crash.

"Fine. I'm going to send some food and drink ashore on the first load," I explained.

Dirk added with a wry grin, "Good luck. Everything was in the bilges."

Facing him I said, "Yeah, I know. I'll send what I find. Hopefully we'll have enough for a day or two."

"No need to worry about having enough to eat, guys," Patrick added. "That fishing village is not far away."

"We ought to check it out soon," said Mike

Bill cautioned us. "Maybe later today or tomorrow. Let's just get this weed ashore for now."

"Yeah. I don't think we want anyone from the village to spot us today," Patrick said wryly.

"Well guys, from what I saw of the load last night, don't expect any good news. There won't be a dry kilo aboard," I said, as Mike joined me in the Avon. He had found one of the oars and began kedging.

"Fish boat!" Mike exclaimed, about halfway out. We stopped a moment to gaze. A fishing boat, about forty-five foot long had come out of the small bay to our south. It was about three-quarters of a mile away and abeam of us on a northwesterly course. No one was visible on board.

"If they're any good, they'll see the boat wreck and radio to the authorities that we're here," I cautioned. "We better get going before someone comes to rescue us while we're running this weed ashore."

"As if we don't have enough problems," Mike said sarcastically.

"Yeah, like ending up in jail! Let's haul ass."

Within moments of spotting the fishing boat we were aboard the *New Mornin*. A chill ran up my spine as I stood in the cockpit. The boat was actually salvageable. If only there was a large crane around. No way. Come high tide the boat would suffer more from the incoming water pushing her ashore. When that happened, I'd be there to witness the destruction.

Below, I was greeted by a mighty mess. The floorboards were under a foot of water, kilos of weed floated freely about—plastic containers full of green, stained water. Drenched clothing was submerged beneath the water, but most all the kilos were still in place in the forepeak and in the quarter berth back aft. They were wet, even though we double wrapped them in plastic; most all the packages were stained green. I picked one up and it weighed several pounds. Mike grinned.

"What else did we expect?" he asked

"Well, if I had taped them up properly, they might have made it through. Right now I'm going to look for my money," I said.

I opened a small drawer below the port bunk, close to the floor boards where I had stashed the last of my cash, some twelve-hundred dollars, all in twenties, neatly stored in a plastic baggy.

Tensing, I cursed. "Shit, it's gone. Oh great, look at this!" I showed Mike the wooden drawer, its frame intact, the bottom missing.

"My money was in here."

After inspecting I discovered that the hull of the *New Mornin* had been eaten away right to the level of the bottom drawer. Shaking my head in anguish, I recalled the strange sensation I had when I put it there the previous week. Subconsciously, I had known it was not a safe spot to stash the only money I had in the world. Ironically, when I opened the drawer above, I found it was fully intact, all the gear in place.

"Had I put the stash of cash there, it would have been safe," I lamented.

"Fuck, really. Maybe it'll wash ashore. You never know," Mike consoled.

"Come on, let's find some food and drink if we can."

Within twenty minutes we had gathered all the available canned food we could find and had tied together several lengths of line. We loaded the Avon with canned food and all the kilos it could hold, and headed to shore with a line tied to the boat. Bill and the rest of the crew had found a solid tie-down and began unloading the contraband. When Mike returned, we once again loaded kilos into the Avon. Once ashore, they were placed on top of the small jib and dragged some two hundred yards into a low spot in the dunes. Working fast and efficiently it took us less than two hours to finish.

When Mike and I came ashore, the last of the load having been dragged into the dunes, my brother and I exchanged angry words.

"What is this, man? You can't be serious? You want to open all the wrappers and dry out the contraband? Bill—the weed is ruined."

The crew backed Bill and had already started the drying process.

"They're wet. That's all. We can salvage them and still get a decent price," Bill insisted.

"God, I don't believe you." I shouted, "Look at 'em. They're completely saturated with water. All the THC has been washed off. They'll rot in a few days. You'd bring this shit up north and sell it?"

"Hey, don't go getting righteous with me, brother. You were the one who put us here."

His stab quieted me for a moment as he continued to instruct the other three on how to proceed.

"You sonofabitch! This is absurd. I'm not going along with this, Bill." I barked, staring him down. "Just for starts, how in the hell are you going to get them up north?"

Bill stared defiantly back at me. "Let me worry about that. You can join us if you want. Dirk is in with me. I'll give a portion to Pat and Mike if they help out."

"You greedy shit. I'll have nothing to do with this. I thought we'd bring this load ashore and bury it right away."

He didn't respond. He was busy opening each soaked and stained bag. It'd take several days to dry them out and they'd still be worth nothing.

I fired another verbal shot at him. "Last night you kindly reminded me my boat was finished, over with, ruined. Can't you see the same is true with this load? It's junk, man. Junk! You'll never get them dry, and if you bury them half-dry they'll rot within a week. Come on Bill, this is madness."

Bill asserted his big-brother status. "No! This load can be salvaged. Dirk has a friend with a boat. We can be back in a very short period and get this load up north. I'm going for it. You got that?"

He continued to open the kilos and I snapped at him. "What about getting out of here safely? Huh? We have two days at most of food supplies and you want to camp out? The fishing boat that came by this morning must have spotted us. They probably radioed the village. Sooner or later someone will show up. Then what? Do we tell them we want to camp out and salvage the boat, or some other ridiculous story?"

Sarcasm didn't sway him. I was consumed with shame, not only from the events of last night, but also with my brother, who wanted to do something ridiculous.

"They're not here are they?" he asked as he turned and faced me. "We'll deal with them if and when they come. As for getting out of here, we can pay someone to drive us to Santa Rosalita on the other side of the Baja. From there we can catch a ferry to the mainland."

"Swell, you've covered everything, haven't you? Now you're running the show because I fucked things up. That's just great, brother. Never mind that we have to worry about getting caught. Just be pig-headed and take a couple of arrogant swipes at me. Well, screw you. You guys can hang with my brother, but I'm not. No way. I'm against this. I want out of here as soon as possible. When are we to leave here, brother, now that you're in charge?"

"Hey cool it," he said, pointing a finger at me, "You're out of hand right now. We're all agreed on this except for you. We'll be out of here in three days. Then you'll change your mind about what we're doing."

"Up yours, Bill." I had half a mind to start a fistfight with him. He was using the boats mainsail to store the contraband. How utterly mindless! If we got caught the evidence pointed directly at me. Nothing I said had any effect. I was a nonentity in the matter, even though the crew overheard everything Bill and I said. Emotionally spent, I headed off down to the beach.

The tide was going out. Standing on the exposed reef, I looked seaward and spotted, for the first time, a kelp bed in the area where we had hit bottom the night before.

I said aloud to no one, "That's why I couldn't maneuver the boat out. We were stuck in kelp."

As I looked over at the *New Mornin*, I wanted to scream. Instead, I started questioning myself again. Why had I chosen to make an in-shore tack at night? No answer came. We were there and that was that. The boat was a total loss and in most ways, so were we. I couldn't stop thinking about the conversation Mike and I had had last night before falling asleep. What had happened on his watch?

"Did you come offshore at eleven?" I asked

"Yes. Just as you instructed." Mike answered.

"What was the wind doing?"

"It had crapped out just before ten."

"Did you turn the engine on as soon as we dropped below five knots?"

"Yes," he said hesitantly. "Yes, I did. We were always above five knots."

"Didn't you see the lights of the village getting close?"

"No... Well, yes, I did" Then a slight hesitation, "Yes I did. Come on, man. I followed your instructions," Mike said defensively.

"Hey, get off his case. He wasn't at fault," Bill said, coming to Mike's defense.

"I'm just going over things with Mike. Sorry! I was the one who told you to come in-shore. I screwed up, no one else but me. I just wanted to make sure."

Still in shock, I initially wanted to blame someone else. But the next day, the reality of our situation was apparent. I had acted alone. I miscalculated, bringing us too far in-shore. Now I would pay the price.

"Come on, man. Get going," I told myself, "Don't let this get you down anymore than it already has. *New Mornin* is lost and I have to find my place and get with it.

As I continued to comb the reef, the sun broke through. Walking across the hard bottom of the reef, I picked up articles of clothing, boat equipment, and more canned food, all of which I piled on the beach. Mostly, I'd been searching for the money that I'd hoped would wash ashore. I came across a pink piece of paper lying face up on a large smooth rock. It was the pink slip to the vessel, registered to me in my false name: Steve Allen Walsh. It was in perfect condition. I picked it up and looked it over, thinking how odd it was to have found it here. Was there some reason I was supposed to find it?

"Think about it, Frank." Folding it, I placed it in my back pocket.

Continuing on, I came across something that shifted my reality another notch. Chicken of the Sea lay dead at my feet. Her face was grotesque, her jaw open, and her tongue out, her eyes showing fear. Before leaving the vessel, I had seen the cat in a panic clinging to the mainsail atop the main boom. I hadn't thought to save her. So she had died, the sea having claimed her. How ironic. How sad.

Then I thought of Sarah. Until that point, I hadn't allowed myself the luxury. Looking down at the grotesque feline, I sank deeper into my anguish. How would I ever find the strength to tell Sarah what I'd done?

In a soft voice, I said, "I'm so sorry, Sarah. I didn't mean to do it. I just got caught up in the way I do things. And you, too, Chicken. I'm sorry you had to die. Ah, Sarah, sweet Sarah, our future is gone. Can you ever forgive me? You don't know what it is that's happened, but you'll soon find out. I need you so badly right now. There's no one else I'd rather be with. I hope you feel the same about me."

As I mouthed the words I realized how pitiful and self-absorbed I had become.

It sickened me to recall how poorly I had acted after the boat was hit by the first series of waves. I had become hysterical and had failed miserably. "Look at what you've done. Look at it good and hard. Store the pictures away to be used someday to understand why this happened."

Picking up Chicken of the Sea, I carried her to shore. On a high dune over looking the beach, I buried her in the soft sand. Satisfied, I headed back to the rocky shelf and earnestly began looking for the friggin' loot.

I scoured the open reef bringing booty back to the beach for over an hour. But I found no cash. Without money, I was dead meat. It meant getting out of there on my own volition. "Where's it hidden? Send the treasure ashore, God. Do me this favor. I'm powerless without the means."

Bill and the crew set up camp to the south of where the load lay drying on the dunes. Dirk and Mike soon joined me. I didn't feel like talking to them, so, I headed for the camp. As I walked up I saw Bill, who was busy turning the clothes over to dry.

I faced him and abruptly admitted, "Well Bill, I blew it all the way, just like you blew doors when you got on our plane. I made a big mistake last night. I screwed up big-time, more so than you did. I'm finished, man. I have no desire to join. Take the load. It's yours. I just want to get out of here safely."

"Hey, I'm with you, brother. We'll get out of here in a couple of days."

"Yeah sure, man, whenever you say it's okay to go."

"You don't need to behave this way. Your ego is shaken by what you've done. You'll get over it. Life goes on. Just don't say things you'll regret." He gave a stare that turned me cold. "You can always change your mind. Remember, we all make mistakes."

"Right, I'm sure you'll remind me of that for a long time to come."

"Come on, man. You're in shock."

"Fucking right I am. I'm in shock by what you're doing."

"I'm being resourceful," Bill pointed out. "There's weed here that's worth money. I can either walk away or try to salvage it. I'm choosing to do the latter. I can see the look of disbelief on your face. Believe me, you're deep into it brother and you're not being rational right now. I know. I've been there before. Try and work your mind into a clear state. It may take a few days."

"I'm dealing with things, thank you. I can tell I'm in shock, but not about certain things, so back off and realize we need to work together to get out of here safely." I turned my heels and headed back out to the beach to look, again, for my precious money.

By one o'clock, we were tired and hungry. We rationed some fruit juice and canned vegetables. Most importantly, we needed fresh water. Tomorrow, we agreed, we'd go to the village for help and to buy supplies, and perhaps even talk to someone about getting out of there. Mike said he was pretty good with Spanish, especially his comprehension of the spoken language.

"Let's get some sleep," Mike suggested.

We awakened around 6:00 a.m. and shared a few cans of vegetables and a can of stew, and talked about our predicament. I had support. The crew was now beginning to realize that getting out safely was paramount. We tossed around a few ideas. The ferry at Santa Rosalita was most popular. I voted for heading to La Paz, breaking into two groups and hanging out a week until things blew over. No one bought my plan. As for how long to leave the contraband exposed, it became a wait-and-see process.

Our spirits lifted a little. Everyone had found their money except me. Once again, I felt powerless, especially when Bill began spearheading another meeting with the crew on how they could salvage the friggin' load. Uncomfortable, I got up and headed for the beach.

With the sun about to set, I walked the high dunes to the north, and stood at the edge of a sand-bluff that overlooked Punta Hipalito. *New Mornin* was directly below me, not more than fifty feet away; the incoming tide having washed her ashore. She lay tilted on her side at a forty-five degree angle, her mast pointing toward the sea. The grinding action of the afternoon tide had eaten away at her planks.

I ached at the sight of *New Mornin*, as she shuddered and tilted in the waves, her guts mangled. I forced myself to look at the vessel so the reality would sink in. What Bill had said earlier in the day—"You're in shock. It may be a few days before you're free of it…"—was true.

Standing there humbled and shaken, I zeroed in on the truth. Bill had made mistakes years ago. He too, had suffered shock. He knew what fools felt. Then Jake had joined his ranks. He was now in jail, and had made a fool of himself for no sensible reason. Manny, our ex-Scientology partner, had also erred. He too was either on the run, or in jail. And Gil and Neal, they had paid with their lives for being dense and uncooperative. And now, I was a member of the club. No matter what the mistake, we had all contributed to our failure. I wanted answers but knew the truth would unfold in time.

As I looked around in all directions, the barren harshness of the desert, an unending, untamed and desolate expanse, punished me. It offered no freedom. It was time to clear out. We were hurting ourselves by staying around, playing yet another stupid game of greed. "My, how the god of money knows how to rule us," I thought. "So do our minds and hearts. Why else would we remain there when all pointed to getting out before it was too late?"

The whole crew was in turmoil, including Bill. None of us were thinking clearly. No one could tell me any different. We were literally just trying to survive, but we faced huge stumbling blocks. We needed to take action before it was too late. If only I could make them realize we needed to march into the village tomorrow to buy ourselves a ride to freedom. But unfortunately, I knew I had lost all credibility in the eyes of the crew.

Mike and Patrick came by as I stood on the dunes. I was really becoming attached to them. They always seemed willing to talk and be friendly. We talked about the previous night's ordeal and I told them I'd committed a serious error. They seemed willing to not pass judgment, as I all but begged them to forgive me. Then we talked about the shock we felt— and agreed that it could further damage us, unless we got over it. We were in this together, and we could get ourselves out starting the next day.

Back at the camp we talked about the plan again. Bill thought tomorrow was too soon.

"Maybe the day after," he said. "Let's get some sleep for now." Our sleeping bags, finally dry, we crawled in and crashed shortly after dark, exhausted and thirsty.

✷ ✷

The next morning we were up early, combing the beach for lost articles. Within a few moments, Mike and I spotted two turtle boats heading toward the reef. We watched as the helmsman of each craft put his boat deftly through an open spot in the reef and headed straight for us. There were some three or four Mexican males of all ages in each craft. The rest of the crew joined us as the two boats neared.

"Mike, can you find out what they want?" I requested. "I'm sure they're here to help."

"Yeah! That's what it looks like."

The Mexicans jumped out of their vessels when they reached shore. Hauling their turtle boats onto the flat bottom of the dry reef, they started walking toward us, a stocky man about mid-thirties leading them.

He smiled. "*Hola, amigos.*"

"*Hola. Buenos días*," we all said and shook hands.

"My name is Pancho," I said in Spanish. Mike did likewise. The apparent spokesman, Jorge, told us they were fisherman from Hipalito, the village two kilometers away. The sudden arrival of the Mexicans unnerved us. Bill said in a whisper, "Lets keep these people preoccupied."

Using what Spanish he knew, Mike did his best to explain our situation. He pointed out that I was the captain of the vessel, and that I miscalculated, which caused us to lose our vessel.

We wanted to create a diversion so I asked Mike to let them know I had insurance, which would cover the boat, and if they wanted, they could salvage what was left. They understood. They were alert, bright, and humble.

They seemed concerned for us as we walked over to the *New Mornin*. Jorge said, "*Sí, es muy triste*," then began talking to his people while looked over the *New Mornin*. Jorge patted the hull and added, "*Muy bonita barque.*"

Knowing that would keep them busy, we were relieved when Jorge sent a man over to one of the boats to retrieve a large plastic container of fresh water, along with oranges and bananas. We graciously accepted his offering, drinking the water hastily. Jorge told Mike that the fishing boat that we had spotted yesterday had radioed him at the village, and that there was a sailboat wrecked on the beach.

As we ate and drank, a large stake-bed truck full of Mexicans came up the lone road to the south. Pulling to a halt but a hundred yards away, the villagers—mamas, papas, and children, all piled out and headed in our direction, some carrying small containers.

"We must have emptied the village," Dirk suggested with a wide grin.

As the villagers walked over I commented to Bill, "I'm sure they're just curious, but they've known since yesterday that we've been here."

"That's okay. It's only been a day and they're here now. Let's just keep 'em busy."

"Yeah. But it's gonna get weird if they start searching around."

"Why don't you and Mike keep them occupied and the three of us will be watchful."

"Let's not underestimate these people. They may be simple, but we're rather obvious, you know, five gringo dudes with long hair and beards. They know what that equals."

"Gotcha!" Bill was serious.

When Jorge offered us some hot burritos, I began to relax. Again, we accepted the offerings. The food was hot and quite tasty. They offered more until we consumed all that was given.

"*Muy rico, Señora. Gracias,*" I said to an old woman who looked me in the eyes for a brief moment, then shied away.

I asked Mike to tell the man once again that it was okay to begin the salvaging process.

"You bet."

We were safe for the moment, the villagers having departed about two that afternoon, along with the diesel engine from out of the *New Mornin*. They had given us a plentiful supply of food and water, but we were far from relaxed. Shortly after the villagers had arrived, two men showed up in a pickup. They had parked some distance away, and then took off abruptly. Their sudden appearance and departure spooked Bill, who asked Mike to see if Jorge, who was still salvaging, would be willing to drive all of us to Santa Rosalita in the morning. We offered him two hundred dollars and he agreed to come pick us up the next morning.

From our camp, anyone approaching was immediately visible. Patrick, on watch that evening, was first to spot a dark blue pickup truck heading our direction about five o'clock— the pickup immediately got our attention. We were even more shaken when five men hopped out wearing navy Federales uniforms. Four of them had M-14 army rifles slung over their shoulders.

As they headed toward us Bill took charge, "Mike, Frank: go greet them. Be cool," he urged.

Mike and I went forward and greeted them. One was a sergeant. The rest were privates. They had come from Ascension, a small cannery town thirty minutes away. Mike struggled with his Spanish, as the tension mounted. Both of us did our best to let them know that we were shipwrecked. He gave the sergeant the details, along with our names. The sergeant then told Mike that he must investigate and do paperwork. His frown told us he wasn't too happy. Mike produced his driver's license. Following his lead, I produced the pink slip. The sergeant spent a few minutes checking them, then handed them back. He looked about a moment, checking out the rest of the crew and my boat some fifty yards away, then announced that all of us would need to come with him to Ascensión to do the report. He was adamant, and stared at us uneasily.

I was beside myself, but remained calm and did all things to look sad— which wasn't really hard to do. "Oh boy, ah… ask him if it's okay if you and I go with him for now. Ah… tell him that we must guard our gear and look for more valuables."

Somehow Mike was able to convince him. The sergeant understood our plight and honored the request. He was satisfied as long as the owner of the vessel would come with him to Ascensión. To make sure all would go well, Mike offered to go along.

Before departing, I hastily conferred with the crew. All of them were beginning to realize that we were pushing the save-the-weed project a bit too far. They agreed to bury the contraband just after dark, and remove all the tracks leading in and out of the area. Mike and I would come back to join them as soon as possible, probably in the morning. We'd leave the area with Jorge, if everything went as planned.

THE CARDINAL RULE

✯ ✯

When we arrived in *Ascensión* we saw a large cannery; alongside it was a long wooden pier with a large steel-hulled vessel tied to it. In the main harbor, several fishing boats were at anchor or on moorings.

The naval sergeant pulled up in front of a small one-story headquarters building, got out and disappeared. We were asked to come inside by the privates and were shown a small room with two cots and some blankets. We could sleep there, they said politely, then pointed at a house up the street where we could purchase a meal.

"*Dónde está Sergente?*" Mike asked a couple of minutes after he had dropped us off.

He went to his *casa*, we were informed.

"We do the report *mañana?*" Mike asked.

"*Sí, mañana, mañana.*"

Everything was *mañana* in Mexico. Put things off today so that you could put them off again tomorrow. Hopefully their *mañana*-isms would help us get out of there soon. With any luck, we'd do the paperwork early the next morning, in time for our immediate departure.

"I guess its okay to go eat. You up to it, Mike?" I asked

"Let's go." When we arrived at the house, we were greeted at the door by a middle-aged energetic Mexican, named Hector. He was as surprised to see us as we were that he spoke such good English.

He exclaimed cheerfully, "*Americanos*! We don't get many of you. A few yachtsmen every once in awhile, but they never come to my *casa*. How are you boys? Come on in." We were boys to him.

For ten pesos, Hector served us a simple Mexican meal. As he prepared our meal, we told him about our disaster and how we had been asked to come to town to fill out a report.

"*Sí.* That is always necessary, but the sergeant is not much for paperwork. No one is around here." He explained that he was the company clerk for the cannery and that if we wished to leave tomorrow, for sixty bucks each, he could get us on the cannery boat, the big vessel that was tied to the pier. "It's going to Ensenada in the afternoon. Just be here at one o'clock."

To appease him, we indicated we were interested, knowing that we'd more than likely take off with Jorge anyway. At least we had another option.

Over the course of an hour we ate a meal well worth the eighty-cents Mike paid for it. After eating we checked out the town and then enjoyed a cold beer while making plans. Around dark we headed back to the headquarters where the privates were playing cards. They told us we could go sleep if we wished—sleep came easy.

In the morning we rose early and told the lone private on duty that we were going to breakfast. After eating at Hector's Mike and I decided not to wait for the sergeant. No one knew when he would show. Rather than wait around to file a report, we needed to let the crew know we could leave by boat that afternoon.

I suggested to Mike, "Let's take a taxi, go back to the beach, and get the rest of the crew and our gear. We don't want to miss the boat if the sergeant is late. We can tell the privates we'll be back soon."

"I'm up for it. We can be back here in an hour and a half, two at most."

"Come on. Let's go for it."

We told the privates that we'd be back in two hours, had Hector prepare three breakfasts to go, and then found a taxi.

Back at the camp, the crew was storing our gear on the flatbed, while Jorge rummaged through the *New Mornin*.

I asked Bill, "How'd it go?"

"No problems. We took care of everything. We got rid of the tracks also."

After telling them what had taken place in Ascensión, we decided to return to town, complete the paperwork, and then take passage aboard the cannery vessel, after the paperwork was done. We told Jorge, paid the taxi, and within minutes, we were in the back of the stake-bed truck.

We cringed as we left the area. The two suspicious men who had come by earlier were parked by the side of the road. They stared at us as we went by. It didn't look good. It was obvious they were waiting for us to leave.

There was nothing we could do to stop them from looking around.

We were soon in the small fishing hamlet of Hipalito. After Jorge parked the truck, he went on an errand. We milled around and were soon surrounded by curious villagers. A minute or so turned into an hour or more.

Suddenly, Jorge showed. After loading the boat gear into a small shack along his house, we climbed in the stake-bed and Jorge headed north to Ascensión.

Ten minutes later, after the truck rounded a large bend in the road, it came to a sudden halt. We rose up and were dumfounded by the scene before us. Spanned out in front of us were some eight to ten Mexican naval soldiers, each of them bearing an M-14 rifle held at the ready. The sergeant, whose truck blocked the road, waved an army Colt 45 in the air and yelled at us in Spanish, "Exit the truck, now!"

CHAPTER TWENTY-THREE

THE ASSASSINATION

MEXICO
JUNE, 1971

WE HAD ESCAPED the treachery of the reef, fooled the good people of *Hipalito* and successfully buried the weed, but we had not prepared ourselves for these guys. We were out-manned, out-gunned, and once again, "out-machoed."

Damn, when were the shock treatments going to stop? A man can only take so much.

The scowling sergeant wasn't rough, he just meant business. He handcuffed us and then his men hauled our butts off to jail. Mack had once said to me, "Don't ever get caught in a Mexican jail, they're the shits." I was about to find out what that advice meant. So were Bill and the rest of the crew.

At the headquarters in *Ascención* they ordered us to remove all our clothes and then searched us. The privates, who had been so nice the day before, now looked askance at us. They were *Federales*; we were the *contrabanistas*. I was bursting with anger and ready to fight them if they harassed us too much. Bill and the others, I was sure, felt the same way, but they didn't provoke us. When they took Mike's money and my gold money-clip, along with my expensive Moon Watch, I knew we'd never see them again. Bill, Dirk, and Patrick had put their money in their socks and hadn't been ordered to take them off.

Then, commanding us to get dressed, we were marched off under guard and deposited in the town jail, a small two-cell cinder-block structure. Each cell had a barred iron gate and each section was an eight-by-eight. There was a concrete floor to sit on, but no toilet. No water, either. It was a bleak building in the middle of nowhere, at the end of a bleak desert town.

We were held in those cells for four full days. Hector, the friendly cannery clerk and restaurant owner, visited us within hours of our arrest.

"They told me you were being kept here. Lots of trouble for you boys, huh? I'll bring you your meals. I will have to ask you to pay for them, five pesos instead of ten. Have you any money?"

We paid him and Hector faithfully brought us our meals and plenty of napkins. With no toilets, we were forced to piss out the cell door. To be polite, we pooped on our empty paper plates, placing them in a pile outside the iron gates. The pile remained there until we were carted off.

On the afternoon of the second day a group of uniformed officials visited us. They interrogated us one at a time in a small office building. Because I was the captain of the crew, they bullied me and tried to frighten me. They had no interpreter, but insisted that I knew how to speak Spanish. I *was* aware that they were asking me where I had gotten the *mota*, but I played dumb, refusing to respond. At their worst they leered at me, and got coarse a couple of times.

Mike had been interrogated first, but I hadn't been able to talk with him when they took me out of the cell. As they stood around excitedly discussing the matter in Spanish, I picked up that they had no other recourse than bullying tactics. They wanted information and they could not get it without an interpreter. Stymied, they took me back to the cell.

The end result was a standoff. Soon, we were back in our cells. We snickered and mocked them as we exchanged stories about their simplistic procedures.

Jorge made a sudden but brief appearance the next afternoon. He shook our hands and passed us a few oranges and apologized. He and his people, he insisted, were not responsible for turning us over to the authorities. He said it was the two *hombres* in the Toyota. We knew he was telling us the truth. Obviously, the men had found the buried contraband as soon as we left, and had quickly returned to Ascención to tell the sergeant. They would probably offer a reward.

Fortune, however, was with us in many ways.

Each time Hector dropped off our meals, he'd stay and talk awhile. If he had his way, we'd be out of there. He was our ally. We learned from a newspaper he passed us that we had been arrested for possession of two tons of weed. We laughed.

Obviously they'd weighed the contraband while it was wet. It was bound to weigh a lot more. Who cared? They had us.

Our real fortune was that they hadn't kept us apart. Bill, Mike, and I were put into the same cell. Patrick and Dirk were right next door and we immediately began to work out a story. A lone guard who was posted day and night only a few yards away, hadn't stopped us from conspiring. Left to our own devices, we came up with a whale of a tale.

At first we squabbled, then came to our senses. We were in this mess together. We could either come up with a sound alibi, or drown ourselves. Bill and I decided to join forces to take any blame off the crew. We realized that we'd be moved from this jail and would ultimately have to face an intense interrogation from Mexican authorities elsewhere. Our strategy was for our crew to claim they had no knowledge that the load was onboard. I was to claim that the weed was locked away in the forepeak by a door that separated it from the main cabin. Who would know other than us? The Mexican authorities, obviously less sophisticated than those in the States, would have to buy the story. Leave the rest to us, we told our crew.

We decided to leave Modesto out of the plot. The crew was unaware of him anyway. Bill and I were as good as dead if we included him; they'd have to torture us first. We even discussed that possibility and then quickly reined in our imaginations. We didn't know if the authorities would stoop to that level.

After some haggling with Bill on our story, I came up with a convoluted, but viable idea. Bill went for it right away. It was to be code-named *"the anecdote"*—hell, it even sounded good to us. Smugly, we figured we could pull it off. The crew agreed.

Every man on the crew was a survivor and they were ready to stand behind us. Maybe, just maybe, a good Mexican attorney could get them off. As for Bill and me, we needed some good luck. There was little we could do to save ourselves from prosecution, unless we paid a huge *mordita*. But where would we get the money? Leaving that aside for the moment, we worked diligently on our new plan and stayed with it. Time would tell if it would work.

The main problem was that the kilos had been buried in my sails. Thanks, Bill. I was fuming about it, but decided no good would come from fighting or arguing at this point. I was in shock and didn't have the stamina or the stomach to confront Bill, or order him to remove all the kilos and find another place to bury my mainsail. Mel and Bill had experienced similar difficulties when the plane had crash-landed in the desert storm in February of 1969. This time, it was Bill and I who were out of touch with reality.

Bill and I were using aliases. The crew suspected as much, but they didn't ask questions. They knew we were brothers with different last names. From the beginning, I had introduced myself as Steven Allen Walsh. Bill was known as Daniel Rattiner. To the crew, we were half-brothers. With his dark hair and the full beard Bill had grown, it was hard for the Mexicans to see the resemblance between us.

On the morning of the fourth day, a special group of high-powered officials visited us just after breakfast. We felt like caged monkeys as they peered in at us and bantered in Spanish. They departed, then returned several minutes later. Two detectives ordered us to come out of our cells and we were handcuffed, then driven in two vehicles to a small airport and put aboard a Piper Navajo. We'd get to know the two very macho detectives who escorted us. One was a tall dude, who insulted us and shoved us around the second we had left the small cells.

Harassing us as we boarded the plane, the jerk ordered us to sit down and handcuffed us to our seats. Bill and Mike were slapped hard in the back of the head for daring to talk. We were *putos* to him: that's "queer" in Spanish. That much I knew, along with several other cuss words. "Mr. Macho," we gathered, was just warming up.

The pilot was a cool dude, a civilian, who spoke good English. Turning to us he said politely, "We're taking you to La Paz. The *hombres* are detectives, mean ones, so take it easy or they'll get rough with you."

He was right. All the way to La Paz the big ape kept proving he was a jerk, throwing us one insult after another while we sat handcuffed to our seats.

"He's just trying to shake us up; don't get into it with him," Bill managed to get out before he was clubbed in the back of the head by the goon detective.

At the airport in La Paz we were pushed, shoved, and kicked by the goofy pig as he ordered us to get into a waiting van. From there they took us to the center of town to a jail that looked all too familiar—a near replica of the citadel that I had the pleasure of visiting in Guymas. Only this one was much bigger.

Bill and the rest of the crew were yanked out, literally, by Mr. Macho. Barring the exit, he yelled at me to stay put.

Suddenly, I was alone and fearful. They drove me a few blocks away, then politely asked me to get out. With several people around, the big boy all of a sudden wanted to show his nice side. Exiting, two men directed me to the lower level of an old office building. The sign above the entry indicated it was the chief prosecuting attorney's office. One of the detectives removed my handcuffs and seated me in front of a large, messy desk.

Two men in suits arrived moments later. One, who was about fifty years old, with dark curly hair, showed me his identification. He was the district attorney. The other, an older man, said he was to interpret. Even though his English was poor, I was starting to feel better; the place did not resemble a torture chamber and the big pig was no longer present. I was offered water and food, which I eventually accepted.

We'd guessed correctly: even these authorities lacked sophistication. Still, they drilled and grilled me for four hours. It was pure nonsense. They should have paid more attention to American crime movies. I even managed to argue and yell at them a few times.

The first order of business was my name. They presented the pink slip to my boat and placed in front of me. It was as though the pink slip, found on the reef, was part of a grander scheme. It was the only identification I had, and to them I was indeed Senor Steven Allen Walsh— the pink slip was proof. Later, I was photographed and fingerprinted. With no proper ID in my possession, they'd have to send my prints directly to the States. No telling how long it would take them to figure out my real identification, and Bill's too, but for now I was *Señor* Walsh. The FBI had no sophisticated computer programs to match fingerprints at the time. This part of the investigation might take months. The universe had thrown us a slow easy ball to hit once again.

"Yes, my name is Steven Allen Walsh," I said. When asked for an address, I gave them a phony one, somewhere in San Francisco, rather than to say I had none. Then the interpreter insinuated that I knew Spanish. We were *Americanos*. We were supposed to know these things. I became irritated with them. He badgered me anyway. That was when he laid things out. I was to tell them the truth—damn that sounded familiar—nothing but the truth. If I would tell them the truth they'd be easy on me. Fine, I'd tell them the truth, nothing but the truth. It was time for the "anecdote" I had cooked up with Bill.

Macho Brains entered for a brief cameo with an 8MM camera. After filming me for about five minutes, he departed with a typical to macho smile.

"Why am I here? What have I done wrong?" I asked, right after he vanished. No one had said anything about what we were being held for.

"You are under investigation, Señor Walsh," the interpreter said.

"What for? Can I have a lawyer?"

"Be patient. First you must tell us everything. Tell us the truth, do you understand? Then there will be no problem," the interpreter relayed.

"What about a lawyer? I'm an American citizen. I don't know your laws."

As the D.A. listened, the interpreter said sternly, "Señor Walsh, there will be no lawyer. You will talk with us and tell us the truth. We will help you if you do this."

I wanted to laugh in his face, but instead faked coming close to throwing a tantrum, insisting that I couldn't talk without my lawyer present. If they were going to work me, I was going to work them, as long as it was safe to do so. I caught myself before they exploded and began playing their game. When the interpreter said something too ridiculous to believe, I knew the truth-for-a-favor deal, would be next on the table.

"The D.A. promises he will get you your boat back, but first you must tell us who gave you the *mota*."

Yeah, sure. I *wished* getting my boat back was an option. In my mind, I talked myself through this sham. "This is second grade stuff, so don't get too cute Frank. Don't create a backfire. Go slow and easy. Let them think they're going to get a big piece of apple pie. That would sweeten them up. Play the dunce act, be sad and be truthful. Above all, don't let them bring in the big pig. First of all, what was the criterion behind the last statement? Prod them. You'll find out."

"I'll tell you who gave me the *mota*, but I want to tell you I don't trust the district attorney. He won't let me have a lawyer and my life is in jeopardy."

Of course the D.A. was unfazed. The interpreter came back with the same line: "Señor Walsh, tell us who gave you the *mota*. We must have the truth."

"What about my boat?"

"If you tell us the truth, the D.A. will give the boat back to you. He promises."

They were actually convinced they could do this, or that I'd be so stupid as to buy their ridiculous story. I didn't need to know where they had gotten their information. I knew differently, so I played the game of I'll-tell-you-who-if-you'll- tell-me-where-the-hell-you-guys-got-your-information from. Really! It was all so absurd, but it was their ballpark and their stupid rules (their "laws," they would say).

I was interested in their absurd offer, so I settled back with a big sigh. They had me, so they thought—I went into a state of compliance that was so good even I was convinced. My life was at stake. Why not deliver unto them what they wanted to hear: *the anecdote*.

I watched the D.A. take notes as the interpreter delivered the story to him in Spanish. I started by telling them that my parents had died in an auto accident. With some inheritance money, I had bought the boat. Sailing to Mexico with Sarah and friends, we had met Daniel Rattiner and had become friends with him. About one month ago, Dan and I met a Señor Maximo, a short, fat, middle-aged Mexican at the waterfront. Knowing I owned the *New Mornin*, he propositioned Bill and me into taking several kilos of *mota* north to Los Angeles. The kilos were placed in my boat just before leaving. Sarah had flown home and knew nothing about the situation. Dirk, Mike, and Patrick were to be paid a crew fee to help Dan and me sail the boat back. Because the kilos were locked in the forepeak, they knew nothing about the contraband.

Finishing the tall tale, I waited for the multitude of questions I figured would come, such as, "Why was the boat wrecked?" Or, "How was it wrecked?" They didn't care about such things. Their only interest was in Señor Maximo.

"How much did you pay for the kilos?"

"Nothing."

"How is this?"

"I was to be paid when I delivered the *mota* to him in Los Angeles."

"Where were you to deliver in Los Angles?"

"At a dock in San Pedro near the California Yacht Basin."

"Where did this Maximo get the *mota*?"

"I don't know. He didn't tell me."

Round and round we went, every question in triplicate. Nothing was asked about Sarah, or the friends who came south with me, or the passage north. Mostly I played the dumb, scared, young *gringo* who was in trouble, never deviating from the story as we went over it again and again.

"I didn't pay for it. He put the *mota* on board and told me to deliver it to San Pedro harbor in Los Angeles. Yes, Señor Maximo would be there waiting for me to arrive. That's why I'm scared. He'll be looking for me."

The lie was all there in black and white. I was sure they knew I would never give them the real truth, but they gave little indication. They never shouted at me, or threatened me. Just tell the truth, they said several times, though the "returning the boat to me soon" became a dead issue. Hard to say what they figured the truth might be. But to me, it was the truth I hoped would save the crew, and eventually Bill and me.

At this point I was led out, photographed, and finger-printed. By this time it was dark, and they offered more food. Doing my best to look defeated and tired, I ate hastily and drank volumes of water. It was crazy. We went around again. It was the same thing all over. The boat was promised again and I acted out the role of a man caught in a bind. Suddenly it was break time. It was also time for another argument. The D.A. left and then returned with sheets of paper he wanted me to sign.

"This is your statement Señor Walsh. It is for you to sign," the older interpreter ordered me as we sat at the D.A.'s desk.

"What is this? I don't understand." I knew full well what they were up to.

"This is the truth of what you say. You must sign it now."

I held the one and a half pages of typed paper in my hand, ready to laugh in their faces again. It was in Spanish. It was my entire confession. All four hours of it, on less than two sheets of paper.

"I can't sign this," I said. "I don't know what this says."

They stared me down for a moment, eyes fixed. The interrogation had lasted too long. They wanted to get going. Bill would be next, I figured. The wall clock read ten-thirty. "Think like a Mexican, act like a man. Challenge them as far as you dare. Piss them off. Make them earn their pay. Entertain them, then sign the confession. Laugh about it later. You'd need the ride. They were in charge anyway."

In the end, they were mighty ruffled. When I decided I finally had the best of them, I signed the stupid sheet of paper. Then I was unceremoniously driven to jail by the big pig and deposited in the citadel. There, I was hustled through the women's sector—mostly prostitutes, who whistled and shook their booties at me. I was led to a cell at the end of a long corridor and through the outside yard. Bill was there, along with this dude Tony, a Mexican inmate. Bill was hustled out as I was hustled in, but I had time to whisper, "All went well," as he passed by.

Tony was glad for the company and offered me a piece of cardboard, which provided a little bit of insulation from the concrete floor. This place was slimy and dank. The pale green paint, cracking and peeling from the walls, sent me into a state of anxiety. I gathered my wits, sat down on the cardboard with my back against the wall and faced Tony, then did my best to relax. Names were exchanged and he wanted to talk, but he spoke no English. What he managed to convey was helpful. Tomorrow, I would be removed from his cell and taken elsewhere.

Moments later, I couldn't help but laugh when I went to piss inside a concrete stall. Everything was concrete, including the toilet, which was a good-sized hole in the floor. As I began to urinate I heard soft laughter. Looking over at Tony, a talkative nut-head, he smiled and pointed at the wall. Looking at the wall in front of me, I spotted a hole about chest high and three-quarters of an inch in diameter. As I fixed my eyes on it, I heard the soft sounds of female giggles, with some squealing in the background. It was the prostitutes. Someone had drilled a hole through the wall for their pleasure. Welcome to Mexican jail, Frank.

I laughed too, as I finished up. Later, Tony entertained them by playing with himself while I tried to sleep on the layer of cardboard. I bet Tony was just sorry that his male member wasn't long enough for the girls to play with.

Bill arrived back in the middle of the night. I gave him half the cardboard. There were no blankets available. Even though La Paz weather was sweltering hot—near a hundred degrees—it cooled off at nights rather rapidly. It was the desert.

Bill and I checked in with each other before going to sleep. All had gone well. He too had refused to sign the confession, but gave in as the pressure mounted. Our stories matched. That was all that we needed to know for now.

We spent much of the next day with Tony. Around noon they let us out into the open courtyard. A lunatic lived in the cell next to Tony's. There was no mental hospital in Mexico, not for poor, insane criminals. All night long, the crazy man had carried on. Once out in the yard, Tony dared to pester him. The lunatic responded by throwing a large turd at Tony, who had to run off to wash it away. Bill and I steered clear of the loony.

Soon enough we were hauled over to the other side to the citadel where the rest of the crew was being held. They had gone through the same kind of questioning and had told their story as we had, and like us, had at first refused to sign the confession, eventually giving in. Bill suggested we hire a local lawyer for the time being. Later, we'd get one through Tambor.

At least this holding tank was large, but it was also made entirely of concrete, side-benches and all. From the cell we could see through the bars to the office and then out to the street. We were about forty feet from freedom. A friendly inmate who worked in the office came by and talked with us in broken English. He told us we were to be held for six days while under investigation. At the end of six days, if the D.A. and the judge had enough evidence against us, we were to be brought over to the main prison and held for trial. Our pictures and the story were in the local papers, he added, as we stood there in quiet shock. The two tons had somehow grown to four tons. We were celebrities of sorts and he treated us with respect, offering to help.

We gave him some money and he ordered plates of food for each of us—warm food from a small restaurant inside the main yard. That was how we got our meals for the next few days. As for sleeping, there was the concrete floor, or the concrete side-benches. What a choice. We were beginning to stink. The shower facility was slimy at best. We had to bear with it.

Later that afternoon the five of us were brought back to the D.A.'s office and allowed to call an attorney. We picked one from a list they gave and called him in to confer. Not much could be done while we were being investigated, but he assured us that he might be able to help us down the line. He informed us about Mexican law: that it is Napoleonic and that you are considered guilty until proven innocent. He also told us that our verdicts wouldn't come down for at least a year and a half, and that our crime, if convicted, would net us from five to eight years—here, in this jail, La Paz, a prison that was over a hundred years old and had at one time been a hospital.

When we returned, we were ready to climb the walls. Sitting became an exercise in futility. Instead, we paced the length of the holding cell with the other inmates: drunks, thieves, the downtrodden and the unquestionably insane.

Sleeping was nearly impossible. Lights were kept on. The inmates were restless and full of rage. We came damn near to fighting a couple of them.

On the third day an American consulate showed up. We were brought to the main office as a group, where he questioned us and gave us information about our rights—which were near to none. He was like a pariah, and we indirectly told him to go away. We offered him little or nothing in the way of information; still, he advised us that he could help us if we told him who to contact in the States. Sure!

On the fourth day, we noticed a lot of movement out on the street when a couple of large army deuces pulled up and some soldiers began to guard the prison. The friendly trustee came by and informed us they had been called in to guard the place against the possibility of a breakout. Whose? Ours, we were told. They had to be kidding!

We were hustled to the main yard around noon on day six. An official and a guard escorted us to our new quarters. Bill was assigned a cell near the gate. Dirk, Patrick, and Mike had cells along the same wall. Lastly, they led me around the exterior of the main structure to a much larger cell, which housed eight or nine inmates.

After the official and guard disappeared, I took stock of my cell. The sleeping quarters were small catacombs in the walls. A friendly man, Carlos, showed me a place to sleep. Depressed, I took off. I sought out Bill for help.

"We'll buy only what we need," he said. "I'll get two thick pads and two blankets. We can cook our food in my cell. I'll get a two-burner hot plate. We can order out for our food like the other inmates."

"Fine. Whatever you say," I thought to myself. What I didn't buy into was his attitude.

He warned me not to get out of hand with money or my ego. "What money—I don't have any—and just exactly whose ego, brother?"

We were federal prisoners and were told we'd be paid six dollars every other week. That was it. We were on your own—amuse yourself, this is jail. No one cared about what we did with our days as long as we behaved and showed respect.

We did have mail privileges, and surprisingly, nothing was to be opened or censored. I acquired writing materials, but then was at a loss as to what to say to my beloved. Attempting to put thoughts to word, my mind went blank. I finally dashed off an emotional note. When I handed it the guard at the gate a deep shame took hold.

We were also allowed phone privileges. The day after I mailed Sarah the letter, I summoned up enough courage to call. After making a request, I was brought to the office and shown a phone. I placed the call and waited, hoping she'd be home. When she answered, I could hardly speak. She knew something bad had happened when I choked up and was unable to express myself. When she became frantic, I knew I had to say something. When the story came out she cried. Not knowing what to say that would comfort her, I said I would write and explain what had happened. We were both lost for words. She was in shock, and mine was renewed.

"Please know that I'm okay and will write you often. Don't say anything, Sarah. Just know that I love you and I'm so sorry that the boat is gone. I want you to forgive me."

Inger paid us a visit. She brought baked goods and words of encouragement, and a lawyer from Mazatlan. Tambor was behind us. The five of us conferred with the new lawyer in the office. He read over all our statements and told us we had done well. He'd be able to help us very soon.

Inger stayed most of the day. She and I were reluctant to talk, so we kept our distance. We were cordial. Nothing was said about what had happened or whose fault it was. Bill may have told her, but he didn't say anything to me. I got the vibe that Inger now hated me. My heart ached for causing such a disaster. Bill told me there wasn't much money, and Inger would have to find a way to support herself and her daughter.

My role in wrecking the boat had grown to new proportions and I struggled within. What would happen to all of us? What would happen between Bill and me? We might go ballistic and have a knock-down, drag-out, end-it-all fight because he wanted to control everything. He sent out daily vibes that it was my fault, entirely. He didn't say it directly, but he implied it with his innuendos and his arrogant disregard for me. When it came down to crunch time, his heart was closed. I knew this might happen but had never felt the full brunt of his ego.

We kept our distance. His demeanor was laced with a cold air of indifference, and some days we'd argue over the smallest of things. He seemed to enjoy what power he held over me. He never asked how I was feeling or if I needed anything. After all, I was to blame for his demise. We'd cook together, but go our own ways to eat. It was ugly, forbidding, and most of all, unnecessary. If he'd open up, so would I. But the chance of that happening was about as likely as our getting out of jail soon.

There were three other Americans in jail, about our ages, all Californians, being held for smuggling hashish into Mexico and then on to the States. They'd been there seven months and had been the first inmates to greet us. They gave us information about litigation procedures and how to survive in jail. They pointed out the killers and cautioned us to stay away from them.

Overall though, these Americans were not all that friendly. Maybe it was because they knew they would be there a long while and wanted to remain private.

We were locked in our cells every evening at six p.m. after roll call. Twelve hours later, the cells were unlocked. We then had free rein of the yard and the showers. Radios started blaring about five each and every morning, without fail. One of the Mexican inmates, Carlos, would smile at me and sing out, "*Buenos días Capitano.*"

Most of them had either read or heard about our misadventures. As I made my way around the yard each day, I'd get a few rounds of, "*Hola, Capitano,*" and then fierce, mischievous smiles. It was a sign of recognition and respect. If nothing else, it made me feel good. As for most of the other inmates, they kept to themselves. Some walked around looking mighty glum.

One morning about a week after we arrived, a friendly inmate accosted me as I was headed to Bill's cell for breakfast.

"*Capitano*, there is more bad news for you in the paper today."

"Oh, really!"

He showed me the front page. Even though it was in Spanish, I understood the gist of the article. Modesto, our good friend and connection in Mazatlan, had been murdered. I held back my shock as he said, "Modestillo, your man, they murder him. It say you and your people are under investigation and that this man is the one who gave you the *mota*."

"No kidding? Well, there's no truth to that," I thanked him for his trouble. I stepped into Bill's cell and asked him to come outside so we could talk in private.

I said, "I was just shown a newspaper by an inmate. Modesto is dead. Someone assassinated him."

"Yes, I know. Did you talk to the guy about it?"

"Hell no! He said Modesto was our man and I told him it was a lie, and walked away."

"Good. We have to be cool about this."

"Yeah, but where's that put us?"

"Modesto's dead. That's all. We have less to worry about."

"Glad you think so."

"What the hell do you mean?"

"Bill, you sent that message to Tambor several days ago. He never got it." While we were in the holding tank Bill had, of his own volition, asked a man who was leaving jail after a night in the drunk tank, to send a message he had written to Tambor. Bill told the rest of us that he had done this—after the fact.

"We've already found out that the guy you gave the letter to was a detective," I said. "They know about Tambor now. I'm sure they've been to see him or at least to talk with the D.A. in Mazatlan; for sure the D.A. there knows Tambor is connected to Modesto."

"How in the hell do you know that?"

"Come on. You know as well as I do that Modesto is famous. They know Tambor too, and his connection with Modesto. They can put that much together. Give them some credit."

"Well, Modesto's dead, so it doesn't matter."

"Bullshit, Bill. We better talk about this right now. Why is he dead within days of our incarceration? Huh? And why did they post all the army guards? They've been out there every day since shortly after our arrival. Who murdered him? And how did he get killed? Shit, he goes around town with three or four armed bodyguards. This is serious shit. You send a letter to Tambor, it's picked off, and now Modesto is a dead man. There's a direct connection to what you did and the shooting."

"Not in my book. Modesto was a hunted man. He was primed to get killed at any time. Maybe his partner Geronimo had him done in. You don't know. You can't say anything until you have more facts."

"Believe me Bill, I'm going to get more."

After breakfast I headed off to think the matter over. We could be in grave danger. If Modesto's people got the notion we were talking or had caused the problem, they'd seek revenge. They might even kill the local D.A. Or, maybe Bill was right about Modesto's partner. Geronimo was a cunning man who gave off unfriendly vibes. We had met him as few times out at the rancho several months back. None of us liked him. He never engaged in pleasant small talk. Tambor had always warned us to be cautious with him. The new developments were unsettling. The extra army guards were removed the next day and Bill was not in the mood to talk about the matter anymore.

We found out from Tambor, two months later, that on the night Modesto was killed he was having a crazy Friday night out on the town. Apparently he got too crazy and started firing his gun, which drew the police. A gunfight ensued and he and a bodyguard were gunned down. But, others said he didn't start a thing and the local police shot him down as he left a nightclub with his four bodyguards. We never got a straight story on how he died—only that it happened shortly after we landed in jail.

We were not long for that jail. The D.A. in Mazatlan won a change of venue because the crime had been committed in his territory: Sinaloa.

On July 5, some thirty days after our capture, we were called to the main office and informed we were to be taken to Mazatlan.

"Go pack," they ordered. "Come back immediately. We want you to wait for two hours and suffer."

We said goodbye to all our new friends and then waited for the officials to get their shit together. Bill and I were rather pleased. The move would bring us home.

Mike, Dirk, and Patrick had already had close friends come down from Los Angeles for a visit. They had brought with them loads of personal items. All of us had collected a few tangibles. Mike, Dirk, and Patrick purchased a good-sized trunk from one of the inmates to transport their goods. Bill and I each came up with bolsa bags. We were ready for the big move.

Who else should show up but our good pal Macho Brains, along with his detective buddy, and a third man, as well as the local D.A. After we carried our goods to an awaiting van, they promptly handcuffed us to each other. We noticed that Macho Brains was moving about at half-power.

We had a long a long wait and were last to board. Hundreds of Mexican passengers, as well as Americans and foreigners were staring down at us as Macho Brains and his crew directed us up the gangplank.

The vessel, five hundred feet in length, had several decks and several comfortable seating areas alongside the hull on the upper decks. We were directed to store our goods on racks then pushed through a bulkhead door out to the seating isles, a place to starboard near to mid-ship. Seated, we were handcuffed to sets of chairs—two abreast—that were bolted down. I was put in the last row. There was a passageway to our left and the ship's metal plating to our right. Mike had an open port above his head, but was warned not to use it. We were told to sit and be quiet.

The D.A. disappeared in short order. We figured he had reserved a posh cabin. His detectives were to do the dirty work, and we expected our guards to start mistreating us about then. But Macho Brains remained in a fine mood, especially when a very foxy young American woman, well dressed and quite glamorous, stopped to talk with us shortly after departure. She was unaware of the detectives resting against the entryway door and she asked us why we were handcuffed. Decked out in shorts, sandals and shirts, as though we were on vacation when actually we were being carted off to jail, Dirk briefly explained the facts, as the rest of us drooled. Feeling sorry for us she smiled and then said, "Can I buy you men a cold beer?"

"Sure." Dirk said, as he squeezed off a big smile, "but you'll have to ask the detective over there, honey."

Turning to Macho Brains, she asked in Spanish if he would be so kind. Much to our surprise, he gave the go-ahead. He was tall, dark and handsome—the perfect gentleman—and all but stepped over himself to accommodate the lovely blond *gringa*.

Moments later she returned with several cold beers, including beers for the two detectives. They refused. They were on duty. She drank one herself as she talked with Dirk and the rest of us for about ten minutes, then left suddenly, wishing us the best of luck.

By then the ship was well out of the harbor and headed toward Mazatlan. While we drank we talked about our arrival time in Mazatlan. We calculated to be there around nine or ten tomorrow. After the detectives brought a meal, which we paid for, we asked if it would be okay for us to have another beer. They gave the green light. Most of the passengers had settled in. Very few came down our aisle as we enjoyed the brew our pals had run off to purchase. As long as it was our money paying for the libation, they kept bringing them. Why they allowed us to continue was a mystery. Maybe they preferred we got drunk. Drinking made us men, not just long-haired, dope-smoking hippies from the States.

Soon we asked to go to the bathroom. The guards uncuffed us, two at a time, and led the pair the short distance to the *banos* and back, their pistols at the ready. This was repeated several times. The others were getting pretty high, but I stopped after two beers. My tab was running.

Around eleven, just after Mike and Bill were brought back from a pee, Bill, who was seated on the outside just in front of me wheeled round and whispered.

"Frank, listen up! The guard put Mike's cuff on real loose. He knows he can slip free. We're going to try something in the morning. We're going to hold our bladders until then. Let's talk more about this later."

"Fine! Sounds good."

"So, you think we'll be in about ten tomorrow?"

"Yes. Figure early morning around eight or ten."

"Good! Enough for now."

They had been handcuffed together, with the chain led through the hollow of the metal armrest. Mike only needed to slip his cuff and both would be free. The opportunity was clear: slip from the cuff, and run. It was worth a shot. It wouldn't take much doing. It'd be a timing game, then a bit of frenzy.

Several minutes later Bill wheeled around again.

"Hey, Frank," he said in a low voice, while the detectives were not paying us much attention. "Tomorrow morning we're going to make a move. We're hoping for a break. We'll only need a couple of seconds when the guards aren't looking. Can you dig it?"

"Yeah. Sounds right to me. How are you going to do it?"

"We'll have to wait for a moment when they're not looking and then

Mike will slip the cuff. I'll run aft, up that staircase there in back of us. It goes to the open deck, then onto the fantail. I'll jump overboard and swim to shore. Mike will go out the porthole. I gave him Tambor's number. If we get ashore, we'll connect up through him. Pat and Dirk know what we're up to."

"You're going to swim with cuffs on?" I whispered, surprised that he'd be willing to put himself at risk.

"That's the least of my worries. If I make it, I'll help you guys get out. Let's keep it cool 'til morning, then we'll talk again."

Now that I knew he and Mike were quite serious, sleep became difficult. I awoke several times during the night. Each time, the lone guard was wide awake and staring at us, as he leaned on or near the passenger exit door. In the morning the guard asked us if we wished to purchase breakfast. We lied and told him we were not hungry.

Bill wheeled round, shortly after he asked an American passenger for the time. "It's eight thirty. We must be real close to the harbor. There's a lot of activity. Beware. Like I say, if we make it we'll get you guys out somehow. Just hope we make it."

As the minutes ticked by, the passengers started carrying suitcases and bolsa bags. The time was getting ripe for action. The D.A. showed up, looking refreshed in a suit and tie, and gave his men instructions. He looked us over then departed as suddenly as he had come. By then, we were certain the ship was in or very near the harbor. Unfortunately, we couldn't see land from our side of the vessel.

Moments later Patrick and Dirk were uncuffed, removed from their seat, recuffed, and then led away by Mister Easy and the third detective. They were supposed to get their trunk and our baggage from the storage locker only a short distance away. While they were being led off through the exit door, Macho Brains stepped through to confer with his detective pals.

For a brief moment, the three of us were completely alone. It was time to escape. Mike grunted as he pulled free. Bill eased slowly from his seat, then bolted aft before Mike could even get to the porthole. As soon Mike reached the porthole, I knew it was a mistake. He should have exited with Bill.

Just as Bill disappeared, Macho Brains came back. Seeing what had happened, he screamed like a stuck pig as Mike was working his way out the porthole, head first, moving as slow as a sloth.

I struggled in my chair as Macho Brains drew his pistol and leveled it at Mike, screaming for assistance. I cringed, waiting for him to pop off a round or two into Mike's rear. Instead of shooting, he put the weapon in his holster and charged Mike, whose legs were flailing. The big brute grabbed and held on. It was just what Mike needed—something to push off from. As the two struggled, Mike thrust one leg against Macho's chest and disappeared out the hole. I was having a major adrenalin rush, and also laughing inside at the absurdity of the scene.

Bill had been gone for at least a decade it seemed, before Macho Brain let out another long stream of screaming, punctuated with curses. He pulled out his pistol again and aimed it directly at my head, trigger cocked. Instincts took over.

"Don't move Frank," I told myself. "Don't even breathe. Above all don't act scared, just stare at him."

While he was still screaming and holding the pistol at my head, out of the corner of my eye, I saw the other two detectives push Dirk and Patrick through the door and back to their seats. I ducked as Brainless backhanded my head, leveled the gun again, and cursed me in Spanish as he checked my cuff to see if it was secure. All the while, he screamed orders to his partners. When Pat and Dirk were recuffed, none too politely, he smacked them in the face a couple of times. He then headed off, leaving the lone reserve man to guard us. Pistol in hand, the reserve feverishly yelled at us in Spanish. All I could figure out was that he wanted us to be still and quiet. We didn't move or utter a word for the next several moments.

With our hearts pounding, we could only hope our two buddies were safe and headed for shore. We listened for sounds of gunfire, but heard nothing, though the vessel stopped. We could feel the engines going into reverse. Not a good sign.

Macho Brains would go ballistic on us if Bill and Mike were successful. We were soon to learn from other prisoners that escaping from jail in Mexico is legal. No additional time is added to a prisoner's sentence for attempting to escape, but those guards or official responsible for letting the escape occur would be investigated. If they were found guilty, *they* would have to spent time in jail based on your sentence! Macho Brains and his detectives would more than likely be in jail for years to come. Napoleonic Code was a setup. Bill and Mike might be shot and there would be little we could do about it.

All I knew at the time was that Macho Brains must have been feeling like a fool. And, maybe the three of us were lucky that Mike and Bill didn't make good on their escape. Unknown to us, the ship was still some five miles offshore. Two lifeboats were put over the side as the ship came to a halt, and Bill and Mike were retrieved from the water. Soaking wet, they were brought back in cuffs and kicked by Macho Brains through the entryway. When they stumbled to the floor, Macho Brains proceeded to kick them. Grabbing Mike by the hair, he rammed his boot into Mike's groin and stomach a few times, then started on Bill while the other detectives joined in, kicking Mike as he held him down. Meanwhile, the three of us began screaming insults in English and doing what we could stop them, but were hampered by our cuffs and the guard holding a pistol on us. Fortunately, the D.A. came in and put a stop to it. Bill and Mike were yanked up by their hair and slammed into their seats.

While we consoled them, Macho Brains yelled at us to keep quiet. We disregarded the warning and kept up. He had lost his grip on us. Dishonored and in tatters, the D.A. called him off again. We were safe for the moment, but knew more rough-housing was in store.

When the ship docked, we were kept in our seats for a long time—we were the last passengers off the ferry. This time they didn't need us to collect our few possessions. They had become the property of Macho Brains and his cronies.

We were driven by van to the public *caracel*, a large prison in the middle of the Colony Juarez—a poor part of Mazatlan. The prison was a full block long and a block wide. Its walls, made of red brick, were at least eighteen to twenty feet high. Two guard towers stood at two ends on the backside. The van parked out front and we filed out. Macho Brains shoved and cursed us as he herded us quickly through the main entrance: a stolid, white wall fronted by a huge, barred, iron gate. Two sentinels, who looked about as dismal as the building, were posted at the gate. We marched past them and into a large office.

We were left to stand there for a moment, as Butthead checked us in with the *Alciadia*, the office buzzing with people, office workers, inmates, and guards. The place was big compared to the La Paz jail, its interior wall painted an ugly pale green that turned my stomach. Shortly, we were led into the *Alciadia's* office. Butthead had no doubt just informed the man there had been an attempted escape, which I'm sure he hadn't wished to report. We knew to stand silent and look humble in front of our new warden.

Finished with his report, Macho Brains signed release forms, leered at us saying something derogatory in Spanish, and then turned and walked out of our lives forever.

As we remained still, the *Alciadia* looked us over. He was an older man, perhaps sixty, short, heavy, and balding. Within seconds he ordered two guards to remove our cuffs and take us away. We were led up a long, wide, concrete ramp then ordered to proceed through another huge barred gate. Entering, we stepped forward into a short, concrete hallway. The gate, once closed, was locked.

We were in the *Grande*. There was no one to tell us where to bunk, or where the toilets and showers were located. In front of us was of one hell of a large dirt yard. What was up? We didn't know, only that they hadn't put us in solitary confinement for the escape escapade. That was a relief.

As we hesitantly stepped into the yard, a few Mexican prisoners stopped and looked us over. Within moments a *gringo* came over and introduced himself.

"Ted Grayson's my name. So, they just threw you in here, huh?" he asked quizzically. We eyed this lanky gringo, shirtless and dressed in shorts and thongs with a tattoo on his shoulder. By the expression on his face, he could either be friendly or trouble.

"Yeah," Dirk spoke first. "We were brought over from La Paz on the ferry."

As they conversed, I gazed around the large rectangular yard. It was forty yards wide and seventy yards long. In the center, going lengthwise, was a group of makeshift tents. At the very end of the yard, against the back wall, were several awnings tied off by poles, along with several prisoners milling around a couple of food vendors. A long corridor was to our right. It housed the cellblocks.

That was where Ted led us. The corridor ran the length of the building. It was ten feet wide, and he directed us to a small restaurant. Along the corridor were barred, unlocked gates, each portal a cellblock. A meal cost five *pesos*. Five were ordered. The food was surprisingly good and we were quite hungry. As we wolfed down the meal, Ted went off and brought back more Americans. There were eighteen in the *Grande*, twenty-four in all throughout the prison. Counting us, we were about eight percent of the main prison population.

We found ourselves surrounded by eight to ten *gringos*, who began asking questions. It was the usual crap: the how-what-where-when details of our bust. Every one of them, being jail-yard lawyers, began painting us a bad picture. One of them told us how his plane, loaded with 1,800 pounds of top-grade *mota*, had crashed on takeoff. He had sustained severe foot damage and some burns. After he was captured, he was made to sit with no medical care until he signed a confession. He got an eight-year term.

"The Mexicans I was working with could have saved me," he whined, "but they were real chicken shits, man. Real chicken shits. Ya know what I mean?" He grimaced, showing us his scars and lamenting about the poor medical treatment he had received, and even had to pay for. I didn't like the guy. His whining drained my energy.

Then someone else chirped in about the D.A.

"There's no paying off the local D.A. He's a real dirt-grinding asshole of a human being. Same with the judges. He's got them under his control. So there's no buying your way out of here, guys."

He too, was an energy drain.

Much to our relief, Ted suggested showing us around. The pilot with the sad tale didn't stop talking.

"Well, good luck, guys. There's not a bunk available in my cellblock. The rest are overcrowded as it is."

Negativity lingered in the air as we got up and headed down the corridor. We entered a cellblock. A toilet was at the entry, and when I peered at the bowl my stomach knotted up. It was full of feces; the stench and the sight over-powering.

What we saw next was even more unimaginable—nothing but rows of metal bunks, army issue, stacked a few feet apart, two high, most all of them enshrouded by blankets or sheets. Even the small passageways between aisles were shrouded. A chill ran up my spine. How would I survive these conditions: little or no privacy, men living on top and across from men, only a sheet and perhaps a yard or so of space between them? It was inhospitable.

Ted showed us his digs, a bunk like all the others enshrouded by sheets. He had a mattress, sheets, a pillow, a small fan, a few books, pens, paper. Not much else. As we crowded around the small space he explained that it was not possible to keep possessions about. Anything of value would quickly be stolen.

"It's like feeding yourself to sharks, guys," he said whimsically.

Mike asked him, "Do you get all your food from the restaurant?"

"Nah. We buy when we can afford to, but we cook a lot of meals in our hut outside. "Gringo Gulch," we call it. Come on out. I'll show you."

He led us outside and into the main yard, where he headed straight for the group of makeshift huts we had first spotted in the center of the yard. As we entered the last one he said, "This is our territory, guys. If any Mexicans enter our domain, we kick their asses, unless we invite them. But that doesn't happen."

The little hut was unbearably hot and depressing. It looked as though no one really used the place, although Ted explained, "We hang out here a lot and cook, talk, and figure ways to escape from this shit hole." He told us that he and a few other *gringos* had started tunneling from the hut toward the gate a few months back. They had gotten about forty feet, when it caved in. They had to pull one poor sucker out before he suffocated. When the officials found out, Ted and his pals were forced to repair the yard themselves.

"Then a couple of us were sent to the hole for thirty days. I'm surprised they didn't put all of you there, too."

Then he told us about the "right to escape" from jail in Mexico and how the guilty party had to do your time if you succeeded. He added, "The guards are only paid fifty *pesos* a day. It's easy to buy them off, but we can't get them to let us escape. Then again, they do bring us our dope."

Ted leered at us with a strange, crooked smile. "I can get you some finger rolls of *mota* for ten pesos. Or a two-hit of heroin for thirty-five *pesos*. It's a good deal stuff."

"No thanks," Bill said.

"Hey, maybe some *mota*," Mike and Dirk chirped.

We found out later several of the inmates, American as well as Mexican, were hooked on heroin—including Ted.

With Gringo Gulch too hot for comfort, we headed for the cooler concrete corridor for a fruit juice. More fellow American inmates were introduced and once again came the questions.

But we were saved when we heard our names being called.

"They want you up at the main gate," Ted said.

We headed off. The guard opened the gate to the *Grande* and ushered us through. He locked it, turned and ushered us to another barred gate. He unlocked it and with a hand gesture, showed us the way in.

It was a much smaller yard, though quite crowded. Stunned, we stood there for a moment, not knowing what to do as we heard the clink of the gate shutting behind us. Within seconds, a tall blond dude about our age, dressed in shorts and sandals, greeted us.

"Welcome to *Correctionalis*," he said, grinning widely. "I'm Steve."

CHAPTER TWENTY-FOUR

CORRECTIONALIS

MAZATLAN
SINALOA, MEXICO
JULY, 1971

Before Steve entered the scene, we had been in our new sector just long enough to get a good picture of it.

There were people everywhere—well over a hundred. A thin Mexican with a big hooked nose, large earrings, and dressed much like a woman was stringing laundry on lines that ran from concrete pilasters to a canopied area at the center of a concrete courtyard that ran eighty by eighty feet. Along three walls were small dwellings, each with a door. It was hard to check the place out with sheets hanging everywhere, but in the far right corner there appeared to be a small store with an opening and a countertop.

The sound of chatter created a dull roar. The place was much like a crowded bazaar one sees in movie scenes, only this one was real, and it was jail—Mexican style. Repulsed, I shuddered and the knot at the center of my stomach tightened. Rod Sterling must have cooked this scene up with a little help from Bosch. Just what was this place, other than unreal? Steve more or less answered the question when he said, "Welcome to Correctionalis." They got that one right. Everything in there needed correction.

Fortunately, Steve distracted us from the maddening scene.

"This is my buddy Walter," Steve said.

Walter was a tall, lanky kid, somewhat younger than Steve, with a long, dark ponytail. Walter had a friendly demeanor, but Steve seemed a bit overzealous. We all introduced ourselves.

"Come to our *caraca*," Steve offered, leading the way to a small hut. Their dwelling was eight feet by sixteen, a virtual palace compared to what we had just seen in the *Grande*. A large, modern, rotating fan whirred away atop a small shelf. There were two wooden cots, a couple of wooden crates with hot plates on them, and some pots with a few utensils. The walls were adorned with posters from a travel catalogue. I felt better already as we crowded in, finding a place to sit, and soaking in the breeze from the fan.

"Jesus, there's five of you guys." Walter observed. "Are you all in for the same thing?"

Now it was time for Steve and Walter to hear our tale.

"Oh boy, so you lost your boat?" Walter asked.

"Yup. The first wave took care of things."

"We were careless too," Steve butted in. "We bought about eight ounces of pot and the asshole turned us in."

"For a reward, no less," Walter said. "We've been here eight months now. We may be out shortly if things go right."

"You think they'll keep us here in this section?" Mike asked, after we told them we had been in the *Grande* for a couple of hours.

"More than likely," Steve replied. "We can find out. I'll send a message to Armando. He's the *Vice-Presidente* of *Correctionalis*. He's a trustee who works in the office."

"Can you? We'd appreciate it," Bill added.

"No problem, man. I'll give a note to the guard. We'll have our answer in a few minutes." He wrote a message on a small pad then left for a brief moment.

Just after Steve returned, we heard a soft knock on the door and a short, pleasant- looking Chinese fellow, dressed in shorts and thongs stepped in. Grinning from ear to ear, he shook our hands.

"Hey, guys. Heard you were here. I'm Fred." He found a place to sit in the crowded room.

We definitely preferred the new sector over the *Grande*. Who wouldn't, after having spent two grueling hours wading in rubble?

"Believe me, it's much nicer over here," Fred confirmed, after catching the gist of the conversation. "I hope you stay. We can use the company. There's one more American here who lives over in the far corner. His name is Joe. He's an older man and keeps to himself, mostly."

Steve interrupted Fred and started schooling us on *Correctionalis*.

"Armando is the man to go see whenever you have a problem. Watch him though. If you purchase some *caraca*, he'll be handling all the deals. If he states a price or asks a lot, talk him down."

"I'm used to that," Bill piped up. "I live in Mexico and I know how to deal with his kind."

"Well, he's an easy guy, but he's cunning. He's at the short end of a four-year term for dope smuggling."

"What else? " Bill sneered. "Everyone here seems to have been into it in some form." We laughed lightly.

"Speaking of dope, is there anyway of getting some *mota*?" Mike asked. "We were offered some for sale in the *Grande*."

"Sure. I have enough to role a joint or two right now," Steve answered. "Walt, can you take care of that?" Turning to Mike he said, "Ten pesos will buy you a finger. Come see me when you want one. I'll take care of ordering for you."

"Who do you place the order with?" I asked, curious.

Steve was evasive. "I have a couple of methods. Any of you guys speak Spanish?" he asked, changing the subject.

"Mike's pretty good at it, and I speak some," Bill replied.

"Good. Learn more." Steve said in a commanding tone, giving us a hard stare. "You're going to be around here a while. Respect goes a long way. Use their language. I've learned a great deal in eight months."

"Well, at least you're getting something out of being here," Dirk said with a strange grin.

"Seriously," Steve said, as he again stared hard. "You can ask for any kind of favor and usually get it if you speak to them in Spanish, especially with the prisoners."

"How about a place to live?" Bill inquired. "Any of the *caracas* for sale? Do we talk to this guy Armando about buying one?"

"Yes and no," Steve replied. "Right now the only place available is the open wall. You could buy a cot or maybe some of these guys will part with their *caracas* (small quarters). Money moves mountains around here."

"Far out. I'd like to check that out and see what we can do to get one," Mike said, as we all nodded agreement.

"We have to find out if you're to stay here first," Steve cautioned. "They're strange. They may call you back to the *Grande*. If you're to stay here, then tomorrow I'll help you to get a good deal. Today is over with. You know, *mañana* rules around here, but I'll ask some of the guys later and see what we come up with. As for food, you can order anything you want as long as you have the money. Every morning the *mandadaros*—the runners—come into the prison and take orders. Just give one of them a list and some *dinero*. I'll show you how in the morning. Tell them who you are, and in a couple of hours he'll be back with a box of groceries. Pay him a few *pesos* for his trouble. The guard puts them inside the gate for you."

"That's cool. Just like that, you have food?" I asked. "Do they ever cheat?"

"Yes." Steve said. "Get to know prices, guys, and you won't have any problems. There's a small store at the end of the wall. The old man is doing nine big ones for growing pot. He's a farmer. Anyway, he's got a lot of stuff: sweets, fruits, cigarettes and such, and there's a restaurant in the main hall outside. You may have seen it when you came up the ramp. Meals are five *pesos*— breakfast, lunch or dinner."

"Here you go, brothers." Walter said, firing up a joint. Sucking in a hit he passed it around.

"Man, I thought we wouldn't be seeing this for a long time," Mike said, as he exhaled.

"There wasn't any available in *La Paz*. We figured the same would be true here," I added, taking a toke and passing it on. Walter fired up a second one.

"What do you do around here?" the quiet one named Patrick asked.

"Again, it's up to you. I read a lot, as does Walt. We sleep some afternoons. I have a girlfriend who lives down here. She visits me twice a week, on Thursday and Sunday. She spends the night with me," Steve said smugly, as though we were supposed to envy him.

"She spends the night here in your room?" I asked, mouth agape.

"You bet. It's one of our privileges, guys. Conjugal visits twice a week."

"Christ, it's enough to make some of these guys want to stay here," I added, chuckling.

"You got it, and if you're gay or a cornholer, like a lot of these guys, there's always Lupe and her troupe. That's the tent alongside our *caracas*. Every so often I have to ask them to keep it down."

Mike grinned. "I hope it doesn't come down to that."

"No one gets butt-fucked around here if they don't want to. Maybe in the States, but not in *Correctionalis*," Steve answered, frowning deeply.

Looking at Bill I suggested, "Hey, you can call Inger. She can come in Thursday and bring Kerstin?" It was Tuesday and I figured he'd be up for it.

"After what we tried today, she'll know we're here," he replied boastfully.

"Yeah. You can bet it'll be in the papers," Mike added, grinning.

After Walter looked puzzled, we explained the aborted escape attempt and our ordeal with Macho Brains.

Bill added with a huff, "Boy, I was never so disappointed. When I got up on the deck and saw that land was so far away, it almost stopped me in my tracks."

"But you jumped anyway?" Steve asked.

"Hell yes. I wasn't gonna give up," Bill said. We all laughed at the absurdity, Bill adding, "Shit, if I hadn't, that ape would have shot me."

"We're lucky they didn't shoot all of us," I said, just as someone called out for Steve.

"That'll be *Armando*. Come on guys. He must have come up from the office to talk directly. Remember, deal with him. Never expect a straight answer from these guys," Steve warned as we headed outside.

Now that the laundry had been taken down, we could see most of the yard. Armando, a short man in his mid-thirties, dressed neatly in khaki pants and a light shirt, greeted us cordially. With wavy hair neatly combed and a pencil-thin mustache, he looked the part of an official.

He smiled and shook our hands as we filed out the door.

"*Hola, amigos. Buenos tarde*. So, you are the boys who caused so much trouble this morning. Good try for you Michael and Dan. They are still laughing about it in the office."

"Same here. Hey, are they going to do anything to us because of that?" Mike asked.

"No. They're thinking of keeping you in here in *Correctionalis*."

"Right on," Mike said with relief. All of us were relieved.

Bill asked, "How can we be sure? We want to see about getting a *caraca*."

Armando began his spiel. "Let me negotiate for you. If you stay, all the *caraca* sales are subject to permission from the office. I am the *Vice-Presidente* here. I am your friend. You can come to me for anything you need. I will take care of you. If you have a problem with another man here, I will help. You are *gringos*. Here in our jail we must make you safe to be here. I will tell the *Alciadia* you wish to stay in *Correctionalis*. *Está bien*."

"*Está bien*," Bill said, without hesitating. We all chimed in.

"*Bueno*. Then I will go to the office and negotiate for you. Remember you are my friends and you come to me when you are in trouble. This is my job. Have you any questions?"

"Yes. Phone calls? Can we make calls out to the States?" Dirk inquired.

"Yes, and you can have your friends call, but not so much."

An hour later, around 5:00 p.m., we were still hanging out in Steve and Walter's *caraca*, when we heard the guard yelling out, "*Yegwa! Yegwa por Correctionalis!*" Then the thunderous noise of human feet running about.

"What's that?" we asked.

"They're feeding the men who have a fifteen-day sentence. They call them *quincados*," Walt replied. "Come on outside. You'll see." Curious, we followed.

"Most of the prisoners here are *quincados*. They're drunks or vagrants," Walt explained.

We watched as they lined up in the center of the yard, pushing and shoving as they fought for a place in line. The line was two deep and wrapped around the washbasin in the center of the yard. A smaller, second line of prisoners formed on the far side. They seemed more at ease and composed. "Those are regular prisoners or the *staters*," Walter mentioned. "You guys are federal, like us. The staters are well-fed compared to the *quincados*."

Just then, two Mexican inmates entered the yard, each carrying a thick wooden pole atop their shoulders; a huge metal caldron balanced in the middle. Struggling, they set down the heavy load and began ladling out broth to the *quincados*, who had small tin cans. Each man was given one ladle of broth and a small stack of corn tortillas. They would find a place to sit and carefully consume the meager meal.

"What are they feeding them, Walt?" I asked.

"*Yegwa*. It's horse bones and beans, mostly just water." He smirked. "They get it three times a day."

"Not very much food for a two-week stay," Pat remarked.

"Yeah, it's a starvation diet from the looks of it," I added.

"Think how many would want to come back if they fed them good," Steve said, as he came out of the *caraca* and hovered over us. Fred headed over, telling us he wanted to get in the staters' line. "I pay for a week's worth every so often. You can't beat the price. *Five pesos for an entire week's worth of food.* And this is a paid week. Be back in a moment."

He headed to his *caraca* and emerged seconds later with a good-sized metal pan. Quickly returning from the line he said, "See what I mean?" He showed us the pot full of beans and a sizable stack of fresh, corn tortillas. "Try some."

I spread a few beans onto a corn tortilla. One bite convinced me. "Great! Yeah, that's good. Add a few veggies and cheese and you're set."

There were enough beans and tortillas for three or four people to snack on so we all indulged.

"Five *pesos* a week," I jested. "Damn! Ya can't beat that."

If Bill ran out of money, and we were only to be paid thirty-five pesos a week, at least we'd get fed. Life might come down to that, I thought. Eight years was a long time. Fred mentioned that they served rice with breakfast in the morning, along with coffee.

As we stood in the yard, the simplicity of our setting was almost touching. The yard was the center of it all—a place to hang out, talk, and eat, but only when the *quincados* were sitting and eating.

Bill approached me and said in a hushed tone, "Steve and I just worked a deal for the small *caraca*, the one to our left nearest the gate." He pointed quickly. "It's an eight by eight. The guys who live there want to sell it for a hundred dollars."

"Right on. That's great." I was surprised by the good news.

"Steve says it's a fair price and subject to approval, but they never disapprove, so he thinks we'll get it tomorrow. I'll pay for it. You can pay me when Sarah sells your car. We'll get some padding for the floor and a fan."

"Yeah, a fan for sure. A good one. We'll need it."

He added, "You can live there with me. I know Inger will come to visit right away. I want it understood that you'll let us be alone when she comes." There was an edge of contempt in his voice. "Steve says Walt sleeps in Fred's *caraca* on visiting days."

"Fine! I'm sure I'll find a place to sleep." I was not in a mood to be nice to him after the tone he used.

"Hey, the crew will more than likely score a *caraca* and you can sleep with them."

"I'm sure they will. We'll talk more about this later. Thanks for the good news." No thanks for the bad act, I said under my breath, heading for the center basin for a cool drink of water. Having seen Walt do the same, I figured it was safe. Later, I found out it was considered a risk, but what the hell. Might as well get conditioned to it now, I figured.

The next day was hot and muggy as usual. I woke up stiff from sleeping on the concrete floor of Steve and Walt's *caraca*. The guard called out morning *lista* so I got up and headed out the door to get in line. The same three officials who had called roll the evening before, began calling off names. There were thirty-five of us regulars. The line filed through as the names were called. We were last and they mispronounced all our names again.

When morning *Yegwa* arrived, I was hanging out with Walt. As I watched the *quincados* push and shove their way into position I asked him, "Do they ever fight for a spot?"

"Not much, but every once in a while they do. Then it's a show. Everyone watches. It's like turning on a tube in a daycare center, only better. No one gets hurt, really. Not that I've seen."

Bill ordered us a five-peso feast from the outside restaurant. Moments later, as I stood in the yard talking with Walt, Fred, and Mike, the daily clean-up began. The five of us had paid the small *mordita* of thirty-pesos to get off clean-up duty. Otherwise, we'd be on the work crew for two weeks.

A stocky fellow, about thirty and with a mean scowl and a crew-cut, ran the show. He bullied the *quincados* with a long, narrow, wooden stick. When he cracked two across the legs they yelped, got back in line, and shut up.

Walt warned, "Whatever you do, stay away from that man."

"What's his problem?" Mike asked, as I listened in.

"He's a killer and he's a bit crazy, as you can see."

"For sure. He looks the part."

"He's *Pedro*, the tank goon," Fred grinned.

"There's one in every tank, isn't there?" I quipped.

The goon lined up his men up and barked out instructions. With buckets, mops, and a hose the crew spent an hour scrubbing and hosing down the entire floor of *Correctionalis,* including the sector's two toilets and showers. This was done once a day, Walt informed us. After seeing the two toilets in the *Grande* the day before, we were glad to learn they kept the place clean.

I added, "And they use plenty of soap. Great!"

We hoped we would get to stay. When I thought about going back to the *Grande,* I shuddered.

Armando came up from the office around ten a.m. and said to Mike, Patrick and me, "The *Alciadia say* you are to stay in *Correctionalis*. If you wish to talk to the men about buying a *caraca,* I think it is a good time."

"Thanks, *Armando*," I replied, as Bill and Dirk joined us.

He gave us further instructions on how to proceed with the purchase and told us to let him know right away which *caracas* we wanted and how much it would cost.

By noon we had closed two deals, with a third one pending. Bill had purchased the small eight-by-eight nearest the gate, which he and I would share. Paying a hundred and seventy five dollars, Mike, Dirk and Patrick moved into an eight by sixteen foot palace at the far end of our row. Two weeks later, Patrick bought the remaining eight-by-eight, sandwiched between Steve and Dirk's *caraca,* and moved in. When the deal was completed we *gringos* owned all four pieces of property along the west wall. No wonder the Mexican inmates didn't have much love for us. We came, we saw what we wanted, and we took over. Money facilitated it all. We lived high and mighty compared to them.

The Mexican inmates, who sold us their *caraca* to support their heroin addictions, moved their cots and few possessions out to the open wall on the south end of *Correctionalis*. They would now have to live out in the elements with only an aluminum awning for protection. There were now six to seven prisoners sleeping outside. The jail was overcrowded, but no one was doing anything about it.

The second night in our *caraca*, I ripped a really fowl fart, just as Bill and I were going off to sleep—unintentionally, of course. Immediately, Bill kicked me hard in the thigh. Jumping up, I told him that if he ever did that again we'd come to blows.

"You didn't have to do it in here. You could have done it outside."

"Sure, like you do. Fuck you. You're the one who does it and expects no one to complain. Just back off, man."

"Do it outside!" he retorted.

"Fine! Then the same goes for you." And that was that. Our sibling rivalry was all but out of hand. We co-existed, cooking, eating and sleeping in the same quarters, but the anger between us was palpable and neither of us would talk about it or give it up. We were typical men, caught up in a typical battle: macho, egotistical garbage.

Inger called the early afternoon of the second day, just after we had purchased the two *caracas*. Bill was called down to the office where calls were received and came back with news: we had made the papers again. One of their friends had told her that we were here and about the attempted escape.

"She'll be here tomorrow with Kerstin. She's bringing some food and a few other items," Bill mentioned, and we talked cordially for a few minutes about how she would directly be able to help us.

About noon, shortly after Inger called, we were ordered to the gate. There was a moment of panic as the guard led us down the long concrete corridor, but it was short-lived. We were cuffed and hauled downtown to meet with the local District Attorney.

This time there were five detectives present. Our infamy obviously preceded us.

One of the detectives warned us not to attempt anything. We complied. They covered us on all flanks as they ushered us politely into a waiting van and then to the office in downtown Mazatlan.

Soon we stood in front of a Señor Coppala, Federal District Attorney for the state of Sinaloa. If our infamy had preceded us, so had his. The

American prisoners in the *Grande* had portrayed him as a monster, a real bad *hombre*. Steve and Walt concurred, and told us what they knew about the man.

Looking him over as we stood in front of him, his left arm in a sling, he did not look the part of a bad dude. He was medium height, pudgy, had a thick mustache, wore glasses, and was balding and approaching middle age. We noticed as he entered the room that he had a pronounced limp.

Greeting us with a nod, an interpreter informed us that Señor Coppala wanted to know if there was anything in our statements that we wished to change. Considering our statements were in Spanish and we didn't have a lawyer present, we had no choice but to say no.

Coppala listened to our answer, looked us over briefly, then said a few words to a colleague sitting next to him, an older man whom the interpreter said was a judge. Then Coppala left the room, followed by two men who we took to be his bodyguards. According to the grapevine, Señor Coppala was on his way home one day after investigating a drug smuggling ring in Culican, when the vehicle he was driving was run off the road by assailants in a truck. They shot several rounds of lead at him and his vehicle. Left for dead, he had somehow recovered from nineteen bullet wounds. We didn't know how long ago the event occurred, or whether it really happened.

He checked us out with a bitter look on his face. Maybe the meeting was his way of figuring out if he really wanted to stick it to us or not. We didn't know, only that we were once again fingerprinted and photographed.

After we were brought back Bill said, "Sure as hell, brother, they're gonna send a copy to Interpol and to the FBI."

"Probably so. But there's nothing we can do to stop them."

We both assumed it would only be a matter of time before the U.S. authorities figured out who we really were. What would happen then, we could only guess. Would our government get the Mexican government to extradite us after we finished our time in Mexico? If it were for murder, yes. In our case, it was too hard to say. We already knew that the Mexican government often escorted undesirables to the border. Extradition wasn't always granted. They could just as simply escort us to the border where

U.S. authorities would then take us into custody.

From the moment we had been captured, we had all talked about escape. La Paz had been a fortress. We were frustrated when none of us could come up with a viable escape plan there. But in Mazatlan, Bill and I were in familiar territory. Bill had plenty of friends to call on for favors, especially Tambor. And there were others. We'd just have to see if any of them would be able to help. Meanwhile, the five of us continued to throw around ideas for escape. We began to collect all the data we could get about *Correctionalis* and the rest of the prison.

We began by grilling Steve, Walt, and Fred for as much information as we could. Within a few days we had come up with a basic plan. We were going to dig a tunnel—but no one knew what to do with the dirt. In time, we'd have a lot more information and perhaps the resources we'd need. We had nothing but time, so we kept on planning.

The first part of this plan was for all of us to agree to be "good boys." No one was to fight or be disruptive in any way. We wanted the officials to have no reason to search or suspect us. Collective chemistry would align us and pull us through as we gathered information.

One of the first things we learned was that the *Grande* was searched fairly often. Here in *Correctionalis*, hardly at all. On the third day in *Correctionalis*, three guards had rushed in on us just prior to *lista* and searched our quarters and scored a couple of kitchen knives and an old deck of cards.

"Funny they didn't search the whole section," I commented to the crew.

We had been put off by the incident. Searches or not, we still conspired as to how we'd go about escaping. We were open to all ideas.

Where to dig the tunnel became the first issue. Someone suggested Fred's *caraca*. The problem was that Fred wasn't in on the discussions and was not yet a part of our group, although his *caraca* along the wall was ideal. Another problem was the twenty-foot high wall—the outer wall.

This formidable obstacle was twelve to fourteen feet from the main wall and ran the length of the prison on our side, including the *Grande*, then at right angles on past the *Grande's* main yard. Essentially, this outer wall was a moat and at the two ends had a catwalk on it for the guards to use while combing the area. Fred's *caraca* was a mere twenty feet from freedom. We soon learned that the entire north wall, both in *Correctionalis* and in the *Grande*, was subject to intensive search. Fred's place was out of the question.

Our second choice for the dig was in Mike and Dirk's *caraca*. It was already everyone's favorite place to hang out. We estimated their *caraca* was thirty-five to forty feet from the outer wall. There was no way to tell how deep we'd have to dig to get under the two main walls. We'd just have to find out when the time came.

Then I mentioned the unmentionable. "What about the water table, guys?"

Someone had just mentioned the fact that the ground, being mainly dirt and small rocks, would be easy enough to break up and was not likely to cave in. It got me to thinking.

"We're about a mile from the river, on low ground," I calculated. "It's the rainy season and you know how it comes down here in the tropics—like rivers. Say we break through the concrete floor, dig down three or four feet and run into water? You guys saw the harbor when we came in. There were no hills or anything of that nature around here. The ground is level and this area might be at sea level. We don't know. It's something we need to consider."

Dirk added, "Yeah, and if we break through the floor and we can't dig because there's water, then we're screwed if they search us."

We realized we still had a lot to consider and more information to collect. To start now would be a big mistake. We were all in accord: it would be best to wait until the monsoon season was over, sometime in late October. In the meantime, we'd continue to collect data and plan.

Inger visited that Thursday, bringing several loaves of home-baked bread and Swedish pastries. She arrived about 10:30 a.m. with two good-sized boxes: one contained kitchen utensils. Now we could begin to cook our own food.

She brought Kerstin, who was now sixteen months old. With her blond hair, blue eyes, and lovely face, it was hard to keep the inmates from doting over her as we walked around the crowded yard.

Armando, whose family had not come that day, especially liked Kerstin. "My family, they live in Culican. I don't see them often," he related, as he held Kerstin. She hardly ever objected to being held by strangers and at that age it was a pleasure to be with her. She would hold my hand as we walked around the yard. She thought everything was just great. The place was full of people who paid attention to her. Her grandmother didn't even know she existed, but that didn't enter my mind as the *quincados* reached out to touch her and say hello.

Inger and I still avoided each other. It was an uncomfortable situation I hoped to rectify. Sooner or later I'd find the right time to cut through the layers of coldness between us.

I noticed, too, that she was not as close to Bill as she once had been. They seemed to be faking their relationship. Perhaps there was love, but there didn't seem to be much trust. Their was no romance; embraces were more civil than emotional.

Nonetheless, she had plenty of spunk and energy. She had mastered six languages, supported herself, raised a child, cared for an imprisoned husband and still found time for her worst habits—prattling, finding the best chocolate in town, and eating as much of it as she could afford. She was a hopeless chocoholic. It didn't seem to affect her a bit. She never gained a pound. But she did complain mightily about the visiting lines—especially the following Sunday.

"Those fucking guards are always bothering us women," Inger complained with her usual flair for salty language and directness. "Never the men. And they always let the men in more than the women. And the matrons, they search us…" She rattled on for a while 'til Bill and I got the picture.

Visiting day was no fun, but she came anyway. She was ruthlessly persistent, as were the guards who were getting to know her.

"Inger, they do it to get your goat; don't allow it," Bill suggested.

"Don't buy into their stuff," I said, backing him up.

Our good advice went by the wayside. She liked to dig at people, and I was on the receiving end of some of the action.

Loving Sarah helped me immensely. We now had a new relationship. She said she still loved me and would forgive me for losing the boat. That was all I needed to hear. I wrote her long letters almost every day, and that helped her know how much I loved her and missed her. I described the jail and all the strange things that happened there, but was careful to leave out anything that might upset her or cause excessive worry.

Then I began to ask favors—lots of them, and some small, some big. I needed money. Could she send some? Any amount would do and I offered as many suggestions as possible: sell my Volkswagen and the extra sails I had stored at her place in Inverness; ask Dale for the two thousand that was given to him as expense money several months ago; call Brother Ray and see if he could send money as a payback for the time I paid his bond; call Joanne and Joan to let them know I was in jail—see if they could help. The list of requests went on and on. I covered all the bases, but never mentioned my desperation. It was a given.

When her letters arrived, I read them over and over. Her emotions had gotten the best of her. She was heartbroken by what had happened to me, the boat, and our kitty who had died at sea. When I wrote her back I gained strength by offering her support and empathizing with the position I had put her in. Though she wrote eloquent words of encouragement, I read through the lines. Sarah, although free and with family and friends, was agonizing about my plight more than I was. I said anything I could think of to lift her out of the misery and depression. She had a job at the restaurant again and planned to work at the local oyster farm shucking oysters very soon.

Instead, she fell sick. It wasn't the flu or a cold. The doctor didn't know what ailed her, but I did. It was the maddening circumstances I had created. There was not much of a future for me, for us. Freedom was years away. She was young and full of vitality. If not for me, she'd have her freedom. We needed to talk.

I encouraged her to come down as soon as she sold the Volkswagen. She could live with Inger and Kerstin for awhile.

"I've never bought or sold a car in my life," she explained over the phone a few days later.

I understood. She was from an affluent family. Everything had been given to her. She'd lived a sheltered life. Without making judgments, I explained how to go about selling a car that wasn't hers or mine. It was registered to a Steve Allen Walsh, who didn't really exist. "Have my friend Dale or someone sign-off on the pink-slip. Nothing will come of the matter. You're in possession of the vehicle. That's all that matters. The DMV doesn't care, as long as someone pays the taxes and the registration. You're not breaking the law. Believe in me."

When Sarah stalled about coming to visit, I began to worry. The people around her in whom she confided were being overly protective. Because she had been with me aboard the boat in Mexico, her friends felt she might be under investigation. She never really said these words, but I deduced her concern. She offered no logical reason about her reluctance to visit, other than her emotional state.

"We're okay down here. Yes, its jail, but it's not the end of the world. Come here. We need to see one another and deal with this."

One day toward the end of July, we finally talked things over. We had a new lawyer now and he said it would be perfectly safe for her to visit.

Still hesitant, she said she'd come down in late August, around our birthdays, although she didn't want to commit to living in Mexico for any length of time. That was fine by me, just as long as she came so we could talk and be together. As I headed back to the yard, my energy sagged. Was I expecting too much from the woman I had let down?

This was the beginning of the end of our relationship. Sarah was a sensitive woman, perhaps hyper-sensitive. Her mysterious sickness continued and she was having difficulty handling all my demands. Joanne, Jake's wife, had always been capable of handling stress and all the problems that came her way. Sarah had come into my life and suddenly my problems were thrown on her: I was a fugitive, for one thing. I was also likely to be in jail for several years. The obstacles seemed insurmountable. The enormous amount of pressure was taking a toll on her. We loved one another, but would that love survive the challenges we faced? I was filled with doubt. I loved Sarah too much to fool myself or selfishly hold on to her at all costs.

The burden began to frighten me. I'd already wrecked my life. Why wreck hers too? If she wanted out of our relationship, I'd let her. I intended to keep these thoughts secret until she came to visit. Meanwhile, I continued sending words of love and encouragement, and committed myself to sorting out why I felt it necessary to give her up.

By now, we'd been incarcerated in the Mazatlan jail for three weeks, long enough to develop a daily routine. Bill and I were even managing to tolerate one another. Under the circumstances, we were all living rather well. We cooked most of our meals and got through the muggy tropical days with the aid of fans and a couple of cool showers each day. We passed our time by writing letters, reading books, and playing cards. Bill joined us in card games on occasion, but inevitably he and I sparred, so he soon bailed out. Mike joined in, but his close pal, Dirk—who was often cheerful in a crude sort of way—was a loner who preferred to read and hang out in his *caraca*, where he could listen to music and read. Their good friends from Los Angeles had once again come down, bringing Dirk a boombox, some good tapes, and lots of wholesome food from health food stores in the States.

Joe Ullery, another American prisoner, was intriguing. He was a short, middle-aged dude with a wealth of fat around his body. He was bald, which was offset with a goatee and mustache. He was an artist and had once been a trumpet player. Joe was a junky. He had been persuaded to come down to

Mazatlan to make a deal that was too good to be true and had been popped. He had a wife and family up in Washington, so he was miles from home.

Getting to know him was difficult. He was an easy-going recluse. At first he warmed to us and even had us over to play cards. Other times, we wouldn't see him for two or three days at a time. He'd just stay in his eight-by-eight *caraca* and not come out. When he did, we'd seduce him into a card game. He loved to talk his stuff to all the younger dudes.

One day in early August while Patrick, Fred, and I were on our way to play cards in Joe's *caraca*, Inger came through the gate and hailed me, saying tersely, "I need to talk with you." It was a Thursday and she was carrying Kerstin, along with a *bolsa* filled with food.

"Okay. You look a bit under the weather today. Here, let me take Kerstin." Taking her daughter I asked politely, "Did you have the usual hassle getting in?"

"Yes, but that's not important. I'm pissed at Bill right now. I know he's done something." Her face flushed, the angry expression compromising her beauty, she set down her *bolsa* and extracted a letter.

"Here, look at this."

She handed me a letter addressed to Bill. It was from a woman by the name of Donna with a Los Angeles return address. Handing Kerstin back to Inger, I opened the envelope and began reading the letter, noting it had already been opened. Soon, I was holding back a smirk. Knowing Inger, she'd read it several times already. Bill and Inger had a general delivery address at a trailer park, north of Mazatlan. Even when they moved around, they kept the address open for friends and relatives to correspond with them.

Knowing Bill's track record with women, I felt she was justified in opening the letter, as any suspecting wife might. The letter was from a woman Bill had met the previous summer, while I was in Guadalajara with him. Bill and I, along with Don and Terry, had taken a short four-day surf and fun trip to San Blas. On the second day, Bill had met Donna on the beach. I suspected they might have had a quick affair. Bill had given her his address in Mazatlan and as I read the endearing note Bill was in deep shit with Inger. There was no confusion about the meaning of the writer's words. But as I finished reading it, Inger asked anyway.

"Did he screw her?"

Communication between Inger and I was already difficult. Any progress we had made would be ruined by this development. Inger wanted the truth, but I didn't know if I could risk it.

Slowly I answered, "I suppose so, Inger. I mean I saw them together. I didn't see them screwing."

"Ohhhh, that asshole. I know he did it. I know it."

"Talk with him, Inger. Don't hang it on him yet."

"No!" she spat out with vengeance. "I know him. He's done this before. There was another woman he screwed. He's a fucking cheat, but he won't get away with it this time. I'm not gonna put up with his crap. I'm leaving him."

In that moment she meant what she said, and I pleaded with her.

"Wait Inger. Calm down a minute."

She was hissing and fuming.

"Calm down."

Desperate, I asked, "Do you love Bill?"

"No. I hate him. He's a cheater." Her face spoke the truth: her voice crumpled me.

"I don't think you really hate him. Come on, Inger, you're angry for sure, but you must care for him, otherwise you wouldn't come to visit like you do. You're hurt and I understand. I know how it feels to have someone cheat on you, believe me. But, try not to be too impulsive. I know Bill is a liar and a cheat. He's also my brother and he's your husband. If anyone can give him a chance it's you and me. Let's use our heads. Put him in his place. Go in there," I pointed to our *caraca*, "and blast him good. He needs it for pulling such a shitty trick on you, but don't tear him apart. I know he'll react. You may be sorry if you act too heavily. If you love him, be cool, be angry—let it show."

"He won't change," she said bitterly. "He'll just do it again."

"Inger, he's my brother. I've put up with his shit all my life. I don't trust him either, but I'm open to building trust, if he's willing. Learn to trust in yourself."

Touching my heart with my right hand I added, "I've been there and back again with him, but I love him and he's my teacher. Believe it or not I've learned through him, and my mother, to believe in myself. Both of them are bad-ass teachers. They teach us to trust in our self. So use your inner resolve. If you can't do that then get it over with and leave him. I'm sure it will crush him. I know it would be hard for me too, with all the help you've given us the past few weeks. You've been an immense help."

"Thank you. I do my best. Perhaps you're right. I know I've got plenty of strength and I do know when to trust myself."

"How about trusting me? You've come in here several times now and this is the first conversation we've had since I left Mazatlan in early June."

"We talk all the time."

"What, like 'hi, how are you, how's the kid?' That's not real talk. That's politeness. No, I'm talking about real talk, like I've had with you in the past. It's like you've been avoiding me."

"Well, things are very difficult right now."

"Inger, you know Bill's a lair. I don't know what he's told you about the boat wreck but you can bet he's withheld a lot of facts. Listen to my story some time. Not right now when matters are tight, but be willing to hear me out. Okay?"

"We can do that sometime—like you say, not right now."

"That's cool. Take care of one thing at a time. Go for it. See what sort of man you've got in there. Bye, Kerstin." I headed off to Joe's *caraca* to play cards.

A few moments later, right in the middle of a game, we heard a rap at the door. It was Bill. As I came to the doorway, Bill stood there with a worried look on his face.

"Can I have a moment with you? It's important."

Stepping out into the busy yard Bill said animatedly, "I'm having trouble with Inger. She's totally blown out, man. She's so pissed she wants to leave me. I need your help. If she leaves, all of us will lose out. Can you dig it?"

I knew Bill was about to manipulate me. He was in deep shit with Inger and as usual would do his best to override me with his powerful ego.

"What's up?" I asked, holding back a smirk.

"Remember Donna, the lady I met in San Blas? She sent a letter. Christ, I never expected her to send one. It's been a year since I saw her. Inger grabbed the letter, you know, from the trailer court and she opened it. She's pissed."

"I imagine she would be."

"I mean real pissed. She wants to leave and take Kerstin with her. Can you cover for me?"

"Please explain."—And dig a deep hole while you're at it, I thought.

"I told Inger I didn't touch her. There's nothing in the letter that says I did. It's all just full of mushy stuff and such. Anyhow, she didn't believe me and I want you to come over and talk with her and tell her Donna was just a very friendly woman and all of us had a lot of fun together, but I didn't ball her. It would straighten things out. Come on. You know what she means to us."

There was truth to this and I gave way to feeling guilty for a few seconds then checked myself and came back with. "Hmmm…so you want me to lie to her about what really happened?"

"I've got to do something to cool her down. She's close to leaving right now."

"You're making a big mistake, man."

"Just this one favor, brother. She'll believe you. I know she will. Talk with her. You have to help me here. We need her."

Disgust replaced another heavy stream of guilt as I stood in front of my older brother. Looking straight at him, I said. "No way. I won't do it. You're making a mistake. Believe me."

"This is for both of us. You know how invaluable she is."

Then it hit me how Bill was turning the tables on me and on his wife.

I didn't have to buy into this deceit. A stream of good energy flooded my entire body as I retorted, "Yes, I do know just how valuable she is, brother, but you don't."

"What's that mean?" he said defensively.

"It means you're a bullshitter Bill, and you're playing Inger and me off against each other for your own fucking gain. Can you dig it?"

"It's just this one time."

"You want me to lie and jeopardize my relationship with her, which is at an all time low, just to save your skin. Come on, man. You're insulting me, and her."

"I'm on the spot. Talk to her. I'll owe you big." He wasn't listening, nor was he being sincere.

"Damn, you're blind." I exploded. "I already did!"

"What are you talking about?" He was annoyed now, but also all ears.

"You're so caught up in your bullshit that you don't see what people around you are doing. She came in and showed me the letter first thing and cornered me. I've already read the letter and I told her that you probably did make love to Donna. That's what."

"For Christ's sake, why did you do that?"

Chuckling sardonically I replied, "Because it's the truth. Remember I said *probably* made love."

"Then go tell her I didn't."

"Jesus, Bill. You're getting in deeper by the minute." At full strength now and ready to topple him, I added. "Tell you what. I'm going to suggest you go back and tell Inger the truth. Deal with that. Meanwhile, you're holding up a good card game. Call your own shots. Good luck." Turning abruptly, I headed back to the game.

"Wait a minute. I have a huge problem here."

"Yes, you do," I replied, turning one last time to face him. "That's why I'm suggesting you tell her the truth. This problem is all yours and you haven't too many other choices. I'm leaving. *Mas tarde*, brother."

I entered Joe's *caraca* feeling like King Kong and announced, "I'm ready guys. Let's get back to this game."

CHAPTER TWENTY-FIVE

MOTHER OF AN ALIBI

MAZATLAN
SINALOA, MEXICO
AUGUST, 1971

Somehow, Bill got Inger to stay. Or maybe Inger goaded Bill to beg, plead, and promise. Who knows? For the time being though, they worked it out.

Then it was *my* turn to run and jump. I did something that brought Armando down on me like a sack of potatoes. He was the last person that I wanted to make mad. It started one morning in early August just after I had just received a box of groceries from a *mandadero* at the *Correctionalis'* gate.

He had an unpleasant look on his face as he headed my way.

I asked him casually, "What's up, Armando?"

He pointed his finger into my chest and said with a thick tongue, "You *amigo*, must learn to stay out of my business or there will be trouble."

"What business are you talking about?" I inquired, slightly shaken. I had an idea, but wanted him to spell it out.

"You know what business I mean. You are not stupid. Stay away. *Comprende?* I must warn you or there will be trouble, much trouble. I do not wish to say this to you again or to the rest of your men. I know you understand. Now I must go to the office. Good day, my friend."

"What was that about?" Bill asked, as he came up to the gate to help receive the groceries.

"Remember the Canadian guys who came in here a couple of days ago that Mike and I helped to get bailed out?"

Two mid-twenties Canadians had been thrown into *Correctionalis* a few nights before, drugged on muscle relaxants they called goof-balls, which they later told us they had purchased at a local pharmacy. Apparently they had taken a few too many, and got "swacked" out of their minds. They didn't know their names, where they were from, or even that they had been thrown in jail. Most of the *quincados* were sleeping when the guard opened the gate and pushed the two lunkheads into the yard.

Those of us who were still awake and saw them started cracking up right away. The Canadians looked like a couple of fools just learning to walk. They hopped around in jerky movements: right leg, right arm, left leg, left arm. I had one of the best laughs I'd had for a long while.

Ignorance might be bliss, but they were starting to annoy others. We were laughing so hard, we had no inclination to intercede and stop the show. They stumbled to the ground but their muscle control was so out of sync they couldn't make it to their feet when they tried. And the look of complete bewilderment on their faces threw us into more fits.

If the *quincados* hadn't been in their way, the Canadians would have come out unscathed, but the *quincados* had had their fill of their antics and our laughter. A couple of the regular prisoners pulled the Canadians into a corner and slapped them around until they behaved.

In the morning they seemed to be all right. Just after *lista*, Patrick, Fred, and I went to talk with them. They seemed like nice guys and were especially glad to see *gringo* faces. They told us they had loaded up on too many goof-balls and beer on the beach. Then the police had come along and hauled them to jail. Their money was gone, as were their wallets. They asked us for help and we obliged by getting a *mandadero* to take a message to their Canadian friends, who were staying at a local hotel. Their friends got them out.

I told Bill the story, then added, "I guess we bypassed Armando and he didn't like it."

"That's the same as a rip-off, man. No more. If these Canadians are stupid enough to get caught, let 'em pay the price," he said officiously.

Coming from Bill, I thought, that's ironic—even hypocritical.

"Hey, you don't have to tell me," I said. "I know. I don't want Armando against us. We need the protection."

The Canadians got bailed out for forty bucks apiece by their friends. Armando, acting as the middleman for anyone thrown in jail, would have charged them twice the amount. Canadians, along with lots of Americans, were thrown in jail all the time: Armando was the bail-master and made money off them as well as his fellow Mexicans. We had interfered with the business he and the *Alciadia* had been running for four years, and we'd beaten him out of eighty bucks. When I saw Armando that evening I apologized. He told me he had already talked to the Canadians and was in the process of arranging their bail, but the Canadian's friends had posted it before he could.

"It won't happen again," I said, "We didn't know better. Now we do."

We shook hands and parted company, but before parting Armando reminded me of the protocol he expected us to follow in "his" jail. I told him we respected his business obligations and understood the need for compliance.

Armando was due to be released around Christmas and someone would take his place. We didn't want to get on anyone's shit list. We were "good" boys. We were quickly learning the system—how to avoid the pitfalls and how to co-exist with a wildly diverse group of people.

※ ※ ※

New prisoners, some Mexicans, some Americans, were thrown in *Correctionalis* every day. The Americans always sought us out. Most had been apprehended with small amounts of pot. And almost always, the *hombres* who had sold them the drug turned them in.

These "maybe not so bright" boys usually arrived at night, and almost without fail, the regulars would rob them while they were sleeping. The regulars stole watches, rings, money and even their clothes, shoes, or pants were taken. By morning, the new prisoners were a mess and god-awful happy to see fellow Americans. Then they'd whine and complain to us about their misfortunes. We knew they'd be released in a few days so we didn't have much sympathy for them, and actually were getting mighty tired of them. Most of them were somewhat questionable characters anyway.

One afternoon a genteel American arrived. He had just had an auto accident involving a Mexican citizen. Mister Genteel, an older family man, said he had auto insurance, but he was terrified that the authorities had thrown him in jail. Surrounded by Joe, Mike, Patrick and me, we educated him about *Napoleonic Law*. We explained that he was to be held here until the matter was straightened out between both companies. Guilty until proven innocent was a new concept to him. We did our best to lessen his fears. Joe allowed him to stay in his *caraca* for two full days while his insurance company took care of matters.

It didn't take us long to be selective with our generosity. After getting ripped off a few times by slime-balls, we stopped giving monetary assistance. We heard "I'll pay you back double as soon as I get bailed," one too many times. They'd never come through. We got wise real quick, and then cynical, but at least we kept our money.

Some of them—the decent ones—were sad to hear we would be sentenced to five to eight years. We'd share meals, talk them down, and even let a few sleep on our *caraca* floors. But none of them helped us out after they went free. Each disappointment made us wary. Our only protection was to band together and against anyone who was a threat to us.

It was Dirk's turn next. He got busted a few days after my encounter with Armando. Dirk's trouble was minor, but it had to be taken care of quickly. It was one more facet of the games that were played out in *Correctionalis*.

It happened on a Sunday when Dirk requested permission to go to the *Grande* for a big festival. Mainly, he wanted to score some good smoke. He purchased three fingers of *mota* and hid them in the heels of his thongs, figuring he'd be home free. A few others did the same. But the *Alciadia* outwitted them. He ordered a search of all inmates leaving the *Grande* that day, wanting to improve his income and his resume at the same time.

Dirk and a few others were thrown into the hole, presumably for a thirty-day tour of duty. We heard it was large, dank, and had toilets like those in the *Grande*. Dirk wanted us to know he was in dire straits, so he sent his main pal, Mike, a message right away.

We headed straight to Armando's *caraca*.

"*Si*, I will go to the office and get him out. First he must spend the night." We knew the stakes were high when he added. "The D.A. must not find out or there will be much trouble. Tomorrow I will go and see what I can do for him."

We were not really worried about the D.A. We were wondering how much money Armando and the *Alciadia* would lift from Dirk's pockets.

Three days and a thousand pesos later, Dirk got out.

"Those sonsofbitches! The two gay dudes who were in there didn't have to pay a cent," Dirk quipped, angry as hell.

We were *gringos*. We paid extra taxes for being stupid. Actually it wasn't a bad system. People got smart real quick. Besides, the gay boys didn't have any money to extort. Dirk got a bargain for eighty bucks, though he didn't think so. His ego was bruised and his wallet drained.

※ ※ ※

"How's it coming?" I asked Dirk, as Patrick and I entered his *caraca* early one Sunday morning. He and Mike were lying down reading.

"I think it's ready. Mike put a bit more yeast in it this time with less sugar so it ought to be ready today," Dirk answered, looking cheerful.

"The balloon shows it's time," Patrick observed, as the four of us peered at the half-full five-gallon glass container.

"He hasn't missed yet. Three tries, three successes, and now this one." I was smirking.

"This should be the best yet." Dirk was right.

"They *do* get better each time," Patrick agreed.

"Yeah! We've got nothin' better to take the edge off," Dirk jested.

"What do you think Mike?" I asked, though I already knew the answer.

Glancing up he replied, "Should be ready this evening," then returned to his book.

We were making pineapple wine: we called it *Pina Vina*—an elixir that took the edge off. Inger had smuggled the yeast in and Mike had ordered out for a case of pineapple juice. The wine-making process was tricky though; without refrigeration, humid, hot climates spoil food quickly. Refrigeration was a luxury none of us could afford, but ironically a few mishaps with spoilage led us to discover our winemaking capabilities. Mike did the honors and turned out a decent product.

Indirectly, the *Alciadia* inspired our wine-making venture. For his own hidden reasons, he had begun cracking down on the inflow of drugs into the prison. Perhaps he wasn't getting his fair share of the profits and wanted to let everyone know who was really running this show.

All we knew was that no drugs had been available. Then suddenly, a few days ago, drugs began flowing again. We were able to purchase our precious fingers. At the same price, no less.

Meanwhile, the "curing" complete, we had two gallons of pineapple wine to consume—just in time for visiting day, which could be depressing. The "blues" would set in because no one had visitors except Bill. So, we eased the pain by getting drunk and playing a boisterous game of poker from dinnertime into the wee hours of the morning. When we could party, life wasn't so bad.

The heroin addicts had it rough. There were several in our sector who were hooked: the ugly gay Lupe with the big hooked nose, and Carlita and Juanita—Lupe's boys. They lived together in a tent made of sheets precariously held up with a wooden frame. Their tent was pressed up against Gringo Row, and centered between Patrick's eight-by-eight and Steve and Walt's eight-by-sixteen. Patrick and Walt would tell us of their episodes of butt humping and the random nightly visitors

There were other gays, like Mario and Bronco, who lived next to Joe along the east wall, also heroin addicts. Bronco dressed cowboy style, which made him look like a clean-cut macho dude. In spite of Bronco's image, Joe assured us they were lovers and that many of the Mexican inmates went for a bit of butt humping. It was a way of life for them while in jail, and we left them alone. In turn, they didn't bother us. After all, this was *Correctionalis*. We were supposed to get things "correct."

One afternoon, Mario staggered out of his room, a screwdriver in his hand, fuming with rage at Bronco who was in the shower. While I was waiting in the shower line, Mario began pounding on the shower door, screaming and cursing at Bronco in Spanish.

Bronco started singing to offset Mario's screaming and cursing. The commotion went on for several minutes, which made me restless; Bronco wouldn't open the door and Mario wouldn't shut up.

His eyes bulging, Mario said in Spanish, "I'll kill that mother-fucker; I'll kill him," as he waved the screwdriver and pounded again on the door.

Bronco simply raised his voice a decibel or two and continued showering. I decided to steer clear and shower later.

The Bronco and Mario havoc happened during the *Alciadia's* crackdown on drugs. By that evening's *lista,* Bronco looked unscathed, but he narrowly escaped having a good-sized screwdriver thrust into his belly.

Once drugs were available, things calmed down. The *Alciadia* either worked out a deal with the guards or gave in, fearing a riot might break out, which could hurt his career. Whatever the case, we were all relieved when the drugs began to flow again. It was definitely the "correct" thing to do from our perspective. Since we were going to spend the next eight years of our lives in prison, maybe we could spend some time contemplating why it was we had needed drugs in the first place.

☆ ☆ ☆

The *Correctionalis'* gays were a creative bunch. They organized parties and made *piñatas* for each event. They were like traditional wives performing "wifely" duties: decorating, cooking, sewing, and doing laundry for themselves and their many friends. They were the prisoners "caretakers."

One morning in mid-August, I noticed a young Mexican, not more than fourteen, among the *quincados*. Having just awakened, still rubbing my eyes, I did a double take as I stood in the *lista* line, "What's a woman doing in *Correctionalis*?" I thought. Then it hit. "Christ, it's a gay dude."

A group of prisoners gathered around the attractive young man, who was dressed in a bright orange dress that came up nearly to his crotch. His long, shiny hair was all ratted up and he wore make-up, earrings, and spiked heels. He looked like a young street-whore. Even his histrionics were feminine: his stance, posture, and demeanor were alluring. We couldn't take our eyes off him, even as we joked from the sidelines and the crowd moved closer around the marvelous wonder.

"Looks like the real thing, doesn't it?" I commented to Fred, Walt and Patrick, who were glaring at the young boy—who was turning on all the inmates, including many of the *quincados*.

"You looking to try it out?" Fred joked.

"I already am. Seeing is believing, isn't it? And I see one foxy bitch over there," I joked.

Before long, the Tank Goon came over. Pedro was never amused and this was no exception. He broke up the mass of inmates and *quincados,* and began talking with the marvel. Then Lupe entered the scene. Somehow, he managed to escort the young "lovely" to tent city, along our wall. We didn't see much them the rest of the day, though Patrick said there was a lot of humping going on that night. A couple of days later, the beauty was gone.

During one of our Sunday night poker games, high on *Pina Vina*, we heard heavy scuffling and loud voices coming from the *quincados* toilet, which was near the *caraca* where we played. A fight was brewing, so Mike, Dirk, Fred, Patrick, and I bailed out of Dirk's *caraca* to see what might be happening. A large crowd had gathered. We tried to push through to get a better look, but we were thwarted. We had to enter the "regular's" toilet and stand on the basin.

From where we peered, a mere five feet from us, we saw four or five of the regular Mexican prisoners beating up on a new inmate, a fellow Mexican, whose head had been shaven. That meant one of two things: either he was a thief or a child-molester, which in most countries is the lowest of low crimes. Here, in Mexico, they especially hate anyone who stoops so low as to prey on children.

The man being beaten was thick-muscled and fat. The punches were doing little physical damage. Mostly they were inflicting emotional damage. We were concerned and we wanted them to put a stop to the brutality.

Bronco stood in the center of the action, attempting to put a broomstick up the prisoner's anus. Four others held him down doggy style over the toilet and beat him. When we started to protest, one of the Mexicans began shouting at us to back off.

Mike said, "The guy's a child-molester. He raped a six year-old girl," so we backed off, though the violence disgusted us, as they continued to assault the man for several minutes. There was nothing we could do to convince them that violence was not the answer. The man needed help, but the system, which was strangely cruel, would be of no help. We never found out what became of this man, only that he was no longer in *Correctionalis*.

The perpetrators of the beating would be ready tonight to take shirts and shoes, whatever, off the newly arriving *quincados*—Mexican, American, whoever. It didn't matter—whatever it took to get that next bag of heroin.

Tambor was lying low and offering little assistance, but was in touch with Inger. She had talked with him directly a few times and relayed to us that he was scared to death. He knew he could be in jail with us if we chose to rat on him. Then again, he didn't want to help much either.

However, he did put us in touch with a lawyer—a young, aristocratic-looking Mexican of Basque descent, who was energetic and passionate for our cause. He had strong connections and could really help, according to Tambor. Modesto's people had used him with great success. Inger asked him to come from Guadalajara, where he lived and practiced law and meet with her.

Huberto arrived in mid-August and arranged for Bill and me to talk with him alone in a small conference room near the center office. Fortunately, he spoke English.

Bill and I were comfortable with him right away and bantered about the ridiculous jail system in Mexico and *Napoleonic law*. Then we got down to business.

"I have read your statements to the D.A. They are very good. My compliments. We can most certainly do something with them."

"How so?" Bill asked.

"We will go to the D.A. and change your statements. This is allowed under Mexican law. We can make a story up that will protect you. There are certain laws here in Mexico which protect the people, and you have made a good start with this Señor Maximo, but we must say that he is from Guadalajara, not from Mazatlan." He looked at Bill and said, "Daniel, your wife Inger tells me you lived in Guadalajara and that Steven here spent some time at your place."

"Yeah. That's true," Bill replied.

"Good. That will be part of the story. That is where you will meet this Señor Maximo. And Maximo will become your friend, but he will force you to do what you did with the *mota*. *Si*."

"Sure. That's no problem," Bill said, as he flashed me a look.

"You want us to build a story?" I inquired.

"*Si*. You must build a story. I will do two things. I will pay a judge in Guadalajara to sign a paper that you came to him. The paper will say that a man, Señor Maximo, threatened your life, held a gun to your wife's head to make you take the *mota* to the U.S. for him. I know a woman with a small apartment house in Guadalajara who will say that you rented it from her for a few months. Your wife will come to Guadalajara and meet her so she will know her. Is this good with you?"

Good? It was hard to believe that a lawyer was really saying this to us. We were ecstatic. It sounded daring, yet possible under the circumstances. It was a risk worth taking and it was the law, he kept saying. All we had to do was to come up with a good story about how we met Señor Maximo and how he had coerced us into bringing up the *mota* to the U.S. Huberto would take care of the judge in Guadalajara—and the woman.

"How much are we talking about?" Bill asked. "We're pretty thin on money."

"Two thousand for all of this: five-hundred for the woman and fifteen-hundred for the judge. The judge only has to sign a statement that we will make up and say that you came to him. That is easy and he will do this for me. The woman will say that you and your wife stayed at her place for maybe four months."

"That's good. Real good," Bill said.

I added, "That's fine with me. I've already come up with something about this Señor Maximo."

"Good. Tell this to me now, then you and Bill tell it to the D.A. when the story is ready. It must be good. *Está bien?*"

"*Está bien*. I'll make it simple. We can say that one afternoon, when I was visiting in Guadalajara and while Bill and I lunched, this fellow, Señor Maximo, overhears Bill and me talking about my sailboat, which was in *Mazatlan* harbor at the time. He came over to our table, introduced himself and wished to talk to us. He said he is interested in buying a sailboat in the States. He can't buy a boat because it's difficult for Mexican citizens to own a boat (I had previous knowledge about Mexican law). He was willing to pay me good money if I'd go to the U.S. and buy him a boat like mine. He also asked me to sail it down to Mexico for him. We agreed and we gave him our address. Later he came over and threatened us. How's that sound?"

"That is very good," our new lawyer and new best friend said.

Bill thought the story had merit and spent several minutes going over it with me. Once we had it refined, Huberto gave us the go-ahead.

"That will do most perfect. Make sure you have the story correct with Inger. In one month, maybe two, I will come back. We will go to Señor Coppala and we will give to him these new statements. I will have the papers from the judge and the women who will say you rented from her."

"Far out! That's terrific. This could work." Bill and I were delighted with the plan. "It will work," Huberto said with a reassuring glance. "One more thing of importance. When we make the statements, you must have someone who can verify that Señor Maximo threatened you. That will be good. Maybe three, four months, after the statements are made, you will go free."

"But wait. Can the D.A. file an appeal?" I wondered.

"*Si*. He may file this appeal. If he does, it will go to Hermosillo. There they have a Tribunal. I have two judges I can go see. This will take time and more money."

"That's a ways away," Bill mentioned, looking at me and then Huberto. "Let's take care of this part first."

"*Si*. It's good that you take care of this first," Huberto agreed. "Be sure to have a good story. When I return, I will go over the story with you. Then we go and tell them to the Señor Coppala. I keep in touch with your wife and hear more of the story when she comes to Guadalajara. I will see you later."

Bill and I stood and shook hands with him.

Back in our *caraca* I said to Bill, "About that witness…I think I know who can pull it off. Do you remember Irv, my good customer, the guy who was in Special Forces?"

"Yeah, that strange dude with the pretty wife."

"Yes, Irv the Perv. I bet he'd come and give a statement. I can have Sarah contact him and get him to call us here."

"Are you sure? He'll have to testify he saw Maximo threaten us."

"Hey, if anyone can, he can. There's no one else that I can think of, but him. He's as outlandish as this story is. He's perfect for the part."

The next day Bill and I perfected the story. Soon we had a solid alibi just the way Huberto had instructed us. Inger was in agreement with the entire matter. She called Sarah for us and Sarah contacted Irv. Waiting for a reply was the hard part.

What a system! We'd never get away with a concoction like this in the States.

That afternoon we told the crew about the plan. We had already told the authorities the *mota* was locked up in the forepeak of my vessel without the crew's knowledge. The new twist would be my statement that I purposely wrecked my boat in order to get free of Señor Maximo, because I feared getting caught by the United States authorities.

The new design had its own logic: why else would I wreck the boat? Why else would Inger have had to move to a new location except to get away from this Maximo fellow? How ironic that all the pieces of the puzzle fit in with our preposterous tale. It seemed crazy to expect the D.A.'s office to believe the story, but they had done such a terrible job investigating us, we knew we had a shot, especially with the judge's help.

Bill and I and the crew had a good laugh over the prospects of getting away with it.

"My God!" Mike chortled. "No one in their right mind would believe this story!"

"Yes, but we'll have the signed affidavit from a judge in Guadalajara that we sought help from him," I pointed out.

Bill said disdainfully with a wild grin, "Hey, it's their laws. It protects people like us from men like Maximo."

"Fine," Dirk added, sitting crossed legged on his cot. "I'll go along. We'll meet with our lawyer and see what he says. Can you give us Huberto's phone number? They'll need to talk."

"I wish we could make it sound a bit more real," suggested Patrick, joining the conversation.

"I hear you, man. Señor Coppola may die of laughter if nothing else when we give our new statements," I chuckled.

"We got to try something to get out of here," Bill replied. "Who cares if it's outlandish?"

"If it doesn't work, we'll bore our way outta' here," Mike proclaimed.

We all nodded in agreement.

※ ※ ※

It was another Sunday. Feeling out of sorts, I headed over to Mike and

Dirk's *caraca* to hang out and play cards with Mike and Patrick. It was hard driving away the doldrums. When Inger arrived, I'd have to lunch with Bill and Inger—absurd. We'd probably have another poker game that night, but just then I wanted company.

As I entered the *caraca* I saw a new face. A tall, lanky male with curly, strawberry blond hair sat cross-legged on one of the cots, talking intently with Mike.

When Dirk saw me he said, "This is the captain of the boat."

When the stranger turned to look at me I was stunned: I recognized him. It was an old friend and a customer of Bill's, a man I had had several dealings with in the old days.

"Michael? Wow! This is unreal!" I exclaimed, before Dirk could introduce us.

Staring at each other in disbelief he uttered, "Christ. Is that you, Frank?"

"Yes. God, I don't believe this. What the hell are you doing here?"

"Apparently you guys know each other," Dirk grinned. "We were just telling him about the boat wreck."

"You didn't get busted, did you?" I asked, as I reached to shake his hand.

Instead, he stood and embraced me. "No. Not at all. Paperwork man! We screwed up. I didn't get the proper papers for my boat so they threw me in here. Penelope and my daughter are straightening it out right now."

"How very Mexican. I can tell *you* some stories. So, you have a boat?"

"Yeah, a thirty-five footer. And your crew here was telling me about yours. Where's Bill these days? Have you heard from him lately?"

Chuckling again, I told him, "He's about fifty feet away from where we stand. He's with his wife and daughter. Boy is he going to blow out when he sees you. Come on. Let's go see him. Besides, I've a few things to tell you."

Once outside, I let him know that Bill and I were fugitives and were using different names.

"Someone told me you guys had gotten busted. Guess they were right."

"Come on. Let's go see Dan."

Knocking on the *caraca* door I said, "We have company." As Bill opened the door, he grinned broadly when he saw Michael.

"Hey Bill, I mean, Dan. How ya doing?" Michael grinned ear to ear.

Stunned, Bill stepped out and embraced his old pal. "Unbelievable. Damn! Where's Penelope? You're never without her."

"Well, she's on the outside and I'm on the inside—for now, at any rate."

We were having one hell of a busy month. That an old friend should show up when we needed outside help was more than just auspicious; it was a godsend. "My, the universe worked wonders," I thought.

We wasted no time bringing him up to date on what had happened, plus our plan to dig our way free. He told us that he and his people would be more than happy to help us. We gave him any information of value we could think of, including how Armando might be able to get him released. Michael insisted Penelope would obtain the proper paperwork shortly.

Inger became very excited and volunteered to interpret for Penelope, adding, "They can stay with me at my place while you're here."

Everything seemed to be falling into place for us. Irv had called. He was set to come down in late September. I lost big at the poker game that evening—a few bucks—but it didn't matter. Michael's promise to help had given me hope. Out in the yard late that night, as the *quincados* slept, I stood near the washbasin, looked into the evening sky and gave thanks.

After a couple of days, Michael was released. He returned as a visitor that Thursday, along with his wife, Penelope, their pretty teen-age daughter Diana, and another friend, named Peggy. We crowded knee-to knee into our *caraca*.

"Like I say, anything we can do to help you guys, we'll do. I have two guys on the outside. They're my crew. They'll help too," Michael said adamantly.

"You don't need to dig that tunnel. We have a plan that's sure to work,"

Penelope said with a grin, as we hung on her words. "Peggy, Diana, Inger and I are gonna get some horses and come riding down the street in the nude right in front of those squally-eyed guards. We'll pull out our pistols and tell them to empty the jail, *pronto*. How about it? Four beautiful Lady Godiva's coming to save you. The pig guards will be looking at our bodies and down the barrels of our guns while you men run free."

"Sounds wonderful. If only I could believe they'd go for it," I said, as we all joined in laughing at the comical image Penelope painted.

Michael and his people had come south to smuggle a few hundred pounds of grass to the States in his boat. "We'll be loading up in a few days. When I'm done, I'll come back. All of us will. Whatever it takes, money, material, transportation, we'll help make it happen."

While Michael and Bill talked, I took Penelope, Diana and Peggy to meet the crew. Peggy was brash. She said, "Hmmm, big, strong, and gorgeous, just the way I like 'em."

Dirk and Mike grinned like Cheshire cats. The women were attractive. Diana kept eyeing us, especially me. Sarah was due in a few days. Thank God. Patrick was his usual cool self and joined in the spirit of the moment, as did Fred, who was now one of us. He planned to help us dig the tunnel whenever we got going.

During the course of the conversation Penelope mentioned that Peggy was Janis Joplin's lover. "Come on, tell 'em about the book you wrote."

"I didn't write all of it," she said, embarrassed. "I got a lot of help."

"What's it called?" Mike came to her aid.

'Going Down With Janis', she said, and then was even more embarrassed.

"Yeah. I've heard of it. Haven't read it," Mike added.

"So have I," Dirk quipped.

All of us had, but Peggy began to get upset, so we cooled it and talked politics.

"Tell me what you know about the Watergate burglary?" I asked. "Ole Tricky Dick and his cohorts are up to something and we never get enough news around here."

Sarah had sold my Volkswagen. Finally, I'd be able to get Bill off my back. Well, maybe. Having wrecked the boat and ruined our weed, I figured Bill would shirk all responsibility for past debts he owed me. Still shamefaced, it was difficult for me to talk with him about the matter. Likewise, he was careful not to mention anything about past debts; present debts were the critical issue now. As for the litigation debts we were incurring, he'd just have to take care of them somehow.

Money for food was the most pressing need. But all I could think about at that moment was that Sarah would arrive on Sunday. She'd be surprised to know we were in good hands and had a good lawyer working on our case. Inger, I was sure, would bring Sarah up to date about the latest developments.

She called Saturday afternoon. "Hi Beast. I'm at Inger's along with everyone else. What a swell group of friends."

"Yes. We're busy these days. There's never a dull moment, sweetheart. I'm sure you've heard some stories by now. How are you, sweet woman?"

"Ready to see you." Her voice was sugary and sincere.

"Good. Let's plan to be together all day. I've special arrangements for us. We'll have our own suite, honey. How about that?"

"My, how nice. I hear they have wonderful beds there. Let's talk more tomorrow, though. I'm tired, Beast. I can see I'm not going to get much rest. They want to take me to dinner."

"Go for it. We'll have our moment tomorrow."

A wave of anxiety ran through me as I hung up. I wanted to see her, but I knew I had to tell her what I felt. My mind hadn't changed about the need to confront Sarah about breaking up. Soon she'd have to decide too. I didn't fully understand why I was considering a breakup; all I knew is that I had to be straight with her.

In the past, I always had the freedom to take a drive or a walk to clear my mind.

Since that was no longer possible, I'd had to make do. I had found place of solace: the area around the washbasin, late at night, when the *quincados* were asleep. It was the center of the courtyard and it afforded the best privacy.

When I arrived there late that evening, I could see the constellation Orion making its way up from the east. Taking a few deep breaths I leaned against the washbasin, waiting for some epiphanies as I gazed at the night sky.

"What are you doing here, Frank?" I asked myself.

"You're here out of choice," my inner voice answered. "You're free to choose what you want to choose."

The answer was always the same. It held truth, yet how could I have chosen to set myself up to end up in jail?

Next, I thought about Sarah. I'd promised to quit the business and go cruising, no matter what. But I had the right to change my mind and had chosen, instead, to make money. I had made a bad decision and it weighed heavily on me. Confused by what had gone wrong with my plans, I was overwhelmed by guilt. Had I stayed with the promise everything would be different. I'd be broke, but with Sarah by my side we'd find work.

Why had I changed my mind? And why, dear God, why had I made an in-shore tack at night when I knew better?

Bill, Manny, and Jake came to mind. Before I had made a mistake and gotten busted, I had plenty of time to think about why these men had self-destructed. Past traumas and greed had a lot to do with their demise. And now I had become what they had become, even though I had endeavored to avoid the karmic path that had led to their demise. What had truly been bothering my mind these past few months was why I had failed myself, as well as Sarah?

As these thoughts coursed through me they cut like knives, leaving me with no way to staunch the bleeding. I was hopelessly lost when it came to dealing with my emotional problems in this present situation. Love—my capacity to give and receive it—was an integral part of my confusion. It would help me overcome the pain that was in my heart. I had to trust that love was indeed the answer—traumas or not—and that somehow in some way answers to my questions would come forth.

Shaken and feeling insecure, I sensed the irony behind my quest. Sarah, my desire for money, the boat wreck—all came back to haunt me as I silently looked to the heavens. I loved Sarah and would go on loving her, but was ready if not eager to back out of that love and let her go. Maybe then I'd gain peace of mind?

Again, I heard the inner voices: "In time, answers will come. Focus on the night the boat crashed upon the rocks, the waves, the feelings of fear and terror that shot through you the instant the first wave hit."

I'd drifted into an altered state and I was shivering, covered in goose bumps. I could feel the panic all over again. So, I did what I could to will away any further thoughts and focused on the dreams I'd been having the past few weeks.

The dreams that had come first were of me being battered around by water, tossed here and there, inside the main cabin of the *New Mornin* as it shuddered and scraped across a rocky bottom.

Lately my dreams had been different: more pleasant, but still frustrating and nightmarish. I'd be outside my boat looking at it from the water as though I were a fish submerged below the surface. The boat, as always, would be sailing along in a smooth, delicious ocean of green liquid. The breeze would be perfect and *New Mornin* would be gliding along effortlessly, when suddenly a rock would appear. The boat would strike it and begin to sink. Then I'd wake up, covered in sweat.

And, as this dream vision ended, other painful recollections came at me with such fury I felt nauseated and immediately shut down all thoughts. It was time to rest so I sought refuge in sleep, hopeful that when Sarah showed up I'd be ready.

When Inger arrived the next morning she announced with a conspiring wink, "Sarah's on her way."

More apprehensive than the night before, I tensed up when the guard's booming voice rang out, "*Recita por Señor Estephen Walsh.*" I turned and saw Sarah enter through the barred gate. She looked terrific, dressed in a pair of Inger's hot pants and a loose fitting white blouse. She did not see me at first, as I stood near the washbasin observing her.

When she spotted me her pace and demeanor changed, as she flowed freely toward me, a smile sweeping across her face, a beam of love so real that nothing else mattered. Our eyes focused on each other as we met near the middle of the courtyard and embraced. We said little, just clung to one another as a crowd of prisoners and visitors milled around us. Gently she drew back, holding my hands, not wanting to let go, a few tears in her eyes. She squinted, pressed her lips together and in her usual whimsical demeanor sang out, "Why didn't you tell me was place was so full of life?"

"But I did, sweetheart."

"Plus, you said you were getting fat."

Seeing her tears I wanted to join her, but not in public. It was a sign of weakness, and survival here depended on one's perceived virility. I held back as dozens of people looked on, discretely wiping a tear away.

"Sorry, sweet thing. I know I said that in the last letter, but it isn't so. As you can see, I was teasing you. It's just that we don't get much exercise in here. We just don't have the room." I motioned my arm toward the crowded courtyard.

She looked about for a few moments, taking it all in.

"Now tell me, did I describe this place accurately?"

"You did, buns. It truly is quite unbelievable. There's so much happening here." Looking at me, her big, blue eyes wide open she admitted, "And, it is everything you said it was—full of life."

"Those guys to our right, those are the gay boys I told you about, Lupe and the gay troupe, but let's not talk about them. Right now I want to be with you. Would you like to join me in our private suite?"

"Nothing would suit me better. Have we far to go?" she teased.

"No sweetheart." Taking her hand I led her toward Fred's *caraca*. "I've never made love on a cot on a hot day. Wanna try it out?"

"Love on a cot! Hmmm, sounds like good story material to me," she said coyly, as we crossed the courtyard.

Stopping in front of Fred's *caraca* I turned and bid her, "Welcome to

Fred's Eight- By." Opening the small entry door, we stepped in.

"Considering what's in the *Grande,* this is as good as a suite at the Playa Del Rey."

When I closed the door, we were in total privacy. Lust overtook me. There was no need to hold back, save for tactfulness.

"Let me undress you," I requested, standing in front of her. "You don't really need clothes on in this climate."

"How true, but be easy, Beast. It's been a long while," she lamented in a soft voice.

In one soft easy motion, her pants were on the floor. Kneeling beside her on one knee, I teased, "Pardon my obsession honey, but I can't make up my mind. Do I love these luscious legs and this fine butt of yours, or do I love your lovely blue eyes and all that comes with them?"

"That's really not much of a problem, sweetheart, you can love it all."

Kissing her softly between the legs, I continued moving up her body to her navel, my hands lightly caressing her skin. I stood up and removed her blouse, and then wondered if I was being too sudden with her.

"Boy, I'm glad you're so easy."

"If I'm easy, you're nasty. That was terrific, Beast. Do it again, more slowly this time. And lots more kisses while you're at it."

Relieved that she was willing, I said, "Then let's play, sweety."

Making love on a small cot on a hot humid day caused a pool of sweat the size of a small lake to form on her abdomen. We laughed and played with it for a while, as though it were a mud puddle, then continued, emotions running high. Though we had both climaxed, I sensed she was not with me. Then again, I was not quite there for her either. Maybe I had pushed her into making love too soon.

"Hey, I know what you'd like right now."

"What's that, you handsome hunk?" Lying beside me she seemed content, but there was an edge of sullenness too.

"Let's do some time in the shower. Our private shower, that is. We can cool off and just touch one another, be together with the water."

"Hmmm... You're on. Let's eat first though. I'm hungry."

"Good sign, sweetheart. Good sign. Let's get up. The shower can wait."

"Okay, but hold on a minute." She grabbed my buttock and held me in place, adding in a somber voice.

"I'm not as 'together' today as you might think."

"Neither am I, sweetheart. Neither am I. What's up?"

"It's hard being here. I just left my parent's place in Pasadena yesterday. They're worried about you and about me. And this place isn't what I expected. Please understand it's not you, it's me. I'm sorry." Tears formed and started running down her face.

"There's a lot for us to deal with, flower. I want you to be comfortable while you're here. It may not be easy, but I love you. We have one another for now."

Stroking my cheeks, and with tears still flowing down hers she said, "Frank, I care so very much, but it's difficult. You don't know what's really happening for me up north. I don't always tell you the truth. I worry. I fret. I cry. I'm not doing the things I need to do. I haven't got the energy."

"That's the very reason I asked you to visit me, Sarah. I want us to be together so that we can get a better picture of what's happening. And now that you're here you can see that things are not so bad. Bill and I and the crew are dead-set about digging a tunnel. And the lawyer we hired, he's determined to get us out of here. You already heard the story. It's far-fetched, but it may work. All we need is money. Michael could help out. But the truth is I'm full of doubts. And that bothers me. I'm afraid, just like you, but you're here and we can talk. In time you and I will come up with a way to work out of these difficulties, not only the ones Bill and I and the crew face, but the ones you and I have to face."

"Yes, my man. I know it's the best thing to do, but sometimes I'm lost, like in a daze."

"Somehow I know we'll come up with some answers and we'll feel better."

"Yes. That's what I want. I want to feel better."

"Then let's go to Mike and Dirk's *caraca*. They're expecting us. We'll show you where we're going to start digging the tunnel and tell you our plans. Come...let's be together."

Michael and his family, along with Peggy, came to visit shortly after we showered. We ate dinner with them then headed back to Mike and Dirk's for a poker game. Although it was illegal to have cards, we had managed to smuggle in two decks. I said to Sarah as we all played, "We do have some good times here, sweetheart."

It was close to ten p.m. Most of the *quincados* were asleep. Sarah replied quietly, "So I see. Would you mind if I go out and talk with some of the gay troopers?"

"Do you need me to go with you?"

"No. I'm okay, really. Life around here is so condensed. It's a mini city, like you said in the letters. I just thought I'd step outside for a moment." The door was open and all was quiet out in the yard.

"I'll join you soon," I offered.

When I stepped out into the courtyard the *quincados* were fast asleep, lying around the perimeter like neatly fallen dominoes. As I made my way to the center basin, Sarah was sitting on a small wooden bench placed in front of the basin. She was conversing in Spanish with *Juanita,* the young gay boy.

As I approached, the boy got up when he saw me and said good night to both of us.

"She's charming." Sarah was in high spirits.

"You mean *he's* charming," I grinned.

"He was born to be a woman."

"I won't argue that, but he was also born to be a thief. That's what he's in for. Although I like him, I don't trust him. Life around here can be that way. Maybe I'm being cynical, but all of us have been ripped off. We learn to watch our backs every second."

"Why are you defending yourself, honey? Come sit down next to me."

"Because I haven't told you what life is really like here and how it affects me, sweetheart."

Facing her, I added, "Maybe that's why you fret and worry. You know that I don't dare tell you the real truth. And the real truth is we may be here a while and this is jail—no matter what it seems like. Things can turn ugly in a second. Fights can break out. I have to live with a brother that despises me and I feel the same about him. A few times we almost came to blows. As for the Mexicans, they have no love for us. We're in the way. They put up with us. If they start a fight, Armando will have them thrown in the hole. When they get out, then what?"

"But most of these guys want to live in peace. Surely you see that. They're friendly and if you spoke Spanish, I'm sure you'd get to know them better."

"Sarah, it's not that easy. Yeah, sure... I want to learn their language, but on the other hand, they piss me off with their stupid gimmicks. The more I talk, the more they hustle. The more they hustle, the more I get turned off," I said, exasperated. "Yeah, I know it's sad, stupid, and senseless. But that's life and they deplete my energy. And that's why I don't care to get too close to them."

"Maybe in time you'll understand their culture. Mexicans are family people. They love life."

"It's not as simple as that, Sarah." I sighed. "I'm not all that sure I can learn their language. Whenever I give it a try, my mind goes blank. The words I learn I can't remember. Not now, Sarah. I haven't the drive. I'd rather be with you right now and talk about our problems."

"Okay. I know you'll eventually find the desire. My love will be there for you. You can find it any time you want to, right there."

She put a hand on my knee and pointed to the evening sky, while looking up at it. "Look. Orion is coming up. Soon the Pleiades will follow, then Gemini, and Taurus."

"I hear you, sweety. Over in the *Grande* they're locked in at night. We have the night sky to look at and I truly appreciate that."

Looking in my eyes she said sincerely, "I'm glad you can do this. It's a way for us to be together. We can look to the sky each night and find each other. We'll find one another no matter what."

"I'd like to believe we can do that. I really would. It seems so simple, but how far will it get us? Things get old; they don't always last so long."

"We can make it last as long as we believe."

Looking away from her, I added again in a somber note, "Sarah, look at the uncertainty I'm faced with. Even if I get out of here soon, I've problems in the States to face. I can't fathom how I'm gonna get myself out of all of this. It's a complete fucking mess and I created it."

"Why are you getting down on yourself? Why don't you see there's a future and that you can be free?"

"Because, right now, I don't have a future, Sarah. I've blown everything to pieces. I don't feel good about what I did: to the boat, to you, to Bill and the crew." I placed a hand on one of hers and held it. "Truth is, I can't make any plans for us."

"I won't let you believe that." She squeezed my hand. "I won't. This new lawyer you have may get you out of here in a few months."

"Please, Sarah. It's a farcical story. We'll do anything to get out of here. No, I'll put my money on escaping first, but that's even a long shot." I purposely chose to be negative with her. I wanted to set things up so that she would face what I had to say to her but it didn't seem to be working.

"Go with it anyway. You've got to make some changes for yourself. Those three men you chose as crew are strong. You can trust them. They're brave and ready for action."

"Yes, I know, but..."

"No buts, my friend. I'll be behind you no matter what." She caressed my cheek.

Suddenly I was full of emotion. Silent for a moment I looked away then said, "The truth is, I've been thinking about letting you go, even though I love you."

She too was silent for a moment. "That hurts, Frank. It really hurts to hear you say that."

I felt like a heel, but I turned to face her. "I want to be real with myself and with you."

"Don't you think I haven't given it thought, too?"

"Yes. Yes I do, and that's why I don't expect you to have to stay with me. I don't want to hold you back from living your life the way you want to live it." My throat was dry. We were both silent for a moment.

"Listen to me. Look at me. Somewhere along the line you have to make the changes that will bring you out of this. You lost your boat. Your self-esteem is somewhere in the clouds. You believe you made a mistake. You think you have no future. I'm saying that's not so."

"I don't see it that way. I made a mistake, more than one..."

"Stop it, Frank. Stop it this minute. Look at me, please. So you made a mistake. I love you. You're the man I want in my life right now. I'm afraid, too. Oh God, I'm afraid sometimes, but I'm here talking to you. I see what you're up against. We'll need strength to handle it. We'll make it through."

"I don't know, Sarah. I just don't know." Staring woefully into her eyes I added, "How can I expect you to remain faithful to me while I'm in here? Can you answer that truthfully? Can you really say you'll be fine after you leave here? Can you? I read your letters. They tell me what I need to know. I feel your sensitivities. I don't think we have the strength to keep this relationship from falling apart. And you're right, my self-esteem is low. I feel like a complete fool sometimes. I don't know if it's wise to keep this relationship alive. I'm a very demanding person. I want all of your love or none of it."

"Yes, you can be demanding. There are times you've been arrogant and have made me mad. And I don't really know if I can say I'll be forever faithful. All I know is I love you, and I want to work through all of this with you. I don't want to end things. I don't. Do I have to break down and cry to prove it?"

Tears were spilling from her eyes, the kind that makes me feel helpless. She was so lovely, so vulnerable, and so was I. We stood and wrapped our arms around each other tightly, and swayed back and forth for a long time.

"This is so difficult Sarah, so difficult. I don't want to give you up, but I don't want to be a fool and make your life miserable. I love you too much to do that to you. Believe me. You're my life. You're everything to me and I want you to understand that."

"Thank you, sweetheart. I want to be with you, too. Don't cut me off. I know you can, but don't. We can have a future. Believe in that," she sobbed.

On Thursday, she came for a second visit. After making love in Fred's small *caraca*, we lay peacefully on the cot. She surprised me by announcing. "Sweetheart, I'm going to be leaving tomorrow and I want to let you know now so you can prepare for it."

Upset, I rose and said as calmly as possible, "But Sunday you said you'd stay another week. What's the reason?"

"There are several, Beast. Believe me. Inger and Jeanie are one. They argue all the time. Inger accused her of stealing something of hers the other day and I'm caught in the middle."

"What did Inger say Jeanie stole?"

Michael and his entourage had departed Inger's and checked into a hotel. That left Jeanie, Steve's girlfriend living there. Inger and she had been roommates for several weeks.

One day, Inger discovered some of her clothes missing. Inger searched Jeanie's suitcases and found the goods. When Inger confronted, her Jeanie said she hadn't put them there and accused Michael and his people of fowl play. Now, both Steve and Walt were distant towards us. I cringed as Sarah described the situation.

"Shit, as if we don't have enough problems," I complained bitterly.

"It's a mess and I don't want to deal with it."

"Stay on Michael's boat for a week. I want you with me."

She rose up from the edge of the cot, reached out, caressed my shoulders softly and said, "It hurts me to visit you. Getting in here is an unbelievable hassle."

"I'm sure it is."

"It would be better if I go now. Please let me do this. My parents are going on vacation come Christmas. They've already hinted at coming here and they'd bring me along. My Dad loves Mexico. I'm sure they'll come. They really do worry about us."

"Aw honey," I said in a huff. "Shit. Dammit all, woman. This is the part of me that is holding on to you." I grabbed one of her hands and pressed it against my heart. "It's crying out right now."

"I'm sorry. I knew this news would upset you," she frowned.

"Yes, you're right. It hurts. It really does. You ask me to fight to make a change, take a stance on the future you say, but you won't even stay another week. Where's your fight?" I argued, but my voice choked up.

Sarah replied, "This is different, Frank, much different. I'll be back soon. I promise."

"No, Sarah. It's not different. Not to me," I said in a controlled voice, my head bowed. "It's demoralizing and I won't argue with you about it anymore. I'll just let go of you first, piece by piece."

She embraced me. "No you won't. I won't let you. I'll prove that I mean what I say. But you have to let me go home. I know how to handle this now that I've seen you. I'll be here at Christmas, even if my parents don't come." She hesitated a moment, then looked me straight in the eyes. "I want to get back into my life. I want to do things differently this time, in Inverness. It's important. And so are you. Let's make a good day of it. I want you to believe in me." She kissed me lightly on the cheek.

"I'll believe the part of you that loves me," I replied, looking intently at her. "That's what is in my heart at this moment. I leave that for you to understand."

CHAPTER TWENTY-SIX

AUGILA: THE WARRIOR

MAZATLAN, MEXICO
SEPTEMBER, 1971

R IGHT AFTER SARAH departed the full brunt of the season's monsoon storms arrived. With the courtyard often awash in torrential rain, we stayed snug and dry in our *caracas* while *quincados* milled around the south wall, discontented, and seeking shelter under the corrugated metal awning that surrounded the yard. There was little else for them to do as they stood packed one against the other, hour after hour. When the rain stopped they would immediately head out into the wet courtyard. Often they'd lie down for a nap, even before it dried.

We preferred to stay in our *caracas* and read when it rained. There were now enough books to pass around that we kept busy.

While locked away in jail, we found safety in holding to a daily routine—something none of us had ever experienced before. No one wanted to toy with the routines, but the rains had changed things around. We were annoyed by the changes and our tempers were on edge.

My relationship with Bill was at an all-time low. We almost came to blows a week after Sarah left. Were it not for the promise we had all made to behave, Bill and I would have fought. From my perspective, our conflict was once again because of his controlling ego.

Jake's wife kept in touch with me by letters. She called in early August to let me know that she and the kids were going to drive down to see me in early September. They arrived and landed at Inger's.

When Bill heard they had arrived he announced, "No way is she coming in here."

"What the hell does it matter?" I argued.

"She's Jake's wife. That's what. They get wind of that and the authorities will know we're here."

"What the hell are you talking about, man? How would the authorities know? She's going to use a false name. I told you this before she came. You know they never check IDs, so get off it."

"It doesn't matter. Things are too tight here. We'll be giving new statements in a couple of weeks."

We went around and around. In the end, Bill had his way. He dug in his heels and at the time, all I could see was that he was trying to control me in ways he never had before. When I told him point blank that he was a control freak, he scoffed at me. When I explained Bill's inflexible position to Joanne on the phone, she was thoroughly disappointed.

Inger sided with Bill on this issue. It was their way of getting back at me for the problems I had created, I told Joanne. She called one last time before leaving.

"I know what they're up to," I confided in her. "It's a nasty game. They want to suck the energy out of us, so let's back away from them for now. Let's let their karma catch up with them. You can bet it will."

She left the next day, having driven all the way from San Francisco to visit me, only to be turned back by Bill and Inger. Inger, who now struck me as an angry and spiteful woman, had driven a wedge into our relationship. That she chose to attack me told me that she was much like all the other people one encounters. In short, I was wary of her now and would carefully consider any future personal interactions.

Reading books and writing letters to Sarah helped relieve my anger.

More so, reading and writing got my creative juices flowing. Before Sarah left she encouraged me to read more and write to her.

"I love your letters," she praised. "They fill up my days. I don't have as much time as you my love, but I'll write as often as possible. But you, my friend, write me daily and record your thoughts and feelings in a journal. Write stories about the people around you, like Augila and that poor American who got thrown in here for three days just because of a traffic accident. He was scared to death and you guys helped him out. Just write, my love. You'll see what I mean."

I did. And, it worked. It empowered me to "hang in" and rise above circumstances I had created. Yet it was difficult to sustain those feelings for long: incarceration in that hell-hole was a constant drain. No matter how busy I kept myself, something always unhinged me.

But I kept writing, telling Sarah my innermost feelings and describing in my journal the crazy people that came and went in *Correctionalis*. Almost every day there were new faces: mostly Mexicans, but also a few Americans and Canadians. A group of five Russian merchant crewmen showed up one morning. They were big men: arrogant, and obnoxious. They wanted nothing to do with anyone. They didn't know a word of English or Spanish. We stayed away from them during their two-day lockup.

One day, an American congressman's son showed up, a young man, crazy as a loon, who had escaped from a mental ward in Los Angeles. We were stunned when he took off all his clothes, not more than an hour after arriving. The *quincados* applauded him as he danced and played in a driving rain. Still in the buff, he proceeded to climb the pilasters, making his way to the corrugated roof. Several of us tried unsuccessfully to talk him down. He was in his own world as he climbed the thick main wall impregnated with broken glass bottles. When the guards removed him we were glad to see him go. He was a healthy-looking, handsome kid in his early twenties, but he was a nuisance to us and to himself.

After Armando told us who this young man was and that he had escaped from a private mental hospital, and somehow had gotten to Mexico I said, "Too bad. He was like a child or an elf. It's strange that he seemed to be okay one moment and then the next moment he'd start dancing and singing. He seemed so free. I don't know, *Armando,* who's the crazy ones, him or us?"

Armando just smiled and winked as he departed.

To the American drug offenders thrown in *Correctionalis*—the usual suspects—who were always frightened out of their minds, we'd counsel them, "If the D.A. calls you in for a statement, you're in trouble. And if you're not out of here in six days, make plans to buy some bedding."

Usually they had less than two ounces of contraband and we knew they'd be deported within three days, compliments of the United States government, who paid the Mexican government to do its work.

"You'll be on their little Green Sheet at the border now," we'd add. They usually complained bitterly that their cars, RV's, money, and possessions had been confiscated.

"What can we say? The Mexicans are running a business down here. Write to your congressman. Let them know."

When Sarah returned home from her visit, she updated my good customer and friend Irving on our situation. At his own expense, he and his wife Tracy flew down. They were planning to stay with Inger.

Irving was my age and had been born and raised in the Bronx—the jungles of New York City. Though he was of medium build he looked fierce due to his dark features and the attitude he packed around. Underneath it all he was a sensitive dude with a contradictable swagger and more brainpower than a Mensa. He told outlandish stories that left his listeners in stitches. Some were actually true, but it was hard to know which ones.

He was *chutzpah* personified, but he never knew when to quit, especially when he was stoned—which was all the time. His wife Tracy would roll her eyes as Irv droned on, unaware that people mostly were laughing at him instead of with him.

Nonetheless, he had come to help us, which said something about his character. He arrived early on visiting day and I spotted him as the guard opened up the gate.

"Irv. Over here, man!" I said loudly, as he swaggered in carrying a book under his arm.

"Go get your brother. I'll growl at these dumb fucking guards and we'll walk you right outta' here. This place is a snap."

We laughed together. "Hey! You're the first one in here today. They didn't even announce you."

"They didn't need to. I was too quick for them," Irv claimed. "They don't know how to handle a guy like me. Besides, I saw what was happening so I made my own line. Just walked up to the guard at the gate at the right time and started talking at him. He didn't understand a fucking word I was saying, but it didn't matter. I just kept talking and sure enough the line formed behind me and I walked in first." We howled over this, then he added, "Here, I brought ya' something you need." He handed me the book he had carried in.

"*The Anarchist's Cook Book*!" I read the title aloud. "Christ, how'd you get this in?"

"How else? I wouldn't let 'em take it away from me." He grabbed it back, flipped to a section titled "Bomb Making" and said, "This one would be easy. I've made this type before. Learned it when I was in the Special Forces. The ingredients are simple. Inger can bring the materials in for you. And on this page is a smoke bomb to go along with it. You can blow the walls away and set up a smoke screen behind you." We laughed heartily.

"Yeah, right, Irv. Same old stuff. Right? Come on, let's get out of the crowd. Bill is waiting in the *caraca*."

Over the next couple of hours, Bill and I helped construct the story Irv and Tracy were to tell the D.A. Two days later, Huberto, our energetic lawyer, showed up in Mazatlan. That afternoon the entire crew was escorted downtown. Señor Coppola was cordial with us as we gave separate statements through an interpreter. Then we were escorted back to jail.

Irving and Tracy gave their accounts the following day.

"No sweat," Irv told us when he came for a visit that Thursday. "You should have seen the look on Coppola's face when I told him about Maximo.

He was ready to shoot me right there. He knew I was lying and there wasn't a damn thing he could do about it. He's a nasty looking asshole."

Their story was simple: my long-time friends, Irv and Tracy, had come to Mexico for a visit. One evening, Señor Maximo showed up on one of his many visits. Irv and Tracy saw him threaten us with a gun as they hid in a back room.

"We'll just have to wait now and see how this comes out. It seems so crazy," I said, as we all sat in our *caraca*.

Inger added, "Huberto said that Señor Coppala will go to Guadalajara to talk with the judge who signed the affidavits and the woman who rented us an apartment."

"At least they're taking it seriously," Bill commented. We chuckled in agreement.

A few days later, Steve and Walt got the surprise they had been long awaiting.

"We're outta' here, man," Walter said to me in the yard, with a smirk on his face that wouldn't go away.

"We just got the news. The *Alciadia* has our release papers. Armando just told us."

"All right, man. That's far out!" I shook his hand.

"We'll be going any moment. God, this is great. I can't tell you. Ten months for a few ounces of weed. We smoked more than that while we were in here."

"They sold it back to you, that's all. You should have smoked it up sooner," I joked.

"Yeah. But who cares? We're getting out. We told Armando you wanted the *caraca*. He said it's OK with him and when he comes up to get us, he'll have it OK'd by the *Alciadia*."

"That's great, Walt. I hope it goes through."

"It will. Don't worry. You can have all our stuff too: the fan, the cots, the hot plates."

They knew we were going to be around a while and would make good use of their donations.

An hour or so after they departed, Armando told me I'd have to pay him one hundred and eighty dollars for this prime piece of property. It took nearly all the money Sarah had brought from the sale of my car to pull it off. Moving in took about two minutes. That night, feeling mighty, I wrote Sarah and told her of my fortune.

"Too hard to believe, dear one. No one in the jail has living quarters as big as mine, an eight-by-sixteen, all to myself. But if an American comes in, he'll have the rights to buy half the place. Why the *Alciadia* hasn't thought to move two guys in from the *Grande*, I don't know."

Right away, I sold one of the cots and bought a small table. That first night, I invited some of the guys over for a game of bridge. We smoked weed and partied until twelve. All of us were glad that Steve was gone. His pal Walter was nothing like him. He was a good man, who'd had the misfortune to join up with a man who liked to control others.

Our crew was now in total control of all the *caraca* along the west wall. Before long, my new dwelling became a gathering place. Fred, Mike, Patrick and I had formed a very tight alliance, one that would help us get out of *Correctionalis*. We no longer had to bother Dirk or Joe for a place to hang out. The four of us not only played cards and talked, we often cooked and got high together.

A few days after I moved in, I invited Joe over to play cards. Inspired by my new digs I suggested, "How about a mural, a decoration of some sort on the wall over there, Joe? Got any good ideas? Nothing too detailed, just something nice to look at. What do you think?"

Tugging on his goatee a moment he answered, "It's harvest time. How about a big yellow sun with a single green stalk of corn... just off center with a clean white background."

Using pastry flour as filler, I smoothed out the rough concrete surface and painted the wall white, then painted a large yellow sun. Joe came over and added the single corn stalk. What a score, an eight-by-sixteen all to myself with custom-designed artwork. Wow! It was my dwelling now and

I wanted to mark it as mine; an act of appreciation and veneration to the perfection of the universe.

The main problem was money. Before Michael left, Bill had invested in a deal with him. We had heard that Michael had made it back to the States with his load of contraband and we were waiting for him to contact us. Once the load was sold, we could pay all our current lawyer fees.

But I couldn't wait any longer for personal funds. I wrote Sarah and asked her to contact my brother Ray. Within a few days he called. I asked him for assistance and he agreed to send me thirty bucks each month. I began to rest easy. There was more time for solitude, a luxury I hadn't had for a long time.

Being free of Bill's constant presence changed my relationship with him. We actually started talking and being friendly. However, he and I and Inger had another falling out around mid-October. It was the same old story: he got married to Inger, had a child, and then started chasing women. This time, I even got blamed for creating the drama.

The previous year, after Modesto had fronted us the load of five hundred kilos, I had to get money safely to Bill, Tambor, and Modesto, by courier. I sent Barbara, Toby's ex-girlfriend, who had also taken care of a very important matter for us by storing our load. We had met Toby, a trusting, easy-going man through Ben. The moment I met his ex-gal, sexual sparks flew. When I asked her out on a date she accepted. We made love that evening. Later, Ben told me she was balling other men to get back at Toby, who she had caught making love to one of her good friends. I was one of Barbara's many conquests, as was Bill who hooked up with her when she came down with the money.

A year had passed. Ben knew we were in jail, but apparently Barbara hadn't found out. Bill, once again, had made the mistake of giving another lover the Mazatlan trailer court address. She wrote Bill a very tasty love letter, mentioning the time they had made love on the beach on La Isla, a deserted stretch of beach to the south of Mazatlan.

After Inger read the letter and confronted Bill, he pleaded with me to save his marriage by concocting a brainless story to convince Inger that he hadn't touched that woman.

Leering at him all I could say was, "Well, was she a good screw?"

"Come on, man. This is it. Tell her Barbara is doing this to get back at you and that she's lying."

Bill had bragged to me several months ago about making it with Barbara and now he wanted me to be part of his conspiracy.

"Forget it Bill," I shot back. "You just don't get it do you? You're the one who's messing around. You're responsible for this situation, pure and simple. If anything, Inger wants you to come clean. Don't drag me into this."

Bill got a reprieve: it was not a visiting day. Inger had come to the prison gate and sent Bill a note, along with the letter from Barbara. She was blown-out angry, but had given Bill enough time to work out a good alibi. I don't know what his alibi was, but he spent a good deal of time trying to convince me to help him out. I calmly refused all his requests. There was no arguing. I was no longer under his control. I felt a certain satisfaction in not giving in to him.

"Tell her the truth," I advised. That's what she wants. That's what you need. Stop the lies."

Somehow they got through the nasty ordeal, but when Inger came for the next visiting day, she got on *my* case.

"You sent that whore down here. It's your fault. If you hadn't sent her this would never have happened."

"Inger, come into my *caraca* and we'll talk about this."

When she left me there was an air of calmness about her. Somehow, I convinced her of the truth. Bill was responsible, and as long as she loved my brother she was also responsible.

Sometime later, through Sarah, I found out Inger had extracted revenge on Bill. On one of his visits to meet with Bill and me, the Basque from Guadalajara had wined and dined Inger. Word had it that they had made love just prior to the second "love" letter that had been sent to Bill at the trailer courts. No more was said about the Barbara incident, but afterwards Inger seemed to walk a bit more proudly. As for me, I believed the nasty trick they had played on Joanne and I had come back at them.

I wished good luck to my brother that no more love letters would arrive. Time would tell. If one more showed up, Bill might lose Inger. That was one more worry for all of us.

Karma nailed me a few days later when I got into a fight with a state prisoner, a fellow named Sandabull. As with many of the prisoners, he had no love for us *gringos*. Buying the eight-by-sixteen only created more envy, which was probably the reason we tangled.

Our problem started one morning while Sandabull was running the clean-up operation for Pedro—as he often did—when I came cruising by in a bit of a stupor. As I walked toward my *caraca*, he threw a buck full of soapy water streaking across the concrete floor right in my path. I realized I had not been paying attention the moment the water splashed across my feet. Still, I knew he had done it on purpose.

I stopped in my tracks and turned in his direction.

"You're totally obvious, Sandabull." I knew he didn't speak English so I added, "You missed you shit. Try again. Make a direct hit this time." I wanted to give him the impression that his antics were silly and that he was pushing things. Thinking I was berating him, he threw another volley of water at me then hacked at me in Spanish, which brought cheers from the *quincados*.

They wanted us to fight, and several dozen *quincados* were standing in back of me. The main yard was clear of people so the washing could take place and I was the lone *gringo* in the yard.

After the water from the second bucket of water washed past, I glared at him as he continued the verbal harangue. When he pointed a finger at me and said something in Spanish, the *quincados* again cheered.

"That's it man. You fucking jerk!" I took a step in his direction. I had to. Both of us were committed. Had I walked away, I'd have been a marked man—such was life in prison. Even though he didn't understand my words he knew my intent.

I was ready for him when he flew at me. I quickly reached out and pushed aside his flailing arms, connected with his shoulders, held tight as I rammed forward, and flung him backwards. He was a couple inches shorter and several pounds lighter than me, so it was easy. He fell to the ground, but quickly gathered himself, readying for another charge.

It never came to pass. Sandabull looked to his right before charging. I was not about to be faked out and paid him no attention. But just then, Armando came into view. He had heard the commotion and in a second, cursed and flew at him. Sandabull was quickly collared and Armando kept cursing and pushing him back.

I was stunned and relieved. I could only imagine what Armando was saying. Sandabull stood a chance of being sent to the *Grande*. He could also be sent the "hole." It was Armando's job to protect us and he was doing his job. Sandabull cowered and backed off. He dared not even look at me or give any sign that he might take the matter up again later. Armando took him away and finished his spiel where few could hear. And just like that, the fight was over.

A friend I had met a few days before, Manual, immediately tried to help me. Manual was one of the few Mexican prisoners I had met who was willing to stand by me. He was my age but was a good six-feet tall and solid. He was a *quincados* who had been here for over a week. He spoke English and had told me about the time he had been in the States as a farm worker—nine years. After the altercation he came up to me and said, "I take two *quincados* off your back."

"Wow! I never felt them. Two?" My adrenaline had been running strong.

"*Si*. They come at you when you push the man, Sandabull. I pull them back very quick."

"Thanks, *Manuel*." I stood there for a moment. "Hey! Are you hungry?"

"*Si*. I be hungry."

I had fed him a few times before and this time we feasted on a breakfast of eggs, vegetables, and tortillas.

Augila, which means eagle in Spanish, was the name of a *quincados* in *Correctionalis*. He had a long aquiline beak of a nose and a crusty, wrinkled, well-tanned face—which had earned him his nickname. Although he was not tall, he was lanky. He was a man of renown at *Correctionalis* who came and went, but never really left for good. A man of sixty, give or take ten years, Augila was known as the town drunk and the clown of Colony Juarez.

Armando told me that in the four years he had spent there, Augila had been coming and going. Because he always returned he was considered a fixture. *Correctionalis* was a home to him, a dwelling place where he found solace.

But not really.

It only took us a few weeks at *Correctionalis* to become familiar with Augila and his sad situation. It was clear that the local police did him a favor by bringing him here where he detoxed and was fed three meals a day: beans, broth, tortillas and coffee—far better fare then he consumed outside jail. At least, that was what we assumed.

However, while he was at *Correctionalis*, his own people taunted him mercilessly. He endured the kind of bashing that would have left most men beaten, tormented into a cocoon. His stays were so frequent that all the *quincados* knew him. Augila's hecklers, especially the *quincados*, could never let him forget his follies. In the food lines he'd be shoved around, knocked down, tripped, pinched, scorned and verbally abused. The *quincados* relished jeering at him, if only to release their own hostilities. He fought back often, but never too seriously.

The chow line scenes lasted several minutes and continued into the meal itself. Sometimes a *quincados* would trip him while he was carrying his food to a safe place. Upended, he'd spill his tray of broth with beans. Most of the time the lowly turd who did the tripping would go free, because

Augila often didn't see the heckler, or have the heart to start a fight. When he did see his heckler, all he could muster was curse words. But the more he shouted, the more his tormentors taunted him. He was the court jester of *Correctionalis*.

The crew and I often found ourselves in the yard at meal time—not because we wanted to watch the show—but because it was the time of day we could enjoy some physical space while the *quincados* were in line or eating. Dirk often walked and exercised. Sometimes we'd join him and end up watching the show between Augila the Warrior and the irreverent *quincados*. Amazingly, he hung in there: he had to, or else succumb to their pranks and merciless ridicule.

One time he lost his cool. He had been tripped, fallen to the ground, and then the lowly *quincados* snatched his tortillas. When *Augila* tried to get back up, his tormentors pushed him back down. Augila fell to the ground again and began crying in earnest. The *quincados'* hearts were so hard that they taunted him all the more, kicking and shoving him around for being a crybaby. He suffered through one indignity after another. The *quincados* stopped at nothing, short of beating him up.

Armando pointed out they were only having fun. Silently, I disagreed. Through it all, Augila the Warrior survived. Each new day meant another day of abuse. I sensed he sometimes enjoyed the harangue. He'd smile and joust, clearly lighting up as the *quincados* who insulted him. It was queer and bothersome to me, but it was reality for this Warrior of *Correctionalis*.

Around eight p.m. each evening the guard at the gate would call out the names of the *quincados* to be released. When Augila's name was called, he was usually given a gala exit. His fellow mates would howl, applaud, and pat him on the back as he exited the barred gate. It was their way of thanking him for all the good times they'd had at his expense. In response, sometimes he'd dance and sing a Mexican ballad, showing everyone he had vigor and the grit to survive. Though often short-lived, it was his moment of glory. Unfortunately, he always returned, often the next day, and the taunting and the ridicule would start all over again.

As I luxuriated in the privacy of my new dwelling, I often thought of Augila. It gave me strength and faith to realize the odds he overcame. When the *quincados* persecuted him, I sent silent energy, always wishing him well, for Augila's struggle reflected my own. We both packed around guilt and shame, but were willing to live as wholeheartedly as we could in the "moment," and thus beyond the guilt and shame. Even if the moment wasn't too great, it was where we were and what we had to deal with. The best we could do was to make the best of it, and not lament what could have been, or might have been.

Since moving into my *caraca* I had been working on this idea of living in the moment, something I'd learned about a few years back. It was a meditation for me to "be in the moment": a way to harness my energy, regain my esteem by exercising free will—which was my path to self-empowerment—and a way to move past the "hurt" of my mistakes and all the negative emotions that crowded my mind and heart.

"Let's make a list of everything we'll need," Fred suggested.

"Number one, a screwdriver to pound through the cement," Mike said.

"We can use it later to break through the dirt," Dirk added.

"Mario has a screwdriver," I said. "He was ready to kill Bronco with it a few weeks ago. Let's see what it will cost to purchase it."

"Don't offer too much," Bill suggested, "or he'll get suspicious."

Sitting in Mike and Dirk's *caraca* we started getting serious about our way to freedom. The *Alciadia* hadn't searched us since two days after our arrival in early July. We'd been patient, had done our homework, and now the time was ripe for us to carry out our plans.

Fred, our Chinese-American inmate whom we all liked and trusted reminded us, "We'll need to make use of our flashlights. All of us can buy batteries."

We all had flashlights because the electricity often went out, especially during the heavy rainstorm—like the night I decided to take a cold shower then found myself in a pitch black arena and had to stumble my way back to the *caraca*. We always needed batteries, especially for Dirk's boombox, so we weren't likely to draw suspicion when we ordered them through the *mandadaros*.

Our list grew longer. Clothesline would be a good substitute for rope. We could purchase a plastic dish tray to carry out the dirt. We also needed a hammer, but a good-sized rock, hard as hell, would suffice. Mike had purchased just such a rock from a *quincados* a few weeks before.

The list completed, we went over procedures. Mike, Dirk, and Patrick would work on breaking through the concrete floor under Mike's cot. Once the top was off, all of us would take turns digging, but only when it was safe. We were careful in our movements to and from the dwelling and monitored our sound level. Dirk's boombox was going to come in mighty handy.

Daily routines at *Correctionalis* were conspicuous, so any deviations would be suspicious. There were certain inmates who would inform on us in an instant, but we could control that element by keeping undesirables out of our *caracas*.

At each step of the project, we began to realize just how delicate the operation would be and all the obstacles that faced us. The first obstacle was the thickness of the concrete floor. Mike suggested we make a small hole to determine the thickness.

Next, we wondered where to put the dirt we would dig up. We were stumped. Mike and Dirk suggested we store it in the grocery boxes we received through the *mandadaros*.

"That's a lot of dirt," Bill pointed out.

Patrick grinned. "Yeah, but we have four *caracas*. Let's make use of them."

"I don't know. One search and we're screwed," Bill complained. Fred and I agreed with Bill's concerns.

Dirk countered, "If they search they're gonna find the floors have been opened anyway, so why not store the dirt? We've got the room."

"True," Fred added. "We can't put it down the drain. It'd clog up in no time."

Finally we agreed to store the dirt in our *caracas*. We were in it together. Besides, there were other considerations, such as, how deep were the two foundations we had to dig under? The unknown obstacles tested our solidarity, but our desire to escape kept us pushing through them.

"Let's start ordering the items on our list so we'll have it on hand," I suggested.

"Let's get a screwdriver first, " Mike said. "I'll pound out a hole and we'll see just how thick the floor is."

We worked out the fine details of masking our daily routines and controlling patterns to and from the *caraca*. Fred suggested we put up a curtain in front of the main door like Armando had on his, so no one can see in when the door was open.

"Slick, Fred. For sure," Mike added.

Next, Bill brought up the idea of visas. "As I told you guys a month or so ago, I've got a good connection to get visas for all of us. It'll cost two hundred pesos apiece. They'll be good for six months. Let's order them now so we'll have them. Inger will take care of getting them for us."

We ran into our first minor obstacle when Mario's screwdriver was unobtainable. Fred had to order out for a good-sized one, about ten inches in length. The guard allowed it to come in with his regular groceries, but to be safe we waited three full days in case the officials had gotten word of it and ordered a search.

After a single day of work, Mike had good news.

"It's less than three inches thick, guys. We're going to cut through the top."

The opening was to be eighteen inches by two feet. They began working and the rest of us went about our regular routines. Bill, whose *caraca* was closest to the gate, handled all incoming messages and picked up mail. Fred and I took turns monitoring the yard.

Progress was slow and tedious; it took the three of them fifteen days to complete the job. We were all smiles when they told us the top was off and that soft, easy-to- remove soil lay underneath. We decided it was time to dig.

Mike was especially eager. "We can dig our way out of here in three or four weeks, tops."

We had all the equipment we figured we'd need, even a ping-pong paddle to use as a scoop for filling the plastic tray full of dirt. Next was the downward leg of our tunnel.

One morning, about an hour after *lista*, the dig began. By eleven, after the crew had gone as deep as they could, we found we had a major problem on our hands. Peering down into the open pit, we could see four to five inches of water in the bottom of the four-foot hole. It sat there like a tiny, unwanted lake.

"Every time I bail, it fills back up right away," Mike stated. As I dropped to my knees to get a good closer look, a vile smell greeted me.

"Damn. That's human feces. This is sewage water."

Bill took a closer look and agreed. "It's shit, all right. There must be a broken sewer pipe nearby. That's rank, man, real rank."

Dirk, sitting dejectedly on the end of his cot added wryly, "I'd say so. The Hole is right in back of this wall and the shitters are close by. I bet there's a broken pipe over there."

"Yeah, and no way can we fix it." Mike plopped down on the far end of Dirk's cot looking discouraged.

Silence hung in the air as we collectively searched for a solution.

On my knees again, looking down into the hole I said, "It may not be a broken sewer pipe."

"What else can it be?" Fred asked, as he stood next to me peering in.

"Like I said a while back, it could be that the water-table level is still high. It's still the rainy season, guys. Maybe we're too soon."

"Nah. I don't think so," Dirk stated flatly, and Bill nodded in agreement.

"Well, think about it. If it's a broken sewer main, there would be no regular flow of water running through the pipe unless someone was cleaning it all the time. And we know they don't do that, not in the Hole. If we bail it out and it comes back right away, that suggests the water-table is high. If Colony Juarez is on low grounds and the tide is high, this will happen. We talked about this a few months ago."

Fred agreed. Now the rest of the crew was ready to reconsider. The rainy season that year had been well below normal: one or two storms in July, a few in August, but several in September. It was now late October. There had only been a few light rains recently. If the water-table was still high, as we expected it might be, then it could be affecting the ground around the toilets, which was the area we needed to dig directly under: the *quincados* toilet.

We concluded both problems might be happening at once. Our venture was now a guessing game, a game of wait and see. While waiting, we'd have to withstand the pressure of a possible search.

"Let's monitor the water level over the next couple of days and see what happens," I proposed.

"Yeah, let's do that," Fred agreed, peering into the hole.

Mike jumped up from the cot springing into action. "I'll put a marker on it right now."

"Good, but what are we to do in the meantime guys, if there's a search?" Dirk asked, disappointed.

We decided to wait three days.

The water level had held at the same level. That afternoon, Mike and Dirk filled up the hole and refitted the concrete top. Using flour, water and dirt to mask the rough edges, Mike did a superb job of concealing the damaged floor. He placed a cardboard box full of groceries over the area as well as his cot. There was nothing else we could think to do but wait, and hope the *Alciadia* didn't order a search. If we were caught, our asses would be thrown in the Hole for a month. Plus, we'd lose all our possessions, including our real estate. More than likely we'd be sent to the *Grande*, and some lucky Americans or Mexicans from the *Grande* would take over our luxury boxes.

"We're just going to have to stay extra cool, guys," Bill advised. We had no choice but to accept our predicament and wait.

"No fights, no commotions, nothing. We gotta be good boys," Dirk advocated, grinning.

The wait-and-see game didn't lessen our motivation. It only added pressure. We were now sitting on a hot potato that could explode at any given moment. In time, we'd take the top off once again and hope the water problem would be gone.

It was a mystery that there hadn't been an inspection for three months. They had inspections in the *Grande* all the time, according to our information. We had seen the five or so inspectors—Goon-Squads we called them—enter the *Grande* a few times. We had no idea how thorough the inspections were, but the conditions at the *Grande* always drew attention. Prisoners were packed in like bats on the wall of a cave. An escape attempt, a riot, or a killing, would send the prison into pandemonium and inevitably, a search would follow.

As the season changed and daily temperatures dropped, we calmly went about our routines. It was now cool enough to sometimes turn the fans off at night. The shower, which was cold water only, was becoming difficult to tolerate. But in the evenings, we could actually get a breath of cool air. The rains had all but stopped; there were only a few lingering thunderheads and showers. The days were mostly clear with brilliant sun-shiny skies. We could only hope that the cooling climate would help keep tempers low as well.

The only tempers that rose came from the *lista* officials when we learned that Ken had escaped.

Ken was a trustee, an American, who lived with several other trustees in a cellblock near the main entrance and front office. Ken was the quintessential diplomat. I admired his self-confidence and how he carried respect for others, and his intelligence.

About our age, he was a healthy, bright man with a full beard, who had been incarcerated for the past eighteen months. We had met him one visiting day when he came to visit Fred. The two had struck up a friendship during Fred's eight-month stay in *Correctionalis*.

When the officials found out Ken could speak Spanish they had put him to work in the office. He had gotten to know the *Alciadia* and the office crew and had become familiar with the politics of running a Mexican prison. The guards were also familiar with him. As a trustee in good standing, all he needed to do was ask the guard to let him through to the *Grande* or *Correctionalis*. He had full reign within the prison.

One morning back in mid-September, just after Sarah had left, the officials taking *lista* were very uptight. As Dirk approached for role call they stopped him and barked out orders.

"They want you to shave off your beard," Joe interpreted. Dirk had been growing one for about a month and Bill had had one for quite some time. He too was ordered to shave his beard off—by evening *lista*, the officials instructed. We were puzzled. Armando cautioned us to be patient and he would find out what was going on from the office.

He didn't have to. Word quickly spread that Ken had escaped. Apparently, the whole time he had been in prison he had been making escape plans. His Spanish was rusty when he first entered, but he quickly brushed up on it when he realized how it could help him. He grew his beard right after getting the trustee position and for the next ten months he did his job well, gaining respect. In return, he escaped by simply walking out.

Fred later confessed to us that he had helped Ken pull off his escape. It was all rather simple. Ken had stolen a lawyer's pass some months back, which went undetected. Luckily, Ken had a suit, a white shirt, and tie, which he stored away in Fred's *caraca* until the given day. On a very busy visiting day, he shaved his beard in Fred's *caraca* and cut his hair. When the guards called for visitors who were not going to spend the night, he showed the guard his pass at both gates and walked away a free man. No one had recognized him. Later, when they pieced together what he had done, everyone with a beard was ordered to shave.

Ken had made fools of the *Alciadia* and his entire staff.

Oddly enough, the *Alciadia* never ordered a shakedown in our sector. Counting the one-month stay in La Paz, we were entering our fifth month of incarceration. The stupid and lazy factor was eating away at us. Who'd win out? No one could put odds on it, but time seemed to be working against us.

One evening, just as darkness was descending, the *quincados* began hooting and hollering while Mike, Fred, Patrick and I were playing a quiet game of cards in my *caraca*. What started out as prattle and laughter soon became a roar. Then we heard the sound of people running, more hooting and hollering, more laughter—then came scuffling. It sounded like a foot race, or a chase. Then there was more laughter and scuffling, and it got increasingly loud.

"What the hell is going on out there?" I asked, jumping to my feet.

"Sounds like a fight," Fred commented.

"We better find out," Patrick said, opening the door.

My first thought was that the inmates were giving Augila a bad time, but I was wrong. A group of *quincados* was chasing a huge rat around the courtyard, while the others cheered them on. The vermin was in a frenzy. Trying to escape his tormentors, he headed for our open door and in a flash the crazed rodent was inside the *caraca*. Patrick, in a whimsical gesture, closed the door.

Some eight inches long, not counting the tail, Mister Vermin ran for cover, settling under my cot. Outside the *quincados* were suddenly quiet. But we were not quiet inside. We were poorly equipped to trap a rat. We were dressed in shorts and thongs and had no desire to have this huge bugger clamp his dirty old teeth in us. We appeared calm, but were really looking for safety. Meanwhile, Mister Vermin was frothing at the mouth, counting the seconds he had to live.

Mike immediately toppled my cot, exposing the frightened rat cowering in the corner. There was nothing to debate and this was no time for deliberation. We were in a Mexican prison with a rabid Mexican rat trapped in the corner of my *caraca*. According to local tradition, rats were despicable, ugly, dirty creatures, to be killed whenever possible. Patrick went to work. Someone handed him the broom. The rest of us stood back laughing, but fearful nonetheless. Using the broom's blunt end Patrick took a stab, but Mister Rat deftly dodged it, heading for another corner. Patrick kept trying, but Mister Rat escaped his blows. Before long we were yelling, cajoling, and jumping about as Patrick calmly continued thrusting and missing. We jumped up on anything we could find.

Patrick aimed and stabbed several more times. Most of the shots looked like sure hits. Mister Rat wouldn't give up running back and forth across the length of the room. We yelled and squealed like frantic women and did our best to assist Patrick by moving objects out of the way so that Patrick could get a good shot. Mike tripped and fell, but was back on his feet before he fully hit the floor, as Patrick continued to aim and miss.

Finally, Mister Rat wanted a time out, but we were merciless. This business of killing a rat was taking way too long. Fred was standing on his footstool giving instructions, while all of us cheered Patrick's efforts. After several more near misses, Patrick finally landed a good blow to Mister Rat, who was just plain wasted. Or, maybe he'd just given in to his ultimate fate.

In a one-two punch, the first hit stunned the rat. Without hesitating, Patrick struck again in a *coup de grace*. Then, without saying a word, Patrick set the broom down and moseyed over to Mister Vermin and picked him up by the tail. Fred got down off his stool, opened the door and Patrick walked out holding up the dead rat for all to see. The clapping was thunderous, the roar of approval ear shattering. He threw the carcass in the middle of the yard and the *quincados* quickly scampered away. Patrick headed back to the *caraca* as the applause reached a crescendo. With finality, we closed the door and resumed our card game.

That night, before I fell asleep, I wondered if the rat episode had been an omen.

What did it mean to trap a rat in your *caraca*? In a Mexican jail? A jail we were about to run from?

Maybe it was best that I not give it too much thought.

CHAPTER TWENTY-SEVEN

PIÑATA

MAZATLAN, MEXICO
NOVEMBER, 1971

OUR GOOD LAWYER Huberto, contacted Inger in mid-November to let her know the local judge would hear our case and hand down sentences within forty-five days, sometime around Christmas. Knowing bureaucrats, we were certain they would postpone until after the holidays. There would be an appeal no doubt. The litigation wrestling match would consume another three to five months. Not to worry. With Huberto's good connections with two tribunal judges in Hermosillo, he once again assured us of an acquittal. He hadn't mentioned how much of a *mordita* we'd have to pay to his Hermosillo Boys, but Bill and I assumed it would cost us a small fortune to sway them our way. We simply didn't have the money. Plus, Huberto wanted payment now for the excellent job he had so far done.

Michael and Penelope, who had yet to contact us, were vital to our financial well-being. Bill and I concluded that Michael was having God-only-knows kind of problems and no doubt thought it best to lie low. All we could do was trust they'd come through sometime soon. Then we'd take care of Huberto and his boys.

As for the tunnel, we were at odds with each other about the matter. Dirk, who tended to be aloof at times and never hung out as "one of the guys," had become rather touchy. More than once he had dropped insinuations that it was my fault that we were there. For that reason, I steered clear of him. I also didn't like his sarcasm with the others. The best policy with him was to go easy and keep the peace. Fred, Patrick, Mike, and I kept to our strong nucleus, which helped keep those negative problems at bay.

Dirk and Mike, being best of pals, were all for starting the tunnel again only two weeks after the sewage water problem. The group consensus was no. Bill and I stood firm. We wanted to hold off a few more days and reopen it right after Thanksgiving. This upset Dirk and he withdrew even deeper into the cocoon he had already formed. It wasn't a truly malicious withdrawal, but it added more pressure. I asked Mike if he would cajole Dirk into cooperation.

"We're all in limbo on this one," I said. "We gotta keep together, and work things out as a group." Mike listened, but I had no idea what he actually said to his pal.

Dirk stayed angry. Still, we all respected him and the great strength he emanated, both physically and emotionally, and my guts told me to hang in there.

A few days before Thanksgiving, as we stood out in the yard one morning, Armando informed me about the holiday festivities in store. He said there would be more visitors than usual.

"You will see. The *putos* love the time of *Navidad*. They decorate the whole yard. You will enjoy this, my friend."

Hearing this, we became more convinced that an inspection would occur, during or after the holidays. In spite of our apprehensions we decided to stick to the plan: open the tunnel after Turkey Day and escape as soon as possible—sometime before Christmas—defying the possibility of a search during the holidays.

Sarah was scheduled to come down just before Christmas and had no way of knowing we'd even started the tunnel. Just as well. If she'd known, she'd probably have been chewing the wallpaper off her bathroom wall. Meanwhile, I wrote to her every day. And every day, my thoughts changed.

Sometimes I was positive and healthy. Other times I was demanding, arrogant, even crude, with cynicism and frustration sandwiched in between. The added pressure, our hot potato, wasn't helping.

I wasn't the only one. All of our moods swung from day to day, like being on an emotional roller coaster. But our strength was building, even through the tension. I felt it. It came and went like waves on a shore. Maybe we were just caught up in self-absorbed thoughts and as soon as Thanksgiving passed, we'd band together as I hoped—as everyone hoped.

What ran strong in my heart was that we were a group. And, even though we all ran hot and cold, on the surface we appeared cool and calm. But, within this matrix our hearts were not always kind. We were prisoners. All of us had closed off certain feelings. Plus, none of us knew one another all that well. I believed we wanted to, but being in such close living quarters we had to create boundaries and withdraw from the constant conflicts in order to survive. Living in a den of thieves, cutthroats, and liars, I longed to be around normal people. Everyone in our group had to feel the same way. But, how did normal people live? And what did "normal" mean? People on the outside, I concluded, were much like those in jail. Some were peaceable and some weren't. Some knew how to work together and some didn't. And if that was so, then all of us had to keep in mind and heart what *we* could do as a group of brothers.

As Thanksgiving approached and the tourist season got underway, *Correctionalis* soon began to swell in population. It was stomach-turning. Up to 150 to 175 *quincados* at any given time were residing in the small quarters we shared with the regulars. *Gringos* came and went like cattle being readied for slaughter.

In a letter to Sarah I wrote: "Tourist season is underway, sweetheart. The price of American meat, flesh and bones included, is down to almost *nada*. In and out they come like flies on shit. We no sooner tell them the ropes, when bang; they're gone—bailed out. They only seem to leave the people we don't want to be left with. Do you think the officials know that? Do you think there's a conspiracy? Wow! There's Larry, Lee, and Wesley right now. Larry, the fragile divorced man, anemic and perpetually coming down from a bender, has some soul to him, but alas he's helpless and interminably broke. But, at least I can trust myself with him and help him.

"Lee, my suspicious mind tells me, is a red-neck caught in our-good-guy-camp. Oh, how nice he pretends to be, with his four strands of top-hair hanging loosely over his brow. He got a whale of a scare from the local bulldozers, the South-Wall Boys, and according to him, he's in here for no reason at all. Can you believe that? He's from the Bay Area, as is Larry, who's grinding up life with his "old lady," he supposes. She, in turn, called the cops to have his ass put in jail. That's why he's down here. My, how guilt works! Now he wants to call her and have money for bail sent down. But Lee, what bail? You have no money. Shit! Get out of here!

"Wesley is from Texas. He lives on an organic veggie farm in Tennessee. Can you see it?—a tall guy with shaggy, dirty hair, a dirty old hippie, popping uppers, who walked right into the local cops. They found some pot seeds and a pack of nicoban in his RV (his "dump" as he calls it), and when they asked him who the 1400 green-backs belonged to he said, 'My friend.' It's funny; his friend said the same thing. Oh well, not all of us were born smart. I recall I'm here for making a stupid mistake as well. Same as the rest. This is a stupid farm, my love. Limbo, signing off."

Having the additional room, I'd often let some of those *gringo* characters sleep on the floor. By now, we'd learned to fend off their pleas. Why deprive them of their lessons in life? Better to make it miserable for them so they get the most out of their time. None of them ever died, or even got sick, except Larry, who was an alcoholic. We kept telling him, "Drink water, man. Drink water and eat the food they give you." Though sick as hell he made it out alive, having survived an epileptic fit the third day there. Life wasn't always fair.

Thanksgiving finally came, along with a small amount of rain. Mostly it was overcast with threatening clouds that seemed to cast a spell of misery on all of us. We made three attempts—the first two of which failed—to get a turkey dinner with all the trimmings. The first attempt was made by the

American consulate, who appealed to the mayor of Mazatlan for permission to provide all the American prisoners with a Turkey Day dinner with all the trimmings. The consulate was promptly refused. The *Alciadia* felt it would incite the Mexican inmates. Just as well. We didn't want a riot either.

The second attempt came close, but had a capricious ending. Rubin, a friend of Tambor's, and also Bill and Inger's, was a very nice Mexican who meant well, and wanted to cook us a turkey feast. We got permission to have the food sent in through Armando. Two days before Thanksgiving, Rubin parked his car in front of his house to unload the groceries and while he was inside his house, two hungry dogs literally made off with our bird. As he came out, he saw the dogs dragging the booty down the block.

We knew Rubin. He was a pacifist and an adamant vegetarian, and when we heard he refused to give chase that was the end of that. Bill and I doubled over and laughed until it hurt too much to carry on.

Inger cooked Bill and I a huge chicken casserole while the rest of the crew ordered up some baked chickens. We felt let down, but that was the least of our concerns.

A few Days before Turkey Day, Armando had informed us that the tap water in *Correctionalis* would be turned off for a day or so to make repairs. Mike checked into the matter and found out that the repair work had taken place in the *Grande* and in the Hole. He and Dirk immediately speculated our problems with the sewage seepage might have been corrected. We decided to wait until just after Turkey Day, and then reopen the tunnel, once the weekend was over.

It was good we waited, because we got a good scare. An incident occurred that shook the fiber of my being—and every man inside for that matter, whether they wanted to admit it or not. We got the story from Armando and read about it in the local paper.

Apparently, the guards brought in a drunken Mexican one night. The guards walked off for some reason and left the man unattended before putting him in the tank. For some insane reason, the drunk picked up an empty coke bottle near the cot of a sleeping inmate and bashed the guy's skull in, killing him. The killer didn't even know the victim. All the inmates were angry with the guards, who were responsible for containing prisoners. And, we realized just how vulnerable we were. Our *caraca* doors had no locks. Anyone could sneak in to our dwellings during the middle of the night, stick it to us, and probably never get caught.

The man who died was the owner of the small restaurant where we often purchased meals. As for the rest of the inmates, we could only hope that the incident wouldn't incite a riot. Not until after we'd finished our tunnel.

"What do you mean you already opened it?" I asked Mike, as we stood inside my *caraca* Friday morning. We were alone. He had come over to tell me his important news.

"Just that! Dirk and I started digging a few days ago. We're already underneath the toilets." His voice was full of defiance, yet still friendly; he was proud of what they had accomplished.

"We're supposed to be in on this together. Who else knows about this?" Part of me was angry at the news—another part elated, but we needed to get the record straight.

"Patrick's been helping us. Hey, we thought it was groovy to go ahead and we did. The water level is no longer a problem." Mike sounded guilty, even though he had an ear-to-ear grin.

"Okay, Mike. Fine, but we can't pull stunts like this in the future. We need to agree on all matters. Come and talk with Dan and me. We're not unreasonable."

"Yeah, I hear you. It's just that we figured you guys wouldn't mind. They repaired the pipes last week and we took a peek. There was no water coming in, so we went for it." Mike was relaxed now that he'd gotten the news off his chest.

"Now that you mention it, I don't mind, but let's pull things off together."

He disregarded my propitious remark and said excitedly, "Come with me. You can take a look at what we've done. We've removed a lot of dirt.

It's been a bitch, but we're under the toilets now.

"Let's go. Now I'm anxious to see it. This is terrific. Maybe we can be out before Christmas?"

"That's the plan, man. That's what we're shooting for, isn't it?"

No one was working in the tunnel when we arrived. After a short talk with Dirk, I donned work shirt and pants before entering the hole. Mike gave instructions on how to enter properly.

"We had to go head first when we started," Mike explained. "It was the shits, believe me."

"How'd you get back out?" I asked.

"Feet first. Whoever was on the outside had to pull the digger back up. Digging out the first few feet was the worst. Now it's simple. There's room to turn around, right beneath the toilets. When you're done, turn around and come out head-first."

"I'm ready."

"Okay. Feet first. Now turn. Lower your body and work your feet in. That's it. Keep going back. You'll be there in no time," Mike instructed.

As I moved backwards an eerie sensation crept over me as the sides of the tunnel closed in. Looking back at the daylight shining down from the entry hole, I wondered how I'd handle working in such conditions. Squirming back some seven or eight feet, I was soon in a more spacious area and I could actually sit up as Mike had said. Swiveling around, I sat with legs tucked in. Shining the flashlight around the entire area, I noticed a clay pipe about four inches in diameter leading down from the *quincado's* toilet. The pipe made a sharp 90-degree bend, then led over toward the regulars' toilet—ours. On the very top of this pipe a chunk of the clay pipe, about three inches by two, had been broken out. It was a clean break and the broken piece of pipe had been wedged in with a good-sized rock. Had someone hit the pipe dead-center, it might have shattered the whole pipe, but it was in good shape. Having seen enough, I crawled forward. Coming to the entry point, I shimmied up, and then pulled myself out. As I stood up, I asked immediately about the pipe.

Mike replied. "Yeah. That was my goof-up. I hit it with the screwdriver, but the main portion is okay."

"It looks fine for now. So does the rest of the tunnel. That's some great work, guys. Let's keep going. I'll go tell Bill what you've been up to and soften him up."

While I changed back into shorts, Patrick came over and checked me for possible mud spots. Then I sat on one of the cots, and we discussed digging further. The three of them, Mike, Dirk, and Patrick were willing to keep on digging as a team.

Dirk added, "You guys can help as we get deeper into the dig, but we prefer to do most of it ourselves right now. You know... too much traffic in and out of here would be a giveaway."

We had discussed this routine weeks before.

"Fine. Whatever it takes. When it's time, we'll all help out on the dig. Besides, it was creepy down there. Are you guys okay about digging in tight quarters?"

"We want out," Dirk replied from his perch.

Mike added, "I'm okay. Patrick hasn't said anything."

"Then I'll update Bill. He and I will take turns listening for any messages. We'll watch the yard also. See you at evening *lista*. We'll talk right afterwards."

After *lista*, we met in my *caraca* for a few moments to go over the next hindrance—the inner wall. Having no idea of the depth of the main foundation, Mike and I suggested digging down at an angle as we approached the wall, which we estimated to be some six feet away from where they had stopped. Once beyond the main wall it was another twenty feet to freedom.

"How long before getting to the main wall?" I asked.

"Hmmm, four or five days," Mike answered.

Dirk chimed in, "Six at the most."

"Damn! Let's hope they didn't put that foundation too far down. Let us know as soon as you get to the wall," I requested.

"Let's not work at night. It's too risky," Bill suggested. "The *quincados* are quiet. If someone goes in to take a shit, they may hear the noise."

"Fred is going to join us," Dirk mentioned. "He comes over here all the time, so it won't look unusual. The four of us are going to do two-hour shifts."

After several days of tedious progress, the dig crew reached the wall, which elated us. Excavating the floor of the tunnel at a slight angle had paid off. "We only have to dig down another few inches to work our way under the footing," Dirk reported.

"It's a bitch working at an angle all the time," Mike added, but they went about their work anyway. After breaching the first wall we could level out and go straight for the outer wall some eighteen feet away.

The plan for "the dig" was working flawlessly. It was a simple, almost comical process. There was a digger and a back-up man: one in the tunnel, one on the outside to retrieve the plastic tray loaded with dirt. Mike had bored two small holes at either end of the plastic tray. The clothesline had been cut in two and a small snap shackle was tied to the end of each line that could quickly be attached and unattached to the small holes of the plastic tray. One end of the line was for the digger, one for the back-up man. The digger would take a screwdriver, ping-pong paddle, and the end of a rope, as well as well as a flashlight and the plastic tray into the tunnel. Once at the worksite, the digger hauled the tray in alongside him near his belly. Breaking the dirt free, he then filled the tray half full, using the paddle as a scoop. When he was ready, he tugged on the back-up line to let the back-up man know he wanted the tray emptied. Hauling the line in, the back-up man unclipped the two lines and carefully lifted the tray, then emptied the soil into an awaiting box. Re-clipping the lines, he tugged the digger's line to let him know to haul the tray back.

Patrick had the whole process down pat when he was doing backup, by tying the tug line to his big toe. This way he could sit and read while working. The first time I saw him doing it, I laughed, then found myself doing the same thing later.

They'd also put together a special work uniform, an old pair of pants and T-shirts. It was quite warm down inside Mother Earth, but it was also damp and muddy. We would often smuggle the muddy pants and T-shirt into the showers and wash them.

The cardboard boxes we had been putting the dirt in were approaching full. All of us decided that in a day or two, we'd have to resort to using Patrick's *caraca*.

All was going well. Our group was functioning as we had intended. Bill and I would soon join in on the dig. Meanwhile, the four of them were making progress.

If there was one thing we knew for sure, problems would arise. Life was full of surprises; we just had to be ready. That was all. Never give in, no matter how insurmountable the problem seemed.

Six days later we had our first problem, though it was only a rumor. Mike got wind of it and called for a meeting. We were full of anxiety when he told us, "I just heard from two different sources that there's going to be a breakout over in the *Grande* tomorrow."

Back in mid-August, just before Sarah had come to visit, a battle between rival Mexican drug dealers inside the *Grande* had broken out. Armando told us about the warring parties one evening just after a prisoner had been sent over to *Correctionalis* to quell the uprising.

The prisoner's name was Piñata. He was an especially big man for a Mexican. He was six-foot-two, muscular and weighed over two hundred pounds. With thick, black, curly hair and a well-trimmed *bigote*, he epitomized "macho."

Armando moved Piñata into his *caraca* the day he arrived. When we asked who the man was, Armando explained the skirmish in the *Grande* and gave us warning: "The other dealers, they try to kill this man. He is a big dealer of drugs. They try to take his business away. The *Alciadia* send him here for protection."

"From the looks of it, he sure doesn't need protection." I said. "He's not only big, he's powerful."

"*Si*. I know this man, maybe two years. He is very brave. Any man who give him trouble know he has '*grande huevos*'."

"I agree, Armando. This man Piñata, he is a bull. I don't know him, but I respect him. He looks fearless," I acknowledged.

As we stood in the courtyard a few feet away from Piñata, Armando smiled respectfully and added, "You get to know him. He is a friendly man. He likes the *gringos*. Come, I will have you meet him."

Even though there was a language barrier, I had gotten to know Piñata. We'd say hello, and greeted one another in a very friendly manner. Before long, I felt comfortable around him.

When Sarah came down a few days later, I pointed Piñata out to her the first evening and told her what I knew about him.

"He's really good looking and he does have strong charisma," she observed.

"He's friendly too. Why don't we invite him to eat with us this evening? I'd like to get to know him. I can tell he wants to get to know us, but he doesn't speak a word of English. If you and Inger could interpret, that would break the ice."

"I think it's a great idea." Sarah seemed amused.

We went to Piñata, who stood leaning against the south wall talking with an inmate. When I introduced Sarah, they immediately started conversing in Spanish.

"He's accepted our invite," Sarah said as she turned to me. "What time and where?"

"Bill's *caraca*. Right after *lista*."

Inger was delighted when she heard about the plan. Bill was a bit put off, but went along anyway.

When Piñata entered the *caraca*, Bill and I had to be patient. Sarah and Inger talked with him almost exclusively. I had to butt in to ask questions, and was beginning to wonder if I had made a mistake by inviting him. Piñata, from the start, was courteous and very much in control. This was his nature and it put me on edge, but I was also pulled in by his composure.

"He's never been married," Inger gushed, her smile was as broad as

I've ever seen it. Bill quietly hid behind his jealousy as his wife flirted.

What impressed me about Piñata was his poise; he used it well by playing indifferent to all the attention the two women gave him. If Bill and I weren't around, I believe they'd have seduced him. Piñata surely must have sensed this, yet he remained respectful and never for a second indicated these two women were attracted to him.

When they asked the big question, "Why aren't you married?" Piñata's answer slayed all of us, at least, it did the women. They gushed with merriment, and the conversation got so completely one-sided I had to interrupt and ask what the hell they were talking about. I got the marriage part, but not much else, only that the girls were beside themselves. I had to admit his reply was first-class.

"I love the American women. They have more freedoms. Mexican woman, they are too frigid and without liberties. In our country, the people are very religious. To the husband, wives are just there to make many babies. They do not know love the way I like them to. Someday I will go to the United States and find many women. But first I must learn to speak English."

Sarah and Inger assured him he would have great success once he had learned English. Then they reproached him for not having learned already. He smiled and they batted their eyes as he let them know that in two years he would go to Los Angeles to live with family and learn to speak English.

A few weeks later, Piñata was sent back to the *Grande*. We hadn't seen him since.

Ted, the American prisoner we had met the first day in jail, was the second person to tell us of the possible breakout. He too had been sent to *Correctionalis* for drug related incidents. He had subsequently become one of the South Wall Boys.

Ted, a low-lifer and a nosey turd, was not to be trusted. Dirk had told him to stay away from us. So far he had, but he'd often stop us in the yard and try to bullshit awhile. We'd have rather avoided him altogether, but he was privy to lots of useful information.

To determine the validity of the rumor, we invited him into my *caraca* for a short talk. His tale matched the one Mike had received from his friend Martin not more than an hour before. Although their facts were sketchy, we figured there was some truth to what the two men said. They had heard that two pistols had been smuggled into the *Grande* recently. Whoever had them was going to incite a massive breakout, tomorrow or the day after.

"They're going to overpower the guards, take their weapons, and force them to unlock the gates," Ted told us with a straight face.

"All the gates, even *Correctionalis*?" Mike asked.

"Yeah. Right to the front gate. They're gonna empty the fuckin' prison, man. That's what I heard."

"That's what Martin told me," Mike said, "that there were guns and the prison would be emptied."

I was vexed. "This could be real or it's a bunch of crap, guys."

"No matter what, we have to take it seriously," Bill directed. "Do you know what time of day they're going to do this?"

"Right before *lista* tomorrow."

We dismissed Ted. This news troubled us. No one needed to tell us what would happen if there were a breakout, or even an attempted breakout. We decided to put our tunnel work on hold until the rumor blew over.

Mike and Dirk planned to put the top back in place and once again use flour and water to conceal the cracks. The boxes full of dirt were monumental problems. All we could think to do was put clothes on top of the boxes to forestall anyone from opening them. We decided to burn incense to mask the earthen smell.

Although I was restless, I did manage to sleep that evening. As for the others, the look in their eyes the next morning told the story. We were all on edge. I tried to write Sarah, but lost focus. Reading didn't help much either. Mike tried to get more news, but came up empty. We just hung out and waited for the inevitable to happen.

About five in the evening we donned pants and shirts, just in case. It had been a long day: minutes felt like hours.

Around 5:30 p.m., tensions inside the yard increased as the hour of doom neared. We left our *caracas* and stood out front in two separate groups. The *quincados*, having just eaten their evening meal, were still mostly sitting around.

Nearly inaudible, sounds of gunshots coming from the *Grande* could be heard in the distance. They sounded like distant pops or fire-crackers, certainly not from the gate leading into the *Grande*, which was no more than fifty feet away from us. Every regular prisoner in the yard, including us, went into full alert.

The shots ceased, followed by a moment of stark silence. Then there was a distinct clamor as the regulars bolted for the entry gate to *Correctionalis* like sharks in a feeding frenzy. We stood back pensively.

Dirk worked his way into the crowd from the right side and was able to see the corridor. He hollered back information to us through the mob at the gate, who were yelling and screaming at the lone guard. Dirk relayed that the *Alciadia* and other officials had come running up the hallway and entered into the *Grande*. At the same moment, the lone guard at the gate came back and yelled at the pack of sharks at the gate to move back and be quiet. The lone guard held his ground until they dispersed.

We also backed away. Fred said, "What a fizzle."

Doubting anyone had gained their freedom, the six of us gathered inside my *caraca*. Whatever had happened in the *Grande* only moments before was history. "Boy, that was a bunch of crap," Bill said with a goofy smirk on his face.

All of us agreed.

Solemn for a moment, Mike broke the ice with another comment.

"Something happened, guys. This doesn't look good."

"You can say that again. How many shots did you guys hear?" I asked.

"Four, maybe five and they weren't very loud," Dirk offered, a wry look on his face.

"Yeah. They weren't anywhere near the gate to the *Grande*," Patrick added.

"It was a botched attempt," Bill concluded.

"I don't agree," Dirk said. "Something big went down. You heard the shots. Even if the attempt failed, they're gonna shake this place down tomorrow for sure."

"You can bet on it," I added. The feeling of defeat deepened around us.

"Well, there's nothing we can do to stop them," Bill said, his grin now gone.

Ready to problem-solve Mike said, "Any suggestions?"

"Yeah. Let's have a tunnel-filling party," I said, attempting to add humor. "It's the only way to hide the dirt."

"Yeah, the dirt," Dirk mused grimly. "They'll find the fucking dirt."

"Let's see if we can get more information," Fred offered.

Lista came late that evening: the officials entered about 7:30 p.m. They wore long faces as they ran us through roll call twice.

Mike went in search of information, but it wasn't until later that evening that Martin had news for him: it was startling, and Mike assured us *Martin* was always in the know, and never lied to him.

Mike said, "He told me several men escaped. He doesn't know how many, only that they went over the far wall in the *Grande.*"

"That's hard to believe, man. Real hard," I commented, as he talked to Bill and me in Bill's *caraca.*

"Could be more Mexican bullshit," Bill added sarcastically.

"I'm going back to my *caraca*," Mike said wearily. "I'll do all I can to doctor up the cracks in the top and hide the dirt better."

I headed back to my quarters, alone with my thoughts. I figured the officials would come in first thing in the morning and search the *Grande*, then *Correctionalis*. We'd be found out and life would really be the shits for a long while. No telling what they'd do to punish us.

As I attempted to settle down for the night, I rolled up a joint. "Might as well as smoke it all up now. Fuck, just what we didn't need—an escape by the guys in the *Grande*. And now once they find us out, we'll more than likely be put in the Hole. What else?" They had no choice but to make a complete inspection of the entire prison. "Might as well get up a card game," I said out loud. "It may be the last one here in *Correctionalis* for us, at any rate."

The next morning, the first surprise was the faces of the men who came in to call *lista*. They were new and they ran us through twice, as had been done the night before. But the big surprise was that the goon-squad had not come in with them.

Fred and Mike, who had gotten up early, had more information. Inside my *caraca* they told me the goon-squad had entered the *Grande* earlier that morning: six to seven federals, along with the new officials. There was more news.

"I ordered a paper. Look at this, man." From inside his shirt Mike pulled out a copy of the local paper, *Notica De El Sol.*

"What's it say?" I asked, looking over his shoulder as he spread out the front page.

"Listen to this. *Grand escape from public caracel in Colony Juarez! Thirty-one escape over the wall!"*

"Thirty-one escape!" I repeated. "Unbelievable, man."

He continued. "Twenty-two federal prisoners and nine state, one American, went over the wall... none have been captured. The local district attorney, Señor Coppala, is investigating the matter... the *Alciadia* and four guards are being held in jail."

"Too much, man. This is crazy. Why didn't they search us this morning?" My head was spinning.

"Maybe they'll come in at *lista* this evening," Mike mentioned.

"Or tomorrow morning," Fred suggested. "Sooner or later they'll show up."

"Let's get more info if we can," I suggested. "We've got a lot to consider. I'll let Bill know what's happening. How do things look with the top, Mike?"

"Great, same with the dirt. I'll go find Martin and see if he knows anything more. We can talk with Armando when he comes up at noon."

"Yeah. For sure. Let's order some breakfast. I don't feel like cooking right now," I said sullenly.

Who could have figured that thirty-one men would make good their escape? The question was soon put to rest when Mike came back with some valuable information. We were always searching for answers and had to rely on numerous sources to get it. Thought it was early, I felt like playing a game of cards to pass time while information was gathered.

Piñata, Mike informed us, had masterminded the entire escape. His plan had been extraordinarily simple. The two .22 caliber pistols smuggled in had been instrumental. We guessed they had been successfully smuggled in by dismantling them and having been brought in by woman visitors, concealed in their private orifices.

Two wooden planks had also been instrumental. One was placed against the west wall to be used as a ladder; the other placed across the outer wall. Piñata, we heard, climbed first. Using one of the pistols, he caught the lone guard by surprise. He coerced the guard to drop his rifle and forced the man to take the second plank and place it across the fourteen-foot expanse to the outer wall. Once the bridge to freedom was constructed, the prisoners began filing across. Thirty-one, all told.

How had the inmates gotten the planks into the prison? The officials must have allowed them in to be used for some sort of construction project the inmates had pitched for.

As for the men who manned the two guard stations—one on the west wall and one on the north wall—Piñata must have waited for them to be out of sight of one another for a few seconds as they patrolled the catwalks.

Piñata and his men, aware of the patrol flaw, only had to wait for the right moment. During the brief lapse, thirty-one men flew over the wall. The shots we had heard had come from the second guard. Having spotted the men escaping, he could only fire warning shots to thwart more prisoners from escaping. During a previous escape attempt, a guard had fired into the crowd wounding an innocent bystander. Their orders as a result were no shooting once the prisoners were on the street.

Piñata probably had a car waiting for him. As for the others, we could only assume the taxicabs near the town center in Colony Juarez must have had a sudden rush of business around 5:30 p.m. that evening.

Piñata had gained his freedom, but in doing so, had jeopardized ours. Nearly ten percent of the prisoners in the *Grande* had gotten out of the yard that day. Essentially, the "emptying of the prison" was the prisoners' answer to correct the gross, inhuman conditions in which they had been forced to live.

The consensus among us was that it was not the public's answer. No way. No community would easily tolerate such a gross mishandling. Their jails were unsafe and there would be a public outcry. They'd want a thorough investigation: what happened and how could it be prevented?

The *Alciadia,* whom we learned was being held in jail along with four guards, would be only one focus of Señor Coppola's investigation. In fact, he too would be questioned, and on down the line until all those responsible were held accountable for the escape. However, this was Mexico. There was no telling what might happen, or how far the investigation would go.

We did know this: the prison now had a new *Alciadia*. An army Colonel was due in any day, Armando told us. We could only speculate he'd be highly motivated to do his job well, especially in the wake of his predecessor's actions. We were certain a major search would take place shortly, not only in the *Grande*, but in *Correctionalis*. We guessed the new *Alciadia* would want to turn the prison inside out to see if there were more pranksters up to no good (like us). He might even try to reform the prison entirely, perhaps by eliminating visiting days altogether.

We discussed every detail as it arose and concluded we were about to be discovered.

The following morning came another surprise: no search at morning *lista*. Once again Mike and Fred had gotten up early. I had joined them that time and was there to witness the goon-squad enter the *Grande*. But they never came into *Correctionalis*. We couldn't believe it. Come noontime, we were still incredulous.

We soon got word that the new *Alciadia* had participated in the search. We also learned that all thirty-one prisoners were still on the loose. Señor Coppola had to be furious. If he had an ounce of revenge in him, he'd order the new *Alciadia* to make a complete search of the entire jail, maybe even participate himself.

On the morning of the third day after the escape our guessing would change. We expected the worst at morning *lista*, but nothing happened.

What gives? Our tension was turning into curiosity. Come noon, we made a decision. We'd wait one more day. The new *Alciadia* might just be playing some sort of twisted game and planned to hit us the following morning. If not, maybe they had no intention of inspecting *Correctionalis*, though it seemed inconceivable.

On the morning of the fourth day, our waiting period was over. We all agreed it was time to reopen the tunnel and dig our way out of there ASAP. Attempting to out-think the authorities for the preceding several days had been draining, but we had won out. There had been no major incidents in *Correctionalis* for the preceding several months. Maybe they felt there was no reason to inspect our sector. Armando might have informed the new *Alciadia* that the inmates in his sector were well behaved, including us *gringos*.

Our decision made, Mike and Dirk went to work. Patrick and Fred were to follow. Bill and I would back them up and remain on call to take messages and watch for unusual activities. Señor Pedro, having just had the yard washed, set off for his next chore. As I stood yard-duty, around ten, Armando came through the gate and headed straight towards me.

"He's never here at this hour," I thought, as he approached. I was reading and got up off the small bench near the water basin to greet him.

"*Capitano*," he said formally, "I have bad news for the *gringos* in *Correctionalis*."

My body tensed, but I asked as calmly as I could, "What's the news, Armando?"

"The new *Alciadia*, he say this to his men and I hear that they move you over to the *Grande* very soon."

"God, really? Boy that would be terrible." I felt a wave of hysteria, making it difficult to project calm.

"*Si*. It is sad. But I am afraid they do this to you. I know you like to be here." He put on a sad face and stared directly into my eyes.

We were standing right in front of Bill's *caraca*. He spotted us, and sensing trouble, came out to see what was up. As Armando told Bill about the problem, I slipped away and rapped on Mike's door. I could see Patrick and Fred, but not Dirk.

"Is Dirk working?" I said in a hushed voice as I entered.

"Yes. What's up?"

"Plenty. Come on out and talk with Armando. Be cool. He says the *Alciadia* is thinking of moving us over to the *Grande*."

The shaken look on their faces reflected the same fear I was feeling. Leaving Dirk in the tunnel, we filed out and marched up to Bill and Armando.

"Please do not worry," Armando said addressing all of us. "I will talk to this new *Alciadia*. He is a very good man. I tell him you are good boys. This will help. I tell him you don't wish to go to the *Grande*. I know this will hurt you. It may take some money. It is necessary. I will go now to the *oficina* and find out for you. I will come back soon."

Patting Bill on the shoulder he departed, leaving the five of us standing there in complete dismay.

"Probably just extortion," Bill said with a hint of sarcasm, though his face was ashen.

"Maybe not. This could be for real," I answered, the rest nodding.

Mike added, "Probably both. Armando's getting out and he's up to his games."

"Yeah. Let's hope it's his last prank," Bill said. "Either way we're going to need some money. We're screwed if they move us."

"Shit, let's hope they don't want too much," I added. "Boy, what a gut-drencher. This sucks."

"Lets hope he's successful." Fred added.

Maybe Armando was acting on his own authority and the new *Alciadia* knew nothing about Armando's money schemes. Armando was scheduled to leave in a few days, and maybe he wanted more than just bus fare home. Either way, all of us were caught in the dilemma. If the *Alciadia* moved us, it would put an end to our escape attempt, plus our plans would be discovered. We'd lose our box-seats and all our possessions, plus be thrown in the Hole for up to a month. The others headed back to work and I was left alone with my thoughts as I resumed my post on the bench. I attempted to read, but the next two hours were excruciating.

Armando returned around noon so I fetched the others as Bill conversed with him.

"I have good news *hombres*," he said as we gathered around him. This time, Dirk, who was on edge, joined the group. "I tell the *Alciadia* you are good men. He will let you stay here. I need two hundred pesos from each man."

As we reached in our pockets and forked over the money, our tension receded. Joe, who had joined us in the courtyard, quipped, "Be sure to give the new *Alciadia* our best regards."

Armando winked at him and replied with his most sincere tone, "I will do that for you. Good day to you, *amigos.*"

Without saying another word, he pocketed the fourteen hundred pesos, turned, and headed off. A collective sigh of relief could be heard as he disappeared beyond the barred gate.

"Like taking candy from a kid," Bill mused. "But this time it wasn't much."

Joe drifted back to his *caraca* as Mike said, "Boy that was cheap. I figured it would be more like a hundred bucks each."

"Yeah. They're slipping," Dirk said snidely.

"You just can't figure 'em out," Fred grinned.

"Who wants to?" I replied coldly.

"Let's get going," Dirk encouraged. "I wanna get some work done while these guys count our loot."

CHAPTER TWENTY-EIGHT

FORGIVE THE TYRANTS

MAZATLAN, MEXICO
DECEMBER, 1971

Despite the problems, we were holding up. The pressure, however, remained a constant. We did what we had to do. The goal was still to be out by Christmas. The six-day delay had thrown our schedule off and we still feared *Correctionalis* would be searched, especially during the holidays. The consensus: we'd rather go down fighting right in the process of digging the tunnel rather than close it down. Our desire and our will for freedom was that strong.

Buoyed by the successful escape of the thirty-one inmates, and having conquered other obstacles that had slowed us, we began to operate in a more fluid manner. No one got out of line or condescended to others. We just did our jobs and helped the next guy by making ourselves available, no matter what the situation. Most matters went smoothly. Nonetheless, I ran into a most unusual situation.

Two days after the reopening the tunnel, the four-man work crew started getting tired. They asked Bill and me to join in on the dig. Donning the pants and shirt that afternoon, I received instructions from Patrick, who'd be backing me up. Entering the hole with the equipment, I shivered. Dirk had just finished showering. The pants and shirt he had handed over were quite wet. Descending into the portal, I crawled backwards toward the turn junction. Rotating around, I shined the flashlight on the work area. As I checked out the entire area, the first bit of apprehension hit me. It was the willies, I told myself. It was only natural. Just get to work and put negative thoughts out of mind's way.

I checked the walls of the tunnel and they seemed stable. The soil, mostly shale, was compact yet moist. The chance of a cave-in was highly improbable. Even so, I felt uncomfortable as I set about working. Crawling to the end of the tunnel, my body was at a slight downhill angle. Pulling the tray into position, I shone the flashlight on the main foundation, my head directly under its massive presence, the far end lying hidden another six inches from being breached.

Shining the light on my work, I stuck the screwdriver into the soil. The tightly packed dirt was surprisingly easy to remove and in a few minutes the tray was half-full. I signaled Patrick. The tray disappeared as he drew it toward him. I kept working the loose soil, concentrating on breathing to offset the strange foreboding anxiety I felt. The tray back in place, I quickly filled it to half-full, and once again tugged the line to signal Patrick. Twisting my body sideways to be more comfortable, I kept a feverish pace going as I worked.

I was scheduled to work two hours in that position, but after only thirty minutes I was sweating profusely. The once cold garments now clung to my body. I filled the tray again and signaled Patrick.

It comforted me to know that Patrick was up there helping, but I soon slowed my efforts to a crawl and began in earnest to breathe deeply, trying to offset the strain on my psyche. I kept thinking, "Just do as the others do, and endure the pressure." But the thought was of little comfort. "Work, dig the soil loose, and put it into the tray; never mind the eerie conditions. Just keep busy. Soon the two hours will pass and you'd have done a good turn, like them," I told myself. It was all rather simple.

Then again it wasn't. Queasiness began to take over. My thoughts ran wild. Muscles went tense. I was fatigued and confused. Filling a tray and sending it off took great effort. Panic and exhaustion were winning.

"Breathe, man, breathe. Don't make this hard. Do not let these absurd feelings gain control."

The tray back in place, breaking soil loose became almost impossible. Something was forsaking me. My energy drained. Lifting an arm was an effort. All the positive imagery that had been used dried up. Head swirling, I gave hope to stilling my fears. Instead, my fears took over. I was fragile and full of remorse. I realized my body and mind were shutting down. I lost all willpower. "Rest this body. Let go of the anxiety," I told myself.

But it did no good. I had no antidote. I fell back in a heap, unable to comprehend what was happening. Then I heard what sounded like a big *whamp*. "Could the tunnel have caved in?" I had lost all control.

Shining the flashlight back toward the entry, I saw a huge pile of dirt lying there, blocking the tunnel. With no way to exit, fear and panic seized me. I cried out to Patrick as softly as I could and pulled on the tow-rope, my head falling back and my eyes closing as I waited for him to reply.

"What's up, Frank?" His voice, clear and calm, brought relief. "Are you okay?"

Eyes still closed, I said in a hushed tune, "The tunnel—it's caved in."

The shine of his flashlight in the entry way was a welcome sight. Rising up, I shone mine in his direction. "No it hasn't. Not that I can see. You're fine."

Staring in disbelief, I could see that everything was fine. I was going insane.

"I got to get out of here, man. I got to get out." Without hesitating, I began the backward crawl. Making the turn at the toilets, I raced for the entrance. I rolled over, pushed up, and Dirk grabbed me by the shoulders. Sitting on the edge of the concrete floor, my feet still in the opening, body covered in sweat, all I could do was pant. Finally, out of harm's way, the cool fresh air began to revive me.

Head bent, I panted, "God, I don't know what came over me. I thought I heard the tunnel collapse. When Patrick shined his light in, I saw that it hadn't. This is weird, guys. I don't think I can handle this. I'm sorry." Shaking my head, I looked over at Patrick, then at Dirk.

"It's okay. Don't worry about it," Dirk said sincerely.

"I can't do it any more. It's too intense."

Dirk handed me a small towel. As I wiped sweat away, I realized I'd been sweating so badly my hair was plastered to my head.

"Hey, some people just weren't meant to get into holes and dig," Dirk added, above the sound of his boombox pumping out a Cat Stevens song. "Come on. I'll help you up."

I staggered toward the cot, light-headed and still breathing erratically. Resting on its edge, I looked up at them again, shrouded in guilt. "I'll pull extra time as back-up man, guys."

"Fine. That's good," Dirk consoled me. "We can use the help. Come on. Move around. Take a shower. Wash the clothes off. Patrick will take a two-hour shift."

"I'll take his place and back him up while he digs," I volunteered right away.

"Fine. Someone has to. Hey, it's okay, man. We'll get the digging done." Standing over me, Dirk appeared enormous. "Come on. Get out of those clothes."

Quickly and quietly, I undressed. Patrick put the clothes on and entered the tunnel. Still in a daze, I decided that no amount of guilt was going to stop me from doing all I could do to help these guys. I stayed there the entire two hours helping Patrick while Dirk quietly read. Because I felt the guys genuinely understood my situation, I let go of my shame. Not everybody was capable of digging underground tunnels. Fortunately, we had four good diggers. Finishing around four that afternoon, I headed for the *caraca* to rest.

Bill took the next shift, but had a peculiar problem himself. He came out of the hole after a while with a badly swollen right hand. When he showed it to me just after *lista*, I thought it looked terrible. Something in the soil must have caused a reaction from a cut he had sustained. As soon as the swelling went down, he'd give the work another shot, he vowed. The swelling diminishing a couple of days later, but he didn't bother to return as a digger. Neither of us could handle the work. Embarrassed, neither of us talked about the matter. Staying as the gatekeeper, he was to collect our mail as usual and monitor the yard.

Mike and Dirk's *caraca* was full to the limit; the entire section underneath of both cots was lined with dirt filled boxes. Owning all four *caracas* made the next chore relatively simple. The four structures had a continuous run of corrugated plastic atop them, set in at an angle. By making use of an eighteen-inch opening at the end along the wall, we could pass the small dirt tray to Patrick's *caraca*. All that was needed was an extra person to sit in his place to receive it. That gave me plenty of work to do. Over the next several days, I'd either be receiving in Patrick's *caraca* or over at Mike and Dirk's, passing the tray to whoever was on duty.

Even though Bill and I were unavailable for digging, the crew didn't falter with its work routine. Each day they made a foot or more of progress. And each day, we found ourselves caught in a paradox: we were euphoric as we made progress, but we would sink at the thought that the Storm Troopers might raid us any day. And every time the crew descended the tunnel I shuddered. How could they keep going without it bothering them? But they just kept taking turns without complaining. Inspired by their efforts, I tried to support them as much as possible.

※ ※ ※

Mid-December rolled around. Inger sent a message to Bill one afternoon that Michael and Penelope had called. She had told them of our progress and that we sorely needed them to come help us. They'd promised to come within a few days, Bill told us with a broad grin. Their timing had been perfect, to say the least. It was the good news we needed. Our collective energy rose up several notches for the next two days.

Then the unexpected happened. It was a stomach-turner. No one, but no one, was quite able to handle the sudden problem—not even the stalwarts, who had managed to dig clear of the main wall and were on level ground, some four to five feet beyond the main foundation.

Mike came over to my *caraca* right after morning *lista* to inform me that we had a peculiar problem. Heading to his *caraca*, he lifted off the cement top and said, "Smell for yourself," with a queer look on his face. I got down on my knees and preparing to look in, I was greeted by a stench so nauseating I wanted to vomit. Shining the flashlight in and extending my head, I saw the problem: on the dirt floor of our tunnel laid a good-sized pile of human feces directly below the toilet pipe.

Springing up, I exclaimed in a hushed tone, "Wow, that's bad. God, you're right! That's more than just a problem. Jesus! Someone's going to have to put that piece of pipe back into place and clean up that shit."

Defeated, Mike agreed. "No doubt about it. The wedge worked loose. I should have checked it." The piece of pipe he had broken loose some weeks back had come loose and had fallen to the ground below.

Patrick, who was standing off to the side added, "There's lots of shit down there."

"And it's piling up," Dirk quickly cut in. "Someone's got to go in and put the piece of pipe back in. How about you, Frank?"

"And clean up the shit?" I queried. A queasy feeling streaked through me. "I don't think so. Let's talk about this."

All of us looked at one another. Nothing was said. Not a soul volunteered. This was the *quincado's* toilet. The piece of broken pipe was causing the *quincados'* shit to wash down onto the floor of our tunnel. The pile of unwanted turds was sure to grow over the next few hours.

I asked, "Does Fred know about this problem?"

"Yes. He doesn't want to touch it," Mike answered, then remained quiet.

One of the six of us had to face this, or a team of two men. There was room for two at a time at the turning juncture just under the shitter, where the problem lay. Suddenly I had a possible solution. At first it seemed crazy then it became clear. "How about asking Ted?" I proposed.

"Ted Grayson!" Dirk looked at me in disbelief. "That junkie know-it-all?"

"Yeah! Why not? Do any of you have a better suggestion?" I looked around for approval.

"Ted, the sore spot. Why not have him fix our sore spot?" Fred, who had just entered, quipped.

We chuckled. Our minds were racing. Dirk was still frowning; we knew he found Ted distasteful.

Mike joined in. "Well, we know it's a job none of us want to consider. And we're running out of time. We have to come to a decision soon, like right now."

"We agreed not to tell him about the project," Dirk stated firmly.

"The guy's everywhere," Patrick countered. "Sooner or later he'll find out about what we're up to."

"I agree," Mike said, eyes beaming. "He may seem unreliable, but if we offer him a deal, maybe he won't be."

"Why not?" asked Fred. "He wants out like anyone else. He's got a long time to go yet and none of us are willing to clean up this mess."

"That's what I figure, guys. He wants out. Think of it this way, Dirk," I said as I turned and addressed him with a grin on my face. "The job is well suited for him."

We laughed a moment and Dirk added, "Maybe so, but I don't want him around here afterwards."

"Hey, let's just see if he'll do it, pal," Mike said, relieved that we had a possible solution.

"Who wants to go get him?" I asked.

In no time, Mike came back with Ted, who was quite surprised when we all greeted him in a friendly manner. We had placed the top back on and given Mike the honor of presenting the deal to him.

"Ted, how much time do you have in here?"

Suspiciously, Ted looked us up and down. "Three years, plus. Hey, what's up? You guys going to dig a tunnel, man?"

"Yes. How'd you like to help us?" Mike continued.

"Hey, you know I dig tunnels. Count me in. I can dig for hours. Have ya started yet?" He looked around the room, eager to get going.

"Let's say we may be out of here around Christmas time," Mike answered.

"That is, if there are no inspections and we keep this to ourselves," I added.

"No shit. Hey, I'll be cool. Really. Mum's the word. I'll dig three, four hours a day. No problem. Just let me know when and where. This is great, man. Great." He checked us out again, grinning like a lunatic.

"We don't need you to dig, Ted," Mike said, looking serious. "We have a special project for you, just one favor. You do it and you'll go free with us. We ask nothing else."

"Remember," Dirk wagged his finger, "do this one job, no questions asked, and you're out of here with us. We'll take care of the digging."

"The job we're going to ask you to do will take most of the day, no more," I added to the mix.

"Yes. A day's work for your freedom," Mike reminded him.

Ted was no dummy. He knew something was up and had a puzzled look. "Fine, a day's worth of work. I can handle that. What's involved? It can't be too bad."

"You're committed then?" Dirk asked, grinding out a commitment.

"Yeah. What's the big deal, guys?"

Patrick and I headed out as Mike and Dirk acquainted Ted with the "big deal." Within an hour I got word that Ted was indeed in the tunnel, doing the job that none of us wanted. Within a few hours, Ted finished, having used a small aluminum pan to pour the shit back down the pipe.

By evening *lista*, we were all smiles. Ted had done a great job. The shit was gone, and our tunnel no longer smelled putrid. The piece of pipe had been put back in place with a rag tied around it so there'd be no more repeats. Ted was as happy as a pig in shit, and promised to keep us informed of anything that we might want to know. Ted, the seventh member of our club, was an added pressure, considering he had an insatiable desire to blab.

Dirk told him straight out, "Tell no one. You'll answer to me if you do."

Some of us gained a renewed respect for Ted as he hit the yard, not flapping his jaw as usual. We had no choice but to believe that he'd stick to his word.

Progress on the tunnel was steady but slow. We held a meeting in my *caraca* on the December 18 to make some decisions. From the beginning, we had calculated digging about thirty-five feet of tunnel. Mike measured the tunnel with a length of clothesline and announced we were twenty-two feet into the dig. We were now less than fifteen feet from our escape. Christmas was one week away. We'd have to remove two feet of dirt a day if we wanted out by then. The diggers were averaging a little better than a foot a day. Dirk and Mike wanted to spearhead a night crew. If we were lucky, and there were no more delays, we'd be out of there by December 25, according to Dirk and Mike's calculations.

Bill, who originally had been against night work, came around. Using Dirk's boombox to muffle the sound, the nightshift began.

That was when Dirk really took over. Though quiet and moody at times, Dirk flat-out worked. His dedication motivated the rest of the diggers and the crew started making a good two feet a day. Everything was falling into place. It was getting down to "when," not "if." The diggers' work ethic inspired the whole group. Each foot of progress marked a new high. Then we'd hit a low spot, though less frequently than before. We just needed to get in the "zone."

Bill and I hardly talked, but we treated each other respectfully during that period of uncommon unity. The crew and I still played a few card games to relieve tension and also to give the illusion of "routine." But there were days when work was non-stop, everyone in good form. Dirk usually started things off with the morning dig.

On the evening of the fourth nightshift, Dirk dug for over three hours. Mike finally sent him a note in the tray that said, "Get your ass out here. It's my turn." Emerging with a grin, Dirk was elated.

All of us were.

Withstanding pressure was now a group activity. Over the next few days, the weather turned nice: fair and warm days, and cool nights with clear skies. The *Correctionalis* population, which had peaked at two hundred, was now lower, but still our sector was over-packed. It all seemed so normal to us now. As for the Americans who showed up from time to time, we knew how to handle them now. That became Bill's territory, or anyone who was available to hold hands and keep them away from the *caraca* at the end of the row. We all worked as a unit. Each crew member was an extension of the next guy—deep feelings lay just under the surface, though no one talked about them, especially me. I marveled at what we had accomplished through solidarity.

By the twenty-first of December, *Correctionalis* had assumed a different look. Lupe and the gay troopers spent hours decorating for the holidays. The south wall was now covered with *Navidad* scenes, the concrete pilasters surrounding the yard were wrapped with red and green crepe paper, and small colorful piñatas hung from the corrugated awnings. Suddenly it was Christmas and the mood of *Correctionalis* was festive. Inmates smiled more and the new officials relaxed a bit.

With *Navidad* around the corner, I was filled with the spirit of love and giving. Knowing I'd soon leave friends behind saddened me. I would miss Joe, a man too big to fit down the entry of our tunnel. He'd have to be left behind, as would many others. If we'd had our way, we'd have found a way to let everyone out with us. But we simply could not do it. Fred, Patrick, and I talked about leaving others behind. We had our regrets, but we agreed unanimously that keeping our number to seven would give us our best shot at success.

Michael, Penelope, and Peggy had arrived. It was a happy moment when we greeted them with hugs. They congratulated us on our achievements and brought with them fresh foods and an assortment of ideas as to how to go about picking us up the night we were to exit. Heading over with Peggy to see the crew I said to her as we entered, "Hug 'em good, Peggy. These guys are the men who are making this project happen."

"Come here, you hunks." She beamed them a big sexy smile and wrapped her arms around each of them. "I'm here to help and to entertain you guys, so let's get going."

She spent the better part of the day helping us unload the trays of dirt.

Meanwhile, huddling at Bill's *caraca*, he and Michael were discussing a new business plan.

They planned to be partners in yet another drug smuggling conspiracy. Bill had been in touch with a chemist who was willing to set up a lab. Bill planned to rent a safe house in Guadalajara, and once they were to set up they would begin extracting THC from cannabis to make hash-oil. Michael would be the transporter and salesman, while Bill would to be the kingpin on his end. I found their conversation annoying, so I left.

Needing solitude, I headed back to my *caraca* to rest. Overhearing Bill and Michael make plans for the future had jolted me. What annoyed me the most was they hadn't bothered to invite me in on the conspiracy. Just as well, I grumbled, still trying to make sense of my anger.

In all the years I'd been in this business—and the time spent as a student of "The Process"—I'd never been a fanatic. During the early days, I had studied the books of an Indian educator and guru by the name of Krishnamurti. His words rang in my mind: "I ask you not to follow me. Make use of your own creative energy."

Following this advice was harder than reading about it. Clearly, if I was angry by Bill and Michael's plans, I still wasn't freely following my own "creative energy." I didn't want to join them, but I still wanted to be invited—included. Life was indeed a test, and being resistant and petulant had landed me here. Now I was being challenged again. But digging our way to freedom flew in the face of being resistant. I was healing myself by letting my creative energy flow, no matter what the outcome

Bolting upright, I came to a decision, and with it, a letting go in my heart. Bill's choice to remain in the business was his alone. Even if he asked me to join him, I wouldn't. There was nothing more to prove to him anymore.

We made tremendous progress over the following two days. As I talked over the construction process with Mike, he let out his frustration.

"We should be at or near the outer wall," he declared that evening. "I can't tell if we're well under it and beyond it or if we've yet to reach the last main foundation."

Measuring and probing the tunnel proved fruitless.

"Then let's dig a small hole at the end of the tunnel and dig up 'til we get to the surface," I suggested

"Yeah. It's the only way, man," Mike agreed, as did Dirk.

The problem was that we were three feet beneath the surface. Still, we had to know.

We asked Inger to purchase two small mirrors. Mike was going to make a periscope.

Sarah arrived in Mazatlan Friday afternoon, along with her parents. The three of them had flown to La Paz, then taken a ferry to Mazatlan. Sunday morning, the twenty-fourth of December, she came for a visit bearing gifts of food and clothes.

Heading for my *caraca* she sat the gifts aside and turned to greet me. "Somehow, I think you won't need the clothes I bought you. At least not here." She beamed a smile and then laughed softly as we embraced, adding, "I've heard about everything, sweetheart."

"Good. How are your parents?"

"Fine. I'm in good hands, Beast. And I'm not upset you didn't tell me about the tunnel." Stroking my hair, she looked intently into my eyes as we clung to one another.

"But I have to admit, I hadn't expected this—the tunnel and how far along you are. It's magnificent. We've been talking about it ever since we arrived Friday afternoon. Everyone's excited and happy, especially my father, who sends his best...I'm beyond excited, buns. We know you're going to make it out. It's part of the plan for everyone who has a hand in building the tunnel. It's why I love you so much," she said, then looked about the *caraca*.

"Hmmm. I see you've upgraded. The amenities keep piling up. I like the wall piece, but you definitely have to do something about the bed, honey. That cot is going to break under pressure. Why don't we do something decadent and make love? If we break the cot you'll have even more reason to get out of here quickly."

"There's always the floor, deary. We can bang on that all we want. There's much more room. It's your choice; just remember I have work to do for the crew, visiting day or not."

"I understand. They'll just have to give you a break for now. Besides it's Christmas Eve and I've brought you more than one present."

Breaking free of our embrace, she backed up and held out her arms, smiling. "All you have to do is unwrap me."

Her warmth was what I needed the most. Anxieties and tensions that had held me in their clutches for three months were no longer present; Sarah was all that was real. We didn't care who heard our lovemaking. We roamed, pleased, and released. Our crumpled position on the small cot was no problem.

A short nap served as an interlude. I wanted to talk when we woke up. "Come, sit up, sweetheart. Let's get comfortable." Placing a pillow against the wall, I wrapped a blanket around her as I got back in the cot and sat cross-legged opposite her.

"What's up, honey?" she asked, gazing at me.

"Plenty, Sarah. Plenty. I have a lot to say and I want you to listen." I began stroking her thighs with both my hands.

"Umm. I'm listening, sweety. Just keep up the hand-play while you talk."

"Have I ever told you that you have terrific legs?"

"Umm, a couple of times."

"Yes, but never enough. Right?"

"Yes, never enough."

"Good, now I can get serious and tell you my plans, Miss Buns."

"Do both, Beast. Stroke me and talk to me about your serious plans," she grinned.

"I know we're going to make it out of here. At least, most of me believes we will go free, and for the past several days I've been pondering what I'd do once I'm free. That's part of it. The other part is, I've been thinking about why I ended up here in the first place. I've come to a very sound conclusion and I need to share it with you—things are starting to come clear."

"They always do, my man. Now tell me about all this serious stuff."

"Sure. Why not? I know you'll be listening, especially when I tell you that I'm just another man consumed by his past."

"No one needs to be consumed, dear."

"Then what else do you call it?"

"Reflections. You're simply making use of what you've experienced in life and you're reflecting on what you did."

She was right, I was reflecting. I sighed and said, "Truth is, I believed that I had to go on with this business, no matter what. Sometimes I'd blame others and sometimes I'd fall in to a victim state—even though I knew I was just as responsible as everyone else for what we did to ourselves and to one another."

Sighing deeply I continued. "I gained a lot of knowledge over the past few years and I want to keep on making use of it. That knowledge came at a great expense. I made money and lost it all, but look at all the experience I gained and will continue to gain—forever. That's the way I see things. I'm going to keep on processing the experiences, especially what happened to me in the past. To me, the past is there as a reservoir of information that I can use, and it will remind me that I was just as much a part of all the problems that came about, no matter if it was Jake or Bill or any of the others who were a part of our smuggling business. Every one of us got caught up in the way we think, and we let ourselves down because we didn't know how to love ourselves or to let love in—something like that. Anyhow, all of us self-destructed in our own way. Now I'm left to pick up all the pieces. What matters now is I have you. Now you're part of this melodrama, if I can call it that."

"You bet, buns. All of this has been a melodrama of passions and wits.

And the main character is caught up in a holy vendetta. Let it be, Frank. Be with me. You're being way too serious right now. Look to the future. We're soon going to be free of all of this."

"Yeah. Then we get to start a new drama series," I quipped, letting go of my seriousness.

"No cot, hun. I want a bed, a real big bed."

"Well, all things considered, I guess I'll just have to wise up. If I do, we'll surely get that bed. If this here protagonist doesn't get his lessons straight, we don't get the bed. Simple as that."

"The bed will come. You can bet on it."

"Great! Then you'll understand what I mean when I say that I want to create a reality for us that makes sense, like the way we make love."

"You said a mouthful, sweetheart. Go on. I like it." She smiled. My pulse raced. How could it not? She was a woman—and I loved her.

"Then let's be happy and feel strong about ourselves and what we do. Even if we make some mistakes down the line, we can adjust and know we'll find an answer to any problems that may face us. Life works this way. Right?"

"Right! Life works this way and we can work with it, for sure."

Sighing deeply again I added, "When Michael arrived yesterday, he and Bill started conspiring almost immediately. They're going to be partners. They want to make hash-oil."

"Really!" She chuckled, and then grinned in a goofy way.

"Yeah! No kidding." Now I was finding it hard to be serious.

"Hmmm. So what?" She leaned forward and grabbed me between the legs.

Removing her hand, I answered, "Yeah. So what. The 'so what' is that they didn't invite me to join them."

"Good. You've had worse things happen to you."

"Hey! Stop using my clichés."

"Now where was I? Ah…yes, the new conspiracy. At first I was angry and full of judgments."

"Get to the point. I know the rest. Give me credit."

"Fine! I turned it down, everything. Let 'em do what they want to do. The short of it is, I'm through with dope smuggling."

"That's another mouthful. And more than that, sweetheart, you've discovered something most men spend a life time looking for and never find."

"What's that?"

Smiling ear to ear, she replied, "*You can live beyond* money. We've talked about this before. Money is important and necessary, but don't get greedy."

"Yes. It doesn't have to be that way, but it often is."

"Perhaps you saw this when you lost the *New Mornin* on the reef, sweety."

"Exactly!" Racked by emotion, I added, "Every fiber of my being feels this, Sarah. I went against the plans I had made with you and myself. I self-destructed and destroyed our dream sweetheart, simply because I was being greedy instead of following my heart."

"Frank, your self-esteem was low, that's all."

"It was more than that. It has to do with my past, sugar."

"But your past is over with."

"Not by a long shot."

"No one needs to get stuck in their past, and I feel that's what you're doing. Let it go, Beast. Live for the future."

"God, I wish I could tell you I am, and that I'm only making use of the past to bring about a healthy future."

"Honey, I wish I agreed with you about this, but I don't."

Disappointed, I took a deep breath, yet I pressed on.

"Somehow I have to come to a resolution about why I ended up where I am. Understanding my past has everything to do with where I am now. And this is the very point I'm attempting to make to you here and now. Can you understand this? Tell me, sweetheart. This is important. Letting go isn't always easy."

"Then begin by believing in yourself. I do. You're the one I love. And I know you have lots of love for yourself and for me. I've got several dozen letters from you that prove this."

Exasperated, I remained quiet for a moment. "Several months ago I asked you to forgive me for what I did. Have you truly done that? Can you say this without a shadow of a doubt?"

"For the most part, yes." She averted her eyes for a second. "Like you say, letting go isn't always easy."

"Do you remember the fire you started on the boat on the way back from our cruise to Jualapa?"

The *New Mornin* had an alcohol stove that had to be primed before turning on the burner. Sarah had misjudged the priming sequence one evening and had turned the burner on full. Not paying attention, she had started one nasty fire. She called out to me, and I had had to use the extinguisher. It made one hell of a mess. I blew my top, hollered, and belittled her for being so stupid. I felt justified at first, then guilt set in later. Eventually the mess was mine to clean.

"How can I ever forget?" she said, suddenly emotional.

"Then let me apologize, sweetheart. I threw a lot of crap at you that day and I'm really sorry, Sarah, for ridiculing you. You made a mistake and I felt superior when you ran off crying. Now I'm asking that you forgive me once again."

Not to my surprise, her tears flowed. "Oh God, that was a horrid moment. I hated you for doing that." Looking into my eyes she added," But, I forgive you, Frank. Really, I do. Please don't ever be that way with me again."

I moved toward her and held her close, and my emotions erupted the moment I touched her. Now tears were flowing in both directions, though I did my best to refrain. Pulling back to look at her I said, "It wasn't really the real me that said all those nasty things to you that day, Sarah. It was what was beaten into me by my mother. I'm not blaming her. She was always that way. Spill a glass of milk and she'd come down on us like Genghis Khan. She always ridiculed us for making mistakes, even simple ones."

"But she's your mother," she replied through a sob.

"Yes, but she was also beaten and mistreated by her stepfather. He was a Teutonic-German, a sheriff, a mean and unreasonable man, from what I heard. She was an illegitimate child and he couldn't deal with that. He must have also been raised by an iron hand. It was common in those days to beat your kids."

I added, "It doesn't stop there, Sarah. My father was one of fourteen children. His parents were so poor he had to live with aunts and foster-parents. He didn't know how to handle my mom and all of her problems, so he split. It was all he could do to save himself. My brothers and I have talked about living with her vengeful ways. Sarah, I know we were not alone with this. Lots of families have problems like this. Your family has problems like this, right?"

Calming a bit she agreed, remembering that I knew that her mother was an alcoholic and often berated her and her brother and sister.

"Then see the true picture, sweetheart. There's never been a time in man's existence upon this earth when we haven't had to put up with problems like this—it's called life. We're all potential tyrants as a result, and it's important to understand this so that the forgiving process can take place. So cry, sweetheart. Cry for yourself. Cry for we humans, who don't understand what the hell we're doing here. Cry out to all those superior assholes who run things, and think that they're right in what they do. All I know is that I love you. I need you to agree that what happened in our past has everything to do with our present and also our future. And Sarah, I've only begun to talk. There's more, much more, but I'll hold off for now. Come on. Let me rest beside you."

We slid back down on the cot and grasped one another, tightly at first, then gently, our bodies, pressed against one another, sending a warm glow through our abdomens.

Upon waking, the first thing Sarah said as we lay together was, "I agree with you. Tyranny does rules us. But, that's not you, Beast. You're not that kind of person. You've learned a lot and I'll be there to support you all the way. What bothers me now is just what the hell are you going to do about your fugitive status in the States?"

"Hmm. That's a tough one. The same way I got into it, I guess." Sighing, I fell silent.

"Well, if anything, it'll be a juggling act of some sort. There's always a way out. Jake and I agreed to this shortly after getting into this business. It helped to keep us from getting too paranoid."

"If there's always a way out, then I'll help."

Teasing her I said, "Good. Then protect me from the DEA boys in the States who want my ass in jail for three years or more."

"Hmm. That's a tall order, buns. Let's just take this one step at a time. For now, you're safe. I can live with that."

"Yeah. One step at a time! Doors will open. The impossible will become possible. Timing and believing are the name of the game. You and I can work together and come up with something magical, and *voila*, life will be different. What are you thinking, sweetheart?"

"Well," she sighed, then frowned and then chuckled. "Damn, it's a lot to think about, considering you're still here in jail. But don't fret. I'll help you figure all this out. Two is better than one, and Dad would say that this is one of life's theorems. We'll get him to inject some of his stuff."

"He'll know, of course, that there's always a portal, an opening of some sort. I don't want the law to own me all my life. Meanwhile, when I get out of here we can work on boats. Both of us know how to paint and varnish. Los Angeles or San Diego would be a good home base; then you'd be close to your parents. How does that sound to you, woman?"

"Perfect, Mister Buns. I also want to explore more of myself and do some writing and get back into my music. I know I'm ready. Southern California just might be a good place, for a while anyway."

"Yes, for now, at any rate. All I need to know is that you're behind me."

"You could do it without me, I know," she said coyly.

"Believe me. I've considered that. But, I don't want to. These past several months in jail have served their purpose. It's time to start letting go of this drama, and all the hurt and anger. Forgiving people is just a starter. Besides, there's a lot more to forgiveness than just saying I forgive you...and today being Christmas Eve, that's my gift to you."

"Thank you, buns. Gift accepted! It's a wise one." Flashing her girlish grin she said cheerfully, "Now, I'm in a predicament. You've done so much talking, I haven't had the time to tell you, but it'll be easy now."

"Easy? Well, tell me."

"Will you forgive me?"

"Yes, of course."

"I promised my parents I'd spend Christmas Eve with them. I'll be leaving just after *lista* on the first call for visitors so I won't be spending the night as planned."

"Oh! Is that all?" I joked, not at all upset.

"Yes. I want to have Christmas with them and Inger. We're going to be together celebrating, rejoicing the eventual victory."

"Well, I'm somewhat put off, but then again, we've work to do. Besides, there's something important I have to ask of you. It's very positive."

"Go for it."

"I have no money to get back to the States once I'm out of here. Will you go to Al at the boat yard or brother Ray—they'd be the best bet—and ask them for...ah, three hundred should do. Then I'll need you to come down here and meet up with me in Guadalajara."

"That's positive and an easy request to fill. Sure."

"Are you coming back tomorrow?"

"Of course. We have a surprise for all of you guys."

"Tell the crew to take a break, would you?" Bill asked me. We were inspecting the food Sarah and Inger had brought to us on Christmas Day: fresh baked breads, stuffing, baked sweet potatoes, a basket of cookies and fruit, along with a turkey.

About two that afternoon, the diggers decided to shut down. Boldly, we brought the booty right to their *caraca*.

The crew planned to dig that night after our guests departed. All of us were still troubled about getting beyond the outer foundation. Would there be an unexpected underground barrier in our way? That was the question on everyone's mind. We were also concerned about our location. We were behind schedule and we didn't know how many more feet of dirt would have to be removed to gain freedom.

Sarah calmed my thoughts, insisting all would go well.

"But you can pretty much figure the footing won't be all too deep, right? My father has already calculated that it won't be all that deep, really. He's gone over all the data. He feels you're as good as out. He even told me to tell you the perfect time to come out the hole would be some time between 3:30 and 4:00 a.m. I believe him. He worked a long time on all of this."

Sarah's father was a physicist who worked on satellite data for the Pasadena Jet Propulsion Laboratory. He even looked the part of a scientist: a tall, happy-go-lucky, pipe smoking, bearded madman. He was the stereotypical scientist who often couldn't find his briefcase, but a welcome addition to our cause.

"Well, you got me there, hon. Your being here helps. I'm just fretting… by the way, the departure date has been moved up to three days from now, sweet thing."

"Yes. Dirk said so. Mike's going to make a periscope, I hear."

"He's going to use it tonight."

CHAPTER TWENTY-NINE

THE RAIN IN NO MAN'S LAND

MAZATLAN, MEXICO
DECEMBER 27, 1971

Things were looking up. A couple of hours after Sarah departed on Monday, Mike descended into the tunnel to try to locate our exact position from the outer wall.

With all our progressions, it was as though we expected a sign for the preceding two days of work. Send us the friggin' wall, God. Maybe we'd unearth the Grail while we were at it. And, maybe one of us would be lucky enough to arrive home with the holy relic.

Mike was proud of the periscope he fashioned out of toilet paper rolls, tape and mirrors—it was crude, but it worked. We had told him not to get too carried away. He was to enter the tunnel, dig a small hole directly up, and if possible, break through to the surface. By extending the homemade device out the open hole, we hoped he'd spot the main outer wall.

He came back no more than twenty minutes later. When he emerged he had a boyish grin on his face the size of a football. "I saw it, man. I saw it. We're right at the outer wall," he said in hushed tones. "It's no more than six inches away. I probed for the foundation and found it. It's not in the way of us getting out of here."

Relief filled the room. We were elated. The problem had been solved.

All we had to do now was to keep on digging and hope the goon-squad kept clear of *Correctionalis*.

"You won't believe it," Mike beamed, stepping out of the opening. "I started digging a hole and all of a sudden I was at the surface. We're only seven to eight inches below the ground in no-man's-land."

"Unreal," Fred marveled.

"That figures," Patrick said sarcastically.

Dirk stayed positive. "That's no problem."

I added blithely, "Does anything make sense around here?" It seemed ludicrous that we were nearly four feet deep at this end and only a few inches deep as we dug across the stretch we had dubbed *No Man's Land*.

We still had a night of digging in front of us. Mike would go first, followed by Dirk. They'd work until midnight. We calculated that less than six feet of dirt needed to come out: two to three feet to get under the wall, and two or so to get beyond.

That evening the diggers worked furiously. They removed over a foot of dirt. Using Patrick's eight-by-eight *caraca* to store the dirt, three feet from the back wall, we placed two large cardboard boxes loaded with soil. The pile of dirt behind this barrier looked bodacious. The flimsy door and a cloth curtain were the only veils hiding the mountain of dirt. Should there be an inspection, well, we were screwed.

Standing over the mountain of dirt that evening I shook my head, chuckling softly each time a tray of dirt was passed over.

The next morning, Bill sent a coded message out to Inger to let everyone on the outside know that we'd reached the outer wall. In two to three days, we'd be out of there.

The next day, after morning *lista* was out of the way, we set to work with great enthusiasm. Once again we worked until midnight. The diggers could actually see the foundation to the outer wall, but the dirt underneath was hard to remove. By night's end, they were a good foot underneath the foundation. Mike and his men were stationed outside from midnight until four in the morning, and were to wait each night, until we got out.

On Wednesday, December 28, *lista* came and went with no searches.

That evening, thick rain clouds formed, but no one paid much attention as we went through another day of digging and packing the dirt over to Patrick's *caraca.*

The next day was a visiting day and we decided it would look strange if none of our guests came. We sent out a message to Sarah and Peggy asking them to come visit us. They arrived just before noon. Peggy headed to Mike and Dirk's *caraca,* while Sarah entered mine, looking bewildered. It had been raining since the previous night and now the clouds looked ominous.

"Honey, it's supposed to rain for the next two days," she exclaimed, as I closed the door to my caraca. "And, it's cold out."

"Yes. The clouds are building. We've been watching them."

"Dad pored over the weather forecast. It's a big storm and it's headed here from the Pacific, all the way from up north. How often does that happen, for God's sake?" She was agitated and befuddled.

"It's almost unheard of this time of year. Rarely do the storms penetrate below the California border, let alone down to the Tropics."

"It's something to reckon with."

"Yeah, no telling what will happen. Hopefully it won't be too severe."

"Gosh, I'm glad I came. I feel better already. How are you, fiend?" She turned, her eyes piercing mine.

Reaching over, I gently drew her face to mine. Kissing her lightly I said, "Better now that you're here. We're all kind of up, down, and sideways."

Coyly she said, "Peggy and I came in to boost morale. She thinks Dirk and Mike are quite the guys. She said she'd like to ball Mike."

"Good! That will make them more productive," I smirked. "In a while I'm going over to Patrick's *caraca* to work. Why don't you join me?"

"We can play too, right?" she asked provocatively.

"Yes, hot lips, I was including that."

Looking more serious, she bowed her head slightly. "I have to admit my fears are overrunning me, too. It's been hard the last two days. My parents are on edge. My mom's hard to be around right now. She and Dad have taken me a few places, but I'd rather be with Inger and the rest of them. I don't know. It's strange. Mom's in a terrible mood."

"That's understandable, honey. Pressure is getting to her. She didn't come down here expecting all this escape business, and you probably feel guilty about not wanting to be with them. They're paying for the entire trip, right?"

"Yes." She shrugged, her head hanging. "I feel guilty."

"Well, I'm here for you, sweetheart. Don't feel guilty. It's her trip. Not yours. Use your energy for better purposes. Let's just be here."

She suddenly perked up, face aglow. "On the way over, I thought about writing some adventure stories. You're giving me a whole lot of material to work with and I have some short stories in mind."

"Good. Write 'em. I need the money," I joked. "Can I send you the bill?"

"Fine. I'll pay you off with good sex. Want a blow job?"

Laughing, I said, "What would your mommy say if she heard you say that?"

"She'd probably say, 'What's a blow job?'"

"You think she's that naive?"

"Not if she's had several vodkas." She was contemplative for a moment. "My mother has a lot of fears. I feel them all the time. It's what makes me want to get away from her."

"I'm the same way with my mother. Fear is contagious, wouldn't you say? It's partly what drives your mom to drink."

"Yes, but how do I get her to stop the drinking? Sometimes I feel like screaming in her face."

"Hmmm. I've had similar feelings with Jake when he'd go into sulking moods. Be resilient. Show your mom some love. That'll help build trust. That's how I appealed to Jake, whenever I had the patience. Have you ever had close, intimate conversations with your Mom?"

"Not really. It's the usual courteous stuff. Real phony."

"Sounds familiar. I live in fear of my mother, too." Sitting sideways, I brushed Sarah's hair back and began massaging her neck and shoulders. "This may sound odd," I said, "but I fear having to face my mother more than I fear being a fugitive. I know that if I confronted her, I'd have to confront my own crap, too. The same is probably true with you and your mom. Her fears are your fears. That's how our past works into these dramas. Does that make sense?"

"I hate having to deal with her. We always argue and run from the problem. I'm always putting the blame on her. She does the same with me, and yes, sometimes I sense that it's me I'm dealing with as I deal with her."

"You can bet on it. That's why I believe we have no choice but to meet people from a space of love."

She began to relax as I ran my fingers over her tight muscles—probably a result of our conversation. I said nothing. My being there was all she needed for the moment.

"It's so nice having you around, baby," she cooed. "Soon, I'll have you around a lot more." Reaching out, she caressed my leg as I worked on her neck. "Then we can work on boats together. It'll be fun, when you get out, of course." She went quiet for a moment and then added, "Funny how things change. Here we are talking as though you're already free, yet you're not, and it all hinges on the tunnel being finished and all of you getting out of here safely."

"Dirk thinks we'll get out tonight. I have my doubts. We'll see. One more day of hanging in together and we ought to have the job done."

Patrick knocked on the door, then entered and stood in front of us. "Well, don't you two look cozy? Mike's done. Dirk is going down next."

"I'm ready. You want me in your *caraca* for now?"

"Yes. Don't bother Mike, though. Peggy's all over him. I think they're ready to get it on." He grinned nonchalantly.

A heavy rain began falling around 3:00 that afternoon as Sarah napped and I read and received trays of dirt from Mike, who was on duty with Peggy. Outside the *caraca*, the *quincados* were restless. They had no blankets and probably wouldn't get any sleep tonight if the rain continued. I started feeling unsettled. Reading became almost impossible.

Sitting on a small folding chair I looked over at Sarah, then over to the enormous pile of earth against the far wall, covered by a single blanket. That and the sound of rain crashing down on the aluminum awning made the whole scene surreal. Sarah, covered with a sheet and a single wool blanket, appeared comfortable, which only added to the irony: she was oblivious to the rain outside.

"Mike, how are things going with Dirk?" I whispered, as he passed me a tray through the gap in the wall.

"Okay, I guess. I sent him a note a while ago to let him know it's raining. Why?"

"The rain, man, it's a bummer. I'm just curious."

"We can't do anything to stop it. We need to keep digging. We expect to crack past the outer wall before *lista*. Then the ground may soften up. There's a chance we can make it out tonight. We'll have to move one hell of a lot of dirt to do that."

"How's Peggy doing?" I asked mischievously.

"She's taking care of business," he grinned, "that's all I can say."

A moment later a chill ran up my spine as I recalled being called to the *Alciadia's* office before Christmas. I thought it was a phone call for me. I was floored when a trustee ushered me into the new *Alciadia's* office.

Suddenly, I was standing in front of a short grizzly man, fifty, with a crew cut. Nothing was said as the new *Alciadia* handed me a bulky letter addressed to me from Sarah. He ordered me to open it. Inside were two letters. He stared up at me officiously and seemed disappointed that he hadn't caught me with contraband or playing cards. He politely excused me and I returned to *Correctionalis*.

I kept thinking all he had to do was give the word and his storm troopers would swoop down on us. With all the holiday visitors coming in we figured it was a good time for a raid. The night before, Dirk had argued forcefully that a search was imminent. Bill had calmed him down by reminding him he couldn't jeopardize our position with his apprehension.

It was a minor miracle that a search hadn't occurred since two days after our arrival in early July. All of us sorely wanted out, but unless a minor miracle took place, tonight was not the night. Would we get out before the inevitable search?

"Hi Beast," Sarah whispered, as I grabbed another tray from Mike.

"Hi, flower. I was going to wake you. It's nearly five."

"Five! Why didn't you?" She sat up and stretched, adding with concern,

"God, it's raining so hard."

"Yes, for about an hour or so and the *quincados* are uptight. Their soup and torts are late and they probably won't get any sleep tonight."

"You sound a bit down."

"I am. I'm worried." I told her about the thoughts that had been crowding my mind for the previous hour or so. "I know I'm feeling paranoid about our situation, and I'm not handling it so well."

"Lie down beside me." She pulled the blanket off for a moment.

"No. I'd rather sit and talk. It would be better." Sitting down on the edge of the cot she hugged me. "This may be the last chance I get to talk with you before we get out of here." Silent for a moment, I croaked, "I can't talk too well right now."

"I'll be patient."

Looking away for a moment to clear my mind, I closed my eyes for a few seconds and sighed. "Just be here, Sarah. Just know that even though you're on the outside, you can still help. Send me your love, no matter what. Tomorrow night will be the night. Then, hopefully, we'll be free of this place."

"Frank, when I leave here this evening, I'll be thinking about all of you. Are you afraid I won't?"

"No. I'm...I'm just afraid, period. This is dragging out. It's raining and I'm kind of coming apart. Maybe this is the worst the rain will get and in no time everything will be fine."

"The other day you told me that life is really a series of tests and learning lessons. Don't you think the rain is a test and the pressure is part of it?"

"In every way, yes. Everything is a test. But this one is eating at me."

"Then see it as that. It's another challenge for all of you to get through.

If you're to maintain what you believe in, then look at it that way. Don't worry if it gets to you a bit, just keep the faith, beast. We'll be on the outside sending you positive energy. That I promise."

"Thanks, sweetheart. I feel kind of humble right now. My energy is mixed, but I'm better. I know you'll be there, no matter what."

As I finished the last word, the evening meal was called. We smiled at each other with a knowingness that went beyond words as we heard the *quincados* shuffling in line for their meal.

She reached out and grabbed my hand. She put it against her heart, then raised it and kissed it lightly. Flashing a subdued smile, her face said, "Come lay with me. We've only a while 'til *recita*."

After Sarah left I headed straight to Mike and Dirk's *caraca*. The rain had lightened up and the diggers were more determined than ever. Peggy had made love with both Mike and Dirk during the course of the afternoon. Patrick and I teased them as Mike told the story—the short version. Mike had made love to her first. Later, when Mike was down digging, he received a note from Dirk and Peggy in the plastic tray asking permission for them to get it on.

"I simply put my 'x' on the yes square and sent it back," he said with an opulent grin.

That evening the crew seemed in good spirits, but the rain was still a burden.

Mike reported that some water, not much, was coming through the hole he had made for the periscope. As for getting out tonight, "Forget it," Mike announced, chagrined. "We're barely past the wall. Maybe seven to eight inches at best."

The goal had been two feet plus a few inches. Around one a.m. we shut down, having made good progress. Dirk was asleep as I helped Mike clean up. We were so close we could almost taste freedom. Six to seven more hours of digging might do the job. Having put in a heavy workday, Mike was weary. He hunched over a large clay pot to clean himself.

I whispered, "Wait 'til morning to wash the work clothes, Mike."

"Fine. I'm pooped out, man. There's a bit to dig out, but we ought to have it by this time tomorrow, no sweat."

"Sure sounds like it, yeah, one more morning *lista*. With this rain the chances of a search are super-low."

"No doubt about it. One more day and we're clear of here. Can you believe it?"

"Yes, San Blas here we come…I'm turning in. See you at morning *lista*, pal."

Sometime during the middle of the night I awakened, my body heavy and damp. I sat up and wiped sweat from my forehead. Outside, the rain was still pouring down. I took a deep breath and fell back on the cot moaning, muscles aching. I cursed out loud, "Fuck, haven't we had enough? This is unbelievable." Lying still, I listened to the *quincados* whispering and to the rain pounding on the metal awnings. I wanted to sleep, but I twisted and turned as the image of *No Man's Land* came into view; the barren stretch fifteen to eighteen feet wide, surrounding the prison on two sides.

With no place for the rainwater to go, how much would enter into the small opening Mike had made the other day? How much would enter the tunnel? Overwhelmed and agitated, I fought off the images and the ragging questions. And, why hadn't we thought to plug the hole?"

Sleep came and went. Each time I woke, I'd rehash the situation, intensified by the torrential downpour, which reverberated off the awning onto the concrete floor.

When the rain finally let up, I slept lightly, sensitive to every peep. I was miserable. As though on cue, my mouth became dry and my saliva bitter.

I shuddered as a torrent of rain hit, clouds burst, and thunder cracked. There was no way to keep the heavens from erupting. I tensed up and lay there listening, wondering, and knowing that all was not well.

"Stop this madness. Stop it!" I screamed inside my head. It was no use. I lay there caught between exhaustion and sleep. Finally I passed out, exhausted, and awoke to light and again the sound of rain—the condemning rain that was sure to spoil our tunnel. I drifted off again until the sound of the guard calling us to *lista* woke me up.

I sat up groggy and tense. Pressing my fingers against my temples, I shook my head in hopes of ridding the tension. Stumbling about, I slipped into shorts and hurried out the door.

Bill and the rest of the crew were in the *lista* line, bleary-eyed and concerned. Nothing was said as the officials called out our names. The fact that there still had been no search briefly crossed my mind. When I entered my *caraca* I went straight to the gap between the wall and the roof and gained Patrick's attention.

"Patrick, have Mike and Dirk come to the wall for a talk," I requested.

Mike appeared at the far wall. "I'm going in to see what's happening with the tunnel," he said softly.

I fell onto my cot and instantly fell asleep. Were it not for Patrick's voice, I'd have slept for hours.

"Hey, dude! Wake up! Come on, wake up! We have a problem in the tunnel," he said with quiet urgency.

He stood on his cot and held on to the large clay urn we had used for washing. He propped it on the edge of the wall, and tried to push it through the small opening, causing a good deal of water to spill to the floor of my *caraca*. The silty water was making a mess. If it leaked into the courtyard, which it surely would, the inmates would soon spot the brown muddy water.

Still in a stupor, I moved as quickly as I could, and grabbed the urn and forced it back, stemming the flow of muddy water. Exasperated, I said, "Stop this, man. This is stupid. What the hell is happening?"

Drawing the urn back, I stared at the mess on the floor, Patrick answered, "Mike's down in the tunnel. It's flooded. He's bailing it out. Dirk put some water in this urn. We have to get rid of it somehow."

"Christ! What does he expect me to do with it?"

"He told me to hand the urn over to your *caraca*. He wants you to pour it on the floor. It's the only way. We've got a big problem in the tunnel."

Spooked by the damage that had already been done, I left my perch and began mopping up the flow of silt on the floor with a blanket.

"We can't do this, man. This is not the answer. Look at the silt. It's going to leak out into the yard in no time. You know what that means."

"We've got to get the water out. Mike said it's pouring in."

Patrick was not getting the picture. He was caught up in the panic, stirred up by Dirk and Mike.

"Goddammit. Tell him to hold on."

"He says we got to get going or the tunnel will be completely flooded."

Pointing a finger at Patrick, I said with heat, "You tell him to stop. I'll be right over. We'll figure this out together."

I called to Bill. When his head appeared I said softly, "We have a huge problem."

"What's up?"

"The tunnel's flooding—Mike and Dirk are in a panic over there. Come to their *caraca* with me. We'll work out what's best to do."

"Meet you there."

Bill and I arrived simultaneously. Dirk gave us a nasty vacant stare. Immediately, he barked out in a muted tone, "We gotta dump this water now!"

"That's why we came over," Bill broke in.

"We've got to figure out a better way," I added sternly. "Call Mike out and let's talk."

"Let's not blow it," Bill cautioned.

Dirk hesitated at first, then knelt down and called softly to his buddy Mike to come to the entry hole.

"You got a better solution?" Dirk asked as we waited, his face sending ripples of tension through my already tense body.

"Yes. Far better than the one you've got," I said sarcastically. I was hot, and he knew it.

Mike appeared at the entry hole and threw an incensed look at my brother and me.

Great! Just what we didn't need—not there, not then.

Bill tried to deflect tension. "Take it easy. Sit tight." As he finished up, Dirk turned up the volume of the boombox to overpower the quarrel.

"No." Mike spat out, hotly, "There's a fucking mess down there and I'm going to keep bailing. The tunnel is flooded. You've no idea how bad it is."

"Cool it man," Bill stated tersely, pointing his finger at Mike.

"You're getting out of hand," I interjected. "You're making decisions for all of us? Is that it, Mike?"

Not bothering to respond to my question, he blurted out, "You guys go sit on your asses. I'm going to work."

"Fine," I responded. "I suppose that you don't want to hear that we have another way to do this."

"Yes. Just hold on and listen," Bill demanded hotly.

Stepping forward I said calmly, "There's more than one way to do this, Mike. Let's make use of the pipe, for god's sake."

"He's right," Fred piped in. "We can take the wrap off the broken pipe. Use the small pan Ted used to bail out the shit with and pour the water down the hole."

"That's exactly what I had in mind, Fred," I said, looking at Mike.

Mike looked around puzzled at first, then beamed, "I hadn't thought of that."

Fred continued, "It's perfect. It's on high ground. I'll come down and help."

"Good. I hadn't thought of that either," Dirk added.

Everyone in the room was calm now. Bill consoled, "We're all tired and pent-up guys. We're not exactly thinking straight."

"I agree." Fred smiled. "We could have figured it out, but we didn't."

"Pressure, guys, pressure will do it every time if we don't acknowledge it," I added. "We gotta keep it together."

"I hear you," Mike concluded. "I'll get the pipe unwrapped. Come on down, Fred. This will be tricky. We don't want any shit sloshing in while we do this."

"Go for it, man. Let's get this done and get the hell out of here," Bill said, lowering his voice, *"tonight!"*

"Tonight!" Dirk repeated the word, giving all of us thumbs up. Everyone chimed in with, "tonight," and gave the thumbs up sign. Patrick, who had been listening at the gap in the wall, joined in too.

As Bill and I headed out the door Fred added, "Far out. We're gonna put Mexican rain water down a Mexican shit pipe so we can finish our Mexican tunnel. I can't wait."

Back in my *caraca*, a good portion of the floor still covered with a dark silt, I grabbed whatever was available and began cleaning up. That in itself was going to be a job. I was elated. We had solved the problem so easily. I had to believe that someone, or something, was looking out for us.

Later, just as I finished breakfast, a ray of sunshine broke through; the storm was coming to an end and the worst was over with. Throughout the remainder of the afternoon the crew worked at bailing the tunnel. Ted helped. Mike told me later that there had been so much water at the tunnel that the far end—which laid lower than the rest—had been eighty percent full. "The tiny hole I made for the periscope is about four inches round now," he said, a goofy grin on his face. "Fortunately the guard can't see it. The hole is right under the catwalk and they won't be looking over that way."

About one that afternoon, Inger and Sarah came to the main gate and sent in food for all of us, two roasted chickens and fresh veggies for us. Bill, as planned, sent out a coded message to them to let Michael and his outside crew know we were ready. They had been waiting in vain for three nights running. Tonight, it was thumbs up.

By early evening the evil rain spell had broken, and only scattered showers remained. As evening *lista* approached we were jubilant. The crew had completely bailed out the tunnel.

Dirk was the first to dig. He emerged just before *lista*. At the evening meal the *quincados* were composed. Augila, their good pal, was not here. They had little to cajole about. Joe was on one of his down cycles, the door to his *caraca* was closed tight. Just as well.

After *lista*, Fred planned to dig next. Mike was to follow. Dirk planned to finish the tunnel. How far and how wide he planned to dig, he didn't know. The last obstacle was his to deal with. Who better than he? The honor was his.

I had the honor of helping out. No way was I going to go to my *caraca* to rest. All of us were running on adrenaline.

Michael and his crew, who would to be outside waiting, had determined that the two outside guards always slept from 2:00 a.m. until just past 4:00 a.m. The footpath along the wall had no foot traffic during those hours. We suspected people would be heading for work about five-5:30 a.m.

When Mike came out at 10:00 p.m., he brought good news. "We're almost two feet beyond the outer wall."

Fred, donning the work clothes said, "Knowing the guards they'll have no problem finding the dirt after we get outta here. They'll have trouble finding the hole in the floor." We laughed at the triteness. Everything seemed farcical.

I stood up on the end of Dirk's cot and peered down at Patrick, who was absorbed in a book. "Here's one more for the mountain," I said as I put the tray on the shelf.

He took the tray and dumped the load, adding, "Pretty ridiculous hump of dirt, man," shaking his head.

"I wonder if they'll put it back in the hole after we leave?"

Shrugging his shoulders, Patrick said, "Hard to say. I'll think about it while I'm reading." We grinned at each other.

Just past midnight, Fred came out of the entry all smiles. "We're real close, more than two feet beyond. If we widen the exit point a bit more, we're there."

Patrick took a turn as Mike, Dirk, Fred, and I hung in. Ted came in later. He wanted to join us. We sent him to over Patrick's *caraca*. We were antsy, but mostly quiet. Out in the courtyard all was serene. The exhausted *quincados* were deep in slumber land. Bill napped in his *caraca* as we gingerly went about our business.

When Patrick emerged around 2:00 a.m. he said, "I think we're ready. It's close."

Dirk, who had been resting, quickly said, "I'll go check." Ten minutes later he sent a note: "Give me one hour."

I had never coped with so much pressure and excitement at the same time. Not even during the hard years. It was strange: I was relaxed and yet falling to pieces. Exhilaration reigned. How did one prepare for an escape?—From a raunchy jail in a third-world country that lacked common sense?

I felt like I was on a mescaline trip: colors seemed more vivid; lights brighter. And the guys seemed larger than life. They attempted to sleep. I couldn't. I was suspended in the moment. I wanted to feel each and every sensation. And everything I observed sent shivers through my body. It all seemed rather inexplicable. It was as though I was receiving energy from an unknown source. I tried to reassure myself that everything would go as planned. "Be calm," I told myself. "Enjoy the ride."

Dirk emerged just after three a.m. and said softly, "We're ready, guys. There's about four inches of topsoil to remove. I'll take the top off once we're in the tunnel. *Let's go home*."

Not much else was said. Everyone knew the plan. As Dirk climbed out of the hole I whispered, "I'll get Bill."

Easing into the courtyard, I stood still for a moment. My only concern was not to be spotted. The scene was surreal. The dim lights of the prison reflected off the walls had a light green aura around them. Stepping over the *quincados* was effortless. I was floating along—not walking. Floating over to Bill's *caraca*, I nudged Bill's door and gave him the thumbs up sign.

Back in my *caraca* I put on an old pair of boots Inger had stored for me, and dark pants and a dark sweater procured for the escape. I scanned the room and thought, "We're going home, back to civilization." I had to leave my possessions that had been vital to our survival behind: fans, cots, clothes and utensils. The Mexican inmates would inherit them; our *caracas* too. Silently, I bequeathed all my worldly property to them. I slipped out the door, ready for my departure.

As I entered I whispered, "Everyone in the courtyard's asleep, guys."

Everyone was present and ready. We quickly reviewed the pre-arranged order of departure: Dirk and Mike, then Patrick, Fred, Bill, me, and then Ted. Bill handed out the *visas* he had been holding for the occasion. Smiles abounded.

It was 3:45 a.m. Our timing was perfect. Dirks said it would take him no more than twenty minutes to finish the job.

"Be sure to roll over when you reach the end of the tunnel. Then push up with your legs," he whispered.

Once we were outside the jail, everyone was to stay along the footpath. From there, we would head west along the wall, then cross the street, stealthily. Michael and crew would be waiting just beyond the corner in the shadows of darkness.

Dirk, dressed in street clothes, entered the exit hole. He turned, smiled, and saluted us. Silently, we saluted back. Mike was next, then Patrick. As my turn came, my heart started pounding. I descended into the tunnel and crawled backwards, turning at the juncture. Crawling forward in complete blackness, I abruptly came upon Bill's feet. Placing a hand on his shoe, I assured myself that when he moved, I'd move.

Lying there in the dark, an eternity passed. Except for the muffled sounds of Dirk working the top loose, I heard little else. I couldn't focus. All my thoughts were fragmented and intangible. The waiting was interminable. I used deep breathing to offset my uncontrollable anxiety. The air inside the tunnel was thin and stale and the smell of earth, water, and body odors stung my nose.

What was taking so long? A half hour or more had passed. Suddenly there was movement in front of me. Bill began crawling, slowly at first, then faster. I scrambled to keep up with him. All that I could hear now was rapid shuffling. Then there was light. Everyone had disappeared. And light now showed the way out. I crawled faster and finally reached the end of the tunnel. Rolling over, I pushed up and rose to my feet. The light coming off the walls was almost blinding.

I stared up at the red brick wall. It seemed immense. I saw Bill. He was three-quarters of the way down the length of the wall, moving quite rapidly. I headed in his direction. My body was weightless. The wall above me looked eerie. There were no guards to be seen. I looked back and saw Ted making his way toward me, grunting and stumbling, making alarming noises.

Bill was already crossing the street as I reached the corner where the guard tower stood. I fixed my eyes on the guard post, then the opposite corner. I hesitated just a second and then headed toward the rendezvous area.

I was soon standing in the shadows of the nearest building with the group. Bill said in a hushed tone, "Michael's not here. They must have just taken off. We're going to take the back streets and go through town."

"Let's haul ass," someone said.

As we headed up the street Bill said, "We'll go to the Pemex station, pronto. I'll call Michael from there."

This was a contingency plan we had had the forethought to put together. We turned the next corner and headed south, Bill leading the pack. We continued at a fast pace toward the center of Colony Juarez, keeping ourselves spread out at varying distances. Occasionally, we grouped up. We were all congratulatory—patting each other on the back, shaking hands, and applauding our efforts. All we could do was laugh about missing Michael and the pickup crew. Won't they be surprised, we thought, when we call and tell them to get their butts down to the *Pemex* Station?

The central square of Colony Juarez was deserted as we approached. No one was in sight and the town center was calm and serene with a few lights to show the way. The park with trees and plants, made me want to stop and feast, but I pressed on. Our paces quickened as we spotted the main boulevard four long blocks ahead.

We walked in the dark shadows for cover. Bill said, "It's a couple of miles or so to the *Pemex* once we hit the main boulevard. Maybe a taxi will come along. If not we'll walk." No one questioned his decision. We had to get out of the area—and fast. Concern for safety was mounting. As we approached the last block, Bill assured us, "Taxi's are up at all hours, guys. With luck, we'll get one."

When we reached the boulevard we crossed, then headed east toward our destination. For the first time we saw signs of life. Up to then, only a few dogs had barked. Now a set of headlights came at us from the opposite direction. The six of us stood back in the shadows as Bill looked ahead. It was a taxi. Bill hailed it loudly. The vehicle almost came to a halt, then wheeled around the divider in the boulevard and headed toward us. The seven of us quickly jumped in. Surprised to see so many passengers, Mike casually let the driver know it had been a long night.

The driver let out an all-knowing chuckle. What he didn't know was that he was an angel from heaven. Bill told him to let us off at the *Pemex* station leading out of town.

It was a short ride. As we bailed out, Bill gave him more than enough. As the cab disappeared into the night we headed to the pay phones. The station, open twenty-four-seven, and was a sight to behold. There were lights everywhere.

Crowding up next to him as he placed the call, I heard Penelope answer in a sleepy voice.

"Hey, sweetheart, we're out. Tell your old man to come pick us up," Bill said, and then laughed heartily.

"Oh God... they're out," she screamed out to everyone in the room. "Where you at?"

"Just tell Michael to come to the *Pemex* station. We'll be there."

"Oh shit! Bill, this is wonderful. He just returned and went to bed. We thought, 'Oh God, something went wrong.' Here he is. Talk to him."

As I stood besides him, sharing the receiver, I could hear everyone in the room screaming and hollering. Sarah, her parents, Michael, and his people, were all staying at the same motel. Sarah would know of our success within seconds.

"Goddamn! All right, brother!" Michael said. "So you did it!"

"Yeah, we did it! We're outta' there! Let's go have a swim."

"Give me twenty minutes. We'll be there."

"No more. Just get here as soon as you can. Okay. Thanks bro. Thanks." Bill hung up, and said, "You heard it. He'll be here shortly. Come on. Let's not hang out here."

We headed back to the others a few feet away and Bill reported, "Michael's on his way." Then he turned to Ted, and said. "You can't come with us, Ted. Why don't you catch a cab and go to the trailer courts north of town in Sabalo."

"I haven't got any money," he whined, looking perplexed.

Bill pulled some bills from his pockets and forked them over to Ted. "Here's two hundred *pesos*. That ought to do the trick."

Snatching the money he pleaded, "Why can't I come with you?"

"We got you out, man. That's all we agreed on. Go to the trailer courts in the Sabalo and find some *gringos*. Tell them your problem. Someone will help you out, man."

"You'll be okay," Mike said, as he patted him on the back.

Ted wasn't happy. I reached out, shook his hand, and thanked him. The others joined in. He turned and walked off. It was a huge station. A cab was waiting for a customer not more than thirty yards away. Ted got in the cab and was gone.

We headed over to a flat spot near a large farm field and settled near a clump of low-lying bushes. Peering up at the sky toward the east, I saw the first light of day. The recent rainstorm had left the air clean and crystal clear. Multitudes of stars splashed above, contrasted by bellowing clouds from the east. I breathed in deeply, welcoming the pungent smell of Mother Earth. I felt invigorated and triumphant, savoring the presence of the men who had made the escape possible.

"You're free now. Look at the spacious earth," I admonished myself. "It needs no introduction. It hasn't changed. Feel the moment, the wonders of your new surroundings. You can head off in any direction you please. The smell of freedom is in the ground, in the field; it's in the darkness, the stars, and the breaking day. Let freedom lead the way. Appreciate it and learn from it."

"Hey, *lista* is in one hour, man," Mike joked, breaking me from my reverie.

"Yeah. I think they're gonna miss us," Dirk mused.

We chuckled quietly.

"Man, that was some ordeal. *It sure did solve a lot of problems though,*" Bill added.

We allowed ourselves to laugh out loud. Nodding in agreement Fred said, "Well put. Hey, thanks again, guys." He stuck out his hand. We gave a round of handshakes for the umpteenth time.

"Nice job, men," I said, grasping their hands firmly, looking them square in their eyes. These would be our final moments together.

Words for how I really felt wouldn't come forth. In a few moments Michael would arrive. The crew, excluding Bill and me, planned to head south, then east to the city of Durango, Mexico. Using their visas, they'd fly directly north to the States. They would soon be leaving my life. They knew nothing of the bad blood that had been building between Bill and me for years. The four of them were my brothers. Seven of us had worked diligently together as a unit of one, in a crafty and well-planned maneuver. It was *Brotherhood in action,* and now that we were free I was as proud as could be to be a part of this scheme. God, how I wished we could be together that day to celebrate our victory. They would have their own stories to tell to their friends and lovers and children. Strange that none of us knew each other well, even with all the time we had spent together. Yet in another respect, they were my dearest friends. Humbled by their presence, I searched for words.

I wanted to run and jump like a kid, but I knew I couldn't. It was not the time or place to create a scene. Just being there was enough. Patrick waited for Michael and crew in shorts and thongs, with his hands in his pockets—Mr. Casual. It was fitting. He smirked. We all did, and the sun inched its way up the sky: the start of a new day.

Fred smiled and bantered with Mike and Dirk. Bill paced as usual. Thirty minutes had passed since the call. Light was eclipsing dark. I fidgeted, inspecting the farm fields which were turning to greens, yellows, and shades of brown. We'd soon see the fiery ball. Yes, it was going to be a fine day—especially after our ride arrived. "Come on Michael. Get in gear. Make the day come together."

"There's Michael," Bill announced.

I swiveled around and was hit by a wave of excitement as two cars pulled up to the Pemex station. Bill walked out a few paces and waved. Spotting us, they headed in our direction. Peggy pulled up and let her door fly open. She screamed shrilly, piercing the early morning air and all but tackled Dirk and Mike.

Anxious to leave, we gave each other our last goodbyes. Everyone rushed for the cars.

Bill and I got into Michael's clunker and we waved to the foursome as they pulled out. Both vehicles were clunkers, but we'd been assured they ran well.

As we took to the road Michael said, "Let's go, dudes. I'll have you swimming in the ocean off San Blas before noon."

"Yes, let's get going. Where's my surfboard, brother?" Bill joked with his pal and soon-to-be partner.

"Some Mexicans stole it on the way over here," Michael gagged.

"Let 'em have it. I've got what I want."

"Right on, brother. Let's finish this escape job. It isn't over yet. Man, this is bitchin'."

"Nothing to it, man," Bill bragged. "Nothing to it."

He craned around and looked at me. I sat in the back seat quiet as a mouse, "How you doing *Pancho*? You okay? You're being quiet."

"I'm here, guys. Right in the place I want to be."

"I'll bet you are," Michael affirmed.

"I'm tired. I haven't gotten much sleep lately," I said.

"How's it feel to be free?" Michael asked.

"Terrific, man. Terrific. I feel like a bird soaring through the sky right now."

"Well, let's start with a nice long ride first," he replied, driving steadily.

As the sun rose, although depleted, I was impassioned, caught up in the moment as I my eyes took in the rich blue sky and the mighty rain clouds stacked up against the distant mountains to the east. The foliage was a bright green. The tropical countryside never looked better. I submerged myself in the beauty. .

Bill told his buddy, "Go slow, we're not to be in a rush." As he settled in he said, "Sure am glad we don't have any Highway Patrol to worry about."

Mexico had yet to establish one. As a precaution, just before departing, Bill had crumpled up a crude map he had made in his *caraca*, leaving it for the Mexican authorities to find. After looking at the map, they'd think we were headed north to Culican to a small airport. Meanwhile, we'd be well south of them and out of harm's way.

"Hey guys, it's time for morning roll call. I sure would have liked to see the looks on the official's faces at *lista* this morning."

"Yes. It's just about time. All hell is gonna break loose!" Bill chortled. We all laughed at the image it conjured up.

Michael added whimsically, "Two major jailbreaks in one month. Too much, man! Too much!"

Bill added with a breath of sarcasm, "Thirty-eight prisoners out the door. That's a mind-blower no matter how you look at it, brother. Simply too much."

"And the D.A.—shit, he's going to hang some butts," I leered.

"Hey, all they had to do was search us," Bill said blithely.

"Yes, and they're going to have to find a new *Alciadia*, " I said, among fits of laughter with the others.

Michael grinned, "The old *Alciadia* and four guards are in jail and after today add another *Alciadia* and a couple more guards. And they have to serve time for you?"

"Hey, it's their law," Bill retorted. "I didn't invent it. Besides, they sure did help us solve a lot of problems," he repeated.

"They sure did," Michael replied.

Within a few minutes, they began conspiring about hash-oil. I withdrew, not wanting to hear about it. It repelled me. All I wanted was to relax and to let go of the last six months.

Besides, my entire body was racked by a soreness that penetrated through to the marrow. I was tired beyond belief. The taste in my mouth was bitter, remorseful. It was time to purge the past. Tomorrow would be another day of freedom, thanks to the slothfulness of the Mexican officials. I was thankful too for the lessons I'd learned. I knew that the best way to start a day was to rise each morning and harness it with all the energy I could muster. Yes, energy was never-ending, and I wanted to work on how to flow with my creative energy source.

One of the first things I wanted to figure out was how to live "beyond" money.

Just what the hell did that mean, now that I had the freedom and time to contemplate the concept? "Always a challenge at hand," I thought, as sleep took me over.

As I awoke from my nap, we were slipping into the small, out-of-the-way hamlet San Blas—a lush, tropical wonder. I was joyous, yet I felt an eerie restlessness creeping in. Damn! Does the search for peace ever end? No matter how many contradictions and questions that came my way, I knew I was on the cusp of finding new meaning in my life.

Arriving in San Blas, we piled out of the car and got us a motel room, paid for by my charming brother and his new partner.

The remainder of the day was a blur of activity. Despite being tired, we purchased swim trunks after breakfast then we headed to the beach to swim and lie in the sun. From there, we headed back to town for feasting and drinking. We crashed, and didn't bother getting up until noon or beyond. The lure of staying indefinitely was compelling, but we decided to leave Paradise as the sun went down.

We arrived in Guadalajara at the home of Bill's friends exactly at the stroke of midnight on December 31—auspicious, I thought. Inger and her two friends opened the doors to greet us with hugs and congratulations, while church bells rang in the distance, announcing the New Year.

EPILOGUE

Jake finished up his three-year jail-sentence two months after I turned myself in. Shortly after his release, I visited with him and his family. He had changed. He was distant and withdrawn. Anguish riddled his face. When I tried to engage him, he wouldn't reminisce about our past, let alone ask me about what I'd been through. He simply greeted me with a handshake, then made busy.

Joanne had warned me he might be remote, but it was still a shock, and I hated the way Jake was treating me—his family too. They needed him and he wasn't there for them. Three years of incarceration and the horrible mistakes that had led him there had taken a heavy toll. "Open up!" I wanted to scream. He remained inaccessible, wallowing in silence. I didn't want to be near him and he made it clear in most ways that I was unwelcome.

It was different with Joanne. She was as friendly as ever, sharing her future plans with me. Jake and family wanted to open a restaurant. They already had a choice location and within a few months they had their business going.

Jake and Joanne came to my sentencing. I wondered if she had spurred him on to attend. Outside the courtroom, he congratulated me on the sentence I received. He had served three years and it must have been disturbing to him to think I'd be serving only six months in a State forestry camp leased by the Feds. He let me know I was getting off too easy.

I kept in touch with Joanne over the years, occasionally dropping by the restaurant for a chat. Jake tended bar, and occasionally sidled alongside where I sat drinking. But he never let go of his bitterness or dark humor.

I dropped in on Joanne one day during the mid-nineties and learned that Jake had broken up their marriage. He had hurt her deeply by telling her he had never loved her and that he loved a much younger woman. The cruel way he had handled it grieved me.

Ironically, Jake confided his problems to me for the first time in years when I ran into to him at the restaurant a few months later. He admitted he was corroding his relationship with his family, but he wanted out of the marriage and had no idea how to do it peacefully. He also admitted that he had carried around a lot of fear during the time we had worked together. When I asked him to talk about the past he refused. He couldn't let go of the inner rage that festered inside him. Stumped, I sat there knowing that I couldn't help him.

Joanne floundered a while but soon managed to pick up the pieces. Today she is doing well, as is her family and business.

✯ ✯ ✯

Bill chose to remain a fugitive, though I did send him a long letter explaining how I had grown and learned. I chose words that ran strong on *Brotherhood*—where it had led us and how it could free us. He ignored my brotherly advice. Over the years, usually during the summer, he'd show up, gathering up the family and making a day or two of it. He missed us and because we hadn't seen him in a year or so, we opened our hearts to him, especially Mom, who finally met her granddaughter.

His marriage to Inger broke up during the late seventies. If you're guessing it was because of another woman, you're right. Inger now lives in her homeland of Sweden, where she teaches at a local university. She married shortly after the breakup and had another daughter.

Kerstin is alive and well. She lives in a major metropolitan city and aspires to be an actress.

EPILOGUE

Victor is alive, but certainly not well. He came into Joanne's restaurant one day in the mid-nineties having gotten news of where to find Jake from an old lawyer friend. I got his phone number from Jake. Over the past few years, I've visited him a few times. He suffers from depression, back pain, internal pain; the list of his ailments is endless. His doctor has him on mood elevators and drugs to alleviate his pain. Each time I visit him, he regales me with drug smuggling stories. His memory is faltering, but at least he's willing to explore his past.

He and Chato remained in business with little success until the mid-seventies. They even served two years together in the *Hermosillo* jail. Once released, Chato was approached by members of a Mexican drug cartel, who offered a small piece of their pie. He refused to work with them so they murdered one of his sons and sent Chato his hands. Desperate, he called his good pal Victor and they agreed to sell the products the cartel demanded.

As payment, they gave Victor several tons of pot. After selling his goods for over a million dollars in profits, he relocated to escape the cartel's grasp. He purchased a ranch style mountain-top home in the California wine country, where he's lived for the past two decades. The view from his house is to die for. At first I was envious. Then I realized I'd rather have my health than the pain and depression that knock him out each and every day.

✯ ✯ ✯

During the mid-nineties I got word about Manny through Brother Ray. While visiting with Manny's brother in Portland, Oregon during the early nineties, Ray learned that during all those years, Manny had never gotten in touch with his family. That left his family, as well as Ray and I, to conclude that Manny had recycled himself, literally or figuratively. Where was Scientology when he needed it?

As for Ray, for the most part he lives the life of a hermit. He married in the early eighties and had a son.

✯ ✯ ✯

Sometime during the mid-nineties, Jake got in touch with Ramon who had gotten into the business of importing shrimp and lobster from Mexico to the States. I visited with him and we talked easily about the old days. However, he didn't even remember I had ripped him off, or other key incidents.

✭ ✭ ✭

The last time I saw Mack was during the mid-seventies. He had just gotten out of jail on a DUI, and was nowhere near the man I once knew. He too was reluctant to talk about the past.

As for Howie and Willy, the two men who had finked on all of us, I heard Willy took to drinking and moved up to Oregon. As for Howie, his wife divorced him. Jake had visited him shortly after getting out of jail and had forgiven him for what he done. So had I, but I had no desire to go see him.

✭ ✭ ✭

Of the three stalwarts who had marshaled the way for our escape, I heard from Mike in a most unusual way. When I came home from work one day in the late-eighties there was a message on my phone machine. The second I heard the voice I knew it was Mike. He had gotten my number from an ad I placed monthly in a free sailing magazine that was distributed both to Northern California and Southern California, where he lives. I had listed my real name, so it was a lucky guess he'd find me.

When I called him back he said he always knew I'd become a boat carpenter. When he saw the ad with my real name, he had to check it out. It was great to talk with him and to find out that he too works as an independent boat carpenter.

A couple of months later, I went to visit with him and his new wife and discovered he'd invited Dirk too. The three of us lunched together. Though Dirk and I had never been close, it was good to see that he was still the stalwart: vibrant, strong, healthy, and more mischievous than ever.

Mike was full of energy and spirits. He talked freely and with passion about our ventures. He knew to use his past mistakes to move forward and

EPILOGUE

live.

Patrick and Fred, Mike told me, had dropped out of sight.

* * *

I connected with Donny, my brother's surfer friend, during the mid-nineties. He too, is a carpenter. He's married and has a swell home with a great view of the ocean. As for talking about past deeds, well, he's a surfer: "What past? Hey, it was all groovy, dude."

* * *

I caught up with Dale and Mary too, after getting out of jail. They had been smart to get out while the going was good and had used their money wisely, buying an old wooden hulled tugboat. Dale spent a few years converting it to a gaff-headed ketch, then they took off and sailed the South Pacific—far off places I had once dreamed about. Eventually they married and had two sons, and Dale is an independent boat carpenter. We have a loose friendship, seeing each other occasionally. For them, the past is the past.

* * *

Sarah had an affair during the time I was in jail. She confessed this shortly after she arrived in *Guadalajara* several days after the escape. On the train trip to the border, she vowed the relationship with this other man was over and that she loved me. Tormented, but understanding because I had put her through hell, I forgave her.

After safely crossing the border, Sarah and I went straight to her parents' house in Pasadena. Completely broke and our future looking bleak, I became sick. A few days later, on a rainy afternoon, we departed with a friend who drove us to the Bay Area. I had Sarah call Joanne and set up a meeting, but asked Sarah not to let her know that I was out of jail. When we met up with Joanne at a park in North Beach, she was angry at first; I had not only surprised her, but had scared the shit out of her. She broke into tears and pounded my chest for being such a sonofabitch and not forewarning her.

After telling her about the jail escape, she got around to forgiving me then filled me in with the latest news. Jake was rotting away in jail. The lawyer we once had ties with had sold the ranch, but had kept the money to pay his lawyer fees. He had also recently sold our plane, but had promised to give Joanne half the money: nine grand. "Guess I'll have to give you half the nine grand, you lucky shit," she jested.

Four days later, money in hand and totally overwhelmed by the good fortune, Sarah and I headed to San Diego in our new, used, VW bus and rented an apartment.

With this money we could start a new life, so we settled in and began looking for anything pertaining to boat work. With Sarah by my side all of this came easily: new friends, painting and varnishing jobs, even a job as sailing instructors on an old, classic wooden hulled sloop. During the next few months our love flourished.

Nine months after setting up shop in San Diego, we moved to Long Beach. We had landed a major refinishing job, and although we had to leave behind all our new friends, Sarah was now closer to her parent's house in Pasadena. She liked that and so did her parents.

I was aware that her parents objected to Sarah's decision to be with me. They didn't want their daughter living with a fugitive. It was understandable that over time they'd do whatever was necessary to protect their daughter and talk sense into her. Over the next several months, her mother began plugging a two hundred and twenty volt power cord into our relationship. When we lived in San Diego, once a month they took us out to a fine restaurant. But shortly after we moved to Long Beach, I became embittered when her parents asked me to stand back while they took Sarah alone out to dinner. Although Sarah insisted her parents wanted to visit with her and nothing out of the ordinary was taking place, I knew better.

Our relationship now in a nosedive, it took a further dive when Sarah informed me that her parents were taking her on a month-long cruise aboard an ocean liner. I pretended to be in favor of the trip, but it unsettled me. Insecurities that had always gripped me began to grow. I fought them off and was able to rebound. But the day she departed I was on edge, and the night she returned became a night much like I endured during the wreck of the *New Mornin*.

She was a different woman; all my senses told me so. And once she was in my arms I felt angst in her, and a searing pain ran through my body. I had rented a motel room for the night in Pasadena, hopeful that her return would bring new life into our relationship. But her guilt-ridden eyes could not hide the anxiety that came from deep within her soul. Then came the moment when she could no longer embrace me: her words cut short as she struggled to tell me what she had done. With head bowed low, she finally confessed to having an affair with a ship's officer the second to the last night of the cruise.

God, how I grieved as she explained away her behavior. The story became a story within a story, a tangle of deceit, which forewarned me that there would be more entanglements to reckon with in the future. Our relationship had just crashed onto a reef. And as we talked on at length, tears flooding our eyes, I was worn thin by her pleas. All I wanted was what she wanted: complete forgiveness and a loving night in bed. I'd spent thirty days in abstinence so I forgave her and took her to bed.

Even though she convinced me she'd be faithful, I was heartbroken by emotions that humbled me as never before. Over the next few days a startling realization crept into my heart: in my desire to keep her at all costs, I had forgiven her under false pretenses. Both of us were living in a liar's den where lies only fester: pretending to be in love, when actually she was trapped in guilt and I was trapped in neediness. Haunted by withholding this truth from her and thoughts of losing her, little by little, my emotions took a beating. Guilt reined in on her because she wanted to leave me, but couldn't because of my fugitive status—at least we were respectful enough not to wield this as a weapon against each other. And indeed I needed her, clutching and hanging on to her, no matter how she felt about me or I about her.

Pretentious love, we'd find out, was a loathsome proposition. There was no longer enough love and trust between us to confront our issues. We ran from them instead. We continued with the pretenses for a while: making love, gaining new friends, and keeping in touch with old friends. But then came a day when she was no longer in bed with me. Her body was there, but her spirit had vacated.

I was an emotional mess and couldn't cope with all the ass-kicking that came into our lives. Unable to sustain trust with her and with my self-esteem ascending one day then plunging deeper the next, I went into a state of catatonic behavior, the likes of which I had never before experienced. Awash in my grief, she became disturbed by my erratic behavior. Completely disabled by her loathing attitude toward me, and her inability to show compassion, I was poorly equipped to deal with the final blow when she announced it was over. She wanted out.

The day she went back to Northern California, I practically fell apart. Before me stood a woman who still fostered a civilized love for me, but who also loathed me because I lacked emotional strength and confidence. I could only agree with her. I had become a wimp, but I too had a loathing for her that ran deep. I felt she had given up in herself and had conveniently added me to her blame list. I felt her insecurities at work, but at this point I knew it was best to stay away from her issues and to move on. It was time to begin repairing my emotional system, which was screaming for relief. After I assured her I'd be okay, even though I was still haunted by being a fugitive, she turned and departed.

All I could do was keep busy and begin surviving the way I had learned the past few years. A couple of days later, when my mind was more at peace, I thought about calling the people I had cruised with to Canada some few years ago. Fortune was with me. They were leaving in a few days and needed one more crew member to help sail the boat from San Francisco to British Columbia. It was mid-May, and I made arrangements to meet them. Finishing up a small job, I took a bus north and joined my sailing pals

During the cruise I had time to heal some of the wounds that had festered, but I was still in a sorrowful state when I headed south on a bus that stopped in San Francisco. Sarah had asked me to stay in touch. I hadn't—so I called her from the bus station.

"Oh God, Frank." Her emotions ran wild and her words tumbled over

EPILOGUE

each other. "I'm so glad you called... I was so worried...and I've got something wonderful to tell you...and you called at a perfect time."

"Why? What's up?"

"You're not going to believe this, but a week ago I ran into a guy I went to school with in Pasadena. He's a lawyer and he works as a clerk for a federal judge in San Francisco. I told my friend all about you and that you were a fugitive. He said that if there was ever a time for you to turn yourself in, this would be it."

The federal Watergate trials were just winding down. In their aftermath, sentences of six months to eighteen months—for crimes like mine—were being handed out like free Coney Island hot dogs on a cool autumn day. Ready to strike a new pose, federal judges across the nation were allowing drug offenders to plead to lesser charges and were handing down lesser sentences.

I had every reason to be excited. The opening I had wished for had come. After returning to L.A., I called the attorney. He laid it all out—get there within four days and the residing judge will O.R. me (own-recognizance). My bail was fifty grand, but the judge would waive it if I showed up before his monthly tenure ended.

Two days later, I boarded a bus for San Francisco. It was a night journey home, but as the sun rose that morning revealing the city in the distance, tears of joy rolled down my cheeks. I was going home.

✯ ✯ ✯

So, I was able to change a few things with my life.

A few days after turning myself in, I returned to my mother's house. My mother and brother John welcomed me with open arms, as did Ray—Bill being the missing son. Deep down, I knew Bill was gone for good and that I had inherited "Older Brother Status." I didn't mind that so much. I loved my younger brothers, even though they were in many ways hard to reach, especially John who was still on medication and under psychiatric care.

Mom had always been a strong-willed woman, but over the next two days I saw her at full strength. She knew I had a long road ahead of me and she promised me that she would stand behind me. I believed her and I was grateful. Stains of guilt ran through me as these and other realizations hit home: Mom had lost all four of her sons over the course of a few years, each of us to different circumstances. I sensed that she had learned a great lesson from this—and was thankful that I had chosen to return home. So was I. Mom was still the same mom in most ways, but she was now more willing to understand what we had been through as a family. This time, it wasn't all about her.

After this bittersweet reunion, I went to Joanie's house in Marin County. She was delighted to have me as a guest; I was delighted by the company. Another gift came along. My good friend Stan was leaving for Hawaii with his wife and two boys. He was an elevator rigger and was to work as a foreman on a new high-rise. I was invited to care-take his home for the next several weeks. All I had to do was rebuild a portion of his kitchen.

I missed Sarah, but not all that much. Twice I visited with her in Inverness and both times I came away frustrated by the condescending way she treated me. She really didn't want me around and I could well see why. I was emotionally bleeding all over. On the second visit, I realized that I no longer had a deep love for her; I was actually caught up in my abandonment issues. I needed to back off.

Life was not going to get the better of me. By choice I would spend only six months in jail and be relieved from any concern about a felony rap. Ironically, going to jail would give me the freedom to think about the life that lay ahead for me. Once free, I'd use my passions to gain better understanding about the universal laws that so endeared me. In time, these pursuits would become a constant.

And over the next several years, I honed my skills as an independent boat carpenter. I also passed from one relationship to another; a hiatus always serving as a means to re-gather myself. Sailing was still a big part of my life as were these relationships, but women, well, I didn't really know how to give them what they wanted, nor did I know what to expect from them beyond what they brought to bed. Some of these relationships were shallow, totally based on good sex. With others, I wanted to win them

EPILOGUE

over, treat them kindly, respect them, be their friend, but many of them complained that I was not there for them. I often felt the same about them.

What helped keep me on course was the wise advice Sarah had given me. She implored me to write my story and gain insight that would cleanse the wounds that were still bleeding. I started writing, but my writing skills were poor. Writing evoked overwhelming emotions, so I let go of the writing project for the time being. Months would pass before a sense of direction took hold.

Sometime during the early 90's, after emerging from another relationship that didn't work out, I began to look at life in a different way after a visit with a psychic therapist. "You're beginning to open up to your feelings and as a result you reached out to this woman to try to heal her wounds. But, she didn't trust you. She feared you and closed her heart to you. This woman didn't match up to *who you really are*," she informed me, adding, "Find someone whose needs are more equal to yours, someone willing to let you in. Someone new will come to you; meanwhile continue to allow your feelings to open."

What bothered me was that no one came, not at first, and most certainly not in the way I had anticipated.

She came when I decided to once again write the book. I didn't own a computer and I needed someone to put my hand written words to type. Calling an ad in the local Yellow Pages, I talked with a woman by the name of Jessica. Her voice was sweet and reassuring and she was happy to help me. She agreed to come to my small in-law apartment in Mill Valley.

I was standing outside when she drove up the driveway that afternoon. As she got out of her SUV, appearing before me was an apparition: a tall, lean, delicate, blonde beauty with emerald green eyes and an enchanting smile.

I had already forewarned her of the content of the book, but it didn't matter to her—she was visibly thrilled to be working on a memoir of this nature. After she departed with a portion of the manuscript, my knees finally regained strength. Ten months later and after several visits and many inspiring and nurturing words from her, the second draft was complete, but the book remained far from finished.

What fascinated me most about Jessica had to do with her heart and sensitivities. I wanted to be like her: aligned, centered and always giving. I also adored the way she treated everyone as equal, so over time she not only became my friend, she became my confidante and my guide to my inner self. Through what was in her heart, I was able to open up to what was in my heart; in short, she was the first and only woman who was able to give me the love and acknowledgement my Mother and all the others hadn't. I wanted Jessica in my life but was frustrated: she was married and had two young boys— but on the other hand, not necessarily happily married.

The day the draft was finished she led me to believe that this would be the last time I'd see her. In a rather coy manner she invited me into her living room and asked if Sarah was still in my life. What threw me off was that Jessica knew Sarah was no longer in my life, but asked anyway, and in a most provocative way, as though Sarah might be someone to compete with. When I assured her she was not, Jessica began to share with me intimacies about her life: problems within her marriage and with her in-laws that she had only spoken of previously in passing. For over two hours she kept my mind and heart captive. It was then that I was able to allow my true feelings to surface: I loved this woman and had been in love with her all along.

My heart was in a deep swoon when I left. It seemed clear from her opening up to me that she too had strong feelings for me. I didn't quite know what to do about this. I wanted to respect her marriage but there was something very powerful connecting us.

So, I wrote her a letter and let her know that I was in love with her, and how much I appreciated and respected her. A month later, after I had returned from a trip to the Caribbean she called me, gushing about how nice it was that someone other than her spouse and her children loved her. When I asked if it would be okay to write more letters, she agreed, although she never directly said that she loved me. I knew she cared for me, but her marriage stood in the way. Over the next few months I sent a few letters, as I moved from place to place—that is, until her husband came across one of them.

He confronted me one day when I came to pay her some money I owed. As I was leaving he stopped me in my tracks and said point-blank, "I want you to stop flirting with my wife—and you know what I mean." I promised to do so, but couldn't help myself and later called Jessica on the phone. She apologized that she hadn't forewarned me, and without much protest, she kept the door open for me to keep writing.

After the discovery of a second letter I cooled it for awhile. I felt a little guilty at first, and later reconciled my feelings by accepting that I loved her unconditionally. But, no matter how either of us felt, I was intruding on their marriage. I was willing to take the back seat, but also longed to have an opportunity to tell her this in person. It never came to pass.

Over the next two years I kept in contact with her by phone and letters. I was living in Mexico for a year and otherwise moving about a lot. My letters were friendly, nothing that would cause her or her husband any grief or anxiety. Every time we spoke, she gave me her full attention. Then, that started to change. She was pushing me away, and I had to face this reality. I gave way to the obvious: I had to let her go, and did so by allowing myself the pleasure of loving her from a distance. This was a good sign; more than just a good sign, this was the turning point in my emotional healing. In spite of our unrequited love, I had experienced giving and receiving unconditional love.

My healing journey reached a pinnacle one day shortly after that when I went for a walk on a beach. It was a cool and invigorating winter day. I was enjoying being alive. I don't know how or why the revelation came, only that it did— it was a like a thunderbolt. In that moment, I knew without a doubt, I was no longer alone. My whole being relaxed into a loving embrace that transcended any physical love I had known. I knew then that even though life may continue to throw me curve balls, I would not have to face them again from isolation or loneliness.

A lifelong pattern had opened to me and it had to do with the Brotherhood values I'd long ago adhered do. Seeds of love had been sown and had somehow come to fruition. I could feel this deep within: I had believed in love and love had set me free.

There is indeed a yin and yang to all of life as Bill had imparted all those years ago: each component complementary to the other and each incomplete alone. And the yin component, the feminine feeling center that resides within all of us, was now beginning to make perfect sense: without feelings how are we to open to our passions? And what is a life without passion?

All of my life I had been afraid to open to my feelings, mainly because I never had a clear understanding about how to "get in touch" with them. When Jessica came into my life, I learned to surrender to my feelings. Letting go and relaxing into love allowed me to enjoy the good moments in life, rather than to remain stuck in tiresome dramas. Dramas would come and go, but unconditional love is eternal.

I'm no master of unconditional love, but I have tasted it and experienced its power to transform and heal. Good fortune has always been with me because even in my darkest moments, I was connected to something greater, guiding me toward love. What I learned on this journey is that "a piece of the action" actually includes everything, even that which we say "no" to. The universal laws provide all the action we could ever want or imagine.

Printed in the United States
132296LV00004B/2/P